Resisting the Holocaust

Resisting the Holocaust

Upstanders, Partisans, and Survivors

Paul R. Bartrop

BLOOMSBURY ACADEMIC
NEW YORK • LONDON • OXFORD • NEW DELHI • SYDNEY

BLOOMSBURY ACADEMIC
Bloomsbury Publishing Inc
1385 Broadway, New York, NY 10018, USA
50 Bedford Square, London, WC1B 3DP, UK
29 Earlsfort Terrace, Dublin 2, Ireland

BLOOMSBURY, BLOOMSBURY ACADEMIC and the Diana logo
are trademarks of Bloomsbury Publishing Plc

First published in the United States of America by ABC-CLIO 2016
Paperback edition published by Bloomsbury Academic 2024

Copyright © Bloomsbury Publishing Inc, 2024

Cover design by Silverander Communications
Cover photos: Group portrait of members of the Kalinin Jewish partisan unit
(Bielski group) on guard duty at an airstrip in the Naliboki Forest. 1941–1944
(USHMM, courtesy of Moshe Kaganovich); Wall (STILLFX/Thinkstock)

All rights reserved. No part of this publication may be reproduced or
transmitted in any form or by any means, electronic or mechanical,
including photocopying, recording, or any information storage or retrieval
system, without prior permission in writing from the publishers.

Bloomsbury Publishing Inc does not have any control over, or responsibility for,
any third-party websites referred to or in this book. All internet addresses given
in this book were correct at the time of going to press. The author and publisher
regret any inconvenience caused if addresses have changed or sites have
ceased to exist, but can accept no responsibility for any such changes.

Library of Congress Cataloging-in-Publication Data
Names: Bartrop, Paul R. (Paul Robert), 1955– author.
Title: Resisting the Holocaust: upstanders, partisans, and survivors / Paul R. Bartrop.
Description: Santa Barbara: ABC-CLIO, LLC, [2016] | 2016 |
Includes bibliographical references and index.
Identifiers: LCCN 2015047024 | ISBN 9781610698788 |
ISBN 9781610698795 (ebook)
Subjects: LCSH: Holocaust, Jewish (1939–1945)—Biography. | World War,
1939–1945—Underground movements—Biography. | World War,
1939–1945—Jews—Rescue—Biography.
Classification: LCC D804.3 .B3637 2016 | DDC 940.53/1832—dc23
LC record available at http://lccn.loc.gov/2015047024

ISBN: HB: 978-1-6106-9878-8
PB: 979-8-7651-2025-5
ePDF: 978-1-6106-9879-5
eBook: 979-8-2161-3890-7

To find out more about our authors and books visit www.bloomsbury.com
and sign up for our newsletters.

Every reasonable effort has been made to trace the owners of copyright materials in this
book, but in some instances this has proven impossible. The editors and publishers will
be glad to receive information leading to more complete acknowledgments in subsequent
printings of the book and in the meantime extend their apologies for any omissions.

To My Students
The Last Generation Able to Say They Met an Upstander,
a Partisan, a Survivor

Never give in, never give in, never, never, never—in nothing,
great or small, large or petty—never give in except to convictions
of honor and good sense. Never yield to force; never yield
to the apparently overwhelming might of the enemy.
—*Winston Churchill*

Contents

List of Entries, ix

Primary Source Documents, xiii

Preface, xv

Introduction, xix

Upstanders during the Holocaust, xxiii

Partisans during the Holocaust, xxv

Survivors of the Holocaust, xxix

Entries, 1

Primary Source Documents, 335

Chronology, 409

Bibliography, 417

Index, 425

List of Entries

Abadi, Moussa
Alice, Princess Andrew of Greece and Denmark
Altman, Tova (Tosia)
Andreas-Friedrich, Ruth
Anger, Per
Anielewicz, Mordecai
Atlas, Icheskel
Bachner, Wilhelm
Baeck, Leo
Bartali, Gino
Baum, Herbert
Beck, Gad
Beitz, Berthold
Benghabrit, Si Kaddour
Bielecki, Jerzy
Bielski, Tuvia
Blaichman, Frank
Bogaard, Johannes
Born, Friedrich
Borromeo, Giovanni
Calmeyer, Hans
Cohn, Marianne
Coward, Charles
Dalla Costa, Elia
Damaskinos, Archbishop of Athens
De Sousa Mendes, Aristides
De Souza Dantas, Luis Martins
Dohnányi, Ernő
Dohnányi, Hans von
Drossel, Heinz
Duckwitz, Georg Ferdinand
Edelman, Marek
Elisabeth, Queen Mother of the Belgians
Errázuriz, María
Feldhendler, Leon
Fleischmann, Gisi
Foley, Frank
Fry, Varian
Gebelev, Mikhail
Gerstein, Kurt
Gies, Miep
Gildenman, Moshe
Glasberg, Alexandre
Göring, Albert
Grüber, Heinrich
Grünhut, Aron

Grüninger, Paul
Guzik, David
Haas, Leo
Helmy, Mohammed
Hirsch, Helmut
Ho Feng-Shan
Hübener, Helmuth
Hulst, Jan van
Israel, Charlotte
Jagendorf, Siegfried
Jonas, Regina
Jospa, Yvonne
Kafka, Helene
Kaplan, Chaim A.
Karski, Jan
Kasztner, Rezső
Katzenelson, Itzhak
Knut, Dovid
Koffán, Károly
Korkut, Dervis
Kovner, Abba
Kowalski, Władysław
Kraan, Willem
Kruk, Herman
Krützfeld, Wilhelm
Lajcher, Berek
Landmesser, August
Langbein, Hermann
Langlet, Valdemar
Leitz, Ernst II
Lichtenberg, Bernhard
Linnér, Sture

Lopatyn, Dov
Lubetkin, Zivia
Luckner, Gertrud
Lustig, Walter
Lutz, Carl
Maltzan, Maria von
Mann, Franceska
Meed, Vladka
Moltke, Helmuth James Graf von
Moszkiewiez, Hélène
Moszkowicz, Daniel
Müller, Filip
Münch, Hans
Norrman, Sven
O'Flaherty, Hugh
Ogilvie, Albert
Pankiewicz, Tadeusz
Pechersky, Alexander
Père Jacques
Père Marie-Benoît
Perlasca, Giorgio
Peshev, Dimitar
Pilecki, Witold
Plagge, Karl
Polonski, Abraham
Preysing, Konrad Graf von
Pritchard, Marion van Binsbergen
Propper de Callejón, Eduardo
Racine, Mila
Rémond, Paul
Ringelblum, Emanuel
Robota, Roza

Rosé, Alma
Rotta, Angelo
Rufeisen, Oswald
Saliège, Jules-Géraud
Salkaházi, Sára
Sanz Briz, Ángel
Schindler, Oskar
Schmeling, Max
Schmid, Anton
Schmitz, Elisabeth
Scholl, Hans and Sophie
Schonfeld, Solomon
Segerstedt, Torgny
Sendler, Irena
Sheptytsky, Andrey
Shirer, William L.
Slachta, Margit
Smolar, Hersh
Sommer, Margarete
Soos, Géza
Sorkine, Charlotte
Stöhr, Hermann
Strobos, Tina
Sugihara, Chiune
Süskind, Walter
Sylten, Werner

Szenes, Hannah
Sztehló, Gabor
Ten Boom, Corrie
Tenenbaum, Mordechaj
Trocmé, André
Ülkümen, Selahattin
Veseli, Refik
Vrba, Rudolf
Wallenberg, Raoul
Wdowiński, Dawid
Wegner, Armin T.
Weidner, Johan Hendrik
Weidt, Otto
Weissmandl, Chaim Michael Dov
Weltsch, Robert
Westerweel, Johan
Winton, Nicholas
Wittenberg, Yitzhak
Wrobel, Eta
Żabiński, Jan
Zilberberg, Rachel
Zimetbaum, Mala
Zuckerman, Yitzhak
Zwartendijk, Jan
Zygielbojm, Shmuel

Primary Source Documents

1. Robert Weltsch, "Wear It with Pride, the Yellow Badge" (April 4, 1933)
2. Armin T. Wegner, Open Letter to Adolf Hitler (April 11, 1933)
3. Interrogation of Father Bernhard Lichtenberg by the Gestapo (October 25, 1941)
4. Resistance Proclamation, Vilna Ghetto (January 1, 1942)
5. Final Report of German Jewish Youth Movement (March 1942)
6. Anton Schmid to Steffi Schmid (April 13, 1942)
7. The White Rose Movement, Second Leaflet (1942)
8. Testimony of Sidney Simon, Forest Partisan (2009)
9. Emanuel Ringelblum on the *Kashariyot* in the Polish Ghettos (May 19, 1942)
10. Dutch Protest at the Deportation of Jews (July 1942)
11. Handbill: Call for Resistance in the Warsaw Ghetto (January 1943)
12. Statement: Call for Resistance in the Warsaw Ghetto (January 1943)
13. Mordecai Anielewicz to Yitzhak Zuckerman (April 23, 1943)
14. Shmuel Zygielbojm to Władysław Raczkiewicz and Władysław Sikorski (May 11, 1943)
15. *The Pioneer* (Warsaw), "The Ghetto Fights On" (May 12, 1943)
16. Unaish Hilari, "The Jewish Partisan" (1954)
17. Tadeusz Pankiewicz: "The 'Eagle' Pharmacy in the Kraków Ghetto"
18. Yankiel Wiernik on the Revolt at Treblinka (August 2, 1943)
19. Call for Revolt in the Vilna Ghetto (September 1, 1943)

20. Alexander Pechersky on the Sobibor Revolt (October 14, 1943)
21. Hirsh Glik, "The Partisan Song" (1943)
22. Ruth Andreas-Friedrich, Diary (March 31, 1945)
23. Kurt Gerstein, Report (May 4, 1945)
24. Statement of Support, Siegbert Lewin, Regarding Otto Weidt (1946)

Preface

This is a book about people who said no to the attempt by National Socialist Germany, between 1933 and 1945, to disenfranchise, dehumanize, and ultimately destroy the Jewish people of Europe. They said no in a wide variety of ways, and for a plethora of reasons. If we were to group them all together, then we would inevitably find ourselves using a single word—resistance—to describe their activities.

Choosing the people featured here was no easy task, and the list could easily have been extended into the thousands. There are so many remarkable stories of men and women who stood up to the Nazis that it would require teams of dedicated researchers to compile them—if details could be found. Locating these has presented a problem: in many cases it has been impossible to compile a full dossier on many of those I would have preferred to include, simply because not enough of the record has been preserved to relate the particulars of their lives.

In addition, my selections here have been conditioned by my preference to choose examples that are representative of the wide range of resistance activities that could have been, and were, undertaken. For every person included here there were dozens more I could have added. Many brave individuals, for the sake of space, had to be omitted. This is unfortunate, of course, though when we realize that tens of thousands of upstanders, partisans, ghetto fighters, concentration camp survivors, rescuers, and others all deserve their place, it becomes clear that as an author I was frequently placed in a dilemma as to whom to leave out. It is my hope, therefore, that readers will appreciate that the people profiled in this book are but a sample of an otherwise enormous range of human beings who, for one reason or another, chose to say no to Hitler. Those not featured in these pages were no less brave, defiant, noble, or righteous than those who are.

One further note of explanation is needed with regard to place names. Europe in the 1930s and 1940s was a continent in flux, in which countries and regions changed borders and towns and cities changed names, depending on who was in charge. As a way to preserve the contemporaneity of the situations under examination, I have preserved the names of the localities by which they were best known within the context of the Holocaust (for example, Vilna), with their modern renditions in parentheses alongside (Vilnius). I hope that this choice will enhance clarity for modern readers and cut through what might otherwise be a confusion of names.

This is not a book about anti-Nazi resistance as such but is, rather, concerned with manifestations of resistance to the Holocaust. While some measure of crossover exists in many cases, the two were not always synonymous, and it is important to emphasize this from the outset.

This book has been written in a number of places. As the names of people were introduced to me—in a variety of ways and in all manner of settings—I would often begin researching or writing about them on the spot. This has therefore been a much traveled project: in addition to my base in Fort Myers, Florida, I have written entries in Melbourne, Hobart, London, Berlin, Reykjavik, New York, Philadelphia, Vancouver, and Los Angeles, among many other places.

In this book I refer a great deal to Yad Vashem, Israel's Holocaust Memorial Authority. It honors non-Jews who risked their lives, and at times those of their families, to save Jews during the Holocaust. Such people are given the title Righteous among the Nations (in Hebrew, *Hasidei umot Haolam*). After an exhaustive investigation process, if a person's actions are deemed to be sufficiently worthy of recognition as Righteous, then the honoree (or his or her heirs) are invited to Jerusalem to receive a plaque and to plant a carob tree in the Garden of the Righteous, in permanent commemoration of the honoree's act. This is generally acknowledged as the highest form of recognition for saving Jews that can be bestowed, and many in this book have been acknowledged in this way.

Sadly, there is at this time no corresponding body or organization that recognizes acts of physical or armed resistance during the Holocaust in quite the same manner.

The following people have provided help in a variety of ways, and I am pleased to acknowledge their help and place it on record: Gotthard Klein, for providing me with the document of Father Bernhard Lichtenberg's Gestapo interrogation, and Lori Boegershausen for translating it into its first-ever English rendering; Kathleen Lee, for adding personal details about Wilhelm Bachner; T. C. Yih, for his assistance with Chinese nomenclature in the entry on Ho Feng-Shan; Elizabeth Snyder, for her help with the chronology and bibliography, and for alerting me to the story of August Landmesser; Amy Simon, for her insights on Herman Kruk and the resistance dimension of diary keeping during the Holocaust; and William (Bill) Gasway, for introducing me to the Leica Freedom Train and Ernst Leitz II.

My friend and colleague David Meola, formerly of Sewanee: The University of the South, provided enthusiastic assistance by bringing his students into the research and writing process. While I am indebted to David for his wonderful initiative, I would like especially to acknowledge the following students for their attention to detail and their keenness: Cameron Mason and Savanna Roaldsand (Gad Beck); Allie Puneky, Cook Carpenter, and Alexandra Huber (Hans Calmeyer); Ned Roberts, Huntre Woolwine, and Evans Ousley (Charles Coward);

Fayyaz Akbari, Drew Mancuso, and Anna Morrow (Archbishop Damaskinos); Molly Elkins, Locke Williamson, and Steve Garcia (Paul Grüninger); Liz Arza, Kyle McCormack, and Noah Day (Johan Hendrik Weidner); James Sweeney and Jaime McDonough (Tova [Tosia] Altman); Mary Gray Stolz and Grayson Ruhl (Chaim A. Kaplan). A number of students also submitted their work anonymously. To everyone, well done and thank you.

My editor at ABC-CLIO, Padraic (Pat) Carlin, continues to provide support in a wide variety of ways, and I remain grateful to him in what has now become a relationship stretching over a number of projects.

My dear friends and colleagues Steven Leonard Jacobs and Michael Dickerman, as ever, were always on hand with advice and support, and I remain proud to call them my friends.

A penultimate vote of thanks goes to my research assistant, Danielle Jean Drew. In so many ways, this has been her project as much as mine; her research skills are superb and have saved me on many occasions. I hope that when the time comes for her to employ the services of an assistant in her own work that she will be as fortunate as I have been. She is, indeed, a fellow historian.

Finally, as in the past, my greatest support comes from my wife, Eve Grimm. There is not a word of this book she hasn't read; barely a dilemma she hasn't thrashed through with me. And her contributions, as always, have made this a much better book than it ever would have been without her input. She, I cannot resist; to her, I could never say no.

Introduction

What constituted resistance during the Holocaust? There were many forms, ranging from armed confrontation to a passive defiance that simply sought to maintain dignity and a sense of humanity. Resistance to the Holocaust also embraced those people who sought to save lives threatened, through rescue, concealment, or any other form of denying Nazis the chance to realize their murderous goals.

In Germany, most Jews were completely surprised by the vehemence of Nazi antisemitism, its uncompromising level of hatred and violence. For the majority, it took years before they understood that they no longer had a future in a country they thought was their homeland. Opposition of any sort, accordingly, was slow in coming. One of the first resistance statements came from Robert Weltsch, the editor of the national Jewish newspaper *Jüdische Rundschau*, who responded to the Nazi-inspired nationwide boycott of all Jewish businesses on April 4, 1933, by writing an editorial—"Wear It with Pride, the Yellow Badge"—which was to be a display of Jewish assertiveness in the face of Nazi provocation.

At other times anti-Nazi resistance surfaced in the way of opposition to the Nazi regime rather than in condemnation of the Holocaust. During the war years, a Jewish anti-Nazi group led by Herbert Baum and his wife Marianne was active. For their attempt in 1942 to disrupt Nazi propaganda in Berlin they were executed. So also were the leading members of the White Rose, one year later.

World War II began with the German invasion of Poland on September 1, 1939. Before the month was out Nazi antisemitic measures had begun in the occupied areas, and during the months that followed Jews were herded into ghettos. With persecution eventually came a response, particularly from Jewish youth. One of the first ghetto revolts took place in Łachwa in September 1942, after a resistance movement had been formed under the leadership of Dov Lopatyn and Isaac Rochczyn. This was but a start. In ghettos throughout Poland, Lithuania, Belorussia, and Ukraine, resistance movements emerged—some more slowly than others, though eventually all over. It has been estimated that more than 100 ghettos spawned underground movements of one sort or another.

The most famous of these included the movements in Vilna, where the Fareynikte Partizaner Organizatsye (United Partisan Organization, or FPO) was led by Abba Kovner; in Minsk, where the resistance was led by Mihail Gebelev and Hersh Smolar; and in Białystok, where the resistance movement was led by Daniel Moskowitz and Mordechaj Tenenbaum, who had formed the Antyfaszystowska Organizacja Bojowa (Anti-Fascist Military Organization, or AOB).

Undoubtedly, however, the ghetto resistance most people recall was the Warsaw Ghetto Uprising of April–May 1943. On April 19 the Nazis attempted to destroy the ghetto and its inhabitants as a birthday present to Adolf Hitler. By that stage, only between 55,000 and 60,000 Jews remained in the ghetto; the vast majority, approximately 300,000, had already been transported to their deaths in the East, mainly at Treblinka.

Earlier, in January 1942, a Jewish resistance organization known as the Żydowska Organizacja Bojowa (Jewish Combat Organization, or ŻOB) had already begun military operations against the Nazis. Comprised largely of Zionist youth and led by Mordecai Anielewicz, Yitzhak Zuckerman, Marek Edelman, Tova (Tosia) Altman, and others, the group planned a resistance effort for whenever it seemed as though the Nazis were about to liquidate the ghetto completely. Dawid Wdowiński led another underground movement in the ghetto, the Żydowski Związek Wojskowy (Jewish Military Union, or ŻZW).

Battle was joined on April 19, with the struggle lasting until May 16—longer than the defense of Poland back in September 1939. The ghetto fighters took the Nazis completely by surprise, and the uprising only ended when the Germans resorted to the technique of burning all buildings in the ghetto, street by street and block by block. On May 8 the command bunker at Miła 18 was destroyed and the ŻOB leadership, including Anielewicz, was dead. Earlier, in a communiqué to Zuckerman dated April 23, Anielewicz wrote that "my life's dream has been realized: I have lived to see Jewish defense in the ghetto in all its greatness and glory."

On May 16 German general Jürgen Stroop reported that the "Jewish Quarter of Warsaw is no more." While the uprising did not materially affect either the outcome of the war itself or the continued annihilation of the Jews, it remains to this day the symbol of Jewish resistance to Nazi tyranny.

In the Nazi extermination camps, resistance was also mounted. The most celebrated of these efforts were large-scale prisoner rebellions at Treblinka, Sobibor, and Auschwitz.

Although Treblinka and Sobibor were extermination camps not designed to house large numbers of people for long periods, some prisoners were selected to act as a pool of labor for the day-to-day chores of camp life. It was these inmates who decided to organize and take on the task of breaking out, an undertaking that would throw the killing machinery into disarray and perhaps ensure the survival of some who otherwise would surely have been killed.

Plans at Treblinka were detailed and precise; every man had a job to do, and responsibility was delegated in such a way that each phase was dependent upon the success of that which preceded it. On August 2, 1943, after building an arsenal consisting of hand grenades and rifles stolen from the camp armory, between 150 and 200 inmates rose in a coordinated action, rushed the fence, and attempted a breakthrough. Others then joined in. Of the 700 prisoners in the camp, only about 200 made it safely into the forests nearby, where they were ruthlessly hunted down by the Nazis and antisemitic Poles. It has been estimated that possibly fewer than 40 survived the war.

The revolt at Sobibor, two months later, was similar to that at Treblinka. Largely the product of careful military planning by Soviet troops who were prisoners—all of them Jews, under the leadership of Alexander Pechersky—the revolt saw hundreds of inmates make a break for freedom. About 80 were killed during the escape, and another 170 were hunted down by the Nazis and killed later, while perhaps 130 did not participate. Best estimates are that only about 53 survived the war.

Both camps were closed down shortly after each of the revolts.

The imminence of extermination was the trigger that led members of the XII Auschwitz *Sonderkommando* to take up arms against the SS and attempt a mass escape. On October 7, 1944, the men working at Crematorium IV rose in revolt. Setting fire to the crematorium, they attacked the SS guards with hammers, axes, and stones. Upon learning that the revolt had begun, the men working at Crematorium II joined in, killing a kapo and several SS men. Then the Hungarian prisoners working in Crematorium III also entered what by now had become a full-scale rebellion in the killing center. The revolt was successful in damaging Crematorium IV beyond repair, and it was never used again. During the revolt several hundred prisoners escaped, though most were caught and killed by the SS. Later that day, an additional 200 prisoners who took part in the revolt were executed.

One month later, on November 7, 1944, the Nazis destroyed the entire gas chamber–crematorium complex, closing down the operation altogether.

Other forms of resistance also took place in the Nazi ghettos and concentration camps. Taken collectively, resistance was an active, ongoing process of opposition to all aspects of life under the Nazis. It could take many forms and arise over any issue. Resistance was as much an attitude as a physical process, and it sought to negate the commands, rules, intentions, actions, statements, and deprivations imposed by the SS. Its numerous forms enabled men and women to take some measure of control over their fate in an environment where survival and success were in no sense guaranteed. Every act of helping, encouragement, and cooperation that took place disproved the claim that an attitude of self-reliance could not be maintained, and individuals, groups, and resistance movements all sought to establish and maintain this attitude.

Beyond the ghettos and camps, partisan groups composed of guerrilla fighters risked their lives fighting Nazis, particularly in the forests of eastern Poland, Ukraine, and Belorussia. They attacked railroads, bridges, and military installations, but they sometimes also cared for nonmilitary combatants—women and children, or those too young, too old, or too sick to fight. Among the most notable of the partisan groups was that associated with the Bielski brothers—Tuvia, Asael,

Zus, and Aron. Other operational commanders included Icheskel Atlas in the Lipiczanska Forest; Moshe Gildenman ("Uncle Misha") in the Volhynia region of Ukraine; and Eta Wrobel, a remarkable woman who commanded a Jewish partisan unit in the forests of central Poland.

In all cases, partisan military operations were essentially based around sabotage and guerrilla tactics rather than direct confrontation. Partisans were mainly active in Eastern Europe, especially after the Nazi invasion of the Soviet Union in the summer of 1941, and their activities ranged widely across Nazi-occupied Europe, extending to France, Belgium, and other places as well as to Eastern Europe.

Physical defiance was the most obvious manifestation of resistance, but spiritual resistance was also paramount, in the form of secret religious observance, artistic and creative endeavors, teaching and learning, and news dissemination. In other contexts, Jews helped each other to escape the Nazis through arranging illegal border crossings, smuggling, forging papers in order to create false identities, and hiding, sometimes for years.

One of the greatest myths of the Holocaust is that the Jews made little or no effort to defend themselves against their Nazi oppressors, though clearly resistance did take place and took many forms.

Upstanders during the Holocaust

An upstander, it might be said, is the opposite of a bystander. For whatever reason, bystanders generally do not get involved in situations in which moral choices need to be made in relation to right and wrong. As a result, it is uncommon for them to take action when confronted with the persecution or the abuse of another.

Upstanders, on the other hand, will intervene in some way, choosing to take positive action in the face of injustice or in situations where others need assistance. Upstanders during the Holocaust were those who resisted the murderous actions of the Nazis, or went out of their way to rescue Jews. Upstanders are those who "stand up" for a cause or belief when they could otherwise have chosen to do nothing; put this way, bystanders are passive and do nothing to help when someone needs it, whereas upstanders actively defend those needing to be defended.

That said, one salient fact is worth remembering: during the Holocaust upstanding was not a soft option, and all too frequently, becoming one was fraught with emotional, moral, and physical dilemmas. It was not easy being an upstander. To stand out from the crowd, to refuse to acquiesce, to not compromise one's own values in order to guarantee personal safety at the expense of others—these were grueling issues for people to confront during this most extreme period in history. Human behavior during the Holocaust, it might be said, was the paradigmatic example of all the best—and the worst—that human civilization carries within it.

Saying no to the Nazis was a choice people made, and it took exceptional courage and commitment to do so. Were, therefore, those who acted as upstanders heroic? It is a difficult question to answer. Certainly, many (possibly most) did not see themselves that way.

We tend to think of heroes as people who act on a grand scale in order to achieve aims that are somehow extra-human. Heroes appear to possess unique qualities beyond what "ordinary" people have. Thus, heroes will be exceptionally brave, display extraordinary courage, and possibly offer themselves for some greater good knowing that their mortality is threatened (if, indeed, they are mortal—and often, the mystique surrounding heroes requires that they be immortal or superhuman). In the face of danger and adversity, a hero will then receive admiration from his or her supporters for the deeds exhibited, and revulsion from those against whom they stand.

While these heroic traits certainly sound familiar, it must be pointed out that the acts of an upstander do not have to take place on a grand scale in order to be effective. Yes, there were *some* exceptionally brave acts on the part of *some* individuals, but it was really in myriad, small ways that the worst excesses of the Holocaust were resisted. As we will see in this volume, people such as August Landmesser, Giovanni Borromeo, Max Schmeling, Torgny Segerstedt, Johannes Bogaard, Charlotte Israel, and Sture Linnér all played a huge role in resisting the Nazis by refusing to acquiesce, or turn a blind eye, or desist from their commitment to the sanctity of human life. So upstanders do not necessarily conform to the heroic stereotype—even though, in so many ways, their actions can be taken as completely heroic, especially in view of what they were facing.

Upstanders during the Holocaust, engaging an enormous variety of helping activities, demonstrated that the intended victims of the Nazis could sometimes find ways out of this most awful of situations.

It must always be remembered, however, that their actions, though outstanding examples of goodness in the face of genocidal evil, managed to save only a tiny proportion of those whose lives the Nazis already considered to be forfeit. Moreover, saving lives was difficult, and sometimes next to impossible. The Holocaust was a time when living space, food, sanitation facilities, and medicine were at a premium, and those who hid Jews from the Nazis risked their own lives as well as those of their families. Given the enormous risks involved in undertaking rescue efforts, it is remarkable that any of these initiatives took place at all. Depending on where one was located, people caught helping or hiding Jews were, more often than not, executed immediately—either on the spot, or later, in public as an example to others.

Perhaps, then, when we ask why there were so few examples of upstanding during the Holocaust, the question could more readily be, in view of everything people faced, how come there were so many?

Further, we often do not know many of the stories surrounding upstanders, for they either were not recorded, or the upstanders themselves did not see a need for them to be remembered or celebrated. In so many cases, such people did not feel as though, by acting to stop Nazi atrocities, they did anything special. For these people, their actions simply constituted what they refer to, over and over again, as "the right thing to do."

A question is often asked: how would I have behaved in the same situation? This is an unknowable question until such time as we are confronted by it, and we must hope that we never have to face what those during the Holocaust had to face. But as the upstanders featured in this book made clear, if we have an idea of how we *should* behave under such (or similar) circumstances, then we might just have the moral compass required to enhance life and confront the forces of awful darkness that so challenged this earlier generation.

Partisans during the Holocaust

According to some estimates, anywhere between 20,000 and 30,000 Jewish men and women fought as partisans against the Nazis and their allies during World War II. Their military operations were essentially sabotage and guerrilla tactics rather than direct confrontation, due to their small numbers in any given location and their limited supplies of weapons, food, medicine, and the like.

Most partisan resistance took place after 1942, once it became clear that the Nazis were murdering every Jew in Europe. Partisan movements were most numerous in the occupied countries and regions of Eastern Europe, where Jews resisted both as individuals and in groups. Armed units operated in Ukraine, Belorussia, Lithuania, Poland, and Russia, among other places, and often formed an important component of local resistance operations. In Lithuania, for example, Jews made up approximately 10 percent of the partisan units.

In Western Europe, Jewish resistance units were established in France and Belgium, where they would engage in clandestine military operations or help their fellow Jews escape across nearby borders. Jews also fought alongside other partisans in Greece, Italy, Yugoslavia, and the Netherlands.

The vast majority of partisans had been civilians before the war, and most were young, with prewar Jewish youth groups forming the foundation for much of the resistance activity in the forests and ghettos. Resistance fighters usually ranged in age from about eighteen to twenty-five, and sometimes children also bore arms. In the normal run of events, most partisan units were small, numbering only a few dozen fighters. Very few had any prior military training, though some, who had served in the Polish or Soviet armies, formed a useful leadership cohort in the areas of strategy and military knowhow.

As forces that began informally, with little-to-no training and no entrenched leadership cohort, partisan groups faced great obstacles. Lack of armaments, conducting operations in a hostile zone, and the members' civilian status were important factors militating against large-scale operations, but many groups were also plagued by a reluctance to leave families behind and a fear of reprisals, together with the ever-present Nazi terror—to say nothing of concerns about their own personal security in a combat situation for which they were underprepared. The generally hostile antisemitic environment, among local people who, often, were their prewar neighbors, further complicated partisan efforts.

Admittedly, in some places Jewish partisans received assistance from local villagers, but often they could not count on such help, partly because of widespread antisemitism, partly because many locals feared punishment should they be caught helping. The partisans lived in constant danger of informers revealing their whereabouts to the Germans. Further, as they were in constant fear of discovery, partisan units were either always on the move or prepared to leave at a moment's notice.

Given this situation, secrecy and concealment were paramount, and as a result most partisan groups were frequently cut off from the world. Other than what they could learn from captured prisoners, newly arrived fighters, or occasional contact with other partisan groups, the partisans knew little of what was happening in the wider world or, more importantly, in the war.

On the positive side, however, geography and topography favored the kind of warfare in which the partisans were able to engage, mounting hit-and-run raids prior to disappearing back into the densely wooded areas where they based their operations. Over time, many Jewish groups were absorbed into the command structure of the much larger Soviet partisan movement, but even here antisemitism and discrimination were frequent.

Jewish partisan groups often moved beyond fighting or sabotage and sometimes sheltered families, women, and children, working to protect Jewish lives at this time of greatest threat. As a result, some groups could number in the hundreds, though with only a small actual fighting strength. These family camps usually consisted of escapees from ghettos or those fleeing from villages in advance of the occupation, and they acted as sites—insecure, to be sure—where those too young or too old to fight hoped to wait out the war.

Fighters in the ghettos and concentration camps, even though not in the forests, can also be included as partisans, even though they enjoyed much less freedom of action than those outside. In many Nazi death camps—including Sobibor, Treblinka, and Auschwitz—large-scale prisoner revolts took place, resulting in huge losses of life but also in the destruction of the Nazis' murder machinery.

Resistance units emerged in more than 100 ghettos in Poland, Lithuania, Belorussia, and Ukraine. Their physical resistance often took the form of sabotage, such as destruction of property, theft of goods, and the like, in addition to open and armed rebellion. Jews resisted when the Germans established ghettos in towns and cities throughout Poland. The best-known example, perhaps, is that of the Warsaw Ghetto Uprising of April–May 1943, which saw the ghetto defenders unsuccessfully attempt to stave off the total obliteration of the Jewish population.

After the war, the fighting partisans, whether in forests, ghettos, or camps, became the symbol of Jewish resistance to Nazi tyranny, though there were, of course, many other ways in which resistance activities could take place without a reliance on armed force. In fact, in order to survive it was often better not to fight back—though every situation had to be assessed on its merits, and when looking at the situation today, the time-and-place circumstances of all resistance activities must always be taken into account.

Survivors of the Holocaust

The question of who might be classified as a Holocaust survivor is, to a large degree, dependent upon resolving the question of how we define the Holocaust itself. A general definition could settle on the Holocaust as being the nearly successful attempt by Nazi Germany and its allies during World War II to exterminate the Jews of Europe in a methodical, sustained, and state-driven operation. To be a survivor, therefore, would of necessity mean that one was Jewish and lived through this operation, outlasting the Nazi regime.

For some, however, this is an incomplete definition. The United States Holocaust Memorial Museum (USHMM), for instance, defines Holocaust survivors as "any persons, Jewish *or non-Jewish*, who were displaced, persecuted, or discriminated against due to the racial, religious, ethnic, social, and political policies of the Nazis and their collaborators between 1933 and 1945" (emphasis added). On the other hand, Yad Vashem, Israel's Holocaust Martyrs' and Heroes' Remembrance Authority, asserts that Holocaust survivors are "Jews who lived for any amount of time under Nazi domination, direct or indirect, and survived."

The difference is important, as the USHMM prefers to be as inclusive as possible—such that *any* victim of the Nazis, Jewish or non-Jewish, is a Holocaust survivor. This demonstrates a certain confusion on the USHMM's part, as it defines the Holocaust explicitly as "the systematic, bureaucratic, state-sponsored persecution and murder of six million *Jews* by the Nazi regime and its collaborators" (emphasis added).

Yad Vashem, on the other hand, has no difficulty focusing its definition exclusively on those who were Jewish. That said, Yad Vashem also acknowledges that Holocaust survivors need not have been targeted directly by the Nazi murder machinery, and it includes Jews who were not confined in ghettos or deported by the Nazis to concentration or death camps, as well as Jews who were forced to leave Germany in the late 1930s.

In another sense, Yad Vashem proposes an extension of the designation "Holocaust survivor" to include "all Jews, anywhere in the world, who were still alive by the end of 1945," and "survived the Nazi genocidal intention." At the same time, the organization acknowledges this definition as being too broad and accepts that "no historical definition can be completely satisfactory."

It is clear, then, that considerable disagreement exists over who might be described as a Holocaust survivor. For some, it is sufficient to say that any Jew who lived for any period of time in a country ruled by the Nazis or their allies is a Holocaust survivor. For others, a Holocaust survivor must be a Jew who was a victim of Nazi persecution and stayed alive beyond the Nazi regime. With this in mind, the questions mount: can Jews who lived in Germany before the outbreak of war in September 1939, but left as refugees for other countries, be counted? Is it appropriate to include Jews from Syria and Lebanon, which was ruled by collaborationist Vichy France; or Libya, a colony of fascist Italy until 1942; or Palestine, which experienced Axis air raids during the war? Can a Jew who lived in hiding, or by passing as a Gentile, or as a partisan in the forest, be classed as a Holocaust survivor?

Indeed, is it sufficient for a Jewish (or any) person from that period simply to define him- or herself as a Holocaust survivor in order to be accepted as one? In whose eyes is survivorship defined? Is it an internal or external form of identity? More than seven decades after the Holocaust experience, these questions still resonate acutely and spark debates among researchers, legal experts, politicians, and those who were there.

Regardless of how it is defined, the Holocaust was far from being some sort of grand social experiment into the nature of human existence. Philosophers and theologians will long argue about the higher elements of the Holocaust experience, and what it signified for the human condition in the long term. Questions as to the nature of revealed truth, the presence or absence of God, and the quality of evil and suffering will be debated ad infinitum. For the survivors, however, all these questions and all the words needed to answer them will be meaningless without an understanding of the human dimensions of the Holocaust at its broadest, and what it meant to those who lived through it.

In a situation where armed resistance was often impossible, the mere act of survival was a form of resistance. For Jews this meant defeating death as much as it meant defeating the Nazis; indeed, the two were essentially the same. Every day in which a person stayed alive meant successfully resisting the Nazis' genocidal ambition. Retaining one's dignity, and sense of what it was to be human, signified a person's defiance. For many, survival did not need to have any deeper meaning beyond this. Quite simply, all Jews in continental Europe who outlived Hitler overcame the fate that he and his regime intended for them, and through that very act they demonstrated an act of resistance stronger than any other.

Abadi, Moussa (1910–1997)

Moussa Abadi was a French Jew from Syria who, along with his future wife, created a Jewish rescue network operating in Nice, France. Between 1943 and 1944 the Marcel Network, as it was called, saved 527 Jewish children ranging in age from babies to teenagers.

Abadi was born on September 17, 1910, in Damascus to Nassim Abadi and Farida Katran. When Abadi was 12 years old his mother died, and his maternal grandparents raised him in a strictly religious environment. Attending school at the Alliance Israelite, he obtained a scholarship to enter higher studies at the Sorbonne, and after arriving in Paris in December 1929 he proved to be an excellent student. In June 1933 he obtained a bachelor of arts and a certificate of child psychology, after which he became a graduate student in theater.

In December 1939 he met Odette Rosenstock, a young Jewish woman who had qualified as a medical doctor during the Spanish Civil War—during which time she supported the Republicans and assisted refugees. The two fell in love and became engaged. With the Nazi occupation of Paris in the summer of 1940 they fled south to the Italian-occupied zone, settling in Nice. Acting as a refuge for Jews, the city hosted many thousands in 1940–1941; here, Abadi taught in a Catholic theological seminary, while Rosenstock practiced medicine until anti-Jewish laws forced her to stop. She then worked as a midwife.

Around the same time, Abadi published an antifascist article under the pseudonym Marcel Samade. He would use the name "Marcel" again in the future.

During his time in Paris, Abadi had begun a doctoral thesis on the origin of fables in the Middle Ages, studying under Gustave Cohen, a French medievalist. After both moved to Nice the scholars were reunited, and Abadi attended a number of Cohen's lectures. At one of these, Cohen introduced Abadi to a French cleric, Bishop **Paul Rémond**.

In 1942, after speaking with an Italian army chaplain fresh from the Eastern Front, Abadi learned that the Nazis were murdering Jews in Poland, Russia, and elsewhere. This gave him pause for thought; if the Nazis had a systematic agenda in place, then it was only a matter of time before they began killing Jews in France, too. Thus, when German troops and Vichy French police began to round up Jewish children in 1942, he decided that the time had arrived to do something about it.

Thus, in November 1942 Abadi and Rosenstock organized a rescue operation to prevent the deportation of the weakest segment of society: Jewish children. There was one important logistical question that needed to be answered, however: how was it to be done?

Early in 1943 Abadi approached Bishop Rémond and asked for his help. Without hesitation Rémond swung into action, giving the young couple official roles within the Church. Rosenstock, under the alias Sylvie Delattre, became a diocesan social welfare representative; Abadi became superintendent of Catholic education under the alias Monsieur Marcel. With this, the Marcel Network was born.

To help facilitate their work, Rémond provided them with the assistance of several priests and with office space at his official residence, where forged papers and baptismal certificates could be produced. He signed a letter of appointment giving them freedom to circulate freely, as well as access to Christian institutions where children could be hidden.

Thus armed, the Marcel Network began. After the Italian surrender in September 1943 the Nazis moved into Nice, and the full force of the Holocaust descended on the Jews of southern France. Abadi and Rosenstock began rescuing Jewish children whose parents had already been deported or were in hiding, and found them safe hiding places among the Church institutions offered by Bishop Rémond.

Abadi also obtained support from Protestant ministers in the area, including pastors Pierre Gagnier and Edmond Evrard, who worked hard to find Protestant families prepared to shelter Jewish children. Throughout this entire time, the lives of the children, as well as of Abadi and Rosenstock, were in constant danger.

While allocating children to welcoming families, the problem arose of how best to camouflage them so they would not give themselves away. Abadi saw that each child would need to undergo a change of identity, with his or her name and personal history altered. Accordingly, these children would have to lose their Jewish identities and learn new, Christian ones. Abadi called this "depersonalization," and he found it one of the more difficult aspects of his rescue initiative—the more so because, when the war came to an end and surviving parents came to collect their children, often a new (and painful) reintegration process would have to begin.

In April 1944 Rosenstock, who continually stayed in touch with "her" children, was denounced. The Gestapo arrested her in May. Tortured during her interrogation, she refused to reveal anything about the Marcel Network. She was first deported to Auschwitz, and then sent on to Bergen-Belsen, where she managed to survive until liberation in 1945. After a period of recuperation she joined Abadi, who had managed to avoid capture in Nice during the final year of the war. Later, they were married.

In early 1948 the couple returned to Paris, where they remained for the rest of their lives. Odette Rosenstock-Abadi resumed her work as a doctor, becoming director of social hygiene, while Abadi spent several postwar years helping Jewish children reintegrate with their families.

In sum, the Marcel Network saved the lives of 527 children who were hidden in sanctuaries throughout southeastern France. After the war neither Moussa nor

Odette Abadi spoke about their work with the Marcel Network, and many people were taken by complete surprise when it was finally revealed.

On September 15, 1997, Abadi died two days short of his 87th birthday and was buried in Montparnasse Cemetery. His wife committed suicide on July 29, 1999, aged 85, unwilling to live a life without her beloved husband.

Alice, Princess Andrew of Greece and Denmark (1885–1963)

Alice, Princess Andrew of Greece and Denmark, born Princess Alice of Battenberg in 1885, was a great-granddaughter of Queen Victoria. Congenitally deaf, she used this disability to her advantage on a number of occasions when, for example, she did not want to accept unwelcome news. A deeply spiritual person, Alice visited Russia in 1908, during which time she talked with her aunt, Grand Duchess Elizabeth Fyodorovna, regarding a new religious order that Elizabeth was planning to establish. This conversation would have a profound impact on Alice's life in later years; she herself became increasingly religious, entering the Greek Orthodox Church in 1928.

Upon her marriage in 1903 to Prince Andrew of Greece and Denmark, Alice moved to Athens. Fluctuations in Greek political life saw the royal family exiled and reinstated a number of times, until the situation stabilized in 1935. In the meantime, Alice was diagnosed with paranoid schizophrenia and spent a number of years undergoing treatment. This condition eventually led to estrangement from her husband, who had received sanctuary in France among those blamed for Greece's military defeat in Asia Minor in 1922.

Alice returned to Athens in 1938 and dedicated her life to working with the poor, a cause that had been one of her core interests from a young age. She did not resume her life in the palace, preferring to live in a tiny downtown apartment. At this time she sent her daughters to live with their relatives in Germany, and her son, Philip, to England, where he stayed with his uncles Lord Louis Mountbatten and George Mountbatten.

When war came to Greece in 1940–1941 the royal family left Athens, first going to Egypt and then Cape Town, South Africa. Alice, however, decided to remain in Athens with her sister-in-law, Princess Nicholas of Greece. She devoted herself to helping the local population, as Greece suffered increasing cycles of starvation; she worked for the Red Cross, organized soup kitchens, and traveled to Sweden to help facilitate that country's aid program—the same program that saw the efforts of **Sture Linnér** bring succor to Greece's starving people. Alice also organized shelters for orphaned children.

At first, the Nazi authorities anticipated that Alice would be pro-German, given that her four daughters were married to German princes. One of her sons-in-law,

Prince Christoph of Hesse, was an SS officer, and another, Berthold, Margrave of Baden, was a German army officer. She did not, however, evince any support for the Nazi occupiers, and she became an object of suspicion when it was learned that her son, Prince Philip, was serving as an officer in Britain's Royal Navy.

Although torn by these family commitments, Alice continued working to undermine the German occupation of Greece, and her efforts extended to aiding Jews, who were hit hard by the Holocaust. During 1943, well over 50,000 Jews were deported from Salonika to Auschwitz, and these measures were accompanied by unanticipated brutality. In September 1943 the Germans occupied Athens, until then under Italian control, and the search for Jews began.

One member of the Greek Jewish community, Haimaki Cohen, a former Member of Parliament who had died before the occupation, was known to the royal family prior to the war. With the occupation his widow, Rachel, and her five children were in danger. When Alice heard of their plight, she immediately offered them shelter, and so, on October 15, 1943, Rachel Cohen and two of her children, Michel and Tilda, found refuge in Alice's apartment.

During the occupation, Alice's behavior inevitably attracted the attention of Nazi authorities. At one point she was even interviewed by the Gestapo, who demanded to know who was living in her apartment. She feigned ignorance and hid behind her deafness, pretending not to follow their line of questioning; with this, the Cohens were able to stay in Alice's residence at the royal palace until Athens was liberated in October 1944.

By this time, her own living conditions had deteriorated. The famine and Nazi occupation had cut deep into Greek society, and Alice had little on which to live. Still, she did her best to ensure that her guests did not go without, despite her own straitened circumstances.

After the war Alice remained in Greece, and in January 1949 she established a nursing order of Greek Orthodox nuns, the Christian Sisterhood of Martha and Mary. This order was a tribute to her aunt, Grand Duchess Elizabeth Fyodorovna of Russia, and their spiritual discussion way back in 1909.

Alice left Greece in 1967. Her daughter-in-law, Britain's Queen Elizabeth II, invited her to live permanently at Buckingham Palace, London, where she died on December 5, 1969. One of her last wishes was to be buried at the Convent of St. Mary Magdalene in Jerusalem, and on August 3, 1988, her remains were accordingly transferred to a crypt below the convent.

In 1993 Yad Vashem acknowledged Alice's wartime actions by recognizing her as one of the Righteous among the Nations. On October 31, 1994, her surviving children, Prince Philip and Princess Sophie of Greece and Denmark, traveled to Jerusalem and planted a tree in her honor at Yad Vashem. In accepting the award, Philip said that his mother was a person "with deep religious faith" who would have considered the need to help the Cohen family as "a totally human action to fellow human beings in distress." His view was endorsed by Jacques Cohen, one of

Rachel's sons. When he had earlier tried to thank Alice, her response was that she only did what she believed to be her duty as a human being.

Altman, Tova (Tosia) (1918–1943)

Tova (Tosia) Altman was an underground leader in the Warsaw Ghetto, where she was a member of the Hashomer Hatzair youth group working alongside **Mordecai Anielewicz** in the Żydowska Organizacja Bojowa (Jewish Combat Organization, or ŻOB) during the Warsaw Ghetto Uprising of 1943.

Born on August 24, 1918, to Anka (Manya) and Gustav (Gutkind) Altman in Lipno, Poland, she was raised in Włocławek, where her father was a watchmaker. At the age of 11, Altman joined the local chapter of Hashomer Hatzair; at 16, she was chosen to represent the movement at its Fourth World Convention, and eventually she became a member of the organization's central leadership in Warsaw. In 1938 she joined the *hachshara* (training) kibbutz at Częstochowa but was soon placed in charge of youth education, postponing her *aliyah*, or migration to Palestine. On August 30, 1939, she was appointed to the Bet (i.e., Secondary) Leadership, a core group of young women who would serve as a substitute governance cohort during an emergency.

With the outbreak of war in September 1939 Altman and several others left for eastern Poland, and she made her way to Rovno. With the midmonth entry of the Soviet army into Poland, the leadership of Hashomer Hatzair decided to relocate to Vilna (Vilnius), where they were able to set up a central headquarters.

The German invasion of the Soviet Union in June 1941 considerably reduced communication opportunities between Warsaw and Vilna. With this development, the Warsaw leadership of Hashomer Hatzair became responsible for the movement across Poland. As reports of the systematic slaughter of Jews throughout the country began to arrive, Altman, then in Warsaw, returned to Vilna, arriving on December 24, 1941. Discussing the situation with local members of Hashomer Hatzair, she reported on the depressing conditions in the Warsaw Ghetto and then sought permission to return to Warsaw in order to work with those remaining.

She thus became the first senior member of the central leadership to return to occupied Warsaw, and upon her arrival she began shaping the movement's different branches for resistance activities. During her travels to many different cities, made easier by her blonde hair and fluent Polish, Altman encouraged young people to become involved in a range of resistance activities. To ease her travel and stay ahead of antisemitic Polish informers, she operated from forged and outdated identity papers.

She then returned once again to Vilna, where she confirmed the rumors of mass killings of Jews in the East, and then visited several cities in eastern Poland before returning to Warsaw. Here, she reiterated the message that Jews all over Poland were being methodically murdered and that the storm would soon reach Warsaw. The warning was difficult to accept, but continual reports gathered independently about the death camps reinforced it.

In July 1942, after the first wave of Jews was deported to Treblinka, the ŻOB was formed. Altman was sent outside the ghetto to consult with members of the Polish underground. The two main underground organizations, the Armia Krajowa (Home Army, or AK) and the communist Armia Ludowa (People's Army, or AL), provided minimal direct support for the ghetto, though Altman and others managed to bring in such crucial armaments as hand grenades and small arms.

Altman continued her travels to other ghettos as an emissary of the ŻOB and was sometimes able to save young men and women from the deportations. In Kraków, for example, she met up with two underground groups, Hechalutz Halohem, led by Aharon Liebeskind, and Iskra, led by Zvi Hersch Bauminger, both of which were effective contributors to the Jewish fighting effort in the Kraków ghetto.

Back in Warsaw, Altman was involved in the ghetto's first armed resistance after the Germans recommenced deportations on January 18, 1943. A party of fighters attacked the Nazis; in the chaos, several Jews were killed and others, including Altman, were captured and taken to the *Umschlagplatz* (collection point for deportation). She managed to escape with the aid of a Jewish ghetto policeman acting on behalf of Hashomer Hatzair.

Placed in charge of maintaining contact with ŻOB members outside the ghetto, she spent a large part of her time on the Aryan side, but always prepared to fight, she returned whenever she heard of an impending roundup.

On April 18, 1943, the final Nazi deportation in Warsaw was launched, and the revolt erupted. Altman relayed messages and information to the ŻOB leaders, reporting by phone to **Yitzhak Zuckerman**. When Anielewicz moved his command structure to a bunker at Miła 18, Altman served as a liaison between him and the other leaders scattered elsewhere. The ghetto was by this stage in flames, so she went out on missions each night to rescue those who were known to be wounded or burned.

As the fighting continued, the fires made the struggle more difficult. When the Nazi forces closed in on Miła 18 and located the bunker, they pumped in gas to compel the fighters to surrender. On May 8, 1943, Anielewicz and most of those with him took their own lives rather than capitulate. Altman was among the tiny group of survivors who managed to get out just in time.

Suffering head and leg wounds, she left the ghetto on May 10, 1943, via the sewers, to the Lomianki Forest. She was found by **Zivia Lubetkin** and **Marek Edelman**, who took her to the Aryan side, where she was hidden in the attic of a celluloid factory. On May 24, 1943, a fire broke out in the factory; Altman, badly burned, was picked up by the Polish police and handed over to the Germans. They, in turn, transferred her to a hospital, where she was cruelly interrogated. She died, untreated, on May 26, 1943—one of the first to resist the Nazis and one of the last to leave the Warsaw Ghetto.

Andreas-Friedrich, Ruth (1901–1977)

Ruth Andreas-Friedrich was a member of an informal Berlin resistance group composed of journalists, doctors, and other professionals.

Born in Berlin on September 23, 1901, she belonged as a girl to the Wandervogel movement, a youth association established in 1896. As a young adult she trained to be a social worker and completed her training in 1922. Both during and after this time, she also wrote reviews and feature articles for several newspapers. In 1924 she married Otto A. Friedrich, with whom she had a daughter, Karin. The couple were later divorced, after which she lived with the conductor Leo Borchard.

Once the Nazis came to power in 1933, Andreas-Friedrich and Borchard founded a resistance group codenamed "Uncle Emil," which, especially during the war years, helped to hide and support Jews who were—increasingly as the Third Reich intensified its antisemitic measures—living underground. The network also ensured that they were supplied with food and, where possible, furnished with false papers. Among the contacts they made was a well-known Jewish forger, Ludwig Lichtwitz, a specialist in the creation of false identity papers. In addition, Uncle Emil gave refuge to political activists and others who were persecuted by the Nazis, in addition to posting anti-Nazi notices and painting slogans on building facades. Throughout this time Andreas-Friedrich continued to work as a journalist and writer in Berlin.

In addition to producing counterfeit identity papers, the couple also worked the black market. In this way they were able to feed and clothe the Jews and other "illegals," whom they saw as their responsibility; at the same time, they moved carefully through Berlin society as regular citizens, surviving Allied bombing raids and avoiding the Gestapo. They would intercede with the authorities when it seemed possible to obtain a fair hearing, and at night they would listen clandestinely to BBC radio.

Much of what is known of Andreas-Friedrich's efforts to rescue Jews was related in a detailed diary she kept before and throughout the war years, published in English in 1947 as *Berlin Underground, 1938–1945*. In the book's foreword we learn something of her motives in writing it, essentially to show that not all Germans during the Third Reich were Nazis, and that some, indeed, did fight back by the simple expedient of saying "no." To a large degree, this also explains her efforts on behalf of Berlin's Jews; they were, as she saw them, such an integral part of German society that there was genuine injustice in their persecution. For her, they were Germans, no better or worse than other Germans. That they were Jewish as well was immaterial to their condition in society.

The diary offers a vivid portrait not only of life in Berlin but also of the attempts Andreas-Friedrich made to ease the lot of those whom Nazi ideology had made less fortunate than she was. She showed the stifling nature of life under the Nazis and just how difficult it was to offer any sort of alternatives. Indeed, while Uncle Emil engaged in activities that were certainly illegal, the movement was far from violent or aggressive; as she showed, their most assertive act was probably a theft from a police station during an air raid. In addition, she provided an excellent picture of what life was like during the Allied air offensives from 1943 through the end of the war and of the nightmare landscape that Berlin became.

Her story continues in a second set of diaries dealing with the aftermath of the war, *Battleground Berlin: Diaries, 1945–1948* (1962). In 1948 she moved to Munich, where she married Walter Seitz, the director of the Munich University Polyclinic. He had also been a member of the Uncle Emil network.

On September 17, 1977, Andreas-Friedrich committed suicide in Munich. In 2002, for her efforts to save Jewish lives during the Holocaust, she was posthumously recognized by Yad Vashem as one of the Righteous among the Nations.

Anger, Per (1913–2002)

Per Anger was a Swedish diplomat stationed in Budapest at the time of the Holocaust, working closely with **Raoul Wallenberg** to save Jewish lives through the provision of visas for Sweden.

Born in Göteborg on December 7, 1913, he studied law at Stockholm and Uppsala Universities, and after graduating in November 1939 underwent a period of compulsory military training. In January 1940 he began his diplomatic career at the Swedish embassy in Berlin; commencing in the trade department, he moved briefly into military intelligence.

In June 1941 Anger returned to Stockholm and resumed his work in foreign trade relations, with a special focus on Hungary. On June 12, 1942, he was appointed second secretary at the Swedish legation in Budapest, beginning his duties there on November 26. The legation was small; the minister was Carl Ivan Danielsson, and although Anger held the formal rank of second secretary he was, de facto, first secretary. The legation included four other members, together with the Swedish Red Cross representative, **Valdemar Langlet**. So long as Swedish neutrality was respected and relations between Sweden and Hungary remained friendly, the posting to Budapest seemed like a straightforward mission.

On March 19, 1944, Nazi Germany invaded Hungary, and everything changed irreparably. Anger had already witnessed Nazi Germany's persecution of the Jews while stationed in Berlin, but after the German occupation of Hungary it took practically no time at all before he became involved in rescue efforts on behalf of Hungary's Jews. At the beginning Anger, along with the others in the legation, had no idea what was going to happen. Within days, however, they saw that routine trade matters would have to be put aside, and the whole legation agreed to concentrate on one thing only—the saving of human lives.

Anger's idea was to issue Swedish provisional passports to protect Jews from internment and deportation. The provisional passport was actually a travel document given to Swedish citizens who had lost their formal documents, and so its legality for Hungarian Jews was extremely dubious. The Hungarian government, however, agreed to recognize bearers as Swedish citizens. With his initiative approved, all Anger needed was an agreement from the Swedish authorities to proceed. His superior, Carl Ivan Danielsson, gave his approval but put responsibility on Anger's shoulders; fortunately, the Swedish Foreign Ministry agreed that the passports could be used, and an initial allocation of 700 was issued. The Hungarian authorities allowed that passport holders would be respected as Swedish citizens but would need to wear the yellow Star of David.

Per Anger, a Swedish diplomat posted to Budapest, Hungary, poses on the roof of the Swedish legation in 1944. He was instrumental in helping to save Jews by granting provisional passports identifying the bearers as Swedish citizens. This initiative was later extended by Raoul Wallenberg, leading to protection for tens of thousands of Jews. (United States Holocaust Memorial Museum, courtesy of Eric Saul)

As word spread among the Jews of Budapest that the passports were available, the number of people seeking a Swedish refuge increased dramatically, and within days hundreds began lining up outside the Swedish legation.

On July 9, 1944, Raoul Wallenberg arrived in Budapest from Sweden with the singular task of finding ways to help Jews. He immediately extended Anger's initiative, introducing a "protective pass," or *Schutzpässe*. To impress the Germans he created a document printed in the Swedish colors of yellow and blue, embossed with the Swedish "Three Crowns" symbol, together with the minister's signature and an array of seals and stamps. The result radiated legitimacy. Although it, like Anger's original provisional passport, was far from legal, it appeared real and was accepted by both Germans and Hungarians.

For Anger, Wallenberg's arrival was a boon. He watched as Wallenberg established a network of safe houses throughout the city, accompanied by welfare and health care facilities. Helpers came forth to assist in the provision of clothing, meals, and medicine. While Wallenberg effectively took over the rescue operation from the moment he arrived, he had much on which to build owing to Anger's initial efforts, and the two men worked together closely. With Wallenberg in charge, Anger went to Stockholm in August 1944 to request further assistance, after which several new officers were sent.

Returning to Budapest, Anger would appear anywhere there was a need for a Swedish presence. At times he would receive a call from Wallenberg asking him to save people from being deported at a train station, or toward the end of the war when the Nazis organized death marches, he and Wallenberg would drive out to meet the prisoners and provide them with sustenance, succor, and *Schutzpässe*, getting them out of the line to safety. They were not alone: diplomats from many other neutral countries did the same thing, complementing the Swedes in their lifesaving work.

As Soviet troops encircled Budapest in November 1944, the Swedish government offered its representatives the opportunity to evacuate, but Anger and Wallenberg, together with several others, opted to remain. In January 1945 the members of the Swedish legation were taken into custody by Soviet troops and detained until orders arrived from Moscow allowing them to return home. Anger was released three months later, and he and the rest of the Swedish legation, except Wallenberg, arrived in Stockholm on April 18, 1945. The last time Anger saw Wallenberg was January 10, 1945; on January 17, 1945, he was taken away by Soviet forces, never to be seen in public again.

After the war Anger continued his diplomatic career, serving in numerous posts including Egypt, Ethiopia, France, Austria, and the United States. He later became ambassador to Australia, Canada, and the Bahamas, but he never stopped searching for Wallenberg, at one point even meeting with Soviet premier Mikhail Gorbachev in the hope of prompting an official and unbiased inquiry. None was forthcoming.

Anger's efforts on behalf of Jews in Budapest during the Holocaust contributed to saving the lives of an estimated 20,000 Jews. In acknowledgment for his efforts, he received a number of awards after his retirement. On April 28, 1981, he was recognized by Yad Vashem as one of the Righteous among the Nations, and in 2000 he received honorary Israeli citizenship. In November 1995 he was honored with the Hungarian Republic's Order of Merit, and in April 2002 Sweden awarded him the nation's highest civilian award, the *Illis Quorum Meruere Labores* (For Those Whose Labors Have Deserved It).

Anger died in Stockholm on August 25, 2002, after suffering a stroke.

Anielewicz, Mordecai (1919–1943)

Mordecai Anielewicz was the leader of the 1943 Warsaw Ghetto Uprising. Born into a working-class Jewish family in Wyszków, Poland, in 1919, he attended a Hebrew high school in Warsaw and was briefly a member of *Betar*, a Zionist youth organization that advocated Jewish self-defense. At the time of the German invasion of Poland on September 1, 1939, he was a leading member of the Warsaw branch of Hashomer Hatzair, a socialist-Zionist youth movement.

On September 7, 1939, Anielewicz fled Warsaw with some fellow members of Hashomer Hatzair and headed east to stay ahead of the German advance. Moving toward Palestine in order to establish an escape route for other young Zionists, he was caught by the Soviet Army at the Romanian border and imprisoned. After release, he went to Vilna (Vilnius), which had just been absorbed into the Soviet Union. The "Jerusalem of Lithuania" was at that time a destination for many Jewish refugees.

By the time Anielewicz returned to Warsaw in January 1940 with his girlfriend, Mira Fuchrer, the Nazis had established ghettos in various parts of Poland. In Warsaw, by the end of November 1939, they had ordered the establishment of a 24-member Jewish Council, or Judenrat, under the leadership of an engineer named Adam Czerniaków. The construction of a wall around the ghetto started on April 1, 1940, and the Germans closed it to the outside world on November 16, 1940. Many Jews then began to die of starvation and disease as conditions worsened.

Inspired to action by **Rachel Zilberberg**, a friend of Mira Fuchrer, Anielewicz became more active in Hashomer Hatzair and set out to transform it into a resistance movement. He established a clandestine ghetto newspaper, *Neged Hazerem* (*Against the Stream*), and organized Hashomer Hatzair into armed resistance cells.

By October 1940 the SS was deporting Jews from the ghetto, and Anielewicz stepped up his efforts against the Nazis. He established contact with the Polish government-in-exile in London, which ordered him to ally with Polish underground forces outside the ghetto; logistics, however, prevented him from doing so. Then, during the spring of 1942, he helped establish a short-lived, unified antifascist group in the ghetto that was dispersed by the arrest of its communist members.

On July 22, 1942, the Nazis began mass deportation of Jews from the Warsaw Ghetto to the extermination camp at Treblinka, 50 miles northeast of Warsaw. More than 5,000 Jews were deported each day until September 1942. During this time, Anielewicz was in southwest Poland on a mission to organize other resistance cells. He returned to Warsaw to reinvigorate armed resistance but found the ghetto devastated by the deportations that had taken place while he was away. Some 265,000 of the ghetto's 330,000 Jews had already been deported.

The members of the Judenrat disapproved of armed resistance for fear of provoking an even more overwhelming German response. In defiance of their warnings, however, Anielewicz, together with another Jewish youth leader, **Yitzhak Zuckerman**, went ahead and established the Jewish Combat Organization (Żydowska Organizacja Bojowa, or ŻOB), with a fundamental aim to resist continued Nazi deportations. In November 1942 Anielewicz became commander in chief of the ŻOB and made immediate contact with the Polish government in London. The ŻOB then officially became part of, and subordinated its activities to, the High Command of the Polish Home Army (Armia Krajowa), which in turn began providing weapons and some rudimentary training.

In early January 1943 Reichsführer-SS Heinrich Himmler visited the Warsaw Ghetto and ordered another deportation, which took place unannounced on January 18. In response, the ŻOB and several other small fighting groups began uncoordinated guerrilla warfare. Anielewicz developed a plan in which his fighters obeyed the deportation orders until they reached a certain part of the ghetto, where they received a signal to attack. Under such circumstances, the Nazis halted the deportation four days later.

This small victory brought only a brief respite. The resistance groups planned and prepared for further combat by procuring arms and building bunkers, and Anielewicz continued to command underground operations. In April 1943 Himmler ordered that the Warsaw Ghetto be cleared of all Jews before Adolf Hitler's birthday on April 20; accordingly, on April 19—the first day of Passover—no fewer than 2,000 Nazi soldiers began the final deportation.

This was the moment for resistance. Approximately 1,500 Jews, armed with 2 machine guns, 15 rifles, and some handguns, hand grenades, and Molotov cocktails, began the attack. The resisters achieved a remarkable victory on the first day, inflicting Nazi losses and forcing a retreat, which left behind weapons that could be retrieved and used again. On the second day, the Nazis returned to drive the fighters from their hideouts with gas, smoke bombs, and flame throwers. The next day they used small patrols for localized street fighting. Although the Jewish resistance was outnumbered and outgunned, the fighters refused to surrender, leading the Germans to develop new tactics. They started burning the ghetto down, block by block, and flooded the sewers so that there could be no refuge or hiding place. After these first few days, Anielewicz moved from the streets to a new headquarters for the ŻOB, deep underground at Miła 18.

After a four-week battle in which the Nazis shelled, bombed, and systematically burned down the ghetto—deporting and killing the remainder of the approximately 60,000 Jews—on May 8 they captured and gassed the ŻOB's headquarters at Miła 18. Anielewicz, Mira Fuchrer, Rachel Zilberberg, and many of the other resisters died. So far as could be ascertained, most had committed suicide to avoid capture. On May 16, 1943, SS General Jürgen Stroop, the Nazi commander, reported that "the former Jewish quarter of Warsaw is no more," and he wrote a 75-page illustrated report that was then bound in black leather and presented to Hitler. The Nazis deported and executed the remaining Jews, with perhaps only about 100 surviving the final assault on the ghetto.

Anielewicz's last communication was a letter to Zuckerman, who had been sent outside in a desperate attempt to attract support from non-Jewish Poles. He wrote: "The main thing is that the dream of my life has come true. I have had the fortune to set my eyes upon Jewish defense in the ghetto in all its greatness." Anielewicz's body was never found; it is generally believed that the Nazis burned it along with all the other Jewish dead. In death, as in life, Mordecai Anielewicz became a symbol of Jewish resistance and is today considered one of the great heroes of Jewish history.

Atlas, Icheskel (1910–1942)

Dr. Icheskel Atlas was a physician who led Jewish partisans to fight the Nazis in eastern Poland, in what later became Belarus.

Born in Rawa Mazowiecka in 1910, he studied medicine in France and Italy. When war began on September 1, 1939, he and his parents were living in Kozłowszczyzna, a small town of no more than 400 Jews in far eastern Poland. Most residents were unassimilated, with only a tiny percentage considering themselves to be Polish. After the Soviet invasion of Poland on September 17, 1939, the Atlas family came under Soviet occupation.

Operation Barbarossa, the Nazi invasion of the Soviet Union, took place on June 22, 1941, and by the end of July the entire region was taken over by the Nazis. In the immediate aftermath of the combat troops came the Einsatzgruppen (special action squads), with the task of wiping out all Jews and communists (which, for the Nazis, equated to the same thing). A small ghetto was soon established.

On November 24, 1941, in a forest just south of Kozłowszczyzna, a group of more than 700 Jews were shot in a mass killing, their bodies buried in six pits that had been dug earlier. Atlas's parents and sister were murdered in this massacre. Having survived, and with no family or community ties, he offered his medical skills to Soviet partisans, basing himself in the village of Wielka Wola. A much larger ghetto massacre on the night of July 24, 1942, saw the Jews of the community of Dereczyn wiped out, with between 3,000 and 4,000 murdered. The survivors, numbering about 250, managed to escape into the forest just before the killing began.

Atlas informed his Soviet commanders that he intended to form an all-Jewish unit to give the Dereczyn survivors an opportunity to exact vengeance on behalf of their murdered families. There was, however, an existing partisan group in the area, composed of Soviet and Polish soldiers commanded by Pavel Bulak and Boris Bulat. Bulak, in particular, scoffed at the idea of a Jewish fighting unit; Jews, in his opinion, did not make good fighters. In addition, his preference was that Atlas be retained for the troops as a medical doctor.

Atlas insisted, and so, as a test, Bulak sent the Jews out on an arms raid. He anticipated a disaster. On August 10, 1942, Atlas attacked the Germans at Dereczyn, watched carefully by Bulak and Bulat. He led a force of 300 partisans (one-third of them Jewish) in an armed assault on the German garrison, taking control of the town, capturing 44 Germans, and killing another 20 during the battle. He then ordered the 44 German prisoners to stand on top of the mass grave outside Dereczyn, where they were lined up and executed. He was reputed to have told his unit after the action, "Our struggle only began with the defeat of the Germans at Dereczyn. Your lives came to an end in the slaughter of the 24th of July. Every additional day of life is not yours, but belongs to your murdered families. You must avenge them."

When the unit returned successfully, Bulak had little alternative but to recognize the potential and legitimacy of a Jewish unit under Atlas's command, and accordingly he authorized its formation. Over the next few months the Atlas unit engaged in actions against German forces at Kozłowszczyzna in September and at Ruda Jaworska in October. Other operations included blowing up a train on the Lida-Grodno line, burning a strategic bridge on the Niemen River, and confronting the Germans in combat on September 15, 1942. The Atlas unit also captured a German plane that made a forced landing in the area on October 2, 1942.

Most Jews in the Atlas unit came from the area in and around Dereczyn. Eventually they numbered some 120 members and included Israel Bogdush, Samuel Bornstein, Chaim Joshua Lipshovitz, Gershon Lipshovitz, and Taibe Lipshovitz. One of those about whom we have details was Eliyahu Lifshovitz Elik, who served as deputy commander. He was a native of Dereczyn. Born on January 1, 1914, Elik studied in a Zionist Hebrew Tarbut school and later served in the Polish army. He was one of those who escaped the massacre in the Dereczyn ghetto and then helped Atlas to organize the partisan unit. When the area was liberated by the Soviet army in 1944 he enlisted as a regular soldier and followed the Nazi retreat all the way back into Germany. Awarded the War of the Homeland medal (First Class), he was murdered by antisemitic Poles on June 1, 1945.

Dr. Icheskel Atlas was wounded in a battle at Wielka Wola—the same village where he first found refuge after the Dereczyn massacre—and died from his wounds in December 1942.

B

Bachner, Wilhelm (1912–1991)

Wilhelm Bachner was born in Bielsko, Poland, on September 17, 1912. His father, Heinrich, who came from Chrzanów, a small village near Kraków, moved in 1905 to Bielsko, where he met and married Helene Buchfuehrer, who worked as a bookkeeper. Later, Wilhelm Bachner described his upbringing (along with that of his two sisters and brother) as being conservative and traditionally Jewish. In this environment, he grew up with German as his first language and Polish his second. As part of his religious education, he also learned and spoke Hebrew.

In June 1931 he went to Brno, Czechoslovakia, to study engineering and in June 1938 graduated with the equivalent of a master's degree. As an observant Jew he faced some obstacles, which he was able to overcome in the relatively liberal climate of interwar Czechoslovakia. For example, as one who could not write on the Jewish Sabbath, his professors permitted him to take oral examinations on Saturdays instead.

In February 1939, after a short stay back in Bielsko, Bachner moved to Warsaw, where in October 1939 he married a local Jewish girl, Cesia Diamant. All members of her family were to be murdered during the Holocaust. After the Nazis invaded Poland in September 1939 the Bachners moved into the Warsaw Ghetto, which was established formally in October 1940.

As a fluent speaker of German, and with an engineering degree from a German-speaking university, Bachner managed to negotiate freely with the Nazis, sometimes leaving the ghetto and camouflaging himself as a Pole or ethnic German. Perhaps equally importantly, he did not "look" Jewish, in accordance with the Nazi racial stereotype. In 1941 this clandestine life became more entrenched as he escaped the ghetto and, still posing as a non-Jew, became a supervisor with a German architectural firm. In this way, Bachner was able to fight against the Nazi occupation in a very unique manner.

Obtaining a pass giving him unrestricted access to the ghetto as an Aryan, he then "employed" some 50 Jewish workers and supplied them with false identity papers and work permits. Most (though not all) of these workers were put to manual labor in the construction of road-and-rail building projects. Utilizing his position, he also spirited some of them out of the ghetto and into hiding. Bachner's forceful character certainly helped to maintain the deception. Having been raised in a German environment provided an excellent cover during his interactions with the Nazis, as it enabled him to bluff his way into their confidence. Further, the development of a solid relationship with a Nazi officer, Oberleutnant Hans Gregor, assisted him in buttressing the deception.

His efforts at masquerade were, however, often fraught with danger. He knew he was taking risks and that he could be exposed any minute. At one point, in fact, a group of suspicious SS men stormed into his office and accused him of hiding Jews. Through bluff and a good measure of audacity he talked them down, however, and they left.

Survival sometimes means becoming aligned with what one hates, and in this regard the case of Wilhelm Bachner might be compared with that of the anti-Nazi SS officer **Kurt Gerstein**, who fought to destroy the evils of Nazism but in doing so became more and more enmeshed in its actions. The closer Bachner got to the Nazis in order to save Jewish lives, the more he appeared to be a German pro-Nazi collaborator. Thus, in what would have been an irony of the first magnitude, Bachner was almost shot by American soldiers after the Nazis surrendered in the spring of 1945.

After the war, Bachner and his wife sought to escape a Poland that was now communist—and in which antisemitism still existed. In 1951 they migrated to the United States, where they settled in California and made new lives for themselves in San Francisco.

In San Francisco they were contacted by Humboldt State University professor of psychology Samuel P. Oliner, who was project director of that institution's Altruistic Personality and Pro-Social Behavior Institute. At first, Oliner was interested in Bachner as a rescued Jew, but as his story came to light through interviews conducted in 1983, Oliner realized that there was much more to his subject than first anticipated. Taking the story further, Oliner and a colleague from Humboldt, Kathleen Lee, extended their range of interviews to include relatives and those who were rescued through Bachner's efforts. They also conducted in-depth documentary research. The result was the book *Who Shall Live: The Wilhelm Bachner Story* (1996), which rescued from obscurity the man who many dubbed the "Jewish **Schindler**."

Bachner's extraordinary story saw him not only survive the Holocaust but also help his wife and his father escape the Warsaw Ghetto and outlive the Nazis. His mother, brother, and sister, however, were murdered. That he managed to save several dozen other Jews was, to say the least, remarkable. Bachner's example is one of quiet resistance to the Nazi regime, to be highlighted and remembered.

Baeck, Leo (1873–1956)

Rabbi Leo Baeck was the undisputed spiritual leader of German Jewry during the years of the Third Reich, providing hope where little was left and standing up to the Nazis through his efforts at maintaining a Jewish communal existence at the time it was under greatest threat.

He was born on May 23, 1873, in Lissa (Leszno), Prussia, the son of Rabbi Samuel Baeck. After attending the conservative Jewish Theological Seminary in Breslau (Wrocław) from 1894, he moved to Berlin to study at the more liberal Lehranstalt für die Wissenschaft des Judentums (School of Jewish Studies) in Berlin. By 1897 he had secured his first post as rabbi in Oppeln (Opole). Here, in 1905, he published *Das Wesen des Judentums* (*The Essence of Judaism*), attracting notice as an up-and-coming rabbi and thinker. The book argued strongly for the continued relevance of Judaism in a changing world and showed Baeck to be a leader for the Jewish people in modern times. In 1912 he went to Berlin, where he worked as a rabbi at the Fasanenstrasse synagogue and taught at the Hochschule für die Wissenschaft des Judentums (Higher Institute for Jewish Studies).

A product of his time and culture, Baeck joined the German army in World War I and served as a Jewish chaplain. In 1918 he returned to Berlin and worked at the Prussian Ministry of Culture as a specialist in Jewish Affairs and Hebrew, while maintaining his pulpit and teaching duties. In 1922 he became president of the Union of German Rabbis (Allgemeiner Deutscher Rabbinerverband) and in 1924 was elected president of the German B'nai B'rith Order.

When the Nazis came to power in 1933 Baeck was elected president of the Reichsvertretung der deutschen Juden (Reich Representation of German Jews), an umbrella organization of German-Jewish groups established in September 1933 to advance the interests of German Jewry under the new Nazi regime. The organization was forced to change its name to the Reichsverband der Juden in Deutschland (Reich Association of Jews in Germany) in 1935 to reflect the Nazi view that there were no "German Jews" but only "Jews in Germany." As president, Baeck saw his role as being one of maintaining the morale of German Jews under the ever-tightening restrictions of the Nazi regime, working to mitigate the effects of antisemitic discrimination and persecution.

On the night of November 9–10, this persecution accelerated with the so-called *Kristallnacht*, or "Night of Broken Glass." Jewish businesses and synagogues throughout Germany, including Baeck's Fasanenstrasse synagogue, were burned and looted. While the Reichsverband under Baeck facilitated a good deal of Jewish emigration from Germany, he refused to leave Germany or his community despite numerous offers of help to do so. He famously was reported to say that he would only leave Germany when he was the last Jew remaining there.

In the aftermath of the pogrom, the Nazis reconfigured Jewish communal arrangements and renamed the organization the Reichsvereinigung der Juden in Deutschland (National Association of Jews in Germany). Baeck remained president until it was forcibly disbanded in 1943.

On January 27, 1943, aged 70, he was deported, along with his family, to the Terezín (Teresienstadt) concentration camp in Czechoslovakia. At Terezín Baeck

Rabbi Leo Baeck, the spiritual leader of German Jewry throughout the years of the Third Reich. He refused to leave Germany or his Berlin community despite many opportunities to do so. Deported to Theresienstadt in 1943, he survived the war and moved to London, where he became a leading member of the Jewish community in Britain. (United States Holocaust Memorial Museum, courtesy of Michael Brodnitz)

became head of the Jewish Council (Judenrat), a position that conferred certain privileges, such as exemption for himself and his family from deportation to "the East." He had slightly better accommodations and healthier food, and could even receive mail, and from this position he was able to provide leadership to those around him. He helped others, gave lectures on philosophy and religion, participated in interfaith dialogue between Jews and Christians of Jewish origin, continued teaching among the youth, and refused to lose his sense of self or dignity. All these measures served to provide those around him with hope and an awareness of self-worth.

While in the camp he also managed to begin a manuscript that would later become his second book, *Dieses Volk: Jüdische Existenz* (*This People Israel: The Meaning of Jewish Existence*).

Although elderly and weakened by his experiences in the concentration camp, Leo Baeck outlasted the Holocaust. Few other members of his family did, with none of his four sisters surviving Terezín by the time the Red Army liberated the camp in May 1945.

After the war, Rabbi Baeck moved to London, where he became president of the North Western Reform Synagogue. He was invited to teach at Hebrew Union College in Cincinnati, Ohio, and became chair of the World Union for Progressive Judaism. In 1955 an institute to preserve the history of German-Jewish culture was established in Jerusalem. Among those behind the initiative were Hannah Arendt, Martin Buber, **Robert Weltsch**, and Gershom Scholem. The resulting Leo Baeck Institute named him as its first president, and it subsequently became an international organization, with Leo Baeck Institutes in New York and London. Also situated in London is the Reform/Progressive rabbinical seminary Leo Baeck College.

Baeck died in London on November 2, 1956, universally recognized as one of the great Jewish leaders of the twentieth century.

Bartali, Gino (1914–2000)

Gino Bartali was an Italian cycling champion who won two Tour de France titles and helped save more than 800 Jews during the Holocaust.

Born in Florence in 1914, Bartali was a devout Catholic whose parents were married by Cardinal **Elia Dalla Costa**. In 1936 and 1937 Bartali won the Giro d'Italia, followed in 1938 with the Tour de France. Thus, before the war Bartali was one of Italy's biggest sports stars and the hero of his nation. Remarkably, he also won the 1946 Giro and his second Tour de France in 1948, ten years after the first.

Following Italy's capitulation on September 3, 1943, and Germany's subsequent occupation, the force of the Holocaust came to bear fully against Italy's Jews. Although the country had a long history of tolerance for its Jews, who formed one of the most assimilated populations in Europe, the Nazi assault built upon Benito Mussolini's antisemitic laws of 1938. These laws prevented Jews from working in government or the education sector, forbade intermarriage between Jews and other Italians, and removed Jews from positions in the media, among other restrictions. By the end of World War II some 7,680 Italian Jews had lost their lives as a result of the Holocaust, with many of those killed in Auschwitz.

Gino Bartali would come to play an important role in the rescue of Jews during this time. When the Germans began the deportations, Archbishop Dalla Costa recruited Bartali into a secret network he was then establishing with the spiritual leader of Florence's Jews, Rabbi Nathan Cassuto, who would be deported and killed by the Nazis in November 1943. The system of rescue involved convents, monasteries, and members of the general public hiding Jews. It ultimately was responsible for saving hundreds of Italian and refugee Jews from territories previously under Italian control, mostly in France and Yugoslavia.

Bartali's role was to act as a courier for the network, hiding forged documents and papers in his bicycle and transporting them between cities. He would do so by concealing them in the seat of his bike, the handlebars, and the bicycle frame. These counterfeit papers, when delivered to their intended recipients, saved many lives. Given an address, Bartali would ride to Jews in hiding and deliver the documents, which often also contained exit visas allowing their recipients to avoid deportation to the death camps. Under the guise of long-distance training, he would ride hundreds of miles across Tuscany and northern Italy to make his deliveries. Italian Fascists, knowing who he was, let him pass without further ado; when he encountered Germans, he asked that his bike not be touched owing to sophisticated calibrations designed to assist him in achieving maximum speed. They always left him alone.

While his many adventures led to the salvation of hundreds of Jews, it was inevitable that Bartali would eventually be identified and forced into hiding. When this happened, he took refuge in a cellar in the town of Città di Castello in Umbria.

Here he hid with a Jewish family, the Goldenbergs, with whom he lived until the liberation of Florence in 1944.

After the war, Bartali never spoke about his exploits in resisting the Nazis by saving Jewish lives, nor did he ask for any kind of reward for what he had done, believing that a person should not perform acts of goodness for a reward. He preferred that people remember him for his performances as a cyclist, rather than for anything he did during the war.

It was, in fact, his son Andrea who led the campaign to have his father recognized. After representations, Yad Vashem began an investigation into this modest hero of the Holocaust. The organization sought testimony through the Italian Jewish monthly *Pagine Ebraica*, and an important contributor came forth in the person of Giorgio Goldenberg, a member of the same family with whom Bartali had hidden in the cellar prior to the liberation.

The result saw an emotional acknowledgment of Bartali at a ceremony in Jerusalem on October 10, 2013. The previous month, Yad Vashem honored him as one of the Righteous among the Nations. Attending the ceremony were Andrea Bartali and Giorgio Goldenberg, representing his family and the survivors whose lives Bartali had secured seven decades before.

Baum, Herbert (1912–1942)

Herbert Baum and his wife, Marianne, founded, at the end of summer 1937, an anti-Nazi resistance group in Germany.

Born in Moschin, eastern Germany, on February 10, 1912, Baum moved with his family to Berlin when he was a baby. Upon leaving school he became an electrician. By 1926 he was an active member in a number of left-wing Jewish youth movements, and in 1931 he joined Germany's Young Communist League. Marianne Cohn, whom he had known since the two of them were young, had joined in 1930. In 1934, after she and Baum were married, they were directed by the Communist party to contact a number of Jewish organizations that Baum had worked with in earlier times. A small circle of friends and acquaintances formed and then grew. Most of them were Jewish, and they met frequently to discuss ways to circumvent Nazi antisemitism. Almost immediately they nominated Baum as their chairman.

By the time of the November 9–10 *Kristallnacht* pogrom, the little group had grown to nearly 100 young Germans, who would attend meetings at various times to discuss their options. After Jewish organizations were banned in 1939 the group grew larger—and, of necessity, more secretive. It retained its leftist and communist identity while recognizing and maintaining its Jewish origin.

In 1940 Baum was drafted into a forced labor unit at the electromotive works of the Siemens-Schuckertwerke, an electrical engineering company based in

Berlin. While there, he engaged in party propaganda, leading to many more recruits from among those at the plant. For some who were communist but not Jewish, the idea of resistance was problematic because of the alliance signed between the Soviet Union and Nazi Germany in August 1939. For the Jews there was little option; they could not afford any political dilemmas.

From 1941 onward, members of Baum's network among the Siemens workers saw that escaping deportation to concentration camps would require mounting some sort of underground resistance while, at the same time, making themselves appear vital to the war effort. Their underground activities at this time focused on the preparation and distribution of anti-Nazi propaganda leaflets rather than physical confrontation.

At the beginning of May 1942 Nazi Germany's minister of propaganda, Joseph Goebbels (who was also the gauleiter of Berlin), organized an enormous exhibition at the Lustgarten, right in the heart of Berlin. This exhibition, entitled "The Soviet Paradise," was intended to dehumanize the Russian enemy and reinforce an anti-Soviet (and, through this, an anti-Jewish) mind-set among the population. Its fundamental goal was to justify the war against the Soviet Union, and well over a million people visited the exhibition.

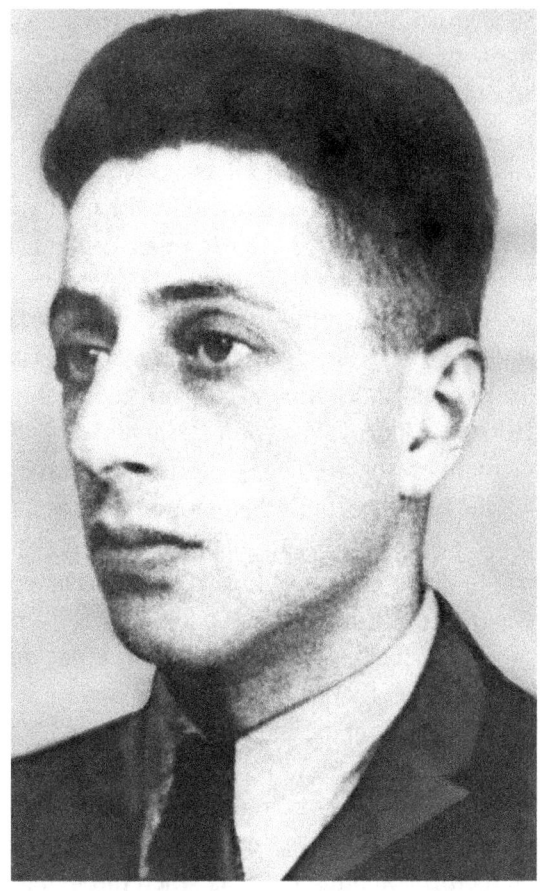

Hebert Baum, leader of a largely Jewish anti-Nazi resistance group in Berlin during the 1930s and early 1940s. Together with his wife, Marianne, and several others, he organized an arson attack against a Nazi propaganda exhibition in Berlin in 1942. Captured, all were subsequently executed; the average age of those in the group was just 22. (Ullstein Bild/Getty Images)

Baum and his circle, recognizing that their actions could always be only symbolic—they could not by themselves topple the Nazi regime—decided to let symbolism confront symbolism. On May 18, 1942, a group of seven Baum members—Herbert and Marianne Baum, Hans Joachim, Gerd Meyer, Sala Kochmann, Suzanne Wesse, and Irene Walther—set a number of fires around the exhibition that were timed to ignite simultaneously. Some members had been cautious about such an action, fearing that Nazi retribution could well see the plan backfire against the Jews of Berlin. Others thought the time was ripe for such an act and that delay would lose the initiative.

Once lit, the fires were quickly extinguished, and within days hundreds of Jewish Berliners, including all seven participants and most of the other members of the Baum group, were arrested by the Gestapo. Marianne and Herbert Baum were arrested on May 22, 1942. He was taken to the Siemens plant and ordered to identify fellow workers who were part of the conspiracy; refusing to reveal anything, he was subsequently tortured mercilessly in Berlin's Moabit prison and died on June 11, 1942. The Gestapo reported his death as a suicide. Marianne Baum was executed in Plötzensee prison on August 18, 1942, along with Joachim Franke, Hildegard Jadamowitz, Heinz Joachim, Sala Kochmann, Hans-Georg Mannaberg, Gerhard Meyer, Werner Steinbrink, and Irene Walther.

Other resisters in the Baum group were caught and tried in succeeding months. Most were executed at Plötzensee on March 4, 1943: Heinz Rotholz, Heinz Birnbaum, Hella Hirsch, Hanni Meyer, Marianne Joachim, Lothar Salinger, Helmut Neumann, Hildegard Löwy, and Siegbert Rotholz. Overall, the deaths of the Baum group members represent a tragic roll call of lost youth and dashed hopes. The average age of those in the group's inner circle was 22; Charlotte Päch, aged 32, was the oldest in the group and nicknamed "Grandma" by the others.

Moreover, not all were Jewish; Franke, Jadamowitz, Mannaberg, and Steinbrink were all non-Jewish communists. Ultimately, of the 32 members of the group who lost their lives, 22 were executed by decapitation, 9 died in death camps, and 1—Herbert Baum himself—was killed through torture. Only 5 members of the Baum group survived the war.

In light of the repercussions of the Baum group's act of resistance to the Holocaust, the question must be asked: was it worth it? The press was forbidden to report on the fire, and no official news was released regarding the Baum group or the fate of its members. Yet the partial destruction of the exhibition at the Lustgarten must have presented something of a shock to Goebbels and the Berlin Nazis. A small but well-organized resistance circle of Jewish communists had challenged a major Nazi propaganda enterprise, in the heart of the German capital, more than nine years after the Nazis had come to power. Little wonder, it might be argued, that the punishments were so overwhelming and devastating. The Baum group, quite simply, rocked the Nazi establishment as few other resistance movements in Germany had up to that time.

Beck, Gad (1923–2012)

Gerhard Beck, born in Berlin in 1923, was a German Jewish homosexual living before and during the Third Reich. He is remembered today as the longest living known male homosexual to survive the Holocaust. Under the Nuremberg Laws, he and his twin sister, Margot, were classified as *mischlinge*, that is, Jews of mixed descent, in that they were the children of a Jewish father and a Protestant mother who had converted to Judaism. Participating in Jewish youth organizations when young, they changed their names to the Hebrew "Gad" and "Miriam" in order to express themselves in a more Jewish way—a form of symbolic resistance to the Nazis.

Beck suffered greatly in his younger years under the Nazi regime. When antisemitism became a part of public education in Germany he was frequently taunted, and his familiar classroom soon became filled with Hitler Youth uniforms. After the "J" stamp was introduced in October 1938, Beck was forced to display a yellow Star of David with that letter on it, singling him out for ridicule among those who had formerly been his classmates. Soon, he was obliged to leave his school and attend a wholly Jewish institution. While he ended up preferring the Jewish school's curriculum (which favored, among other things, foreign languages), he was eventually forced to drop out because his family could no longer afford the private school's much higher fees.

As Beck entered young adulthood and became aware of his homosexuality, he developed a gay lifestyle despite the potential risks this carried under the Third Reich, which had passed harsh anti-gay laws. Homosexuals were persecuted heavily under the Nazis' extension of Paragraph 175, a provision of the German Criminal Code dating from May 15, 1871. In defiance of this law, Beck took his first lover, another Jew, Manfred Lewin; this relationship did not last long, however. The Nazis captured Lewin and his family and then deported them in 1942. In another act of defiance, Beck borrowed a Hitler Youth uniform and gained access to the place where Lewin was being held prior to his deportation, in the hope of saving him. With this ruse, Lewin would in fact have been able to walk out of the holding area with the disguised Beck, but he decided to remain with his family. All the Lewins were later murdered at Auschwitz.

The act of trying to help Lewin propelled Beck to participate in resistance activities against the Nazi regime. He began this in earnest during 1943, when Propaganda Minister Joseph Goebbels sought to declare Berlin free of Jews in time for Adolf Hitler's birthday on April 20. Beck and his father were arrested and held in the former Jewish community building on Berlin's Rosenstrasse, where protests by women outside eventually secured the release of all the other men being held captive.

After this, Beck went underground with Chug Chaluzi (Clan of Pioneers), a Zionist youth group in Berlin dedicated to helping Jews and *mischlinge* escape Germany. The group's activities included educating members in Jewish traditions and religion. Beck's most important underground accomplishments came during his time in Chug Chaluzi, when he and his friends were all actively involved in helping others escape. As a result, Beck spent much of the war dodging the Gestapo, taking huge risks by smuggling rations, money, and clothes to fellow Jews in hiding.

During 1944 Beck became the leader of Chug Chaluzi. The group itself was very small, comprising only about 40 young Jewish boys and girls, with 8 of those, including Beck, making up the inner circle. Their actions helped many Jews flee to safety in Switzerland through the provision of forged papers. The nature of Beck's resistance activities focused more on teaching culture and providing help, such as hiding Jews, enhancing Jewish values, and assisting with escape attempts, rather than on violent acts of retaliation.

His activities came to an end when a Jewish spy working for the Gestapo betrayed Beck and some of those around him, leading to their arrest in the spring of 1945. They were sent to a transit camp in Berlin, where they awaited transport to an unknown destination. In his cell, Beck narrowly escaped death, suffering a number of broken bones after he became pinned under debris during an air raid. He was liberated by Soviet troops after the capture of Berlin.

In 1947 Beck moved to Palestine, helping Jews migrate to the new homeland then being established. He lived in Israel for several years, until he began traveling and giving lectures on his life experiences. For a short time Beck participated in youth work through the Jewish community in Vienna. He moved back to Berlin in 1979, served as director of Berlin's Jewish Adult Education Center, and became a prominent gay activist.

Beck retired after 10 years of work at the Center, where he taught students about the Jewish culture that had once flourished in their country. During this time he gave many interviews and participated in numerous documentaries, in addition to writing his own memoir, *An Underground Life: Memoirs of a Gay Jew in Nazi Berlin*. Gad Beck died on June 24, 2012, just six days before turning 89. He was survived by his partner of 36 years, Julius Laufer.

Beitz, Berthold (1913–2013)

Berthold Beitz was a German industrialist who saved hundreds of Jewish workers during the Holocaust by declaring them to be essential employees at the Beskidian Oil Company (later renamed the Carpathian Oil Company) at Borysław (Boryslav), in Poland's eastern Galicia.

Born on September 26, 1913, in the German city of Zemmin, Beitz trained to become a banker like his father. In April 1938 he found employment with the Royal Dutch Shell Oil Company in Hamburg, which led to a military deferment when war broke out in September 1939. He remained an employee of Shell during the first years of the war.

In 1939 Borysław was annexed by the Soviet Union, but in the summer of 1941, with Operation Barbarossa, it came under German control and was attached to the newly formed Generalgouvernment. Beitz's expertise in the oil industry led to a wartime commission as manager of oil supplies in the Borysław oilfields.

This position gave him the opportunity to identify which residents to employ as "essential to the war effort." As the area around Borysław had a large Jewish population with many Jews employed in the oil industry, it was inevitable that Beitz would employ Jews as local workers, and he used his office to create superfluous positions that saved hundreds of Jews and Poles from deportation to death camps. While he certainly engaged professionals able to assist in oil production, he also hired a large number of Jews who were unqualified, in poor physical condition, and unable to make any contribution to the company. He would later say that while he should have employed more professionals, he instead chose "tailors, hairdressers and Talmudic scholars," issuing work cards that classified them as "vital petroleum technicians."

In his managerial capacity Beitz was part of a regional network of senior Nazis, and through his connections he could learn of impending anti-Jewish actions. Soon after arriving in Borysław, for example, he witnessed atrocities perpetrated by the Einsatzgruppen (special action squads), whose sole task was the murder of Jews and other racial and ideological enemies of the Reich. He was notified in advance when any anti-Jewish measures were being planned, and so he took it upon himself to choose which Jews were to be saved once they had all been assembled for transport. In this way, in August 1942, he took 250 Jewish men and women off a train heading for the Bełzec extermination camp; for him, they were needed for the oil industry and thus were "vital war workers."

Earlier that same month, on August 7, 1942, he witnessed an SS action in which the Jewish orphanage of Borysław was viciously "evacuated"; babies and toddlers were thrown out of windows, and children were driven barefoot to the train station in the middle of the night. Seeing this, he decided to act; so from this point on, whenever he could, Beitz issued false work papers and hid Jews in his home. He also tipped off local Jews whenever he learned of an impending anti-Jewish action.

It helped that the oil industry in Borysław was such a focused location for Jews. After the region was taken over by the Nazis, management passed to the Carpathian Oil Company, which stationed its workers and their families in segregated work camps. A special badge bearing the letter "R," identifying the wearer as a *Rüstungsarbeiter*, or armaments worker, was sewn onto their clothes. The work camps provided Beitz with a ready reservoir of employees and a location that he could watch should knowledge of any new pogroms come his way.

In an interview with the *New York Times* in 1983, Beitz explained his motivations as having nothing to do with politics. He did not act because he was opposed to Nazism or fascism, and he did not see himself as part of any organized resistance movement. "My motives," he said, "were purely humane, moral motives." His main concern was to save endangered lives.

Because of this approach, Beitz is credited with saving up to 800 Jews. He remained at his post in Borysław until March 1944, when he was drafted into the army. While he did not see himself as a resister, by going out of his way to deliberately save the lives of Jews, Beitz opposed one of the most sacred principles of

National Socialism, for which he could have been denounced and arrested, at the risk of his own life, at any moment.

After the war, Beitz became one of the leading industrialists in postwar Germany, playing a critical role in rebuilding the country into an industrial powerhouse. In the 1950s he became the head of the powerful steel conglomerate ThyssenKrupp and helped in the reindustrialization of the Ruhr Valley. While these were immense achievements, his work on behalf of Jews during the Holocaust was well remembered and garnered him a number of important awards. These include the Leo Baeck Award, the highest honor bestowed by the Central Council of Jews in Germany, awarded to Beitz and his wife, Else, in 2000. He also received awards from Poland.

On October 3, 1973, however, the highest recognition came to Beitz when Yad Vashem named him as one of the Righteous among the Nations for his work in saving Jewish lives. His original nomination for this award received strong support from most of the survivors from Borysław. Upon further research and deliberation, Else Beitz was also recognized as one of the Righteous among the Nations on February 5, 2006.

On July 30, 2013, at the age of 99, Bernhard Beitz died at his holiday home on the island of Sylt, off Germany's northern coast.

Benghabrit, Si Kaddour (1868–1954)

Si Kaddour Benghabrit, rector of the Great Mosque of Paris, saved Jews and resistance fighters during World War II. This is a little-known event, in which Benghabrit and a handful of anti-Nazi Muslims fought for the French Resistance using the Great Mosque of Paris as their base of operations.

An Algerian deeply loyal to France, Benghabrit was born into a prominent family in Sidi Bel Abbes in 1868. In 1892 he was appointed as a diplomatic interpreter, serving in a liaison capacity between North African officials and the French Ministry of Foreign Affairs. In 1916 he went to the Arabian Peninsula to assist pilgrims making the hajj to Mecca, and in 1917, upon his return to Algiers, he established and worked with organizations designed to help North African Muslims make the pilgrimage from French territories.

During World War I Benghabrit was honorary consul-general for Morocco in addition to serving the religious needs of Muslims in the French army. Afterward he worked in the French Ministry of Foreign Affairs. In 1920 Benghabrit initiated a plan to build a mosque in Paris that would serve as a memorial to the 100,000 French Muslims from North Africa who had died fighting for France during World War I. As a result, the Great Mosque of Paris was built in 1926, and he was appointed rector, a role in which he would serve simultaneously as guide, director, and community leader.

Both because of the war and a need for labor to rebuild the country, large numbers of North Africans migrated to metropolitan France during the 1920s. By 1940 the population numbered some 100,000—and of those, most were from Algeria. When war broke out in September 1939, many enlisted voluntarily in the French army; then, when France was defeated, divided, and occupied by Germany, some became involved in the French Resistance movement.

In Paris, the Great Mosque came to serve as a secret refuge for Jews escaping persecution from the Nazis and their Vichy French collaborators. Under the guidance of Benghabrit, the mosque provided Jews with shelter, safe passage, and fake Muslim birth certificates. In most cases, should they be captured, the certificates would enable their owners to escape arrest and deportation. Numbers vary as to how many were saved. Well over 1,000 resistance fighters found refuge in the mosque at one time or another, while hundreds of Jews are believed to have been saved. The French official figure is put at around 500; eyewitnesses have claimed that more than 1,000 Jews were saved by Benghabrit and his helpers.

During this time the Nazis suspected Benghabrit of aiding Muslim resistance agents and helping North African Jews by giving them false identity certificates, though they could never pin anything on him precisely. In most cases, when fugitives were captured, Benghabrit's counterfeit documents enabled their owners to avoid deportation.

Si Kaddour Benghabrit served the Great Mosque of Paris until his death in 1954. The mosque remains a testament to those thousands of French Muslim soldiers who paid the supreme sacrifice during two world wars, but in many respects it also serves as a legacy to Benghabrit's bravery and his sense of common decency, of brotherhood, and of true humanity. His actions, and the actions of those around him, are a shining story of human solidarity in the face of Nazi oppression. He is buried within the same walls that safeguarded so many Jewish and Christian lives from the Nazis.

Bielecki, Jerzy (1921–2011)

Jerzy Bielecki was a Polish social worker best remembered as a prisoner who escaped from Auschwitz in 1944 with his German-Jewish girlfriend, Cyla Cybulska.

Born on March 28, 1921, in the town of Słaboszowie, near Kielce, he was finishing school in Kraków just at the time war broke out in September 1939. With the rapid Polish defeat, he decided to join the Polish army then being reestablished in France. While crossing into Hungary on May 7, 1940, with five friends, however, he was arrested by the Gestapo. At first he was incarcerated in prisons in Nowy Sacz and Tarnow, but on June 14, 1940, he was sent in the first transport of 728 Polish political prisoners to the newly created concentration camp at Auschwitz, registered as prisoner number 243. For the next 18 months he worked on *aussenarbeit* (work outside the camp), in particular at a mill in Babice, where his excellent German language skills enabled him to move freely among the other workers. It was under these circumstances that he came into contact with members of the Polish resistance.

In the fall of 1943, while working at a grain warehouse, he met a Jewish prisoner named Cyla Cybulska. She came from Łomża, a town about 50 miles from Białystok, and had been a prisoner at Auschwitz since January 19, 1943. Her family had been murdered upon arrival. Despite the strict separation of the sexes in Auschwitz, the two fell in love and began to meet in secret. Bielecki promised her that he would find a way to survive Auschwitz by escaping.

On July 21, 1944, wearing a stolen SS uniform, he masqueraded as a guard and "ordered" Cybulska to come with him. Armed with forged documents "authorizing" him to take the prisoner away, he marched her out of the camp through the front gate. The daring escape went undetected, and they managed to get away.

They then walked, mostly by night, for the next 10 days. Exhausted, they reached the village of Przemęczany, where Cybulska was hidden in the home of Bielecki's uncle. After a short while, she was placed with the Czernik family, friends of Bielecki's living in the village of Gruszów. She remained there until the end of the war. Bielecki joined the Armia Krajowa (Polish Home Army) and fought as a partisan. They promised each other that they would meet again after the war, but sadly their separation became permanent. Cybulska was told that Bielecki had been killed in guerrilla fighting, while he heard that she had gone to Sweden and died there.

After the war Cybulska moved to the United States, settling in New York. In May 1983 she learned from a Polish woman who cleaned her family's apartment that Bielecki was alive; the woman learned this from watching a television documentary in which he told his story. Cybulska then found Bielecki's phone number in Poland; they spoke, and on June 8, 1983, she traveled to meet him. He greeted her with a bouquet of 39 roses, one for each year of their separation.

In the meantime, since the end of the war, Bielecki had cofounded and become honorary president of the Christian Association of Auschwitz Families, an organization bringing together former prisoners, their families, and those interested in the history of Auschwitz. In 1985, for his work in helping Jews during the Nazi occupation, he was recognized by Yad Vashem as one of the Righteous among the Nations and accorded a further tribute by receiving Honorary Citizenship of the State of Israel. In 2006 he was one of 32 former prisoners who met with Pope Benedict XVI at the so-called Black Wall in the courtyard of Block 11 at Auschwitz.

Bielecki's escape from Auschwitz with Cybulska has been the subject of several documentaries and books, including Bielecki's own autobiography, *Kto ratuje jedno życie . . .* (*He Who Saves One Life . . .*), published in 1990. In 2011 the couple's story was made into a feature-length movie in Germany, *Die verlorene Zeit*

(*The Lost Time*), directed by Anna Justice and starring Alice Dwyer and Mateusz Damięcki. The movie was released in English as *Remembrance*.

Bielecki died in Nowy Targ on October 20, 2011, at the age of 90.

Bielski, Tuvia (1906–1987)

Jewish partisans fighting the Nazis in the forests of Belarus, Ukraine, and Poland (among other places) faced considerable obstacles to both survival and success. One celebrated case among many is that of Tuvia Bielski and his brothers Asael, Alexander (known as Zus), and Aron.

The children of David and Beila Bielski from a family of 12 (10 boys and 2 girls), theirs was the only Jewish family in Stankiewicze, a small village then situated in eastern Poland, between the towns of Lida and Navahrudak. Born in 1906, Tuvia Bielski learned to speak Polish, Yiddish, and German. Recruited into the Polish army in 1927, he married after demobilization and opened a store in the small town of Subotniki, which was occupied by the Soviets in September 1939. Here, after the Nazis invaded in June 1941, the Bielski brothers Tuvia, Zus, and Asael were called up for home defense against the invaders. In early July 1941 the Nazis moved Jews from across the region into a ghetto in Nowogródek, but the brothers hid instead. After they learned that the rest of their family had been killed in the ghetto in late 1941, the brothers fled into the forest.

Together with 13 neighbors who had also survived the initial Nazi assault, they established the nucleus of a partisan combat group in the spring of 1942. Originally this consisted of some 40 people, but it grew quickly once word got around that the group refused to turn away Jews. In the forest, however, there was a great deal of uncertainty. Should they fight back through joining a partisan unit, or create one of their own? And what form would such fighting take? Further, what would be the objectives of such a unit? Eventually the Bielskis established a community of fighters that also cared for nonmilitary combatants, women and children, and those too young, too old, or too sick to fight.

As commander of what became known as the "Bielski *otriad*" (partisan detachment), Tuvia Bielski's priority was to save Jews rather than kill Germans, and in pursuit of this he sent emissaries to infiltrate ghettos in the area and recruit new members to join the group in the Naliboki Forest. Hundreds of men, women, and children, individually or in small groups, eventually found their way to the Bielski camp. At its peak 1,236 people belonged to the *otriad*, with up to 70 percent of its membership consisting of women, children, and the elderly. Fewer than 200 actually engaged in armed operations.

The partisan community was housed in underground dugouts (*zemlyankas*) or bunkers. In addition, several utility structures were built: a kitchen, a mill, a bakery,

One of four brothers (with Asael, Zus, and Aron), Tuvia Bielski led a Jewish partisan unit in the Naliboki Forest of Belorussia (Belarus) from 1942 until 1944. At its peak, the Bielski group numbered 1,236 people, of whom 70% were women, children, and the elderly. Pictured is a group portrait of former Bielski partisans from Nowogródek taken in the Foehrenwald displaced persons camp in April 1948. (United States Holocaust Memorial Museum, courtesy of Jack Kagan)

a bathhouse, a medical clinic for the sick and wounded, and a quarantine hut for those who suffered from such infectious diseases as typhus. A small herd of cows supplied milk. Artisans made goods and carried out repairs, providing the combatants with logistical support that later served Soviet partisan units in the vicinity as well. More than 125 workers toiled in the workshops, which became famous among partisans far beyond the Bielski base: tailors patched up old clothing and stitched together new garments; shoemakers attended to footwear; and leather workers labored on belts, bridles, and saddles. A metalworking shop repaired damaged weapons and constructed new ones from spare parts. A tannery, constructed to produce the hide for cobblers and leather workers, became a makeshift synagogue owing to the fact that several of the tanners were observant Jews. Carpenters, hatmakers, barbers, and watchmakers served the community, nicknamed "Bielsk" in honor of the leadership. The camp's many children attended class in a *zemlyanka* set up as a school. The camp even had its own jail and rudimentary court of law.

The Bielski group's partisan activities were aimed at the Nazis and their collaborators, such as Belorussian volunteer policemen or local inhabitants who had betrayed or killed Jews. They also conducted sabotage missions. In 1943 the Nazis led major clearing operations against all partisan groups in the area, and some suffered major casualties. The Bielski partisans, however, fled safely to a more remote and impenetrable part of the forest and continued offering protection to noncombatants. They raided nearby villages to seize food (like most other partisan groups), and on occasion locals who refused to share were subjected to violence, generating hostility toward the partisans from peasants in the villages.

The Bielski partisans eventually became affiliated with Soviet organizations in the Naliboki Forest. Several attempts by Soviet partisan commanders to absorb Bielski fighters into their own units were resisted, and under Tuvia Bielski's command the Bielski *otriad* retained its separate identity. This allowed him to continue protecting Jewish lives as well as engaging in combat. According to partisan documentation, Bielski fighters overall killed a total of 381 enemy troops, sometimes during joint actions with Soviet groups. Only 50 members who sought protection with the Bielski *otriad* did not survive.

Immediately after the war, Tuvia Bielski returned to Poland; later he moved to Palestine, which became the State of Israel in 1948. Eventually, he and his brother Zus settled with their families in New York, where they built and maintained a successful trucking business over the next 30 years. In 2008 a major motion picture focusing on the Bielskis, *Defiance* (directed by Edward Zwick), was released to critical acclaim around the world. It stars Daniel Craig as Tuvia, Liev Schreiber as Zus, Jamie Bell as Asael, and George MacKay as Aron.

Blaichman, Frank (b. 1922)

Frank Blaichman was a partisan in the forests around the village of Kamionka, eastern Poland, fighting alongside Soviet troops and other partisan units.

Ephraim Blaichman (or, in the Polish variant, Franek or Franciszek Blajchman) was born in Kamionka on December 11, 1922, one of seven children. His father was a merchant who bought grain from local farmers and sold it in nearby towns and the city of Lublin. Prior to the outbreak of war in September 1939, the several hundred Jews who lived in Kamionka enjoyed relatively trouble-free lives, with little antisemitism intruding upon their daily activities.

With the arrival of the Nazis a wide range of orders was issued to the people of Kamionka. These orders isolated the Jews, deprived them of their livelihoods, and dispossessed them of their businesses, property, and valuables. Travel was limited, and Jews were required to identify themselves by wearing Star of David armbands.

The 16-year-old Blaichman took risks to help feed his family. He defied the restrictions, riding his bicycle around the neighborhood to obtain a variety of foodstuffs. Like most males of the village, he was assigned work, in his case, performing agricultural labor for two days a week. He bought his way out, however, and used the days to continue his black market activities.

By 1942 Germany and the Soviet Union were at war, and the "Final Solution" was about to hit Kamionka hard. The Jewish community was already victimized on a daily basis by harassment and random violence, and shootings were frequent. In October 1942 the Jewish Council (Judenrat), established by the Nazis to oversee the running of the Kamionka ghetto, informed the residents that they were to be resettled in the larger Lubartów ghetto, not far from the village.

Blaichman, unwilling to surrender his freedom, fled Kamionka and hid. A farmer, Aleksander Głos, gave him temporary shelter, and while living on the farm and sleeping in the barn, Blaichman learned from Głos that Kamionka's Jews had not been relocated to the Lubartów ghetto, but instead had been placed on trains to another, unknown, destination. He never saw his family or neighbors from the village again.

After two days with the Głos family Blaichman learned that other fugitive Jews were hiding in the forest; he left the security of the farm, entered the forest, and eventually located a group of more than 100. He told the group what had happened to the Jews of Kamionka and that they were in danger should they just sit there waiting for something to happen. Although only 19, Blaichman suggested that the men make arrangements to defend the group, even though at that time they did not possess any weapons.

A corps of 12 stepped forward to take up the challenge, and with this the nucleus of a partisan group was formed. One who had military training through service in the Polish army was appointed as commander. Within a month Blaichman had convinced another local farmer that he was himself a partisan officer sent from Moscow; this bluff secured the unit's initial arsenal: six rifles, a pistol, and ammunition.

In early 1943 the unit merged with men and women from the town of Markuszow, bringing the unit's strength to some 60 Jewish fighters. In the spring of that year they met up with another Jewish partisan group commanded by Samuel Gruber. Many of Gruber's men had served in the Polish army and were able to impart advanced military knowledge and training to Blaichman's group. As a united force, they began small acts of sabotage and light skirmishing in the neighborhood, as well as identifying and killing collaborators. By September 1943 the unit had attracted attention from the underground People's Army (Armia Ludowa, or AL), which began providing arms and supplies to assist the partisans in their fight.

Partisan warfare was not always successful. Resistance units were often the object of German surprise attacks and ambushes, often as a result of tipoffs from local peasants keen to appease the occupiers. Such attacks could result in substantial loss of life; in one such attack on the group, Blaichman was one of only 22 survivors. To avoid ambush, the unit split up into smaller platoons, staying away from larger populated areas and moving deeper into the forest or onto secluded farms, a strategy that met with some success.

In early 1944 Blaichman's unit was ordered by the AL to move further east and combine with another Jewish partisan unit operating in the forests around the town of Parczew—a town that had been decimated by the Nazis in late 1942. Yehiel

Grynszpan commanded the larger unit, numbering some 400 partisans. Gruber was appointed deputy commander, with two platoon commanders, one of whom was Blaichman, now age 21. In July 1944 Soviet forces moved in from the east, entering the forest around Parczew and affording some measure of relief to the partisans. Soon Lublin fell, and the long German retreat back to Berlin began.

Once the war ended, Blaichman encountered a young woman named Cesia Pomeranc, whom he first met in the forest as her two brothers fought with him in the Parczew area. The two married, and six years later they settled in the United States and raised a family.

In 2009 Blaichman published an account of his years as a partisan, *Rather Die Fighting: A Memoir of World War II*. It was translated into Polish and published a year later as *Wolę zginąć walcząc. Wspomnienia z II wojny światowej*.

Bogaard, Johannes (1881–1963)

Johannes Bogaard was a Dutch farmer who rescued 300 Jews during the Holocaust. Coming from a devout Christian family and taught by his father to respect the Jews as the people of the Bible, Bogaard—with only a poor formal education—nonetheless felt a responsibility for helping Jews who were fleeing from the Nazis.

Born in 1881 in the small farming community of Nieuw Vennep, not far from Amsterdam, Johannes Bogaard, known as Hannes, was raised in a Calvinist family where the Jews were considered to be God's "chosen people." In view of that, he had little difficulty in recognizing his duty when the Nazis began deporting Jews from the Netherlands in July 1942. Unhesitatingly, Bogaard and his family decided to find a way to help Jews escape deportation. They would do this by hiding Jews on their farm and prevailing upon their relatives and neighbors to do likewise.

Before the war, Bogaard had only a very limited experience of Jews. He was acquainted with only one Jewish family, the Mogendorffs, who lived in Amsterdam. Knowing them to be in danger, he took a train—for the first time in his life—and visited them in Amsterdam. He offered them a refuge, initiating a series of actions in which he contacted other Jews and made the same offer. He began making the trip to Amsterdam more frequently, once or twice a week, and shuttling the Jews back to Nieuw Vennep. He also visited Rotterdam and other cities, repeating the process. So keen was he to collect as many people as possible that at one time he harbored as many as 100 Jews.

The help he provided extended beyond simply hiding Jews. He also organized ration cards, money, and false identity papers, and he arranged for most of the Jews to be moved to safer locations afterward. Two of Bogaard's brothers, Antheunius and Willem, were responsible for ensuring a supply of rye, wheat, and other food to the refugees.

The rescue network Bogaard created operated for a year and a half, quite independent of any institutional support from the organized Dutch resistance movement. This came to an end in November 1942, however, when Dutch Nazis raided his farm, finding and deporting 11 Jews. Over the next few months the farm was raided twice more, with other Jews captured. The raids pointed to the extent to which rescuing Jews was a Bogaard family affair. The hidden Jews were to a large degree cared for by Bogaard's daughter, Metje, and by his sister, Aagje. Most of the Jews were concealed at the farm of Bogaard's father, the 77-year-old Johannes "Grandpa" Bogaard Sr.

On October 6, 1943, the farm was again raided, with 34 people found and deported. During the raid, Willem Bogaard managed to save a large group of Jewish children, who were hidden elsewhere by his brother Antheunius once the SS men had left. All of them save one subsequently survived the war. Metje Bogaard managed to save another group during the raid. However, the Jews who were hidden with another of Bogaard's brothers, Pieter, were caught.

Grandpa Bogaard was arrested and detained for 10 weeks at the Amstelveenseweg prison in south Amsterdam. The Gestapo offered him freedom only if he agreed not to repeat his offense, but this he refused to do. It would cost him his life; sent to Sachsenhausen, he was murdered there on February 15, 1945. Pieter Bogaard died at his home on September 15, 1944, after months of imprisonment at Holland's Vught concentration camp.

After this, Johannes Bogaard went into hiding, but his family members continued their efforts on behalf of Jews. His wife, Klaasje, continued his work by hiding four Jews on the farm. She was, however, denounced, forcing her to flee and join her husband. The Jews she was shielding were killed, along with other members of her family. Although Johannes and Klaasje Bogaard survived the war, their family structure was devastated. On the positive side of the ledger, however, estimates place the lives of some 300 Jews directly at their feet. The number of their descendants by now can be measured in the thousands.

Johannes Bogaard died on May 31, 1963, at the age of 82. On October 22, 1963, Yad Vashem recognized him as one of the Righteous among the Nations for his selfless actions in saving the lives of Jews during the Holocaust. Several years later, on August 15, 1974, Antheunius and Willem Bogaard were similarly recognized. The example set by this family, who refused to acquiesce to the Nazi horror, is inspirational and serves as an outstanding witness to their religious faith during the darkest of times.

Born, Friedrich (1903–1963)

Friedrich Born was the chief delegate of the International Committee of the Red Cross (ICRC) of Switzerland in Hungary. Between May 1944 and January 1945 he issued thousands of Red Cross letters of protection to the Jews of Budapest.

He was born on June 10, 1903, in Langenthal, Switzerland. Going initially to Budapest as a member of the Swiss Federal Department of Foreign Trade, he was living there as a businessman prior to his ICRC appointment. He took up his position in May 1944, just as the Nazi deportation of Hungary's Jews was beginning.

Born began taking personal initiatives to save Jewish lives. He "recruited" several thousand Jews and provided them with employment papers, as well as issuing up to 15,000 Red Cross letters of protection (*Schutzbriefe*). These saved their bearers from deportation and almost certain death.

He designated several buildings as ICRC-protected homes, in which he concealed up to 6,000 Jewish children. At Born's direction, two sections dealing with children were established: Section A, led by a Hungarian Zionist leader, Ottó Komoly; and Section B, led by **Gabor Sztehló**. In these homes—of which up to 60 were functioning at times—Born not only rescued Jewish children but also supplied them with food, medicine, and fuel. In addition, he managed to extend ICRC protection to adults locked in ghettos.

A third unit, Section T, was responsible for transportation. It also engaged in rescue and relief operations, while Born further extended the remit of the ICRC to include hospitals, old-age homes, and many other public utilities by the simple stratagem of installing signs outside with the words "Under the Protection of the International Committee of the Red Cross."

Born also used his position to negotiate with diplomatic representatives of various countries stationed in Budapest. Thus, for example, he worked with the Swiss vice-consul, **Carl Lutz**; the Vatican's apostolic nuncio, **Angelo Rotta**; and the Italian stand-in for the Spanish ambassador, **Giorgio Perlasca**, who in reality did not possess any official standing at all. He worked with them in creating documents to place the Jews under their own national jurisdictions, and in finding ways to negotiate extraterritorial status for the buildings in which people were housed. Between them, they also brought back thousands of Jews from deportation camps and death marches, with the justification that they were protected people who should never have been arrested in the first place.

Overall, Friedrich Born is credited with rescuing between 11,000 and 15,000 Jews in Budapest. Those who knew him and witnessed his actions have testified that there were occasions on which he risked his life to help Jews, commenting on the outstanding efforts he made despite Nazi and Hungarian Arrow Cross antisemitic measures. And, remarkably, he was not censured by the ICRC or recalled on disciplinary grounds, even though he worked more often than not on his own initiative and in clear violation of standing rules regarding neutrality and impartiality.

After the war, Born was ordered to leave Hungary by the occupying Red Army. He returned to his normal life and rarely spoke about his actions in Budapest. On January 14, 1963, he died practically unknown—and certainly unrecognized—for his deeds in rescuing thousands of human beings. Twenty-four years after his death, on January 4, 1987, Yad Vashem designated him as Righteous among the

Nations. Up to that point he was the only Red Cross worker to have been awarded that honor, though two years later, on May 7, 1989, another Swiss delegate, the nurse Roslï Näf, was also recognized for her part in rescuing Jews and saving lives during the Holocaust in Hungary.

Friedrich Born had the courage to face both Hungarian and German Nazis, and he stood up to them in demanding that the deportations be stopped. When this did not work, he looked for more direct ways in which to resist, taking matters into his own hands. So far as can be ascertained, his motivation was one of simple humanitarianism in spite of the temptation—to which he never succumbed—of doing nothing or looking the other way.

Borromeo, Giovanni (1898–1961)

Giovanni Borromeo was an Italian medical doctor responsible for hiding hundreds of Jews after fabricating a so-called "deadly" disease that kept the Nazis away from the hospital in which he was working.

Born in Rome on December 15, 1898, he came from a line of distinguished physicians. When Italy joined World War I in 1915 he was already enrolled in the Faculty of Medicine at the University of Rome, and at the age of 18 he joined the Italian army. During the war he won a Bronze Medal for bravery. With peace he returned to his studies, and at the age of 22 graduated with honors. When he turned 30 he became chief physician of the United Hospitals of Rome.

Refusing to join the Fascist party during the 1920s—a move which reduced his career possibilities—he was appointed in 1934 to the Fatebenefratelli hospital, located in the *San Giovanni Calibita* church complex on Rome's Tiber Island. With the help of the prior, Father Maurizio Bialek, he worked to transform the hospital (then being used as a hospice) into the most modern and efficient hospital in Rome.

Under Borromeo's direction, the Fatebenefratelli hospital became a safe haven for Jews after the introduction of Italy's antisemitic laws in 1938. At first, this was on a small scale. One of those protected was Dr. Vittorio Emanuele Sacerdoti, who was able to work in the hospital on false papers. By late September 1943, after Nazi Germany had occupied Italy and initiated severe antisemitic measures against Rome's Jews, Sacerdoti, with the approval of Borromeo and Father Maurizio, arranged for Jews to be brought into the hospital and admitted as "patients." Many of these were from the Jewish hospital, not far from the Fatebenefratelli, which also became a haven for others: police, partisans, and antifascists.

On October 16, 1943, the Nazis raided the Jewish ghetto in Rome, and a major *razzia*, or roundup, took place. Desperately seeking to escape, many Jews managed to get to the hospital, where they were admitted. From this point on, Borromeo began announcing that these "patients" were diagnosed with a new strain of fatal disease, which he called "*Il Morbo di K*." Just what this illness might be was open to interpretation, but for the most part the German occupiers decided to play it safe and refused to intervene. Not only did the fake disease scare the Nazis off but it also prevented them from entering and searching the hospital. In this way, Borromeo saved many people—by some accounts, at least 100, but perhaps more.

The deception meant that the Jews inside the hospital had to play their part, too. The "patients" were instructed to cough and appear sick so that any inspectors would be terrified by what they saw. Coughing, in particular, was an important device: it made it seem that *Il Morbo di K* might have some relationship to tuberculosis, which was particularly frightening. Throughout this time the hospital also served as a place for genuine patients. It has been suggested that Borromeo's designation of "K" for the Jewish refugees was a way of marking them off from those who were actually sick—"K" being an inside joke relating to German general Albert Kesselring, who commanded the German troops in Rome.

Borromeo did not restrict his efforts only to sheltering Jews. He and Father Maurizio also resisted the Nazis through the installation of an illegal radio transmitter and receiver in the basement of the Fatebenefratelli, placing them in continuous contact with local partisans—particularly one of Borromeo's personal friends, Italian air force general Roberto Lordi.

Borromeo (with Father Maurizio's help) did not act alone. Many of the young doctors who served on the staff of the hospital volunteered to assist in the deception, and all knew that one slip-up could cost them dearly. Given that reality, a shuttle service was created to ferry certain "patients" to safe houses when possible. They would remain for a few days, in the hope that new hiding places would be found quickly, the better to ensure that they would not be vulnerable targets should the Nazis decide to raid the hospital—which actually happened at the beginning of May 1944. On that occasion, however, such was the care with which the ruse was carried out that only five Jews, all refugees from Poland, were taken.

After the war, some who knew of Borromeo's work questioned his motives, arguing that his chief concern was to protect partisans, not Jews, and that his protection of them was unintended. This does not, however, sit well with his earlier care for Jews facing fascist persecution before the war. Moreover, the fact that he did not turn Jews away—which he could easily have done in order not to jeopardize his partisan activity—was something that never seemed to occur to him.

After the war, Borromeo received a number of honors from the Italian government, including the Order of Merit and the Silver Medal of Valor. He was also made a Knight of the Order of Malta. On August 24, 1961, at the age of 62, he died at his own Fatebenefratelli hospital in Rome.

He was not, however, forgotten by those he had helped during the Holocaust. Several of those whose lives he had saved kept his memory alive, and two in particular, Claudio and Luciana Tedesco, alerted Yad Vashem as to how their family had been sheltered at the hospital. Other families also furnished proof of their own salvation owing to Borromeo's efforts. As a result, on October 13, 2004, Yad Vashem posthumously recognized Giovanni Borromeo as one of the Righteous among the Nations for resisting the Holocaust and saving Jewish lives.

Calmeyer, Hans (1903–1972)

Hans Georg Calmeyer was a renowned German lawyer who utilized his position within the Nazi regime to save thousands of Jews during the Holocaust. Known in some circles as the "Dutch **Schindler**," he was neither Jewish nor did he have an ulterior motive for saving Jews besides his own moral code.

He was born on June 23, 1903, in the German city of Osnabrück, Saxony. His father was a judge, providing the young Calmeyer with a comfortable upbringing. Relatively little is known of his childhood, though it is recorded that two brothers perished in World War I. Because of his father's profession, the concepts of law and justice, as well as notions of morality, were instilled in him at an early age. Inevitably, Calmeyer followed in his father's footsteps and studied law, later opening his own practice in Osnabrück.

It was not until the Nazis came to power in 1933 that Calmeyer's straightforward and contented life began to change. His legal practice took on many cases concerning communists, resulting in the regime questioning and closely monitoring his work.

Soon after the passage of the Nuremberg Laws in 1935, there were many small areas in which restrictions against Jews in public life were implemented. One of these saw a rule banning Aryans from employing Jewish assistants. Calmeyer's small practice had only two employees, one of whom was Jewish. When he refused to dismiss her, he attracted the attention of the Nazi regime, and his practicing license was revoked for a year.

Called up for the army in May 1940, Calmeyer took part in the invasion of the Netherlands. A friend from Osnabrück then offered him a job with the occupation authorities in the General Commissariat for Administration and Justice in The Hague. His duties would involve examining and adjudicating "doubtful" racial cases, and ruling on the appropriate classification of the people in question, declaring them either fully Jewish, partly Jewish, or Aryan. From the moment he started on March 3, 1941, he realized that the position would afford him the opportunity to prevent Jews being persecuted. He would, however, have to be careful and avoid arousing any suspicion that he was acting outside of Nazi-imposed rules.

The team he built around him comprised several dependable local lawyers who helped draw up false credentials, as well as German assistants, such as Gerhard Wander, who later joined the Dutch underground.

Contrary to the position of the Nuremberg Laws, Calmeyer argued that the legitimacy of Jewish heritage should not be based on a person's membership in the Jewish community, but rather determined from tangible evidence, including birth and baptismal certificates. The distinction made all the difference in the world for the Jews on whose cases he was to adjudicate. It created a legal loophole, leading to a deception that allowed Calmeyer to save thousands from deportation. Of the 4,787 cases brought before him, he decided that 42 percent were to be considered half-Jews (*mischlinge* first degree), and another 18 percent one-quarter Jews (*mischlinge* second degree), creating a total of 60 percent who were thereby exempt from immediate deportation.

He referred to his work as "building a lifeboat" not only to help Jewish families remain together but also to provide them with a sense of hope. With the help of only his closest and most trusted friends, he turned a blind eye to fabricated baptismal certificates and falsified documents in order to save Jewish lives, or at the very least stall their deportation to Auschwitz. Conforming to his reputation of being "rigorously correct and incorruptible," Calmeyer was not personally involved in any of the forgeries. In fact, he sidestepped any personal contact with lawyers who approached his department on behalf of Jewish clients to avoid the suspicion of being overly sympathetic. Further, he did not attempt to intervene personally on behalf of Jews in any official capacity. The SS leadership was nevertheless highly suspicious of Calmeyer's work and constantly urged Reichskommisar Arthur Seyss-Inquart to close down his operation. Seyss-Inquart, however, permitted Calmeyer to continue. Playing for time, Calmeyer added more names to his special list and tried to find ways to extend its purview.

In June 1943 Calmeyer's team was put under close inspection after SS Police Chief Hanns Albin Rauter asked for a complete reexamination of the "Calmeyer Jews." While Rauter had been suspicious of Calmeyer's work for some time, there had been a series of internal power struggles in the Nazi establishment that had delayed Calmeyer's evaluation. The committee appointed to investigate included a Dutch SS member, Ludo Ten Cate, who had been appointed in early 1942 to the position of Official Representative for Genealogical Certificates. Eventually, however, Ten Cate became involved in a vehement quarrel with other Nazi experts, leading to his dismissal in August 1944 and his transfer to the Eastern Front. After Ten Cate's removal, the SS continued to investigate Calmeyer's practice and kept a close eye on every document that passed through his hands. The following year Calmeyer was openly confronted about trying to save Jewish lives through swindling and deception.

He persevered to the end, however, and through his efforts at least 3,000 Jewish lives were saved, the majority as a clear result of his judicious manipulation of the rules.

Calmeyer died in 1972 at the age of 69. On March 4, 1992, Yad Vashem recognized him as one of the Righteous among the Nations, and on January 2, 1995, his son, Peter Calmeyer, together with the ambassador of Israel to Germany, Avi Primor, were present when the town of Osnabrück honored Calmeyer with its most prestigious award, the *Moesermedaille*. In 2011 a new organization, the Calmeyer Foundation, was established with the aim of encouraging people to follow his lead in accepting and respecting difference, stating its primary objectives as raising Holocaust awareness, fostering Jewish-Christian cooperation, and furthering laws respecting life and liberty.

Hans Georg Calmeyer had both the moral determination and a position in the Nazi apparatus that enabled him to bring about real change. He is an example of a humanitarian leader during a dangerous period; his leadership saved the lives of thousands of Jews, in an act of resistance all too rarely replicated during the period of the Third Reich.

Cohn, Marianne (1922–1944)

Marianne Cohn saved Jewish children during World War II as a member of the French-Jewish resistance, and lost her life doing so.

Born on September 17, 1922, in Mannheim, Germany, she was the eldest child of Dr. Alfred and Grete (known as Radt) Cohn. The family was Jewish but not religiously observant. In 1929 they moved from Mannheim to Berlin, and in 1934, one year after the Nazi seizure of power, to Spain. With the onset of the Spanish Civil War in 1936, they moved again in 1938, this time settling in France.

When World War II started, Cohn's parents, as German nationals, were detained at the Gurs internment camp, and she and her sister were sent to a farm. In 1940, after the fall of France, she became subjected to Nazi-imposed antisemitic legislation and took refuge in a home for Jewish children in Moissac. She was informally taken under the care of the Eclaireurs Israelites de France (the Jewish Scouts), and in 1941 she joined the Mouvement de la Jeunesse Sioniste (Young Zionist Movement, or MJS), which brought her into resistance activities.

In 1942 Cohn was active in producing forged passports for the MJS, and she began to smuggle Jewish children out of France. This led inevitably to her arrest, though after three months' detention in a Vichy prison in Nice she was released. It was during this period of imprisonment that, in early 1943, she wrote her famous poem "I Shall Betray Tomorrow." This has become an immortal statement of defiance in the face of the Holocaust:

> I shall betray tomorrow, not today.
> Today, pull out my fingernails,
> I shall not betray.
> You do not know the limits of my courage,
> I, I do.
> You are five hands, harsh and full of rings,
> Wearing hob-nailed boots.
> I shall betray tomorrow, not today.

> I need the night to make up my mind.
> I need at least one night,
> To disown, to abjure, to betray.
> To disown my friends,
> To abjure bread and wine,
> To betray life,
> To die.
> I shall betray tomorrow, not today.
> The file is under the window-pane.
> The file is not for the window-bars,
> The file is not for the executioner,
> The file is for my own wrists.
> Today, I have nothing to say,
> I shall betray tomorrow.
> —Anny Latour, *The Jewish Resistance in France (1940–1944)* (New York: Holocaust Library, 1981), pp. 164–165.

At the end of the war one of the children saved by Marianne Cohn passed the poem to the head of MJS. It is a testimony of courage, and one of the great poems of the resistance.

In 1943 Cohn was living in Grenoble. Volunteers known as "*passeurs*," who escorted Jewish children to Switzerland, undertook hazardous missions under constant risk of detection by Nazis or French collaborators. When one of the *passeurs*, **Mila Racine**, was captured on October 21, 1943, Marianne was sent by the MJS to replace her. Using the false identity of Marie Colin, she then undertook nine further transfers of children, escorting groups of about 30 into Switzerland on each occasion.

In January 1944 Cohn began working with another resister, Rolande Birgy, with whom she ferried groups of up to 20 children across the southern border into Switzerland. Birgy, who had earlier teamed with Mila Racine, was known as the "Blue Beret" in resistance circles. In 1984 Yad Vashem recognized her as one of the Righteous among the Nations.

By the start of 1944 Cohn had taken hundreds of children to Switzerland, but on the evening of May 31, 1944, a German patrol arrested her near Annemasse, just 200 meters from the border. She was at this time escorting a group of 28 children ranging in age from 4 to 15, and they were held at the local Gestapo jail, known as the Prison de Pax. The Vichy-appointed mayor of Annemasse, Jean Deffaugt, who sympathized with the resistance (and was later also recognized as one of the Righteous), intervened on behalf of the children. The younger ones were sent to local orphanages, while Cohn and the older children were paroled to work in Annemasse during the day, provided they returned to the prison at night.

This worked for a short time, but the resistance knew that Marianne was in extreme danger; not only this, but the whole escape operation was in jeopardy.

A plan was arranged to rescue her, but she refused to leave the children, fearing reprisals.

The underground then sent a message to the Gestapo, threatening to kill its members if the detainees were harmed, but the Gestapo began its interrogation nevertheless. On July 3, 1944, a special squad was sent to Annemasse from Lyon with the assignment of removing six of the prisoners, including Cohn. In her defiance, she refused to hide behind her alias and revealed her true identity; for her rebelliousness, she was tortured horribly. She did not, however, speak—other than to say that she had no regrets for her actions.

On the night of July 7–8, 1944, only three weeks before the liberation of Annemasse, she was taken to the nearby Ville-la-Grand and murdered along with two other prisoners; it is recorded that the Gestapo continually hit them with shovels and kicked them until they were dead. They were buried hastily, and their mutilated bodies were discovered after the war. The 28 children imprisoned with Cohn were all saved and released with the liberation in August.

When Marianne Cohn was murdered, she was just 22 years old.

Marianne Cohn, a young Jewish woman who shuttled Jewish children across the border between Vichy France and Switzerland until her brutal death at the hands of the Gestapo in July 1944. This image is her official identification photograph taken while she was still a teenager in Germany, in which she was forced to expose her "distinctively Jewish" left ear. (United States Holocaust Memorial Museum, courtesy of Marianne Roberts)

Coward, Charles (1905–1976)

Charles Joseph Coward was a British prisoner of war who became known as the "Count of Auschwitz" after he helped save the lives of at least 400 Jews working in slave labor camps.

Born in England in 1905, he enlisted in the British army in June 1937 and rose to become quartermaster battery sergeant major. On May 25, 1940, he was captured by the Germans at Calais and made two escape attempts before reaching a prisoner of war camp. While at the camp he made numerous further escapes. On one occasion, he even received the Iron Cross while posing as a wounded German soldier in an army field hospital. He was recaptured on each occasion.

In December 1943 he was sent to Auschwitz III (Monowitz). Here he was placed in the E715 labor detachment camp (administered by Stalag VIII-B), where British POWs were detained. Upon discovering that a fellow British prisoner was confined in the Jewish labor section of the camp, he smuggled himself into the camp for one night in an attempt to meet with this man and witness the conditions under which he was imprisoned. He could not locate the British POW, but witnessed the gas chambers, malnutrition, cramped living quarters, and SS treatment of the prisoners, and saw it as his humanitarian obligation from now on to resist the brutality confronting the Jews.

Due to his fluency in German, Coward was named the Red Cross liaison officer for the British prisoners. Acting as the go-between for the prisoners and the guards, he used the limited freedom this position provided to engage in resistance activities. He and other British prisoners smuggled food and assorted items to the Jewish inmates, and through letters addressed to his deceased father back in England he smuggled reports to the British War Office regarding camp conditions and other information that he believed had military value. Coward's wife received these letters; the information they contained was later used as evidence during the Nuremburg Trials. In addition, he witnessed the arrival of trainloads of Jews for extermination.

Coward's greatest achievement at Auschwitz was his liberation of hundreds of Jews. British POWs received packages from the International Red Cross containing Swiss chocolate, and Coward used these as bargaining chips with the SS to obtain the corpses of dead non-Jewish prisoners. He had these placed in ditches along the paths employed for slave laborers on their way to and from work. The Jews would then slowly drop out of the group and hide in the ditches; Coward would swap their clothing and identities with the corpses and give the healthy Jews the documents and clothes he had taken from the corpses. The Jews then adopted these new identities and were smuggled out of the camp to freedom. It has been estimated that through this scheme Coward saved up to 400 Jewish lives.

In December 1944 he was sent back to the main camp of Stalag VIII-B. He was finally liberated in January 1945, in Bavaria.

After his liberation, Coward remained active in his opposition to the Nazis. He acted as a witness during the I. G. Farben Trial at Nuremberg in 1948–1949, and attested to the sadistic treatment of Jews. In his court statement, he mentioned that during his imprisonment in the labor camp I. G. Farben workers would openly admit that they knew about the gassing and were fully aware of the role they were playing in the war.

In 1954 a British author, John Castle, published a biography of Coward, *The Password Is Courage*, which records his wartime activities. This book was then made into a movie of the same name in 1962, directed by Andrew L. Stone. Coward was portrayed by Dirk Bogarde, and his humanitarian efforts were recognized; however, as the film does not fully illustrate the terror of the Holocaust and the pain and suffering endured by the Jewish prisoners, it does not sufficiently acknowledge the fullness of Coward's feats.

Charles Coward's exploits were a product of his unwavering devotion to human life, rather than to his duty as a soldier. In 1963, in recognition of his nonviolent resistance during the war, he was named as one of the Righteous among the Nations by Yad Vashem. Then, after his death in 1976, the Department of the Righteous at Yad Vashem released a statement commemorating Coward's righteous and brave actions as a humanitarian. He received appreciation and respect from his home country when, in 2010, he was posthumously named a Hero of the Holocaust by the British government.

Dalla Costa, Elia (1872–1961)

Elia Dalla Costa was the Catholic archbishop of Florence between December 19, 1931, and his death on December 22, 1961, and a cardinal from 1933. During the Holocaust he played an important role in establishing a network to rescue Jews in Italy.

He was born on May 14, 1872, the youngest of five children, in the small northern Italian town of Villaverla, and was ordained on July 25, 1895. In 1923 he was appointed bishop of Padua, and then archbishop of Florence in December 1931. Pope Pius XI elevated him to the cardinalate on March 13, 1933.

During the Holocaust, Dalla Costa spearheaded the rescue of hundreds of Jews in Florence with an operation initiated by two leading members of the city's Jewish community, Rabbi Nathan Cassuto and Raffaele Cantoni. Dalla Costa embraced the role the Church could play in helping the Jews of the city. Seemingly without hesitation, he offered to participate in, and help organize, a new rescue network to save the Jews of Florence. He recruited those who would assist from among his own clergy, assigning his personal secretary, Father Giacomo Meneghello, to administer the program. Father Meneghello called Father Cipriano Ricotti, a Dominican friar from San Marco monastery in Florence, to an audience with Cardinal Dalla Costa on September 20, 1943. Dalla Costa asked Ricotti whether or not he would be able to dedicate himself to the rescue of Jews. Upon Ricotti giving his assent, Dalla Costa then gave him a letter to pass on to the heads of monasteries and convents throughout Tuscany, asking that they open their gates to Jews. Father Ricotti later wrote that the letter was crucial to the sheltering of Jews in the convents and monasteries "which otherwise would not have opened their doors."

Cardinal Dalla Costa also sheltered Jews in the archbishop's palace, where they would often stay overnight until taken to different convents in the city the next morning. He also searched his congregants for those willing to help. Among those in the forefront of efforts to save Jews was the national Italian cycling champion **Gino Bartali**, who as part of the rescue program helped save more than 800 Jews through his own efforts. And the rescue network was a truly Jewish-Christian project, at least until the arrest in December 1943 of the Jewish members—most of whom were subsequently murdered.

Following these arrests, Cardinal Dalla Costa continued his rescue campaign, encouraging, cajoling, and generally forcing the Church to persevere in its efforts to rescue Jews. Some clergy paid the supreme sacrifice in pursuing their cardinal's wishes, suffering arrest, torture, and murder at the hands of the SS. For all this, however, and as a result of their work, the network managed to save hundreds of local Jews as well as Jewish refugees from territories that had previously been under Italian control, mostly in France and Yugoslavia.

After the war, many people came forward to testify on Dalla Costa's part. One, Giorgio La Pira, an antifascist politician who later served as mayor of Florence, described his archbishop as "the soul of this 'activity of love'" that "aimed to save so many brothers." In his memoirs, Father Ricotti wrote that due to Dalla Costa's efforts "a real organization to help Jews was set up" in Florence, the result of which saw many hundreds saved through the Church, and hundreds more through individual efforts inspired by the lead of the Church.

On December 22, 1961, at the age of 89, Cardinal Archbishop Elia Angelo Dalla Costa died as a result of an acute pulmonary condition in Florence. He was buried at the Cattedrale di Santa Maria del Fiore (the Duomo di Firenze, or Florence Cathedral). At the time of his death, he was the oldest member of the College of Cardinals. Twenty years later, on December 22, 1981, a beatification process in his name commenced.

Proceeding from the example started by Cardinal Dalla Costa, Jerusalem's Yad Vashem subsequently launched investigations into a number of Florence-based clergy who were known to have saved Jews during the Holocaust. The results, over a lengthy period, saw several recognized as Righteous among the Nations. They included Father Cipriano Ricotti (December 10, 1972); Mother Marta Folcia, Mother Benedetta Vespignani, and Enrico and Luigina Sergiani (all December 13, 1994); and Mother Sandra Busnelli (July 31, 1995).

On November 26, 2012, Dalla Costa was himself recognized as one of the Righteous among the Nations.

Damaskinos, Archbishop of Athens (1891–1949)

Dimitrios Papandreou, as Father Theophilos Damaskinos, was archbishop of Athens during World War II.

Born in Dorvista, Greece, in 1891, Damaskinos was educated as a lawyer at the University of Athens, and upon graduating he enlisted in the Greek army and served during the Balkan Wars as a private. After this he was ordained as a priest of the Greek Orthodox Church, and the Greek Holy Synod soon thereafter appointed him abbot of the Penteli Monastery in Athens. In 1938 he was elected archbishop of Athens, but due to the opposition of Premier Ioannis (John) Metaxas, his appointment was voided, with Bishop Chrysanthus appointed instead. After the Germans invaded Greece in April 1941, the city of Athens was handed over to the Italians, and Damaskinos was reappointed as archbishop.

On March 23, 1943, when the Nazi deportation of the Greek Jews began, Damaskinos sent an appeal to Prime Minister Constantinos Logothetopoulos to halt the deportations. As these requests were continually denied, however, Damaskinos was forced to take a different approach and appeal to the Germans directly. Therefore, the next day, March 24, 1943, he published a letter composed by the famous Greek poet Angelos Sikelianos that was signed by 29 prominent Greek citizens. He also sent a petition to Günther Altenburg, the Reich plenipotentiary for Greece.

The letter protested the treatment of Greek Jews, stating that it was contrary to the Nazis' own rules that all Greek citizens, without distinction of race or religion, were to be treated equally. Damaskinos appealed to the Germans by explaining the history of the Jews in Greece, praising their citizenship and the integral role they had played in the country's economic and military development. Damaskinos wanted to emphasize the unity between the Jews and the Orthodox Christians, and on this basis he refused to allow them to be deported without taking a stand.

The letter enraged the German military commandant in Athens, SS General Jürgen Stroop, who threatened Damaskinos with death by firing squad if he persisted with his criticisms. In response, Damaskinos voiced his opposition that "according to the traditions of the Greek Orthodox Church, our prelates are hung and not shot. Please respect our traditions!" His boldness might also have led the way for other resisters to stand up to the Nazi regime. It can even be conjectured that by showing this level of communal leadership Damaskinos helped initiate a Greek movement to resist the German occupation.

In order to help save as many Jews as he could, Damaskinos also convinced Angelos Evert, the Athens police chief, to resist. Evert, who was later named one of the Righteous among the Nations by Yad Vashem, ordered that thousands of new identity cards bearing Christian names and specifying the holder as a Christian be issued to Jews. Evert later testified that he drew his inspiration from Damaskinos.

As the Nazi measures against the Jews intensified, Grand Rabbi Elias Barzilai was ordered to compile a list of all the Jews residing in Greece. He sought help from Damaskinos for how to proceed, and so, following the archbishop's advice, he destroyed important documents pertaining to the Jewish community and encouraged all Jews to flee Athens.

Damaskinos stalled the Nazis in order to give Jews time to flee the city and find refuge in the countryside. He urged religious leaders and citizens across Greece to aid Jews by providing them with shelter and protection, and he ordered convents and monasteries in Athens to hide Jews within their walls. With his help, more than 250 Jewish children were protected by the Orthodox clergy. Damaskinos also aided Jews through the provision of falsified government documents, and he instructed priests to spread the word to their congregations that Greek Jews needed to be helped by other Greeks if they were to survive.

At the end of the war, due to the work and dedication of Archbishop Damaskinos, the remaining Jews in Athens were left to rebuild their community. In the political vacuum that followed the removal of German and Italian control in 1944, fighting broke out between pro-royalist Greek soldiers and communist partisans; in order to bring some semblance of order to the country Damaskinos appointed himself prime minister, and he was then proclaimed regent until the return of King George II from exile. After the monarchy was restored in September 1946 Damskinos resigned as regent and commenced a quieter lifestyle, focusing less on politics and more on his clerical duties until his death in Athens in 1949.

For his role in aiding Jews to escape Nazi rule in Greece, Archbishop Theophilos Damaskinos was recognized as one of the Righteous among the Nations by Yad Vashem on May 27, 1969.

De Sousa Mendes, Aristides (1885–1954)

Aristides de Sousa Mendes was the consul-general of Portugal in Bordeaux, France, during World War II, responsible for issuing visas to thousands of refugees (including about 10,000 Jews) fleeing the Nazis during spring and summer 1940. In doing so he deliberately defied the orders of Portuguese dictator António Salazar.

He was born in Cabanas de Viriato on July 19, 1885. His father, José de Sousa Mendes, was a judge. Studying law at the University of Coimbra, he graduated in 1908. The same year, he married Maria Angelina Coelho de Sousa, with whom he had 14 children. As a young diplomat he was posted to such assignments as Zanzibar, Brazil, Spain, the United States, and Belgium. In 1938 he was assigned as consul-general in Bordeaux.

With the outbreak of war in 1939 the Portuguese capital of Lisbon became Europe's refugee capital and principal port of embarkation for sanctuary in the New World. Salazar's government did not accept many Jews for permanent residence, preferring to act as a temporary haven; Jews were allowed to remain only until they could arrange passage elsewhere. Most refugees arrived in Lisbon on a two-week transit visa, issued in the refugee's home country by the local Portuguese consul upon presentation of a valid entry permit for a third country. Many of these third-country entry permits were fictitious, elicited through bribes involving vast amounts of money or precious gems. Portuguese consuls throughout Europe were only too aware of the traffic in bogus entry permits, but in many cases they turned a blind eye to the practice and processed transit visas regardless.

Following the Nazi invasion of France in May 1940, the population of Bordeaux swelled as refugees from across the country fled the advancing Nazis. Cities all over southern France began to overflow with desperate refugees. On June 17, 1940, France surrendered, and de Sousa Mendes told his family: "From now on I'm giving everyone visas. There will be no more nationalities, races or religions." Announcing that "the only way I can respect my faith as a Christian is to act in accordance with the dictates of my conscience," and seeing the terrible plight of the refugees, he set up an assembly line process in the consulate. With help from two of his sons and several volunteers, he began issuing entry permits; those who could not pay the visa fees, he said, would receive the documents without charge.

In issuing these visas, de Sousa Mendes deliberately and knowingly disobeyed his own government's decree. As a devout Christian, he saw that his actions were the right thing to do in accordance with his religious obligations.

During the period June 15–22, 1940, de Sousa Mendes issued a total of 1,575 visas, working nonstop for days and nights at a stretch—but this was only the beginning. Leaving Bordeaux for the far western port city of Hendaye, on the border with Spain, in order to provide visas to those stranded there, he was not at the consulate when two cables arrived from Lisbon ordering him to stop issuing more visas. Adding to the ever-increasing numbers, he also directed the honorary vice-consul for Portugal in Toulouse, Emile Gissot, to issue transit visas to any who applied.

De Sousa Mendes's actions were clearly known back in Lisbon; they could hardly have been missed. On June 24, Salazar again ordered de Sousa Mendes's immediate return to Portugal, and this time two detectives were sent to escort him back. Starting the journey, and deliberately moving slowly, he continued issuing Portuguese visas as he went. As they passed the Portuguese consulate in Bayonne, he entered and ordered the local consul to issue visas to hundreds of people lined up outside. He stamped the visas personally, adding in handwriting, "The Government of Portugal asks the Government of Spain kindly to allow the holder of this document to cross Spain freely. The holder of this document is a refugee from the conflict in Europe and is en route to Portugal." He then personally escorted the refugees to a Spanish border post and made sure they crossed safely.

When the party returned to Hendaye, de Sousa Mendes learned that the visas he had previously issued in that town were not being honored. He ordered his driver to slow down and waved those bearing such visas to follow him to a border checkpoint without telephones. The border officials there, unable to phone in for verification, had no alternative but to recognize the diplomatic entourage they now encountered, and de Sousa Mendes led the refugees across the border.

The disgraced consul-general arrived back in Portugal to face charges on July 8, 1940. In Lisbon he was brought before a disciplinary panel, and on October 19, 1940, was found guilty of "disobeying higher orders during service." On October 30, 1940, Salazar decreed that de Sousa Mendes would be subjected to "a penalty of one year of inactivity with the right to one half of his rank's pay, being obliged subsequently to be retired." His career in tatters, he was stripped of his title and assets, and became an outcast. The public dishonor that followed reduced him to poverty, led to the fracturing of his family, and brought on lasting health problems.

While some scholars have disputed the generally recognized figure of 30,000 people saved as a result of de Sousa Mendes's actions—of whom perhaps 10,000 were Jews—it is clear that the number of refugees granted visas on his watch came to many thousands. Those reducing the number often only consider his efforts in Bordeaux, omitting the actions he took in Hendaye (twice), Bayonne, and Toulouse, among other places.

In 1945 Aristides de Sousa Mendes suffered a stroke that left him partially paralyzed. Clearly, the strain of the previous few years was a contributing factor and also played a role in his early death on April 3, 1954. He died in poverty and obscurity, with one of his nieces the only person present.

The rehabilitation of his reputation only began after his death. On October 18, 1966, Yad Vashem recognized him as one of the Righteous among the Nations, the first diplomat to be so honored. Within Portugal, his children worked to clear his name, but it was only on March 18, 1988, that the Portuguese government gave some measure of recognition, when the Parliament dismissed all charges and posthumously restored him to the diplomatic corps. In 1995 President Mário Soares declared de Sousa Mendes to be "Portugal's greatest hero of the twentieth century."

De Souza Dantas, Luis Martins (1876–1954)

Luis Martins de Souza Dantas was a Brazilian diplomat who illegally granted diplomatic visas to hundreds of Jews in France during the Holocaust, thereby saving them from certain death.

Born in Rio de Janeiro in 1876, he was a career diplomat with a long record of service in France even before the outbreak of war in 1939. After the fall of France in 1940 and the establishment of a collaborationist French government in Vichy, de Souza Dantas was retained as Brazilian ambassador, though formally retired by that stage.

Soon, he requested permission from the Brazilian Foreign Ministry to issue migration visas to a small number of French citizens. At the time he did not specify that they were Jews, which was already against the rules; Brazil had a closed policy regarding Jewish immigration. Despite this, he ended up granting diplomatic visas to hundreds of Jews while at the same time masking their Jewish identity.

He would often pre-date these visas to ensure that any subsequent ban on their use would be negated. In January 1941 a passenger ship, the SS *Alsina*, set sail from France with a large number of Jews carrying forged visas. Prevented for several months by the British navy from landing in Dakar, Senegal (controlled by Vichy France), the *Alsina* was forced to land in Casablanca. By this stage, the visas had expired, but de Souza Dantas arranged for them to be renewed, and the Jews managed to move on to Rio de Janeiro.

De Souza Dantas applied himself to the task of rescue through subterfuge. He would grant diplomatic visas to those holding passports without going through the usual laborious application processes. He would write on the documents in French rather than Portuguese for greater ease of egress at the ports of departure, though he followed all other official procedures for ensuring that the documents would be acceptable. Often, he assisted with the provision of visas for Jews seeking entry through other embassies, interceding personally to claim Brazilian "citizenship" for those who were actually refugees.

In short, he granted diplomatic visas for hundreds of people to enter Brazil who, from the perspective of Brazilian immigration policy, were considered undesirable. They were Jews, communists, and homosexuals.

The actions of de Souza Dantas flew in the face of Brazil's dictator Getúlio Dornelles Vargas, whose regime tolerated antisemitism. It was not long, therefore, before de Souza Dantas became the object of official inquiries in Rio de Janeiro. He knew his actions were illegal, but nevertheless continued to work on behalf of Jews whenever—and for as long as—he could. Recalled to Brazil for disciplinary hearings, he defended himself on grounds that he was motivated by "Christian feelings of mercy" regarding the persecuted Jews.

When Brazil's Ministry of External Relations (known colloquially as the Itamaraty) opened the investigation into his behavior, the charge was one of granting irregular visas. In his defense, de Souza Dantas stated, falsely, that he had not done so after he had been told to desist, and no visas had been issued. The hearing found him guilty of contravening Brazil's immigration policy regarding Jews, but he escaped punishment on a technicality: since he was theoretically retired and only working for the government as a special favor during the period in which he forged the visas, he was not bound to the same standards as a full-time permanent representative. It was a technicality, but it saved him from severe punishment.

Unlike other Latin American diplomats at the time, who had an unenviable reputation for corruption when it came to granting visas, de Souza Dantas did not grant visas for personal gain, nor did he discriminate in favor of (or against) specific groups. Travel itself was not the major problem, as ships still plied the Atlantic until 1942. The greatest obstacle for the refugees was obtaining the necessary permits for the countries they sought to enter. At great personal risk, de Souza Dantas worked to overcome this obstacle, at least insofar as his own responsibility was concerned.

After the war, de Souza Dantas returned to Paris, where he lived out his days in obscurity. His career as a diplomat was long over, having ended ignominiously after his recall. The memory of his actions on behalf of those persecuted during the Holocaust was forgotten for several decades, recalled only by those whose lives he had saved. He died in Paris on April 14, 1954.

Overall, Luis Martins de Souza Dantas saved the lives of more than 800 people, including 425 confirmed Jews. In the eyes of some, he was the Brazilian equivalent of the German rescuer **Oskar Schindler**, though in entirely different circumstances. The most important feature linking the two men was the duty each felt toward the saving of human lives, and for this, on December 10, 2003, de Souza Dantas was recognized by Yad Vashem as one of the Righteous among the Nations.

Dohnányi, Ernő (1877–1960)

Ernő (Ernst) Dohnányi was a Hungarian composer and conductor who, in the late 1930s and early 1940s, used his considerable influence to protect Jewish musicians from the Holocaust.

Born in Pozsony (modern-day Bratislava) on July 27, 1877, he was a musical prodigy who began studying at the age of 8. When he was 16 he moved to Budapest and enrolled in the Royal National Hungarian Academy of Music, studying under István Thomán and Hans von Koessler. In June 1897 he took his final exams before his 20th birthday and obtained his diploma as a composer and pianist.

Dohnányi performed as a pianist in various concert halls throughout Europe and the United States until 1908, at which time he became professor of piano at the Berlin Hochschule. From 1919 to 1944 he conducted the Budapest Philharmonic Orchestra, and in 1934 he became director of the Budapest Academy.

There were several occasions on which Dohnányi openly defied the Nazis, including blocking the creation of a Hungarian Chamber of Music that would have excluded Jews from the music profession, as the infamous *Reichsmusikkammer* did in Nazi Germany. Dohnányi also resigned his position as director general of the Franz Liszt Academy of Music instead of carrying out orders to fire Jewish instructors. As conductor of the Budapest Philharmonic, Dohnányi disbanded the ensemble rather than dismiss its Jewish members.

In addition to these public acts of defiance, Dohnányi assisted a number of individual Jewish musicians. Such names included music promoter Andrew Schulhof, whose migration from Germany to the United States in 1939 Dohnányi helped to facilitate. After Dohnányi wrote a letter declaring the pianist Lajos Hernádi and his hands to be irreplaceable national treasures, Hernádi was discharged from the labor service. A noted violinist, Carl Flesch and his wife were in grave danger of being deported to a concentration camp, and when Dohnányi learned of this he helped reinstate their Hungarian nationalities; this enabled them to return to Hungary from Germany and ultimately find safety in Switzerland. In 1941 Dohnányi threatened to resign as director of the Budapest Academy in protest at having to dismiss his favorite Jewish pupil, György Farago.

Dohnányi also personally saved the pianist György Ferenczy and his wife, as well as several other Jewish musicians, from deportation to Auschwitz in 1944. Another Hungarian composer, Zoltán Kodály, later reported that Dohnányi had signed dozens of documents that saved Jewish lives during the Holocaust. In *Ernst von Dohnányi: A Song of Life* (2002), Dohnányi's widow, Ilona Zachár, placed that number in the hundreds. Jewish violinist, violist, and composer Tibor Serly, a student of Kodály, extolled Dohnányi's resistance to the Holocaust with the conclusion that "not one Jewish musician of any reputation living in Hungary lost his life or perished during the entire period of World War II."

As with many people in positions of influence during the Third Reich, Dohnányi could only do so much to assist people in need—and even then there were times when he was forced to make compromises with the regime that was oppressing those he wanted to help. As a result, he was accused of being a Nazi collaborator in the years after World War II.

One such accusation was that he did not save the Jewish composer Leo Weiner from losing his job or from being incarcerated in the Budapest ghetto. Of greater significance was an accusation that in 1943 Dohnányi demanded that no Jews be admitted into the Budapest Academy's master class. Whether it was for this or other reasons—possibly even because of Dohnányi's actions in helping Jews, within a regime that was increasingly antisemitic—Hungary's Minister of Education and Religion, Jeno Szinyei-Merse, forced Dohnányi's resignation as director of the Academy.

Dohnányi did, however, continue to lead the Budapest Philharmonic until late 1944, when the exigencies of war led to the orchestra's dissolution after the Soviet Red Army's siege of the city. In December 1944 he left Hungary.

With the war over, Dohnányi and his wife Ilona moved around: first to Austria, then to Argentina and Mexico, before settling in the United States. Repeatedly defended by prominent Jewish musicians who had worked closely with him in Hungary during the Nazi regime, he was investigated for collaboration and cleared by Allied tribunals on a number of occasions. In 1949 he took up a teaching position at Florida State University's School of Music, and in 1955 he and Ilona became American citizens. Ernst Dohnányi's last public performance was on January 30, 1960. On February 9, 1960, he died of pneumonia in New York. He was buried in Tallahassee, Florida.

His son, **Hans von Dohnányi**, who was arguably even more renowned as an anti-Nazi resister and rescuer of Jews than his father, was murdered by the Nazis for his resistance activities in 1945.

Dohnányi, Hans von (1902–1945)

Hans von Dohnányi was a German lawyer who rescued Jews during the Holocaust and was active in the German resistance to Nazism.

He was born in Vienna on January 1, 1902, to Hungarian composer **Ernő Dohnányi** and pianist Elisabeth Kunwald. After their divorce young Dohnányi grew up in Berlin, where he went to school with Dietrich and Klaus Bonhoeffer, two brothers who

Hans von Dohnányi, a German lawyer (and son of renowned Hungarian composer Erno Dohnányi). An active anti-Nazi resister during World War II, he worked as an intelligence operative for the Nazi regime but was actually a double agent who utilized his position to save two Jewish families in 1942. Dohnányi was executed by the Nazis at Sachsenhausen concentration camp in early April 1945, just weeks before the camp's liberation. (Ullstein Bild/Getty Images)

would also become resisters to Nazism. Between 1920 and 1924 he studied law, earning a doctorate in 1925. In that same year he married Christel Bonhoeffer, Dietrich and Karl's sister. He assumed the Germanic aristocratic form of his name, "von Dohnányi," while still young.

Furthering his career, Dohnányi became a prosecutor with the Reich Ministry of Justice from 1929 onward. Moving through various offices, he became an adviser in 1934 to Minister of Justice Franz Gürtner, a non-Nazi conservative whom Hitler retained to reassure the German people that the law remained impartial. Dohnányi stayed in this position until 1938 and was welcomed into the inner sanctum of the Nazi hierarchy, advising such leaders as Adolf Hitler and Joseph Goebbels.

After the bloody party purge in 1934 known as the Night of the Long Knives, Dohnányi became disillusioned with the Nazi regime, seeing the purge as an illegal use of authority by the state. To get him away from the party where his criticisms could do damage, Martin Bormann, the head of the Chancellery, had Dohnányi transferred out of Berlin to Leipzig; to protect him, Minister of Justice Franz Gürtner had him appointed to the Supreme Court, thinking it safer for him than the Ministry of Justice.

By way of response, Dohnányi made connections with people in the German resistance movement and began keeping confidential and compromising files of what he saw as the Nazi regime's crimes in office.

Just before the outbreak of war in 1939, General Hans Oster, deputy head of Germany's military intelligence bureau, the Abwehr (and, as it was to turn out, a leading figure of the German resistance), called Dohnányi in for a meeting. By the time war broke out, he had been conscripted to serve in the Abwehr's information department. The Abwehr, under Admiral Wilhelm Canaris, became a clandestine focus of anti-Nazi resistance, and knowing that Dietrich Bonhoeffer had been preaching against the regime, Dohnányi arranged for him also to be brought into the Abwehr, where he could be protected.

In September 1942 Dohnányi utilized his position to initiate the rescue of two Jewish lawyers from Berlin, Friedrich Arnold and Julius Fliess, who, together with their families, escaped to Switzerland before being sent to concentration camps. Dohnányi organized this under cover of a clandestine operation codenamed U-7, involving deployment of all 13 in the two families disguised as Abwehr agents. Dohnányi's brainchild, the operation included people who were elderly and disabled as well as children, and in order to coordinate the escape he had a number of meetings with Friedrich Arnold beforehand. He had known Arnold before the war, and, recognizing the danger he faced, worked this out as a means to save him and his family. Once the operation had been completed successfully, Dohnányi made a secret visit to Switzerland to see that the group had been satisfactorily looked after upon reception.

On April 5, 1943, Dohnányi was arrested by the Gestapo on suspicion of anti-Nazi activity. He was initially charged with foreign currency violations, which he performed in order to transfer the rescued Jews' funds to a Swiss bank. At the same time, Dietrich Bonhoeffer and Christel Dohnányi were also arrested. Christel Dohnányi was quickly released, and after a time so also was Hans von Dohnányi for lack of evidence. Bonhoeffer, however, remained imprisoned.

Dohnányi was rearrested shortly before the July Bomb Plot to assassinate Adolf Hitler in 1944. (His involvement in the conspiracy only came to light after its failure.) During their investigations the Gestapo located some of the anti-regime records and files he had saved and hidden during the 1930s, which automatically declared his hand as a conspirator and enemy of the Nazi state. He was sent to Sachsenhausen, where the Nazis determined to destroy him as part of their final purge prior to their own defeat. On the express orders of Adolf Hitler, he was condemned to death by order of an SS judge on April 6, 1945, and was hanged with piano wire on April 8 (or 9), 1945.

On October 26, 2003, at an official ceremony in Berlin, Yad Vashem recognized Hans von Dohnányi as one of the Righteous among the Nations for his actions in saving the Arnold and Fliess families, at risk to his own life. His children Klaus von Dohnányi, Barbara von Dohnányi-Bayer, and Christoph von Dohnányi were on hand to accept the posthumous award on behalf of their father.

Drossel, Heinz (1916–2008)

Heinz Drossel, born in 1916, was a German army officer during World War II who helped Jews escape persecution at the hands of the SS. He managed to finish his law degree just before war broke out in 1939 but was denied entry to the legal profession when he refused to join the Nazi party. In November 1939 he was drafted into the German army and in 1940 served during the Battle of France.

In the summer of 1941, at the time of Hitler's invasion of the Soviet Union, Drossel's resistance to the demands of Nazi ideology began when he refused to execute a Russian officer as ordered. Instead, he led the officer into the forest and sent him back toward Soviet lines. This was not an isolated incident. When his unit captured a Russian officer, Drossel defied orders to take the man back to headquarters—where he knew the prisoner would be shot—and turned him loose instead, saying "I am no killer. I am a human being."

On medical leave in Berlin in 1942, Drossel encountered a distressed young Jewish woman, Marianne Hirschfeld, about to leap from a bridge. Learning that she was Jewish and afraid for her life, Drossel took her to his family's empty apartment, provided her with money for sustenance and safe shelter before he returned to his unit, and then left. He risked immediate court-martial and likely execution by doing so, but this had also been the case on the Eastern Front; Drossel's concern was with the welfare of human beings, not the rules that could get him into trouble.

In early 1945 Drossel continued his helping activities on behalf of Jews. While visiting Senzig, Brandenburg, where his parents had sought safety from Allied bombing raids, he was informed by a local Nazi supporter that a number of Jews were living in the community on forged papers. Drossel offered immediate assistance to Jack and Lucie Hass, their daughter Margot, and her friend (and later husband), Ernst Fontheim. Without hesitation, he took Jack Hass and Ernst Fontheim back to the empty apartment in Berlin, while he found a safe house for Lucie and Margot Haas. Again, by helping Jews he placed himself at considerable risk, but their lives were saved.

In the spring of 1945 Drossel was sent back to what was left of the Eastern Front. On May 4 he was ordered by a Waffen-SS commander to lead his troops in a suicidal attack on Soviet positions, and rather than sacrifice his men on a hopeless task, he point-blank refused to obey. When threatened with the consequences of his refusal he, in turn, ordered his troops to open fire on the SS. He was immediately arrested and sentenced to death, but while awaiting execution was freed by advancing Soviet troops, who captured him as a prisoner of war. By the end of the year he was released from Soviet captivity and returned home.

In a freak encounter on the streets of Berlin, Drossel later met Marianne Hirschfeld, the Jewish woman he had saved in 1942. After he had hidden her in his parents' apartment, she had survived in hiding. Saved by the actions of this reluctant German officer, she was practically the only member of her family to escape the Holocaust. A relationship developed; in 1946 they married and began to raise a family.

Drossel then sought to rekindle his legal career, which had been cut short by his refusal to join the Nazi party in 1939. He was appalled by what he saw in the legal profession, as many former Nazis were given leave to continue their careers. Over time he progressed and eventually became a successful lawyer and then a judge. In 1981 he retired, respected by all those around him.

Though he never spoke about his resistance to the Nazis during the war, those whom he had helped did not forget him. In 2000 Yad Vashem honored him as one of the Righteous among the Nations for his efforts to save Jewish lives. In receiving the award in May 2000 at the Israeli embassy in Berlin, Drossel spoke for the first time about his actions during World War II. A year later, he was similarly honored by the German government; this opened up a new path for Drossel, who then began speaking to German schoolchildren regarding those awful days during the war.

In April 2008 Heinz Drossel died in Simonswald, Baden-Württemberg, at the age of 92. His story was that of a Wehrmacht officer who refused, at great risk to his own life, to abandon the courage of his convictions in the most extreme circumstances. When the safety of others was threatened, he showed that the value of their lives was paramount, despite orders or the destructive ideology that sought to destroy his ideals of what was right.

Duckwitz, Georg Ferdinand (1904–1973)

Georg Ferdinand Duckwitz was a German maritime attaché, stationed in Denmark during World War II, who warned the Jews in Denmark of their imminent deportation at the hands of the Nazis in 1943. This action saved almost the entire Jewish community.

He was born on September 29, 1904, in Bremen. After finishing commercial college, he pursued a career in the international coffee trade. He became a member of the Nazi party in 1932, and in 1939 the Nazi Foreign Ministry assigned him to the German embassy in Copenhagen as an expert in maritime affairs.

When Germany occupied Denmark in April 1940 there were no immediate threats to the Danish Jewish community, but things seemed about to change in 1942 when a new Nazi plenipotentiary, Werner Best, was appointed to Denmark. Best, a former deputy chief of the Gestapo and hard-core Nazi ideologue, was known for his ruthlessness in planning a new Europe on racial lines. After his appointment to Denmark, however, he chose at first to retain a policy of moderation.

August 1943, after an increase in resistance activity, a state of emergency was declared across Denmark, paving the way for the Nazis to move against the country's Jews. In September Adolf Hitler approved their deportation, with the operation to commence at 10:00 p.m. on October 1, 1943. Two German passenger ships were ready to move approximately 5,000 Jews to Germany, while buses would take the remaining 2,500. The destination of all was to be Terezín (Theresienstadt).

Duckwitz learned from Best of the deportation plans on September 11, 1943. In a state of shock, he flew to Berlin two days later to try to have them stopped, though he was, predictably, unsuccessful. Two weeks later he flew to Stockholm and contacted Prime Minister Per Albin Hansson with the request that Sweden receive Jewish refugees from Denmark should they be smuggled across the Øresund sound. Two days later, Hansson responded in the affirmative.

Returning to Denmark on September 29, 1943, Duckwitz leaked news of the deportation order to a leading Danish Social Democrat, Hans Hedtoft, who later recalled that Duckwitz made his announcement in a state of "indignation and shame." Hedtoft immediately warned Carl Bertelsmann Henriques, the head of the Jewish community, and Rabbi Dr. Marcus Melchior, the acting chief rabbi of Denmark. They took immediate action and spread the warning, realizing that the deportation was to begin on the Jewish holy day of Rosh Hashanah. By October 2, when the Gestapo set out to implement its plans, almost no Jews were left to deport.

In what became a national underground project, both the organized Danish resistance movement and everyday citizens worked to evacuate as many members of the Jewish community as possible. Phone calls were placed, homes were opened as safe houses, and Jews were spirited to hiding places in the countryside while arrangements were made to move them across the Sound. From all walks of life and in all parts of the country, Danes felt that the persecution of minorities was an intolerable breach of Danish culture.

Once the Jews were out of the gaze of the Nazis, a safe passage was arranged across the water to Sweden. While some were transported in large fishing boats, many others—individuals or families—were ferried to freedom in much smaller vessels, even rowboats. A mass escape of more than 7,200 Jews and 700 of their non-Jewish relatives thereby took place. Only 500 Jews, many of whom were elderly and sick, were caught and deported to Terezín.

Once in Sweden, the Jewish refugees remained protected by their Danish neighbors back home, who oversaw the protection of their property in their absence. For those who were captured and deported, the Danish government arranged for food, medicine, clothes, and other supplies to be delivered, and the government prevailed upon the Nazis to allow the Red Cross to regularly inspect their conditions. Although, tragically, there were some fatalities, by the end of the war most of those who had been captured returned to Denmark.

Once Duckwitz had tipped off the Jewish community and witnessed their rescue, he resumed work as Germany's maritime attaché to Denmark. He kept his head down for the rest of the war, conscious of possible exposure to the Gestapo and knowing full well the severe consequences if he were caught—especially since he was a member of the Nazi party himself. Certainly, the likelihood of death or a concentration camp was ever present.

After the war, Duckwitz remained in the German Foreign Service and became West Germany's ambassador to Denmark between 1955 and 1958. Later, he became ambassador to India, and in 1966 he was appointed secretary of state in West Germany's Foreign Office until his retirement in 1970. On March 29, 1971, Yad Vashem recognized Georg Ferdinand Duckwitz as one of the Righteous among the Nations for his efforts to assist the Danish Jews in escaping to Sweden. He died on February 16, 1973.

Edelman, Marek (1919–2009)

Marek Edelman was a leader of the Jewish fighters during the Warsaw Ghetto Uprising of 1943.

It is unclear in which year he was born, though September 19, 1919, is the date quoted most often. Born in Homel (now Gomel, Belarus), he was an only son. Both his parents were socialists: his father, Natan, was a member of the Socialist Revolutionary Party, and his mother, Cecylia, was an activist in the Jewish Labor Bund. Orphaned by the time he had turned 14, he had already been thoroughly indoctrinated into socialist ways; as he grew to maturity, he became an active member of the Bund.

After Germany invaded Poland in September 1939 Edelman, barely 20, found himself herded into what became the Warsaw Ghetto. On July 22, 1942, the Nazis began deporting Jews from the ghetto at a rate of 6,000 a day. In response, Edelman and other young Jews—among them **Mordecai Anielewicz**—formed a resistance group determined to confront the Nazis. Composed largely of youth groups that anticipated the Nazi intention to liquidate the ghetto entirely, the members created what became known as the Jewish Combat Organization (Żydowska Organizacja Bojowa, or ŻOB).

The ŻOB was a formation that united three usually incompatible groups: Zionists, communists, and Bundists, and given the ideological gulf separating them it proved difficult for ŻOB to mobilize the inhabitants of the ghetto for the struggle to come. Still, this did not hold Edelman back from trying to develop a viable and effective force. As an employee of the ghetto hospital, he was able each day to visit the *Umschlagplatz*—the square in Warsaw where the Nazis concentrated Jews for deportation to Treblinka—carrying passes that authorized him to take people who were too ill to travel off the trains. He took advantage of this to save fit younger Jews who could be recruited to fight.

By September 1942, after wholesale deportations had taken place, only 60,000 Jews remained. In advance of the anticipated confrontation, the ŻOB began acquiring whatever weapons it could obtain for a possible revolt—not, as Edelman said later, in order to defeat or destroy the Nazis, but to at least give those who were already doomed the opportunity to choose how they were to die.

On January 18, 1943, ŻOB fighters opened fire, forcing the Nazis to withdraw and suspend the remaining deportations. Then, when it seemed certain that the final liquidation of the ghetto was about to take place on the eve of Passover (April 19, 1943),

Marek Edelman, one of the leaders of the Jewish Fighting Organization in the Warsaw Ghetto, and, as such, a key participant in the Uprising of April–May 1943. After the death of Mordecai Anielewicz on May 8, Edelman assumed overall command and survived the war by escaping through Warsaw's sewers. At the time of his death in 2009, he was regarded as the last surviving leader of the Warsaw Ghetto Uprising. (United States Holocaust Memorial Museum, courtesy of Benjamin [Miedzyrzecki] Meed)

the ŻOB struck. Firing from every vantage point, they forced the Germans onto the defensive and obliged them to retreat in what became the most extensive act of armed urban resistance in Nazi-occupied Europe.

The ŻOB could only muster 220 men and women as their fighting strength. This was ranged against Nazi units numbering a daily average of more than 2,000 troops, backed by tanks, artillery, and aircraft. The ghetto fighters were largely untrained, woefully underequipped, and lacking in food and clean water. Edelman led the medical teams assisting the wounded in a constant struggle to alleviate pain caused by gunfire, falling masonry, and above all burns after the Nazis decided to reduce the ghetto by fire.

When Anielewicz lost his life during the fighting at Miła 18 on May 8, Edelman—who had been one of three subcommanders—took over as leader of the ŻOB. Overall, the resistance struggle with the Germans lasted three weeks. While the fighters took some German lives and wounded many others, the Jewish losses were significantly greater—and this was to say nothing of the remaining civilian population, which was deported in the tens of thousands. As the fighting intensified, the Nazi military, led by General Jürgen Stroop, decided to clean out the ghetto block by block. Instead of fighting for the buildings, Stroop ordered that they be burned, leaving the remaining fighters with nowhere to turn for cover.

The scorched-earth tactics worked. The remnants of the ŻOB—only about 50, by most estimates—fled through Warsaw's sewers with the help of couriers from the Polish underground outside the ghetto. Edelman then joined the left-wing People's Army (Armia Ludowa), fighting alongside the Polish Home Army (Armia

Krajowa) in the equally ill-fated Warsaw Uprising that began in August 1944. After the failure of the Warsaw Uprising, Edelman and other ŻOB fighters hid in the ruins of the city before being rescued and evacuated.

After the war Edelman elected to remain in Poland, where he studied at Łódź Medical School. Upon graduation he specialized in cardiology and became one of Poland's leading heart specialists. He maintained an active interest in issues relating to social justice and workers' rights, and in 1976 he became an activist with the Workers' Defense Committee. He was an early member of the Solidarity free labor union movement and was among those interned when General Wojciech Jaruzelski declared martial law in 1981. After the fall of communism in Poland in 1989, Edelman became a member of various centrist and liberal parties.

In recognition of his activities as a fighter against Nazism, Edelman was awarded Poland's highest decoration, the Order of the White Eagle, on April 17, 1998. Before his death in 2009 at the age of 90, Marek Edelman was recognized by all as the last surviving leader of the Warsaw Ghetto Uprising, and a hero to the memory of those who fought back during the Holocaust.

Elisabeth, Queen Mother of the Belgians (1876–1965)

Queen Elisabeth, Duchess in Bavaria, was Queen of the Belgians as the wife of King Albert I. She was born in 1876 and married Prince Albert, then heir to the throne of Belgium, on October 2, 1900. When he was crowned in 1909 she became queen. In 1934 King Albert died in a climbing accident in Belgium's Ardennes region, and Elisabeth became Queen Mother upon the accession of her son, Leopold III.

After Belgium's surrender to Nazi Germany on May 28, 1940, Elisabeth worked to assist the Jews of Belgium, now faced with immediate threat of deportation. To facilitate their occupation, the Germans created a Jewish Council, the Association des Juifs en Belgique (Association of Jews in Belgium, or AJB), which all Jews were required to join. In May 1942 Jews were forced to wear a yellow star to mark them out in public, and the persecution of Belgian Jews escalated.

On August 1, 1942, Elisabeth held an audience at the royal palace in Brussels, called at the request of the AJB. Those attending were Eugène Hellendaal, Salomon Van den Berg, and Lazare Liebmann; together, they informed her of the atrocities then being committed against Belgium's Jews, giving harrowing descriptions of conditions at the Mechelen/Malines transit camp. Throughout the summer of 1942 the Nazis made preparations to deport the Jews, and after August 1942 two transports, each loaded with about 1,000 Jews, left the camp every week for Auschwitz-Birkenau. Because of this, Mechelen was known as the "Antechamber of Death." Conditions were especially brutal, a point not lost as the delegates spoke with the

Queen Mother. They also described the conditions facing the elderly and the children. Elisabeth promised that she would apply herself to stopping the deportations.

Immediately, she called upon her German background and wrote to Adolf Hitler, asking that the deportations be stopped; she made this appeal through the military governor of Belgium, General Alexander von Falkenhausen, with the backing of the Italian royal family and the International Committee of the Red Cross. Von Falkenhausen, in turn, sent his civilian deputy, an SS officer named Eggert Reeder, to Berlin to clarify the policy with Reichsführer-SS Heinrich Himmler. Deferring to Elisabeth's position (and probably to prevent inflaming public opinion against the occupation), concessions were then made. A telegram from Berlin promised that Jews with Belgian citizenship would not be deported or separated from their families. Those currently being held at Mechelen/Malines awaiting deportation, moreover, could receive visitors. It was also agreed that Jewish men over the age of 65 and women over age 60 would not be deported.

This response was passed on to members of the AJB, who received the news with gratitude. The Queen Mother's secretary, Baron Edouard de Streel, however, cautioned that, given the changing fortunes of war and the Nazi regime, the promise might be transitory.

His warning was accurate. On October 30, 1942, the Germans arrested children at an orphanage in Wezembeek, not far from Brussels. Again, however, Elisabeth intervened, insisting that they be released, and again she was successful. In May 1943 Elisabeth visited a hospital in Borgerhout, Antwerp. Shocked by what she heard when she was there—that the Nazis were about to clear out the Jewish patients—she once more protested. This resulted in up to 80 elderly and sick Jewish patients being allowed to remain in the hospital. Then, in June 1943, she again protested against the imprisonment of Belgian Jews in Mechelen/Malines, resulting in about 300 being released.

The constant intervention of Queen Mother Elisabeth in Jewish issues resulted in suspending the mass deportation of Jews with Belgian citizenship for a full year. On September 3, 1943, however, the Nazis made a concerted attempt to organize deportations to Auschwitz of all Belgian-born Jews in one fell swoop. Hundreds from Antwerp were arrested and taken to Mechelen/Malines, and once again, Elisabeth protested. She was supported at this time by the Catholic cardinal (and archbishop of Mechelen) Jozef-Ernest van Roey. In frustration, Reeder ordered their release. Thus, the most intensive attempt to mass deport Belgian Jews was a failure.

This is not to say that deportations did not take place; transports continued to leave Mechelen/Malines throughout the entire period. Overall, possibly some 29,000 out of the 65,000 Jews in Belgium (Belgian-born and foreign refugees) were murdered during the Holocaust.

In addition to her larger expressions of protest, Queen Mother Elisabeth also intervened in a number of individual cases, frequently successfully. Her many interventions in the Nazis' anti-Jewish measures, whether on a large or small scale, saved people's lives. Like **Princess Alice of Greece**, she was not prepared to stand by and allow the mass deportation and murder of her own subjects. And, as with Alice, the intervention on behalf of Jewish citizens by a member of a royal family in Europe (albeit not at that point on the throne) was so uncommon as to be without parallel.

On May 18, 1965, in recognition of her efforts in standing up to the Nazis and resisting their campaign to annihilate the Jews of Belgium, Yad Vashem recognized Queen Mother Elisabeth as one of the Righteous among the Nations. She died in Brussels a few months later, at the age of 89, on November 23, 1965.

Errázuriz, María (1893–1972)

María Errázuriz was a Chilean woman who worked with the French Resistance during the Nazi occupation in World War II, saving Jewish children at considerable risk to her own life.

Born in Santiago to an aristocratic Catholic family in 1893, she was the daughter of Agustín Edwards Ross, who served as the president of the Chilean senate between 1893 and 1895. At a young age she married an aspiring diplomat, Guillermo Errázuriz Vergara, who was a nephew of renowned artist José Tomás Errázuriz and a member of an elite family from central Chile. The young couple moved to Paris, where Errázuriz Vergara had been sent to take up a diplomatic post. In 1922, however, he committed suicide. Deciding to stay in Paris, María Errázuriz remained in France from this point on, and she stayed after the Germans arrived in 1940.

During the occupation Errázuriz, who was a social worker by profession, volunteered as a nurse at the Rothschild Jewish hospital. After 1942 one of the hospital's primary aims was to conceal as many Jews as possible from the Nazis, and Errázuriz would often risk her life to rescue Jewish children who had been separated from their parents. Some of the hospital buildings had been enclosed to become a de facto internment camp, where patients who recovered were detained prior to being sent to the transit camp at Drancy and then deported to Auschwitz.

Another social worker, Claire Heymann, who was Jewish, organized a number of escapes alongside Errázuriz, who used her wealth to assist those in distress. Heymann had worked at the Rothschild Hospital as a social worker since March 1932 and is today considered an unsung hero for organizing the escape network from the hospital throughout the war. Along with others, these two supplied false papers for Jewish children, arranging for them to be sent to friendly non-Jewish families for sanctuary. To the children in their care, they were known universally as "Auntie Claire" and "Auntie Marie." In February 1943 Errázuriz participated in a celebrated escape and transfer (organized by Heymann) of 16 children from the Rothschild orphanage to safe houses and convents in Paris and the province of Touraine.

In 1944 the French collaborationist police arrested Errázuriz as a resister. Handed over to the Gestapo for interrogation, she was tortured repeatedly as her persecutors sought knowledge of the whereabouts of French Resistance fighters and of Jews who were in hiding. It was reported later that she was subjected to the so-called "ice bath" torture, where her head was held under ice water until she nearly drowned. She never broke and was eventually released owing to her background as a Chilean national and through the intervention of the Spanish ambassador in Paris on her behalf.

On September 2, 1953, the French government awarded María Errázuriz the Legion of Honor for bravery and her contributions to the resistance during the war. In 1960 she returned to Chile, marrying her second husband, the French writer Jacques Feydeau. In 1972, at the age of 79, María Errázuriz died, but on October 27, 2005, she was recognized posthumously by Yad Vashem as one of the Righteous among the Nations. Present at the ceremony were her granddaughters Barbara, Solange, and Maria Victoria.

Feldhendler, Leon (1910–1945)

Leon Feldhendler was one of the two leaders of the prisoner revolt and breakout from the Nazi death camp at Sobibor on October 14, 1943.

The son of a rabbi, born in 1910, Feldhendler had been head of the Nazi-imposed Jewish Council (Judenrat) in his village of Żółkiewka, Poland, prior to his deportation in early 1943. At Sobibor he was put to work in the provisions warehouse and sometimes had to help out working with the Bahnhofkommando, the unit responsible for unloading trainloads of deportees being brought to their death.

In late September 1943 a train arrived from Minsk carrying a detachment of Soviet Jewish prisoners of war. Their officer was Lieutenant **Alexander Pechersky**. Already, back in July, the prisoners had organized a Jewish underground, but without trained leadership they were uncertain of how to proceed. They recruited Pechersky and placed him in command, along with their liaison—and now, second-in-command—Leon Feldhendler.

He and those around him had previously proposed a number of different plans for an escape from the camp, but all proposals were either stymied by SS discovery or proved to be impractical. The arrival of Pechersky turned things around, and with Feldhendler and a few others the prisoners put together an escape plan that did have a chance of succeeding. The plan saw the camp's SS personnel killed, with the Soviet prisoners of war raiding the camp armory. The telephone wires and electricity lines would then be cut, prior to a general insurrection that would storm the wire and the front gate.

Pechersky ran the operation in Camp 1, while Feldhendler commanded the operation in Camp 2. Just before 4:00 p.m. on October 14, 1943, the first SS soldier was killed with an axe. Soon, 10 more SS men, together with a number of Ukrainian guards, were also dispatched. Within an hour, the insurrection had taken place. Of the 600 prisoners who were in the camp, 300 managed to escape through the minefields that ringed the perimeter. Some 150 were killed by gunfire or by mines, and 170 were recaptured in the nearby forest and murdered. About 150 sick prisoners, together with those from Western Europe and Germany whom the underground had not managed to inform in time about the revolt, were also killed, as were all those who had stayed in the camp.

Some who were caught within the camp perimeter were shot immediately. The others, including those in the gas chamber complex who had not taken part in the uprising, were shot the next day when one of the leading senior officers in

Operation Reinhard, SS-Sturmbannführer Hermann Höfle, arrived in the camp from Lublin.

Among those who managed to get away, some looked for and joined partisan units, while others sought shelter among sympathetic Poles. Leon Feldhendler was one of the latter. He made his way to Lublin, where he survived in hiding until the city was liberated by the Russians in July 1944. After this, he shared a house on Kowalski Street 4 with two fellow survivors, Chaskiel Menche and Meier Ziss.

On April 2, 1945, however, he was shot and seriously wounded in suspicious circumstances that have never been fully resolved. One interpretation is that he was shot through the closed door of his apartment; another is that he was shot in an armed robbery. Other commentators have argued that he was shot by members of the right-wing Polish National Army who were actively hunting Jews. Taken to the hospital, Feldhendler died three days after the shooting.

In 1987 Feldhendler was portrayed by Alan Arkin in an award-winning movie, *Escape from Sobibor* (directed by Jack Gold). Thomas ("Toivi") Blatt, a survivor of the uprising, served as a technical consultant.

Feldhendler and those around him—other than the Soviet Jewish soldiers—were not trained combatants. They were forced to fight due to the imminence of their own deaths, with a desire for revenge against those who had killed their families, and a hope that through their actions they could so upset the killing process that more lives would be saved. Afterward, many of the survivors provided comprehensive firsthand accounts of the mass murders at Sobibor, making available valuable details that would probably otherwise never be known.

Fleischmann, Gisi (1892–1944)

Gisi Fleischmann was a leader of Slovak Jewry during the Holocaust and one of the heads of the Bratislava Working Group, an underground organization dedicated to helping Jews through (among other things) the payment of large bribes to German and Slovak officials.

The eldest of three children, she was born in Pressburg (Bratislava), Slovakia, in 1892 (her year of birth is also variously given as 1895 and 1897), to Julius Fischer and Jetty Elinger. She only had eight years of schooling, but when she had the chance taught herself German literature, history, and art history.

Slovakia, which was a Hungarian possession, became one half of the new state of Czechoslovakia in 1918 and a Nazi-imposed "Protectorate" in March 1939. When World War II broke out in September of that year, Fleischmann was away in London. She returned home to her husband and two daughters, sent the girls to Palestine, and then decided to remain in Bratislava, where she would be able to assist the Jewish community.

A Zionist possessed of considerable natural leadership abilities, she found herself heading up HICEM, a Jewish immigrant aid organization formed in 1927 by the merger of three earlier Jewish migration associations: HIAS (Hebrew Immigrant Aid Society), ICA (Jewish Colonization Association), and Emigdirect. She was able to function in this capacity through Bratislava's *Ústredňa Židov*, or Jewish Council.

In the summer of 1942 Gisi, working with the ultra-Orthodox rabbi **Chaim Michael Dov Weissmandl**, started the so-called "Working Group" as a secret organization for rescuing Jews. The time was now long past for emigration; sheer survival was the current objective. Part of her activities involved liaising with the American Jewish Joint Distribution Committee (known colloquially as the Joint), a task made difficult since the United States had become involved in the war against Nazi Germany in December 1941; as a result, financial transfers were nearly impossible to arrange. Nonetheless, Fleischmann arranged to conduct a clandestine correspondence, in code, with numerous other Jewish organizations, particularly with Hechalutz (an association of Jewish youth whose aim was to train its members to settle the land in Israel), and with representatives of the Jewish Agency for Palestine stationed in Istanbul. To these and other organizations she provided alarming reports on the Jewish situation in Central and Eastern Europe. In 1943 she also directed rescue operations for Polish ghetto survivors, working to ferry groups of orphans across the borders of Poland, Slovakia, and Hungary.

Arguably the most important initiative of the Working Group was an audacious attempt to save Jewish lives that became known as the Europa Plan—which, though it did not succeed, would have rescued large numbers of Jews from Nazism.

In pursuit of the plan, Rabbi Weissmandl and Fleischmann negotiated an agreement with the Nazis in late 1942 in which a ransom of up to 2 million dollars would be provided to stop many of the transports heading to "the East"—which signified, in the eyes of those with insider knowledge, certain death. The idea was that Dieter Wisliceny, one of the key Jewish experts working for Adolf Eichmann, would receive the bribe. The promise of an initial payment (with more to come) seemed to work, and the deportation of Slovak Jewry was held back for a considerable period. In the long term, however, the plan failed; the bribe was pitched to Slovak officials rather than to the Nazis, and it was the Slovak officials who checked the deportation process—something they could not do indefinitely.

Another ingredient marking the unfeasibility of the Europa Plan was the reluctance of the Joint and Hechalutz to devote moneys which would, directly or indirectly, go to the Nazis. The representative of the Joint in Switzerland, Saly Mayer, was especially wary about such a scheme, to say nothing of the legalities—of which he was all too aware—of how currency transfers in a time of war transgressed the Trading with the Enemy Act.

There was one area in which the Working Group was, however, successful; its distribution of the "Auschwitz Report" detailing the workings of the Auschwitz killing machinery as revealed by two escapees, **Rudolf Vrba** and Alfréd Wetzler. Escaping on April 7, 1944, the two made their way to the Slovak Jewish Council in Žilina and presented their report and evidence. It was then copied and given to **Rezső Kasztner**, head of the Zionist Aid and Rescue Committee in Bratislava, who passed it on to Weissmandl and Fleischmann.

Weissmandl forwarded his version to a member of the Hungarian Foreign Ministry; from there, it reached George Mantello, a Jewish diplomat working for the Salvadoran consulate in Geneva. Through her own contacts, Fleischmann ensured that the report reached the press, and in the spring of 1944 she was therefore responsible for conveying the first eyewitness testimony on the death camps to the wider world.

On October 15, 1944, during the mass deportations of Jews taking place at that time, the SS arrested Gisi Fleischmann. At first she was taken to the concentration camp at Sered and offered her freedom if she gave up the names of all the Jews she then knew to be in hiding. When she declined to offer any names she was tortured but still refused to divulge any information. On October 17, 1944, she was sent on the last transport from Slovakia to Auschwitz. SS-Hauptsturmführer Alois Brunner, assistant to Adolf Eichmann, ordered that the words "return undesirable" be placed on the deportation directive alongside her name. When the train arrived at Auschwitz on October 18, Fleischmann's name was called, and two SS officers immediately took her away to the gas chambers. She was never seen again.

Foley, Frank (1884–1958)

Francis Edward ("Frank") Foley was ostensibly head of the British Passport Control Office (PCO) in Berlin before World War II, though in reality he was Britain's most senior spy there. During his time in Berlin, he is estimated to have saved 10,000 German Jews in the years following 1933.

Foley was born on November 24, 1884, in Highbridge, Somerset; his father was a railway worker whose family was originally Irish. He received a Jesuit education before being sent to study classics at the Université de France in Poitiers. During World War I he served as an officer in France, where he was wounded and invalided back to Britain. There he was recruited into an intelligence unit, which saw him appointed as PCO in Berlin after the war—though in reality he was head of the British Secret Intelligence Service in that city. He was stationed in Berlin from 1922 until the outbreak of World War II in 1939.

As chief PCO, Foley constantly bent the rules in order to help thousands of Jews escape Nazi Germany. He assumed that he possessed wide latitude to decide on the admission of migrants into the British Empire. After passage of the Nuremberg Laws in 1935, a growing number of Jews applied for permits to enter the United

Kingdom or other parts of the British Empire, and these came directly to Foley's office. His ingenuity in helping facilitate their entry knew few bounds. While British immigration regulations were tight, Foley exploited procedural loopholes wherever possible, based on his understanding of what he could get away with.

After the *Kristallnacht* pogrom of November 9–10, 1938, Foley utilized legal means whenever possible. Thus, in one case, when entry to Palestine required a surety of £1,000 in landing capital, and the person in question could only produce £10, Foley issued the permit upon a promise that the balance of £990 would be paid once the subject landed at Haifa. On another occasion, Foley accepted a guarantee in writing that the sum would be available once the applicant had crossed the border safely into the Netherlands. In such myriad ways, Foley issued up to 10,000 visas for Palestine.

Foley and his wife, Katharine, also took Jews into their home overnight to shield them from Nazi search parties and then facilitated their escape the next morning. Included among such people was the spiritual leader of Berlin Jewry, Rabbi **Leo Baeck**.

One of the problems Foley faced—and which he ignored—was the fact that he did not possess diplomatic immunity and ran a serious risk of arrest and imprisonment if his actions were questioned by the Gestapo or denounced to the authorities by the British Foreign Office. Yet knowing this seemed to make him only more audacious. Not only did he forge passports—as a Secret Intelligence Service officer he had skills that most others did not—but he also entered the Nazi concentration camp at Sachsenhausen and presented such documents to the camp authorities in order to have Jews released. Of course, by forging these documents and presenting them as official he was also breaking British laws and clearly exceeding any official position he might have possessed.

Finally, when war broke out in September 1939, Foley left behind a considerable number of pre-approved visas that could be utilized by those seeking sanctuary after his departure. This, too, was completely illegal, but it saved even more lives.

Once he arrived back in London he assumed full duties as a Secret Intelligence Service officer. In 1941, for instance, he was given the responsibility of interrogating Hitler's deputy, Rudolf Hess, after Hess's abortive flight to Scotland. When the war ended Foley was sent back to Germany to continue his work, which included the search for former SS officers charged with war crimes and crimes against humanity.

Upon his retirement in 1949, Foley retreated to a much quieter life in Stourbridge, in the West Midlands. He rarely spoke about his exploits in saving Jewish lives, and he did not seek any recognition for what he had done. He died at Stourbridge on May 8, 1958.

Owing to accounts from those he had rescued, Yad Vashem decided to research Foley's exploits. After considerable discussion and in view of the vast number of people he saved—and the fact that he operated without any apparent ulterior motives—on February 25, 1999, Yad Vashem recognized Frank Foley as one of the Righteous among the Nations.

This honor began a wave of appreciation. On November 24, 2004, the 120th anniversary of Foley's birth, a plaque was placed on the house where he was born; in May 2005 a statue dedicated to him was unveiled; on May 31, 2009, a garden was dedicated in his memory at London's Sternberg Centre for Judaism (a campus area housing a number of Jewish institutions); and in 2010 Foley was named a Hero of the Holocaust by the British government.

The level of resistance shown by Foley to the Nazis ensured the survival of thousands of Jews prior to the outbreak of war. While some rescuers saved more Jews during the Holocaust itself, none were as successful as Foley beforehand, underscoring the achievement of this remarkable man.

Fry, Varian (1907–1967)

Varian Mackey Fry was an American rescuer of Jews during the Holocaust. Born in New York on October 15, 1907, Fry attended Harvard University, where he studied classics. He began his working life as a photographer, but in 1940 he went to Marseille, France, as a representative of an American refugee organization called the Emergency Rescue Committee. While there, he worked hard to secure passports and visas enabling refugees to leave Vichy France and reach safety.

Fry's academic background fitted him well to take on the role he assumed in later years. An exceptionally bright student at Harvard, he started a career in journalism while there, establishing the literary journal *Hound & Horn* with fellow student Lincoln Kirstein. On June 2, 1931, Fry married Eileen Avery Hughes, an editor at *Atlantic Monthly*.

Fry first visited Berlin in 1935. On this visit he saw SA men assaulting Jews in the city's streets, and from then on knew he could not remain indifferent. When he returned to the United States he decided to act. In 1935 he wrote in the *New York Times* about the Nazi treatment of the Jews and used other venues to raise awareness of the issue at a time when American isolationists preferred not to know.

After Germany invaded France in June 1940 the Emergency Rescue Committee, a private American relief organization, sent Fry to France to aid anti-Nazi refugees who were in danger of being arrested by the Gestapo. He landed in Marseille with a fighting fund of US $3,000, hoping to use his American citizenship and neutral status as a way to evade French measures for refusing exit visas. He had no previous experience with the kind of underground activities he would have to undertake to obtain the necessary papers, but by the end of his mission he had saved upward of 4,000 people from the hands of the Nazis.

Fry and a group of accomplices composed a list and created clandestine escape routes for the refugees under imminent threat of arrest by the Gestapo and Vichy French police. His organization had a very specific focus: the rescue of intellectuals, artists, musicians, and others in the creative core of European culture. All those opposing the Nazis—whether Jewish or not—were legitimate targets for Fry's efforts. Among those rescued were Marc Chagall, Hannah Arendt, Pablo Casals, Heinrich Mann, Lion Feuchtwanger, Franz Werfel, Konrad Heiden, Max Ernst, and many others.

Fry's strategy was to hide those he was saving at the Villa Air-Bel in Marseille until they could be smuggled across the border to Spain. From there, they would move to Portugal, and then to the United States. He did not work alone—his companions at the villa included Miriam Davenport, Mary Jayne Gold, and Hiram Bingham IV, the U.S. vice-consul in Marseille who was sympathetic to the plight of the Jews and helped Fry obtain the necessary visas for those on his list to enter the United States.

Varian Fry, an American rescuer of Jews in 1940 and 1941. With no prior experience in underground activities, he worked clandestinely to save the flower of European cultural life. In this capacity, through his Emergency Rescue Committee, he saved artists, intellectuals, musicians, and many others. Recalled to the neutralist United States in shame, he lived out the rest of his life in obscurity until his death in 1967, at the age of 59. (United States Holocaust Memorial Museum, courtesy of Annette Fry)

Fry also established contacts with the French underground, hired professional forgers, bribed border guards, and even consorted with Corsican mobsters. His front organization, the American Relief Center, used all manner of illegal means, such as black-market funds, forged documents, secret mountain passages, and sea routes, in order to move endangered refugees from France.

When Fry's resources for procuring visas dried up, he smuggled the refugees into Spain. For this, and for acting without a valid passport of his own, he was arrested by Vichy police and deported to the United States in September 1941. He had been in France for 13 months, during which time he was under constant surveillance and was, more than once, detained and questioned. Upon his return to the United States he was reprimanded by the State Department for his illegal activities. No recognition was made for his outstanding humanitarian rescues.

After the war Fry continued his work as a journalist and editor, but he became increasingly distressed by the memory of what he had seen and experienced during the war. He lived out the remaining years of his life in obscurity, developed ulcers, and was diagnosed with manic depression. On September 13, 1967, while in the midst of revising his memoirs, he died of a cerebral hemorrhage.

Shortly before his death, the French government recognized his contribution through the award of the *Croix de Chevalier de la Legion d'Honneur*. In 1991 the United States Holocaust Memorial Council posthumously awarded Fry the Eisenhower Liberation Medal, and in 1994 he became the first U.S. citizen to be recognized as one of the Righteous among the Nations by Yad Vashem. Varian Fry's remarkable efforts on behalf of Jews and the cultural elite of Europe was also related in *Varian's War* (directed by Lionel Chetwynd, 2001), an award-winning movie starring William Hurt in the title role and Julia Ormond as Miriam Davenport.

For his work in saving thousands, Fry is frequently mentioned alongside other major rescuers, such as **Oskar Schindler** and **Raoul Wallenberg**. Indeed, there are some in the United States who have referred to him as "the Oskar Schindler of America."

G

Gebelev, Mikhail (1905–1942)

Mikhail Gebelev was an anti-Nazi resistance leader in the ghetto of Minsk. Born on October 15, 1905, in the Jewish *shtetl* (village) of Uzliany, he later moved to Minsk and worked there as a clerk and public servant.

After Germany invaded the Soviet Union and occupied Minsk on June 28, 1941, Gebelev went into hiding. He had good reason. Within days of the occupation, Einsatzgruppen squads massacred 2,000 Jewish leaders and intellectuals; additional murders of Jews henceforth became a daily occurrence. Within the first few months of the German occupation, at least 20,000 Jews were slaughtered.

On July 20, 1941, the Minsk ghetto was created, to be managed by a Nazi-appointed Jewish Council (Judenrat). At this time, the total population of the ghetto was about 80,000, of which some 50,000 were prewar inhabitants; those remaining were refugees forcibly resettled by the Germans from smaller villages nearby. In August 1941 activists led by Isay Pavlovich Kazinetz, a Jewish engineer, established an underground group in which members forged documents, set up a radio receiver, and aided Soviet resistance in the area. This was one of the earliest expressions of Jewish resistance after the invasion of the Soviet Union.

Having escaped the clutches of the Nazis, Gebelev made contact with Kazinetz, who appointed him as liaison officer between the communist resisters on the Aryan side and the ghetto fighters, whose leader was a Polish Yiddish writer from Białystok, **Hersh Smolar**.

Together with another resistance leader, Matvey Pruslin, Gebelev quickly emerged as the unstated head of the ghetto underground due to his charisma and ingenuity, and he played a key role in Kazinetz's plans to stage large-scale simultaneous uprisings throughout Minsk to drive out the Germans and hold the city until the Red Army arrived. These uprisings would be conducted by communists, ghetto fighters, and Soviet prisoners of war incarcerated in the city. The proposed rebellion did not take place, however, owing to its plans being leaked to the Nazis. Kazinetz was among those ultimately hunted down. Before he was taken, however, he shot two Germans; wounded and captured, he then held out under torture and refused to reveal any names or information, even after one of his eyes was put out. On May 7, 1942, Isay Kazinetz and 28 other underground fighters were publicly hanged in the center of Minsk. It is recorded that his last words were "Death to the Nazis!"

Despite this huge setback, the resistance movement in the ghetto remained largely intact owing to Gebelev's leadership and the support of the head of the Judenrat,

Moshe Yoffe. In the period that followed, Gebelev organized mass escapes from the ghetto to the forests outside Minsk, where the escapees formed (or joined) partisan units. The underground's main objective was to save as many Jewish lives as possible, realizing that all were condemned to death in any case. At night, under extremely dangerous conditions, couriers led small groups of prisoners out of the ghetto. There were as many as 300 active members of Gebelev's underground organization, and through their efforts perhaps up to 10,000 Jews achieved their objective of escaping the Minsk ghetto, with many joining the partisans.

It was said of Gebelev himself that on the numerous occasions he was encouraged to flee his reply was always that "I am here in the line of duty!" In August 1942, however, he was arrested by local collaborators while preparing the escape of a group of Soviet prisoners of war. He was handed over to the Gestapo, and, like Kazinetz before him, brutally tortured while refusing to provide any names or information. On August 15, 1942, he was hanged in the Nazi prison in Minsk.

The ghetto itself was liquidated on October 21, 1943. Those Jews still remaining in the city at this time, including Moshe Yoffe and Mikhail Gebelev's 80-year-old father, Liev, were murdered, with most being deported to the extermination camp at Sobibor. Several thousand were massacred at a camp that had been established on the outskirts of Minsk, Maly Trostenets. By the time the Red Army retook the city on July 3, 1944, only a handful of Jewish survivors remained.

Hersh Smolar did manage to escape just prior to the final liquidation of the ghetto, and in 1946 he produced a memoir of Minsk, *Fun Minsker geto* (published in English as *The Minsk Ghetto: Soviet-Jewish Partisans against the Nazis*, 1989). In the book he describes in some depth Gebelev's role in the resistance movement, highlighting both his initiatives and his heroism in the face of immense obstacles and constant danger.

Gerstein, Kurt (1905–1945)

Kurt Gerstein, born in 1905, was simultaneously a senior SS officer intimately connected to the Nazi mass murder of the Jews at Auschwitz and other death camps, and, paradoxically, a man unremitting in his resistance to the Nazi extermination program, who sought ways both to stop it and publicize it to the outside world.

Recalled through at least two biographies, two plays, a novel, and an award-winning movie, Gerstein's life and efforts prompt key questions even now: how could this man be both a major actor in the murder machinery and a resister to it? Should he be awarded the status of Righteous among the Nations? Were his activities carried out because of his understanding of the plight of the Jews, or did he operate from other motives? And if so, does the difference matter? Did his efforts ultimately save anyone?

Gerstein was a deeply devoted Christian from Westphalia, a low-ranking officer in the SS, and a member of the Waffen-SS Institute for Hygiene. In the 1930s he served two periods of detention for defying Nazi authority on the grounds of his Christian principles (one of them in Welzheim concentration camp, near Stuttgart), and he was dismissed from membership in the Nazi party before being reinstated.

In early 1941 he joined the SS and because of his technical abilities in both chemistry and engineering rose quickly to become Head of Technical Disinfection Services. In this capacity, on August 17, 1942, he went to Bełzec death camp, where he witnessed the gassing of some 3,000 Jews; the next day he went to Treblinka and saw a repetition of the killing process. He was then given responsibility for ordering vast quantities of Zyklon B gas to use in the mass murder of Jews at Auschwitz.

On the night of August 20–21, 1942, on his way back to Germany, Gerstein traveled by train from Warsaw to Berlin. Deeply disturbed by what he had seen at Bełzec and Treblinka, he was desperate to unburden himself; fate intervened in the person of the secretary to the Swedish legation in Berlin, Baron Göran von Otter, who was on the same train. Engaging him in conversation, Gerstein exclaimed: "Yesterday I saw something appalling." "Is it to do with the Jews?" von Otter asked, and the conversation—more like a monologue—began. In a feverish conversation lasting 10 hours, Gerstein poured out the whole story, crying and smoking incessantly. He related all he had just seen and begged von Otter to inform the Swedish government. Von Otter later recalled that Gerstein gave him details, names, and how he had come to be involved. He was determined to act as a witness to the Nazi atrocities, not anticipating that he would himself be drawn inextricably into the murder machinery. He pleaded with von Otter to inform the Allies and the outside world so that the

Kurt Gerstein, head of Technical Disinfection Services in the Waffen-SS Institute for Hygiene. Responsible for ordering vast quantities of Zyklon B gas canisters needed for the annihilation of the Jews, he sought every opportunity to alert the world to the Nazi extermination program and to mitigate its effects. (AP Photo)

Allied air forces, acting on Swedish information, would drop millions of leaflets over Germany. The German people, horrified, would then rebel against Hitler.

This was not the only occasion on which Gerstein sought to draw attention to what he had witnessed. He attended upon the papal nuncio in Berlin, Archbishop Cesare Orsenigo, but was turned away; he also saw numerous members of the Confessing and Lutheran churches, and opponents of the Nazi regime. In fact, he spoke to anyone who would listen, and often to those he did not even know, in his eagerness to get the message out.

Apart from the Swedish authorities, the Allies, and the Vatican, Gerstein also tried to convey his message via a friend, J. H. Ubbink, in the Netherlands. In February 1943 Ubbink received a message from Gerstein about the gas chambers, which he passed to the Dutch resistance. Skeptical, they decided not to forward the report or circulate it publicly. Another Gerstein attempt to let the world know thus failed.

While attempting to raise consciousness, he also took practical steps to negate, or at least minimize, the devastating effects of his office. As the war progressed, a despairing Gerstein ordered that shipments of Zyklon B gas canisters be buried on the pretext that they had spoiled in transit and posed a risk to German soldiers and civilians. He tried, unsuccessfully, to have a chemical removed from the gas compound that caused severe irritation, so that death would be less painful for the victims. In addition, he fought with his superior officers who demanded that ever-larger consignments of Zyklon B be dispatched, arguing that storing large amounts was extremely hazardous. If hit by Allied air raids, the result would be a catastrophic loss of life throughout the region where the gas was stored.

His efforts saw only small returns, despite an inner turmoil that aged him prematurely, brought on clinical depression, and led to a suicide attempt. Finally, on April 22, 1945, he defected to the Allies, making his way to French lines in the occupied town of Reutlingen. He was well received and given the opportunity to write a full report (actually, three) of what he had done and seen. Later, he was transferred to the Cherche-Midi military prison in Paris, where he was treated as a war criminal. On July 25, 1945, while still in French custody, he was found hanged in his cell, an alleged suicide.

Many questions have been asked as to why Gerstein behaved as he did. Moved to join the SS in early 1941 "to see things from the inside," he was shocked and outraged at the death of his sister-in-law, a victim of the so-called T-4 euthanasia campaign. Accordingly, he sought both to change the direction of Nazi policies and to publicize the crimes being committed. He saw himself as acting the way a committed Christian should. As a covert anti-Nazi, he had a very special mission—nothing less than infiltrating the SS in order to expose the atrocities it was perpetrating.

Gerstein's actions pose a major dilemma, however. Increasingly drawn into the very system he was trying to overthrow, he realized at every stage what he was doing and found himself incapable of extricating himself from its grasp. In view of this, how can he be recognized for his efforts? Moreover, bearing in mind that he was an SS officer whose name appears on receipts for large orders of gas canisters, is it even proper that he should be?

On the one hand, Gerstein sought desperately to save Jewish lives, at enormous personal risk, through alerting people to the Nazi measures and through the destruction of the very gas he was compelled to order. On the other hand, a critic must ask: what, ultimately, did he achieve, other than his own sad death, the destitution of his family, and a place in the annals of those who tried to combat the Nazi state from the inside?

On August 17, 1950, a denazification court in Tübingen concluded that Gerstein was a Nazi offender for his assistance in the production and delivery of Zyklon B. His widow, Elfriede, was denied a pension, though in January 1965, after a long battle, Baron von Otter and others managed to restore Gerstein's reputation, and he received a posthumous pardon.

His report became perhaps the most horrifying eyewitness account of the Holocaust. After he had witnessed the gassing at Bełzec, he was told by the commandant, SS Major Christian Wirth: "There are not ten people alive who have seen or will see as much as you." Gerstein worked to ensure that as many people as possible "saw" what he had seen. Although much of his report is unscientific and exaggerated, many other Nazis verified after the war the basic facts he recounts. In its essentials, the report gets much right. SS colonel Dr. Wilhelm Pfannenstiel, who was with Gerstein at Bełzec on the fateful day he witnessed the gassing, testified in court on June 6, 1950, that the account given by Gerstein was basically correct.

Gerstein's self-appointed mission was to expose the horrors of Nazism to the world and mitigate the suffering around him. His is the story of a remarkable and highly complex man who refused to surrender his conscience in the face of mass murder. He realized that he was continuing to commit the very acts he repudiated, albeit via legally enforceable orders in accordance with the law of the land at that time. To disobey those orders would have put him totally beyond the pale and back in the concentration camp—and, thus, completely unable to achieve the results he sought.

The situation in which Kurt Gerstein found himself—the conflict between legality and morality—was one that probably could not have been resolved; and that, perhaps, is the essence of his tragedy.

Gies, Miep (1909–2010)

Miep Gies was an Austrian-born Dutch citizen who hid Anne Frank and her family, along with several other Jews, in Amsterdam between 1942 and 1944.

She was born Hermine Santruschitz on February 15, 1909, in Vienna. In 1920 she was sent to Leiden, in the Netherlands, to escape the unrest and food shortages of post–World War I Austria, and was taken in as a foster child by the Nieuwenburg family. As a girl she was given the nickname "Miep."

In 1933 she went to work for Otto Frank, a German Jewish businessman who had fled Germany with his family to escape the Nazis. Soon thereafter, she met Jan Gies, a bookkeeper. The two grew fond of the Frank family, with whom they developed a close friendship.

In 1941 German occupation officials in the Netherlands insisted that she join a Nazi women's association. When she refused, her passport was canceled, and she was ordered to be deported to her native Austria within 90 days. By way of response and in haste, Jan Gies married her on July 16, 1941, so that she could obtain Dutch citizenship and thereby avoid deportation. Then, as German occupation officials and Dutch collaborators began to persecute Jews and deport them to unknown destinations in "the East," the Gieses decided to keep the Frank family safe. In July 1942, after some consideration as to method, they hid the Franks, along with several other Jews, in a small second-story apartment above Opekta, Otto Frank's spice company located at Amsterdam's Prinsengracht 263.

At considerable risk to her own safety, Miep Gies supplied the Franks with food and medicine. The hiding place was only a short distance from her home, and Gies continued to work in the office below the apartment so as to prevent unwanted intrusion by anyone seeking access to the second floor. Throughout the period in which the Franks were in hiding, Opekta had to continue operating in order to protect the family, as any change in routine could have led the Gestapo to investigate. Therefore, Gies and those around her kept things running smoothly to maintain the charade that nothing untoward was happening.

On August 4, 1944, as Gies worked at her desk, a police official walked into the office, pointed a gun at her, and demanded that she show him the secret room. Somebody had tipped the police off about the Franks. Within minutes, the Franks and other people hiding in the second-floor apartment were arrested and taken away. Gies escaped only because the police officer had been a native of Vienna and understood her situation. The Franks were eventually sent to death camps.

Gies saved and hid Anne Frank's diary, the whereabouts of which she kept secret until the end of the war. In 1945 Otto Frank, who had survived Auschwitz, returned to Amsterdam and was reunited with Miep and Jan Gies. It was then that he learned of Anne's death at Bergen-Belsen. Determined to let the world know about his family's ordeal, he permitted the diary's publication in 1947.

Gies hid the Frank family for more than two years. Although devastated by their arrest, she had sufficient presence of mind to ensure that she too was not picked up at the same time, enabling her to continue her work as a resister.

After the war, Gies developed into something of a celebrity, a status she eschewed. She always held that she did not do anything remarkable, preferring to believe that she only did what anyone in the same position should have done. In her view, although risking arrest every day for two years, what she did was simply her human duty. She developed her ideas around this theme in her memoir, *Anne Frank Remembered: The Story of the Woman Who Helped to Hide the Frank Family*. In 1947, when she and her husband moved to a new home at Jekerstraat 65, they allowed Otto Frank to move in with them.

Gies received many honors recognizing her efforts to save Jewish lives during the Holocaust. In 1994 she was awarded the Order of Merit of the Federal Republic of Germany, and in 1995 she was recognized as one of the Righteous among the Nations by Yad Vashem. In 1997 she was knighted in the Order of Orange-Nassau by Queen Beatrix of the Netherlands; on July 30, 2009, she received the Grand Decoration of Honor for Services to the Republic of Austria.

On January 11, 2010, just short of her 101st birthday, Miep Gies died after a fall in a nursing home in Hoorn, a town outside of Amsterdam.

Gildenman, Moshe (1898–1958)

Moshe Gildenman ("Uncle Misha") was a Jewish partisan commander in the Volhynia region of Ukraine. Born in Korets (then in Russian Poland) on January 1, 1898, he was an active member of the Jewish community until the outbreak of World War II in September 1939.

Soviet forces entered Korets on September 17, 1939. When Germany invaded the Soviet Union on June 22, 1941, some 500 Jews managed to escape Korets before German troops entered the town on July 2, 1941. On August 8, 1941, Jewish men were called up for forced labor, only to be murdered on the outskirts of the city. Others were killed as the year progressed, and additional antisemitic measures were introduced. When winter came, the community suffered from hunger and disease.

On May 21, 1942, the Germans carried out an action against the Jews of Korets, and more than 2,200 people, including Moshe Gildenman's wife and 13-year-old daughter, were killed near the village of Kozak. About 1,000 survivors were then concentrated in a ghetto, where a Judenrat (Jewish Council) was established under Moshe Krasnostawski. The Judenrat, in turn, maintained contacts with a small Jewish underground movement of about 20 fighters that Gildenman, by this stage known generally as "Uncle Misha," and his son Simkha had established. Their arsenal consisted of one pistol, five rounds of ammunition, and some butchers' knives.

On September 25, 1942, when the Nazis ordered the final liquidation of the Korets ghetto, Moshe Krasnostawski directed that it be set on fire, during which many people escaped. Gildenman led his small team, now numbering only 11, to the forests north of the town. There, after working their way through the woods for about two weeks, the team members met and took in the survivors of a group of

Jewish fighters and created a partisan unit. They were armed only with weapons they managed to capture, but in this they were effective; they ambushed a unit of policemen and captured six rifles, two pistols, and several hand grenades, and then attacked small police stations in the area and seized more weapons. From these beginnings, they fought both German *Volksdeutsche* and their Ukrainian collaborators.

In January 1943 the group joined up with General Alexander Saburov, one of the leaders of the Soviet partisan movement in Ukraine and western Russia. Gildenman's men aligned themselves with Saburov's partisans, setting up an all-Jewish combat unit. In view of the fact that Soviet policy did not permit segregated Jewish partisan units, other fighters, of Ukrainian origin, joined Gildenman's ranks. The Jews in the unit became a minority, though it was always known specifically as Uncle Misha's Jewish group.

The partisans launched numerous operations in the Zhitomir area, setting mines and engaging in sabotage until the region was liberated by Soviet troops in October 1943. Some 500 survivors returned to Korets after the liberation. Many realized that there was little future for them in remaining under Soviet rule, and most of the survivors left subsequently for destinations in Israel or the West.

Gildenman and his unit volunteered to continue the fight against the Germans. Now a soldier and no longer Uncle Misha, Moshe Gildenman was given the rank of captain and attached to an engineering corps. He and his son Simkha stayed together, fighting with the Soviet army during its advance across Poland and Germany, until the capture of Berlin on May 2, 1945, and Germany's surrender six days later.

With the war over, Simkha Gildenman returned to Korets. Upon identifying the Ukrainian who killed his mother and sister, he shot the man on the spot.

Moshe Gildenman—Uncle Misha—received a number of military decorations for his efforts during the war; these included the Soviet Order of the Red Star, the "War of the Homeland" medal, and the Polish Order of the Cross of Grunwald. In 1950 he settled in Rehovot, Israel, where he died in 1958.

Glasberg, Alexandre (1902–1981)

Father Alexandre Glasberg was a French Catholic priest who saved the lives of Jews during the Holocaust.

Born to a Jewish family in Zhitmomir, Ukraine, in 1902, Glasberg was baptized along with his brother, Vila (later to be known as Victor Vermont), when they were both children. In 1921 Glasberg went to Vienna to escape anti-Jewish pogroms in the aftermath of the Russian Revolution, and while there undertook religious studies. In 1933 he moved to France, where he entered the seminary of Moulins prior to being ordained in 1938. He was appointed vicar of the parish of Notre-Dame de Saint-Alban, a poor suburb of Lyon, whose pastor, Father Laurent Remilleux, was a pioneer in providing welfare and relief to refugees.

After the Nazis occupied France in 1940, Glasberg was appointed by Cardinal Pierre-Marie Gerlier of Lyon as delegate to the Committee to Aid Refugees, and from there he began playing an active role in the French Resistance. He started by hiding political refugees from the Nazis but extended this to working with the Oeuvre de Secours aux Enfants (OSE), a Jewish organization dedicated to rescuing Jewish children.

In early 1942, alongside Father Pierre Chaillet, Jean-Marie Soutou, and a young student, Germaine Ribière, he founded the resistance group Amitié Chrétienne (Christian Friendship), whose purpose was to help Jews and victims of Nazism from being interned in French camps. He created a network of five absorption centers stretching throughout southern France, and he established shelters that took in hundreds of Jews who had been released from French internment camps.

In the summer of 1942, with the start of large-scale arrests of Jews in southern France, Glasberg began forging the identities of those he was trying to rescue and stepped up the pace of his activities. He actively participated in the rescue of 180 Jewish children held in the camp at Vénissieux, near Lyon, while moving others through various safe houses. He also worked with Jewish rescue associations and made sure that Jews living in his shelters were not pressured into converting to Catholicism.

In December 1942 he was forced to go into hiding after French police and the Gestapo tried to arrest him. Soon thereafter, in early 1943, Pierre-Marie Théas, Bishop of Montauba, created a fictitious position for him under the false name of Father Elie Corvin. He was appointed pastor of the Honor-de-Cos in the hamlet of Léribosc, in the department of Tarn-et-Garonne. During this period he was an active member of the French Resistance, occupying a position within the Departmental Liberation Committee chaired by Paul Guiral.

While he was in hiding, his brother, Vila Glasberg, took charge of rescue activities, but on August 16, 1943, the Gestapo, mistaking Vila for his brother, arrested, deported, and murdered him. Father Alexandre Glasberg continued to evade the Gestapo and survived the war in hiding.

After 1945 Glasberg helped facilitate the emigration of Holocaust survivors to Palestine, participating in the activities of *Aliyah Bet*, the illegal campaign helping Jews migrate from Europe to what was then still Mandate Palestine under the British. He was closely involved with the ship *Exodus 1947*, a celebrated case in which some 4,515 Jewish refugees and displaced persons forced their way into Palestine under the guns of Britain's Royal Navy. Glasberg and Rose Warfman, née Gluck, a survivor of Auschwitz and member of the French Resistance, made false identity papers for the passengers, the easier to facilitate their arrival in Palestine upon landing.

After the establishment of the State of Israel on May 14, 1948, Glasberg also worked with the Israeli intelligence organization Mossad in assisting the migration process. Beyond this, he used his position as a Catholic priest to enable Israeli soldiers to maintain communication through East and West Jerusalem during the War of Independence, and he was one of those responsible for purchasing weapons in Czechoslovakia and facilitating their transit through Corsica to Israel. In 1951 he participated in Operation Ezra and Nehemiah, the airlift organized by Mossad to evacuate Iraqi Jews, and assisted in the mass emigration of Jews from Morocco and Egypt.

Father Alexandre Glasberg died in France in 1981. In 2004 he and his brother Vila were both recognized as Righteous among the Nations by Yad Vashem. Many observers at the time argued that if the brothers were still alive then they would probably want to be identified as Jews rather than those "among the nations." In that case, however, because the status of "righteous" is only awarded to non-Jews, Yad Vashem could not have recognized them for their work.

Göring, Albert (1895–1966)

Albert Göring was the younger brother of Hermann Göring, head of the German Luftwaffe (air force), who was, for a lengthy period, the second most powerful man in Germany after Adolf Hitler. Unlike his brother, however, Albert Göring was bitterly opposed to National Socialism and worked to save Jews and anti-Nazi dissidents.

Göring was born in Berlin on March 9, 1895, the fifth child of Heinrich Göring, former governor of German South-West Africa, and his wife, Franziska "Fanny" Tiefenbrunn. The Görings were an elite household with many extended family connections in Germany, Switzerland, and Austria; they could count among their relatives such names as Zeppelin, Grimm, Burckhardt, and Merck, among others. Because Heinrich Göring was absent from his family for long periods on state duties, the children spent a lot of time with their godfather, Baron Hermann von Epenstein, who took on much of the responsibility for raising them. Ironically, as it would turn out, von Epenstein was of part-Jewish background, and rumors abounded for many years that it was he who actually fathered both Hermann and Albert during a long-term affair with their mother.

Unlike his brother, Albert Göring evinced no interest in politics, preferring to live the high life as a spoiled child of the near-aristocracy. With the ascent to office of his brother's party in 1933, however, he proved to be a committed opponent of deep moral conviction. Moving to Vienna, he worked in a film studio and lived for a time on an allowance from von Epenstein and often spoke out against Adolf Hitler. Once Austria was absorbed into Germany in March 1938, this opposition marked him out for harassment from the Gestapo, but he was protected by his brother Hermann, who ensured that Gestapo attention would always be deflected.

An early example of the assistance Göring could provide related to his former employer, the Austrian film producer Oskar Pilzer. A well-known member of the Jewish community in Vienna, Pilzer was arrested by the Gestapo immediately after the *Anschluss* of Austria and Germany. Göring not only used his influence to arrange for Pilzer to be freed but also helped him and his family to escape Germany; they went first to Rome, and then Paris.

Testimonies from those who survived the Holocaust provide ample evidence that Göring saved many Jewish lives and provided support in other ways. One example among many relates to his intervention when he saw a group of Jewish women forced to scrub the street. Göring joined them, and the SS officer on the scene, upon realizing who this man was, ordered that the scrubbing cease.

As the anti-Jewish measures intensified, Göring decided to act. Seeing the danger facing the Jews, he often forged his brother's signature on transit documents, or helped Jews escape Vienna by obtaining legitimate hard-to-obtain travel documents. On one occasion, in the fall of 1943, he took the completely unauthorized step of signing passports with his own hand for a Jewish family he had befriended. Using his influence at another time, he persuaded SS chief Reinhard Heydrich to release Czech resistance fighters who had been captured by the Gestapo.

Göring's doctor since 1939, Laszlo Kovacs, later stated that Göring provided him with money to establish a bank account in Switzerland, which Jewish refugees could access in order to fund travel to Lisbon. Later, after the German occupation of Italy in the fall of 1943, Göring wrote out a special pass to enable Kovacs to reach safety.

It was clear that, despite their diametrically opposed ideological differences, the two brothers were very fond of each other. Hermann Göring, in particular, seemed to be always on the lookout to keep his brother out of trouble. Albert Göring was arrested by the Gestapo several times but was on every occasion released due to his brother's intervention. Perhaps, however, this family loyalty only went so far. Richard Sonnenfeldt, chief interpreter of the American prosecution team at the International Military Tribunal at Nuremberg, later recalled how Hermann Göring enjoyed displaying his power to his brother by freeing Jews from the concentration camps when asked to do so. While Albert Göring continually brought newer and newer cases to his brother—and there were more than 100 verifiable names of those saved at his insistence—Hermann Göring permitted the releases just to demonstrate how important he was.

Albert Göring, however, possessed a degree of influence on his own. He often helped people in need financially and on the strength of his name alone.

Göring intensified his anti-Nazi activity when he was made export director at the Czech Škoda Works. In this capacity he saved many employees, among them the director, Jan Morávek, and his family. Morávek, as it turned out, was an important member of the Czech resistance movement—and he was not the only Czech resister looked after through Göring's efforts. At Škoda, Göring also encouraged minor acts of sabotage, and it was said that he even refused to return the Nazi salute when officers visited Škoda. When he learned of the imminence of an action involving Jews or captured resisters, he sent trucks to nearby concentration camps with requests for slave labor, only to have them stopped before arriving at the factory so that those on board could escape.

After the war, Göring was questioned during the Nuremberg Trials, but on the strength of the many people who came forward to speak on his behalf, he was not prosecuted. He was also arrested by the Czechs but was again saved through the intercession of many Jewish families he had saved.

The postwar years were anything but kind, however. His name alone dogged him for the rest of his life, leading to many years without employment. He worked for a time as a designer in a construction firm in Munich and also found occasional work as a writer and translator, but he lived out his remaining years on a government pension. Although a devout Catholic, he married four times, and when he died on December 20, 1966, he was survived by his fourth wife, Brunhilde Seiwaldstätter.

Grüber, Heinrich (1891–1975)

Heinrich Grüber was a German Protestant theologian and anti-Nazi opposed to National Socialist antisemitic racial hatred, risking his life to offer active assistance to the Jews of Germany.

Heinrich Karl Ernst Grüber was born on June 24, 1891, in Stoleberg, Germany, the eldest son of a teacher, Dr. Ernst Grüber, and his wife, Alwine Cleven. His mother, who came from Limburg, gave her son an early knowledge of the Dutch language and culture, while he learned French from his father, who had been raised in France. After initially studying philosophy, history, and Protestant theology, he undertook his first theological exam at Easter 1914 before seeing front-line service as a volunteer in the German artillery during World War I.

After the war, he was ordained in 1920 as a pastor in Berlin, and he obtained his first pulpit in Dortmund-Brackel before moving in 1926 to Brandenburg as director of a home for boys with psychological illnesses at Templin.

In early 1933 he joined the Nazi party, though his membership was short lived as Grüber soon became a dissident. He joined the Pfarrernotbund (Emergency Association for Protestant Pastors), formed in September 1933 by Pastor Martin Niemöller as a protest against the introduction of Nazi antisemitic legislation into the Church.

As a result, he was dismissed by the Nazis from his position at Templin and did not find employment again until February 1934. As a member of the Confessing

Church, Grüber now found himself in constant conflict with his parish council, which was for the most part dominated by conforming "German Christians" who fell in behind the regime. He was given responsibility for the Dutch community in Berlin, but in May 1938 he assumed a new role—establishing an "auxiliary body for non-Aryan Christians," which looked after Christian families of Jewish background as determined by the Nazi racial laws. This body became known as the Büro Grüber (Grüber Bureau) and opened in central Berlin just three weeks after the *Kristallnacht* pogrom of November 9–10, 1938. Its core function, as Grüber saw it, was to help organize the emigration of Jews facing imprisonment in concentration camps. It would soon become one of the more important rescue offices for racially persecuted Jews.

Grüber ran his office without any formal authorization from the Church, but his work was supported by the Nazi authorities on the ground that by facilitating Jewish emigration he was actually helping the Third Reich remove Jews from Germany. Further, over time the line between "non-Aryan Christians" and Jews became indistinct, and Büro Grüber found itself working more and more closely with the representative body of German Jewry, the Reichsvereinigung der Juden in Deutschland (Reich Association of Jews in Germany), established by the Nazis on July 4, 1939, under the presidency of Rabbi **Leo Baeck**.

Overall, until its dissolution in December 1940, Büro Grüber helped to facilitate the emigration of between 1,700 and 2,000 Jews. Pastor Grüber was able to achieve this remarkable feat through exploiting his status as an Aryan minister with connections to government departments that had the same objective as he did, albeit for different reasons. It was those reasons, however, that made all the difference for Grüber's eventual fate. He did not simply attempt to expedite the emigration of Jews from Germany; he also tried to make the lives of those remaining as sustainable as possible. This, in the government's view, only acted as an incentive for Jews to stay. Moreover, with each successive antisemitic move from the regime, Grüber became more and more vociferous in his protests.

Finally, on December 19, 1940, he was arrested by the Gestapo and taken to Sachsenhausen. From there, he was transferred to Dachau in 1941 and incarcerated in the so-called "Pfarrerblock" (priest barracks). Over the next two years he endured severe beatings from Nazi guards together with psychological torments. He witnessed the suffering of his former assistant (and protégé) **Werner Sylten**, who was deported to the "euthanasia" plant at Hartheim Castle in Austria and murdered in August 1942. The Büro Grüber was dissolved, and most of its staff was deported to death camps.

Grüber was released from Dachau on June 23, 1943, after suffering a series of heart attacks. Later, with the war over, he became dean of St. Mary's Church in Berlin. He spent much of his remaining energy trying to bring about a meaningful and lasting dialogue between the government of West Germany and the State of Israel, in whose cause he remained a constant advocate. He was a witness for the prosecution at the 1961 trial of Adolf Eichmann in Israel, which necessitated him traveling to the Jewish state.

For his wartime work in opposing the Nazis and rescuing Jews he was honored widely in the years that followed. Just a few of his awards include the establishment of a Heinrich Grüber forest in Jerusalem on October 18, 1961; a knighthood of the Order of Oranje-Nassau, bestowed by Queen Juliana of the Netherlands on June 21, 1966; and, also in 1966, election to the position of honorary president of the German-Israeli Society. Of greatest significance, perhaps, was his recognition by Yad Vashem on July 28, 1964, as one of the Righteous among the Nations.

Heinrich Grüber died of a heart attack in Berlin, on November 29, 1975, at the age of 84.

Grünhut, Aron (1895–1974)

Aron Grünhut, a Slovak Jewish merchant from Bratislava, born in 1895, sold goose liver and other goods before World War II. A member of the local Chamber of Business and Industry, he was also active in the Orthodox Jewish religious community as a leading member of the Chevra Kadisha (burial society) and the board of Bratislava's Jewish hospital.

There was little to suggest in Grünhut's early life that he would take an active role in the saving of Jewish lives, but after the Sudetenland crisis of September 1938, at which time Nazi Germany occupied the German-speaking regions of Czechoslovakia, he saw it as his duty to save people in danger. During the winter of 1938–1939 he made contact with a staff member of Czechoslovakia's Ministry of Slovak Affairs. It was he who tipped off Grünhut that a pogrom was about to take place against Bratislava's Jewish quarter. Grünhut, who had earlier worked with Jewish youth groups in techniques of self-defense, organized these youths to put up a robust resistance in the neighborhood, and they turned back an antisemitic mob.

Grünhut then traveled to Vienna, where he met with a Gestapo lawyer in order to secure the release of Bratislava clothing merchant Juda Goldberger, who had been kidnapped and transported across the border.

One of his most dramatic rescues took place in July 1939, when he arranged for an illegal transport of Jewish refugees to Palestine. He chartered two steamships to sail the Danube River from Bratislava to the Black Sea, where he had a freighter waiting to take some 1,365 Jews to Palestine. He then negotiated with a former British consul to Bratislava to ensure that the refugees would obtain permission to enter Palestine legally. The trip took 83 days, but these Jewish refugees—from Czechoslovakia, Hungary, and Austria—were saved.

Grünhut's actions caused the appointed Jewish community leaders concern, as they did not like the idea of this maverick undertaking rescue missions on his own initiative. When his transport was due to depart they tried to have him arrested; when he returned to Bratislava, they accused him of having led those in his care to exile and death. Only upon learning that the refugees had arrived safely in Palestine did they change their opinion, and then they asked him to consider organizing additional transports. This was to be the start of half a dozen further rescues that would ultimately save more than 2,000 lives.

With the onset of war in 1939, Grünhut decided to remain in Czechoslovakia. Eventually he moved to Budapest, Hungary, where he and his wife, under false names, went into hiding with other Jewish refugees in the cellar of the former Czechoslovak embassy. He was helped by a firefighter named Emanuel Zima. Because of Zima's bravery, all survived until the arrival of the Red Army in 1945.

Yet even in this situation, Grünhut worked to save Jewish lives. During his period in exile and hiding, he helped charter a train to take Jewish children from Budapest to Tehran. He bribed the engineers to detour the train to Palestine during its journey, saving another 350 Jewish lives. He then managed to make contact with the British humanitarian **Nicholas Winton**, who was responsible for the *Kindertransport* that brought Jewish children from Slovakia to Britain in 1939. In an operation organized by Winton, a few of the children from the Tehran train were taken to England, among them one of Grünhut's five sons, Benny.

After the war, Grünhut returned to Bratislava, but the communist takeover in 1948 and the establishment of the State of Israel that same year persuaded him to leave Czechoslovakia for the last time. In Israel, Grünhut helped Slovak Jews reintegrate their lives, and he became chairman of the Association of Bratislava Jews.

Aron Grünhut died in Israel in 1974. Sadly, although he was remembered with fondness and admiration by his community, he was largely unrecognized outside of those whose lives he had touched directly. In September 2014, however, an exhibition celebrating Grünhut's life and achievements was mounted by Slovakia's Ministry of Culture. His sole surviving son, Benny Grünhut, was present to pay respects to this remarkable Holocaust survivor, rescuer, and resister.

Grüninger, Paul (1891–1972)

Paul Grüninger was a Swiss police commander whose actions on the Swiss-German border before World War II saved several thousand Jews who otherwise would have been refused sanctuary.

Born on October 27, 1891, in St. Gallen, the son of a cigar shop owner, Grüninger lived a fairly simple lifestyle and was not especially involved in matters outside of his hometown. During World War I, when Switzerland was neutral, he served in the Swiss army as a lieutenant. After the war he joined Switzerland's border police, rising to the rank of colonel; by 1919 he had become commander of the border police for St. Gallen Canton.

When the Nazis came to power in Germany in 1933 many Jews fled to neighboring Austria, but with the Austrian *Anschluss* on March 12, 1938, Jewish persecution began there immediately. As a result, Jews from Austria sought sanctuary in Switzerland, which responded by closing its borders in August 1938 to those without proper entry papers. A few months later in October, the Swiss government asked Germany to stamp the letter "J" on all Jewish passports so that Swiss officials might more easily identify Jews. In 1939 Switzerland decided not to admit religious or racial refugees, thereby denying Jews access.

It was in this context that German and Austrian Jews seeking asylum approached Paul Grüninger every day, and as he heard their stories, he could scarcely believe the things they told him. When faced with choosing between following state laws or staying true to his moral code, his sense of compassion made it nearly impossible for him to turn the Jews away. Many border commanders, similarly torn, simply forced subordinates to deal with the refugees. Grüninger realized that he could easily follow the commands of his superiors, or he could put himself at risk by doing what was humane and right. Ultimately, he believed that saving lives was far more important than preserving his job, and as a result he admitted more than 3,600 Jews—by falsifying their passports and entry papers or turning a blind eye when required. He even used his own money to buy winter clothes for refugees who were forced to leave all their belongings behind.

In addition, he would record the Jews' date of entry into Switzerland as prior to March 1939, when Switzerland further tightened its borders, enabling the arrivals to be treated as legal refugees. They would be taken to a camp established at Diepoldsau on the Austrian frontier, where, aided by Jewish organizations, they could await permits for a temporary stay in Switzerland or their departure to a final destination.

On April 3, 1939, Grüninger arrived at work to find a young cadet, Corporal Antón Schneider, blocking his way into the office. Schneider had not been informed of the reason for his order to deny Grüninger entry to the building, which came directly from the office of the commander in chief. Grüninger, however, knew why he was being stopped.

A friend working at a border post in Bregenz, Austria, informed him that he was on the Gestapo's blacklist for having helped a Jewish woman, whom he had already assisted in escaping from Austria, to recover her jewels. She had left them at a hotel in Bregenz, and Grüninger contacted Ernest Prodolliet of the Swiss consulate in Bregenz to collect the jewels for her. Prodolliet and Grüninger had worked together on missions similar to this before. The woman was so grateful for Grüninger's help that she wrote about his kindness in a letter to some friends. The Gestapo intercepted the letter, imprisoned the hotel owner, confiscated the jewels, and began to keep an eye on Grüninger. This news did not, however, dissuade him from continuing to falsify Jewish passports in order to save Jews.

Soon after this incident, the Swiss authorities learned of Grüninger's illegal activities and dismissed him. He was placed on trial in January 1939, in proceedings that would last for two years. In March 1941 the court found him guilty of a breach of duty; he was imprisoned, had his pension revoked, was forced to pay trial costs, and was fined. Although the court accepted that his actions were honorable, they declared that as a state official he should have followed his orders, refused entrance to Jews, and not falsified official documents.

Grüninger was publicly humiliated and lived the rest of his life with a prison record, making it practically impossible to find steady work. He did not seek redress or recognition for his actions, instead focusing on surviving and supporting his family. In 1954 he claimed that "my personal well-being, measured against the cruel fate of these thousands, was so insignificant and unimportant" that he never took the consequences of his actions into consideration.

When Paul Grüninger died at the age of 81 on February 22, 1972, his family was still living in near poverty.

In December 1970 the Swiss government sent Grüninger a letter of apology, but at the same time still refused him his pension. Then, a year before his death, Israel's Yad Vashem recognized him as one of the Righteous among the Nations. Any other recognition that Grüninger received came posthumously. In 1994 the Swiss government published a Declaration of Honor for him, before finally annulling his conviction one year later. In 1998 the Parliament of St. Gallen Canton agreed to compensate Grüninger's descendants, and his family put the money into the Paul Grüninger Foundation, an organization that works to reward outstanding acts of humanity and courage that align with Grüninger's actions. Although most recognition came after Grüninger's death, his decision to save those in need has served as a model of moral behavior for the world today.

Between 1937 and April 1938, Paul Grüninger is estimated to have saved approximately 3,600 German and Austrian Jews from death or deportation to concentration camps. By doing so he risked his career and safety to help others, even though he had no apparent Jewish connection in Austria or Germany. He was an upstander to Nazi persecution who used his position as a Swiss civil servant to save as many Jews as he could, against direct orders.

Guzik, David (1890–1946)

David Guzik was the Warsaw director of the Joint Distribution Committee (JDC), a worldwide Jewish relief organization based in New York. He was born on November 3, 1890, in Warsaw and began working with the JDC in 1918, serving as an accountant and finance director. After World War II broke out in September 1939, he became one of the four JDC directors in the Warsaw Ghetto, working alongside Isaac Giterman, Isaac Bornstein, and Leib Neustadt.

Soon after the war began, Giterman was imprisoned in Germany. Guzik, as his deputy, took control of JDC activities. As an officer of an American organization he had some freedom of movement denied other Jews, and in 1940 Guzik and Neustadt traveled to Belgium to meet with JDC representatives from the United States, discussing currency transfers to Poland that would not breach wartime monetary regulations. While in Brussels they arranged for food to be shipped into Poland, after which they returned to Warsaw.

On another occasion Guzik visited Portugal to collect money to assist Warsaw's Jewish population. Through his efforts he raised funds that assisted in financing welfare services, providing medical help, and fostering cultural and underground activities in the ghetto. He also obtained and smuggled black market goods onto the open market, with all proceeds transferred to the JDC for community use. By the fall of 1941 it was reported that he was providing for some 250 soup kitchens across the ghetto, from which many thousands of Jews received sustenance each day.

To help his fellow Jews he worked long, hard hours on behalf of the JDC, but when the United States entered the war in December 1941 the office was forced to close down. Unperturbed, Guzik continued his work of fund-raising, in particular securing loans—which would never be paid back owing to the destruction of the ghetto and the murder of most of its residents. These loans continued the work of providing soup kitchens and medicine, as well as helping to finance **Emanuel Ringelblum's** Oneg Shabbat archive.

On July 22, 1942, the Nazis began a major mass extermination operation of Jews from the Warsaw Ghetto entitled *Grossaktion Warschau* (Great Action Warsaw). In the period that followed, Jews were terrorized in daily roundups and concentrated for what was euphemistically termed "resettlement in the East." Most were transferred to the death camp at Treblinka, including Guzik's wife, daughter, and one of his two sons.

The day after the operation began, Guzik consulted with other ghetto organizations to consider what response to take. This included a discussion of possible resistance activities, and it soon became clear that he would be a supporter of the ghetto underground. With the establishment of the Żydowska Organizacja Bojowa (Jewish Combat Organization, or ŻOB), Guzik immediately aligned himself with the group and left the ghetto to collect funds for the resistance. On January 21, 1943, together with Dr. Ignacy (Yitzhak) Schiper, Menachem Kirschenbaum, Yochanan Morgenstern, and Josef Sak, he signed a petition that was sent to the Polish government-in-exile in London, desperately calling for assistance to stop the annihilation of Polish Jewry. Then, in the spring of 1943, while still on the Aryan side of Warsaw, he sent whatever money he could raise to help finance the Warsaw Ghetto Uprising.

Surviving the revolt, Guzik fled once more to the Aryan side, where he remained in hiding for the duration of the war. While there, he developed and maintained connections with the Polish Warsaw underground. The work in which he was engaged was dangerous, and on one occasion he was actually arrested, but by a judicious use of bribes he managed to obtain his release.

Throughout most of the war years there was no direct contact between Guzik and the headquarters of the JDC in New York, but in May 1945, completely out of the blue, a cable from Guzik arrived expressing his readiness to continue working on behalf of Jews, noting that urgent care was needed for the 40,000 or so survivors then being liberated from concentration camps across Europe. He was immediately appointed as the director of JDC Polish Operations and began to find ways to care for survivors and help in the rebuilding of the Polish Jewish community.

The work in which he was engaged came to an immediate halt, however, when on March 5, 1946, he lost his life in a plane crash at the Prague airport while returning to Poland from a conference in Paris. On board the same plane was another JDC worker, Gertrude Pinsky, who held the same office as Guzik relative to the Netherlands. It was a terrible dual blow for the JDC at a time when it needed all the institutional experience it could muster. David Guzik was survived by his remaining son, who participated in the liberation of Europe with Palestine's Jewish Brigade and later settled in France.

H

Haas, Leo (1901–1983)

Leo Haas was a Czech Jewish painter, printmaker, draftsman, and caricaturist whose work as an inmate of the Terezín (Theresienstadt) concentration camp during World War II came to symbolize the nature of artistic resistance.

A Slovak, he was born in 1901 in Opava, the eldest of four children. A prodigy in artistic endeavors, he was encouraged at school to pursue his skill, which he did by moving to an art academy in Karlsruhe, Germany. In 1921 he relocated to Berlin to further his studies. In 1923 he traveled to France for further education and inspiration, before moving in 1926 to Vienna. He then returned home to Opava, married Sophie Hermann in 1929, and became a well-known portrait painter.

After the Munich Agreement of September 1938, Opava, located in the Sudetenland, was taken over by Germany. Haas, who was known to the Nazis as a painter of so-called "degenerate art," was imprisoned during the Nazi takeover. Then, after the *Kristallnacht* pogrom of November 9–10, 1938, during which time Opava's synagogue was destroyed, he and his wife moved out of their home and went to live with her parents in Ostrava.

In October 1939, after the outbreak of war, thousands of Jews from the region, including Haas, were sent to a Nazi-imposed Jewish "reservation" in Nisko near Lublin, where they were put to hard labor. Haas's work, among other tasks, was as a wagon driver bringing food and construction materials from Lublin. In whatever free time he had, he painted portraits of SS men, and in return received such privileges as better food and fewer restrictions over movement. This gave him the opportunity to draw the building sites, portraits of other prisoners, transports arriving and leaving, and the general life of the camp.

After the Nisko initiative came to an end, Haas returned to Ostrava. He decided to stay there, but his marriage collapsed because his wife could not believe that by remaining in Ostrava she and Haas would see an end to persecution. Haas, remaining in Ostrava, soon met Erna Davidovitc, whose family was involved in smuggling Jews to Poland. Haas became involved in this activity in 1941, and Davidovitc became his second wife.

In August 1942 he was arrested by the Gestapo but released after a short period. He had, however, been noticed, and he was rearrested when the next transport to Terezín was organized a month later. Haas and his extended family arrived at Terezín on October 1, 1942, and were immediately separated. In no time at all, Haas was put to hard labor.

His skills as an artist recognized, he was transferred to a technical drawing unit, the object of which was to develop plans for Terezín's expansion. Several other well-known artists worked in the unit as well, including Otto Ungar, Ferdinand (Felix) Bloch, and Bedřich Fritta, who became a friend and leader of the team.

Working in the graphics department gave its inmates certain privileges, such as being able to visit other parts of the camp. Using this opportunity, they all made secret drawings documenting ghetto life. Haas used the chance to draw anything and everything: inmates searching for food and waiting to be transported, the nature of the buildings, and the elderly, the sick, the dying, and the dead. He made portraits of his colleagues and portraits of other inmates. Haas and his comrades risked their lives by making such drawings. Together, and in complete secrecy, Haas, Fritta, and Ungar created a large body of work illustrating all aspects of life in Terezín.

The secrecy was an obvious form of resistance, and the Nazis, keen to ensure that the truth about Terezín did not get out, launched numerous searches of the graphics department. All the artists had to find hiding places for their works: Fritta buried his pictures in the ground inside a metal box; Ungar hid his paintings in a depression in a wall; and Haas hid his in an attic. The necessity of doing so took on urgency when a delegation of the Red Cross visited Terezín on June 23, 1944, to inspect living conditions in the ghetto.

Several days before the visit, the group was detained and interrogated by none other than Adolf Eichmann. The artists maintained their silence and were imprisoned with their families in what was known as the "Small Fortress." Haas was confined for three and a half months, and the artists were again employed at hard labor. On October 25, 1944, Haas and Fritta were condemned for distributing "atrocity propaganda" and deported to Auschwitz. They arrived on October 28; Haas, although Jewish, was branded a political prisoner with the number 199885. Fritta died of blood poisoning eight days after arrival.

At Auschwitz, Haas resumed his artistic work, producing sketches for Dr. Josef Mengele, the "Angel of Death." In November 1944, however, he was transferred with other artists to Sachsenhausen and given another new number, 118029. Here, the artists were again segregated, and they joined a team of prisoners who had been working for the past two years on Operation Bernhard, a secret plan by Nazi Germany to destabilize the British economy by flooding it with forged currency. Haas's group was given the job of counterfeiting American dollars.

At the end of February 1945, with the war coming to an end, the members of the group were transferred to Mauthausen. Then, on May 5, 1945, they were moved again, this time to the camp at Ebensee, where they were liberated the next day by American troops.

After his liberation Haas returned to Terezín and was reunited with his entire art collection of more than 400 drawings; in addition, he located many of Fritta's works. It was then that he learned that most of his friends and family had perished, though his wife Erna had survived. Fritta's son Tomáš also survived, and the Haases adopted him. Erna Haas died in 1955 from the effects of medical experiments conducted on her while in Auschwitz. After her death, Haas moved to East Berlin, where he worked as an illustrator for a number of magazines and newspapers.

Leo Hass's resistance work was of a very special kind. Employing his artistic skills, he did what he could to chronicle what he saw and whom he met. In this way he worked under the most trying of circumstances to bear witness to the Nazi atrocities and reveal these images to people outside the wire. The record that he and his comrades created was a vital contribution to the knowledge that later generations would possess about the Holocaust.

Helmy, Mohammed (1901–1982)

Mohammed Helmy was a Berlin-based medical doctor who helped save Jews during World War II. Born in 1901 in Khartoum, Sudan, to an Egyptian father and a German mother, he moved to Berlin in 1922 to study medicine. He worked in the field of urology at the Robert Koch Hospital until 1938, rising to be head of the department. Due to Nazi racial laws, however, he was dismissed from his position because he was not an Aryan. In 1939 he was arrested for speaking out against Nazism, along with many other Egyptian nationals living in Germany. He was detained for more than a year but was discharged on health grounds.

After his release a young Jewish patient of his, Anna Boros (later Gutman), sought his help. By way of response, and notwithstanding the great danger, he hid her in a cabin on the outskirts of Berlin from March 10, 1940, until the end of the war. At times he had to shuttle her around to the homes of various friends to escape detection, but the cabin remained her core hiding place throughout most of the war years. With the help of Frieda Szturmann, a German woman he knew, Helmy also arranged for three members of her family—her mother, Julie; her stepfather, Georg Wehr; and her grandmother Cecilie Rudnik—to be hidden. He also provided the family with medical care. All survived the war and later migrated to the United States.

Helmy did all he could to assist Boros during her long period in hiding. Documents in German and Arabic were later found revealing just how far he was prepared to go. These included a certificate from the Central Islamic Institute in Berlin (headed by the antisemitic Haj Amin al-Husseini, Mufti of Jerusalem) attesting to her having converted to Islam, and a certificate saying that she had married an Egyptian in a ceremony that was held in Helmy's home.

After the war, Helmy remained in Germany and married his prewar fiancée, Emmi. It was later said that the couple decided not to have any children, given the type of world they would be brought into. Frieda Szturmann, who had provided great assistance in saving the lives of Boros and her family, died in 1962. Mohammed Helmy died in 1982, at the age of 81.

Several years later, Jerusalem's Yad Vashem learned of Helmy through letters written by several Jewish survivors he had helped. An investigation took place, in which researchers from the Department of the Righteous searched for as much information as could be found and spoke to a number of people, including Anna Boros-Gutman. With no known next of kin, Yad Vashem asked the Egyptian embassy in Israel for help in tracking down any relatives. It was known, for example, that Helmy had been visited from time to time in Germany by nephews from Egypt in the decades after the war.

The result saw a decision, on March 18, 2013, to recognize Mohammed Helmy and Frieda Szturmann as Righteous among the Nations. It was a momentous decision, as Helmy was the first Arab rescuer to be so recognized.

Yad Vashem made contact with Helmy's great-nephew in Egypt in order to present the award, but he rejected it on the grounds that it was an honor bestowed by the state of Israel. Mervat Hassan, speaking on behalf of her husband, was quoted as saying: "If any other country offered to honor Helmy, we would have been happy with it. . . . But not from Israel." The rejection was met with some measure of consternation at Yad Vashem, where a spokesman said that in Nazi Germany, which was in a state of "total moral collapse, there was a small minority who mustered extraordinary courage to uphold human values. Bystanders were the rule; rescuers were the exception. Helmy was one of them." The level of disappointment was intense, particularly in view of the fact that this recognition, of a Muslim Arab who rescued Jews, had come in honor of his individual goodness, not his national background.

It was indeed an ironic situation. The man who some news outlets dubbed the "Arab **Schindler**" received due acknowledgment for saving Jewish lives during the Holocaust, at risk of his own life and in the face of Nazi persecution, but he did not have the honor recognized by his own family in his home country for political—not moral or humanitarian—reasons.

Hirsch, Helmut (1916–1937)

Helmut Hirsch was a German Jew who took part in a plot to destabilize Nazi Germany by bombing Nazi party headquarters in Nuremberg in December 1936.

Born on January 27, 1916, in Stuttgart, Hirsch and his younger sister, Kaete, were the children of Siegfried and Marta Hirsch, née Neuburger. Siegfried Hirsch had lived in the United States for a decade prior to his marriage in 1914 and became a naturalized American citizen before returning to Germany. During World War I he lived with his wife and two children in the then German state of Alsace. His

U.S. citizenship was revoked in 1926 because he had left to live abroad, rendering the entire family stateless.

In 1935, after Germany introduced the Nuremberg Laws on race, which among other things excluded Jews from German universities, Helmut Hirsch moved to Prague to study architecture at the Deutsche Technische Hochschule (German Institute of Technology). His family joined him in 1936, after his sister graduated from high school and faced the same situation as Hirsch had in not being able to enroll at a German university.

While in Prague, Hirsch became closely involved in the Black Front, an anti-Nazi organization of German expatriates. His mentor in the organization was Eberhard Köbel, who went by the codename Tusk. Hirsch belonged to a youth movement known as the Bündische Jugend, a union comprising a number of different youth associations. Tusk belonged to one of these, the Deutsche Jungenschaft. From this tenuous link, Tusk made his original contact with Hirsch.

Through Tusk, Hirsch met Hitler opponents Otto Strasser, who had been expelled by the Nazi party in 1930, and Heinrich Grunow, a Prague publisher. Over time, they met repeatedly, and Hirsch was sucked deeper and deeper into the Black Front, becoming a willing tool in their hands. Black Front leaders worked on his idealism and vulnerability, appealing to his hurt sensibilities as a Jew and arguing that he must act to show that Jews were not afraid to stand up for themselves. Tusk, for his part, left for London later in 1935 after the Deutsche Jungenschaft, of which he had been a leader, was banned. This left Hirsch without his mentor; he kept his involvement with the Black Front from his family, and in his naiveté had no idea that the organization was riddled with pro-Nazi agents.

Mesmerized by the allure of making a difference on behalf of the Jewish people, Hirsch decided to proceed with some sort of action against the Nazis. The plan called for him to take bombs placed in two suitcases and blow up the Nazi Party headquarters in Nuremberg—or, failing that, the offices of the antisemitic newspaper *Der Stürmer*. On December 20, 1936, he took a train to Germany from Prague, not realizing that German agents had probably been watching him for some time already, or that the Gestapo was informed when Hirsch entered Germany. The mission was unclear and relatively unformed. Hirsch knew he was supposed to bomb something, but it was left up to him as to just what that would be.

He did not stick to the plan from the outset. Instead of going to Nuremberg, he passed it by and went to Stuttgart, where he hoped to meet a friend who would give him the resolve he needed—either to go ahead with his quest, or abandon it altogether. Hirsch arrived late on the evening of December 20, but his friend did not turn up. Hirsch checked into a hotel, only to be picked up by the Gestapo in the middle of the night on December 21 and charged with treason. There is little doubt that he and his planned action were denounced by a double agent in the Black Front.

Hirsch was interrogated in Stuttgart then transferred to Berlin's Plötzensee prison, where he was held in solitary confinement for nine weeks. His trial began in March 1937 before the Volksgerichtshof (People's Court). Hirsch admitted his guilt, adding that he would have even killed Adolf Hitler if he'd had the chance. It took the court little time to find him guilty and sentence him to death. The trial proceedings were conducted in secrecy.

It was only when the verdict and sentence were made public that Hirsch's family learned where he was and what he had been doing for the past three months. At this, they immediately began a campaign for clemency, using his father's lost U.S. citizenship as their trump card. Hirsch had not been born in the United States, of course, and his father's citizenship had been revoked, but the case became a cause célèbre in any case. Hirsch's American cousin, George Neuburger, engaged an American lawyer to petition for Siegfried Hirsch's citizenship to be reinstated. The petition was granted, and on this basis Helmut Hirsch was also declared to be an American citizen on April 22, 1937. The U.S. ambassador to Berlin, William E. Dodd, met with a number of senior German officials in an effort to obtain a pardon, but his efforts proved fruitless.

Other attempts for clemency came from the International Committee of the Red Cross, the Society of Friends, and the Norwegian government, which offered Hirsch asylum. The matter was brought before the League of Nations and the British Parliament, all to no avail.

On the eve of his execution, Hirsch composed a final letter to his parents in which he wrote that "in these last months I have really found the way to myself and to life. Real beauty must stand before unswerving honesty. You know that I have lived every moment fervently and that I have remained true to myself until the end. You must live on. There can be no giving up for you. No becoming soft or sentimental. In these days I have learned to say 'yes' to life."

Hitler refused all entreaties, and at 6:00 a.m. on June 4, 1937, Helmut Hirsch was executed by decapitation at Plotzensee prison. He was 21 years old.

Ho Feng-Shan (1901–1997)

Ho Feng-Shan was one of the first diplomats to save Jews by issuing them visas to escape the Holocaust. Between 1938 and 1940 he was responsible for saving thousands of Jews in Nazi-occupied Austria.

He was born into a poor family in rural Yiyang, Hunan province, on September 10, 1901. His father died when he was seven years old, and his family was assisted by the Norwegian Lutheran Mission, which enrolled him at its school. An excellent student, he received there the foundation for further study—first at the College of Yale-in-China, and then at the University of Munich in 1928. By 1932 he had earned a PhD in political economy, graduating magna cum laude.

In 1935 Ho began his career as a diplomat representing the Republic of China, with an initial posting to Ankara, Turkey. In the spring of 1937 he was placed as first secretary to the Chinese legation in Vienna, but when Nazi Germany invaded Austria in March 1938 and the country became absorbed into the German Reich, the legation was transformed into a consulate. In May 1938 Ho Feng-Shan was appointed to the post of consul-general. The staff comprised Ho and one other officer, who had the title of vice-consul.

Ho found the Vienna posting an ideal location. Fluent in both English and German, he was an active participant in the social scene and was often called upon to speak in public about Chinese culture and customs. He developed a wide circle of friends and acquaintances, many of whom, given the groups among whom he was associating, were Jewish.

After the *Anschluss*, however, Austria's Jews became subjected in the space of six weeks to all the same antisemitic measures that had befallen German Jewry during the previous five years. Desperate to leave the country, Austria's Jews began looking for any country that would accept them, at a time when few were prepared to do so.

The situation then intensified to major crisis proportions after the November pogrom, known as the *Kristallnacht*, of November 9–10, 1938. Ho was shocked by the nature of Nazi violence, and he experienced something of the Nazis' racism himself when he was held at gunpoint by Nazi thugs searching for Jews. He recognized that the Jews of Austria were in extreme danger and that he could help to get them out.

The government of China was far from convinced that this was a matter requiring Chinese involvement; in fact, China's leader, Chiang Kai-shek (Jiang Jieshi), flirted with Germany's Nazi government throughout the 1930s. He employed German military advisers in his struggle against both Japanese invaders and Chinese communists and purchased large quantities of weapons from Germany.

Against this background, it was perhaps not surprising that Chiang Kai-shek wanted to maintain good relations with Germany and did not oppose Hitler's racial policies. Accordingly, the Chinese ambassador to Berlin, Chen Jie, instructed Ho Feng-Shan in Vienna that he was not to issue visas to Jews. Ho, however, acting against Chen Jie's explicit orders, began issuing visas for Shanghai. Although he was convinced that most would not actually go there, he knew that possession of such a document was enough for Jews to purchase a ship ticket and leave Austria.

His efforts were assisted by contributions made by American relief organizations, which at that stage were trying desperately to assist Jews in getting out. Ho was forced to maintain contact with these organizations covertly, as he had been forbidden from helping Jews.

For continuing to issue visas despite a direct order not to do so, a black mark, or "demerit," was entered into Ho's personnel file in 1939. He continued issuing visas, however, until he was recalled to China in May 1940. It is not known how many visas he actually authorized before he left. He issued his 200th visa in June 1938 and signed number 1,906 on October 27, 1938. There is solid room for speculation, therefore, that in the ensuing months through to his departure from Vienna, many, many more, probably numbering in the thousands, would have been issued.

Ho went on to represent China in a number of diplomatic posts, including Egypt, Mexico, Bolivia, and Colombia. In 1949 he chose to remain loyal to the Republic of China rather than recognize the newly victorious People's Republic of China. He retired in 1973 and moved to the United States, settling in San Francisco. There he became a founding member of the Chinese Lutheran Church and wrote his memoirs, *Forty Years of My Diplomatic Life*, published in 1990. Explaining his actions in helping the Jews of Austria against the instructions of his own government, he expressed the view that "I thought it only natural to feel compassion and to want to help. From the standpoint of humanity, that is the way it should be."

Ho Feng-Shan died at his home in San Francisco on September 28, 1997, at the age of 96. On August 7, 2000, he was recognized by Yad Vashem as one of the Righteous among the Nations for his courage in issuing Chinese visas to Vienna's Jews.

Hübener, Helmuth (1925–1942)

Helmuth Hübener, a youthful opponent of National Socialism, was executed for his anti-Nazi stance at the age of 17—one of the youngest opponents of the Third Reich to be judicially sentenced to death and executed as a result.

Born on January 8, 1925, Hübener came from a religious family in Hamburg and was a member of the Church of Jesus Christ of Latter-day Saints (LDS), whose adherents are often known as "Mormons." He had been a Boy Scout, but when the Nazis banned the scouting movement in 1935 he joined the Hitler Youth at the age of 10. Three years later, when the *Kristallnacht* pogrom occurred in November 1938, he broke with the Hitler Youth on the grounds that its violence against Jews was unacceptable.

Hübener's stance went against LDS policy. In 1937 the World LDS president, Heber Grant, visited Germany from the United States and counseled members not to react negatively against the Nazi regime. In the aftermath of *Kristallnacht* Grant arranged for all non-German Mormon missionaries to be evacuated from the Third Reich, leaving dissidents like Helmuth Hübener dangerously exposed. Local branch president Arthur Zander, for example, was an enthusiastic Nazi, who in 1938 posted notices on LDS churches stating "Jews not welcome." In Hübener's own congregation, Jews were barred from attending services. Hübener came to be viewed as a young troublemaker by some other LDS members.

In 1941 Hübener finished middle school and entered as a trainee at the Hamburg Social Authority. His circle of contacts widened, and he learned more about the world outside through exposure to BBC radio at the home of a friend. In the summer of 1941 he learned that his older brother Gerhard, at that time serving in the German army, had a shortwave radio, which enabled private listening sessions at home. Listening to the BBC, of course, was a crime; and Hübener, armed with "new" information, began to write leaflets opposing the government. He drew attention to the regime's criminal activities with regard to human rights generally, and the Jews in particular. He wrote about how the war was destroying Germany, with defeat inevitable, and distributed copies in the vicinity.

As 1941 unfolded, Hübener drew two of his fellow LDS members—Karl-Heinz Schnibbe and Rudi Wobbe—into his project, together with Gerhard Düwer, whom he had met at work. The more they learned, the more horrified they became, particularly concerning the situation (as they understood it) facing the Jews. Together, they listened to BBC radio and worked on the leaflets. Hübener, Schnibbe, and Wobbe then began distributing the 60 or so pieces Hübener had produced.

On February 5, 1942, less than a month after turning 17, Helmuth Hübener was arrested by the Gestapo. Heinrich Mohn, a Nazi with whom he worked, saw him trying to translate his pamphlets into French and then denounced him. On February 15, 1942, acting on orders from the Gestapo, the LDS excommunicated Hübener. Over the next few months he was brutally interrogated and tortured in Gestapo prisons in Hamburg and Berlin before finally being brought before Judge Otto Georg Thierack of the People's Court (Volksgerichtshof) in Berlin on August 11, 1942.

Hübener's performance during the trial would have been remarkable for anyone standing in such a situation; for a 17-year-old, it was phenomenal. Tried as an adult despite his age, and having been deprived of his civil rights, he was found guilty of conspiracy to commit high treason and advancing the cause of the enemy. His friends, Schnibbe and Wobbe, were also found guilty and given sentences of 5 and 10 years at hard labor, respectively. Hübener, as the ringleader of the group, received the death penalty. Witnesses said that after the sentence was read he turned to Judge Thierack and shouted, "You have sentenced me to death for telling the truth. My time is now—but your time will come!"

Appeals for clemency proved fruitless; it was to be two months from the time of sentencing to the execution. When his death appeared imminent he wrote a number of farewell letters to family and friends. In one of them he wrote: "My Father in Heaven knows that I have done nothing wrong." On another, penned the day of his execution, he stated that: "I know that God lives and He will be the Just Judge in this matter."

On October 27, 1942, the Nazi Ministry of Justice upheld the verdict and sentence. Hübener was told of the Ministry's decision at 1:05 p.m. on the scheduled day of execution, and at 8:13 p.m., in Berlin's Plötzensee prison, he was beheaded by guillotine. At the age of 17, he was the youngest person ever to be sentenced by the People's Court and executed for conspiracy to commit treason against the Nazi regime.

In 1946 Helmuth Hübener was posthumously reinstated in the LDS Church and ordained an elder, and he was rebaptized on January 7, 1948. Since then, he has been honored many times as a hero of the resistance against Hitler, and an exhibit focusing on his resistance, trial, and execution is located in the former guillotine chamber at Plötzensee prison.

Hulst, Jan van (b. 1911)

Jan van Hulst was the principal of the Hervormde Kweekschool te Amsterdam (Reformed Teacher Training College in Amsterdam) and personally involved in saving the lives of hundreds of Jewish children. Born in Amsterdam on January 28, 1911, he studied psychology and pedagogy at the Vrije Universiteit Amsterdam (VU University).

A strictly Calvinist (*Gereformeerd*) Protestant, van Hulst worked as a teacher in a number of Dutch cities before becoming principal of the Hervormde Kweekschool—an office he held from 1942 to 1960. He was at the same time a patriot and a pedagogue opposed to any watering-down of children's education. Thus, both he and a majority of other faculty members rebelled in the early summer of 1942, when Dr. Jan van Dam, secretary-general of the Nazi-controlled Ministry of Education, tried to force the academy to close down by withholding its subsidy. Preferring to keep the doors open, the faculty continued to teach in spite of government pressure and with little to no money.

In response, the principal at the time resigned, and on September 1, 1942, van Hulst became the new principal of the Hervormde Kweekschool. The school now came into play as a crucial location for the saving of Jewish children. It was situated at 27 Plantage Middenlaan, only two buildings away from a Jewish crèche from which, since January 1943, children had been smuggled out and hidden at addresses outside Amsterdam.

Much of this activity was orchestrated by one of the leaders of the Nazi-imposed Jewish Council (Joodse Raad), **Walter Süskind**; an administrator with the Hollandsche Schouwburg (Dutch Theater), Felix Halverstad; and the director of the crèche, Henriette Henriques Pimentel. Together, they created a means for Jewish children to be rescued. The children would be brought secretly to the Hervormde Kweekschool and, with van Hulst's assistance, passed through the garden and into the Dutch Theater. They would then be moved from the crèche over the low fence and temporarily hidden in one of the rooms at the theater until they were collected by rescuers, who would take them to safe places outside the city.

In this way, the organizations managed to smuggle at least 100 Jewish children through van Hulst's school. On his own initiative, he helped save another 100, who were taken away by his students.

On the morning of June 19, 1943, however, it seemed as though van Hulst's operation was about to collapse. An inspector from the Ministry of Education,

Mr. Fieringa, had been sent to the college to oversee the matriculation exams, and seeing the children, he asked whether or not they were Jewish. Conceding that they were, van Hulst was terrified as to what might happen next, but Fieringa simply shook him by the hand and wished him well with the caution, "In God's name, be careful."

When the Nazis ordered that the crèche be cleared out in late September 1943, the principal, Virrie (Virginia) Cohen—the daughter of David Cohen, president of the Joodse Raad—went to van Hulst and told him that the children were about to be taken away. Faced with the agonizing task of choosing only some who could be rescued, van Hulst took 12 of the children, between the ages of 5 and 12, to safety.

After this, it seemed as though van Hulst's options to do more had come to an end, but he continued to find ways to help people in hiding, and he managed to keep the college open until the end of the war. With just three weeks left before the Netherlands was liberated, he was forced to go into hiding. Upon later reflection, he asserted that he had no regrets, but he would have preferred to save more children than he did.

Jan van Hulst had a successful life after the liberation, becoming a politician with the Christian Historical Union (CHU), a political party that merged into the Christian Democratic Appeal (CDA). He served as a senator between July 3, 1956, and June 10, 1981, and as senate leader of the CHU from December 10, 1968, until June 8, 1977. When the CDA was formed, he became senate leader there until June 10, 1981. He was also a member of the European Parliament between 1961 and 1968. Throughout this time, he remained a professor of pedagogy at the Vrije Universiteit in Amsterdam and is now, as a centenarian, an emeritus professor.

In view of his work in facilitating the rescue of hundreds of Jewish children during the Holocaust, Yad Vashem recognized Jan van Hulst as one of the Righteous among the Nations on March 8, 1972.

Israel, Charlotte (b. 1910)

Charlotte Freudenthal Israel was a demonstrator against the Nazi regime during the Rosenstrasse Protest in Berlin between February 27 and March 6, 1943, in which a large demonstration of non-Jewish women protested outside the local Jewish community building at Rosenstrasse 2-4. Inside this building, some 2,000 Jewish men married to non-Jewish partners, together with their male children, were detained by German police.

Charlotte Freudenthal was born in Berlin in 1910. She dropped out of school in order to pursue a trade, becoming a seamstress. Her family had decidedly pro-Nazi sentiments; her brother was a party member, and her brother-in-law was an SS officer. In 1933 she married Julius Israel, who was Jewish.

On February 27, 1943, the day of the so-called "Factory Action" (*Fabrikaktion*), Propaganda Minister Joseph Goebbels ordered a "Jew-free" Berlin, and the SS and Gestapo began seizing Jews wherever they could find them. Julius Israel attended the local police station to obtain a work permit and was arrested upon arrival. He and several others were loaded onto trucks and taken to the three-story former Jewish Social Welfare building at Rosenstrasse 2-4, in central Berlin. The operation called for the capture of Jews with German spouses and their children of mixed background, known as *mischlinge*. Up to this point, such Jews had not been targeted by the Nazis.

Julius Israel was among 1,500 men rounded up on February 27, 1943. Charlotte Israel, not having heard from her husband, contacted the police only to be told that he had been arrested and taken to Rosenstrasse. By the time she arrived, a crowd of non-Jewish German women also concerned about their husbands had spontaneously begun to assemble. They brought with them food and other personal items to pass to their loved ones, but they received no confirmation that their husbands or children were actually inside. As a result, the rapidly growing crowd refused to go home until they were given some indication as to the fate of their men.

Armed SS men guarded the building's only entrance from the women, who stood from dawn until dusk chanting, "Give us back our husbands." Inside, crammed into 40 rooms, the men waited. Some could see their wives and children outside, while others managed through various ruses to send messages out. Julius Israel sent his wife a message on the back of his potato-ration card saying, "I am well."

By the second day, more than 600 women were protesting; by the third, SS troops were given orders to train their guns on the crowd but to fire only warning shots. On March 4, and with no end in sight, the frustrated SS officers aimed their rifles at the women. Many ran for cover, but others, including Charlotte, remained. They now shouted their defiance even more loudly. The unnerved SS had expected complete acquiescence; they lowered their weapons, in what was rapidly becoming an unprecedented phenomenon in the heart of the Nazi capital.

Throughout the week of the protests the SS threatened several times to shoot the demonstrators, and from time to time, when they opened fire in the air, they scattered the crowd into nearby doorways—only to see them soon return and continue their chants of "Give us back our husbands." Inside the building, one SS officer, impressed by this showing, commented to those detained that the women were showing "true German loyalty" to their men.

The protest eventually expanded to include German women and men who were not in mixed marriages, with numbers overall nearing 1,000. Joseph Goebbels, who was also gauleiter (Nazi administrative chief) of Berlin, tried to staunch the demonstration by closing down public transport to the area, but this had no effect; women simply walked the longer distance in order to get to the protest. After a week of demonstrations, he saw no alternative but to let the prisoners go, and on March 6 most of the imprisoned Jews were released, including Julius Israel. Some 35 Jews who had already been sent to Auschwitz were returned to Berlin on a regular passenger train.

At Rosenstrasse, confronted by popular protest in the capital, the regime hesitated before finally capitulating to what would later be termed "people power." It was, as someone observed, the day Hitler "blinked." The regime that terrorized occupied Europe was challenged within its own capital.

The very act of protesting was radical and came as the culmination of a history marked by Jewish humiliation, discrimination, intimidation, and threats of violence dating back to the Nuremberg Laws of 1935. Quite simply, once their Jewish husbands and children were taken from them, the German women of Berlin said that enough was enough, and they let the Nazi regime know it in the most strident manner possible at the time. Goebbels and those around him knew, moreover, that if they did not accede to the women's demands on this occasion, then a culture of popular protest could develop. It was either that, or they would have to shoot the women down—something that certainly would not be tolerated by the citizens of Berlin.

On March 6, 1943, the Israels were reunited with Julius, and the remaining prisoners were released the following day. Her experience of resistance, like that of the other women, was completely spontaneous and unplanned. In that sense, she is representative of hundreds of others who, tested beyond endurance, decided to do something when confronted by what they considered to be the ultimate in indignity and personal torment. Those who were present at Rosenstrasse showed that even under totalitarian conditions, successful resistance is sometimes possible.

Julius Israel died in 1976. After the war, Charlotte Israel spoke on a number of occasions to schoolchildren and other groups about the days of the Rosenstrasse protest, and her testimony was an important link to those days. In the mid-1990s she was still active in providing her account of what happened, but soon thereafter she dropped from view. All subsequent attempts to locate her proved unsuccessful.

Jagendorf, Siegfried (1885–1970)

Siegfried (Schmiel, or Sami) Jagendorf managed a factory in Mogilev, Romania, through which he saved thousands of Jewish lives during the Holocaust.

Born on August 1, 1885, in the northern Bukovina village of Zviniace, he was the youngest of four children and the only son of Abraham Jagendorf and Hannah Bassie Offenberger. The Jagendorfs were Orthodox Jews; Abraham Jagendorf owned and operated a flour mill and ran a small herd of livestock.

After completing school, the young Jagendorf enrolled in a three-year mechanical engineering course at the Technical Trade-Museum in Vienna. There he joined a student Zionist organization. He completed his engineering qualification on May 31, 1907, at the Technikum Mittweida, near Dresden, specializing in tool making and, around this time, adopting the German name "Siegfried." On May 9, 1909, he married 21-year-old Hinde ("Hilda") Feller in Radantz, Bukovina.

Jagendorf's service as an officer in the Austro-Hungarian army during World War I earned him the Order of Franz Joseph, the empire's highest military decoration. After the war he was employed at the Siemens-Schukert Werke in Vienna and was transferred to Cernauti, Bukovina. In 1923, after just one year in Bukovina, Jagendorf resigned from Siemens-Schukert Werke and for the next four years served as general director of Foresta, the society of Bukovina's lumber industry. In March 1938, when German forces entered Austria, Jagendorf found himself trapped in Vienna. He managed to escape by bribing his way back into Romania.

Shortly after arriving back in Cernauti, Jagendorf was drafted into the Romanian army. He served until September 2, 1940, when he was demobilized owing to an antisemitic purge in the military.

In August 1939 Hitler and Stalin had signed a pact containing a secret provision that returned Bessarabia to Soviet rule. Ten months later the Soviet foreign minister Vyacheslav Molotov demanded the evacuation within 48 hours of all Romanian forces from Bessarabia; at the same time, the Soviet Union took over northern Bukovina, and the local Romanians blamed the Jews for this humiliation.

On July 4, 1940, King Carol II of Romania appointed a pro-Nazi, Ion Girgurtu, to head the government and declared an amnesty for the fascist Iron Guard. Girgurtu enacted harsh antisemitic legislation, dismissing Jews from the army and civil service and from editorial posts and corporate boardrooms, and he restricted Jews from practice in the legal and other professions. The definition of "Jews" was based on the Nazi Nuremberg Laws categorizing Jews as a race rather than a religion.

Girgurtu resigned in August 1940 and was replaced by Marshal Ion Antonescu. On September 14, 1940, Antonescu appointed the leader of the fascist Iron Guard, Horia Sima, as vice president. The Iron Guard conducted murderous rampages, and on January 2, 1941, Sima attempted to overthrow Antonescu in an unsuccessful coup. This degenerated into a pogrom in Bucharest. Two hundred of Bucharest's most distinguished men and women were taken to the abattoir on the edge of the city, stripped, forced to kneel on all fours, and put through all stages of animal slaughter until the beheaded bodies, spurting blood, were hung on iron hooks on the wall. Antonescu finally crushed the rebellion, after which the Germans took Sima and 300 of his Iron Guard to Buchenwald, where they were kept in a special section of the camp.

When the Romanian and German armies invaded the Soviet Union in the summer of 1941, a rumor circulated that the Jews had sheltered Soviet spies and shot at Romanian soldiers. Antonescu used this as a pretext to order the execution of 50 Jews for every Romanian killed. In the pogrom that followed, more than 10,000 Jews were murdered. The Nazis, ironically, disparaged this pogrom as barbaric.

Antonescu called for the Jews of Bessarabia and Bukovina to be deported to Russia. The entire state apparatus—army, gendarmerie, police, civil authorities, prefectures, city councils, and tribunals—joined together to implement this ethnic cleansing. Some 140,000 to 150,000 Jews from Bessarabia, Bukovina, and Dorohoi were deported to Transnistria in western Ukraine.

On October 12, 1941, Siegfried and Hilda Jagendorf were deported across Romania's eastern frontier, and the leaders of the Jewish community asked Jagendorf for assistance in organizing the exodus. He was assured that no more than 40 people would occupy the cattle cars evacuating the Jews, but more than 100 families were instead crammed into them. After a two-day journey they were offloaded at Atachi, Bessarabia—the last station in Romania, where Ukrainian gangs competed with Romanians in pillaging the deportees. A group of Jews, including the Jagendorfs, reached the eastern bank of the Dniester River, avoided the gendarmes, and entered the city of Moghilev-Podolski unmolested. Jagendorf found shelter and set out to find the local German commandant.

Jagendorf dressed in his Romanian officer's uniform before the meeting. With the aid of a letter identifying him as a former director of Siemens-Schukert Werke, he was eventually ushered into the commandant's office. Once inside, he asked immediately what the Germans planned for the evacuees and where he could find food and shelter. In reply he was told that the area was now under Romanian control and that the Germans had no official role to play. Moghilev was out of bounds to Jews; the city was devastated and had no electricity or other vital services.

Jagendorf realized that the group's fate was in Romanian hands. The Jews would have to become indispensable. As the city was without electricity, he decided that the Jews could provide the technical expertise and manpower necessary to repair the power station, and perhaps even rebuild Moghilev's shops and factories. He realized that he would have to sell this idea to the local town prefect, Colonel Ion Baleanu.

He found an empty movie theater, applied at police headquarters for permission to use the building, and persuaded the police chief that confining several thousand Jews in one place would ease his task when the evacuation orders arrived. The chief thereupon instructed his officers to allow anyone Jagendorf designated to occupy the theater. When the theater reached capacity, the police put several damaged houses at Jagendorf's disposal. At that point Jagendorf took responsibility for the fate of Romania's banished Jews.

To meet Baleanu, Jagendorf was clean-shaven and wearing a white shirt, a clean suit, and gloves. Baleanu told Jagendorf that he had granted the interview because he needed his services. With the power station incapacitated, he asked Jagendorf to select four or five electricians and mechanics, and to set up a machine shop. Jagendorf then sent scouts into Moghilev to find an abandoned machine shop, and on November 3, 1941, they found a large disused foundry. Jagendorf told Baleanu that he could not do the job with the limited workers at his disposal but instead needed at least 100 men; there was no other way to restore the foundry and get electricity to Moghilev. This became the Turnatoria foundry.

Baleanu ordered that the requisite authorizations be issued. Jagendorf then presented a list of 116 names and asked that the men's families be allowed to remain with them. Each man claimed 10 or more dependents; nearly 1,200 authorizations were issued. Jagendorf billeted the workers and their families in a school building, repaired with materials taken from bombed houses. The electrical engineers and mechanics worked on the municipal power station and restored the power to Moghilev within two weeks. Baleanu then ordered Jagendorf to repair the city's damaged government buildings; to do so, Jagendorf requested hundreds of additional authorizations, which Baleanu routinely signed, and Jagendorf repaired the lumber mill, flour mills, and wineries.

Over time, the Germans saw that restoration of food production in the district would alleviate food shortages on the battlefront. By this time more than 10,000 Jews were engaged in unpaid productive labor. Jagendorf asked for authorizations for doctors, dentists, barbers, tailors, cooks, and shoemakers. With official approval the Jewish specialists could work in essential manufacturing enterprises.

Baleanu was eventually dismissed because he was seen as too soft on the Jews. The new, harsher arrangements imposed on Jagendorf required him to impose tougher discipline on those in the foundry. He demanded complete obeisance and tolerated no dissent. This attitude was needed—at least two serious typhus epidemics threatened the community, while Jagendorf could still not prevent Jews from being taken into forced labor battalions outside.

Jagendorf left Transnistria for Romania just days before Soviet troops arrived in Moghilev in March 1944. Of the approximately 150,000 Jews deported to

Transnistria, some 50,000 were still alive. At least 15,000 of those who survived could put their fate down directly to Jagendorf's efforts.

When the war ended Siegfried Jagendorf became one of the chief witnesses for the Romanian government in local war crimes trials, though he did not stay long. He and his wife soon emigrated, arriving in the United States on December 23, 1946, where they were met by their daughters. Jagendorf died of cancer in California, on September 8, 1970.

Jonas, Regina (1902–1944)

Regina Jonas was a woman unique anywhere on the globe—during the 1930s she was the first (and, to that point, only) female rabbi, anywhere. She was born in Berlin on August 3, 1902, the daughter of Wolf and Sara Jonas, and grew up in the Scheunenviertel, a poor, mostly Jewish, neighborhood. Her father was a merchant; when Regina was 11, he died of tuberculosis, leaving her mother to take care of herself and her two children, Abraham and Regina.

At high school, Jonas's passions for Jewish history, the Bible, and Hebrew led to her interest in what at the time was unthinkable for a girl: she wanted to become a rabbi. She spoke about it often with her fellow students and studied hard in order to be able to teach. She enrolled in Berlin's Hochschule für die Wissenschaft des Judentums (Higher Institute for Jewish Studies) and took courses designed for liberal student rabbis.

Several people supported her along the way, leading Orthodox rabbis among them. She was even tutored in a weekly *shiur* (study session) by Rabbi Max Weyl, until his deportation to Theresienstadt during World War II. In 1924 she graduated as an "Academic Teacher of Religion," along with her fellow female students. She then became the only woman who hoped to go one step further and be ordained a rabbi.

The thesis that followed would, in the normal run of events, have been required as one of the important steps leading to ordination. Supervised by Professor Eduard Baneth, who was responsible for rabbinic ordination, her thesis was entitled "Can a Woman Be a Rabbi According to Halachic Sources?" Submitted in June 1930, this was the first known attempt to find a basis in Jewish religious law to allow for female ordination. Her conclusion was that there was no prohibition *in law* holding women back from being ordained.

Her work received a grade of "good," which should have paved the way for ordination. Shortly after the thesis was passed, however, Professor Baneth died, and his conservative successor, Rabbi Hanoch Albeck, refused to ordain her because she was a woman. Jonas graduated as a teacher of religion—but only that.

After the Nazis came to power in early 1933, there was an increased demand for Jewish religious teachers. Jewish children were forced out of public schools and into Jewish establishments, and "Miss Jonas" worked hard to impart both Jewish knowledge and *Ahavat Yisroel* (a love of the Jewish people) to her pupils.

Throughout the years following she continued to pursue ordination, until finally, in 1935, Rabbi Max Dienemann agreed. On December 27, 1935, she became Rabbinerin Regina Jonas. She began working as a chaplain in various Jewish organizations, although because she was a woman congregations across Germany denied her a pulpit. The spiritual head of German Jewry, Rabbi **Leo Baeck**, endorsed her ordination after the fact, though he refused to assist in the process leading her to the rabbinate on the grounds that a female rabbi, at that particular time, would cause massive and unnecessary complications within the Jewish community.

In the years that followed, Jonas threw herself into pastoral work. Although she did not have her own pulpit, she spent long hours visiting the sick in Berlin's Jewish Hospital and cared especially for elderly Jews whom circumstances—whether through age or finances—had left in a precarious position. With the onset of war she became a roving rabbi, ministering to Jewish communities in towns that no longer had one. In 1941 she led special services in lieu of regular worship, which was no longer viable in smaller communities where large-scale emigration had taken place. Her messages were always positive, emphasizing the need to remain true to Judaism and a Jewish identity despite the horrors taking place outside.

On November 6, 1942, Jonas and her mother were deported to Theresienstadt. Two days beforehand she was forced to fill out a declaration listing all her property, which was all then confiscated by the state.

At Theresienstadt she continued working. As well as counseling older Jews, she spent a lot of her time and energy preaching to children about the glory of being Jewish and the privilege of doing God's work. She also helped the renowned Austrian Jewish psychoanalyst Viktor Frankl to establish a department of mental hygiene as a means to prevent suicide attempts. Working without a break for two years, she lectured, preached, counseled, and gave hope constantly to those around her. Being a "woman rabbi" was never a concern to her; being a rabbi, per se, was. She was aware of her unique status but considered that to be only a temporary uniqueness; her hope was that she would be the harbinger of more to follow.

On October 12, 1944, time ran out. Jonas and her mother were deported to Auschwitz and probably killed that day or the next. There is no certainty, however; it could even have been as late as December of that year.

Among her papers, found in 1991 by Dr. Katharina von Kellenbach from St. Mary's College of Maryland, was a sermon that could have been Jonas's epitaph: "May all our work be a blessing for Israel's future (and the future of humanity).... Upright 'Jewish men' and 'brave, noble women' were always the sustainers of our people. May we be found worthy by God to be numbered in the circle of these women and men.... The reward of a mitzvah is the recognition of the great deed by God."

Jospa, Yvonne (1919–2000)

Yvonne Jospa was a founder, with her husband, Jewish communist Hertz Jospa, of a Belgian resistance organization known as the Comité de Défense des Juifs (Committee for the Protection of Jews, or CDJ). Born in Romania in 1910 with the name Have Groisman, the third of four girls, she came from a background that was traditionalist in its adherence to Judaism. Her father was one of three judges in their hometown, and her mother was actively involved in the work of the local Jewish school.

Yvonne Jospa—a nom de guerre in the Belgian resistance—attended school in Kishinev (Chişinău) before moving to Belgium to study social work at the University of Liège. In 1933 she married Hertz Jospa, a pharmaceutical chemist. Straight after their wedding, the couple joined the Communist Party of Belgium, and in 1934 they became Belgian citizens. Prior to the outbreak of World War II they worked with child refugees from the Spanish Civil War and organized the passage through Belgium of Romanian antifascist volunteers going to Spain to fight with the International Brigades.

During 1935 and 1936 Yvonne Jospa also took care of Jewish refugees from Germany and Austria. After the *Kristallnacht* pogrom of November 9–10, 1938, her work intensified dramatically. She would often shield illegal immigrants in her house prior to smuggling them out of the country.

On May 10, 1940, Nazi Germany invaded Belgium, which capitulated on May 28. At this point, Jospa stopped work in order to devote herself fully to social and relief matters. As one who was Jewish, communist, and anti-Nazi, she knew that she was in extreme peril if her activities led to her arrest, and as a result she and her husband moved around constantly with false names and papers. In September 1942 they established the CDJ, with Jospa as head of the branch working to rescue Jewish children. Through her efforts, more than 3,000 Jewish children were saved from deportation and placed with sympathetic non-Jewish Belgian families.

The means by which the CDJ operated was simple. Committee workers, with two subcommittees in play—one for adults and one for children—would separate the children from their parents to make it easier to hide them. For the adults, the committee's problems were twofold: finding places to stay, and providing them with subsistence. Children presented other difficulties. They were farmed out to carefully chosen Belgian families, but those who took them in had to be people the parents did not know; moreover, the parents could not know the family's name or where their children had been sent.

Overseeing the children's committee required considerable organizational skills. A staff of 16 volunteers worked tirelessly to ensure the operation's success, and it is to Jospa's credit that no one was arrested for harboring Jewish children. The committee maintained three sets of documents: in the first were the real names of the children; in the second were the children's places of sanctuary and their false names; in the third were codes that connected the two other books, and for security each of the three sets was kept separately and apart.

Survival, however, came at a price. In order to be saved, the children had to live as Belgians, abandon their Jewish identity, and assume new names and identities—even going to school as Belgians. Friendly priests prepared false baptism certificates so that the children could be registered in their new schools, and parents and children were able to maintain mail contact through the introduction of an underground mail system. Ration cards and stamps for Jewish children in hiding were organized through partisans stealing documents.

In June 1943 Hertz Jospa was arrested while meeting with a courier who was identified as Jewish. He was deported as a political resister, not as a Jew, which saved him from being sent to Auschwitz. After a period of detention in Belgium, he was deported in May 1944 to Buchenwald. Yvonne Jospa lost contact with him and thought he had died, but he returned on May 8, 1945, after the camp was liberated. When he returned he was but a shadow of what he had been prior to his arrest, emotionally and physically exhausted and very sick. It took a long period of convalescence for him to return to health.

When peace and liberation came, there were inevitable problems of reintegration for the children and their parents—some of whom had not seen each other for years. In some cases, rescuing families did not want to give the children back; in others, where parents did not return, serious questions arose within the Jewish community regarding the children's future. Some Zionists held that they should be moved to Palestine; Jospa's position was that they should not be moved out of Belgium until they were old enough to decide their own futures. Ultimately, a series of compromises saw some moved overseas, and some remain in Belgium.

All the members of Jospa's family who remained in Romania were murdered during the Holocaust. A sister who stayed with her in Belgium survived. No one, however, other than those with whom she had the closest contact during the war, knew of her accomplishments on behalf of Jewish children. In 1964, in order to keep alive the community of resisters she had played such an important part in facilitating, Jospa cofounded the Union des Anciens Résistants Juifs de Belgique (Union of Former Belgium Jewish Resistance Members). She remained honorary chair of this organization until her death in Brussels in 2000.

K

Kafka, Helene (1894–1943)

Helene Kafka, better known as Sister Maria Restituta, was the only German nun to be condemned to death in a court of law under Germany's National Socialist regime.

She was born on May 1, 1894, in Husovice (not far from Brno) in the Austro-Hungarian Empire, the sixth daughter of a Catholic shoemaker, Anton Kafka, and his wife, Maria. When she was two years old her family moved to Vienna. She was raised in the Austrian capital, becoming a ward sister (and eventually, head nurse) at the Lainz General Hospital, working with the Franciscan Sisters of Christian Charity. In early 1914, at the age of 19, she entered the convent (despite her parents' opposition) and took the name Maria Restituta, after a fourth-century Christian martyr. From 1919 until 1942 she served at the hospital in Mödling, Vienna, where she became a surgical nurse and anesthetist.

She quickly developed a reputation for radiating Christian love and kindness, regardless of the origin or beliefs of the patient. Whether Christian or Jewish, or of any political viewpoint, all patients received her equal devotion and care. She was viewed not only as a skilled nurse but also as one who stood up for the poor, the persecuted, and the oppressed.

With the *Anschluss* of Germany and Austria in March 1938, one of the Nazis' first actions was to close more than 1,400 religious—primarily Catholic—institutions, including more than 200 monasteries, all Catholic associations and youth organizations, and countless societies. Maria Restituta was allowed to continue her work, but the Mödling hospital was placed under the direct control of staff known to be loyal to the new government.

With her commitment to equality and personal freedom, Sister Restituta was vocal in her rejection of the new regime, even going so far as to call Adolf Hitler a "madman." She reaffirmed religious freedom and refused to remove the crucifixes hanging in each hospital room; not only that, but when a new wing of the hospital was built, she hung crucifixes in *all* the new rooms. The Nazis demanded that they be removed and threatened her dismissal—but they were not removed. At one point she even defied the Nazis by secretly leading a child for baptism. She was staunch in her opposition to the Nazi persecution of the Church, to the oppression of the Jews, and to all forms of political repression. In short order, she was soon regarded as an enemy of the regime. She continued to pray with the dying, however, ensuring that they received the last sacraments.

Her downfall came when she asked a secretary to copy an anti-Nazi leaflet from the White Rose resistance movement. Two female members of the hospital staff witnessed her act and reported it to an SS doctor, Lambert Stumfohl. He had long been aware of Sister Restituta's insubordination and had been seeking an opportunity to remove her from the hospital. Armed with this new information, he turned her in to the Gestapo on Ash Wednesday, February 18, 1942, for "favoring the enemy and conspiracy to commit high treason." She was accused not only of having deliberately and rebelliously placed the crucifixes, but also of writing a poem ridiculing Hitler.

On October 29, 1942, the People's Court (Volksgerichtshof) condemned her to death by beheading, and she spent her last days caring for other prisoners, giving away most of her rations to those who needed them more. She was offered better conditions, and even release, if she renounced her vows, but she refused.

Several requests for clemency were made, including one from the archbishop of Vienna, Cardinal Theodor Innitzer. All were rejected. Martin Bormann, head of the Reich Chancellery, saw her death as "an effective deterrent" to any future episodes of disobedience, and as a consequence all appeals for mercy were vetoed. On March 30, 1943, the sentence was carried out. She went to the guillotine with her hands tied behind her back and wearing a paper shirt. The prison chaplain, Father Ivanek, followed her to the door of the execution chamber, and just before her death she asked him to make the sign of the cross on her forehead. Her last recorded words were: "I have lived for Christ, I would die for Christ." She was killed along with three communists who were also beheaded. Prior to her death she saw it as her role to provide comfort for them, rather than to dwell on her own imminent sacrifice.

In order to ensure that she would not be revered as a martyr, the Nazis refused to hand over her body and threw it into a mass grave. At the time of Sister Maria Restituta's death she was 48 years old.

On June 21, 1998, Sister Maria Restituta was beatified in Vienna by Pope John Paul II during his papal visit to Austria.

Kaplan, Chaim A. (1880–1942)

Chaim Aron Kaplan was an educator and diarist of the Holocaust who resisted the Nazis by chronicling the day-to-day events of the Warsaw Ghetto, making a record of life there under German occupation.

Kaplan was born in 1880 in Gorodishche (Horodyszcze), a village in Belorussia in the Russian Empire. He was educated at the famous Mir yeshiva, and later studied at the Vilna teachers' college. In 1902 he moved to Warsaw, where he established an elementary Hebrew school; he would remain there as principal for the next 40 years. In 1921 he visited the United States, and in 1936 Palestine, with the idea of joining his two children. As he saw little economic future for himself there, however, he returned to Warsaw.

Kaplan devoted his efforts to education and writing. He began keeping a diary around 1933, and in September 1939, at the start of World War II, he decided to detail Jewish life in Warsaw and thus preserve a record for posterity. This was to become Kaplan's *Scroll of Agony*. His very first entry, on September 1, 1939, was prescient: "This war will indeed bring destruction upon human civilization.... I doubt that we will live through this carnage. The bombs filled with lethal gas will poison every living being, or we will starve because there will be no means of livelihood."

After Warsaw's surrender to German forces on September 27, 1939, Kaplan wrote: "the Nazis' objective was to eliminate the Jews physically through a slow choking process." By the time the ghetto was established formally on October 12, 1940, roughly 375,000 Jews (nearly a third of Warsaw's population), along with many refugees, were squeezed into a ghetto that took up 2.4 percent of Warsaw's surface area. To make matters worse, Jews in the ghetto were only allotted one-tenth of the required caloric intake and were subjected to forced labor, disease, and slaughter. Kaplan commented on the frequent murder of Jews and the horrific treatment they experienced, explaining that: "The Aryans are put to death after a short period of arrest; the Jews are killed without even a pretense of arrest." He further detailed how the Nazis carried out many of their violent acts: "The murderers burst into a home in the middle of the night and put an end to a life."

Scroll of Agony would become one of the most powerful and inspiring testimonies from the Holocaust period. Kaplan recorded his diary in small notebooks and focused primarily on daily experiences. He attempted to remain objective despite the dire conditions and saw his mission as preserving a record for posterity, focusing strictly on facts and situations as they appeared. The diary recorded the events and experiences Kaplan witnessed himself, or those told to him by members of the ghetto community. He set down his own thoughts as well as conversations with friends and with those he met in the streets, and sought out firsthand information to provide immediacy and authenticity.

Keeping a diary or any sort of written testimony during the Holocaust created many risks; however, Kaplan did not fear being caught. He felt that recording his experiences was a responsibility. He continually expressed the hope that the diary would be saved, realizing its significance for future generations. As he moved from place to place, and as the Nazis seemed to be intensifying their murderous activities, he worked faster, often writing several times a day in order to include every detail of the horror surrounding him.

This sense of duty was emphasized in the January 16, 1940, entry, when Kaplan wrote: "Anyone who keeps such a record endangers his life, but this does not frighten me. I sense within me the magnitude of this hour, and my responsibility toward it, and I have an inner obligation that I am not free to relinquish. . . . My record will serve as a source material for the future generation." In essence, he wrote his diary so that others would someday be able to understand the Holocaust and never forget the Jews' experiences during it. In 1942 conditions in the Warsaw Ghetto worsened, as Kaplan wrote in his diary: "The Jewish section of Warsaw had become a city of slaughter."

Kaplan was not as concerned about his own future as he was about the future of his diary. He knew he had to get it out of the ghetto if there was any chance that his observations, so carefully chronicled, would survive. Thus, in late 1942 he gave his diary to a Jewish friend to whom he refers only as Rubinsztejn, who did forced labor each day outside the ghetto. Rubinsztejn smuggled the notebooks out and delivered them to a Pole, Władyslaw Wojcek, who lived in the small village of Liw, near Warsaw. In the early 1960s, Wojcek moved to the United States, where he sold the notebooks. Eventually, they were edited, translated, and published, and the diary has since appeared in English, German, French, Danish, and Japanese.

Kaplan's final entry was made on August 4, 1942: "If the hunters do not stop, and if I am caught, I am afraid my work will be in vain. I am constantly bothered by the thought: If my life ends, what will become of my diary?" The diary did survive, but Kaplan and his wife did not. They were deported to Treblinka, and it appears they were murdered in December 1942.

Karski, Jan (1914–2000)

Jan Karski was a member of the Polish underground. He documented and publicized the plight of Polish Jews during World War II, having infiltrated the Warsaw Ghetto and other places in order to report firsthand what he had seen.

He was born Jan Kozielewski on April 24, 1914, in Łódź, Poland. A Christian, he was raised in an integrated and tolerant neighborhood where there were many Jews. He received part of his education in a military college, graduating with high marks in 1936. At the same time he also studied at the University of Lvov, from which he obtained a law degree in 1935. Joining the foreign service as a trainee diplomat, he served in Germany, Romania, Switzerland, and Britain. He gained a First in Grand Diplomatic Practice, and on January 1, 1939, started work with the Polish Ministry of Foreign Affairs.

Karski served as an officer in eastern Poland after World War II began in September 1939, seeing action against Soviet troops following the invasion of September 17, 1939. Taken prisoner, he pretended to be a private soldier rather than an officer, and the Soviets handed him over to the Germans because his birthplace was Łódź, in the German zone. In November 1939 he escaped and joined what was later to become known as the Home Army (Armia Krajowa, or AK). Beginning in January 1940 he undertook a series of daring missions as a courier and spy for the Polish government-in-exile, crossing enemy lines and national borders between France, Britain, and Poland on numerous occasions. In July 1940 he was arrested by the Gestapo in Slovakia and severely tortured during interrogation. Smuggled out by the resistance, he returned to active service after a short period of recuperation.

In 1942 the London-based Polish government-in-exile selected Karski for a new mission in which he was to ascertain the extent of German atrocities in occupied Poland and report back. On at least two occasions he was smuggled incognito by Jewish underground leaders into the Warsaw Ghetto, where he witnessed firsthand the brutality of the Nazis' policies.

In addition, Karski visited what he thought was the death camp at Bełżec, though indications are that he confused his visit with a particularly brutal ghetto at Izbica, from which Jews were deported to Bełżec. The first mass deportation to Bełżec took place in mid-March 1942, and it is possible that Karski witnessed this and conflated the horror of the two events in his understanding of what was happening.

Jan Karski, a Polish soldier and member of the Armia Krajowa (Home Army). In 1942 he undertook a mission to infiltrate the Warsaw Ghetto and report his findings to authorities in London and Washington, where he attempted to raise Allied awareness of what was happening to the Jews of Poland. He was, however, unable to convince anyone to make defeating the Holocaust a priority in military planning. (United States Holocaust Memorial Museum, courtesy of Jan Karski)

In the fall of 1942 Karski visited London and personally briefed leaders of the Polish government-in-exile, together with such Allied officials as British foreign secretary Anthony Eden, about the horrors of the Warsaw Ghetto and the Nazi death camps. He also produced hard evidence of anti-Jewish atrocities, contained in microfilm he had carried with him from Poland. On the basis of this information, Polish foreign minister Edward Raczyński could provide the Allies with some of the first information available about the Holocaust. Karski implored Western leaders to stop the killing, but Allied leaders gave greater priority to other issues related to the war effort.

In the early summer of 1943 Karski traveled to the United States, where he engaged in a whirlwind campaign publicizing the plight of the European Jews. He met with American politicians, conferred with senior religious leaders from several religious denominations, and gave lectures around the country. On July 28, 1943, he met with President Franklin D. Roosevelt in the Oval Office. There he presented a detailed account of his experiences, though it was later reported that Roosevelt did not ask a single question about the Jews. Of all the influential political leaders to whom he spoke, Karski was unable to convince any to make the Holocaust a priority.

In 1944, with the war still raging, he published a book entitled *Courier from Poland: The Story of a Secret State*, which told of his exploits with the Polish underground. As an indictment of the Nazi occupation of Poland, the book was a revelation to many Americans and became a runaway best seller. Within a year, it had sold more than 400,000 copies. The book was rereleased in 2013, educating an entirely new generation.

After the war, Karski settled in the United States. He earned a doctorate in international relations from Georgetown University in 1952, became an American citizen in 1954, and spent the next four decades at Georgetown teaching political science and international relations.

On June 2, 1982, Karski was recognized by Yad Vashem as one of the Righteous among the Nations for his work in bringing the Holocaust to the world's attention. In 1994 he was made an honorary citizen of the State of Israel. Among the many other awards he received were Poland's Order of the White Eagle and the *Virtuti Militari*, Poland's highest military decoration for bravery in combat. In addition, he was nominated for the Nobel Peace Prize.

On July 13, 2000, Jan Karski died of heart and kidney disease in in Washington, D.C.

Kasztner, Rezső (1906–1957)

Rezső (Rudolf) Kasztner was a controversial Jewish rescuer of Jews in Nazi-occupied Hungary. Born in 1906 to Yitzhak and Helen Kasztner, he was raised with his two brothers in Cluj (Koloszvár, Klozenberg), Transylvania. He was well educated, with a qualification in law. A linguist, he was fluent in Hungarian, Romanian, French, German, Latin, Yiddish, Hebrew, and Aramaic.

Early in his career, he worked as a journalist for the Zionist newspaper *Uj Kelet*. A committed Zionist, he edited the youth periodical *Noar* (*Youth*) from 1926 to 1928, and then worked in Budapest between 1929 and 1931. In 1934 he married

Elizabeth Fischer, the daughter of Dr. Jósef Fischer, a member of Parliament, president of the Jewish community of Kolozsvár, and member of the National Jewish Party. By 1942 he was fully ensconced in that city and opened the local office of Keren Hayesod, the United Palestine Appeal. From 1943 until 1945 he was the deputy chairman of the city's small Zionist Organization.

After the German invasion of Hungary in March 1944, he and Jewish rescue worker Joel Brand found themselves interacting with SS Lieutenant Colonel Adolf Eichmann, who had come to Budapest specifically to establish the Reich Security Main Office and implement the Final Solution in Hungary. However, the very idea of them negotiating with the Germans was controversial, both during the war and afterward.

While the Nazis were imposing the Final Solution, they were clearly bent on the destruction of Hungary's Jews; but at the same time, they were also the only authority with whom Jews could negotiate if rescue were to be achieved. As Kasztner was trying to work within this genocidal regime, the fundamental topic of conversation settled on an initiative that became known as the "Blood for Goods" ("*Blut für Ware*") proposal. According to this agreement, Nazi Germany would receive certain quantities of supplies for the German war effort from neutral countries (with the help of international Jewish bodies) in exchange for the survival of the Jewish population and their transfer from German-occupied territories to safety abroad, particularly Palestine.

This meant Kasztner had to deal face-to-face with Eichmann and other Nazis in his capacity as head of the Vaada Etzel Vehatzalah (Jewish Relief and Rescue Committee). The negotiation ultimately led to the Nazis releasing a trainload of 1,368 Jews, which included Rabbi Joel Teitelbaum, founder of the Satmar Hasidic dynasty, as well as members of Kasztner's own family. The train left Budapest on June 30, 1944, but instead of heading directly to Switzerland it was diverted to Bergen-Belsen on July 9. Then followed months of delay, during which Kasztner worked to negotiate the Jews' release. They were segregated from the other inmates and given a subsistence diet. Prior to their release in two batches—some in August and others in December—several died.

By this stage, no war matériel had yet been transferred to the Nazis; the release was an initial gesture of good faith in the expectation that the relationship would hold and that these goods would be forthcoming at some stage soon thereafter.

Kasztner and his committee arranged for a diverse group of Jews to be assembled for the rescue. People of all ages and of all social classes were included: Zionists and non-Zionists, Orthodox and ultra-Orthodox, 972 females and 712 males. Baron Fülöp von Freudiger, director of the Orthodox congregation in Budapest, selected 80 rabbis and other prominent figures and paid for their inclusion on the passenger list.

It was, however, because of 150 seats that were auctioned off to wealthy Jews that Kasztner's name was vilified—and they were to cost him his life several years later. He was criticized not only for charging wealthy Jews but also for rescuing some of his family members at the expense of others in the Jewish community.

His successful arrangements for the transfer of these Jews to Switzerland would later be viewed as both self-serving and evidence of his collaboration with the Nazis. Later, at his trial in Israel, Eichmann said that Kasztner had "agreed to help keep the Jews from resisting deportation—and even keep order in the collection camps—if I would close my eyes and let a few hundred or a few thousand young Jews emigrate to Palestine. It was a good bargain."

The story of the Kasztner Train quickly became a controversial episode in the history of Jewish rescue during the Holocaust. As things turned out, the train was unique; it was a "life train," as distinct from the death trains that had been conveying Jews to their fate in the extermination camps up to that point. Overall, some 1,670 Jews survived as a result of Kasztner's negotiations with Adolf Eichmann, which is about 400 more than **Oskar Schindler** saved through his famous list. The difference between Kasztner and Schindler, however, is that some viewed Kasztner, a Jew, as having sold out vast numbers of other Jews in order to save his own life and the lives of his family members and favorites, whereas Schindler, a Gentile, has been recognized for his unconditional goodwill toward Jews.

After the war, Kasztner and his family remained in Europe before emigrating to Israel. Upon his arrival, he was welcomed into the ranks of the Mapai (Labor) Party, which led pre-state Palestine and later governed Israel. He twice stood unsuccessfully for election to Israel's Knesset.

Kasztner's role in working with the SS made headlines in 1953, when he was accused, in a pamphlet produced by Malchiel Gruenwald, of collaborating with the Nazis. It said that his actions enabled the mass murder of Hungarian Jewry, and that Kasztner also partnered with Nazi officer Kurt Becher in the theft of Jewish property—and then saved Becher from punishment after the war. Kasztner sued Gruenwald for libel, in a trial that was turned around and became an action exposing Kasztner's behavior during the war. In his ruling, Judge Benjamin Halevi acquitted Gruenwald of libel on the first, second, and fourth counts. The Israeli government appealed on Kasztner's behalf, and the Supreme Court of Israel overturned most of the original judgment against him in 1958.

This was not the end of Kasztner's ordeal, however. Soon after midnight on March 4, 1957, he was shot in Tel Aviv by Ze'ev Eckstein, a veteran from the pre-state right-wing militia Lehi (known also as the Stern Gang), who, with his accomplices Yosef Menkes and Dan Shermer, accused Kasztner of selling out the Jewish people for his own convenience. Kasztner died on March 12 and was buried on March 17, 1957. Together, his assassins were found guilty of murder and given life sentences, but seven years later they were released.

To this day, despite the rescue of more than 1,600 Jews and the subsequent birth of many thousands of their descendants, Kasztner remains a divisive figure among survivors. He is, in short, seen as a hero in some circles and as a hated collaborator in others, with a legacy that is still highly disputed and controversial.

Katzenelson, Itzhak (1886–1944)

Itzhak Katzenelson was a Hebrew and Yiddish poet and dramatist in Poland, who was active in cultural resistance to the Holocaust.

Born to Hinda and Jacob Benjamin Katzenelson on July 21, 1886, in Karelichy (Korelichi), a small town near Minsk, he received his early education from his father. He was a descendant of a long line of rabbinical and Talmudic sages and scholars dating back to the great Talmudic commentator, Rabbi Yom-Tov Lipmann Heller.

Katzenelson was raised in Łódź, where the family moved soon after he was born. He was considered a literary prodigy, and by the age of 12 had already written his first play, *Dreyfus un Esterhazy*. As a young adult before World War I he opened a secular Hebrew school and created a network of such schools in Łódź from kindergarten to high school, which functioned until 1939. He also became known for his Hebrew textbooks and books for children, which were the first of their kind.

In addition, Katzenelson wrote Yiddish comedies (translated into Hebrew), and in 1912 he founded the theatre Habima Halvrit (The Hebrew Stage), which toured Poland and Lithuania. Several of his Yiddish plays were performed in Łódź before World War I. His first volume of poetry, *Dimdumim* (*Twilight*), appeared in 1910.

Beginning in 1930, Katzenelson belonged to the Dror Zionist movement in Łódź and also to Hechalutz—which, with emigration to Palestine as its goal, operated a training commune, Kibbutz Hakhsharah. During the period between the wars, Katzenelson was conditioned by his belief that Jewish life in Poland was without hope due to the ingrained antisemitism of the Polish masses.

Nazi Germany invaded Poland on September 1, 1939, and eight days later Łódź was occupied. Katzenelson's school was immediately closed down, later serving as the city's Gestapo headquarters. Urged on by his family, Katzenelson fled to Warsaw in late November 1939. Once settled, his wife, Hanna, and their three children followed. She and their two younger sons, Benjamin and Ben Zion, would be deported to their deaths in Treblinka on August 14, 1942.

In the ghetto, Katzenelson entered his most creative period, writing poems and articles in the underground Zionist press, as well as approximately 50 plays. He wrote poems reflecting the contemporary suffering of the ghetto, masked through Biblical or historical themes. His descriptions were his responses to the wretched conditions in which the Jews of Warsaw found themselves, and through his plays he hoped to improve ghetto morale. His Yiddish play *Iyov* (*Job*) was published on

June 22, 1941, possibly the only Jewish book published in the ghetto during the German occupation.

On July 20, 1942, just before the Nazis began their mass deportations of Jews from the Warsaw Ghetto, **Mordechaj Tenenbaum**, one of the leading members of Dror and a founder of the Jewish Combat Organization (ŻOB), concealed some of Katzenelson's writings in an underground hiding place. Some of these survived the war. In April 1943 the Jews of the Warsaw Ghetto began a revolt that would last for the next 27 days. The day after the start of the revolt, to save his life, friends smuggled Katzenelson and his surviving son Zvi out of a bunker at Leszno 50, and into the Aryan part of the city.

They went to the Polski Hotel, from where they obtained documents from Katzenelson's friend **David Guzik** of the Joint Distribution Committee, certifying that they were citizens of Honduras. In possession of his new passport, they were transferred in May 1943 to the French internment camp at Vittel, where the Nazis held Allied citizens and nationals of neutral countries for possible later prisoner exchange. It was here, on October 3, 1943, that he wrote possibly his greatest Yiddish work, *Dos Lid funem Oysgehargen Yidishn Folk* (*The Song of the Murdered Jewish People*). He completed this epic, a poem in 15 chapters describing the horrors of the Holocaust, on January 18, 1944. Its lines include:

> And it continued. Ten a day, ten thousand Jews a day.
> That did not last very long. Soon they took fifteen thousand.
> Warsaw, the City of Jews—the fenced-in, walled-in city,
> Dwindled, expired, melted like snow before my eyes.
> Warsaw, packed with Jews like a synagogue on Yom Kippur, like a busy marketplace
> Jews trading and worshiping, both happy and sad
> Seeking their bread, praying to their God.
> They crowded the walled-in, locked-in city.
> You are deserted now, Warsaw, like a gloomy wasteland.
> You are a cemetery now, more desolate than a graveyard.
> Your streets are empty—not even a corpse can be found there.

The poem ended with the words "Woe unto me, woe."

Katzenenlson made two copies of the poem, one of which he gave to Ruth Adler, a German Jew from Dresden who had a British Palestinian passport. In the spring of 1944 she received permission to leave the country in a prisoner exchange and smuggled out one of the copies, taking it to Palestine. Katzenelson buried the other copy in bottles under a tree at Vittel with the help of a fellow prisoner, Miriam Novitch, who retrieved it after liberation. The poem was first published in May 1945. Extracts have since been published in numerous languages, and a stand-alone volume has also appeared.

In the early spring of 1944 the Jews interned at Vittel were declared stateless, and on April 18, 1944, those of Polish origin were transported in three railroad cars to the Drancy transit camp near Paris. In late April 1944, Itzhak and Zvi Katzenelson were sent on a transport to Auschwitz, where they were murdered on May 1, 1944.

In Israel, the Ghetto Fighters' House (Beit Lohamei Hagetaot) has been named in Katzenelson's honor as the Itzhak Katzenelson Holocaust and Jewish Resistance Heritage Museum. The museum was founded in 1949 by Holocaust survivors, former ghetto fighters, and veterans of partisan units. Its aim is to serve as a place of testimony relating the story of the Jewish people in the 20th century, and in particular during World War II. As a further lasting monument, the museum has made extensive efforts to collect as many of Katzenelson's manuscripts as can be located, and to translate his works into English and other languages.

Knut, Dovid (1900–1955)

Dovid Knut was a Russian Jewish poet and member of the French Resistance. He was born Duvid Meerovich Fiksman in 1900 in Orgeev (Orhei), Bessarabia—the Romanian-speaking region of Russia (now Moldova). The son of a grocer, and from an observant Jewish family, he was raised in Kishinev (Chişinău) and found an early interest in poetry. At the age of 14 he began publishing his poems, and by 1918 he was editing the magazine *Molodaya mysl'* (*Young Thought*). At this time he adopted the literary name Dovid Knut.

After the annexation of Bessarabia to Romania in 1920, he moved to Paris where he took a number of odd jobs. At night he studied French at the Alliance Française, and he opened a restaurant where he employed his sisters and a younger brother. Over time, as he became more and more familiar with his new surroundings and language, he took courses in the Department of Chemistry at the University of Caen (Normandy), and also worked as an engineer.

Paris at that time served as a magnet for exiles from the Russian Revolution. A complete Russian cultural life included cafés, restaurants, shops, and newspapers solely for Russians. Schools conducted classes in Russian, and life-cycle events were conducted according to Orthodox religious rites. Knut participated actively in this cultural life. He contributed poems to many émigré publications, and his first collection, *Moikh tysyachiletii* (*My Millennia*), appeared in 1925. A second volume of poetry was published in 1928.

In late 1934, having divorced his first wife, Sarra Groboys, he began a relationship with Ariadna Scriabina, daughter of the Russian composer Alexander Scriabin. Scriabina associated herself with the Russian émigré community and married Knut, who would be her third husband. They both became committed Zionists, and in 1940 Scriabina converted to Judaism and took the name Sarah—demanding that she be called only by that name from then on. Her conversion was viewed as a betrayal by the non-Jewish Russian immigrant community. For Scriabina, however, identification with the Jewish people became an obsession. She became intolerant of even the slightest manifestations of antisemitism, a characteristic that would condition her and Knut's attitude toward Nazism once France was overrun in 1940.

In the years prior to that, however, they both visited Palestine (August–December 1937), where the newspaper *Haaretz* published one of Knut's poems in Hebrew. Back in France, in early 1939, the couple began to publish a Jewish newspaper, *L'Affirmation*, aimed at awakening the Jewish national consciousness. Knut served as both editor and reporter, and the paper was used as a vehicle to combat antisemitism. In August 1939, in recognition of their work on behalf of the Jewish people and of Zionism, the couple was invited to the XXI World Zionist Congress in Geneva.

One week later Germany invaded Poland, and World War II began. Knut was mobilized into the French army, and the newspaper had to close. He was deployed in the defense of Paris, but with the advance of the German army his unit was sent to the south of France. Shortly before the country fell and the Germans entered Paris, his wife joined Knut in Toulouse. It was here, in January 1942, that they, together with **Abraham Polonski**, his wife Eugénie, and the socialist Lucien Lublin, established the Armée Juive (Jewish Army, or AJ).

At first, the Armée Juive was called the Mouvement des Jeunesses Sionistes (Young Zionist Movement, or MJS); later, it evolved into the Organisation Juive de Combat (Jewish Combat Organization, or OJC). Its intentions were twofold: to protect Jews threatened by the Nazis, and to develop military skills that could then be used to help in the establishment of a Jewish State in Palestine. As the war progressed, the peak strength of the Armée Juive eventually numbered some 2,000 fighters. During the winter of 1943–1944, its escape network helped some 300 Jews flee to Spain through the Pyrenees; most of them then migrated to Palestine. The Armée Juive's military actions were essentially limited to using weapons supplied through British air drops.

Knut was forced to escape to Switzerland in December 1942, when the Gestapo, in an attempt to destroy the Armée Juive, came close to apprehending him. His wife stayed behind in Toulouse, where she gave birth to Knut's son Joseph (Yosi) in May 1943. While holding an AJ meeting at her apartment one day in July 1944, she was ambushed and killed by members of the Milice (French militia), a paramilitary force created by the Vichy regime to help fight the resistance.

Knut returned to Paris in the fall of 1944. He worked at the Centre de Documentation Juive Contemporaine (Contemporary Jewish Documentation Center), which had been established in 1943 as a clandestine organization with the objective of documenting the Holocaust by gathering together all the information and documentary evidence collected by various Jewish organizations during the war.

His role was to serve as editor of the Center's *Bulletin du Centre de Documentation Juive Contemporaine*.

In 1946 he became editor of the magazine *Le Monde Juif* (*The Jewish World*), and in 1947 he married a 19-year-old half-Jewish actress, Virginia Sharovskaya, who converted to Judaism and became Leah Knut. In 1947 he published a book, *Contribution à L'Histoire de la Résistance Juive en France 1940–1944* (*The History of the Jewish Resistance in France, 1940–1944*), and in 1949 he published his *Selected Poems*. In October of that year, Knut and his family migrated to Israel, settling in Tel Aviv, where he taught Hebrew. He died in 1955 from a brain tumor.

Koffán, Károly (1909–1985)

Károly Koffán was an artist, art teacher, and professor at the Hungarian Academy of Fine Arts, Budapest. Born in 1909, he founded Budapest's Open School of Art, where from 1944 onward hundreds of Jews and other victims were hidden and saved from the Nazis. He also arranged for the creation of false papers, often doing the artwork and signatures himself.

From 1934 until 1939 Koffán and his wife, Keska, lived in Paris, where he enjoyed the cosmopolitan atmosphere, painting, sculpting, and building a puppet theater. He joined the Communist party but was not especially zealous or politically active. After the Nazi occupation of Paris in 1940, however, he returned to Hungary and established the Open School of Art in an attempt to replicate the environment he had enjoyed so much in Paris. Those who gravitated toward the Open School were Lajos Szentiványi and students André Mészáros, László Ridovics, and Sandor Kovács, among others.

Nazi Germany invaded and occupied Hungary on March 19, 1944. Although his previous personal history gave little indication that he would engage in any form of resistance activities, Koffán decided to do something to help those who needed it, and so, together with Szentiványi, he concluded that the art school (and, eventually, his home on the top floor of the same building), located on Erzsebet Square, could serve as a hiding place. Among those who were arrested, and whom the group could not save, was Szentiványi's father, who was sent to Mauthausen concentration camp in Austria.

The artists' resistance activities were entirely spontaneous and unstructured. They did not belong to any formal underground movement; had neither diplomatic immunity nor access to the resources of a large organization; did not have a plan to follow; and did not keep records of their activities. More often than not, they helped people on the basis of personal acquaintanceship, motivated by humanitarian feelings. Koffán and Szentiványi ran the group's rescue activities, while the students carried out the missions to save people.

Mészáros, Ridovics, Kovács, and others brought forged documents to Jews, rescued people from ghettos and transports, and smuggled them into hiding places. They also brought food into the ghettos and liberated Jews by presenting themselves as soldiers. Later on, still masquerading as soldiers, they went into the transit camps where Jews were sent before being transported to Auschwitz, and they took people out. Early in the morning, before classes at the art school, students would take the refugees to nearby hiding places, or if this were not feasible, then to the school itself. People from all social circles, including artists, intellectuals, communists, clerks, and officers, met regularly at the school in the evenings, and sometimes up to 20 people stayed overnight.

Keska Koffán hid the visitors in plain sight by giving each one an art book, and when Nazi or Hungarian Arrow Cross forces came looking for victims, they appeared to be students in an art class.

Using their creative skills, Koffán and Szentiványi forged papers, filled in stolen blank documents, and faked official stamps. Preparing these documents was not an easy task since proof of identity had first to be established. This was facilitated through one of the artists at the school, who worked in a government office and managed to obtain blank baptism certificates. Szentiványi and Koffán then forged signatures and other details. Cleverly, they often manipulated the places of birth on these certificates by writing in towns and villages that were already under Soviet control.

The students would then courier the documents to those who needed them, scattered around Budapest or in hiding. Eventually, the artists managed to obtain and distribute Swedish and Swiss *Schutzpässe* (safety passes) to the Jewish community, which came from **Raoul Wallenberg** and **Carl Lutz**. The Nazis usually accepted these passes as legitimate and did not deport those holding them. It is not known how many people the Koffán group managed to save, as nothing official was ever kept. The figure would most certainly run into the hundreds, however.

After the war, Koffán's earlier membership in the Communist party in France held him in good stead. Under Soviet control, he was able to continue painting, and he taught at the Hungarian College of Fine Arts. After taking part in the 1956 Hungarian Revolution, however, he lost his position and status. He became instead a photographer, particularly of bird life. The Soviet authorities, concerned lest they lose control over such an eclectic bunch, also kept a close eye on Szentiványi and the others in the years following the liberation. Koffán died in 1985.

Members of the Koffán group knew how to distinguish between right and wrong in the darkest era of humanity, and they were willing to rescue their friends and strangers, even at the risk of their own lives. Their attitude was that they were simply doing their humanitarian duty. At least one of the rescuers, André Mészáros, was recognized as one of the Righteous among the Nations by Yad Vashem in 2006. As of this writing, more detailed investigations are being made into the actions of other group members, foremost among whom are Károly Koffán and Lajos Szentiványi.

Korkut, Dervis (1888–1969)

Dervis Korkut, an ethnic Albanian Muslim, was known for his sympathetic literature on the oppression of minorities, specifically Jews, and for saving both a book—the Sarajevo Haggadah, a sacred Jewish text—and a "person of the book," Mira Papos, when the Nazis invaded Bosnia during World War II.

The details of Korkut's early life are meager. He was born in 1888 in Travnik, Bosnia, and his father was an *alim*, an Islamic legal scholar who was often looked upon as a judge in Islamic law. His brother, a professor of Arabic, allegedly made the first widely used translation of the Qur'an into the Serbo-Croatian language. Korkut studied theology at Istanbul University and Near Eastern languages in Paris at the Sorbonne. His career in religious studies included serving as the senior official in Yugoslavia's Ministry of Religious Affairs, prior to an appointment as honorary consul for France.

It is clear that Korkut was an intellectually gifted and cosmopolitan theologian. He was capable of navigating between, and perhaps even straddling, cultures, as suggested by his very dress. He wore handsomely tailored Western-style suits topped off by the fez that always adorned his head. Perhaps his rare blend of cosmopolitan intellectual outlook and personal religious faith encouraged him to empathize with Sarajevo's Jews, and ultimately to protect the Sarajevo Haggadah.

Korkut was also interested in the affairs of lower-class citizens and minorities and, in response to Yugoslavia's increasing antisemitism in 1941, wrote an essay entitled "Anti-Semitism Is Foreign to the Muslims of Bosnia and Herzegovina." In this, he argued that antisemitism is "only the lightning rod used to draw the people's attention away from their real problems." He debunked what he saw as the main premise of antisemitism, that Jews are the "predatory financial manipulators of propaganda," by pointing out that most Bosnian Jews were indeed part of the lower class.

By the time war came to Bosnia, Korkut not only was interested in protecting Jews from persecution but he also held great respect for the contributions of the Jewish community. Back in the 1920s, he had published, in a local Jewish newspaper, a translation of an Ottoman-era document that recorded the lives and contributions of prominent Bosnian Jewish families. With that background, he saw that it was not the Jew who was the "stranger" to Bosnian society—it was the antisemite. As Nazi Germany and the collaborationist fascist Croatian state began to assault Bosnian society, Korkut constantly refused demands to join groups such as the Ustashe, despite the personal risks in not doing so. He was singular in his actions—being raised in a family of scholars, together with his knowledge and appreciation of different cultures, made him thoroughly accepting in his treatment of those his countrymen condemned.

As a linguist, translator, cultural emissary, and librarian, Korkut established himself as a preserver and transmitter of traditions long before the Nazis began their assault on the Jewish community of Sarajevo in April 1941. Their assault began with the pillaging of the city's eight synagogues and extended to literary works, artifacts, and other culturally significant Jewish items. One such important item, stolen and never recovered, was the Sarajevo *pinkas*, a complete record of Sarajevo's Jewish community, which was likely used as a source of information against the Jews when deportations began. Korkut rightly feared that the Bosnian National Museum's collections might be among the next places ransacked by the Nazis. To Korkut's irritation, in 1942 General Johann Fortner, commander of the 718th Infantry Division and a notorious antipartisan general, paid a visit to the Bosnian National Museum, where Korkut worked as chief librarian. It was apparent to Korkut that Fortner planned to confiscate any Jewish artifacts housed by the museum, and he was especially worried that the museum's prized possession, the Sarajevo Haggadah, would be among the works seized.

The Sarajevo Haggadah, written in 1350, was used during the Passover ritual to tell the story of the Jewish exodus from Egypt. It was (and is) one of the best-known and oldest surviving illuminated Hebrew manuscripts in the world. Rather than wait for Fortner to stumble upon it, Korkut took action, hiding it under his coat to protect it from the fate he had already seen befall Torah scrolls destroyed by Nazis on Sarajevo's streets. Korkut's efforts paid off. After Fortner failed to notice the secret Korkut was hiding in his waistband, Korkut slipped out of the museum and entrusted the Haggadah to an imam who lived in the country. The imam hid the Sarajevo Haggadah in his mosque's library, where it sat alongside sacred Muslim texts until the end of the war.

Later in 1942, Korkut came home with something new to hide—Mira Papos, a Jewish resident of Sarajevo who was in danger of being captured by the Nazis and deported to a concentration camp. Her family had been murdered by the Nazis in 1941, but she had escaped to the forest where she lived for a year among partisans. Moving back to Sarajevo, she had the good fortune to encounter a janitor who had once worked in her father's office. He, in turn, knew Korkut and took Papos to see him in hopes that he could help her. Without hesitation Korkut moved Papos in to live with his family, a measure that put Korkut, his wife, Servet, and their newborn child in danger. Yet the Korkuts decided to hide Papos "in plain sight" by dressing her in traditional Muslim clothes, changing her name to Amira, and passing her off as a new nanny for their baby. For the next five months she lived with the Korkuts; in August 1942 her aunt arranged for Papos to be smuggled out of Bosnia with a rail ticket and a forged passport.

After the war, Korkut was imprisoned by the communists, who falsely accused him of collaborating with the fascist militia. Following six years of imprisonment, he was saved from execution by Jewish friends who spoke on his behalf.

During the Holocaust, Korkut's scholarly, cosmopolitan background, coupled with what was a singularly acute sense of morality, inspired him to assert his humanity by preserving both the lives of Jews and their history. His wife would later recall his words upon bringing home Mira Papos: "This is a Jewish girl. We have to keep her safe here." For Dervis Korkut, there was no hesitation in trying to save her, despite not being Jewish himself. Paralleling the imam who hid the Sarajevo Haggadah among the Qur'an and other sacred Muslim texts, Dervis and Servet Korkut hid Papos among the members of their own family.

Korkut died in 1969, and his wife died in 2013. In 1994, largely due to the efforts of Mira Papos, Yad Vashem recognized both as Righteous among Nations in Jerusalem.

Kovner, Abba (1918–1987)

Abba Kovner, renowned in postwar Israel as a poet and cultural hero, was a leading partisan in Vilna (Vilnius) during the Holocaust.

Born on March 14, 1918, in Sevastopol, Crimea, his parents were Rachel (Rosa) Taubman and Israel Kovner. When he was a child the family moved to Vilna, where he was educated at the Hebrew high school and the school of arts. Like many young Polish Jews of his generation, he became a Zionist and joined the youth movement Hashomer Hatzair.

Living in Vilna during World War II, he found his life initially dominated by the Soviet occupation of eastern Poland, but on June 24, 1941, two days after Germany launched its surprise attack against the Soviet Union, everything changed. The Nazis occupied Vilna; Kovner, together with other members of Hashomer Hatzair, escaped and hid for a time in a Dominican convent outside the city. The convent, under the direction of Anna Borkowska (known as Mother Bertranda), gave shelter to Kovner and 16 other young Jews, for which in 1984 she was recognized by Yad Vashem as one of the Righteous among the Nations.

Kovner did not stay in hiding for long. Returning to the ghetto, it took him no time at all to see the dire circumstances facing the Jews, with oppression—and liquidation—beginning almost immediately. In July, less than a month after the Germans occupied Vilna, 6,000 Jewish men were rounded up by the SS and taken to the forest at Ponary, just outside the city, and shot. At the end of August, supposedly in retaliation for an attack against the Germans, a four-day killing spree took place in which another 8,000 men and women were shot at Ponary. After this, tens of thousands of Jews from surrounding areas were crowded into Vilna, and the ghetto became filled to the bursting point.

Kovner realized that a revolt would be necessary, if not to stop the killing, then at least to hinder the Germans. He started building a ghetto defense force, and in December 1941 a number of meetings were held in which a resistance movement was established. The defenders decided to remain in the ghetto and fight rather than try to escape. On New Year's Eve, before a gathering of 150 Jews at Straszuna 2 in a public soup kitchen, Kovner proclaimed:

> Jewish youth!
>
> Do not trust those who are trying to deceive you. Out of the 80,000 Jews in the "Jerusalem of Lithuania" only 20,000 are left. . . . Ponar is not a concentration camp. They have all been shot there. Hitler plans to destroy all the Jews of Europe, and the Jews of Lithuania have been chosen as the first in line.
>
> We will not be led like sheep to the slaughter!
>
> True, we are weak and defenseless, but the only reply to the murderer is revolt!
>
> Brothers! Better to fall as free fighters than to live by the mercy of the murderers.
>
> Arise! Arise with your last breath!

Three weeks later, on January 21, 1942, a meeting was held at the home of Josef Glazman. Representatives from the major youth groups met: Kovner, from Hashomer Hatzair; Glazman, from Betar; **Yitzhak Wittenberg** and Chyena Borowska, representing the communists; and Nissan Reznik of Hanoar Hazioni. Other groups came into the movement soon after.

Kovner's assertion that Hitler wanted to kill all the Jews of Europe was the first time such a conclusion had been reached by Jews in occupied Europe, and it sounded a tocsin for Jewish communities throughout Poland. That the groups had agreed to unite, given the fractious nature of Jewish communal politics before the war, was an indication of just how serious the matter was, and Kovner played an important role in the unification process. The groups formed themselves into the Fareynikte Partizaner Organizatsye (United Partisan Organization, or FPO), with multiple aims: to prepare for mass armed resistance; perform acts of sabotage; join the partisans where possible; and convey the message to other ghettos that they, too, should revolt. Wittenberg was appointed commander, with Glazman and Kovner his staff officers. The FPO was one of the first ghetto resistance organizations to be established.

As a poet—something for which he would later receive the prestigious Israel Prize—Kovner was inspirational at this time. His poems were published by Hashomer Hatzair in Vilna, and in 1943 one was smuggled out of Poland and made its way to Palestine, where it was published in the newspaper *Haaretz*.

In July 1943 Kovner became the leader of the FPO after Wittenberg was arrested at a meeting with the head of Vilna's Jewish Council (Judenrat), Jacob Gens. Six weeks later, the Nazis decided to liquidate the ghetto. The FPO issued a call for the Jews not to participate in the deportations, proclaiming that the time had come for the ghetto residents to "Defend yourselves with arms!" and not to go "like sheep for the slaughter!" Sadly, most did not pay attention and were sent to labor camps in Estonia, where they were eventually killed by the SS.

On September 1, 1943, the FPO rose in revolt but had little support, and in short order its members saw that they were fighting alone. Escaping to the forests through the sewers, some created a partisan group of their own, and others joined those already under Soviet command. Kovner, with Vitka Kempner and Rozka Korczak, commanded a partisan group called the Avengers (Nokmim) in the forests near Vilna. There they engaged in sabotage and guerrilla attacks against the Germans and their local collaborators, operating from September 1943 until the arrival of the Soviet army in July 1944.

On May 8, 1945, Kovner helped to found a secret postwar organization called Nakam (Avengers), which built on the earlier Nokmim partisan group. The 50 or so members of the group, including Rozka Korczak and Vitka Kempner, decided to dedicate their lives to avenging the 6 million Jews who were murdered by the Nazis. To do so,

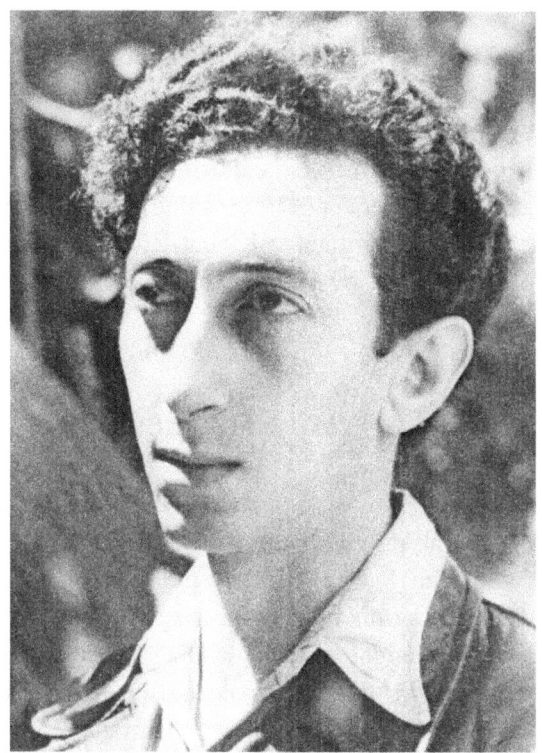

Abba Kovner, one of the founders of the resistance movement in the Vilna ghetto. Calling on the Jews of Vilna not to go to their deaths "like sheep to the slaughter," he was among the fighters who rose in revolt on September 1, 1943. He survived the revolt and escaped into the forest, where he founded a partisan unit that operated until the arrival of Soviet forces in July 1944. (United States Holocaust Memorial Museum, courtesy of Vitka Kempner Kovner)

they planned to undertake an extensive program of revenge against the people of Germany; one plan called for the extermination of 6 million Germans through poisoning the water supplies of Hamburg, Frankfurt, Munich, and Nuremberg. Another was to kill SS prisoners held in Allied POW camps, and in April 1946 Nakam operatives actually broke into a bakery where bread was being prepared for the Langwasser internment camp near Nuremberg. The bread was poisoned, and more than 2,200 of the German prisoners fell sick, but no deaths ensued.

With the end of the war, Kovner looked to a future that would be built on the ruins of the Holocaust. He was one of the prime movers behind the movement known as Bricha (Flight), an underground operation conducted between 1944 and 1949 to move Jews from Europe to Palestine/Israel. In July 1945 he traveled to Palestine via Italy, and in 1946 he married Vitka Kempner, his partner in the FPO.

They settled, with other former partisans, at Kibbutz Ein Hahoresh. Kovner joined the Haganah in December 1947, serving as an officer in the Givati Brigade of the Israel Defense Force during the War of Independence in 1948. At the end of the war he returned to his kibbutz and devoted most of his time to poetry, publishing two prose volumes and collections of poems. In 1961 he gave important testimony about his experiences in the Vilna ghetto at the trial of Adolf Eichmann.

Abba Kovner died at Kibbutz Ein Hahoresh on September 25, 1987, at the age of 69, survived by his wife Vitka Kempner.

Kowalski, Władysław (1895–1971)

Władysław Kowalski was a Polish military officer who, between 1940 and the end of the war, risked his life to save the lives of some 50 Jews.

Born in 1896 in Kiev, he studied in St. Petersburg, where in 1915 he earned a degree in agronomic engineering. With World War I raging, he enlisted in a Polish brigade fighting for Poland's independence; at the same time, his parents were murdered by the Bolsheviks. After World War I he joined the Polish army; he served until 1935, retiring with the rank of colonel. He then took a job in Warsaw with the Dutch electronics firm Philips.

On September 1, 1939, Poland was invaded by Nazi Germany, and Kowalski, called back to the colors, was given command of a brigade defending Warsaw. When continued resistance seemed hopeless and his commander ordered him to surrender, Kowalski refused. He continued fighting after the fall of the city until he was captured by the SS and taken to a prisoner-of-war camp for Polish officers. He was eventually paroled due to the fact that he was an agent for Philips, a foreign (and neutral) company.

The first Jew Kowalski rescued was 17-year-old Borel Bruno, who in the summer of 1940 stumbled upon Kowalski, a stranger. In desperation he said: "I am a Jew." Kowalski took him home, looked after him, and acquired a forged Polish passport for him. On seeing that he was safe, he arranged a more permanent place for Bruno to live and organized a job for him at the Philips plant.

Then, in August 1941, Kowalski was walking past a ruined building in Warsaw when he heard the sound of someone in distress. It was a Jewish lawyer named Phillip Rubin, who begged for Kowalski's help. Kowalski took Rubin, together with his brother and sister, home.

With a permit to enter the Warsaw Ghetto owing to his work with Philips, Kowalksi was able to move about freely, and he used this privilege to smuggle weapons and medicine to the underground. This was to prove important later, for in 1943, during the Warsaw Ghetto Uprising, the support he had provided (and continued to provide) gave the fighters some hope that they would be able to mount an effective resistance.

Moreover, Kowalski persevered with his rescues, helping a woman named Leah Bucholtz to leave the ghetto with her son and find refuge with a Polish woman on the Aryan side. This was not an isolated incident; he also brought seven other Jews out of the ghetto in similar circumstances. He continued to hide Jews in his own home and helped at least a dozen others financially. With the war coming to an end—and in view of the fact that he had been watched by the Gestapo for some time (and was even arrested on numerous occasions)—he decided to hide with 49 Jews in his homemade bunker while awaiting liberation by the Soviets in January 1945. So closely did he identify with the persecuted Jews that he even underwent circumcision, though he held back from converting to Judaism, knowing it was a capital crime for any rabbi caught performing the ceremony.

With the end of the war, Kowalski returned to the job for which he was qualified, working with the Polish Ministry of Agriculture. In 1947 he married Leah Bucholtz, the woman he had saved during his early days of rescue work. In 1957 they, together with Bucholtz's son, migrated to Israel. By this stage of his life, at the age of 61, the move proved difficult. He moved around the country doing a variety of jobs, and eventually his marriage fell apart. For a time, he worked part-time in the documentation department at Yad Vashem in Jerusalem.

His efforts during the Holocaust were hardly known for many years, but in 1961 he addressed a conference of immigrants in Tel Aviv with the words: "I did not do anything special for the Jews, and I do not consider myself a hero. I only did my duty as a human being toward people who were persecuted and tortured. I did not do this only because they are Jewish, but rather I helped every persecuted person without regard to race and origin."

In 1963 Yad Vashem recognized him as one of the Righteous among the Nations, but his story was far from over. On February 3, 1971, he died in Jerusalem at the age of 75, leaving instructions that he was to be buried "alongside Jews." The rabbinate, which governs life cycle events in Israel, refused to allow this, arguing that in Jewish religious law it was prohibited for a Christian to be buried in a Jewish cemetery.

With no certainty as to what would happen next, Kowalski's body lay in a Tel Aviv morgue for five days, and a cemetery could not be found that would agree to his final request. A solution was finally found when Yad Vashem and Chief Rabbi Yedidya Frenkel of Tel Aviv arranged for him to be buried at Kibbutz Yad Mordecai in southern Israel. It was fitting that this be his final resting place, as the kibbutz was named in honor of **Mordecai Anielewicz**, the commander of the Jewish Combat Organization during the Warsaw Ghetto Uprising. Kowalski was laid to rest on February 10, 1971. Engraved on his tombstone is the image of the Righteous among the Nations medal he received from Yad Vashem.

Kraan, Willem (1909–1942)

Wilhelmus (Willem) Johannes Kraan, a road worker with the Amsterdam city council, was a leader of an otherwise spontaneous strike in 1941 that shut down the port of Amsterdam just as the Nazis were commencing their deportation of the city's Jews.

Born in Amsterdam on August 2, 1909, Kraan was a member of the Communist party of the Netherlands (Communistische Partij Nederland, or CPN). Along with his friend Piet Nak, a worker in the sanitation department and also a CPN member, Kraan made the decision on Sunday, February 23, 1941, to initiate a strike in protest of the German treatment of the Dutch Jews.

In early 1941 the persecution of the Jews of Amsterdam had begun to intensify. Already there had been protests against the occupation, and on February 19, 1941, a group led by Ernst Cahn and Alfred Kohn, two German Jewish émigrés, raised their voice against the Nazis. Cahn and Kohn were business partners, proprietors of the popular "Koco" ice cream parlors in the city. Cahn was arrested for fomenting dissent, becoming the first resister executed by the Nazis in the Netherlands. The February strike that followed was a direct outcome of the Koco protest.

On Saturday, February 22, the Germans raided Amsterdam's Jewish Quarter, and more than 400 Jews were arrested. A second raid took place the next day. Kraan witnessed firsthand the Sunday arrests, returning home with tears in his eyes; many other citizens of Amsterdam had seen the same events and were outraged. In response, Kraan spoke to Nak, and together they decided that strike action was needed to paralyze the city so that the arrests and deportations would stop. They began approaching workers in the street and on the docks, asking them to strike in protest on behalf of the Jews. Extending the notion, they also sought the cooperation of the public transport workers, who would strangle the city and stop all movement.

On Monday evening Nak made a speech in front of between 300 and 500 workers at the Noordermarkt (North Market). Another CPN colleague, Dirk van Nimwegen, also made a speech, in which he emphasized that the Dutch people should not be seen to behave like the Germans. The speeches inspired those attending to agree to the strike action. The strike call was now disseminated through the CPN. Posters were made and distributed throughout the night, along with thousands of handbills. By Tuesday, all municipal and government services in Amsterdam and nearby were on strike, with tens of thousands not showing up for work. News of the strike spread through the city like wildfire.

With this, the only widespread strike against a Nazi antisemitic action had become reality. The strike only lasted two days, however, before it was called off on February 25, 1941. The Germans then introduced draconian reprisals: the mayor of Amsterdam was threatened with punishment and dismissal; 4 strikers were executed, 22 were imprisoned, and another 40 were taken as temporary hostages; and the city of Amsterdam was fined 15 million guilders.

The Germans then sought desperately to find and apprehend the organizers. One of those arrested was Piet Nak, who was beaten severely even though the Germans were unaware of the extent of his involvement. Upon his release he went underground for the next two months, but in November he was picked up again and interrogated under torture for four months on the nature and extent of the Dutch communist resistance. Eventually he was freed, but in May 1943 he was once more arrested on charges of helping Jews, and then released again in June.

On November 16, 1941, Willem Kraan was also arrested and imprisoned. His fate was to be different from that of his friend Nak. After a brutal period of imprisonment, Kraan, together with 32 others, was executed at the Soesterberg airport on November 19, 1942.

In 1966 a monument to the strike and the memory of Willem Kraan was unveiled in the newly renamed Willem Kraanstraat. The bronze statue was supposed to be of Kraan but was, instead, of an anonymous dockworker. Its appearance caused consternation among many of the survivors, particularly Piet Nak, who emphasized that the strike was organized by municipal workers, not dockworkers. The monument—entitled *De Dokwerker*—was cast in 1952 by Mari Andriessen and was based on a 1930s volunteer from the Spanish Civil War. Nonetheless the monument, located in Jonas Daniel Meier Square, is the focus of an annual commemoration to the February strike.

On May 31, 1966, Yad Vashem recognized Willem Kraan and Piet Nak as Righteous among the Nations for their efforts in resisting the Nazis and thus trying to save the lives of Jews in Amsterdam. Piet Nak died in Haarlem on December 16, 1996, a few days before his 90th birthday.

Kruk, Herman (1897–1944)

Herman Kruk was a Jewish diarist of the Vilna ghetto, who resisted Nazi persecution through his writing and his passion both for keeping alive Jewish culture and for recording Nazi measures against the Jews.

Born on May 19, 1897, in Płock, Poland, he became involved in politics through the Jewish Labor Bund early in his adult life. He moved to Warsaw after World War I, becoming director of the Yiddish Grosser Library at the Kultur-lige (Culture League) there. He began publishing articles in his monthly library journal and around town.

After the outbreak of war on September 1, 1939, Kruk, like most other intellectuals and local leaders, left the city and headed east. He made his way to Vilna, which had only recently been ceded to the Soviet Union.

During the war Kruk became very involved in the cultural life of the Vilna ghetto. He diligently continued his participation in and activism for the Bund, while building a ghetto library. He did all he could to rescue as many Jewish books as possible, determined to preserve the remnants of Yiddish culture for future generations. Running the library was also a public service, and after 100,000 books had been borrowed Kruk declared a public holiday to commemorate the occasion.

As head of the library, Kruk was ordered by the Nazi occupation authorities to plunder repositories from across Vilna in order to acquire cultural materials for the Reichsleiter Rosenberg Taskforce (Einsatzstab Reichsleiter Rosenberg), a continentwide Nazi project dedicated to appropriating cultural property in all the occupied areas. Named for Alfred Rosenberg, head of the Foreign Policy Office of the Nazi Party, it operated between 1940 and 1945 and was responsible for looting vast amounts of Europe's cultural heritage. Kruk's task in Vilna was to acquire books that would be added to Rosenberg's Center for the Study of Jewry without Jews (Judenforschung ohne Juden), located in Frankfurt. Here, Jewish scholars sorted and catalogued the books into what was intended to become the largest Jewish library in the world—recognition of a lost civilization.

Kruk took advantage of the freedom of movement his mission gave him to steal and smuggle Jewish secular and religious texts to safe places. His work thus became one of cultural resistance, as he and those around him tried to retain the most important Yiddish books, documents, and artifacts for a Jewish future.

In addition to his communal work as head of the ghetto library, Kruk began keeping a diary soon after his arrival in Vilna. He began with the German attack on Poland and an account of his flight from Warsaw, but he mostly chronicled the daily life of Vilna's inhabitants—first under the Soviets, and later after the Nazis invaded eastern Poland and forced the Jewish community into the ghetto. Kruk's decision to stay in Vilna after the Nazi invasion was conditioned largely by his determination to endure whatever might befall the community. At one point he wrote: "I'm staying . . . [and] if I'm going to be a victim of Fascism, I shall take pen in hand and write a chronicle of a city. . . . I shall record it all. My chronicle must see, must hear and must become the mirror and the conscience of the great catastrophe and of the hard times."

As a political activist, Kruk was concerned about the destruction of the intricate social and cultural life of European Jewry, and with this in mind the diary is from the first a chronicle of political life—but it is also much more than that. In the ghetto he saw the tragic destruction of Eastern European Jewish culture, prompting a passionate interest in rescuing the history of an entire people and their way of life. With such a self-declared mandate, he became a resolute and meticulous chronicler of day-to-day ghetto life under the Nazis.

He wrote continuously from June 23, 1941, to July 14, 1943. There followed a break in the chronology, but Kruk maintained the diary and continued chronicling his experiences after he was transferred to the Klooga concentration camp in Estonia. Surviving letters starting in September 1943 have been found, and a portion of his diary from Klooga (and another camp at Lagedi, where Kruk was transferred on August 22, 1944) remains from July 7 to September 17, 1944. On that final day he wrote: "I bury the manuscripts in Lagedi, in a barrack . . . right across from the guard's house. Six persons are present at the burial." This was to be Kruk's last entry.

The next day, September 18, 1944, Kruk and the other prisoners were forced to carry logs to a pile, spread them in a layer, and lie down on them; they were then shot. The bodies were burned in a massive pyre. One day later Soviet troops arrived. There was only one witness from the six who had watched Kruk bury his diary, and he returned later to retrieve it.

The diary—it was never in complete form, and pages were located in a number of different places in succeeding years—was redacted and published in Yiddish by the YIVO Institute in New York in 1961. An expanded and annotated English translation, *The Last Days of the Jerusalem of Lithuania: Chronicles from the Vilna Ghetto and the Camps, 1939–1944*, was edited and translated into English by Barbara and Benjamin Harshav in 2002. This huge volume of 614 pages was one of the first full-length diaries of life in the Nazi-created ghettos and is an important chronicle of daily existence under Nazi rule. Its very existence is also an intimate expression of cultural resistance to the Holocaust, and its value cannot be underestimated.

Krützfeld, Wilhelm (1880–1953)

Wilhelm Krützfeld was the chief of police precinct number 16, Hackescher Markt, in the center of Berlin, and in that capacity he was instrumental in stopping the attack on the New Synagogue (Neues Synagoge) during the *Kristallnacht* pogrom of November 9–10, 1938.

Born on September 12, 1880, in Horndorf, a small village in the district of Segeberg, Schleswig-Holstein, Krützfeld was a career officer who joined the police force in 1907 after a period in the army. After serving in the National Police Office, he became the senior officer at police station 65 in the Prenzlauer Berg, followed in April 1937 by assignment to station 16 at Hackescher Markt.

The infamous Nazi pogrom on the night of November 9–10, 1938, was called, euphemistically, the "Night of Broken Glass," or *Kristallnacht*. It was supposedly a spontaneous protest against Germany's Jews in retaliation for the assassination of the third secretary of the German embassy in Paris, Ernst vom Rath, by Herschel Grynzpan, a Polish-Jewish teenager. In reality, it was a carefully orchestrated assault on Jewish life in Germany, carried out by the SA, the SS, and civilians who were Nazi sympathizers. According to Nazi figures, more than 30,000 Jews were arrested, 815 shops and 29 department stores owned by Jews were destroyed, hundreds of synagogues and cemeteries were vandalized and burned, and 91 Jews were killed outright (with many others in the concentration camps later). These figures are all certainly underestimates.

The New Synagogue was situated on Oranienburger Strasse 29-30, Berlin-Mitte—right within Krützfeld's precinct. It was the largest synagogue in Germany, and arguably the most beautiful. It had been built between 1859 and 1866, the year of its consecration. Designed in the Moorish style and resembling the Alhambra in Spain, it was intended to serve the growing Jewish population of Berlin, in particular, immigrants from the East. It was built to seat 3,200 worshipers and was dedicated in the presence of Otto von Bismarck and many other Imperial and Prussian dignitaries. Ornate and imposing on the Berlin skyline, the New Synagogue had been granted legal protection by Kaiser Wilhelm I. It was this document of protection that was the key to Krützfeld's defense of the building on the night of November 9–10.

When the SA storm troopers arrived, they invaded the synagogue and desecrated whatever they could find. Furniture was destroyed, Torah scrolls were torn up, and anything that could be set on fire was ignited. Police station 16, located on the corner of Rosenthaler Strasse and the Spandau Bridge, was very close to the scene, and one of Krützfeld's officers, Lieutenant Otto Bellgardt, was quick to arrive. Stopping the assault before the fire got out of hand, Bellgardt pulled out his gun and, facing down the Nazis, ordered them to leave. Acting on the strength of local knowledge, he knew the building was a protected historical landmark and said as much to the assailants, affirming that he would uphold the law that underwrote its protection.

With this, he called in the fire department and permitted them access to extinguish the fire before it could spread, despite the ban on fighting fires that were burning on Jewish properties. From this time on, the building was under round-the-clock police protection. As Bellgardt's superior, Senior Lieutenant Wilhelm Krützfeld was directly responsible for his actions, but rather than rebuke his subordinate he supported his action and covered up the full extent of what he had done to save the synagogue. The next day Berlin's police president, Wolf-Heinrich Graf von Helldorf—who was not only a member of the SA and an ardent antisemite, but also the man who orchestrated the *Kristallnacht* events in Berlin—summoned Krützfeld to his office for an explanation. Krützfeld took full responsibility for his department's actions and did not betray Bellgardt. Von Helldorf reprimanded Krützfeld but, surprisingly, took no further action on the matter. Krützfeld was neither arrested nor dismissed; in 1940 he was transferred to another police station, and in 1943 he took early retirement.

Krützfeld and Bellgardt—and, so far as can be ascertained, other members of the precinct—already had a history of anti-Nazi activity before the November pogrom. Indeed, Bellgardt reputedly stamped forged identity cards, while both he and Krützfeld warned Jews in the neighborhood when orders came in regarding new antisemitic measures. It is also clear that they provided **Otto Weidt** with appropriate time to organize himself in advance of Gestapo raids on his brushmaking factory, also within the precinct's boundaries, where he employed and shielded a number of deaf and blind Jews.

The New Synagogue, for its part, remained intact—one of two synagogues, along with the Rykestrasse Synagogue in Berlin's Prenzlauer Berg district—not destroyed during the *Kristallnacht*. The damage was repaired by the congregation, and it remained a place of worship until the beginning of April 1940, when the Nazis prohibited any further services. The synagogue was formally declared closed to Jews on April 8, and the German army subsequently took the building over as a place for the storage of military uniforms.

Little is recorded regarding the life or fate of Otto Bellgardt, though it is believed he died at the end of the war in 1945. Wilhelm Krützfeld survived the war and died peacefully in Berlin on October 31, 1953.

Lajcher, Berek (1893–1943)

Berek Lajcher was one of the principal leaders of the prisoner revolt at Treblinka death camp on August 2, 1943. A Polish Jew born in Częstochowa in 1893, he fought for Poland while still a student and became an officer during the Polish-Soviet War (1919–1921). In 1924 he graduated as a physician from Warsaw University's Faculty of Medicine. By the time of the Nazi invasion of Poland in September 1939 he was a medical practitioner living in Wyszków.

On September 4, 1939, almost immediately after the invasion, all the Jews of Wyszków were expelled by the Nazis to Węgrów, in eastern Poland. Several months later, Lajcher, as a medical doctor, was approached by the Nazi-imposed Jewish Council (Judenrat) and asked to help in establishing a hospital. In February 1941 the Węgrów ghetto was sealed, and hunger began to emerge along with disease. This placed Lajcher in an important position in the community, and with very few means at his disposal did what he could to alleviate suffering.

On April 26–27, 1943, the Węgrów ghetto was liquidated, at which time Lajcher's wife and 13-year-old son were murdered. Those who survived the ghetto clearance, including Lajcher, were sent to Treblinka, where they arrived on May 1, 1943.

While Treblinka was not a concentration camp in the usually accepted sense of a place where prisoners were "concentrated" in large numbers for long periods, there were a few whom the Nazis allowed to survive the initial killing process in order to maintain the camp infrastructure. Lajcher, one of these, was put in charge of a small infirmary for the SS. An underground group, hopelessly underresourced and comprising only a few prisoners, had earlier formed under the leadership of a former Jewish captain of the Polish army, Dr. Julian Chorążycki. A medical doctor like Lajcher, Chorążycki was betrayed by a Ukrainian guard he had tried to bribe, and to avoid capture he swallowed poison on April 19, 1943. The leadership of the group then approached Lajcher to assume a command position.

After a period of preparation, though with full knowledge that any escape would be unlikely to rescue everybody, the group stole some weapons from the camp arsenal and launched an uprising on August 2, 1943. Most of the camp became involved. Buildings were set ablaze, and those prisoners with weapons attacked the main gate. While a number of Ukrainian guards were killed, most of the prisoners died through machine-gun fire and explosions. Of the approximately 200 Jews who managed to make their escape out of the compound, only 40 are known to have survived the war. Berek Lajcher, leading the revolt, was killed in the fighting.

During the camp's remaining two months, gassings continued to take place, though orders were received that it should be closed down at an early date. Further, with a number of former prisoners on the loose who were likely to spread news about the killing processes at Treblinka, it was decided in Berlin that the evacuation of the remaining prisoners—those who had not escaped or been killed during the rebellion—should take place to camps further west.

When the site was finally overrun by Soviet troops in July 1944, they found little there of the former camp. The gassing facility had been dismantled, the landscape was leveled, and a farm had been built on the site. A former member of the Ukrainian guard detachment named Oswald Strebel had been assigned the task of remaining to oversee the area after the camp closed. He applied for permission to bring his family, so as to complete the fiction that they had been long-term farmers on the site. Treblinka's last commandant, Kurt Franz, survived both the war and a subsequent period of imprisonment, and died in Düsseldorf in 1998.

The death camp at Treblinka was constructed as part of Operation Reinhard—the Nazi plan to carry out the murder of European Jewry in the area known as the Generalgouvernment. Overall, the operation marked the deadliest phase of the Holocaust. Treblinka, operating between July 1942 and October 1943, saw the mass murder of at least 850,000 men, women, and children, most of whom were Jews. It was the major destination for the Jews of the Warsaw Ghetto; indeed, the Treblinka resistance movement arose as a direct result of large numbers of Warsaw Jews being transported to Treblinka during the Warsaw Ghetto Uprising in the spring of 1943. In a grisly accounting, more Jews died at Treblinka than at any other Nazi extermination camp, with the exception of Auschwitz.

Landmesser, August (1910–1944)

August Landmesser worked during the 1930s at the Blohm & Voss shipbuilding and engineering works located in Hamburg. He is best remembered for an act that has become renowned as one of the starkest acts of resistance in Nazi Germany—on June 13, 1936, among thousands of others with their hands raised in the Hitler salute, he was pictured with his arms folded in direct protest of the Nazi regime.

Landmesser was born on May 24, 1910, the only son of August Franz Landmesser and Wilhelmine Magdalene, née Schmidtpott. In 1930 he joined the Nazi party, thinking it might improve his job prospects at a time when the Great Depression was destroying the German economy. There is no evidence that he was committed to Nazi ideology; in fact, in 1934 he did what no committed Nazi would ever do—he met and fell in love with Irma Eckler, a young Jewish woman.

Within a year they were engaged; immediately, he was expelled from the party, and their application to be married was rejected in accordance with the Nuremberg

August Landmesser, a shipyard worker in Hamburg who, on June 13, 1936, was pictured in the defiant action of standing with his arms crossed while all those around him had theirs outstretched in the Hitler salute. He is shown here in the photograph that captured the moment, circled. His act was reinforced by the fact that it took place in the presence of Adolf Hitler and Hitler's deputy, Rudolf Hess. (Heritage Images/Corbis)

Laws of 1935. One of these laws, the Law for the Protection of German Blood and Honor, prohibited Jews from marriage with other Germans. Sexual relations were also prohibited and referred to as *Rassenschande*, or "race shame"—in effect, "defiling the Aryan race." Once the laws began to be applied systematically across Germany, the crime became a capital offense. Nazi ideology held that "race mixing" would weaken the "purity" of the Aryan race, especially if children resulted from the union. It was hardly a surprise, therefore, that when the couple had a baby girl, Ingrid, on October 29, 1935, it alerted the Gestapo to their existence, after which they were watched closely.

It was perhaps with this in mind that Landmesser, who by now must have harbored no little dissatisfaction with the regime, took his famous action at the shipyard on June 13, 1936. The occasion was the launch of a new naval vessel, the training ship *Horst Wessel*, a ceremony filled with significance. In the presence of Adolf Hitler, his deputy, Rudolf Hess, gave a speech, and the mother of Horst Wessel christened the ship with a bottle of champagne. Wessel, of course, was an SA man who was killed in the early Nazi struggle for power, and he wrote the song that became the Nazi anthem played or sung on every official occasion after the Nazis assumed office.

Refusing to give the Nazi salute was Landmesser's ultimate protest against the Nazis. He was probably unaware that his action was photographed, or that he stood out to the extent that he did. Afterward, more than ever, he was watched by the authorities. For this single act of resistance he could well have been arrested; that he was not said much about his luck in snubbing the regime at this time.

In 1937 his wife was again pregnant, and the little family attempted to flee to Denmark. Their flight, however, was unsuccessful, and they were arrested near the border. Landmesser was charged with "dishonoring the race," and in July 1937 he was imprisoned in accordance with the Nuremberg Laws. In the trial that followed, both he and his wife argued that neither of them knew she was Jewish, as she had been baptized in a Protestant church after her mother remarried. Accordingly, on May 27, 1938, Landmesser was acquitted for lack of evidence. He was warned that he would be subjected to very harsh punishment if he were ever arrested again for the same offense.

Almost as if to dare the Gestapo to follow through on their threat, the couple continued their relationship in the open. On July 15, 1938, Landmesser was arrested again, and this time he was sentenced to hard labor for two and a half years in a concentration camp. It was to be the last time he saw his family.

The Gestapo also detained Irma Eckler on the basis of a law allowing for the arrest of Jewish wives of Aryan men who had "dishonored the race." She was held for a time at the local prison in Hamburg, Fuhlsbüttel, where she gave birth to a second daughter, Irene. From there she was sent to the concentration camp at Lichtenburg, and then transferred to Ravensbrück. She was compulsorily (and permanently) separated from her two daughters. It is known that she was still alive in January 1942, as letters from her exist up to then, but in February 1942 she was relocated to a Nazi "euthanasia center" at Bernburg, Saxony, where she was gassed to death. She was one of 1,400 women from Ravensbrück murdered in Bernburg by the spring of 1942. In 1949 she was pronounced legally dead.

Landmesser was probably unaware of this. He had been discharged from prison on January 19, 1941, and sent to work as a foreman for a transport company stationed in the seaside resort town of Warnemünde. In February 1944 he was drafted into a penal unit, the 999th Fort Infantry Battalion, which saw service in Greece and other parts of the Balkans. He was killed during fighting in Croatia on October 17, 1944; at the time he was declared missing in action, but in 1949 he, like his wife, was pronounced legally dead.

After their mother's arrest, Ingrid and Irene Eckler were taken to Hamburg's city orphanage. Ingrid was later permitted to live with her maternal grandmother, but the infant Irene was removed from the orphanage and nearly sent to a concentration camp when, at the last moment, she was picked up by someone known to the family and sent to temporary safety in Austria. Upon her return to Germany she was hidden in a hospital where her Jewish identity was suppressed, and she was able to escape detection until the end of the war. Both children lived with foster parents after 1945.

In 1951 the marriage of August Landmesser and Irma Eckler was recognized retroactively by the Hamburg Senate. In the fall of that year, Ingrid took her father's surname, Landmesser, though her sister Irene continued to use the surname Eckler.

The story of August Landmesser's defiant action in the Blohm & Voss shipyard in Hamburg achieved widespread coverage after March 22, 1991, when the German weekly newspaper *Die Zeit* published the photograph taken on June 13, 1936, and Landmesser was identified by one of his daughters. Then, in 1996, Irene Eckler published a book, *Die Vormundschaftsakte 1935–1958: Verfolgung einer Familie wegen "Rassenschande"* (*The Guardianship Documents, 1935–1958: Persecution of a Family for "Dishonoring the Race"*), in which she chronicles, with documents, how her family had been destroyed in the aftermath of her father's solitary act of resistance and how her parents' love for each other transcended racial ideology and a brutal totalitarian regime.

Langbein, Hermann (1912–1995)

Hermann Langbein was an Austrian stage actor imprisoned in a number of German concentration camps for being a communist and enemy of National Socialism. He was also a leading member of various resistance movements.

Langbein was born in Vienna on May 18, 1912. Upon leaving high school he became an actor at Vienna's Deutsches Volkstheater. In 1933 he joined the Communist party of Austria (Kommunistische Partei Österreichs, or KPÖ), and in 1937 he volunteered for the Spanish Civil War, fighting with the International Brigades as part of the Republican army.

After the fascist victory in Spain he fled with many others to southern France, where he was arrested and transferred to a number of different French internment camps. With the invasion and defeat of France by Germany in the spring of 1940, émigrés such as Langbein were in a particularly vulnerable position, and he, together with other Austrian prisoners, was handed over to the Germans in April 1941. Sent to Dachau, he arrived on May 1, 1941, and assigned to the camp *revier*, or sickbay, where he became clerk to the SS chief doctor, Dr. Eduard Wirths, after another communist prisoner of longer standing in the camp recommended Langbein to an SS man he knew.

In August 1942 he was transferred to the camp at Auschwitz to help combat an outbreak of typhus, where his administrative skills were considered useful. A month later he was joined by Wirths, who had been made chief SS doctor at Auschwitz. Langbein again became his personal secretary and saw immediately that he could exploit this position to his fellow prisoners' advantage. One of the initiatives he took, for example, was persuading Wirths to stop killing sick prisoners with phenol injections. On other occasions, he managed to convince Wirths to examine sick Jews and find treatment for them rather than sending them to the gas chambers. Medical treatment and the care of patients in the prisoner infirmary improved significantly.

Remarkably, Langbein also managed to convince the SS to permit Jewish doctors and orderlies to work at the Auschwitz *revier*, and soon such privileges extended to Birkenau and other subcamps of Auschwitz. This development broke through a racial barrier, as prior to this change only Poles and Germans could serve in a medical capacity.

Another way in which Langbein resisted Nazi measures took place on January 20, 1944, when a "selection" took place in the hospital. Some 1,800 Jews were marked for the gas chambers, but Langbein put the argument to Wirths that sick prisoners, to avoid execution, would feign that they were well—and when this happened, the likely spread of disease through the camp would be increased. He asked Wirths to request camp commandant Arthur Liebehenschel not to proceed with the action. The commandant agreed, on the condition that only those known to be terminally ill would be murdered.

By the end of 1942, with Auschwitz a camp for prisoners from all over Europe, a number of resistance cells had formed, for the most part along national and ethnic lines. There was a Jewish resistance organization, together with others from France, Belgium, Russia, Yugoslavia, Austria, and Germany—the latter two essentially made up of communists and socialists with a long history of imprisonment.

Under the leadership of **Witold Pilecki**, a Polish soldier who had been smuggled into the camp in 1940 with the aim of fomenting resistance, a Polish underground movement, the Związek Organizacji Wojskowej (Union of Military Organization, or ZOW) had formed long before Langbein's arrival. In 1942 the ZOW and other smaller groups formed a single organization associated with the Polish Home Army (Armia Krajowa, or AK). In 1943 Langbein and others formed Kampfgruppe Auschwitz (Auschwitz Combat Group), an international resistance organization with a broad-based membership that, in early 1944, joined with the AK to form an overall Auschwitz Military Council to coordinate resistance.

By this stage, Langbein was well known among both prisoners and guards. He had been in trouble a number of times. On two occasions he was jailed, and once he was even slated for execution but managed to avoid it. None of this deterred him, however, and he remained an important member of the camp resistance movement.

It was generally acknowledged among all the prisoners that they could not hope to destroy the entire edifice of Auschwitz, but the main objective of the resistance movement was not to do so. Rather, it sought ways to help prisoners survive, as well as to organize escapes and collect information that could be useful in bringing the Nazis to justice once the war was over. Only as a last resort—and only if the total annihilation of all the prisoners seemed imminent—was the resistance prepared to mount a general camp uprising.

On August 25, 1944, Langbein was transferred to a subcamp of Neuengamme. He was later sent to other camps, until he escaped from an evacuation transport in April 1945.

After the war he worked to punish Nazis who had committed crimes in Auschwitz, and he fought for compensation payments from the firms that had benefited from slave labor. At his initiative, an important trial of Nazi war criminals took place in Frankfurt, and afterward he published a major book documenting the trial. In 1954 he became general secretary of the International Auschwitz Committee, a group formed by Auschwitz survivors in 1952 to fight racism and antisemitism and serve as a support network.

Immediately after the war, Langbein wrote his first account of Auschwitz, initiating a career in writing and speaking about the Holocaust. Over time, he wrote several books about his experiences in the Nazi concentration camps and collaborated with others to enhance the message he wished to convey.

He also continued his Communist party work on both sides of the Iron Curtain during the Cold War. On April 4, 1967, in recognition of his many acts of resistance throughout World War II, Yad Vashem recognized Hermann Langbein as one of the Righteous among the Nations. He died in Vienna on October 24, 1995, at the age of 83.

Langlet, Valdemar (1872–1960)

Valdemar Langlet was a Swedish journalist and publisher who, with his wife Nina (1896–1988), lived in Budapest from 1932 onward. Together, they saved thousands of Jews through the provision of fabricated Swedish Red Cross "Letters of Protection" that gave Jews a modicum of safety until something more formal could be arranged.

Born in Lerbo, Sweden, on December 17, 1872, he qualified as an engineer before turning to journalism, serving as editor of numerous Swedish newspapers. His first wife, Signe Blomberg, died in 1921, and in 1925 he married Nina Borovko, a woman of Russian background. In 1931 Langlet taught Swedish at Budapest University. He also became an honorary cultural attaché at the Swedish embassy, while at the same time working with the Swedish Red Cross. His wife gave piano lessons. They both learned Hungarian and moved within the wide social circle of the Hungarian elite.

When the Germans invaded Hungary on March 19, 1944, Langlet was 71 years old. From the first day, he worked to help those in danger. He remained working at the university and the Swedish embassy, and at first helped his own acquaintances as they came knocking at his door. It was not long, however, before word spread that he would not turn anyone away, and soon he and his wife found themselves welcoming into their home anyone in need, regardless of language, nationality, religion, or citizenship.

As the occupation intensified, Langlet managed to have himself appointed chief operations officer in Budapest of the Swedish Red Cross. After May 1944, when Jews began to be deported, he issued Red Cross protection letters to thousands of Jews and arranged for them to go into hiding. These letters possessed no standing in international law, and they were printed on plain paper without embossing or watermarks. Langlet initially went to the Hungarian government—now overseen by the German occupiers—which agreed that 400 letters of protection could be issued and would be accepted. Instead, Langlet issued 4,000 and distributed them liberally. Given the way in which the document was produced, it was also easy to forge, an act that Langlet encouraged.

The ruse worked. Both the Hungarian police and the Germans accepted the letters, and even the Hungarian Nazis—the Arrow Cross—respected Langlet and his bogus documents. The fact was, however, that these letters were issued entirely on his own initiative, and without the permission of the Swedish Red Cross. As his position was honorary, it did not authorize him to do anything officially, but Langlet did not allow this technicality to stop him. He actually took things further, developing another scheme on top of the protective letters in which he created "protected houses." These sheltered Jews under the protection of the Swedish government, and although they had no basis in international law, the houses, like the letters, were respected by the Hungarian authorities.

Per Anger, second secretary at the Swedish legation in Budapest, gave his support to Langlet's efforts, even though the minister, Carl Ivan Danielsson, could not provide any official endorsement of his own.

Throughout this time, the Langlets continued searching for places to house Jews, whom they were now saving in the thousands. Any accommodation they could arrange gave people the opportunity to avoid deportation, and so apartments and homes were rented while orphanages were given over as safe houses under Swedish protection. They could not work alone—over time, Langlet developed a large volunteer network of helpers who did much of the day-to-day work required in such an operation.

Langlet was also supported by the organized Budapest Jewish community, whose leaders clearly valued the work he was doing. Through them he received the Auschwitz Report compiled by **Rudolf Vrba** and Alfréd Wetzler, two escaped prisoners from Auschwitz. He translated this report into Swedish; eventually, it made its way to King Gustav V, who in turn wrote to the Hungarian regent, Miklós Horthy, demanding that the deportations be stopped. Eventually, they were—not only because of this one act, though Langlet's effort certainly played its part.

Langlet was far from finished, however. He requested that the Swedish Foreign Ministry send an emissary to Budapest to help organize further humanitarian activities, and so, on July 9, 1944, **Raoul Wallenberg** arrived in the Hungarian capital.

Following Langlet's lead, Wallenberg began issuing Swedish embassy letters of protection, while at the same time Langlet convinced the extremist Hungarian government that his earlier initiatives had official sanction.

Eventually, the Swedish government closed down Red Cross operations in Hungary. Langlet then began to act independently, working through another organization, the Swedish-Hungarian Association. This carried nothing like the same authority as the Red Cross or the Swedish embassy, and there were times when he had to go underground in order to avoid arrest.

Overall, we see through the life of Valdemar Langlet that those who resisted the Nazis always faced dangers, and it often took ingenuity and daring—and no little amount of bravery—to be successful. There is little doubt that Langlet risked his life to shelter Jews and create both false papers and a network of volunteers to distribute them. He did not receive any pay or support for his actions, and he employed his own resources to save those he saw as his charge.

All this came at a price beyond money, however. His health suffered due to the demanding work in which he was engaged, and this, together with the advanced age at which he began his rescue work, led to Langlet's repatriation to Sweden on May 31, 1945. Upon his return, he learned that he had received the Hungarian Republic's Order of the Cross for his wartime work, and in 1946 he was awarded the Swedish Red Cross Medal.

In retirement, however, he was largely forgotten by a Swedish population who barely knew him in the first place. He and his wife spent their remaining years in poverty. Valdemar Langlet died on October 16, 1960, in Stockholm. Nina Langlet, who was 24 years his junior, died in 1988. In 1965, in the ultimate recognition of their work to rescue Jews in Budapest, both Valdemar and Nina Langlet were recognized as Righteous among the Nations by Yad Vashem.

Leitz, Ernst II (1871–1956)

Ernst Leitz II was the owner of the German Leica Camera Company, through which he and his daughter, Elsie Kuhn-Leitz, mounted a remarkable rescue effort known as the Leica Freedom Train, in which hundreds of Jews were smuggled out of Nazi Germany before the Holocaust.

Born in 1871, he was the second son of Ernst Leitz I, who founded an optics company in the Hessian town of Wetzlar in 1869 and turned it into a company of world renown. The family was Protestant, with a social conscience ahead of its time. Ernst I, for example, instituted an eight-hour workday long before it became mandatory in Germany, accompanied by pensions, sick leave, and health insurance. When Ernst I died in 1920 his son, Ernst II, became head of the E. Leitz optical company and remained in charge until his own death in 1956.

The Leitz family supported democratic causes in the interwar years and had no time for Nazism. Certainly, as it became clear that Nazi antisemitism was an integral part of the party's raison d'être, Leitz distanced himself as much as possible after the Nazis took power in January 1933. His political sense told him, however, that he should join the party, and as a result he became a member soon after Hitler took office.

Within days, Leitz began retraining a group of young Jewish apprentices from Wetzlar in preparation for transferring them to New York. There they would work in the Leica showroom on Fifth Avenue, or with distributors across the United States. In this way, he felt, he could rescue them from what he anticipated would be a horrible fate at the hands of the Nazis. In other instances, he learned that certain of his employees were related to Jews by marriage; to these he also held out the hand of affiliation with the company and worked to ensure that they, too, would be taken care of.

One of the Leica refugees was a camera mechanic, Kurt Rosenberg. Leitz not only paid for his journey to New York in 1938 but also helped him obtain a U.S. landing visa, aided by the fact that a job was waiting for him at the Leica showroom on Fifth Avenue. This was but a start.

Leitz established what became known over time as the Leica Freedom Train, a secret means of allowing his Jewish workers and colleagues to leave Germany in the guise of Leitz employees being assigned overseas. The Train would be at its most active during 1938 and early 1939, with groups of Jewish refugees disguised as Leica workers sailing to New York every few weeks. In addition, Leitz moved others to places elsewhere in Europe—for example, to France or Britain. He was even known to arrange for his Leica "employees" to be sent to Hong Kong as salespeople or camera technicians. Everyone in Leitz's care would be supplied with a Leica camera, as it could be exchanged for cash if needed. They were also paid a small allowance until they could find regular work.

Not everyone in this scheme was an employee, nor was everyone involved in the camera industry. Still, many were—whether as designers, repair technicians, salespeople, marketers, or writers for the photographic press. Leitz worked to ensure that everyone would be looked after, but this care extended beyond employees to retailers, family members, and even friends of family members. As a way to get them out of Germany Leitz "employed" them and then watched carefully as they were dispersed to various sales offices around the world.

With the invasion of Poland on September 1, 1939, Germany closed its borders, and the transports were stopped. By then, hundreds of German and Austrian Jews had escaped to havens outside. An accurate number is not known, but if both the workers and their families are counted then it would certainly have run to 300 in the United States alone, with hundreds more elsewhere.

In order to engage in his lifesaving work Leitz ran considerable risks—not only for himself but also for his family. He was openly defying the Nazis by trying to save Jewish lives, and taking matters into his own hands rather than waiting to be told what to do. From time to time, this defiance backfired. A senior executive, Alfred Turk, was jailed when caught trying to help Jews, and he was freed only after Leitz paid a large bribe. On another occasion, Leitz's daughter, Elsie Kuhn-Leitz, was imprisoned by the Gestapo after she was caught at the Swiss border helping Jewish women cross to safety. Interrogated, she was eventually freed—but not until after the Gestapo had given her the obligatory beating in custody.

How could such a public figure as Ernst Leitz II and the Leica Camera Company pull off this remarkable and sustained rescue operation? The answer is straightforward: the Nazis were dependent on the military optics produced at Leitz's factory. The importance of having the Leitz Company maintain production often outweighed the potential value of arresting and removing him from the workplace. Moreover, the Leitz name carried cachet overseas and was an important face in the international marketplace. Executives were convinced that this was enough in itself for the Nazis to leave the company alone, as it brought in hard currency from overseas at a time when it was desperately needed. They knew, too, that Leitz's single biggest market for optical goods was the United States.

Both before and after the war, the Leitz family did not seek any publicity to recognize or celebrate its heroic efforts under the Nazis. Ernst Leitz himself never spoke about what he had done, considering that he was only doing what any decent person in his position would have done. Those he had saved, however, knew and did not forget. On February 9, 2007, the Anti-Defamation League (ADL) recognized Leitz posthumously with its Courage to Care Award, presented in honor of those who rescued Jews during the Holocaust. His granddaughter Cornelia Kuhn-Leitz accepted the award at the League's National Executive Committee Meeting in Palm Beach, Florida.

As of this writing, an investigation is taking place at Yad Vashem in Jerusalem over whether or not Ernst Leitz II should be accorded Righteous among the Nations status.

Lichtenberg, Bernhard (1875–1943)

Bernhard Lichtenberg was a German Catholic priest who resisted Nazi antisemitic and racial doctrines by preaching against them from the pulpit, before his arrest and subsequent death during transport to Dachau concentration camp.

The second oldest of five siblings, he was born on December 3, 1875, at Ohlau (Oława), some 30 kilometers southeast of Breslau (Wrocław) in what was then the Prussian province of Lower Silesia. The merchant family from which he came was part of a Catholic minority in what was, at the time, a predominantly Protestant city.

Lichtenberg obtained his *Abiturium* (school-leaving exam) at the local high school and decided to become a priest. He studied theology in Breslau and

Father Bernhard Lichtenberg, Catholic provost of St. Hedwig's Cathedral, Berlin. An opponent of Nazism, he preached from the pulpit against Nazi antisemitism, and took charge of the Relief Office of the Berlin episcopate assisting Catholics of Jewish background. In October 1941 he was denounced by two students who heard him pray publicly for the Jews, and was arrested by the Gestapo. He died on his way to Dachau concentration camp in November 1943. (AP Photo/KNA-Archiv)

Innsbruck and was ordained in 1899. In 1900 he began his ministry in Berlin as pastor of the Heart of Jesus community, Charlottenburg, where he remained for more than a decade. The remainder of his career focused on Catholic activities in and around Berlin.

With an interest in Catholic politics, Lichtenberg served from 1913 until 1920 as a representative of the Center party in the District Assembly in Charlottenburg, and between 1920 and 1930 he was a member of the regional assembly of the Berlin district of Wedding. During World War I he served as a military chaplain, after which he became a member of the Peace Association of German Catholics (Friedensbund Deutscher Katholiken). In 1929 he was elected to the board of the Inter-Denominational Working Group for Peace (Arbeitsgemeinschaft der Konfessionen für den Frieden).

In 1931 he was appointed rector of St. Hedwig's Cathedral, Berlin, a position he took up in 1932. Even at this stage, before the National Socialist party had attained power, Lichtenberg had shown himself to be opposed to their ways of thinking. In 1931 he underwrote an invitation to Catholics to view the American antiwar film *All Quiet on the Western Front* (directed by Lewis Milestone, 1930), which led to a personal attack on him in the Nazi newspaper *Der Angriff*.

Then, on March 31, 1933, two months after the Nazi takeover, Lichtenberg arranged for the Jewish banker Oskar Wassermann to meet with Adolf Cardinal Bertram, archbishop of Breslau and president of the German Episcopal Conference, in a vain attempt to convince him to intervene in the antisemitic boycott of Jewish businesses planned by the government for the next day. Cardinal Bertram, however, held that the matter lay outside the Church's sphere of activity, and no action was taken. Still, with this action Lichtenberg marked himself as an opponent of Nazism who needed to be watched in the future.

In 1937 Lichtenberg was elected cathedral provost, a role which thrust him deeper into helping Berlin's Jewish community. In August 1938 he was put in charge of the Relief Office of the Berlin episcopate, assisting Catholics of Jewish descent who wished to emigrate from Nazi Germany. When the *Kristallnacht* pogrom of November 9–10, 1938, took place, Lichtenberg spoke out against Nazi brutality, and he prayed publicly for the Jews during services—one of only a few who did so.

After the outbreak of war in September 1939, Lichtenberg continued his protests in another area, this time writing to the air raid authorities to remonstrate against an order dated December 14, 1939, that decreed racial segregation in Berlin's air raid shelters.

While the Nazi authorities initially dismissed Lichtenberg as a nuisance, he was nonetheless warned that he should be careful lest he be arrested. He continued with his protests, however, condemning the Nazi euthanasia program and even organizing demonstrations outside concentration camps. He was finally denounced by two female students who had heard him pray publicly for Jews and concentration camp inmates, and he was arrested on October 23, 1941, by the Gestapo. In their search of his home and possessions they found incriminating evidence—a pulpit proclamation in favor of Jews to be read in the cathedral that Sunday, in direct defiance of a police order.

Lichtenberg refused to retract his words during his interrogation, even going so far as to condemn Hitler's *Mein Kampf* as antithetical to Christianity. In May 1942 he was duly sentenced to two years' imprisonment; when asked if he had anything to say upon sentencing, he asked that no harm should come to citizens who pray for the Jews.

Toward the end of his prison term he was given the opportunity to remain free provided that he refrain from preaching for the duration of the war. The offer was conveyed to him by Berlin's Bishop **Konrad Graf von Preysing** on behalf of the Gestapo. In response, Lichtenberg requested instead that he be allowed to accompany the deported Jews and Jewish Christians to the Łódź ghetto, where he would serve as a priest.

With little other alternative, the Nazi authorities ordered that he be sent to Dachau, where all anti-Nazi priests were imprisoned. On November 5, 1943, while in transit and awaiting his final transport to the camp, he collapsed and died.

Father Bernhard Lichtenberg was beatified as a Blessed Martyr by Pope John Paul II on June 23, 1996. The beatification ceremony took place in Berlin during a Mass celebrated at the city's Olympic Stadium. Lichtenberg's tomb is situated in the crypt of St. Hedwig's Cathedral in Berlin. On July 7, 2004, Jerusalem's Yad Vashem recognized Bernhard Lichtenberg as one of the Righteous among the Nations.

Father Lichtenberg was one who "lived" his faith and the teachings it espoused. He listened and responded to the voice of his conscience as he witnessed the growing power of Nazism and its anti-Jewish ideology. Driven by his faith, he was a courageous resister who lost his life in the cause of stopping an evil he identified as detrimental to all humanity.

Linnér, Sture (1917–2010)

Sture Linnér was a Swedish delegate to the International Committee of the Red Cross, stationed in Greece during World War II. The son of a merchant, he was born in 1917 in Solna, just outside of Stockholm, and studied at Uppsala University from which, in 1943, he earned a doctorate. Soon thereafter he became a professor of Greek language and literature. In Greece he met Clio Tambakopoulou, whom he married in 1944.

In 1943 he went to Athens as part of a Swedish Red Cross delegation sent to administer a vital relief operation. Since the Nazi invasion of Greece in 1941, the country was in the midst of a famine. This epidemic was so intense that an estimated 300,000 people may have died by the end of the Nazi occupation in 1944. The alleviation of this distress quickly became Linnér's primary concern.

In February 1942, however, long before his arrival in Greece, an Allied naval blockade of the country was lifted so that supplies could be landed under Red Cross supervision, with Sweden offering to take a lead in the plan to send 15,000 tons of Canadian wheat. By the end of 1942, a steady supply of foodstuffs was arriving.

Linnér saw the food aid as a means to save lives in another way—it could be used as a form of barter to save Greece's Jews, who were at that time in the process of being deported to Auschwitz and other places. Indeed, the Jews were being rounded up in Salonika on the very day he arrived.

In Salonika, the Germans established a ghetto into which they concentrated as many Jews as they could find. The ghetto served as a holding pen for those awaiting transportation to the Nazi death camps in Poland. Linnér, sensing an opportunity to help the Jews, sought a way to smuggle them out to some of the Greek islands, using the food supplies that had been entrusted to his care as a form of trade. Approaching a fisherman at the Salonika docks, he suggested that perhaps he could take some Jews onto his boat in exchange for food and other supplies. On this occasion, he received a rebuff—not because the man refused to save the Jews but because he would not hear of doing so for payment. Then, over the next few days, this fisherman smuggled out, by Linnér's estimation, about 200 Jews by cover of night to offshore islands.

Questioned about this incident later, Linnér said that he was prepared to use his role as a Red Cross delegate for purposes other than bringing food relief, but as it turned out, he did not have to do so on this occasion. He also noted that he knew he was breaking rules, but he was chiefly concerned "about the fate of those human beings." Further, he said, "when human lives are at stake and you are the only one, for various reasons, who might save those human lives, then I would act exactly the same way today. The primary concentration must be, in my mind, to save lives threatened by death."

While it was often impossible to intervene directly to save lives in any official capacity, Linnér was determined that what he witnessed should somehow be recorded for posterity, and he used his camera widely to show the extent of the suffering caused through Nazi measures. Thus, his formal neutrality as a Swede, and as a Red Cross delegate, remained intact throughout—though his measures on behalf of the Jews would certainly have aroused hostility back in Sweden as well as in Geneva.

Linnér's opposition to the Nazis occurred in other ways as well. During a short stay in Munich in 1942–1943, before he even arrived in Greece, Linnér met **Hans Scholl** and his sister **Sophie**, and undertook some activity with their resistance movement, the White Rose.

After the war and his return to Sweden, Linnér worked on various projects with the United Nations (UN), alongside the UN secretary-general (and fellow Swede) Dag Hammarskjöld. He was handpicked by Hammarskjöld to serve as head of the UN's civilian operations during the Congo crisis of 1960–1961, and he would have perished with Hammarskjöld in a plane crash on September 18, 1961, but for a last-minute change of itinerary.

As an expert on Greek history and culture, he wrote numerous academic studies and in the 1980s sought a way to reestablish and rescue the history of Egypt's ancient library in Alexandria, destroyed in 391 CE.

In 2004 the Greek government appointed Sture Linnér as its ambassador for Greek culture, and in 2006 he was awarded the Swedish Academy's highest award, the Grand Prize. On January 29, 2008, he was also awarded the Serafim Medal by King Carl Gustav XVI of Sweden for his lifetime of extraordinary national and international work. This medal is the equivalent of a knighthood in the Swedish honor system.

Sture Linnér died on March 21, 2010, in Stockholm.

Lopatyn, Dov (d. 1944)

Dov Lopatyn was a Zionist leader who headed the Nazi-appointed Jewish Council (Judenrat) in Łachwa, Poland (now Lakhva, Belarus) during the period 1941–1942. He was a medical doctor and a respected elder of the community with ties to Zionist youth movements in the ghetto, but little else is known about his past prior to his incarceration.

In the 1930s the town of Łachwa, then in eastern Poland, had a majority Jewish population. After the Nazis invaded the area during Operation Barbarossa on June 22, 1941, the Jews were confined to a ghetto, which was so overcrowded by April 1942 that each resident had only about one square meter of living space. Lopatyn, together with two rabbis, comprised the Judenrat. As early as August and September 1941, Łachwa was already receiving news of anti-Jewish massacres in the surrounding towns, and under such conditions it was not long before a resistance movement was formed.

Beginning in January 1942, the Jewish youth of Łachwa organized a number of underground groups, with the first unit of five youths coming together under the leadership of Isaac Rochczyn, head of the Revisionist Betar movement. In time, numerous other groups of five were formed in a resistance movement that also included the ghetto police. These groups established contact with outside partisan units in order to secure funding and weapons, though such units were largely antisemitic and gave little effective support to the movement.

Dov Lopatyn served as one of the leaders of resistance activities at Łachwa, and he played a crucial role in the uprising that took place there. In August 1942 the people of Łachwa heard from Jews on *aussenarbeit*—forced labor outside the ghetto—that nearby communities in Łuniniec and Mikaszewicze had been liquidated. On September 1, 1942, two underground leaders—and through them, the population of the Łachwa ghetto—learned that some nearby farmers had been ordered by the Nazis to dig large pits outside the town. They could see, moreover, that German Einsatzgruppen soldiers, together with hundreds of local militia troops in a supporting role, had surrounded the ghetto.

On September 2 Lopatyn was ordered by the Nazis to organize the 2,000 Jews of Łachwa for deportation. He refused. When the German-appointed administrator of the town, a *Volksdeustcher* named Koch, then informed him that although the ghetto was about to be liquidated he could save the Judenrat, the ghetto doctor, and thirty skilled workers, Lopatyn told him, "Either we all live, or we all die." Isaac Rochczyn and the youth underground saw little other option but to attack the ghetto wall at midnight. The Jews would then flee to the forest nearby, and in this way the entire population could be saved. Lopatyn vetoed this suggestion on the grounds that it would place the elderly and the children in a vulnerable position, and he refused to abandon them. To buy time, he asked that the attack be postponed until the morning. At first light, the ghetto inhabitants were ordered to gather for deportation.

At this point Lopatyn and Rochczyn made the decision to resist, and the underground fighters rose in revolt and began to fight the Nazis with axes, clubs, Molotov cocktails, and even their bare hands. Lopatyn set the Judenrat building on fire as a signal to the people that the revolt had begun. Rochczyn killed a Gestapo officer with an axe and jumped into the river in his attempt to escape, but he was shot and killed. Elsewhere, the fighters broke through the ghetto gate, allowing large numbers to rush through to the outside. Perhaps up to 100 Nazis were killed or wounded in the battle, but those remaining recovered their composure sufficiently to mount a counterattack, and many of the escaping Jews were shot down.

Łachwa lost the majority of its people during the revolt, with more than half the ghetto population killed. Another 300 were captured, many of them women and old men, and they were taken to nearby pits and shot by the early afternoon of September 3. In the first few days after the escape many were hunted down by the Germans and killed, or betrayed by local non-Jewish farmers and handed over to the Nazis.

Of the approximately 1,000 Jews who escaped the confines of the ghetto, some 600 made their way to the Pripet Marshes. Many of these tried to join partisan units, but at least 120 died or were captured before contact could be made. Eventually, only about another 120 of the survivors, including Dov Lopatyn, managed to assemble in the forest. Of these, 25, armed with two rifles, were accepted into the ranks of the Soviet partisans. Lopatyn joined a communist partisan group, the "Stalin" unit. He did not survive the war, as he was killed on February 21, 1944, when he stepped on a mine.

At the end of the war, only 90 of the escapees from the Łachwa ghetto were still alive. Dov Lopatyn left a legacy of his courage and leadership, however. His refusal to allow his community to die without resisting saw the Jews of Łachwa stand up to their oppressors, in what was one of the earliest ghetto uprisings of the war.

Lubetkin, Zivia (1914–1976)

Zivia Lubetkin was a leader of the Jewish underground in Poland and one of the founders of the Jewish Combat Organization (Żydowska Organizacja Bojowa, or ŻOB) in Warsaw.

She was born in Beten (Byteń), Poland, on November 9, 1914, to Ya'akov-Yizhak and Hayyah Lubetkin, née Zilberman. An affluent family, the Lubetkins had six daughters and a son. Both parents and four of Zivia's sisters perished in the Holocaust, while her brother Shelomo and sister Ahuvah, who had both managed to migrate to Palestine, survived.

Lubetkin studied at a Polish government school. From early childhood she was a member of the Zionist-Socialist youth movement Freiheit (Freedom), which gave her a solid grounding in Jewish communal life and a sense of duty. She also joined and worked with the Hechalutz youth movement in Warsaw as a coordinator. In 1938 Freiheit joined Hechalutz to form one movement, Dror, and Lubetkin became a member of its executive council. In 1939 she traveled to Geneva for the 21st Zionist Congress, returning to Poland just before the outbreak of war.

After Nazi Germany attacked Poland on September 1, 1939, the movement decided to send its leadership cohort east, away from the fighting. Then, when the Soviet Union invaded eastern Poland on September 17, Lubetkin went to Lvov to help organize Dror underground activities. During the winter of 1939 she and other members left the Soviet zone and returned to German-occupied territory to continue their resistance work. In January 1940 they reached Warsaw. As the ghetto was forming, Lubetkin's tasks included organizing the movement and facilitating communications with those outside the ghetto. During this period she also met and fell in love with another underground leader, **Yitzhak Zuckerman**.

By the fall of 1941 there could be little doubt that the Jews were being exterminated, though the precise means were still unknown. Lubetkin, realizing that the Jews had little hope if they sat by passively, decided to resist. On July 28, 1942, during the first mass deportation from Warsaw, she was among the founders of the ŻOB as well as a member of the ŻOB's political arm, the Jewish National Committee (Żydowski Komitet Narodowy, or ŻKN)

Lubetkin became the only woman on the ŻOB's high command, and her first name in Polish, "Cywia," became the code word for "Poland" among resistance groups on both sides of the ghetto wall during World War II. In January 1943 the Germans launched a new wave of deportations, and the ŻOB's resistance network decided to act. Fighting a limited action against the Nazis, the ŻOB turned the Germans onto the defensive, and the deportations were brought to a temporary halt. Lubetkin was among the fighters in this initial resistance operation.

In April 1943, when the final liquidation of the ghetto began, Lubetkin was instantly involved in the combat that followed. While the first few days of fighting seemed to offer some measure of success, it was inevitable that the Nazis' overwhelming firepower would tell in the long term. As the resistance began to falter, Lubetkin, while keeping her combat command role, also acted in a liaison capacity with the various groups of fighters and maintained contact between them. On May 8 the ŻOB command in the bunker at Miła 18 sent her to find a way out through the sewers leading to the Aryan side. She was successful, and on May 10 she navigated the sewer system with the last of the fighters. The remaining fighters in the bunker—**Mordecai Anielewicz**, Mira Fuchrer, **Rachel Zilberberg**, and nearly 50 others—were either killed or took their own lives to avoid capture.

Until the end of the war Lubetkin remained on the Aryan side, continuing to serve in the underground. She fought with the remaining ŻOB units during the Warsaw Uprising from August to October 1944, and then, together with the last of the fighters, she surfaced during November 1944. She was one of only 34 Jewish fighters from the Warsaw Ghetto to survive the war. After the liberation of the city by Soviet troops on January 17, 1945, she once more met up with her beloved Yizhak Zuckerman.

After the war Lubetkin was active in organizing Bricha (Flight), an organization helping Jewish survivors migrate to Palestine. She herself wished to go as quickly as possible, and on March 1, 1945—even before the war was over—she attempted to do so by going to Romania with another resistance fighter, the partisan **Abba Kovner**, and members of his group. Unable to proceed beyond Bucharest, however, she returned to Warsaw.

While there, she was hardly inactive. Together with Zuckerman and a survivor of the Białystok ghetto, Chaika Grossman, she created an infrastructure to enable survivors from the Soviet Union to migrate to Israel. She and Zuckerman finally left for Palestine in May 1946 and were married in 1947. That same year they met with other ghetto fighters and partisans to start the process that would lead, by April 19, 1949, to the establishment of Kibbutz Lohamei Hagetaot. A museum focusing on Jewish resistance, Ghetto Fighters' House, was created on its grounds. The Zuckermans built their home and raised their two children at the kibbutz, where Lubetkin preferred to live as an ordinary member without fanfare. In 1961, however, she was among the principal witnesses at the trial of Adolf Eichmann, and she provided important evidence relating to the destruction of Polish Jewry.

On July 11, 1978, at the age of 64, Zivia Lubetkin died; she was buried at the kibbutz the next day. The year of her death saw the birth of a granddaughter, Roni. In 2001 Roni Zuckerman became the first female fighter pilot in the Israeli Air Force.

Luckner, Gertrud (1900–1995)

Gertrud Luckner was born as Jane Hart on September 26, 1900, in Liverpool, England. Following the early death of her parents, and having no other family, she was sent to live with foster parents in Germany. They adopted her as a young adult, and she acquired German citizenship. She studied economics, with a specialization in social welfare, at the Universities of Königsberg, Birmingham, Frankfurt, and Freiburg, from where, in 1938, she earned her doctoral degree.

Raised as a Quaker, she converted to Catholicism in 1934. She developed an early and abiding interest in social welfare, and the year before her conversion was already working in Freiburg with the Catholic aid organization Caritas. She was also a member of the German Catholics' Peace Association.

Luckner was one of the first Catholic lay leaders to identify the true meaning behind Nazi antisemitic measures, and she saw that her position as an officer in an international organization provided her with the opportunity to save lives. As a result, she utilized her international links to find a way out of Germany for refugees. She organized assistance networks for Jews, helped many to escape, and worked with such anti-Nazi priests as **Bernhard Lichtenberg** and Alfred Delp.

After the outbreak of war in 1939 she continued her work for the Jews through Caritas, attempting to establish a national underground network. In 1941 the archbishop of Freiburg, Conrad Gröber, invited her to help those who were being persecuted, leading to her organizing a special "Office for Religious War Relief" (Kirchliche Kriegshilfsstelle) within Caritas, further supported by the president of Caritas, Benedikt Kreutz. The new office became the instrument through which Freiburg Catholics helped racially persecuted "non-Aryans" (both Jews and converted Christians of Jewish background). It also provided Luckner with increased financial and travel possibilities, which she used intensively for her underground activities.

She henceforth transmitted messages, requested and obtained forged passports, and helped refugees escape from Germany, ensuring that the relief effort would be successful. The covert funds she received from Archbishop Gröber were used to smuggle Jews over the Swiss border. From 1940 onward she sent packages to Jews deported from Stettin to Lublin, and she continued this scheme for Jews originating in Baden who had been deported to the French internment camp at Gurs—a remarkable situation in which the Jews of Baden (mainly women, children, and the elderly) were evacuated from Germany in October 1940 and incarcerated under French administration.

Luckner also exploited the Caritas network to establish contacts with people from other religious traditions. In addition, throughout this time and beyond, she remained in close contact with Rabbi **Leo Baeck**, the Berlin-based spiritual leader of German Jewry, until his arrest and deportation to Terezín (Theresienstadt) in early 1943.

In a totalistic police state such as Nazi Germany, secret activities such as Luckner was performing could not be maintained without attracting unwanted attention, and the Gestapo eventually learned of her various endeavors. She was kept under surveillance, and Gestapo headquarters in Düsseldorf assembled a detailed dossier about her activities. On March 24, 1943, she was arrested for "activity in favor of Jews and contacts with groups against the state" and transferred to the Gestapo detention center in Düsseldorf. She was interrogated and tortured by the Gestapo for a number of months but refused to disclose anything about her actions on behalf of the Jews. Eventually, she was released but watched closely, and on November 5, 1943, as she was about to transfer 5,000 marks to the last remaining Jews in Berlin, she was arrested by the Gestapo and sent to Ravensbrück, where she spent the rest of the war until the camp's liberation on May 3, 1945.

After the war she rededicated herself to building bridges of understanding within the Christian-Jewish relationship, a cause that had formed so much of her life through the dark years of the Third Reich. She returned to social work, assisting the victims of persecution in other contexts. In 1948 she established a journal, *Freiburger Rundbrief* (*Freiburg Circular*), which she used to promote Christian-Jewish dialogue, and then, at the invitation of Rabbi Leo Baeck, she visited Israel in 1951—one of the first Germans to do so. She remained active in Christian-Jewish discourse until her death, working also to enhance relations between Germany and Israel.

On February 15, 1966, in acknowledgment of her involvement in the German resistance and for rescuing Jews during the Holocaust, Yad Vashem recognized her as one of the Righteous among the Nations.

Luckner was honored frequently in Israel for her activity in favor of Jews, and she reciprocated by showing her unconditional solidarity with the state of Israel. When the Yom Kippur War broke out in 1973, she immediately flew to Israel. When the conflict was over, she initiated the establishment of a physiotherapeutic pavilion in the rehabilitation home for wounded soldiers on Mount Carmel.

She also took on another humanitarian problem: the fate of Christian women who had helped Jews to survive under Nazi rule and married Jewish men contrary to the Nuremberg Laws. Many of these women had converted to Judaism after the Holocaust and migrated to Israel with their husbands. When their husbands died, these women remained alone and lacking sufficient means. Luckner threw herself into finding a way to assist them, eventually establishing a residence where they could retire in safety.

On August 31, 1995, Gertrud Luckner died in her hometown of Freiburg. Her deep Christian sense not only sustained her personally during the period of the Third Reich but also gave her inspiration to live her faith, resisting an evil she viewed as antithetical to everything in which she believed.

Lustig, Walter (1891–1945)

Dr. Walter Lustig was the medical director and chief administrator of the Berlin Jewish Hospital during the period of the Third Reich. The hospital—remarkably—not only remained open and viable as a key medical facility right up until Berlin capitulated to Soviet forces in May 1945, but it also served as a tiny haven of Jewish presence right in the heart of the Holocaust.

Throughout the war years, Lustig was obliged by the Nazis to compile lists of patients and hospital personnel for deportation—to Terezín (Theresienstadt), at first, and then ultimately to Auschwitz. While doing so was reprehensible and a crass betrayal of those around him, Lustig was able to placate the Nazis (who saw him as a pliable tool bending to their will) and thereby keep the doors of the hospital open. This provided some measure of relative safety to those who had not yet been deported. By the time of the liberation, the Berlin Jewish Hospital had remained an island in which some 600 Jews survived, deep in the Nazi capital.

Born in 1891, the son of a Jewish merchant, Lustig converted from Judaism to Christianity while young. At the outset of World War I, before he had finished his medical studies at the University of Breslau, he volunteered for the German army in the medical corps, and served throughout the war. In 1920 he became a medical officer in Koblenz. In 1927 he moved to Berlin, and by early February of that year had joined the Berlin police as an administrator. He moved through a number of offices in the police department, essentially with responsibility for health care in schools and homes—a kind of police medical welfare officer.

This lasted only until the Nazi seizure of power in 1933. The Law for the Restoration of the Professional Civil Service, passed on April 7, 1933, was intended to restructure the civil service in such a way that tenured civil servants could be dismissed if they were not of "Aryan descent." As a World War I veteran Lustig was at first exempt from the ban, but by October 1933 he was dismissed. His exemption was rejected on the grounds that he did not see frontline service during the war but had, rather, stayed behind as a military doctor in Breslau. With little alternative but to work in Jewish enterprises, he was employed by 1936 in the Jewish community administration in Berlin. In July 1939 he became responsible for health care within the organized community's Department of Welfare.

Berlin's Jewish Hospital, which was already well over two centuries old by the time the Nazis came to power, saw a major change after the advent of the Nuremberg Laws on Race in 1935. From that point, the treatment of "Aryans" at the hospital was forbidden, and non-Jewish employees were forced to look elsewhere for work. It truly became a *Jewish* hospital, in more than just name. In the years that followed, the hospital was repeatedly threatened with closure. Looting of hospital stores was frequent, and medical supplies were increasingly difficult to obtain. In December 1941 the Nazis began pressuring hospital administrators to keep detailed lists of everyone inside the walls: medical staff, auxiliary staff, and patients. With this list, they would have a ready-made pool of possible Jewish deportees should the order ever come through to close down the hospital and move the Jews out.

On October 20, 1942, Walter Lustig became medical director of the Jewish Hospital, which, over time, became a de facto ghetto for Berlin's Jews. Lustig worked to keep the hospital viable and aimed to ensure the medical staff was seen to be useful.

The Nazis had a different set of agendas, however, with the hospital employed for a hodgepodge of purposes during the war, some having little to do with medical treatment. In order to weaken the bonds of marriage between Jewish husbands and non-Jewish wives, Jewish men were forcibly interned there. Some, thinking that the hospital could serve as a kind of Noah's Ark, bought their way in. Jews who fell ill or were injured in police stations, prisons, or concentration camps were brought to the hospital by the Nazis, only to be murdered once their health was restored.

Through it all, however, the Nazis demanded that numbers be kept at a constant low. The hospital, which came under the direct supervision of Adolf Eichmann's office, was watched very carefully. Indeed, Eichmann visited the hospital on many occasions and personally selected patients and staff to be deported.

These deportations were frequent, and actions to clear a certain number of Jews from the hospital were a constant reality. Realizing what the raids held in store for those being deported, the staff sometimes allowed elderly patients to die, while helping instead younger or more robust patients, who had a better chance of surviving the camps. Transports, which left Berlin on a weekly basis, always had some patients from the Jewish Hospital on board. Sometimes, in order to avoid deportation, staff performed unnecessary elective surgery; pregnant women and new mothers with babies, however, were never spared. Sometimes, in order to deceive the victims, Jewish doctors and nurses were sent along with the patients. No hospital staff ever returned, their fates the same as those of the patients in their care.

On February 27, 1943, the so-called *Fabrikaktion* (Factory Action)—the roundup of the last Jews still in Berlin—began. In order to ensure that the entire hospital was not closed down and the whole population removed, Lustig arranged for some 300 hospital employees (with their families) to be sent to concentration camps. This is possibly the clearest example of him intentionally sacrificing some in order to save a larger number of others. However, as 300 Jewish employees and their families might have totaled up to 900 or even a 1,000 people, it is not necessarily clear that his decision served a greater good, to say nothing of whether or not the sacrifice was ethically justified.

Lustig's decisions regarding who was to be deported and who was to be saved also pose a problem. Believing that careful selection would keep the hospital viable, he spread the impact among the various medical departments so that none would be completely emptied out. Yet personal favoritism and sexual politics governed at least some of Lustig's choices. Allegedly a notorious womanizer, it was said that he had mistresses among the nursing staff and, it is rumored, among some of the longer-term patients. Possibly he used the threat of deportation as a way of obtaining sexual favors; it has also been claimed that he allowed his mistresses to guide his choice of whom to deport. Lustig himself was exempt from deportation owing to his mixed marriage; his father, however, was deported to Terezín.

The *Fabrikaktion* was just the beginning. In June and November 1943 patients were again deported, and from early March 1944 the hospital's pathology building was used as a collection point for Jews—no longer patients—who were deported from there to Terezín, then Auschwitz. All the while, the Nazis expected Lustig to make up the deportation lists.

His authority was boosted from the end of 1942 onward, when he also belonged to the board of the Reichsvereinigung der Juden in Deutschland (Reich Association of Jews in Germany), the Nazi-appointed body responsible for internal Jewish self-government. When the Reichsvereinigung was closed down on June 10, 1943, and the leadership deported to Terezín, Lustig was the only senior member remaining. Further questions are thus posed: why was he, alone, spared? And over what did he preside? Sadly, this was to be only a rump organization, now answerable directly to the SS.

When the Red Army fought its way into Berlin in 1945 it found the Jewish Hospital intact, with some 370 patients, nearly 1,000 internees, 93 children, and 76 prisoners held in police custody. It seemed impossible to believe—and, at first, the only explanation seemed to be that Lustig, in collaborating with the Nazis, was a Nazi himself. Looked at more carefully, however, it soon became apparent that Lustig was far from being a Nazi. An ambitious, assimilated Jew in Berlin's professional class, baptized and married to an Aryan, Lustig nonetheless had his medical license revoked under the Nuremberg racial laws and had few options open to him other than working within the Jewish community as permitted by the regime.

Despite his situation, some of those around him vilified Lustig as an unscrupulous sociopath bent only on his own self-preservation. There is no doubt that by choosing some Jews for deportation he proved his (temporary) indispensability to the Nazis by doing their work for them. And herein lies a major dilemma when assessing Lustig's actions, as he found himself drawn more deeply into the Nazi scheme of manipulating Jews through deception.

Walter Lustig was appointed by the Gestapo to preside over the hospital in the last years of the war. His personal characteristics made him a suitable candidate for both hero and villain. He showed his courage in standing up to the SS on a number of occasions and was aware of the byzantine internal dynamics of the German bureaucracy, which gave him the opportunity to exploit the system. The hospital's status as an exclusively Jewish institution thereby held fast throughout the war almost until the very end, and it was not until the last days of the war that wounded non-Jewish patients were treated at the hospital.

For his part, Lustig remained director. The Soviet occupying forces were hardly convinced that he had acted honorably, and he was last seen leaving the hospital with two Soviet officers at the end of June 1945. Opinions differ as to his fate. The most common account is that he was murdered by the Soviets. Another possibility is that he might even have staged his own disappearance. The bottom line must be that the fate of Walter Lustig remains as much a mystery as do his actions during the war. On October 19, 1954, the District Court of Berlin-Wedding gave his official death date as December 31, 1945.

The story—and the enigma—of Walter Lustig still stirs heated debate today between the families of those deported to the camps at his order and those who were saved in the hospital through his negotiations. It is truly a "gray area" of upstanding (or connivance) with the Nazis, and determining how it should be assessed is likely to be one of the last areas for discussion and resolution coming out of the Holocaust.

Lutz, Carl (1895–1975)

Carl Lutz was the Swiss vice-consul in Budapest between 1942 and 1945. Through his actions, tens of thousands of Jews were saved from deportation and death at the hands of the Nazis following the German invasion of Hungary in March 1944.

He was born in Walzenhausen, Switzerland, on March 30, 1895, and migrated to the United States as an 18-year-old, working in a number of places before attending college at Central Wesleyan College, Missouri. In 1920 he joined the Swiss legation in Washington, D.C., and while there completed his education at George Washington University. In 1926 he worked at the Swiss consulate in Philadelphia before moving on to the consulate in St. Louis, where he worked until 1934. That year he was appointed as vice-consul in Jaffa, Palestine, serving there for the next eight years.

His next appointment was as Swiss vice-consul to Budapest, where he arrived in January 1942. As chief of the Department of Foreign Interests he represented some 14 countries then at war with Hungary. Additionally, given his experience of the past few years, it was not long before he began cooperating with the Jewish Agency for Palestine to help in facilitating Jewish immigration through issuing Swiss safe conduct documents, which enabled almost 10,000 Hungarian Jewish children to emigrate.

Germany invaded and occupied Hungary on March 19, 1944. Almost immediately, the Holocaust arrived in the form of SS-Obersturmbannführer Adolf Eichmann, who brought with him a team of experts to oversee the ghettoization and eventual deportation of Hungary's Jews. Lutz began to help the Jews by trying to persuade the Hungarian government to stop the deportations. He then negotiated a special deal involving both the Hungarian government and the Nazis, obtaining permission to issue protective letters to 8,000 Hungarian Jews for emigration to Palestine. By the time he had finished, almost 50,000 Jews had been put under Swiss protection as potential immigrants to Palestine, all having received letters of protection (*Schutzbriefe*) guaranteeing their safety from persecution until they left for Palestine. As a way of hiding this vastly overinflated number, Lutz repeated numbers 1 through 8,000 with each new batch of visas and grouped each batch of 1,000 names together into one Swiss collective passport.

In like manner to his Spanish contemporary, **Ángel Sanz Briz**, he also established safe houses around the capital—some 76, in fact, all bearing the Swiss consular seal declaring them as extensions of Swiss diplomatic territory. One of these was the property known as the "Glass House," where, at one time, around 3,000 Jews found refuge. As an engaged Christian, Lutz felt he had to find every means possible to protect the people he considered to be in his care. Within the houses, Lutz's wife, Gertrud, played an important role in providing food and finding medical treatment. Lutz possessed only paltry financial resources, but his attitude was that if assistance was needed, a way could always be found to provide it.

He worked closely with others in the diplomatic community, including such men as **Raoul Wallenberg** of Sweden, Carlos de Liz-Texeira Branquinho and Sampaio Garrido of Portugal, **Angelo Rotta** from the Vatican, Ángel Sanz Briz and **Giorgio Perlasca** from Spain, and **Friedrich Born**, the Swiss delegate of the International Committee of the Red Cross. Lutz, with his longer experience in refugee relief, instructed Wallenberg and the others on the best use of the protective letters, and he provided his colleagues with information as to whom they should approach in Hungarian official circles.

During the death marches of November 10–22, 1944, Carl and Gertrud Lutz followed the Jews. Whenever possible, they pulled prisoners out of the line by producing documents declaring the Jews to be under Swiss protection and demanded that the guards allow the prisoners to return to Budapest.

The Swiss minister in Budapest, Maximilian Jaeger, supported Lutz thoroughly until the government in Bern ordered him home as the Soviet army approached in late 1944. Help and support for Lutz then continued at the hands of Harald Feller, who took over after Jaeger's recall. As the Soviet siege of Budapest intensified during December 1944, when all diplomatic and consular missions except Sweden's had left the Hungarian capital, Lutz remained at his post. He risked his life to continue saving Jews, and for a period of nearly a month he and his wife remained in a bunker under the residence of the former British embassy with a group of Jews they had rescued. Finally, when the Soviets took over in January 1945, Carl and Gertrud Lutz returned to Switzerland.

After the liberation a Swiss inquiry into Lutz's wartime activities took place. He was criticized for exceeding his authority and endangering Swiss neutrality, despite the fact that he had saved the lives of tens of thousands of people. As a result, his career suffered and he was denied opportunities to advance. His reputation was only restored in 1958, when Switzerland reconsidered his role during World War II. At this, Lutz became something of a national hero in the eyes of the public, the more so when people realized that he was responsible for helping 62,000 Jews survive. He finally retired in 1961.

On March 24, 1964, Yad Vashem recognized Lutz as one of the Righteous among the Nations, making him the first Swiss national to be so named. Fourteen years later, on February 13, 1978, Gertrud Lutz was similarly recognized.

Carl Lutz died in Bern, Switzerland, on February 12, 1975, a few weeks short of his 80th birthday.

Maltzan, Maria von (1909–1997)

Maria von Maltzan was a German aristocrat who saved the lives of many Berlin Jews during the Holocaust while acting as a member of the German resistance.

Born into a family of eight on an estate in Silesia on March 25, 1909, she studied science upon leaving school and in 1933 earned a doctorate. Because she could not find a position in her chosen field of biology, she went instead to work for the Innsbruck-based Catholic weekly magazine *Weltguck* (*World Look*), as a result of which she became politically active. In 1943 she completed a degree in veterinary medicine.

As a Silesian countess, von Maltzan was a patriotic German keen to uphold the old order. With the outbreak of World War I, when she was just five years old, she joined her brothers and sisters in seeking the murder of their French governess. Her rebellious temperament was turned against the Nazis from the moment they seized power. Opposed to Nazism's radical nationalistic ideology, she joined different resistance movements from as early as 1933. Where Jews were concerned, she sought to assist those in need by responding to any calls for help that came her way, and she took Jews into her Berlin home from 1935 onward. That same year she married a cabaret artist, Walter Hillbring, but the marriage soon failed. Once in Berlin, she decided to stay rather than return to Silesia.

While von Maltzan was writing for the *Weltguck*, Father Friedrich Muckermann, a Jesuit priest opposed to the Nazis, worked alongside her in seeking to publicize overseas the true nature of the regime. Because the *Weltguck* was printed in Innsbruck, Austria, von Maltzan was able to smuggle out artwork and encrypted messages from Father Muckermann and others, and to promote the anti-Nazi cause through the paper.

Her opposition went further, however, as she was involved with various anti-Nazi aristocrats, artists, and communists. After 1939 the circle within which she moved distributed leaflets, obtained and passed on classified information, and freed political prisoners. On at least one occasion she rescued a Jewish woman by smuggling her across Lake Constance to Switzerland, and on another she was present at the arrest of the resistance leader Hanna Solf, whose release she then tried to obtain. Erik Myrgren, pastor of the Swedish Church in Berlin, referred to von Maltzan as the "Lioness of Berlin" and testified after the war that she hid Jews in freight trains being sent to Stockholm after first smuggling them out through Berlin's municipal sewer system. He recalled that von Maltzan was the complete resister, knowing judo, swimming, riding "like a man," and handling a gun if needed.

Throughout the war von Maltzan provided a safe haven for more than 60 Jews, for whom she arranged escapes in trucks that she often drove herself. She also falsified official visas and other documents.

In 1942 Maria saved the Jewish author Hans Hirschel, the former editor of *Das Dreieck*, an innovative German literary journal, by hiding him in her Berlin apartment. She had known Hirschel since before the war and soon took him as her lover. To protect him, she provided a special hiding place inside a couch in the living room of her apartment. She even became pregnant with his child, though the baby did not live because the hospital where its premature birth took place was bombed. After the war they were married, though the marriage did not survive peacetime. They separated after two years but then remarried in 1972.

The postwar years were not kind for von Maltzan. In many respects, her life was in ruins. As an aristocrat and part of the German elite she was prosecuted, had her license to practice veterinary medicine withdrawn, and endured a denazification hearing. The strains of war had told on her nerves, too, and she became a drug addict. Her registration as a veterinarian was periodically revoked, and at one point she was admitted to a psychiatric hospital, where she was forced to scrub floors in order to earn her keep.

Later, after Hans Hirschel died in 1974, Maria decided to rebuild her career as a veterinarian in Berlin. She settled in a lower-class neighborhood, where she catered to pet owners—often immigrants—who could not normally afford care for their animals.

In 1986 she published *Schlage die Trommel und Fürchte Dich Nicht* (*Beat the Drum and Fear Not*), her autobiography, from which she became known to the wider public. Soon after, her story was also the subject of a movie. Across the years, the Jews she saved remembered her, even though her efforts were largely unknown beyond a small circle. Due to her efforts, Yad Vashem recognized her in 1987 as one of the Righteous among the Nations.

On November 12, 1997, Maria von Maltzan, known to some as "the rebel Countess," died in Berlin, at the age of 88.

Mann, Franceska (1917–1943)

Franceska Mann was a Jewish dancer from Poland who expressed her resistance to the Nazis in a particularly dramatic way immediately prior to her murder at Auschwitz in October 1943.

Born on February 4, 1917, she was based in Warsaw, where she studied dance at the Irena Prusicka dance school, one of the city's three largest dance academies.

When the war broke out she was renowned as a beautiful performer at the Melody Palace nightclub and seen as one of the most promising dancers of her generation. It was not long before she moved into the Warsaw Ghetto, but she managed to leave again holding a foreign passport, probably obtained from the Hotel Polski on the Aryan side. In July 1943 the Germans arrested the 600 Jewish inhabitants of the hotel. Some were sent to Bergen-Belsen, while others were sent to Vittel in France to await transfer to South America. Franceska Mann was one of those on the Bergen-Belsen transport.

On October 23, 1943, a train with some 1,700 Polish Jews carrying foreign passports was transported out of Bergen-Belsen and sent to Auschwitz. They had been led to believe that they were going to a transfer camp called Bergau, near Dresden, from where they would continue on to Switzerland to be exchanged for German POWs; but this was a ruse to get them to cooperate. Told that they had to have showers and be "disinfected" prior to moving on to Switzerland, the prisoners were taken into a room next to the gas chamber and ordered to undress.

At this, in a famous and often-quoted episode of camp lore, Mann attacked two SS men, the roll call officer, SS Sergeant Major Josef Schillinger, and an SS sergeant named Emmerich. Having come from Warsaw, where stories of the mass killing of Jews had already been circulating for some time, it did not take long for those in the transport to realize what their fate would be. They soon became, in the words of **Filip Müller**, a *Sonderkommando* worker who was there, "restless," knowing, it would seem, "what was up." As the Jews began to disrobe, the two SS men were attracted by Mann's beauty. Schillinger ordered her to undress completely, and noticing that the men were staring at her, Mann launched into what appeared to be a seductive striptease act. The SS men, fascinated by her performance, paid little attention to anything else. On seeing that they had momentarily relaxed, she acted, it was recalled later, "with lightning speed"; as she was taking off one of her shoes she sprang at Emmerich and slammed the heel into his forehead; at the same time she grabbed his pistol and fired two shots, point-blank, into Schillinger's stomach. Then she fired a third shot that wounded Emmerich.

A panic broke out among everyone present; the SS retreated to safer ground, and the *Sonderkommando* managed, with difficulty, to lock the doors of the gas chamber before a riot took place. Reports vary as to what happened next. According to one, the shots served as a signal for the other women to attack the SS guards; to another, an SS man had his nose torn off, and another was scalped. Elsewhere, the only victims referred to were Schillinger and Emmerich.

Auschwitz commandant Rudolf Hoess rushed to the scene with reinforcements carrying machine guns and grenades. A report stated later that the women were removed from the scene one by one, taken outside, and shot. Another view, from Filip Müller, is that all the women not yet inside the gas chamber were mown down by machine guns; yet another states that they were pushed into the chamber and then gassed.

Given the various conflicting accounts, it is unclear what happened after the incident, but some things can be confirmed. Josef Schillinger died and Sergeant

Emmerich was wounded at the hands of Franceska Mann, who refused to be a passive victim; all the Jewish women were subsequently murdered, and the incident prompted a panicked response from the SS command. In view of this, it could be said that Mann's subsequent death was bought for the Nazis at a high price, emphasizing that not all Jewish victims were prepared to walk to their deaths without resistance.

Meed, Vladka (1921–2012)

Vladka Meed was a member of the Jewish underground in the Warsaw Ghetto from its inception.

Born Feigele Peltel in Warsaw on December 29, 1921, to Shlomo and Hanna Peltel, she was educated in Yiddish but picked up Polish readily and became fluent while still young. At the age of 14 she became active in Zukunft, a youth movement connected to the Jewish Labor Bund.

Meed and her family were forced into the Warsaw Ghetto once it was established in 1940. Over time, her father died of pneumonia and her mother, sister, and younger brother Chaim were sent to their deaths at Treblinka. With few other alternatives, Meed decided to become part of the resistance movement in the ghetto, and she joined the Żydowska Organizacja Bojowa (Jewish Combat Organization, or ŻOB) soon after it formed in 1942. She was inspired to join after hearing a Bund leader, Abrasha Blum, speak about the need for armed resistance. Blum was a member of the Jewish coordinating committee, a body that sought to unite the diverse political factions of the ghetto. At this time she assumed the resistance code name of Vladka, which she kept for the rest of her life.

Owing to her flowing red locks and typically "Aryan" appearance, and her fluent Polish, Meed passed as a non-Jew outside the ghetto. Her major assignments involved working as a courier, mainly of money, arms, and intelligence information. One of her most important missions was to smuggle a map of Treblinka out of the ghetto and into the hands of resisters outside, who would, it was hoped, forward it on to the Allies. This information was also vitally important in the ghetto itself, as news spread more widely about where the deportations ended up. The upshot was a determination on the part of the ŻOB to resist further deportations by force, leading in April 1943 to the Warsaw Ghetto Uprising.

Meed also helped children escape the ghetto and arranged for them to be sheltered in Christian homes. In addition, she acted as an information conduit for Jews who were searching for news about their relatives in labor and concentration camps or fighting with the partisans in the forest, and she assisted other Jews hiding on the Aryan side; having survived the uprising, she continued supplying money and papers to help them stay alive.

During her time in the Warsaw underground she met another courier living under false papers, Czesław (Benjamin) Miedzyrzecka (Meed). Accounts differ as to when they were married—dates are given variously as 1943, 1944, and 1945. Known with certainty is that they were among the first survivors to reach the United States after the end of World War II, arriving in New York on May 24, 1946.

Soon after her arrival, Meed was approached by American Jewish organizations with a request to provide lectures to the American public about her experiences; these would form the basis of a book published in Yiddish in 1948. An early firsthand account on the subject of what later became known as the Holocaust, her book was published in English as *On Both Sides of the Wall* in 1972, with translations into other languages (including German and Polish) coming later. The work was highly condemnatory of Warsaw's non-Jewish population, who, Meed asserted, did little to help the Jews in the ghetto.

In 1962 Meed and her husband, with a group of several other survivors, established the Warsaw Ghetto Resistance Organization for the purpose of raising awareness among the next generation about what they had experienced. Meed traveled and spoke widely about the Warsaw Ghetto Uprising and the Holocaust generally. Immediately after the World Gathering of Jewish Holocaust Survivors in Israel in June 1981, an American Gathering of Jewish Holocaust Survivors was established to prepare for a second gathering, to be held in Washington, D.C., in April 1983. On this occasion Benjamin Meed was in the forefront of the organizing process, though his wife also played a key role.

In recognition for her work in Holocaust education, Meed received an award in 1973 from the Warsaw Ghetto Resistance Organization, and the Morim Award from the Jewish Teachers' Association in 1989. These honors were followed by the 1993 Hadassah Henrietta Szold Award, and the 1995 Elie Wiesel Remembrance Award. She also received honorary degrees from Hebrew Union College and Bar Ilan University.

Benjamin Meed died of pneumonia in Manhattan on October 24, 2006; Vladka Meed died a little over six years later, from Alzheimer's disease, at her daughter's home in Paradise Valley, Arizona, on November 21, 2012.

Moltke, Helmuth James Graf von (1907–1945)

Helmuth James Graf von Moltke was an aristocratic resister to the Nazi regime, executed for treason in January 1945.

He was born on March 11, 1907, on the family estate at Kreisau, Silesia. His mother, Dorothy, was a British subject from South Africa. He was the great-grandnephew of Helmuth von Moltke the Elder, one of Prussia's outstanding military commanders during Germany's wars of unification, and grandnephew of Helmuth

Johann Ludwig von Moltke the Younger, who served as chief of the German general staff between 1906 and 1914.

Von Moltke's parents were Christian Scientists, though their son became an Evangelical Christian when he was 14. He studied law and political science between 1925 and 1929, moving between universities in Breslau, Vienna, Heidelberg, and Berlin. In 1928 he became involved with an organization called the Löwenberger Arbeitsgemeinschaften, or Löwenberg working groups, in which college teachers, youth movement leaders, young unemployed workers, students, and young farmers were brought together in a voluntary work camp in Silesia, where all could learn from each other and discuss matters of mutual social and political interest.

In 1931 he married Freya Deichmann, who had begun her own studies in law at the University of Bonn. She also attended seminars at the University of Breslau, where she worked for a time as his research assistant. On October 18, 1931, they were married in Cologne, and they moved into the family estate at Kreisau before relocating to Berlin, where he finished his law degree; at the same time, Deichmann also studied law, receiving her degree from Humboldt University in 1935.

The same year he was given the chance to become a judge but declined on the grounds that he would have to become a member of the Nazi party. His personal beliefs regarding democracy held him back; there had been times in earlier years when he had expressed open criticism of Hitler, and he was known to oppose the regime in office. Rather than join a system of which he disapproved, he opened up his own legal practice in Berlin. Between 1935 and 1938 he undertook additional legal training in the United Kingdom in hopes of joining the British Bar. This plan was stymied with the outbreak of war in September 1939.

During the war he was drafted into German military intelligence (the Abwehr) within the armed forces high command in Berlin. It was there that he first began to demonstrate his opposition to the Nazi regime, advocating humane treatment for prisoners of war and the observance of international law, and acting to undermine human rights abuses in German-occupied territories.

In early 1940 Helmuth and Freya von Moltke and another aristocrat he had known since 1938, Peter Graf Yorck von Wartenburg, began to gather around them an informal group of around two dozen opponents of Nazism, many of them also aristocrats, to imagine a new and better Germany. What emerged from this was the Kreisau Circle, centered on von Moltke's estate at Kreisau, though meetings also took place in Berlin. The group became one of the main foci of German opposition to the Nazi regime; small though it was, it comprised many elite members of society. Through his contacts, von Moltke reached out to Protestant and Catholic Church leaders, as well as to what was left of the social democratic movement.

In a voluminous correspondence with his wife and others, he asked many questions about where Germany was heading and what degree of responsibility each person would bear after the war. In one of his letters from October 1941, referring to the slaughter of the Jews in Russia, he wrote: "Certainly more than a thousand people are murdered in this way every day, and another thousand German men are habituated to murder.... What shall I say when I am asked: And what did you do during that time?" In October 1941 Jews in Berlin began to be deported. In the same letter, von Moltke wrote: "Since Saturday the Berlin Jews are being rounded up. Then they are sent off with what they can carry.... How can anyone know these things and walk around free?"

He hoped that he could use the law and his social contacts to bring some sort of humanitarian dimension to military events, and he knew that he was not alone; others, such as Admiral Wilhelm Canaris and General Hans Oster, both his superiors in the Abwehr, felt the same way. Throughout the war, he pleaded for the Geneva Conventions to be respected, and after Operation Barbarossa in the summer of 1941 he wrote a controversial legal opinion urging Germany to adhere to international law. He also ordered the removal of Jews to countries offering a safe haven, possibly not realizing that few states were prepared to accept them. In addition, he attempted to reduce the scale of mass murder by writing reports drawing attention to the psychological problems faced by German soldiers who witnessed and/or participated in the wholesale shootings accompanying Einsatzgruppen operations.

From his own perspective, knowing about these things only served to reinforce his own opposition to the war and the Nazi party. Pursuant to this, one of his actions was to disseminate confidential information on Nazi war crimes to those outside the Nazi party, in the hope that it would be passed on to the Allies.

Of course, rejection of orders placed him at risk, and on January 19, 1944, he was arrested by the Gestapo, which discovered that he had warned members of another resistance group, the Solf Circle, that they were about to be rounded up and prosecuted. (The Solf Circle was an informal resistance gathering of German intellectuals who were arrested and executed in September 1943.) Only later was it discovered that von Moltke was also involved in the failed coup attempt of July 20, 1944, against Hitler—something about which he had very mixed feelings, fearing that Hitler would become a martyr if he was assassinated.

Facing Judge Roland Freisler before the People's Court (*Volksgerichtshof*), von Moltke found himself in a delicate position, fighting for his life. No evidence, however, could be found that he had actually participated in any conspiracy to bring about a coup. Freisler therefore was forced to concoct a new capital charge; looking over the record of the Kreisau Circle, he determined that discussions of a future Germany based on moral and democratic principles met the criteria for the death penalty. As von Moltke noted in a letter to his wife, this judgment signified that he was going to his death for his ideas and not for anything he had done—a damning indictment against the regime he was opposing.

In what was an inevitable judgment, von Moltke was sentenced to death on January 11, 1945, and executed on January 23 in Berlin's Plötzensee prison.

Von Moltke was not a pacifist, but he believed strongly in international law and the laws of war as essential tools to protect the innocent and reduce the brutalities that conflict generates. In one of his final letters, written to his sons while awaiting execution, he gave his reasons for acting the way he did, declaring that ever since National Socialism came to power he had attempted to make its consequences "milder for its victims and to prepare the way for a change. In that, my conscience drove me—and in the end, that is a man's duty."

Moszkiewiez, Hélène (b. 1920)

Hélène Moszkiewiez was a Belgian Jewish resister during the Holocaust who infiltrated Gestapo headquarters in Brussels and managed to organize the escape of Jewish prisoners and Allied POWs.

Born in 1920, the daughter of a tailor, she resisted manifestations of antisemitism from an early age. With the arrival of the Nazis, one of her first acts of defiance occurred when her family was forced to carry their heavy radio to the city center and hand it over to the occupying authorities. While delivering the radio, Moszkiewiez purposely dropped it. She then told the Germans that they could fix the radio with their highly trained technicians. This act of defiance would be the first of many.

In 1937, at the age of 16, Moszkiewiez had met François, a Belgian officer who had an on-and-off relationship with her until he disappeared in 1939. Then, in 1940, Moszkiewiez and her mother saw a German soldier named Franz at a café; he revealed himself as the François whom she had dated previously. He met up with her again and introduced her to his friend Jean, who thought Moszkiewiez would be a great candidate to join their resistance group based on her linguistic skills, good looks, and motivation to defy the Nazis.

Before beginning her underground missions, however, Moszkiewiez obtained a false identity from Jean and Franz allowing her to sell newspapers in the German barracks. She got to know certain German soldiers, setting the stage for her first major mission. She began "dating" a Nazi officer named Alfred, who always carried with him a briefcase containing important documents. One night she was invited for dinner at Alfred's home. After multiple glasses of wine, he passed out, creating the perfect opportunity for her to get the briefcase. Inside she found documents, including classified maps, and immediately brought them to the underground leaders.

After numerous missions and another false identity, she was set up to meet the head of the Gestapo secretariat in a café. Infiltrating the Gestapo would be her most significant and daring mission yet. She persuaded him to get Franz a job at the Gestapo office, after which Franz, in turn, hired Moszkiewiez as his assistant, and they begin to receive information on Gestapo activities. Eventually, a promising young Nazi officer was set to become the next leader of the Gestapo office, and Franz and Moszkiewiez, seeing him as a threat to their operation, decided there was no alternative but to kill him. After a great deal of planning, Moszkiewiez was chosen to carry out the deadly mission. She struggled with having to commit the awful act but eventually found justification after learning about the murder of her parents. She carried out the brutal stabbing successfully and fled with Franz until she could return to her secret work at the Gestapo offices.

Over time, however, she realized that Franz was actually a double agent, prepared to sacrifice her life to protect his identity. The danger in which this placed her was mitigated only by the fact that her quick wit and luck enabled her to not only survive but also to rescue prisoners, warn intended victims of impending raids, and work closely with the resistance.

None of this came without cost. From her position at Gestapo headquarters, for example, Moszkiewiez learned that her parents had been deported on the last train to leave Belgium for the concentration camps; she also learned the fate of her husband of one week, who was another victim of the Holocaust.

As the Allied advance neared the Belgian border, the German civil administrator Josef Grohé ordered a general evacuation of German occupation forces on August 28, 1944. On September 4, 1944, the Allies liberated Brussels. After a wide variety of missions and rescues, Moszkiewiez, standing in her now abandoned office in Gestapo headquarters, found a list of all the informants who had betrayed Belgian Jews during the war. Selecting 25 of the worst offenders from that list, and accompanied by other members of the underground, she then paid each of them a visit and dispensed appropriate justice.

With the war drawing to a close, Moszkiewiez's secret life slowed and eventually ceased. A few years later she married and began to put her life back in order, and eventually she moved to Canada. There, she wrote a memoir, *Inside the Gestapo: A Jewish Woman's Secret War* (1985), outlining the multitude of activities in which she had been involved to thwart the Nazis. In 1991 the book was used as the basis for a movie, *A Woman at War* (directed by Edward Bennett), starring Martha Plimpton.

Moszkiewiez's wartime acts were courageous and heroic, though she also often had doubts—such as when she feared her resistance activities might cause the capture of a young Jewish girl through a poorly timed operation intended to help her. Even with these personal fears, she found the courage to resist and ultimately help save numerous lives. She provided a powerful example of individual defiance during the Nazi occupation of Belgium.

Moszkowicz, Daniel (1905–1943)

Daniel Moszkowicz was a Jewish resister who, with **Mordechaj Tenenbaum**, was one of the principal leaders of the Białystok ghetto uprising of August 16, 1943.

A member of Poland's Communist party, he was born in 1905 and was a merchant before the war, when he began serving as a noncommissioned reserve officer in the Polish army. With the outbreak of war in September 1939 and the rapid defeat of Poland, however, his hometown of Białystok was taken over by the Soviet Union. After the commencement of Operation Barbarossa, Białystok was occupied by the German army on June 27, 1941.

A ghetto, governed by a Nazi-imposed Jewish Council (Judenrat) led by Efraim Barasz, was established between July 26 and early August 1941. Just as elsewhere, overcrowding was the order of the day, with 56,000 Jewish residents crammed into a small space. The Judenrat cooperated with the Nazis in helping to run textile and arms factories, making the ghetto a cheap and viable concern that served the economic interests of the Reich. Moreover, the Białystok Judenrat, unlike those in many other ghettos, was trusted by the inhabitants. Barasz had been a respected Zionist and community leader before the war and was well known. His likable personality gave his interactions with the Nazis some measure of acceptability.

Daniel Moszkowicz found himself trapped in the ghetto after the Nazis arrived; he then worked in various occupations to try to keep body and soul together.

Between February 5 and February 12, 1943, Nazi Einsatzgruppen (mobile killing squads) rounded up and deported some 10,000 Jews from Białystok, who were sent to the extermination camp at Treblinka and annihilated. During the same action, 2,000 others were murdered in Białystok itself, while around 7,600 were relocated to other parts of the ghetto. Those fit to work among the relocated were sent to Majdanek. The ghetto was then raided again, until the population was so reduced that it seemed all hope was lost for those remaining.

In January and February 1943 a resistance movement, the Antyfaszystowska Organizacja Bojowa (Anti-Fascist Military Organization, or AOB), was created in Białystok. Daniel Moszkowicz immediately became a member, though so long as all remained quiet in the ghetto, and Barasz enjoyed the confidence of both the ghetto residents and the Germans, armed resistance was slow in coming. The Germans had promised Barasz that the ghetto was essential to the war effort as long as it kept producing, and thus, even into the summer, he remained certain that the ghetto would not be liquidated. The underground itself had decided to hold back from any military action until it was clear that the Germans intended to liquidate the ghetto in its entirety.

However, on the evening of August 15, 1943, Barasz was summoned to Gestapo headquarters and informed that the workers of Białystok and their families would be transported to Lublin the following morning. It was now apparent that the final round of deportations was about to take place.

At approximately 2:00 a.m. on the morning of August 16, a lookout observed that a heavy military presence was encircling the ghetto. A hurried meeting of the ghetto fighters took place to decide what should be done. They were as much in shock as Barasz; no one had foreseen that the Nazis would take such a step at this time. Mordechaj Tenenbaum, who had come from Vilna to Białystok because it was so quiet, and had himself developed a good relationship with Barasz, was prepared to lead the fighters in a last-ditch stand. The decision was made to launch the armed insurrection that had been delayed for so long.

There were between 200 and 400 fighters, but the arsenal with which they went into battle was poor. They had about 25 rifles, perhaps 100 pistols, 3 or 4 submachine guns, 1 heavy machine gun, Molotov cocktails, and bottles filled with acid. The objective of the revolt was to enable as many Jews as possible to break out of the ghetto and flee into the Knyszyn Forest.

The best they could hope to achieve, given the speed of events, was an attack against the irresistible German forces and their Latvian, Ukrainian, and Belorussian allies. They threw their Molotov grenades and their bottles of acid from windows and balconies, and fired their guns in the direction of the enemy. One of the resisters was Chaika Grossman, a woman with links to the Vilna ghetto and a friend of the Warsaw Ghetto resister **Rachel Zilberberg**. A group from the Betar youth movement, led by Yitzhak Fleischer, joined the insurgents, but all were quickly overwhelmed. The battle ended when the ammunition ran out, and most of the fighters, including Mordechaj Tenenbaum and Daniel Moszkowicz, were killed. A widely held view was that Moszkowicz, surrounded by Germans and with no chance of escape, took his own life rather than be captured. Chaika Grossman was one of the few to survive.

The sacrifice did not stop the planned deportations, which went ahead without delay. Around 10,000 Jews from Białystok were sent to Treblinka, Majdanek, and Auschwitz, while up to 1,200 children were sent to Terezín (Theresienstadt) before further deportation to Auschwitz. Around 150 of the fighters succeeded in breaking out of the ghetto and making it into the forest. Here they joined other Jewish guerrilla groups, doubling the number of Jews fighting as partisans in the area.

It is clear that, having already confronted Jewish resisters in the Warsaw Ghetto Uprising earlier that year, the Nazis knew better how to deal with Białystok. Rather than the Germans being taken by surprise, it was the Jews on this occasion who had no inkling that the Nazis were about to liquidate the ghetto. Thus, when the uprising happened it had no chance whatsoever of success; the best it could deliver was that the Jews would die in combat rather than in Nazi camps. Even that, however, went awry. Of almost 60,000 Jews who lived in Białystok before the war, only a few hundred survived the Holocaust.

Daniel Moszkowicz was not one of these. After the war, he was posthumously awarded the Order of the Cross of Grunwald by the Polish government in recognition of his efforts to resist the Nazi onslaught.

Müller, Filip (b. 1922)

Filip Müller was a Czech Jew from the city of Sered, born in 1922. In April 1942, at the age of 20, he was deported to Auschwitz and became prisoner number 29236.

Placed in a work group responsible for the construction and maintenance of the crematoria, he was destined to be one of the very few *Sonderkommando* workers to survive Auschwitz.

Originally an SS term for units assigned to special tasks, primarily killing Jews, the word *Sonderkommando* later came to mean those Jewish prisoners in the death camps assigned to the gas chambers and the crematoria. These prisoners would help the victims with the removal of their clothing, shave their hair, and later, after the victims had been murdered, inspect their bodies for hidden coins and jewels, remove any gold teeth, and then take the bodies from the gas chambers to the crematoria. Their job was also to stoke the crematoria and do the "heavy work" involved in such operations.

The life of the *Sonderkommando* prisoners was short, as they themselves would be murdered after approximately three months. As witnesses to the most ghastly expressions of the mass murder operations, the Nazis saw no other way to ensure secrecy. The knowledge possessed by the *Sonderkommando* men was far too sensitive for anyone in the outside world to know, so the Nazis would regularly gas the men of a *Sonderkommando* unit and replace them with a new team. The first task of the incoming group would be to dispose of their predecessors' corpses.

Müller was a member of Birkenau's Twelfth *Sonderkommando*. On October 7, 1944, the men working at Crematorium IV rose in revolt. Setting fire to the crematorium, they attacked the SS guards with hammers, axes, and stones. Upon learning that the revolt had begun, the men working at Crematorium II joined in, killing a kapo and several SS men. Then the Hungarian prisoners working in Crematorium III also entered what by now had become a full-scale rebellion. The revolt was successful in damaging Crematorium IV beyond repair; it was never used again. During the revolt, several hundred prisoners escaped from Birkenau, though most were caught and killed by the SS. Later that day, an additional 200 prisoners who took part in the revolt were executed.

One month later, on November 7, 1944, the Nazis destroyed the entire gas chamber-crematorium complex, closing down the operation altogether.

Filip Müller did not choose to be, or remain, a member of the *Sonderkommando*. The grisly work in which he was engaged was forced upon him, and he had no alternative but to continue with it. At one point, feeling unable to go on, he tried to take his own life by joining a group of Czech Jews entering the gas chamber, but he was talked out of it by one of those condemned—he had a responsibility, she told him, to stay alive in order to bear witness. The drive to expose the truth of the murderous Nazi program ultimately became Müller's sole raison d'être, resulting—decades after the event—in the appearance of his astonishing memoir, *Auschwitz Inferno: The Testimony of a Sonderkommando* (U.S. title, *Eyewitness Auschwitz: Three Years in the Gas Chambers*). In this book, Müller gives one of the most detailed accounts of how the gas chambers and crematoria operated, from one who observed as a witness-participant.

Müller's testimony was remarkable in that it was one of very few *Sonderkommando* accounts from any of the Nazi camps; it was even more extraordinary in that he survived the revolt. He provided clear evidence regarding the Nazi extermination process, describing in detail how the cremations were reduced to mathematical equations whereby certain combinations of dead bodies—some still with fat, some, reduced by starvation, with little or none—were found to produce a more efficient cremation process. These "experiments" were undertaken in order to "find a way of saving coke." Compounding the criminality of the Nazis' actions was the deliberation accompanying them—they were observed by civilian technicians employed by Topf and Sons, the firm that had manufactured and installed the cremation ovens. Müller believed that the technicians were there to ensure a measure of quality control and look for any improvements that might be made.

Filip Müller resisted the Nazis in two distinct ways. In the first place, he was both a witness and a participant in the *Sonderkommando* revolt, and he lived to bear witness to what happened on that occasion. Secondly, he resisted the Nazis through the very act of surviving—not with regard to the revolt, but in relation to the grisly work he was assigned in the crematoria. In living through the ordeal, he became an eyewitness to the almost unbearable treatment of 1 million human beings. From this, he was to provide one of the most important pieces of evidence damning the regime.

Conscious of the responsibility conferred on him, Müller gave his first testimony in 1945, while still recovering in the hospital. In 1966 his account was published in *The Death Factory*, a book in English written by two other Holocaust survivors, Erich Kulka and Ota Kraus. In 1964, during a series of war crimes trials held in Frankfurt between December 20, 1963, and August 19, 1965, Müller provided further testimony about the crematoria and the *Sonderkommandos*. As a survivor-participant-witness, then, Filip Müller is a very special type of Holocaust resister, one whose very endurance marks him as unique.

Münch, Hans (1911–1989)

Hans Münch was an SS doctor stationed at Auschwitz between 1943 and 1945. His is a classic case of a conflicted Nazi who was committed to doing his duty, but who at the same time drew an ethical line when it came to the mass murder of Jews. His resistance to the dictates of Nazi ideology was selective, but for the Jews he saved it was vitally necessary.

He was born in 1911. Having studied at the Universities of Tübingen and Munich, Münch became associated with the Nazi party as a student, conscious that alignment would be necessary for his employment prospects. Accordingly, he joined the National Socialist German Students' League in 1934. Three years later, in May 1937, he joined the Nazi party, and in 1939 he qualified as a medical doctor.

At the start of World War II he sought to enlist in the German army, but this was denied on the grounds that the civilian need for medical practitioners had to be met. As a result, he worked as a doctor in rural Bavaria, covering for other doctors already serving. Denied the opportunity of serving in a combat unit, he was persuaded by a friend, Dr. Bruno Weber, that if he really wanted to serve he could do so by joining the SS. Upon his successful application in June 1943, he was ordered to report to a Waffen-SS unit stationed at Kraków. He was not expecting, nor was he aware, of the existence of Auschwitz, nearby.

Münch was assigned to the SS Hygiene Institute in Raisko, outside the Auschwitz main camp. Here, he was assigned to undertake bacteriological research, especially involving typhus, under the direction of his friend Dr. Bruno Weber. As a medical doctor, he was also responsible for general health in the barracks, meaning that from time to time he was obliged to visit the camp itself. When visiting the camp, he was called upon to make "selections" of prisoners when trainloads arrived. This involved a cursory medical inspection to see who was fit enough to work, and who would be consigned immediately to death in the gas chambers. The chief of the medical staff at Auschwitz, Dr. Josef Mengele, told him that his cooperation in this task was mandatory. Shocked, Münch went to Berlin immediately and spoke to the head of the SS Hygiene Institute there, saying that he would not undertake this assignment, "regardless of the consequences." The result was that his superiors in Berlin interceded, and he was absolved from making selections.

Münch's action placed him in the category of an unusual Nazi within the SS structure at Auschwitz. Moreover, he showed himself to be friendly toward the prisoners, with a personal interest in those around him. Despite his rare attitudes and demeanor, in mid-1944 he received promotion to SS-Untersturmführer (second lieutenant).

Although he refused to conduct selections at Auschwitz, Münch did continue with his human experimentation. He soon realized that within the camp female prisoners were the most vulnerable; once experimentation on them was completed, they were very quickly expendable. Münch could not accept that human beings should be disposed of in this way. His approach was to expand the scope and duration of the experiments, such that the women involved could be kept alive for longer periods of time, and thus, perhaps, escape a sudden and horrible death. He also tried to make prisoners' lives more bearable. He would sometimes visit those who were sick and in the infirmary and, on other occasions, find ways to add to their stocks of food.

In January 1945, with the war coming to an end, Auschwitz was evacuated. Münch was reassigned to Dachau, in his home state of Bavaria. The surviving prisoners who had known him were also taken to Dachau, where Weber and Münch compiled a list of former Raisko Institute workers who accompanied them. Within days, the workers were moved to a less crowded barrack, and a laboratory was established where they resumed their former duties. Upon learning that there might be a further transfer to yet another camp, Münch spoke with the prisoners about a possible escape. One of his ideas was that he would take them through the main gate and then provide them with SS uniforms. Another idea, from the prisoners themselves, was that they would accept going on the new transport train and later escape into the mountains near Switzerland. Münch, remarkably, gave the prisoners a revolver and ammunition for protection in the event of a shootout. He then shook hands with each of the prisoners and wished them good luck and an early freedom. Survivors from that attempt later vouched for his efforts on their behalf.

With the end of the war, Münch went home. He surrendered to the occupation authorities in 1946 and spent nearly a year in prison while awaiting and undergoing a trial in Kraków. Many former prisoners testified in his support, with letters confirming that he set up false experiments and prolonged them in order to save prisoners' lives, and that he did not make selections. The court duly acquitted him on December 22, 1947. Of the 40 Auschwitz staff on trial in Kraków, he was the only person acquitted of war crimes.

On January 27, 1995, on the 50th anniversary of the liberation of Auschwitz, Münch returned to Auschwitz at the behest of Eva Mozes Kor, a survivor of Mengele's experiments on twins. Münch took the opportunity to prepare and sign a document verifying that the gas chambers had existed:

> I . . . hereby attest that as an SS physician on duty in Auschwitz in 1944, I witnessed the selection process of those who were to live and those who were to die. Other SS physicians on duty in the camps made selections at the barracks. I was exempt from performing selections because I had refused to do so.
>
> I further attest that I saw thousands of people gassed here at Auschwitz. . . .
>
> I am signing this paper of my own free will to help document the cruel intolerance of my fellow SS.
>
> I, a former SS Physician, witnessed the dropping of Zyklon B into simulated exhaust vents from outside the gas chambers. Zyklon B began to work as soon as it was released from the canisters. The effects of the gas were observed through a peephole by an assigned doctor of the SS officer on duty. After three to five minutes, death could be certified, and the doors were opened as a sign that the corpses were cleared to be burned.
>
> This is the nightmare I continue to live with fifty years later.
>
> I am so sorry that in some way I was part of it. Under the prevailing circumstances I did the best I could to save as many lives as possible. Joining the SS was a mistake. I was young. I was an opportunist. And once I joined, there was no way out.

Dr. Hans Münch was a Nazi who resisted the Holocaust. Known to those around him as "the Good Man of Auschwitz," he was celebrated in *The Nazi Doctors*, a book by author Robert Jay Lifton, as "a human being in an SS uniform." It could be concluded that, in Auschwitz, Münch was placed in a thoroughly dishonorable position—and he did what he could to remain honorable. His actions demonstrate, moreover, that at times there were ways in which one could defy Nazism without suffering severe consequences.

Norrman, Sven (1891–1979)

Sven Norrman was the head of the Warsaw office of the Swedish engineering company ASEA during the German invasion in 1939.

Born in 1891, Norrman, before the war, enjoyed the life of a business executive in a foreign mission. A fluent speaker of Polish, he collected Polish art, was well liked by his staff, and loved hunting. At the time of the German invasion in September 1939 he was based in Stockholm, though he visited Poland every two to three months.

The Nazi occupation saw Norrman and other Swedes in a similar position living relatively comfortable lives. It was in Germany's interest to ensure good relations with Sweden, which provided such goods and services as matches, ball bearings, and technical equipment to which Germany did not have ready access. At first, as the bombs rained down on Warsaw, the so-called "Warsaw Swedes" lived much of their time in a bunker at the Swedish embassy, but over time life resumed to a fairly normal condition. Norrman even fell in love with his secretary, a young Polish Jew named Gizela "Iza" Zbyszynska.

From their elevated standing, the Warsaw Swedes witnessed the unfurling Holocaust before their very eyes. It began with antisemitic violence, in which Jews, singled out through the compulsory wearing of a Star of David, were beaten in the streets and humiliated in various ways. Norrman photographed such examples of oppression in October 1939 in Włocławek, in northern Poland, which became the first European town in which Jews were required to wear the star. He was also witness to Jews being banned from using the sidewalks. In Warsaw, Norrman entered the ghetto itself, where he secretly took thousands of photographs.

All this, however, was but a prelude to other, more vital, acts of opposition. Norrman noticed that Jewish acquaintances were disappearing in increasing numbers—whether through death in the ghetto, deportation, or (less likely) imprisonment—and he became more and more anxious as to where developments were heading. Swedes like Norrman could move around Warsaw as well as to and from Sweden, and he saw that an opportunity existed for him to make the horrors of Poland known more widely. Eventually, he and other Warsaw Swedes began smuggling documents and photographs back into Sweden; not only that, but he brought money back into Warsaw, with which the resistance movement could buy arms.

Both the Polish government-in-exile in London and the Armia Krajowa (Polish Home Army, or AK) in Warsaw saw the use that could be made of the Swedes' willingness to help. On May 16, 1942, the AK's commander in chief, General Stefan Rowecki, observed that the Swedes were a valuable resource that needed to be protected; a few days later, on May 21, Norrman took one of the most important consignments of documents to Stockholm thus far, with full particulars of the annihilation of 700,000 Polish Jews. His secret package included thousands of negatives documenting Nazi crimes in Poland.

Within a few weeks, all this information had been passed on to London, and on June 9, 1942, Poland's exiled premier, Władysław Sikorski, made a broadcast over the BBC revealing all the details Norrman had smuggled out. This was the first time that the world heard news of the Nazi crimes against the Jews in any detail. Some news had previously been revealed, but never on such a scale.

In response, the Gestapo began rounding up the Warsaw Swedes, instinctively aware that they were the only way in which information could have been smuggled out. On the direct order of SS chief Heinrich Himmler, seven Swedes were arrested by the Gestapo: Nils Berglind, Carl Herslow, Sigfrid Häggberg, Tore Widén, Einar Gerge, Stig Lagerberg, and Reinhold Grönberg. By a quirk of fate, Sven Norrman was in Stockholm at the time of the arrests. His mistress, Iza Zbyszynska, managed to get a message to him just before he was due to return. Four of the men, Berglind, Herslow, Häggberg, and Widén, were sentenced to death in July 1943, though all seven were eventually released in the fall of 1944 and returned safely to Sweden. It is likely that intercession by Sweden's King Gustav V, who wrote to Adolf Hitler seeking an amnesty, led to their releases.

For her part, Iza Zbyszynska was taken into custody. Although she had lived as a Christian on the Aryan side in Warsaw, the Gestapo became aware of her Jewish identity once she was captured, and she was sent to the Moabit prison in Berlin, where she survived until the end of the war. Upon her liberation, she and Norrman were reunited in Warsaw; Norrman then divorced his wife in Sweden and married Zbyszynska. In 1974 the Polish government awarded him the Armia Krajowa Cross in recognition of his services for the Polish people during the war.

Norrman explained his motivation in an interview several years after the war, in words that left little room for doubt as to why he acted as he did: "During my entire life I was a businessman. I liked my job and I was good in my field. I joined the struggle because I wanted to do something that was not for profit for once in my life."

Sven Norrman died on February 8, 1979, in Stockholm. His actions led to the world possessing the first detailed knowledge of the Holocaust while it was taking place, and for this action, undertaken at the risk of his life, he should be remembered with honor.

O'Flaherty, Hugh (1898–1963)

Monsignor Hugh O'Flaherty was an Irish Catholic priest stationed in Rome during World War II. There he organized an escape operation for Allied prisoners of war and Jews that ultimately saved more than 6,500 lives. Evading all attempts on the part of the Gestapo to capture him, he became known as the "Scarlet Pimpernel of the Vatican."

He was born on February 28, 1898, to James and Margaret O'Flaherty in Kiskeam, County Cork, and raised in Killarney, where his father worked at a golf course. In his youth he witnessed the Irish War of Independence and saw both sectarian and state violence during which friends were killed. In 1918 he began studying for the priesthood and was ordained in Rome on December 20, 1925. He then remained at the Vatican, where he earned doctorates in divinity, canon law, and philosophy. He served as a diplomat in a number of different locations in the 1920s and 1930s, and in 1934 Pope Pius XI bestowed upon him the title of monsignor in recognition of his diplomatic work on behalf of the Holy See.

With the outbreak of war, O'Flaherty began visiting Allied prisoners held in Italian prisoner-of-war camps, and he provided succor to Jews suffering under the anti-Jewish laws of Italian dictator Benito Mussolini. By the fall of 1942, with the war starting to go badly for Mussolini, the fascist regime began to crack down on prominent Italian Jews as well as aristocratic antifascists. O'Flaherty knew many of these people, having mixed with them socially before the war. Realizing the danger they faced, he decided to hide them—in monasteries and convents, in his former college, and even in his own residence. This would be the start of a major rescue operation lasting for years.

The fall of Mussolini on July 25, 1943, followed by Italy's surrender on September 8 that year, precipitated a German invasion and occupation of the country. The Vatican remained neutral, permitting O'Flaherty to save more people in need. During the spring of 1943 he helped escaped British prisoners of war and Allied airmen who had been shot down, and he developed a network of safe houses throughout Rome where they were able to hide.

In addition, he built a rescue organization comprising a number of able collaborators: other priests, French resistance agents, and senior British officers on the run from the Nazis, among others. Together they hid thousands of escapees and Jews. When Allied soldiers and airmen arrived looking for sanctuary, he provided it; when he learned of Jews who were in danger, he secretly left the Vatican to find them, and bring them to safety.

This latter activity was personally risky. A Vatican diplomat originally from a neutral country, O'Flaherty had long surrendered his neutrality so far as the Nazis were concerned, and after they learned—to their surprise—that the head of the rescue network was an Irish priest, efforts were made to capture him. On at least one occasion an attempt was made to assassinate him. The Nazis could not enter the Vatican, a neutral state; however, when O'Flaherty went outside the Vatican precincts, he was often disguised, earning the title "Scarlet Pimpernel of the Vatican."

When SS lieutenant colonel Herbert Kappler, head of German police and security services in Rome during World War II, learned about Monsignor O'Flaherty, he ordered that a white line be painted around the perimeter of St. Peter's Square, ordering his troops to shoot O'Flaherty if he was caught outside it.

While much of O'Flaherty's activity involved rescuing and hiding Allied military personnel, the work he did on behalf of Jews was significant. Before the start of the war, Rome had a Jewish population nearing 10,000. During the war, just over 1,000 Jews were sent to their deaths at Auschwitz. The majority were hidden by priests like O'Flaherty, and while he was not responsible for saving most of them, his efforts and his example saved many—just how many will never be known owing to the clandestine nature of the work, which was often ad hoc and informal. In addition, O'Flaherty ensured that their religious needs were met. Jewish services, for example, were conducted in the Basilica di San Clemente, at that time under Irish diplomatic protection arranged through Monsignor O'Flaherty.

When Rome was liberated on June 4, 1944, thousands of surviving prisoner-of-war escapees, Allied personnel on the run, and others trying to stay ahead of the Nazis had been protected through the efforts of such upstanders as O'Flaherty, who put themselves out on the basis of a common humanity. This figure does not include Jews who were in O'Flaherty's personal care. After the war O'Flaherty traveled to Jerusalem to visit many of the Jewish refugees he had saved through his own efforts, and who were known to him personally.

For his work in saving lives during the war, O'Flaherty received a number of awards, including Commander of the Order of the British Empire (CBE) and the United States Medal of Freedom with Silver Palm, together with honors from Canada and Australia.

In 1960 Monsignor Hugh O'Flaherty suffered a stroke and returned to Ireland to convalesce. He moved to Cahersiveen, County Kerry, where he lived with his sister until he died, at the age of 65, on October 30, 1963. In 1983 his wartime exploits were portrayed in a movie entitled *The Scarlet and the Black* (directed by Jerry London), starring Gregory Peck as O'Flaherty and Christopher Plummer as his nemesis, Herbert Kappler.

Ogilvie, Albert (1890–1939)

Albert George Ogilvie was the premier of the Australian state of Tasmania between 1934 and 1939, and a rescuer of Jews from Nazi Germany prior to World War II. Born in the Tasmanian capital city of Hobart on March 16, 1890, he was educated at one of Australia's prestigious Catholic colleges, St. Patrick's in Ballarat (Victoria), and at the University of Tasmania, where he graduated in law. Admitted to the bar in 1914, he soon developed a reputation as a successful barrister defending criminal cases.

Ogilvie was elected to the Tasmanian Parliament in 1919 as the Labor member for the seat of Franklin (he was the youngest member of the House), and in 1928 he became leader of the Labor party. He led the party into government at an election in 1934, and as premier moved quickly into action to implement the many plans he had for the future of his state. A highly energetic and domineering leader, Ogilvie was determined to modernize Tasmania, expand the population, and improve the state's infrastructure.

In 1935, together with his minister for health, John Francis ("Stymie") Gaha, Ogilvie took a trip to Europe to see firsthand how other countries were dealing with the effects of the Depression, visiting Britain, Italy, France, Belgium, Switzerland, Germany, Poland, and the Soviet Union. As a Labor politician his impressions of the latter country were highly favorable, but he evinced horror at what he saw in Italy and Germany. In the Nazi state he met with officials from the German foreign office and also with the president of the Reichsbank, Hjalmar Schacht. In discussion with foreign office representatives, mention was made of the

Albert George Ogilvie, premier of the Australian state of Tasmania from 1934 until his death in office in 1939. A champion of human rights and an advocate of Jewish refugee admission to Australia, he was motivated by the idea that no one can remain a passive bystander in the face of suffering. As such, he was arguably the only executive office bearer in the country prepared to oppose the federal government's otherwise restrictive stance regarding Jews from Nazi Germany. (Daily Mail/Rex/Alamy Stock Photo)

Jewish issue, with which Ogilvie had been apprised through the British and Australian press. He was disgusted by what he learned from the Nazi officials with whom he spoke.

Upon his return to Australia he was driven to help Jews who applied to his state for refuge—even though, as a state premier, he had no say over immigration policy at a time when the federal government in Canberra was applying policies to restrict Jewish refugee admissions. Ogilvie pleaded with his federal colleagues to allow Jews to enter Tasmania, working from the premise that as an island state it would be easy to restrict Jewish entry to the mainland, if that was the federal preference.

The volume of mail his office received from German and Austrian Jews seeking refuge was huge, with large numbers believing that Tasmania was a country separate from Australia, like New Zealand. Numerous applications for entry came straight to Hobart because the refugees believed that the state controlled its own immigration policy. The frustration Ogilvie experienced caused him considerable distress—all his government was able to do, in the usual run of events, was forward these requests on to the Department of the Interior in Canberra, which dealt with migration matters. More often than not, applications for entry were denied.

Given this situation, Ogilvie often found himself affronted by the federal government's dismissive attitude. On more than one occasion he interceded with the progress of refugee applications, contacting the responsible minister in Canberra, the United Australia party's Hattil Spencer Foll, and requesting, as a personal favor, that Jewish refugees be allowed entry to his island home. As Ogilvie came from the opposite side of politics to Foll, and was a state premier rather than a federal politician, Foll rarely gave Ogilvie's appeals a second thought (though there were occasions when the premier's efforts did manage to soften the heart of the otherwise tough minister for the interior).

As a result, there were frequent instances of Jewish rejection before the full facts of a specific case were known. An example can be seen in the case of a Warsaw Jew, Mordka Nejman. His brother-in-law, Norman Seidel, had migrated to Australia several years earlier and had settled in Hobart, where he soon became established in soft goods manufacture. In 1938, owing to the situation prevailing for Jews in Poland, Nejman decided to sell his flourishing electrical business and move to Australia. Seidel arranged employment for him that would not displace an Australian, and with an assured landing capital of £500, together with Seidel's maintenance guarantee, Nejman made his application to come to Australia.

The application was refused without the Department of the Interior providing any reasons. Ogilvie took up the case personally, and in a letter to Prime Minister Joseph Lyons—a fellow Tasmanian—on March 14, 1939, he asked whether the Department could favorably reconsider Nejman's application. On May 26 the premier received news that upon further reflection the application for the admission of Nejman, in addition to his wife and children, had now been approved. In view of the ease with which reconsideration was given to the case, it is possible to speculate that with a little more care the application would have been approved in the first place.

For Ogilvie, this was only the tip of the iceberg. Overall, he pursued some 15 separate cases of Jewish entry to his island state, and was successful in 10. Most of these related to Jews seeking refuge from Nazi Germany and Austria. He also put forth proposals for block Jewish settlement on Tasmania's offshore King Island, and he went to great lengths to oversee the progress of individual applications from refugee applicants. For the most part, sadly, his entreaties rarely softened the position of the federal immigration authorities in Canberra.

On June 10, 1939, Ogilvie collapsed and died of a heart attack in Melbourne while attending a federal loan council meeting. It has been suggested that the pressure under which he had been working on behalf of Jewish refugees was a contributing factor to his death. Of course, he had many other matters to attend, but it could be argued that the tragedy of the refugees did little to ease his tension. His untimely death left unfinished a matter on he would have sought completion ahead of many others.

Albert Ogilvie was arguably the only executive office-bearer in Australia during the 1930s to advocate refugee entry in spite of existing regulations or policy considerations. He was not only prepared to oppose the federal government's restrictive immigration policies but he also did so on numerous occasions. That no more than a handful of Jewish refugees made it into Tasmania is not his failure; the lives he saved through his intervention, rather, demonstrate his success.

The main principles for which Ogilvie fought throughout his life sprang from the premise that no one can remain an innocent bystander in the face of suffering. This stance was abundantly demonstrated in his activities on behalf of Jewish refugees from Nazism.

P

Pankiewicz, Tadeusz (1908–1993)

Tadeusz Pankiewicz was a Polish pharmacist widely credited with helping Jews escape from the Kraków ghetto during World War II. Born on November 1908 in Sambor, Poland (now Sambir, Ukraine), Pankiewicz studied at the Jagiellonian University in Kraków, and in 1933 he assumed control of the Apteka Pod Orłem (Under the Eagle) pharmacy established by his father, Jozef, in 1910.

While the pharmacy had long been a place catering to both Jews and non-Jews, in March 1941 the Nazis demanded that Pankiewicz and all other non-Jewish inhabitants in the ghetto district of Podgórze leave, as it was being closed off for Jews only. When the other non-Jewish pharmacists in the area complied with the order and moved to the Aryan side of the city, Pankiewicz remained the only dispensing chemist in the ghetto. He persuaded the Nazi administrators to allow him to stay there so that he could continue selling medicine. He could also live on the premises in the ghetto, even though he was not Jewish. His three employees, Irena Droździkowska, Aurelia Danek-Czort, and Helena Krywaniuk, were given permits enabling them to enter and exit the ghetto on workdays.

It did not take long for Pankiewicz to see the opportunities for good that could arise from his pharmacy's doors staying open. As a place where people were coming and going all day long, it became a clandestine meeting place for those working in the underground movement, and it evolved into a hiding place for ghetto dwellers on the run from Nazi raids. Information was exchanged by couriers, to be collected as people came and went. As a clearinghouse, the pharmacy was especially useful for trading information about possible escape routes out of the ghetto.

On a more down-to-earth level, Pankiewicz helped Jews by supplying often-scarce pharmaceutical medications and other products, frequently free of charge. Such items were vital in helping to maintain the Jews' standard of living and life chances. For example, Pankiewicz would regularly supply various hair dyes to the ghetto inmates in order to help disguise their identities. On other occasions he would provide tranquilizers to keep children quiet during Gestapo raids, when silence could mean the difference between life and death.

For two and a half years the pharmacy remained open, during which Pankiewicz and his staff risked their lives constantly to undertake frequent covert operations. Not only did they keep the store open but they also smuggled food and passed on information, often not waiting for the couriers to arrive. Perhaps even more remarkably, Pankiewicz also created a secret vault beneath the pharmacy premises, where Torah scrolls and other religious artifacts were stored for safekeeping. If detected, any of these activities would certainly have resulted in instant death for Pankiewicz and his dedicated staff.

On the night of March 13–14, 1943, the liquidation of the Kraków ghetto was carried out under the command of SS-Untersturmführer Amon Goeth. Those Jews considered fit for slave labor were transported to the nearby Płaszów labor camp, of which Goeth was the commandant. Death in the ghetto was the fate of those not considered fit for work. Pankiewicz was thus a direct eyewitness to the destruction of the ancient Kraków Jewish community.

In 1946 Pankiewicz appeared before the Nuremberg Tribunal as a prosecution witness, and in 1947 he wrote a memoir of his wartime experiences entitled *Apteka w getcie krakowskim* (*The Cracow Ghetto Pharmacy*). He continued working as a pharmacist until his retirement in the 1980s.

During the period 1941–1943, Pankiewicz and those around him resisted the Holocaust through their refusal to remain indifferent to human suffering and by helping those in need. In recognition of this, on February 10, 1983, Yad Vashem recognized Tadeusz Pankiewicz as one of the Righteous among the Nations for his bravery in the saving of Jewish lives. Later that same year, in April 1983, his premises in the Apteka Pod Orłem building were transformed into a Polish national heritage museum, and to much acclaim, Pankiewicz was at its inauguration. In the 1993 Academy Award–winning film *Schindler's List* (directed by Steven Spielberg), set in the Kraków ghetto, the pharmacy is featured in scenes of ghetto life.

Tadeusz Pankiewicz died in 1993 of kidney failure and was survived by his wife, Selena. He is buried in Kraków's Rakowicki Cemetery.

Pechersky, Alexander (1909–1990)

Alexander "Sasha" Pechersky was a Jewish soldier in the army of the Soviet Union and the leader of the Sobibor revolt on October 14, 1943, the most successful uprising and mass escape of Jews from a Nazi death camp during the Holocaust.

The son of a lawyer, he was born on February 22, 1909, in Kremenchuk, Ukraine. In 1915 his family moved to Rostov-on-Don; after graduating from university with a diploma in music and literature, he managed a small school for amateur musicians.

On June 22, 1941, the day of the German invasion of the Soviet Union, Pechersky enlisted in the Red Army with the rank of lieutenant. In October 1941, during the Battle of Moscow, he was captured by the Nazis and became a prisoner of war. After a period of sickness, escape, recapture, transfer to different camps (during which the Nazis learned that he was Jewish), and incarceration in the Minsk ghetto, he was eventually sent to Sobibor on September 22, 1943, together with other Jewish soldiers and approximately 2,000 Minsk Jews. Almost everyone in the convoy was gassed on arrival; Pechersky and about 80 others were selected to live and work as slave labor.

The arrival of the Soviet soldiers at Sobibor was a huge morale boost for the prisoners already there. They had devised a number of plans for escape or revolt but did not have the strategic expertise to put any of them into practice. A military presence, it was hoped by many, could now possibly change things for the better.

The prisoners at Sobibor realized that time was of the essence if they were not all to be wiped out and the camp liquidated. The biggest question was whether to engage the guards in battle, or to force a mass escape in the hope that at least some people would survive and bear witness. Within five days of Pechersky and his men arriving at Sobibor, the Polish Jews, led by **Leon Feldhendler**, approached Pechersky about his ideas for an escape plan. Pechersky saw that the choice was clear—a mass escape should be mounted, with as many prisoners as possible getting away while SS officers and Ukrainian auxiliaries were killed. As a soldier, he also had a goal of his own—to join up with the partisans and continue fighting the Nazis.

He began by studying the camp carefully, learning its layout and routine. Once he saw how the place operated, his plan was to surreptitiously kill a maximum number of SS officers—rendering the auxiliaries leaderless—and then start the escape by rushing the fence and the main gate. The prisoners would have obtained weapons prior to eliminating the auxiliaries. The plan was timed to begin at 4:00 p.m. on October 14, 1943, but the revolt began a little ahead of time owing to one of the SS officers learning of the plan and starting to shoot Jews. Prior to this a number of other SS had already been dispatched individually, in different locations around the camp.

With no time to lose, a general uprising started on Pechersky's command. There was a wild rush to the main gate and fences all around the perimeter, with prisoners breaking out and running through the surrounding minefields in a mad scramble to reach the woods outside. In the chaos, huge numbers of prisoner-escapees were shot down.

The uprising led to a grisly accounting of death. Eleven SS officers and an unknown number of Ukrainian auxiliaries were killed; from an approximate number of 550 Jewish prisoners, 130 did not participate in the uprising; about 80 prisoners were killed during the escape; and another 170 were hunted down by the Nazis and killed in a bloody aftermath. Best estimates are that only about 53 of those who escaped from Sobibor survived the war.

It had only taken Pechersky 22 days from the time of his arrival at Sobibor to lead, with Feldhendler, the biggest death camp revolt of World War II. Having survived the breakout, Pechersky was joined in the forest by a group of about 50 prisoners, most of them soldiers who had arrived in camp with him. Over several days they split into smaller groups, with Pechersky and his men continually heading east in the hope of meeting up with Soviet partisans. On the night of October 19, 1943, they crossed the Bug River, and after encountering other partisan units they eventually met up with a detachment from the famous Voroshilov regiment. From this point on, they became part of the formal resistance movement.

Alexander Pechersky's tribulations were far from over, however. The Soviet attitude was that prisoners of war were cowards and traitors who deserved to be punished. Although fighting with the partisans, Pechersky was denounced and sent to a Soviet prison for several months, prior to being drafted into a punishment battalion and sent in the first wave of a series of near-suicidal attacks toward the end of the war. Not only did he survive combat but he was also promoted to captain and received a medal for bravery.

After the war, Pechersky returned to his hometown of Rostov-on-Don, but in 1948 he was arrested by the Soviet authorities during Stalin's campaign against Jews suspected of pro-Western leanings. He was only released after Stalin's death in 1953.

Regardless of his status as a free citizen or as a prisoner, however, Stalin's government forbid him to testify at any of the postwar international trials related to the Holocaust—such as at Nuremberg, where the prosecution had hoped he would appear as a witness. In like manner, he was sought after as a witness for the trial of Adolf Eichmann in 1961, but he was forbidden to travel to Israel. He did, however, appear as a witness during the Soviet trial in 1963 of 11 former Ukrainian guards at Sobibor. All were convicted, and 10 were executed.

In 1987 a movie was made about the Sobibor revolt, featuring Dutch actor Rutger Hauer in the role of Alexander Pechersky and Alan Arkin as Leon Feldhendler. *Escape from Sobibor* (directed by Jack Gold) won or was nominated for several awards, with Hauer receiving the Golden Globe for Best Supporting Actor. Pechersky, however, was forbidden from leaving the Soviet Union to attend the movie's premiere.

Alexander Pechersky died just short of his 81st birthday on January 19, 1990, and was buried in Rostov-on-Don.

Père Jacques (1900–1945)

Père Jacques de Jésus, OCD, was a Carmelite friar and teacher responsible for accepting several Jewish children into his school for refuge. For his efforts he was arrested and imprisoned in a number of Nazi concentration camps. The combined effect of these experiences cost him his life.

Born Lucien-Louis Bunel in 1900, he was the third of seven children from a hardworking family in Normandy. Inspired by his father's deep piety, strong sense of social justice, and commitment to work, he decided to become a priest. In 1925 he was ordained in the diocese of Rouen and served in the St. Joseph seminary in

Le Havre. He combined prayer and seclusion with social activism and was noted for his sermons and preaching. As a teacher of religion and English, he employed modern approaches to classroom management and was renowned for his intellect and sense of humor.

His longing for solitude and a life of contemplation, mixed with service to the poor, led him to consider joining a monastery. In 1930, upon deeper reflection, he entered the novitiate of the Carmelite Order and took his vows as Père Jacques three years later. In 1934, at the suggestion of his superiors, he opened a new Carmelite boarding school for boys, the Petit Collège Saint-Thérèse de l'Enfant-Jésus in Avon, Seine-et-Marne.

Père Jacques remained at the school as principal until 1939, when he was called up for military service. When France surrendered to Germany in June 1940, however, he had little intention of resuming a quiet life. Returning to the school, he became an active member of the French Resistance.

He decided to resist in a novel way—not through physical confrontation, but through the act of rescue. He made the school a refuge for Jews and opened its doors to young Frenchmen seeking to avoid conscription for forced labor in Germany. In January 1943 he enrolled three Jewish boys—Hans-Helmut Michel, Jacques-France Halpern, and Maurice Schlosser—as students. A fourth, Maurice Bas, was hidden in plain sight as a worker at the school, while a local villager protected Maurice Schlosser's father. When Lucien Weil, a distinguished botanist from the National Museum of Natural History in Paris, sought sanctuary, Père Jacques placed him on the faculty. In addition, he sought every opportunity to place Jewish children with Catholic families so that their lives might be spared.

On January 15, 1944, however, these initiatives came to an end. A former member of the school had been captured and tortured by the Gestapo into revealing what Père Jacques had been up to, as well as the hidden Jews' whereabouts. On February 3, 1944, the three students—Michel, Halpern, and Schlosser—together with Lucien Weil, his mother, and his sister, were taken to Auschwitz and gassed. Père Jacques was also arrested, and the school was immediately shut down. One of the students in the school was Louis Malle, who grew up to become an Academy Award–winning film director. He later remembered that as Père Jacques was led away he turned to the watching students and said: "*Au revoir et à bientôt*" ("goodbye and see you soon"). This farewell was to be the inspiration for Malle's celebrated autobiographical film from 1987, *Au Revoir les Enfants*.

At first Père Jacques was interned in the prison at Fontainebleau, but he was moved to a brutal German "reprisal camp" at Neue-Bremm, where he remained for three horrendous weeks, during which 44 of the 51 prisoners who arrived with him perished. On April 22, 1944, he was transferred to Mauthausen and immediately set about the task of trying to help others, sharing his rations, hearing confession, and bringing whatever comfort he could. On May 18, however, he was sent to Gusen, a subcamp of Mauthausen. When the priests imprisoned there were transferred to the "priest block" at Dachau, Père Jacques hid his identity in order to remain at Gusen so that he could continue ministering to the prisoners.

The 18 months of his captivity left him sick and exhausted. When American troops arrived to liberate the camp on May 5, 1945, Père Jacques, suffering from tuberculosis and weighing only 75 pounds, tried to restore order among the prisoners and help organize the relief effort. On May 20 he was moved to a hospital near the Carmelite friars in Linz, but he succumbed several days later and died on June 2, 1945, at the age of 45. His body was returned to France and buried in the cemetery of Avon.

On January 17, 1985, Yad Vashem recognized Père Jacques as one of the Righteous among the Nations for his efforts in hiding Jewish students and saving their lives in his school during the Holocaust. Within the Catholic Church, he was honored further when the cause for his canonization was opened in 1990.

Père Marie-Benoît (1895–1990)

Père Marie-Benoît was a French Catholic priest credited with saving several thousand Jews from near-certain deportation and death during World War II.

Born Pierre Péteul on February 5, 1895, in Bourg d'Iré, western France, Père Marie-Benoît saw action during World War I as a medic's assistant and was wounded at Verdun. After the war he became a friar with the Capuchin Franciscan order. Ordained a priest, he undertook advanced studies in Rome, where he earned a doctorate in theology. Until 1940 he lived in the Capuchin monastery in Rome, but when war between France and Italy seemed inevitable he returned to France and moved into the Capuchin monastery at Marseille.

Aware that thousands of Jewish refugees in the region hoped to flee to the relative safety of Spain or Switzerland, Père Marie-Benoît began a major operation to provide for the transportation of these people out of France. In the basement of his monastery he set up an elaborate assembly line producing bogus baptismal certificates, identification cards, passports, and other documents for Jewish refugees. He received aid from members of the French Resistance, as well as members of other religious organizations (Protestant, Greek Orthodox, and Jewish), and built solid (though illicit) relationships with local border guides, or *passeurs*. Through them, and utilizing the false documents he had engineered, he managed to smuggle thousands of refugees into the neutral countries. As his reputation grew, it was said that the waiting room in his monastery was always full, and that the printing press in the basement worked overtime.

In November 1942 the Germans moved into what had, until then, been unoccupied France. This included Marseille, which jeopardized Père Marie-Benoît's rescue activities. In order to continue rescuing Jews, therefore, he moved to Nice, which was at that time still under Italian occupation. There he met with Guido Lospinoso, the Italian commissioner of Jewish affairs, whom Mussolini had handpicked to ensure that there would be no special deals for Jews. Instead, Père Marie-Benoît negotiated a deal with Lospinoso to permit the passage of Jews through the city so they could seek refuge in Switzerland. He also successfully lobbied the Italians not to deport or harm the many French Jews living in Nice.

In July 1943 Père Marie-Benoît went to Rome in the hope of soliciting the Vatican's help in transporting Jews from France in northern Italy. While he was in Nice, Père Marie-Benoît met Angelo Donati, a leading Italian-Jewish banker. Donati had a plan for relocating the Italian Jewish population to North Africa. Such a huge operation, however, would require the support of the Italian government, which meant the cooperation of the Vatican. In April 1943 arrangements were made for Père Marie-Benoît to meet with Pope Pius XII to discuss the plan. According to one report, Père Marie-Benoît received a cold reception from the Pope, who declined to assist. Besides, when the Germans occupied northern Italy and the Italian-occupied zone of France, the idea had to be shelved.

Vatican officials did, however, provide an alternative source of help. Père Marie-Benoît returned from Rome to France in order to facilitate the transportation of French Jews to safety in neighboring Spain, proceeding from an arrangement made with the Spanish government that allowed at least 2,600 French Jews to enter by offering "proof"—using the priest's falsified documents—that they were of Spanish extraction.

In addition to helping Jewish refugees materially, he also attended to their spiritual needs, often comforting children as they awaited transport out of France, and he worked hard to find safe houses to protect Jews from deportation. When his supporters became concerned toward the end of the war that the Nazis and their French collaborationist allies were about to uncover his activities, Père Marie-Benoît fled France and took up residence in northern Italy under the alias "Father Benedetti." In Rome, he was elected to the board of Delasem (Delegazione Assistenza Emigranti Ebrei, or Delegation for the Assistance of Jewish Emigrants), the main Jewish welfare organization in Italy. When the Jewish president of Delasem was arrested, Père Marie-Benoît was named acting president.

He immediately transferred the organization's headquarters to the International College of the Capuchins, where he recommenced the forging of documents for Jews. He contacted the Swiss, Romanian, Hungarian, and Spanish embassies, and obtained from them documents enabling Jews to circulate freely under false names. He also obtained ration cards from the police, asserting—deceptively—that they were meant for non-Jewish refugees. None of this escaped the attention of the Gestapo, and in early 1945 his office was raided several times. Most of the Delasem leadership were arrested, tortured, and executed.

Soon after this, Père Marie-Benoît went into hiding. Until the end of the war, however, he persisted in his efforts to save Jews.

When Rome was liberated in June 1944, the Jewish community held an official synagogue ceremony in honor of Père Marie-Benoît. Then, on December 1, 1966, Yad Vashem in Jerusalem recognized him as one of the Righteous among the Nations, and he was presented with the award in person at a ceremony in November 1967 at the Israeli embassy in Paris.

Père Marie-Benoît died in France on February 5, 1990, recognized by many in the Jewish community, fittingly, as *Père des juifs*—the Father of the Jews.

Perlasca, Giorgio (1910–1992)

Giorgio Perlasca was an Italian rescuer of Jews during the Holocaust in Hungary, posing as the Spanish consul-general during the winter of 1944–1945 and saving 5,218 Jews from deportation and certain death.

Perlasca was born in Como, Lombardy, in 1910 and raised in Maserà, Padua. Swayed by the ideals espoused by Italian poet and nationalist Gabriele D'Annunzio, Perlasca supported the fascist regime of Benito Mussolini. He fought in the Italian army during the invasion of Abyssinia in 1935 and was a volunteer during the Spanish Civil War in 1936 on the side of Francisco Franco. After his return to Italy he deserted fascism, replacing his former belief with a more general patriotism and loyalty to his king, Victor Emmanuel III.

After World War II broke out Perlasca became a procurement officer and was sent as an emissary to Eastern Europe with the task of purchasing meat for the Italian army. In the fall of 1943 he was appointed as an official of the Italian trade commission in Budapest, Hungary. Wider developments in the war then took over. On September 8, 1943, Italy surrendered to the Allies, and on October 13, 1944, he was interned by the Hungarian government—an Axis ally—as a diplomatic detainee. Eventually, on medical grounds, he was granted parole and sought asylum in the Spanish embassy. He changed his name from Giorgio to the Spanish Jorge, and owing to his earlier service during the Spanish Civil War was granted the rights of a Spanish citizen.

Seeking work through the embassy, he spoke with the Spanish chargé d'affaires, **Ángel Sanz Briz**, who had been issuing protective passes to Budapest Jews since the spring of 1944. Sanz Briz gave Perlasca responsibility for safe houses sheltering Jews under Spanish protection.

Toward the end of 1944 Sanz Briz was ordered to leave Hungary because of Spain's refusal to recognize the new pro-Nazi government of Ferenc Szalasi. On November 30, 1944, Perlasca learned that Sanz Briz had gone to Switzerland, and that he had been invited to accompany him on a diplomatic passport. Perlasca chose to remain in Hungary, however, and informed the Hungarian authorities that the embassy had not closed and that he had been appointed as charge d'affaires.

He did not possess any official documentation to that effect, but he managed to convince the Hungarian minister of the interior that Sanz Briz would return shortly from a period of leave and had appointed him as temporary successor.

Haste was needed; the Hungarians, believing that official Spain had left, saw this as an opportunity to take over the Spanish embassy and the safe houses where Jews were hiding under Spanish protection. Over the next few months, Perlasca worked actively to hide, feed, and transport thousands of Budapest Jews. He obtained medicine and food on the black market and developed a system of safe conduct passes using a Spanish law dating from 1924, which allowed Spanish-born Jews full citizenship and protection. This was then extended to all Jews of Sephardic origin, including those who were the descendants of Spanish and Portuguese Jews expelled from Spain in 1492 and 1497.

Across the winter of 1944–1945, Perlasca worked to save the lives of Hungarian Jews alongside Sweden's **Raoul Wallenberg**, apostolic nuncio **Angelo Rotta**, and the Swiss Red Cross delegate **Friedrich Born**. It has been calculated that Perlasca was responsible for saving the lives of more than 5,200 Jews by the time the Soviet army accepted the surrender of Budapest in February 1945.

After the war, Perlasca returned to his family in Padua and lived a quiet life. For 30 years he did not speak about his actions while in Hungary; not even his family knew of his exploits. In 1987, however, a group of Hungarian Jewish survivors who had been trying to trace his whereabouts for several years finally found him, and he began telling the world of his heroic deeds during the dark years.

Perlasca eventually became well known around the world. In 1991 an Italian journalist, Enrico Deaglio, wrote a best-selling biography, *La banalità del bene: Storia di Giorgio Perlasca* (1991), which was later published in English as *The Banality of Goodness*. This, in turn, was used as the basis of a movie, *Perlasca—Un eroe Italiano* (2005, directed by Alberto Negrin), starring Luca Zingaretti in the title role.

Giorgio Perlasca received many honors for his heroic acts of resistance during World War II. Among his decorations are Israel's Medal of the Knesset (1989); Hungary's Star of Merit (1989); the Town Seal of Padova (1989); the United States Medal of the Holocaust Museum (1990); Italy's *Grande Ufficiale della Repubblica* (1990); Spain's *Orden de Isabel la Católica* (1991); and Italy's Gold Medal for Civil Bravery (1992). In 2011 a 10,000-tree forest was planted in his honor in Israel's Galilee, following his recognition as one of the Righteous among the Nations by Yad Vashem on September 6, 1988.

Giorgio Perlasca was a man who continually risked his life to save others. He had the option to leave the danger zone in exchange for his personal safety, yet he chose to remain and provide aid to the Jews for whose lives he had assumed responsibility. He died at home of a heart attack on August 15, 1992, and was buried in his hometown of Maserà, outside Padua. He expressed the wish that the words "Righteous among the Nations" be written in Hebrew on his tombstone.

Peshev, Dimitar (1894–1973)

Dimitar Peshev was a leading Bulgarian politician in the 1930s and 1940s, and a major actor in resisting the pro-Nazi government of Premier Bogdan Filov. Through this opposition he prevented the deportation of Bulgaria's 48,000 Jews to the death camps of Nazi Germany.

Born in 1894 to an affluent family in Kyustendil, a town in far western Bulgaria, he studied languages in Salonika and law in Sofia and became a magistrate after having fought in World War I and completing his law degree. In 1935 he was appointed minister for justice and was elected deputy speaker of the Sobranie (Parliament) in 1938.

Like many other Bulgarian political figures, Peshev favored Bulgaria's alliance with Nazi Germany, signed by Tsar Boris III and Adolf Hitler in 1940. This worked well for Bulgaria; after the German conquest of Yugoslavia in April 1941 and the country's partition, Bulgaria expanded at Yugoslavia's expense. Given that he thought the alliance would bring prosperity to Bulgaria and its people, Peshev was blind to the real goals of the Nazi government.

One of the costs of the alliance was that Bulgaria would develop antisemitic laws in line with those of the Nazis. On January 23, 1941, Peshev's party enacted the Law for the Protection of the Nation, restricting Jewish participation in the country's economic and social life. The law ordered such controls as Jews being compelled to change their names, new rules regarding Jewish places of residence, confiscation of Jewish possessions, exclusion from the public service, and a prohibition on economic and professional activity. Other measures included a prohibition on marriages between Jews and Bulgarians, special taxes, and requirements that all Jews wear a star and that male Jews be drafted for forced labor. Peshev supported this new law, seeing it as only a temporary expedient that would soon pass and could be controlled. Of interest was that most Bulgarians actually opposed the law, though this did not alter the new realities in view of the authoritarian nature of the government.

In the spring of 1943 the Bulgarian government signed a new law whereby all of Bulgaria's 48,000 Jews would be deported through Kyustendil on March 10, 1943, and sent to Nazi death camps in Poland. Jews in the Bulgarian-occupied territories of Thrace and Macedonia would also be rounded up and deported. When the Jews of Kyustendil learned of their imminent deportation, they attempted to have the order overturned through the intercession of one they knew as a friend: Dimitar Peshev.

On March 8, 1943, a local delegation, including a personal friend of Peshev's, Jakob Baruch, spoke with him about the government's deportation plan. Peshev had not previously known of this plan but upon confirmation of it decided that the deportations had to be stopped. He traveled to Kyustendil and met with the assistant chief of police, who described to him how the deportations were to take place. Peshev felt that acquiescence to the Nazi demands was no longer an option. He saw all too clearly the consequences of the alliance with Hitler and decided that it was his responsibility to act.

Next, he and his close friend and colleague (also from Kyustendil), Petar Mihalev, went to Parliament and burst into the office of Interior Minister Petar Gabrovski, insisting that he cancel the deportations. Explaining the gravity of the situation, and after a fierce argument, Gabrovski called the governor of Kyustendil and instructed him to stop preparations for the Jewish deportations. By 5:30 p.m. on March 9—just one day after Peshev had learned about the planned action against the Jews—the deportation was cancelled.

Despite the minister's assurance, however, Peshev needed further guarantees, especially after he learned that the Jews in the occupied territories of Thrace and Macedonia were already being deported. Most of the Jews of Thrace were deported to Treblinka (with some going to Auschwitz), while almost all the Jews of Macedonia were deported to Auschwitz, the last transport leaving on March 29, 1943.

Peshev decided to bring the matter to the Sobranie. On March 17, 1943, he wrote a letter of protest and had 42 parliamentarians sign it. In disregard of Prime Minister Filov's instruction not to subject the letter to a vote in the House, it was discussed in caucus on March 23, 1943. So as not to have his authority undermined, Filov demanded that each of the signatories stand and announce their support of Peshev's letter. Under this pressure, only 30 of the original 42 confirmed their support, and when a final vote was taken the party decided to censure Peshev. The next day he was forced to step down as deputy speaker.

After Bulgaria was knocked out of the war by the Soviet invasion of September 1944, Peshev was arrested as a member of the former Bulgarian collaborationist government, charged with antisemitism and collaboration. Facing the death penalty, members of the Jewish community from Kyustendil, led by Joseph Nissim Yasharoff, testified on his behalf. He was sentenced to 15 years in prison at forced labor, with all his property turned over to the state. After a year and a half, however, he was released once the court reviewed his case and confirmed his key role in saving Bulgaria's Jews. Upon his release, he was forced to live in isolation, without a job or a means for sustenance. His deeds during the war went unrecognized.

In January 1973, however, Yad Vashem recognized him as one of the Righteous among the Nations for his role in saving the Jews of Bulgaria. A few weeks later, on February 20, 1973, he died—a Holocaust resister recognized by his home country only after his death.

Pilecki, Witold (1901–1948)

Witold Pilecki was a Polish cavalry officer who infiltrated Auschwitz as a volunteer in order to start a military underground movement there.

He was born on May 31, 1901, in the Karelian town of Olonets, close to the border with Finland. A subject people under the Russian Empire, the Poles rebelled in 1863–1864; after the uprising's suppression, Pilecki's grandfather Józef Pilecki was exiled to Siberia. The family, then subject to internal exile and forcible resettlement, made their new home in Olonets. In 1910 they moved to Vilna (Vilnius), and in 1916 the teenage Witold Pilecki relocated to Orel, southwest of Moscow. After Poland's independence from Russia in 1919, Pilecki joined the Polish army and fought in the Polish-Soviet War of 1919–1920. He remained in the army, becoming a junior cavalry officer in 1926. On April 7, 1931, he married Maria Pilecka, née Ostrowska, with whom he had two children, Andrzej and Zofia.

With the invasion of Poland by Nazi Germany on September 1, 1939, Pilecki's unit was heavily engaged until forced to withdraw to the south. It disbanded after the Soviet Union invaded on September 17, and Poland surrendered.

On November 9, 1939, Pilecki, together with Jan Henryk Włodarkiewicz and Władysław Surmacki, founded one of the first Polish underground movements, the Tajna Armia Polska (Secret Polish Army, or TAP), which by 1940 comprised some 8,000 men. In 1942 it was incorporated into the Armia Krajowa (Home Army, or AK).

In mid-1940 Pilecki sought operational permission to infiltrate the newly constructed concentration camp at Auschwitz after it was established for Polish political prisoners. In a report written after the war, Pilecki stated the aims of the movement he intended to create: keeping up fellow prisoners' spirits by supplying and spreading news from outside; organizing extra food and dividing clothing among TAP members; sending reports outside; and, above all, preparing for a takeover in the event of an assault on the camp from outside.

Receiving permission to proceed, he was given forged papers and a new identity as "Tomasz Serafiński." He let himself be taken prisoner in a Warsaw roundup and arrived in Auschwitz on September 22, 1940.

To create his organization, Pilecki reasoned that only a system based on the strictest secrecy could have any hope of success. He decided to base the movement in two main areas, the *revier* (infirmary) and the *Arbeitseinsatz* (office responsible for labor distribution), as he saw these as the most likely places to start a program of camp welfare. He named his secret network the Związek Organizacji Wojskowej (Union of Military Organization, or ZOW).

At the same time Pilecki was establishing his resistance movement, Stanisław Dubois, under the direction of the Polish Socialist party, was forming another. Within a short time, a third group was formed by right-wing Polish nationalist elements. It was not until December 1941 that the three groups came together as some sort of federated movement, but by that stage it no longer represented all sections of the camp. Until the middle of 1941 the camp had only housed Poles; by the end of the year, however, other national groups had appeared, and these, too, had organized their own resistance movements. After considerable difficulties, Pilecki's organization managed to unify with the most important of these other groups—the Czechs, Russians, and later the Austrians—under the leadership of a communist, **Hermann Langbein**.

The ZOW soon became the major resistance movement at Auschwitz. Some smaller national groups still persisted, and inmates occasionally held dual membership within their own group as well as the ZOW. This enabled a small group of communists and socialists led by the Austrian Langbein and a Pole, Józef Cyrankiewicz, to break with the ZOW and form a new movement, Kampfgruppe Auschwitz (Auschwitz Combat Group), on May 1, 1943. The internal politics thus generated played out several years later and contributed to Pilecki's death.

The ZOW provided the Polish underground with invaluable information about the camp, and from October 1940 it smuggled reports to Warsaw. As early as March 1941, via the Polish authorities in London, Pilecki's reports informed the British government of the atrocities taking place in Auschwitz, and these reports intensified as gassings of Jews increased. In 1942 the ZOW was broadcasting from a secret radio station and providing up-to-the-minute details of the number of transports, arrivals, and deaths in the camp. These reports were, for a time, the main source of Allied intelligence about Auschwitz, and Pilecki hoped that action would be taken to attack the camp and bring its operations to an end.

In 1943, after nearly two and a half years at Auschwitz, he made the decision to escape so that he could testify in person and force the AK to mount an assault on the camp. On the night of April 26–27, 1943, he and two comrades overpowered a guard and broke out. Making his way to Warsaw, he reached AK headquarters but was unable to convince anyone to mount the hoped-for attack. He did, however, compose a detailed report of more than 100 pages, which was transmitted to London; it was the first sustained intelligence report on the Auschwitz concentration camp. Through this, Pilecki confirmed for the Allies that the Holocaust was indeed taking place. "Witold's Report," as it came to be known, was the first insider documentation confirming the Holocaust.

After this, Pilecki resumed his role as an officer with the AK, staying loyal to the London-based Polish government-in-exile. On August 1, 1944, the Warsaw Uprising broke out, and he fought as a private until assuming a command role later in the revolt. When it was defeated he went into captivity as a prisoner of war. He returned to Poland in October 1945 to engage in undercover work for the Polish government-in-exile, but on May 8, 1947, was arrested as part of a prosecution of AK members who still gave their allegiance to the government-in-exile. Among those presenting evidence for the State was Józef Cyrankiewicz, who was in Auschwitz at the same time as Pilecki and a member of the leftist Kampfgruppe Auschwitz. On March 3, 1948, a show trial took place, and Pilecki was convicted of various crimes against the newly installed communist government. On May 15, 1948, he was sentenced to death, with the sentence carried out on May 25.

After the end of communism in Poland, Witold Pilecki was rehabilitated on October 1, 1990. In 1995 he was posthumously decorated by the Polish government with the Order of Polonia Restituta, and in 2006 he received the highest Polish decoration, the Order of the White Eagle.

Plagge, Karl (1897–1957)

Karl Plagge was a German military officer who joined the National Socialist party in 1931 out of a conviction that the Nazi social and economic platform offered prosperity for Germany's future.

Born on July 10, 1897, in Darmstadt, Plagge saw service for Germany during World War I, and in 1924 he graduated from the Technical University of Darmstadt with a degree in engineering. As a member of the Nazi party he felt confident that Hitler was the man to lead Germany, though he could not agree with Nazism's racial theories. This stance led to a falling out with the local party leadership in 1935 and denied him any future senior positions within the party hierarchy.

At the beginning of World War II he was drafted into the German army, and in July 1941 was sent to Vilna (Vilnius) to command an engineering unit. Once there, he witnessed severe anti-Jewish measures, and similarly to another Wehrmacht solider, **Anton Schmid**, was conscience-stricken by what he had seen. He thereupon decided to help Jews in the ghetto through the granting of lifesaving work certificates. He issued some 250 such permits, covering about 1,000 men, women, and children, between 1941 and mid-1944. In addition, Plagge obtained extra food rations, warm clothing, medical supplies, and firewood for his workers.

Between August 6 and September 5, 1943, more than 7,000 Jews were deported to their deaths from the Vilna ghetto, which was itself then prepared for final liquidation. (This happened under the direction of SS-Oberscharführer Bruno Kittel on September 23–24, 1943.) In response to these developments, Plagge sprang into action on September 16, 1943, having managed to establish a Jewish slave labor camp, HKP (Heereskraftpark) 562, located on Subocz (Subačiaus) Street. Officially an SS camp, it was run by Plagge's Wehrmacht unit. As a specialist camp, HKP 562's main task was to repair military vehicles damaged in combat. Plagge transported more than 1,000 of his Jewish workers and their families from the ghetto to HKP 562, where they remained in relative safety. Plagge ensured that the work conditions were bearable, with adequate food supplies. The guards, operating under Plagge's orders, did not engage in prisoner abuse.

On March 27, 1944, the SS carried out an action against the children of the camp (*Kinderaktion*) while Plagge was away on home leave in Germany. They entered the camp, collected most of the camp's 250 children, and then deported them.

On July 1, 1944, Plagge addressed the prisoners, tipping them off to the likelihood of their imminent relocation under the SS to another site further west, and saying that the days of his protection were coming to an end. Spurred on by this warning, at least half the prisoners hid prior to the arrival of the SS on July 3, 1944. Those who remained, some 500, were murdered immediately. Subsequently, the SS located half of those who had gone into hiding and shot them, too. When the area was liberated by Soviet troops a few days later, the 250 hidden Jews crept out of their various safe places. They were the largest single group of Jewish survivors in Vilna.

It has been estimated that Plagge's efforts, overall, might have saved up to 1,240 Jewish lives, though no one will ever know the precise number. What is known is that he took in as many prisoners as he could, as forced labor, to work for him—thereby giving them a much better chance of survival than if they were deported to the forests of Ponary and summarily shot.

With the end of the war, Plagge returned to Darmstadt. In 1947 he was put on trial as part of the postwar denazification process. Like many of those who worked on behalf of others during the Holocaust, he blamed himself for not having done enough to save more lives, and his feelings of guilt as a former member of the Nazi party and an officer in the Wehrmacht led him to seek classification from the tribunal as a "follower" or "collaborator" with the Nazis. When some of his former prisoners, then languishing in a displaced persons camp in Stuttgart, heard that he was facing denazification proceedings, they testified on his behalf. This swung the outcome positively in his favor, and the court awarded him the status of an exonerated person. His preference to be named as a Nazi collaborator remained, and the court had no alternative but to classify him as a *Mitläufer*, or "follower."

After the trial, Plagge lived the final decade of his life quietly in Darmstadt. In the decades that followed, survivors of the Vilna ghetto and their families tried to locate the man who had done so much to save Jewish lives by resisting the Holocaust from within the system. Relatively little was known of his identity, and even less of his motivations. Survivors of HKP 562, moreover, who had moved to various places around the world, never forgot his many kindnesses, and some began a campaign to have his work on their behalf recognized in some way.

On June 19, 1957, Karl Plagge died in Darmstadt. His efforts were finally acclaimed, posthumously, when Yad Vashem in Jerusalem recognized him as one of the Righteous among the Nations in 2005. Then, in February 2006 a German military base in Pfungstadt, not far from Darmstadt, was named in his honor as the Major-Karl-Plagge-Kaserne—a similar award was bestowed on his contemporary in Vilna, Sergeant Anton Schmid, who lost his life in 1942.

Polonski, Abraham (b. 1913)

Abraham Polonski was a founder of the French Jewish resistance movement. Born in Russia in 1913, he moved to France before World War II and worked as an electrical engineer in Toulouse. In August 1940, after the French surrender on June 22, he and his wife, Eugénie, together with **Dovid Knut** and his wife, Ariane, and Lucien Lublin, built a secret underground organization called La Main Forte (The Strong Hand). Its aim was to establish a movement that would defeat the Nazis before moving on to take control of Palestine and establish a Jewish state.

Polonski (whose resistance code names were "Pol" and "Maurice Ferrer") and the others were committed Zionists. On January 10, 1942, they (and others with an equal commitment to the same ideals) established an underground Jewish militia, the Armée Juive (Jewish Army, or AJ). The first members of the AJ were recruited from a Torah study group led by Rabbi Paul Roitman. The organization received funds from a refugee group based in Switzerland, the Zionist Organization of France.

Polonski and Lublin directed most Armée Juive activities, which were undertaken by the most committed members of the various Zionist youth movements. Through to the summer of 1942, Polonski and Lublin recruited militants from Toulouse, Montpellier, Nice, Grenoble, Lyon, and Limoges. They, in turn, fought in their own cities as well as in Paris, attacking informers and Gestapo collaborators.

The oath that new members of the Armée Juive had to recite was straightforward. Placing their right hands on the blue and white Zionist flag and the Bible, they would say:

> I swear fidelity to the Jewish Army
> And obedience to its leaders.
> May my people live again,
> May Eretz-Israel be reborn.
> Liberty or death.

In May 1942 a new resistance organization, the Mouvement de Jeunesse Sioniste (Zionist Youth Movement, or MJS) was created by Simon Levitte and Dika Jefroykin. Together with another member, Leonardo Zupraner, they brought into the Armée Juive a number of new resistance members. Recruitment standards were severe, with secrecy and obedience mandatory. The primary purpose of the organization was to resist when success seemed likely, in addition to rescuing Jews by the provision of false papers, assisting with border crossings, and the like.

During the winter of 1943–1944 the escape network of the Armée Juive helped around 300 Jews flee successfully to Spain, from where most moved on to Palestine. The Armée Juive was assisted substantially by such outside bodies as the Jewish Agency for Palestine and the American Jewish Joint Distribution Committee, with tens of millions of francs being disbursed to help procure arms and border crossings.

The Armée Juive later evolved into the Organisation Juive de Combat (Jewish Combat Organization, or OJC). At its height, it was believed to have more than 2,000 fighters and other operatives. On May 21, 1944, Polonski entered into discussions with the National Liberation Committee (Comité français de Libération nationale), which led to the OJC being recognized as an official movement within the French Resistance, with its operational district centered in Toulouse.

In June 1944 Polonski narrowly escaped capture—and possible death—at the hands of a local collaborationist militia group in Toulouse. Although he escaped through the roof of the building where he was located, the assault prevented any activities from the Armée Juive that day. Polonski then had to go on the run, and he moved to Lyon, where he maintained operations until August 1944. When the Germans surrendered Paris to the Allies on August 25, 1944, Polonski and several of his fighters were present to help achieve the city's liberation.

After the war, Abraham Polonski went on to became a commander of the Haganah in Palestine, with responsibility for assisting illegal Jewish immigrants traveling from France and North Africa to the Middle East. After the creation of Israel in 1948, he retired to a quieter life.

Overall, the Armée Juive carried out almost 2,000 actions against the occupying Germans and their collaborationist allies. Many Jews fought in other units as well, often in leading positions. While Jews comprised just 1 percent of the French population, they constituted almost 15 percent of the French Resistance movement.

Preysing, Konrad Graf von (1880–1950)

Konrad Graf von Preysing was the Catholic bishop of Berlin from 1935 until his death in 1950, and for much of this time he was a leading opponent of Nazism.

Born into an aristocratic Bavarian family on August 30, 1880, von Preysing was one of three brothers, all of whom became priests. In 1898 he became a law student at the University of Munich, before moving to the University of Würzburg in 1901. He entered the Bavarian civil service in 1906 but chose instead to become a priest, and he was ordained in Munich on July 29, 1912. In 1913 he earned a doctorate in theology from the University of Innsbruck. He was soon appointed personal secretary of the archbishop of Munich, Cardinal Franziskus von Bettinger, and continued to work in the Munich Archdiocese until 1932, when he became bishop of Eichstätt.

Immediately after the Nazis came to power in January 1933 he expressed criticism of the confidence that Catholic bishops, clerics, and believers placed in the new regime, quickly becoming one of the most consistent senior Catholics to oppose it. These feelings were more than reciprocated by the Nazi regime, though this did not stand in the way of von Preysing being named bishop of Berlin on July

6, 1935. He was critical of the approach of Adolf Cardinal Bertram, the chair of the Fulda conference of German bishops, who refused to protest the Nazi boycott of Jewish businesses in March 1933 on the grounds that it was a purely economic matter—and also because, in his opinion, the Jewish press had kept silent about the persecution of Catholics. Von Preysing spoke out against Bertram in public sermons and at various high-ranking ecclesiastical conferences, arguing that the Church should mount strong opposition to the Nazis.

On March 14, 1937, Pope Pius XI issued *Mit Brennender Sorge* (*With Burning Anxiety*), an encyclical reinforcing the inviolability of human rights and accusing the Nazi government of "systematic hostility" toward the Church and what it stood for. Von Preysing was part of the five-member commission that prepared the encyclical, an anti-Nazi statement couched in diplomatic language.

On August 24, 1938, he cofounded the Hilfswerk beim Bischöflichen Ordinariat Berlin (Welfare Office of the Berlin Diocese Office). Through this he made himself personally responsible for the care of Catholics of Jewish descent as well as of unbaptized Jews. In 1940 and 1941 he also protested against the Nazi euthanasia program, in which those with mental and physical disabilities and incurable diseases were murdered by the state. He sent numerous letters to his priests urging them to protest similarly.

Von Preysing worked very closely with the rector of St. Hedwig's Cathedral, his seat in Berlin, Father **Bernhard Lichtenberg**. Expressing opposition to the Nazis was something von Preysing could do with relatively little fear of recrimination due to his high position, but Lichtenberg enjoyed no such protection. From 1938 onward Lichtenberg conducted prayers for Jews and others imprisoned in Nazi concentration camps; arrested in 1941, he died while in transit to Dachau in 1943. After this, another opponent of Nazi antisemitism, **Margarete Sommer**, took on the role Lichtenberg had left. While assisting all those persecuted by the government, she also gathered intelligence on deportations of Jews as well as other anti-Jewish measures, and from 1942 onward she wrote reports outlining her findings.

There was little doubt that von Preysing was apprised of the unfolding Holocaust. A letter he wrote to Pope Pius XII in January 1941 indicates that he was aware of how bad the situation was for European Jews, and he pleaded with the Pope for some sort of assistance to alleviate their distress.

Von Preysing also worked with leading members of the German resistance, particularly Carl Goerdeler and **Helmuth James Graf von Moltke**. In pastoral letters issued in 1942 and 1943 he expressed a decidedly anti-Nazi message, one of which was broadcast in German by the BBC in London. Finally, in 1944 he met with resistance leader Claus von Stauffenberg prior to the failed July Bomb Plot, an assassination attempt on Hitler. Von Preysing blessed von Stauffenberg and wished him well in his endeavor, though at the same time he expressed misgivings as to whether killing Hitler would be permitted under Church law.

Several months after the end of the war, in 1946, Konrad von Preysing was elevated to the position of cardinal by Pope Pius XII, a position he held until his death, in Berlin, on December 21, 1950. He was buried in St. Hedwig's cemetery, but on February 12, 1968, his remains were transferred to the crypt of St. Hedwig's Cathedral—the same location as Father Lichtenberg, who was beatified as a Blessed Martyr by Pope John Paul II on June 23, 1996.

Pritchard, Marion van Binsbergen (b. 1921)

Marion van Binsbergen Pritchard was a member of the Dutch resistance and a rescuer of Jewish children during the Holocaust.

Born Marion van Binsbergen in Amsterdam in 1921, she was the daughter of a Supreme Court judge and an English mother. In 1940, soon after the Nazi invasion and occupation of the Netherlands, she was a student at Amsterdam's school of social studies when she and a friend were arrested, while studying, on suspicion of contact with members of the Dutch resistance. Although her friend had such contact, van Binsbergen did not, but she was considered to be guilty by association and subsequently imprisoned for seven months.

In the spring of 1942 van Binsbergen saw children between the ages of two and eight loaded onto trucks and taken away by Nazis. Shocked by what she had witnessed, she decided to commit herself single-mindedly to rescue work.

Initially in her work as part of the Dutch underground she provided essential items, such as food and clothing, to Jews in hiding. Assuming a more active role, she agreed to deliver a package handed to her by a stranger—a baby girl—for safekeeping. On reaching her destination with the child, she learned that her contacts had been arrested. Another couple, who were not originally part of the operation, took the baby off her hands, and van Binsbergen's new role as a smuggler of children began.

One Saturday in 1942 van Binsbergen was asked by the head of the social welfare organization where she was working if she could find a safe place for a two-year-old Jewish boy named Jan Herben. Sheltering a Jew—even a child—was a criminal offence, but she immediately took the boy to her parents' apartment until she found a safer place. Her rescue activities increased rapidly.

At the end of 1942 Pritchard moved to Huizen, North Holland, where she lived in a house belonging to a friend of her parents. Asked if she could shelter a Jewish family, Fred Polak and his three children, she obliged. The house, which was secured by the Dutch resistance movement, was 150 miles outside Amsterdam, and the Polaks stayed there until the end of the war. A friendly farmer brought them supplies of milk every day. Van Binsbergen successfully hid them in a safe place dug under the floor; in the event that the Nazis launched a raid, the baby would be given a sedative to keep it quiet.

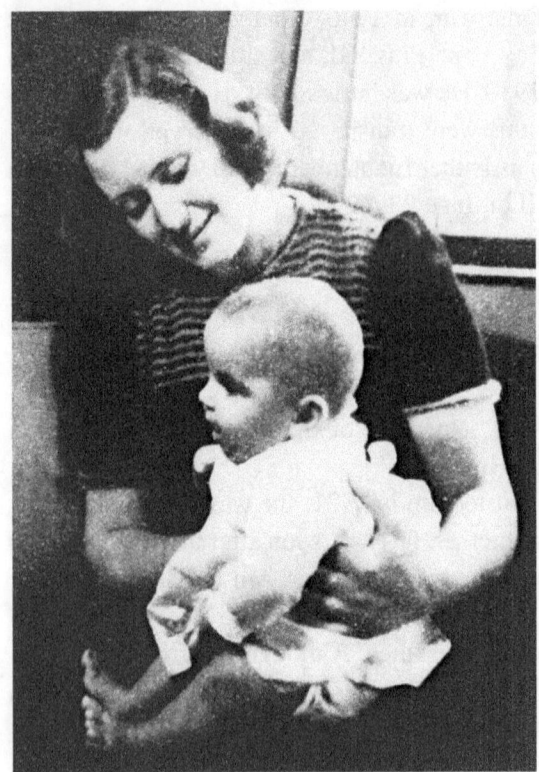

Marion van Binsbergen Pritchard, a social work student and member of the Dutch underground, provided essential items to Jews in hiding before starting her own program of hiding Jewish children. In 1944 she shot and killed a Dutch Nazi whose investigations threatened to expose the Polaks, a Jewish family she had concealed. Here she poses with Erica Polak, the family's infant daughter. (United States Holocaust Memorial Museum, courtesy of Marion Pritchard)

Late one night in 1944 a suspicious Dutch Nazi entered the house looking for Jews after a tipoff from a neighbor. Van Binsbergen, aware that if the family were found they would be sent to a concentration camp, reached for a revolver hidden close by and, without hesitation, shot and killed the officer. Her neighbor and friend Karel Poons, a Jewish ballet dancer, came quickly to her aid. He walked to the village and arranged for the baker to collect the body, while others, including a butcher and an undertaker, also got involved. The body was buried, the Polak family was safe, and there was no follow-up from the authorities.

Van Binsbergen then placed 25 Jewish children with families in an area known as Het Gooi—a place near Hilversum characterized as the home of the rich and famous. On another occasion she pretended to have a child of her own born out of wedlock and registered this Jewish child at the city hall—a deception she repeated on a number of occasions in different towns and cities. Once, when staying as a house guest, van Binsbergen was given a little girl to place with a family. Taking a nap, she awoke to find the woman of the house changing and feeding the baby, without asking questions or giving any sign of denunciation. It underscored van Binsbergen's sense that an underlying sense of right and wrong still prevailed at the time, particularly with regard to protecting innocent children.

During the Holocaust, van Binsbergen safeguarded the lives of between 125 and 150 Jews, most of them children. She used whatever means were at hand; by 1945 she admitted that she "had lied, stolen, cheated, deceived, and even killed."

After the war she moved to Germany to work in displaced persons camps, hoping to learn the fate and possible location of Jewish friends who might have survived the war. It was in one of the refugee camps that she met (and later married) Tony Pritchard, a former U.S. army lieutenant. In 1947 they moved to the United States, where they settled in Vermont and raised a family. There, she lectured extensively about her experiences during the war.

On March 31, 1981, Yad Vashem recognized Marion van Binsbergen Pritchard as one of the Righteous among the Nations, and in 1991 she was made an honorary citizen of Israel. In 1996 she was awarded the Wallenberg Medal from the University of Michigan, **Raoul Wallenberg**'s American alma mater, placing her alongside such other rescuers and upstanders as **Jan Karski**, **Miep Gies**, **Per Anger**, **Heinz Drossel**, and **Nicholas Winton**.

Propper de Callejón, Eduardo (1895–1972)

Eduardo Propper de Callejón was a prominent Spanish diplomat who played an important role in saving a large number of Jews in France during the Holocaust.

Born in 1895, Propper de Callejón came from a mixed background—his Jewish father, Max Propper, was a banker who came from the Czech lands during the time of the Austro-Hungarian Empire, and his Catholic mother, Juana Callejón, was the daughter of a Spanish diplomat. Living in Spain, they raised their children as Catholics.

Joining the Spanish Foreign Ministry at the end of World War I, Propper de Callejón became a diplomat serving in a number of overseas missions, including Brussels and Vienna. His wife, Hélène, was Jewish, the daughter of a banker and related to the Rothschild family. When Spain became a republic in 1931 he left the diplomatic service and remained loyal to the monarchy. During the brutal and bloody Spanish Civil War, waged among various factions between 1936 and 1939, he supported the right-wing nationalist forces of General Francisco Franco. Resuming his diplomatic career after Franco's victory in 1939, he was immediately appointed as first secretary to the Spanish legation in Paris.

France surrendered to Nazi Germany on June 20, 1940. The French government had left Paris, as had the foreign diplomatic corps. Propper de Callejón, along with his wife and children, went to Bordeaux, where the Spanish consulate doors were locked and the consul had left. Thousands of refugees milled around in front of the consulate, hoping to obtain visas to enter Spain and leave France.

Propper de Callejón opened the consulate and began issuing transit visas to the refugees, which would enable them to enter Spain temporarily before moving on to more permanent sanctuaries. He worked nonstop from June 18, 1940, until June 22, 1940, stamping and signing thousands of passports. At one point members of his family visited him in his office only to see him stamping visas with both hands. His son Felipe and daughter Elena recalled their mother putting cold compresses on their father's hands after a marathon day of signing to relieve cramping, and Elena later recalled him saying that these were the most important days of his life.

Throughout the later part of July 1940 Propper de Callejón also worked alongside Portuguese consul-general **Aristides de Sousa Mendes** in Bordeaux, and together they issued tens of thousands of transit visas that would enable Jews to cross Spain and reach Portugal. Moving back to Vichy from Bordeaux, Propper de Callejón continued to provide visas at the newly reestablished embassy there.

Propper de Callejón defied Spanish Foreign Ministry instructions not to issue such visas without prior approval. In doing so he risked his life on account of his Jewish background. In March 1941 Spain's foreign minister, Ramón Serrano Suñer, learned that Propper de Callejón was still issuing visas despite the direct order from Madrid to stop. In response, Serrano Suñer informed José Lucresia, Spain's ambassador to France, that Propper de Callejón would be transferred to Larache, in Spanish Morocco. Lucresia attempted to have the order overturned, citing the fact that Propper de Callejón had been honored with a decoration from the president of Vichy France, Marshal Philippe Pétain. Suñer acted; Propper de Callejón was demoted, and while he would never again hold the rank of ambassador, he continued to serve in the Spanish Foreign Ministry, receiving postings to Rabat, Zurich, Washington, D.C., Ottawa, and Oslo.

Eduardo Propper de Callejón retired in 1965 and died in London in 1972. He never gained public recognition for his heroic acts during his lifetime. A campaign spearheaded by his sister-in-law, Baroness Liliane de Rothschild, and supported by Archduke Otto von Habsburg, led Yad Vashem to investigate his record, and on August 6, 2007, he was recognized as one of the Righteous among the Nations.

The exact number of people he saved will never be known. Records of the Spanish consulate in Bordeaux did not survive, and figures from the Spanish embassy are not recorded. Yad Vashem director Avner Shalev (who called Propper de Callejón the Spanish **Raoul Wallenberg**) has estimated that the figure of both Jewish and non-Jewish he saved would be at least 1,500.

R

Racine, Mila (1921–1945)

Mila Racine was a Jewish resister in France who saved the lives of Jewish children and others by smuggling them across the border from France into Switzerland.

Born on September 14, 1921, in Moscow, she was the daughter of Georges (Hirsch) Racine and his wife Berthe (Bassia). One of three children, she had a brother, Emmanuel, and a sister, Sacha. Fleeing the Soviet Union and a climate of pogroms in the aftermath of the Russian Revolution, the family relocated to France, settling in Paris.

After the Nazi invasion, partition, and occupation of France, the Racine family moved into the Vichy Zone. Mila joined the Resistance on January 5, 1942. While her parents were in a safe house in Nice, Racine and her siblings worked for Éducation Physique (Physical Education), part of the Mouvement de la Jeunesse Sioniste (Zionist Youth Movement, or MJS), as guides helping children reach safety.

Racine, operating under the alias of Marie Anne Richemond, came from a Zionist background and had been an active member of the Women's International Zionist Organization (WIZO). In the summer of 1943 she was given command of a unit of the MJS in Saint-Gervais-Le Fayet (Haute-Savoie) in the Italian zone, covering a region that included Toulouse, Gurs, Saint-Gervais, Nice, and Annemasse, under the overall command of Netanel "Tony" Gryn.

Her activities, particularly around Annecy, saw her working in the "underground railroad" smuggling Jews to Switzerland. After Italy surrendered to the Allies on September 3, 1943, Jews in the alpine region took refuge in Nice. This provided Racine with the opportunity to drive convoys of children and adults to Annemasse, from where they could reach the Swiss border. From then on, she helped hundreds of families and children who fled into her area. From her base in the French Alps, and often working close to German patrols, Racine and the other members of the MJS received children sent from French cities, often many miles distant. In order to protect them, they organized the children into small groups and then accompanied them to the border, where they would be helped by Christian rescuers.

On October 21, 1943, she was conducting a convoy that included 30 children from the city of Nice, accompanied by a male member of the MJS, Roland Epstein. Logistically, this was a difficult group. It comprised children, an older couple, a young mother with a baby, and another couple with a small child. Without warning, they were intercepted by Germans with police dogs at Saint-Julien-en-Genevois. Gunshots rang out; one woman was killed, and another wounded. Racine, Epstein, and the children were taken to Annemasse and incarcerated in the Pax Hotel, the prison at Gestapo headquarters.

Suffering the torment of continual Nazi torture, Racine divulged nothing as they sought information regarding the smuggling operations. The mayor of Annemasse, Jean Deffaugt, managed to visit the prison and arranged with the Nazis to allow some of the children, including a baby of 14 months, to be freed and placed in a nearby children's home. Through the underground movement, he also managed to provide Racine with an escape plan. This was not something she could accept, however, as she had an instinctive feeling that the children (or, perhaps, Deffaugt) would be punished—or worse—if she were to escape.

Racine and Epstein were transferred to the prison at Fort Montluc in Lyon. From there, Epstein was sent to the transit camp at Drancy and then deported to Buchenwald. He lived to see the end of the war. Racine was deported, via the Royallieu transit camp at Compiègne, to Ravensbrück. From there, she was sent to Mauthausen, where she was put to hard labor repairing railways destroyed by Allied bombing. On March 22, 1945, on the eve of liberation, a British air raid targeted Mauthausen. Racine, on *aussenarbeit* (work outside the camp) at the time, was killed by shrapnel.

The work of Mila Racine did not end with her arrest, however. After her capture the MJS sent another resister, **Marianne Cohn**, to replace her in saving the lives of Jewish children. When Cohn, in turn, was captured on the evening of May 31, 1944, she was replaced by **Charlotte Sorkine**. Such importance did the MJS place on the work of these young women that the organization's leaders allowed nothing to stand in the way of their rescue activities, even at the risk of their very lives.

After the war, Racine was posthumously awarded the *Medaille de la Resistance* and the *Croix de Guerre* by the French government. It is perhaps fitting that the recognition she received in Israel, many years later, was for a kindergarten and nursery in Tel Aviv to be named in her memory.

Rémond, Paul (1873–1963)

Paul Rémond was a French Catholic clergyman who rose to become bishop of Nice from 1930 until his death in 1963. During the Holocaust, he continually protested against Nazi antisemitism.

Born on September 24, 1873, in Salins-les-Bains, Franche-Comté, he came from a deeply Catholic family and was the eldest of seven children. He studied at the College of the Brothers of Mary of Besançon before going on to university at the University of Besançon and the University of Freiburg. He earned a doctorate in philosophy in 1899 and a PhD in theology in 1900 at the French Seminary in Rome. In 1899 he received his ordination.

With the outbreak of World War I in 1914 he was mobilized and received rapid promotion, becoming the highest-ranking cleric in the French army. In 1921 he was appointed chaplain general of the Army of the Rhine, and moved to Mainz, Germany. He was appointed bishop of Nice on May 20, 1930.

On April 9, 1933, very soon after the Nazis assumed office in Germany, Rémond delivered a sermon at the Sacre Coeur Cathedral in Paris condemning what he termed "persecution on account of religion," and affirmed his desire to "soften the pain" of the German Jews. In subsequent years he would put these early words into practice time and again.

In May 1940, with France in the thick of the fighting, Rémond visited a number of camps where foreign Jews had been interned, and on the ground that they were refugees and not "enemy aliens," he managed to secure a number of releases. Then, in July 1940, when France capitulated and a new collaborationist government was installed under Marshal Philippe Pétain at Vichy, a majority of French bishops, including Rémond, rallied to the new regime and urged their congregations to support it. This proved to be difficult, in one sense: Rémond was deeply anti-Nazi and thoroughly opposed to the anti-Jewish policies of the Vichy regime. This conflict was never resolved, other than through him constantly supporting initiatives to help Jews while at the same time paying lip service to the regime.

After the establishment of the Vichy regime, antisemitism became institutionalized. On August 26, 1942, 655 Jews of foreign origin were rounded up and interned; 560 were deported to Drancy internment camp on August 31, 1942, from where the majority were deported to Auschwitz. In November 1942 the Italians occupied Nice, but by that stage Rémond was already involved in the rescue of Jews, particularly children. During the summer of 1943 he was approached by **Moussa Abadi**, a Parisian Jewish refugee in Nice, who was in the process of creating a rescue scheme called the Marcel Network. Abadi had learned from an Italian officer about the mass murder of Jews then taking place in Eastern Europe, and he feared it was only a matter of time before German forces occupied Nice and deported the city's Jews. He conveyed this information to Rémond, who immediately agreed to help by offering up the resources of the Church to ensure that all Catholic institutions in the diocese would open their doors, especially to Jewish children.

At the same time he appointed Abadi, under a false name, as inspector-general of diocesan schools. By the time the Germans occupied Nice on September 9, 1943, an arrangement for the rescue of Jewish children was already in place. This led to the rescue of some 527 Jewish children, many of whom were sheltered in the dormitories of Catholic schools. Rémond also intervened personally in helping to save Jews through issuing false baptism certificates.

As anti-Jewish persecution intensified throughout 1943–1944, increasing numbers of children continued to arrive seeking sanctuary. This made it more difficult for the Marcel Network to function efficiently; making the situation even more hazardous was the fact that the Gestapo was aware of Bishop Rémond's activities.

He did not stop his efforts, however, and on one occasion, warned of the situation by one of his priests after a tipoff, he forged additional certificates of baptism and communion, accompanied by a handwritten letter in which he declared himself prepared to intercede with the Gestapo in person to release detained children.

After the liberation of France, Rémond received a number of honors and awards for bravery and humanitarianism in the face of the Nazi terror. These included the *Légion d'Honneur*; the *Croix de Guerre avec Palmes* and two gold and silver stars; and an Order of Leopold from the Belgian government.

Paul Rémond died on Wednesday, April 24, 1963, in Nice, at the age of 79. On December 2, 1991, in one final honor, Yad Vashem in Jerusalem recognized him as one of the Righteous among the Nations.

Ringelblum, Emanuel (1900–1944)

Emanuel Ringelblum was a Polish-Jewish historian best remembered for creating the Oneg Shabbat Archive (also called the Ringelblum Archive) in the Warsaw Ghetto.

He was born in Buchach (then in the Austro-Hungarian Empire) on November 21, 1900. He moved to Nowy Sącz in 1914, and under the influence of two friends, Raphael Mahler and Artur Eisenbach—both of whom would also become noted historians—Ringelblum joined Poale Zion (Workers of Zion), a Marxist-Zionist Jewish workers' movement established across Russia at the start of the 20th century. After the party split in 1920 he moved further to the left and played a major role in the organization's Yiddish cultural work.

In 1927 he earned a doctorate in history from the University of Warsaw, focusing on the history of the Jews of Warsaw during the Middle Ages, and he developed a reputation as an expert on Polish Jewish history from late medieval times to the 18th century. After completing his thesis he taught history at Yehudiya, a private secondary school for girls, before working for the Joint Distribution Committee (JDC).

In November 1938 he was sent by the JDC to the Polish border town of Zbąszyń, where 6,000 Jewish refugees from Germany were huddled with nowhere else to go. They had been expelled from Germany but were forbidden from entering Poland. Ringelblum's task was to coordinate relief efforts for these people—a duty leaving him to reflect on the nature of good and evil, and on helping those in need. He later wrote a book, *Notes on the Refugees in Zbąszyn*, giving a detailed perspective on the situation there.

After the Nazi invasion of Poland in 1939, Ringelblum and his family were forced into the Warsaw Ghetto. It took him little time to realize what he needed to do; he would collect information in secret regarding every facet of life in the ghetto to serve as a comprehensive and permanent record of what the Nazis were doing to the Jews of Warsaw and, by extension, to Poland. He recruited a number of Jewish writers, scientists, and other citizens to work with him in collecting diaries and documents. He organized studies and sent younger people out into the streets to gather posters and announcements pasted around the ghetto.

This all came together under the aegis of what Ringelblum called the Oneg Shabbat (or Sabbath Pleasure) Archive, which he founded in November 1940. He would coordinate and collect materials by day and spend his evenings writing. Overall, his archive would eventually comprise nearly 30,000 individual sheets of data relating to towns, villages, the ghetto, and the resistance movement, as well as whatever was known about other ghettos, the Chełmno and Treblinka death camps, and the effects of starvation and disease on artificially confined civilian populations.

While engaged in these activities, Ringelblum remained active in the day-to-day life of the ghetto, working for the Żydowska Samopomoc Społeczna (Jewish Social Aid), which had been established to assist those suffering from starvation. He organized welfare programs and soup kitchens, and tried to find other ways in which to help combat deprivation. At the same time he also cofounded, with Menahem Linder, the Yidishe Kultur Organizatsye, a society to maintain and advance Yiddish culture in the ghetto.

The gathering of materials for Oneg Shabbat continued at least until late February 1943, when other events overtook the project. The resistance movement had already begun to fight back against the Nazis the month before, and the liquidation of the ghetto seemed imminent. Ringelblum saw that he should attempt to escape if he was to continue his work. Before he did so, however, he made sure that the archive would be protected. It was placed into three large milk cans and several metal boxes. These containers were buried and placed in various parts of the ghetto.

In March 1943 Ringelblum took his family into the Aryan section of Warsaw. After the uprising began on April 19 he returned to the ghetto; captured, he was deported to the Trawniki labor camp, but in August 1943 he managed to escape, helped by a Polish man and Jewish woman. He hid in an underground bunker with his wife, Yehudis; son Uri; and 34 others at Grójecka 81. While in hiding, Ringelblum worked around the clock writing a history of Polish-Jewish relations during World War II, together with essays on key members of the Jewish intelligentsia. These writings, now known as *Notes from the Warsaw Ghetto*, survived and were published after the war.

On March 7, 1944, the Germans discovered the hideout and apprehended all those inside. A few days later Ringelblum, his family, and the other Jews with whom he had been hiding were taken into the ruined ghetto and murdered. Overall, only three members of the Oneg Shabbat survived the war: Hersh Wasser and his wife, Bluma, and Rachel Auerbach.

After the war, people searched for Ringelblum's Archive in the ruins of the ghetto, with mixed results. In September 1946 ten metal boxes were found, and in

December 1950 two of the milk cans were located. Despite repeated searches, the rest of the archive, including the third milk can, was never found.

The Jewish Historical Institute (Żydowski Instytut Historyczny, or ŻIH) is a research establishment in Warsaw dealing primarily with the history of the Jews in Poland. Created in 1947, it was renamed in 2009 in honor of Emanuel Ringelblum. The centerpiece of the collection, the Warsaw Ghetto Archive, is the legacy of Ringelblum's work with Oneg Shabbat, containing about 6,000 documents composed of nearly 30,000 individual sheets. The archive, as well as Ringelblum's own writing, constitutes the most comprehensive repository in existence dealing with the daily experience of the Jews in Warsaw during the Holocaust.

Robota, Roza (1921–1945)

Roza Robota was one of four women hanged at Auschwitz for their role in the revolt of the XII *Sonderkommando* on October 7, 1944.

She was born in 1921 in Ciechanów, Poland. As a youth she was a member of the Zionist youth movement Hashomer Hatzair, and she engaged in underground activities of the movement during the Nazi occupation. When the liquidation of the Ciechanów ghetto was carried out in 1942, she was deported with her family to Auschwitz. She was the only member of the family to survive the selection process; the others were sent directly to their deaths upon arrival. At first she was assigned to the women's camp at Auschwitz I but was transferred to Birkenau later in 1942.

She was assigned to the clothing shed in the Kanadakommando, right next to Birkenau's Crematorium III. Here, the belongings of Jews transported to Auschwitz-Birkenau were sorted before being transported back to Germany for use by German citizens in the war effort. The name "Kanada" was given by the prisoners to this area rich in all manner of items, such as clothing, jewelry, and foodstuffs, because to them the country of Canada symbolized wealth and abundance.

In view of her past membership in Hashomer Hatzair, and given that she was known to some of those working in the Auschwitz underground, Robota was recruited to smuggle a form of gunpowder—*schwartzpulver*—to the men working in the *Sonderkommando* in Crematorium III. She was one of many such women brought into the resistance movement. Others, such as Estusia Wajcblum, Ala Gertner, and Regina Safirsztajn, had already been smuggling small amounts of gunpowder, at enormous personal risk, from their workplace at the Weichsel-Union-Metallwerke, a munitions factory in the Auschwitz complex, to those in the camp proper.

Robota established contact with about 20 women in the Union plant who were willing to cooperate, and over a period of several months they smuggled in the *schwartzpulver*. There were risks—prisoners were often searched when returning from work on *aussenarbeit* (labor outside the camp), though each day they were able to pass on tiny amounts to the men of the underground in matchbox-size quantities.

It took a year and a half of careful preparations before the revolt took place, but there was, unfortunately, never a large enough quantity of powder to enable the prisoners to stage a revolt of sufficient strength. When the men of the *Sonderkommando* rose in rebellion on October 7, 1944, however, enough powder had been accumulated to enable the resisters to blow up Crematorium IV.

The *Sonderkommando* uprising was unexpected, breaking out before a hoped-for general camp revolt. In the chaos, around 600 of the *Sonderkommando* workers broke through the fences separating the crematorium from the rest of the camp, though ultimately all those who escaped were caught and shot.

The Gestapo was brought in after the revolt had been crushed, with the express purpose of tracing the source of the explosives used in the revolt. They were tracked back to the Union plant, and several suspects were arrested. In subsequent days, Robota, Gertner, Wajcblum, and Safirsztajn were arrested and placed in the notorious Block 11, where the kapo Yakov Kozalchik managed to sneak in the occasional visitor. Under brutal torture, they were then subjected to weeks of interrogation. They refused to reveal the names of others who had participated in the smuggling operation and were duly hanged on January 5, 1945—Wajcblum and Safirsztajn at the morning roll-call assembly, and Robota and Gertner in the evening. The executions, only two weeks before the camp was liberated, were held in public, as a warning to the entire camp.

According to some eyewitness accounts, Roza Robota and her comrades shouted "*Nekamah!*" ("Revenge!") to the assembled inmates before they died. Robota's last message was a note in Hebrew, scratched on a piece of paper she managed to smuggle from her cell: "*Chazak V'amatz*"—"Be strong and have courage."

When Roza Robota was executed, she was just 23 years old.

Rosé, Alma (1906–1944)

Alma Rosé, the niece of composer Gustav Mahler, was a renowned virtuoso violinist who resisted the Nazis while appearing to collaborate with them as the driving force and conductor of the women's orchestra at Auschwitz. Through her commitment to excellence and precision, she created an aura of indispensability around the women's orchestra, thereby ensuring the survival of its members—even though this effort was ultimately at the cost of her own life.

She was born in Austria in 1906; her father, Arnold Rosé, led the Vienna Philharmonic Orchestra and the Vienna State Opera orchestra, and a career in violin was mapped out for her from an early age. In 1932 she founded the woman's orchestra Die Wiener Walzermädeln (The Waltz-Girls of Vienna), and in 1930 she married a Czech violin virtuoso, Váša Příhoda (1900–1960), from whom she was subsequently divorced in 1935.

The annexation of Austria by Nazi Germany in March 1938 caught the completely assimilated Rosé family by surprise. Alma Rosé went to London with her father but returned to the Continent and continued performing in the Netherlands. In 1940 she fled to France and went into hiding. She attempted to get to Switzerland but was betrayed and arrested in late 1942. In July 1943 she was deported, via Drancy, to Auschwitz.

In August 1943, in view of her former public profile, she was given the task of leading the Mädchenorchester von Auschwitz (Girl Orchestra of Auschwitz), which had earlier been formed under the leadership of a Pole, Zofia Czajkowska. The orchestra was the initiative of an SS officer, Oberaufseherin Maria Mandel. In recognition of her new role and Mandel's fondness for her pet project, Rosé requested special living and working quarters for the orchestra and demanded an end to playing in all weathers. She also managed to have additional sheet music provided. After her appointment, she began to work on the orchestra's performance. Weaker musicians were removed, though not fired; in order to ensure that they would not be sent back to the barracks, she sought to retain them in auxiliary roles as helpers. The musicians themselves were subject to a strict practice schedule, with entire days given over to rehearsal when they were not performing.

Although the orchestra included two professional musicians—cellist Anita Lasker-Wallfisch and vocalist/pianist Fania Fénelon—it comprised essentially amateur musicians playing a variety of instruments. The orchestra played classical pieces at the main gate each morning when the work gangs went out, and again in the evening when they returned. It also gave weekend concerts for the prisoners and the SS, and entertained at SS functions. It is inconclusive whether or not the orchestra was required to play during gassings, though it is possible the Nazis would have employed their services in order to ease tension among newly arrived prisoners, thereby making the task easier for the SS killers.

As conductor, Rosé had a higher status than the other prisoners, and she was given privileges and comforts such as extra food and a room of her own. She knew that by playing for the Nazis the members of the orchestra were providing a service that extended their lives; she thus worked hard to ensure the highest possible musical standards, the better to retain SS patronage.

A perfectionist, her creative temperament was sometimes taken for egotism and personal ambition. One account, written by Fania Fénelon, controversially portrays Rosé as a coldhearted disciplinarian who abused those around her and bowed before the Nazis. Others, however, have strongly disputed this image, claiming that her ultimate interest was to protect the well-being of the women in her orchestra. This demanded not only that she establish and maintain high musical standards but also that she satisfy the Nazis. Her sponsors among the SS included such camp luminaries as Maria Mandel, camp commandant Josef Kramer, and the infamous Dr. Josef Mengele.

Under her leadership, the orchestra underwent rapid improvement. Rosé varied the program according to the sheet music she had available and wrote orchestrations for the various instruments from memory. Classical works from the great German and Austrian composers were introduced, as she recognized the attraction that the music could have for the camp personnel. This, in turn, could help to guarantee lives; the longer the orchestra was viable and wanted, the greater the possibility that the musicians could stay alive. While the Nazis saw the prisoners as less than human, the prisoners, seeking to retain their humanity in spite of their circumstances, showed that they were not prepared to succumb to the Nazis' designs. Rosé knew this and acted accordingly.

It is understood that all those in the orchestra under Rosé escaped death at the hands of the SS. Among those who survived to recall their experiences, Rosé was generally remembered as a heroine who forced her musicians to work hard in order to save their very lives. Through her actions in conducting this, the only female musical ensemble in the Nazi camps, she was able to save the lives of nearly 50 women.

On April 4, 1944, Alma Rosé died, having fallen ill at a concert given for the SS two days earlier. Speculation surrounds her death; while the most frequently given explanation is food poisoning, typhus has also been offered. Fania Fénelon alleged later that Rosé was deliberately poisoned. In her honor, the SS allowed a service of remembrance to be held on her behalf.

In 1980 a movie was made about the women's orchestra of Auschwitz, *Playing for Time* (directed by Daniel Mann and Joseph Sargent). Based on the memoir of the same name by Fania Fénelon, it stars Jane Alexander as Alma Rosé, Vanessa Redgrave as Fania Fénelon, and Shirley Knight as Maria Mandel.

Rotta, Angelo (1872–1965)

Angelo Rotta was the apostolic nuncio in Budapest when the Holocaust came to Hungary in 1944. An Italian originally from Milan, he was born on August 9, 1872. After attending high school he studied philosophy and theology in Rome and was ordained in 1895. He then held a number of positions in the Church until 1922, when Pope Pius XI appointed him an archbishop. In 1925 Rotta was part of a papal delegation to Costa Rica, Honduras, Nicaragua, Panama, and El Salvador, and later that same year he was apostolic delegate to Istanbul.

With the onset of World War II in September 1939, Rotta began rescue activities immediately. Polish soldiers and Jewish civilians escaping the Nazi onslaught began flooding into Hungary, where they were frequently arrested and imprisoned prior to repatriation back to Nazi-occupied Poland. He began a diplomatic campaign to prevent this, visiting the camps where they were being held in order to demonstrate his support publicly.

Over time, increasing numbers of refugees from the war inundated Hungary, coming from countries all over Eastern Europe. In 1942 Rotta learned of a group of Jewish children who were about to be deported to Poland. Rushing to the camp where the children were being held, he established an orphanage on the spot to protect and hide them. He nominated this as a place "for the children of Catholic Polish officers," knowing that, because they were now under his protection as "Catholic" children, they would be safe—even though they were, in fact, Jewish. Everyone, it seemed, knew of the deception, but when he demanded that the Hungarian authorities provide the children with new, non-Jewish names, they did so without demur. Later, as Vatican representative for Church interests in Bulgaria, he issued false baptismal certificates and visas for Jews to travel to Palestine.

Monsignor Angelo Rotta, apostolic nuncio in Budapest in 1944. After the Nazi invasion of Hungary he organized a covert network of priests and nuns prepared to help Jews. He then played a leading role with other members of the foreign diplomatic community in establishing an "International Ghetto" designed to save Jewish lives, and defied Pope Pius XII by publicly condemning the Nazi treatment of the Jews. (United States Holocaust Memorial Museum, courtesy of Eric Saul)

Before 1944 Rotta's reports to the Vatican provided very detailed intelligence regarding Hungarian antisemitic measures, as well as the level of German interference in the affairs of its Hungarian ally. In 1944 he became nuncio representing Pope Pius XII in Budapest, and he devoted his attention to protecting the Jews. As dean of the diplomatic corps, he actively protested Hungary's mistreatment of the Jews, and after the German invasion of Hungary in March 1944 worked with the Pope to lobby the Hungarian regent, Miklós Horthy, to stop their deportation.

When it became known that Rotta was sympathetic to the Jews, people began besieging the Vatican embassy in the hope that he and his staff might be able to give them assistance. While this was happening, he organized a covert network of priests and nuns prepared to help—knowing that by doing so they were placing themselves at risk by hiding Jews.

Among the activities Rotta undertook was a leading role in a combined Swiss, Swedish, Portuguese, Spanish, and Vatican initiative, together with the International Committee of the Red Cross (ICRC), to establish an "International Ghetto" comprising dozens of apartment buildings into which large numbers of Jews were brought. These became safe houses once the various embassies placed their respective countries' coats of arms on them, and eventually some 25,000 people were saved. The enterprise was the brainchild of the Swiss vice-consul, **Carl Lutz**, and involved such figures as **Giorgio Perlasca, Friedrich Born, Raoul Wallenberg**, and **Ángel Sanz Briz**.

When Freidrich Born from the ICRC asked Rotta if he could find a way to organize some pre-signed blank identity papers bearing the Vatican stamp, these were not only forthcoming but came with Rotta's full backing. Eventually, he was responsible for issuing more than 15,000 safe conduct certificates to Jews and Jewish converts to Christianity. He issued hundreds of baptism certificates to Jews in labor camps and elsewhere, set up and personally protected numerous safe houses throughout Budapest, and even hid two Jews in his own house.

Moreover, he was unceasing in his protests against the deportation and murder of the Hungarian Jews. On November 19, 1944, the Vatican, through Rotta, joined the four other neutral powers in a further collective protest to the Hungarian government, on this occasion calling for the suspension of deportations. Perhaps surprisingly, the call was successful, even though the Hungarian fascists, the Arrow Cross, ignored the government's commitment. They raided the International Ghetto and murdered Jews, even as Soviet forces approached Budapest. Rotta went directly to the Arrow Cross leadership and demanded that the party take control over its members and desist from attacks, deportations, and atrocities against the Jews.

Angelo Rotta utilized his diplomatic position to protest actively against the Holocaust. He was simultaneously an upstander and a resister, on many occasions going directly against the preference of his own cardinal primate, Jusztinián György Serédi, in making public statements condemning the deportations and antisemitic violence. His stance also ran counter to the preferred position of Pius XII, who, it was said, shunned Rotta upon his return to the Vatican in 1945.

With the arrival of Soviet troops, Rotta was expelled from Hungary. He returned to Italy and lived in retirement in the Vatican while serving as a member of the Secretariat of Christian Unity. When Angelo Roncalli, an old friend and colleague, became Pope John XXIII, Rotta was offered a position as a cardinal, but he declined on the grounds that, in his mid-80s, he was too old. He died at the Vatican on February 1, 1965, at the age of 92.

In 1997, more than three decades after his death, Yad Vashem honored him as one of the Righteous among the Nations. Only then did his many acts on behalf of Jews during the Holocaust become public and well known.

Rufeisen, Oswald (1922–1998)

Oswald Rufeisen was a resister in the Mir ghetto in eastern Poland, whose actions led to the escape and survival of more than 200 Jews. He was born as Shmuel Rufajzen in 1922 to a Jewish family living in Zadziele, a small village in Upper Silesia near Oświęcim (Auschwitz), not far from Kraków. As a teenager he belonged to B'nei Akiva, a nonsocialist religious Zionist youth movement.

When Nazi Germany invaded Poland in September 1939, Rufeisen fled with his brother and some friends to eastern Poland, where there was a large Jewish population in Vilna (Vilnius). The country was about to be invaded by the Soviet Union, but beforehand large numbers of Zionist youth arrived from Poland in the hope that they could somehow use the country as a staging post for later migration to Palestine.

After the Soviet takeover, Rufeisen decided to stay. At that point, some visas were made available to nonresidents to leave the country; with a choice to make, Rufeisen gave his place to his younger brother and remained.

In June 1941 Germany launched Operation Barbarossa against the Soviet Union, invading through Soviet-occupied Poland and the Baltic States. Rufeisen was drafted for forced labor, chopping wood in the frozen Ponary Forest just outside the city. Seeking escape, he slipped away quietly with the help of a Polish peasant farmer and began to walk. Finding himself in the small town of Mir in November 1941, and carrying false identity papers, he told the German military police occupying the town that he was a *Volksdeutscher*, that is, an ethnic German. He then talked his way into a job.

At the same time, he also made contact with those who had not fled from the local Jewish community. They had been concentrated in an improvised and sealed ghetto, and Rufeisen informed them of forthcoming Nazi measures. Before this, they had no idea of what was happening outside. He also made contact with the tiny ghetto underground and smuggled in a few weapons from police headquarters.

When he overheard the planned date for the ghetto liquidation, Rufeisen warned his friends inside and falsified his translations in order to get the police out of town; while this was happening he arranged a mass escape for those in the ghetto to flee to the forest, where many joined the partisans. About 200 of the 850 still alive on the night of August 10, 1942, made it into the woods. The rest were slaughtered.

Having been exposed as a Jew and not an ethnic German working for the Nazis, Rufeisen was arrested. Finding a way to escape, he fled the police station and received sanctuary at a nearby convent run by the Sisters of the Resurrection. He hid there until December 1943, on occasion even dressing as a nun when the convent was forced to relocate to another building or when he had to go out in public. While in the convent he decided to convert to Catholicism.

During the winter of 1943–1944 he left the convent and joined a partisan unit in the Naliboki Forest, a large area that was a hotbed of anti-Nazi partisan activity and the center of operations for, among others, **Tuvia Bielski**. He provided a valuable service by translating between the fighters and their German prisoners. At first he was suspected by Soviet partisans, who knew that he had not only cooperated with the Nazis but also had worn a German uniform, but he was saved through the intervention of those he had helped escape from Mir—they identified him and helped clear his name. He then returned to the area just as the Red Army drove out the Nazis and was instrumental in identifying collaborators. This, in turn, led to his involvement with prosecutions against these same collaborators. He also testified against Nazi war criminals. Later, he was decorated by the Soviet Union for his partisan activities.

With the war over in 1945 he returned to his native Poland and began to study for the priesthood. He became a Discalced Carmelite friar, taking the name Brother Daniel, and eventually became a priest. Anti-Jewish measures during and after the Stalinist period of the early 1950s persuaded Rufeisen (who still saw himself culturally as a Jew) to leave Poland. In 1958 he made his way to Israel and applied for citizenship under the Law of Return, which gives Jews the right to immigrate and gain automatic Israeli citizenship. Here he reunited with his brother and survivors from the Mir ghetto.

The Israeli government denied Rufeisen's request for citizenship under the Law of Return on the ground that he was now a Christian and had denied his status as a Jew. Rufeisen appealed the case to Israel's Supreme Court, in what became a celebrated test case regarding Jewish identity. This brought the rabbinate into the equation, as it was the body that adjudicated legal issues relating Jewish identity. The rabbbinate ruled that Rufeisen/Brother Daniel should be given citizenship as a Jew because, having been born to a Jewish mother, his identity remained Jewish irrespective of any faith decisions he had made. The Supreme Court disagreed, ruling in 1962 that a person could not be both a Catholic priest and a Jew. Rufeisen lost his case, and the government's original decision stood.

Nevertheless, he was given permission to enter Israel as a regular immigrant. He later became a naturalized Israeli citizen, and in 1965 he founded the Stella Maris Carmelite Monastery in Haifa; there, he would spend the rest of his life. It was said that from the moment he arrived in Israel those who originally came from Mir accepted him as one of their own.

Oswald Rufeisen died in Haifa in August 1998.

S

Saliège, Jules-Géraud (1870–1956)

Jules-Géraud Saliège was the Catholic archbishop of Toulouse between 1928 and 1956, and he served as a cardinal from 1946 onward. He resisted the Nazi occupation of France and rescued Jews in his region, with the result that he was later honored as one of the Righteous among the Nations by Yad Vashem.

He was born in Saint-Flour in the Auvergne on February 24, 1870, and ordained on September 21, 1895. After a number of junior teaching and canonical roles, rising in position and influence on each occasion, he was called to the colors in 1914 as a military chaplain. In 1917, however, he was caught in a gas attack and had to be discharged. On October 29, 1925, he was appointed bishop of Gap, in the archdiocese of Marseille. Then, on December 17, 1928, he became archbishop of Toulouse.

Immediately after Hitler's accession in 1933 to office in Germany, Saliège began to denounce the antisemitism he witnessed across the border. With the Nazi occupation of France in 1940 he became known for his opposition, condemning the deportation of Jews, compulsory labor service for French citizens, and all other Nazi outrages. His attempts at raising awareness were hampered, however, by the muzzling of a free press, meaning that the only way he could spread his message was through the pulpit and word of mouth.

In mid-August 1942 a meeting was arranged between Saliège and a Jewish communist resistance leader, Charles Lederman. What Lederman told Saliège steeled the archbishop's resolve to do more to help the Jews. Lederman pointed out the existence of the camps, the kidnappings, and the deportations that were being carried out against the Jews of France. This led Saliège to make a firm stand, and on August 23, 1942, he read out a pastoral letter in church and directed that all the parishes of his diocese do the same thing. The text read:

> My very dear brothers,
>
> There is a Christian morality, there is a human morality that imposes duties and recognizes rights. These rights and these duties are the nature of man. They come from God. They cannot be violated. No mortal has the power to remove them.
>
> Children, women, men, fathers and mothers are treated as a vile herd, that members of the same family are separated from each other and shipped to an unknown destination. It was reserved for our time to see this sad spectacle.

Why is there no longer the right of asylum in our churches?
Why are we the defeated?
Lord have mercy upon us.
Our Lady, pray for France.

In our diocese, scenes of horror took place in the camps of Noah and Récébedou. The Jews are men, Jewish women are women. Foreigners are men, foreign women. Everything is not permissible against them, against these men, these women, these fathers and mothers. They are part of the human race. They are our brothers, like so many others. A Christian cannot forget it.

France, beloved fatherland France, you hold for all of your children the tradition of respect for the human person. France chivalrous and generous, I have no doubt, you are not responsible for these horrors.

Receive, my dear brothers, the assurance of my respectful dedication.

Personal Letter from Cardinal Jules-Gérard Saliège. Yad Vashem Archives, O.9/239 (p. 5). AIU, CC-26, CDJC, CCXVIII-72. Reproduced by permission of Yad Vashem Publications.

It was later said that these words gave inspiration to many other members of the Church, such as the Capuchin monk **Père Marie-Benoît**.

The Vichy prime minister, Pierre Laval, ordered that the letter not be published lest the Germans cast doubt on the ability of the Vichy regime to regulate its own affairs. Nonetheless, it was read in several parishes, appeared in *The Catholic Week*, and was broadcast by both Vatican radio and, on August 31, 1942, the BBC. Hundreds of thousands of copies were made and circulated by members of the resistance throughout France, and the address became a call to action across the country.

This notwithstanding, Saliège's resistance to antisemitic persecution was far from widespread in an environment that remained largely loyal to Vichy. Indeed, only five other bishops initially followed his lead, though his statement did signal the start of an opposition movement within the Church in France. By 1943 a number of priests were involved in helping Jews through providing false baptism certificates in their parishes.

While Saliège spoke on numerous occasions condemning Vichy and Nazi antisemitism, he also counseled against acts of physical aggression toward the German occupying forces, arguing that an armistice had been signed in 1940 that—regardless of the political ramifications—should be respected. This was not enough to help him in the long run. On June 9, 1944, the Gestapo arrested him for his pro-Jewish statements, though due to poor health he was released soon after. His arrest was enough to galvanize support around him, however, and he became a further source of inspiration for French anti-Nazis.

On August 7, 1945, he was awarded a *Compagnon de la Libération* medal by the leader of the Free French forces, General Charles de Gaulle, even though he had never been a member of the organized resistance movement. Then, in February 1946, upon his appointment as cardinal, Saliège received another honor, the *Ordre de la Libération*.

Archbishop Jules-Gérard Saliège died in Toulouse on November 5, 1956, and was buried in Saint-Étienne Cathedral, Toulouse. On July 8, 1969, Yad Vashem recognized him as one of the Righteous among the Nations for his leadership and statements on behalf of Jews during the Holocaust.

Salkaházi, Sára (1899–1944)

Sára Salkaházi was a Hungarian Catholic nun who saved the lives of approximately 100 Jews during the Holocaust.

She was born Sára Schalkház in Kassa (Košice) in the Slovak-speaking area of the Habsburg Empire on May 11, 1899. She was the second of three children, and her father died when she was still an infant. A thoughtful and religiously devout child, she began to write plays and short stories as a teenager. As a young adult she earned an elementary school teacher's degree, which was the highest available qualification for women in education at the time. She taught school only for one year, leaving to become a book-binder. Later still, she learned millinery. After this, she turned to journalism.

Politically, she joined the Christian Socialist party of Czechoslovakia and worked as editor of the party newspaper with a specific focus on social problems, especially as they pertained to women. Over time, however, she felt that something was missing until she found solace in religion.

Only after a long personal journey did she decide that her life should be spent in the service of others. In 1929 she entered the Society of the Sisters of Social Service in Budapest, a religious order founded in 1923 by **Margit Slachta** devoted to charitable, social, and women's causes. At Pentecost 1930 she took her first vows, choosing as her personal motto the words "Here am I! Send me!" (Isaiah 6:8). She took her final vows in 1940.

In 1941 Sister Sára, as she was now known, went to Budapest to serve as the national director of the Hungarian Catholic Working Women's Movement. She became editor of the movement's publications and through these cautioned members against the growing influence of Nazism. She also established a network of Working Girls' Homes in order to create a safe environment for working single women.

With the onset of war, political conditions in Budapest became less clear-cut than they were in earlier times. The Arrow Cross party, the Nazi-inspired antisemitic movement in Hungary, began persecuting Jews, and the Sisters of Social Service, in response, commenced a program of providing safe havens for Jews fleeing from harassment. Salkaházi opened up the order's Working Girls' Homes as places of refuge under increasingly dangerous circumstances, and her efforts also extended to the provision of food and other vital goods.

As conditions worsened, she saw by 1943 that there was only one possible option for her to consider; in order to truly live up to the example set by Jesus, she offered her life for the Society of the Sisters of Social Service and its mission. She pledged herself to God as a willing sacrifice to ensure that the other sisters and the order were not harmed. With the intensification of anti-Jewish persecution during 1944, Salkaházi redoubled her efforts to save as many people as she could. Ultimately, the Society sheltered up to 1,000 Jews, with Salkaházi personally responsible for approximately 100 of these.

On the morning of December 27, 1944, armed Arrow Cross troops came to one of the Girls' Homes under Salkaházi's care, looking for Jews. They took four Jewish women and children and a religion teacher, Vilma Bernovits, into custody. Salkaházi was not present at that time, but when she arrived at the home she was immediately detained. Later that night the little group was driven to the Danube Embankment, stripped naked, and shot into the river. It was said that as they were lined up Salkaházi knelt and made the Sign of the Cross. Her body was never recovered.

In 1969, after her nomination by the daughter of one of the Jewish women killed alongside her, Salkaházi was recognized by Yad Vashem as one of the Righteous among the Nations. Further recognizing her martyrdom, Pope Benedict XVI beatified her in a proclamation on September 17, 2003, in the first beatification to take place in Hungary since that of King Stephen in 1083.

In an ongoing tribute to her martyrdom, the Sisters of Social Service hold an annual candlelight memorial service on the Danube Embankment every December 27, the anniversary of Salkaházi's death. It is generally acknowledged that her sacrifice for the Society saved not only many Jews suffering persecution but also the order itself.

Sanz Briz, Ángel (1910–1980)

Ángel Sanz Briz was a Spanish diplomat serving as chargé d'affaires in Budapest between 1942 and 1944. Acting without formal orders from his government, he used all possible resources to save thousands of Jews from being deported to their deaths.

He was born into a merchant family in Zaragoza on September 28, 1910. After studying law in Madrid, he earned a degree in the study of diplomacy in 1936. With the outbreak of the Spanish Civil War that year he enlisted with the rebel Nationalists; in 1939, with the end of the war, he received his first diplomatic posting to the Spanish legation in Egypt. He was later posted to Budapest, arriving in 1942.

While he considered the persecution of Hungary's Jews to be severe at the time of his arrival, he was outraged by their treatment after Germany invaded in March 1944. He offered to supply Jews of Spanish origin with Spanish passports and to negotiate with the Hungarian government for their protection, basing his action on a law made under the Spanish constitution of December 20, 1924, that allowed all Spanish Jews in Europe to apply for Spanish citizenship. Without anything in the way of an official brief, all he had to rely on was a vague instruction from Spanish foreign minister José Félix de Lequerica, who urged Sanz Briz to save "as many as he could." Forced to improvise a plan of his own, therefore, and without the approval of the Spanish or Hungarian governments, he developed a means whereby he could grant Spanish citizenship to Sephardic Jews in Greece, Hungary, Bulgaria, and Romania—all locations in which the Holocaust was playing out.

In the first instance, he offered to give Jews of Hispanic origin Spanish passports. In many cases, "Hispanic" dated back to the expulsion of the Jews from Spain in 1492, but if lineage could be demonstrated satisfactorily then it would be respected. Sanz Briz negotiated with the Hungarian government for the distribution to Jews of 200 Spanish passports, but he changed this unilaterally to 200 *families*, thereby increasing the number of individuals covered substantially. As the situation worsened, he surreptitiously increased this number several times. He adopted the simple expedient of not issuing any documents with a number higher than 200, thereby multiplying the original number many times over. He then finessed this system by adding letter sequences (1A, 1B, 1C, and so on) so that members of the same family, if arrested, would each have an individual permit number.

The next problem he addressed was where to send those protected once their safety was, for the time being, secured. Sanz Briz rented several apartment buildings in Budapest, which he placed under the Spanish flag, marking these buildings as belonging to the Spanish legation. As such, they were protected places, and to reinforce the point he erected signs stating that the buildings were part of the Spanish diplomatic mission. In these "Spanish Houses" he accommodated Jews. As they were forbidden from leaving the buildings, he also provided them with food and other necessities. At the same time, to further safeguard their well-being, he prompted **Friedrich Born** of the International Committee of the Red Cross to place signs in Spanish throughout Budapest wherever there were Jews living under Red Cross aegis, such as on hospital buildings, maternity clinics, and orphanages. The inference here was that these, too, were under Spanish protection.

Through his various efforts, Ángel Sanz Briz, who became known as "the angel of Budapest," saved some 5,200 Jews. Only a minority of these were actually of Spanish origin, as there were only about 500 Sephardic Jews in Budapest prior to the Nazi invasion. He swelled the range of those rescued by including Ashkenazi Jews as "Spanish citizens," first placing them into the "Spanish Houses" and then organizing rudimentary Spanish language lessons so that, if challenged, they could affect a vague Sephardic identity.

Sanz Briz did not act alone in the Budapest diplomatic community; he worked alongside others who were equally determined to save Jewish lives. These included, but were not restricted to, **Raoul Wallenberg** of Sweden; **Angelo Rotta**, apostolic nuncio from the Vatican; and **Carl Lutz** of Switzerland. They were all in constant touch with one another and liaised closely in organizing their various rescue activities.

With the advance of the Red Army on Budapest toward the end of 1944, Sanz Briz was ordered by the government in Madrid to relocate from Budapest to Vienna, and from there move to neutral Switzerland. On December 20, 1944, he left secretly. Before he left, however, he delegated authority to **Giorgio Perlasca**, an employee of the Spanish embassy. Perlasca, an Italian who had fought in the Spanish Civil War, continued the work of Sanz Briz and extended the scope of the rescue operation into 1945. Sanz Briz did not close the embassy—which would have meant that the Jews in the "Spanish Houses" and elsewhere would have immediately lost their protection—but, instead, worked out a plan with Perlasca whereby he was named Spanish consul in situ. The houses remained open, and Perlasca's efforts then guaranteed the lives of their inhabitants. In this way, Spain's record of rescue in Budapest can claim two courageous figures: Sanz Briz, who began the process of saving Jewish lives, and Perlasca, who assured their continued safety.

After the war, Sanz Briz continued his diplomatic career. He worked in a variety of other missions around the world, in such places as San Francisco, Washington, D.C., Bayonne, Guatemala, The Hague, Brussels, and China.

On October 18, 1966, Yad Vashem recognized Ángel Sanz Briz as one of the Righteous among the Nations for his unwavering efforts to save Jewish lives. In 1976 he received his final diplomatic posting when he was sent to Rome as Spain's ambassador to the Vatican, and there, on June 11, 1980, he died at the age of 79. In 1994 the Hungarian government posthumously awarded him the Cross of the Order of Merit.

Schindler, Oskar (1908–1974)

Oskar Schindler is perhaps the best-known rescuer of Jews during the Holocaust by virtue of the multi-award-winning movie *Schindler's List*, made by filmmaker Steven Spielberg in 1993. At his enamelware and munitions factories in Poland, and later in Bohemia-Moravia, Schindler saved more than 1,200 Jews from extermination at the hands of the Nazis.

Born to Johann and Franziska Schindler, née Luser, on April 28, 1908, in Zwittau (Svitavy), Austria-Hungary, Oskar Schindler had an unsettled education which carried over to his early adult years. On March 6, 1928, he married Emilie Pelzl. An opportunist and womanizer, always interested in get-rich-quick schemes that inevitably failed, and with little else going for him, he joined the Abwehr, the German military intelligence network, in 1936. He applied for membership in the Nazi party on November 1, 1938, and in February 1939, five months after the German annexation of the Sudetenland, he was accepted.

Following the German invasion and occupation of Poland, Schindler moved to Kraków in October 1939. Taking advantage of the German occupation program to "Aryanize" businesses in the so-called Generalgouvernment, he purchased an enamelware factory in November 1939 from its Jewish owner, Nathan Wurzel, and reopened it as Deutsche Emalwarenfabrik (German Enamelware Factory), or, by its shortened version, Emalia. He employed Jewish slave labor, at extremely exploitative rates payable to the SS, which he brought in from the Kraków ghetto. After the ghetto's liquidation in March 1943 the Jewish workforce was relocated to the concentration camp at Plaszów, under the command of Amon Goeth.

Oskar Schindler, a German industrialist, war profiteer, and Nazi party member. He saved more than 1,200 Jews from extermination by employing them as forced labor in his factories in Poland and Bohemia-Moravia. Arguably the best known of all rescuers, Schindler is pictured here with his horse at his enamelware factory in Kraków. (United States Holocaust Memorial Museum)

Schindler went to great lengths to ensure the survival of "his" Jews, or *Schindlerjuden,* as they came to be called. Though they were still subject to the draconian and deadly rules and regulations of the concentration camp (and the whims of Goeth's erratic regime), Schindler made constant intercessions on the Jews' behalf, seeing to it that they were neither deported nor killed. He repeatedly demanded that they not be harmed on the grounds that they were essential to the war effort, and with the assistance of his Jewish accountant Itzhak Stern, he managed to keep the prisoners in one place while making it appear as though the factory were performing valuable war work.

It was no surprise at first that Schindler was only interested in making money from his enterprise, but as he witnessed the brutal treatment Jews were experiencing he became more and more disillusioned with Nazi ideology. Over time he became transformed, from the moneygrubbing opportunist he had always been to a humanitarian with a desperate desire to save Jewish lives. The underlying reason for this change of heart has eluded historians, but it can be said with certainty that Schindler was never part of any organized resistance movement or rescue organization, and that he acted from motives that were his alone.

Protecting his workers came at a huge financial cost, but the money Schindler had made as a war profiteer he spent in bribes and expensive presents to Nazi officials. Eventually, he lost count of how much he had spent in protecting "his" Jews. Certainly, it was many millions of Reichsmarks. In trying to ensure that his workers would survive the war, he was prepared to spend all his money. Incurring huge costs in order to protect his workers, Schindler had to engage in illegal business dealings on the black market, for which he was arrested on three separate occasions. He was also twice arrested for *Rassenschande*, or "race shame," after kissing Jewish girls—one of them on the cheek as a gesture of affection and gratitude.

With the advance of the Eastern Front during 1944, many of the concentration camps located in eastern Poland began to close down. Seeing the prospect of this happening to Plaszów, a Jew working as Goeth's personal secretary, Mietek Pemper, informed Schindler that all factories not directly involved in the war effort, including his factory camp, were at risk. He then proposed that Schindler would be more secure if he were seen to be producing armaments instead of pots and pans. Accordingly, in October 1944 Schindler sought permission to relocate his factory to Brünnlitz (Brněnec) in Moravia and resurrect it as an arms factory, taking as many of his "highly skilled workers" as possible with him. Permission was granted, and the factory became reestablished as a subcamp of Gross-Rosen.

Pemper then compiled a list of people who, it was argued, had to go to Brünnlitz. The names were provided by a corrupt member of the Kraków Jewish police, Marcel Goldberg, who identified 1,000 of Schindler's workers and 200 from the textile factory of a Viennese businessman in Kraków, Julius Madritsch. The lists were typed up by Goldberg; contrary to popular wisdom, Schindler was not present when this took place. Nonetheless, all were sent to Brünnlitz: 800 men deported by the SS from Plaszów via Gross-Rosen, and just over 300 women who went from Plaszów via Auschwitz, were rescued at the last moment from gassing by the timely arrival of Schindler's secretary, Hilde Albrecht, who came armed with bribes of black market goods, food, and diamonds.

Once the Jews were relatively safe at Brünnlitz, compared to the fate that would likely have greeted them at Plaszów, Schindler worked at ensuring that his charges remained secure by continuing to bribe the SS and other Nazis, some of whom had an eye for profit; others had an ideological commitment to keep the Jews working unto death.

By the time Brünnlitz was liberated by the Russians on May 9, 1945, Schindler was bankrupt, and as a member of the Nazi party who was perceived as a war profiteer and exploiter of slave labor, he was on the run. He smuggled himself and his wife, Emilie, back into Germany, where they settled in Regensburg and kept a low profile.

They stayed there until 1949, when they migrated to Argentina. There, just as before the war, he failed in his business ventures. His marriage broke down, and in 1957 the couple separated. In 1958 he returned to Germany alone.

On July 18, 1967, for his efforts in rescuing more than 1,200 Jews during the Holocaust, Schindler was recognized by Yad Vashem as one of the Righteous among the Nations. His wife was similarly recognized on June 24, 1993. Oskar Schindler died, penniless, on October 9, 1974, in Hildesheim, Germany. Later, he was buried in Jerusalem on Mount Zion. He was the only member of the Nazi party ever to be so honored.

In 1980 Australian novelist Thomas Keneally learned about Schindler from Leopold (Poldek) Pfefferberg, a Schindler Jew. The result was a fictionalized account of the story, *Schindler's Ark*, which appeared in 1982. In the United States the book was published as *Schindler's List*. The book was later adapted for the screen by Steven Spielberg using the American title, to immense critical and popular acclaim. The film won seven Academy Awards, including Best Picture, and Liam Neeson was nominated as Best Actor for his portrayal of Schindler.

Because of the high profile accorded Schindler as a result of the movie, and a vast array of books and documentaries that followed, his name has become a byword for rescue during the Holocaust—such that one of the highest accolades given today to a rescuer is that he or she is "the Oskar Schindler" of a given situation.

Schmeling, Max (1905–2005)

Max Schmeling was a German heavyweight boxer who risked his life to save two young Jewish brothers by hiding them in his hotel room, and then helping them escape Germany during the *Kristallnacht* pogrom of November 1938.

Of modest background, the son of a sailor, Maximilian Schmeling was born in Klein-Luckow, Germany, near Hamburg, on September 28, 1905. From a young age his life was to be that of a boxer. He turned professional in 1924 at age 19 and won the German light heavyweight title two years later. On June 19, 1927, he won the European light heavyweight title, and then the German heavyweight crown. He soon went to the United States, where he had his first American fight at Madison Square Garden against Joe Monte on November 23, 1928. He won by knockout. The following year, also in New York, Schmeling signaled his intentions by defeating a pair of top heavyweights, Johnny Risko and Paulino Uzcudun.

With these victories, he moved to the number-two ranking and a shot at the heavyweight title. At that time the crown was vacant, and Schmeling met Jack

Sharkey to settle the title. They met on June 12, 1930, and Schmeling won when Sharkey was disqualified in the fourth round after delivering a low blow. This became the only occasion in boxing history when the heavyweight championship was won by disqualification.

In April 1933, not long after Adolf Hitler became chancellor of Germany, he summoned Schmeling—by now his favorite athlete—for a private dinner meeting with himself, Hermann Göring, Joseph Goebbels, and other Nazi officials. In discussion, he told Schmeling that when he was in the United States he should inform the American public that reports of Jewish persecution in Germany were untrue. When Schmeling arrived in New York he complied, saying that there was no anti-semitism in Germany and emphasizing the point that his manager, Joe Jacobs, was Jewish. Few were convinced, particularly as Hitler had banned Jews from boxing soon after he and Schmeling had met.

In July 1933 Schmeling married a blond, beautiful Czech movie star, Anny Ondra, and the two became Germany's most glamorous couple. The same year, Schmeling lost the title in a rematch with Sharkey after a controversial 15-round split decision, followed by defeat at the hands of Max Baer before a crowd of 60,000 at Yankee Stadium in June 1933. His loss was deemed a "racial and cultural disgrace" by the Nazi propaganda newspaper *Der Stürmer*, which considered it outrageous that Schmeling would even have deigned to fight a "non-Aryan." Baer's father was Jewish, and Baer himself fought wearing shorts emblazoned with a Star of David.

By this stage Schmeling was viewed as a something of a Nazi puppet, when not being accused of sympathizing with Nazism. On March 10, 1935, he fought and knocked out American boxer Steve Hamas in Hamburg. At this, the 25,000 spectators spontaneously stood and sang the *Horst Wessel* (the Nazi anthem), with arms raised in the Hitler salute. This caused outrage in the United States, with Schmeling now being publicized in Germany as the very model of Aryan supremacy and Nazi racial superiority, something he would detest all his life.

During the 1936 Olympics in Berlin, Schmeling requested from Hitler a promise that all American athletes would be protected, which Hitler respected. Around this time, the German dictator also began pressuring Schmeling to join the Nazi party, which would have made a wonderful propaganda coup for the regime. Not only did Schmeling refuse but he also turned down every inducement to stop associating with German Jews or to fire Joe Jacobs as his manager.

Nonetheless, the German propaganda machine still found enough traction in Schmeling to retain him as a propaganda model of Aryan supremacy. The U.S. public also wanted Schmeling, but for the opposite reason. Rather than celebrating him, many in the United States hoped he would come back for another fight, and lose—this time to the young American hero, the "Brown Bomber," Joe Louis. As Schmeling's record of late had not been strong, he went into the fight a 10-1 underdog, and many people thought that at 30 years of age he was past his prime.

On June 19, 1936, the fight took place at Yankee Stadium. Schmeling had studied his opponent's technique closely and found a weakness in his defense. In the 12th round, he scored what some consider the upset of the century, when he sensationally knocked Louis out. In Germany, the Nazi press—to Schmeling's dismay—boasted of the victory as representing white Aryan supremacy. When he returned to Berlin, he was invited by Hitler to join him for lunch.

A rematch at Yankee Stadium, on June 22, 1938, was arguably the most famous boxing bout in history. The fight had huge implications, plain for all to see. It became a cultural and political event, billed as a battle of the Aryan versus the Negro, a struggle of evil against good. Held before a crowd of more than 70,000, the match saw a determined and highly motivated Joe Louis knock Schmeling out within two minutes and four seconds of the first round. Schmeling later said that although he was knocked out in the first round and shipped home on a stretcher with a severely damaged spine, he was relieved that the defeat took Nazi expectations off him. It made it easier for him to refuse to act as a Nazi, and he was shunned by Hitler and the Nazi hierarchy for having "shamed" the Aryan Superman ideal.

Max Schmeling, German heavyweight boxer and world champion from 1930 to 1932. In an illustrious career, he twice fought the American Joe Louis (1936 and 1938), for one win apiece. He incurred the wrath of Adolf Hitler by consistently refusing to join the Nazi party, and rejecting demands to fire his American-Jewish manager, Joe Jacobs. (Bettmann/Corbis)

On the night of November 9, 1938, as antisemitic mobs were sacking Jewish property throughout the Reich, Schmeling's opposition to Nazism was tested as never before. One of his friends, a Jew named David Lewin, was a tailor at Prince of Wales, the shop where Schmeling bought his suits. As the *Kristallnacht* intensified throughout the night, Lewin asked Schmeling to shelter his two sons, Heinz and Werner, ages 14 and 15, respectively. Without hesitation, Schmeling took them to his room in the downtown Excelsior Hotel and kept them there for three days. He told the desk clerk that he was ill and must not be disturbed. After things settled down, he drove them to his house for further hiding; waiting another two days, he then delivered them to their father. In 1939 Schmeling helped the family to flee the country altogether. They went to the United States where one of them, Henri Lewin, became a prominent hotel owner in Las Vegas.

For his part, Hitler never forgave Schmeling for losing to Louis, especially given the circumstances, or for refusing to join the Nazi party. During World War II he saw to it that at the age of 35 Schmeling was drafted as an elite paratrooper into the Luftwaffe, where he served during the Battle of Crete in May 1941. It was said that the Führer took a personal interest in sending the former champion on suicide missions.

After the war, Schmeling tried to reinvigorate his boxing career. He fought five times, but in May 1948 he was beaten by Walter Neusel, whom he had defeated in a classic match several years earlier. This was his last fight. Across his career, Schmeling's record read as 70 fights for 56 wins (40 by knockout) and 4 draws.

In retirement, Schmeling became one of Germany's most revered and respected sports figures. He remained popular not only in Germany but also in America. He was awarded the Golden Ribbon of the German Sports Press Society and became an honorary citizen of the City of Los Angeles. In 1967 he published his autobiography, *Ich Boxte mich durchs Leben*, later published in English as *Max Schmeling: An Autobiography*.

In 1957 he bought a Coca-Cola dealership, from which he derived much financial success. This enabled him to become one of Germany's most beloved philanthropists. He became friends with many of his former boxing opponents, in particular Joe Louis. He would often help out Louis financially, and their friendship lasted until the American's death in 1981, when Schmeling, in a final tribute, paid for the funeral.

On February 28, 1987, Schmeling's wife of 54 years, Anny Ondra, died. In 1992 he was inducted into the International Boxing Hall of Fame, though sadly he was never honored by Yad Vashem as a Righteous Gentile for his actions during the *Kristallnacht* of November 1938. No one, it seems, ever nominated him.

Max Schmeling was a man in conflict with both the Hitler regime and the racial policies of Nazism. The degree of resistance he showed was built around a sense of what it was to be a decent human being. On February 2, 2005, he died at the age of 99, at his home in Hollenstedt, near Hamburg.

Schmid, Anton (1900–1942)

Anton Schmid, an Austrian soldier serving in the Wehrmacht during World War II, resisted the Holocaust through the saving of Jews—and was executed as a result. He was born in Vienna in 1900, married his wife, Stefi, and had a daughter. An electrician by trade, he owned a radio shop and lived a comfortable life in Vienna by the time he reached early middle age.

Having been drafted into the German army after the *Anschluss* with Austria, he was mobilized upon the outbreak of war in September 1939. He was sent first to Poland, and then, after the Nazi invasion of the Soviet Union in June 1941, to Nazi-occupied Lithuania. By the autumn of 1941, promoted to sergeant, Schmid was stationed near Vilna (Vilnius).

Witnessing the creation of the Vilna ghetto in September 1941, Schmid soon learned what the fate of the Jews was to be. Mass killings had already been taking place since July 1941, and they continued throughout the summer and fall. By the end of the year, Einsatzgruppen units and their Lithuanian allies in the Ponary Forest near Vilna had murdered some 21,700 Jews. Schmid was appalled, particularly as he saw children being beaten in front of him. From his perspective, it was unthinkable not to find a way to go to the Jews' aid.

Schmid's assignment in Vilna saw him commanding a unit responsible for reassigning soldiers who had been separated from their detachments. He was based at the Vilna train station; from there, he saw a great deal of the treatment meted out to Jews, and he lost no opportunity in using his position to ease their situation. He took them off the trains and employed them as workers, arranged for some to be released from prison, organized new papers for others, and even—at immense personal risk—sheltered Jews in his office and personal quarters.

Among those he hid were Herman Adler and his wife, Anita, both members of Vilna's prewar Zionist movement. Through them, Schmid met with a leader of the nascent Jewish resistance movement in the ghetto, **Mordechaj Tenenbaum**. The result saw him smuggling Jews out of Vilna to other Jewish cities such as Białystok—places where it was thought the Jews could have a better chance of survival. Schmid also acted as a conduit enabling various resistance groups to establish contact with each other.

Ultimately, Schmid's actions in hiding Jews, supplying them with false papers, and arranging their escapes managed to save the lives of up to 250 men, women, and children. Within resistance circles, news of his activities on behalf of Jews spread; inevitably, he began to be watched more closely by Nazi authorities. The knowledge that he could be found out only emboldened him to work on behalf of Jews with greater determination and audacity. Inevitably, though, he was found out. In the second half of January 1942 he was arrested and on February 25 was summarily court-martialed for high treason. The death penalty was only the possible outcome of such a trial, and on April 13, 1942, he was duly executed by firing squad.

Anton Schmid was an extremely brave human being. He clearly knew that he was placing himself in danger through his actions, and that, if caught, his fate would be sealed. For all that, however, he did not see anything particularly special in what he did. In his last letter to his wife, Stefi, written from his prison cell prior to execution, he claimed, "I only acted as a human being and did not want to hurt anyone." His actions had an unfortunate outcome for his wife—she lost not only her husband but also his income, his pension, and the benefits of a war hero's death. When word got back to Vienna, her neighbors shunned her, referring to her husband as a traitor and socially ostracizing her. At one point her windows were smashed.

The lifesaving deeds of Anton Schmid had another outcome, however, when, on May 16, 1967, Yad Vashem in Jerusalem recognized him as one of the Righteous among the Nations. Stefi Schmid received the award personally, having flown to Jerusalem for the occasion.

Then, on May 8, 2000, the German government named a military barracks in Schmid's honor in Rendsburg, northern Germany, as the Feldwebel-Schmid-Kaserne. At the naming ceremony Germany's defense minister Rudolf Scharping said: "We are not free to choose our history, but we can choose the examples we take from that history. Too many bowed to the threats and temptations of the dictator, and too few found the strength to resist. But Sergeant Anton Schmid did resist."

Schmitz, Elisabeth (1893–1977)

Elisabeth Schmitz was a German Protestant anti-Nazi resister, mainly remembered for writing an important memorandum in 1935 on the situation of the German Jews, in which she predicted accurately their fate under the Nazis.

She was born on August 23, 1893, in Hanau, Hessen, the youngest of three daughters of August Schmitz, a schoolteacher, and Clara Marie, née Bach. She was educated in Hanau and Frankfurt am Main, and then went on to study at the Universities of Bonn and Berlin until, having studied under the noted historian (and antisemite) Friedrich Meinecke, she graduated in 1921 with a doctorate in history. She was also a first-rate student of theology. While her preference would have been to become a pastor, this was not an option available to women at the time, and so, frustrated, she instead became a teacher. She lived in Berlin between 1915 and 1943, witnessing firsthand in the German capital World War I, the fall of the Imperial monarchy, the Weimar Republic, the rise of National Socialism, and World War II.

On April 1, 1929, she was hired to teach at the elite Luisengymnasium Berlin. After the ascent of the Nazis to office in 1933, the school's socialist director was dismissed, and Schmitz was appointed in his place. Because of her own rejection of National Socialist ideas, however, she landed in trouble and was discharged as director in 1935.

As early as 1933 it was clear to her where Nazi antisemitism was leading, and through the Evangelical Church she attempted to raise awareness of this potential. Her philosemitism stemmed from her recognition that Judaism was the essential foundation of Christianity and that for this, if for no other reason, the Jewish people needed to be respected and protected.

In 1934 Schmitz became a member of the Confessing Church. Earlier, she had conducted a correspondence with the Swiss theologian Karl Barth, a correspondence that continued for several years. She also paid him several visits in Switzerland. Her major focus was on persuading him to make a public statement on the Jewish question and to condemn Nazi antisemitism, but he declined on the grounds that the Jewish question was just one part of a much bigger issue, the very nature of Nazism itself.

In 1935 she wrote a memorandum on the overall situation of the Jews under Nazism and urged the Church to stand up to antisemitic discrimination. She completed it in September 1935, providing numerous examples of the plight of the Jews and exposing how extensively their persecution had penetrated German society. She showed how antisemitism had become both institutionalized and socialized, involving government agencies at all levels, together with neighbors, colleagues, business partners, and teachers. She wrote: "For the past two and a half years a severe persecution has been inflicted on a portion of our people because of their racial origin, including a portion of our own parish membership. The victims of this persecution have suffered dreadful distress both outwardly and inwardly but this is not widely known, which makes the guilt of the German people all the more reprehensible." To reduce the risk of persecution against those found with the memorandum in their possession, she wrote it anonymously but directed it at the senior members of the Church hierarchy.

The memorandum was unique on several levels, not the least of which was that it was written by a woman calling for opposition to the Nazis' anti-Jewish agenda. Written early within the span of the "Thousand Year Reich," it blatantly charged Church members with assuming their moral responsibilities under the teachings by which they professed to live. Finally, the Schmitz memorandum referred not only to Jews who had been baptized but also to all persecuted Jews regardless of their religious status.

In attempting to submit the memorandum to the Third Confessing Synod on September 26, 1935, she aimed to cause such a stir that a public protest against antisemitic persecution would follow, but the issue was not discussed until she had written an addendum in the aftermath of the Nuremberg Laws, passed earlier in September. When the new version was presented on May 8, 1936, drawing attention to the devastating consequences of these new laws, it failed to gain any support and achieved no practical effect in Church policy.

Due to the memorandum's anonymous authorship, it was ascribed for many years to another philosemitic (and outspoken) member of the Confessing Church, Marga Meusel. It was not until 1999 that Schmitz's authorship was recognized, after a large packet of hitherto unseen documents (including the original first draft) was discovered in Hanau following her death.

After the November Pogrom took place on the night of November 9–10, 1938, Schmitz saw the writing on the wall. She knew instinctively that her days as a schoolteacher were numbered since she refused to compromise her educational standards in favor of Nazi classroom indoctrination. Neither the Nazis nor Elisabeth Schmitz was capable of accommodating the other. As a result she resigned her duties as a teacher, and at the age of 45 asked to be allowed to take early retirement. The request was granted, and she was even awarded a small pension.

From then on, Schmitz sought to make a difference in other ways—mostly by giving short-term refuge to Jews needing a safe house overnight. One such refugee was Karl Mühlfelder (later Charles C. Milford), whose father had been picked up and detained in the former Jewish community center at Rosenstrasse in February–March 1943, and whose mother had joined the protests there. For others, she provided money and donated her ration cards. She tried to provide any assistance she could to protect Jews from the threat of deportation, particularly from the spring of 1943 onward, when the Jews of Berlin were especially targeted.

In 1943 Allied bombing destroyed her apartment, and she was evacuated from Berlin back to her parents' home in Hanau. She stayed there after the war and resumed teaching, finally retiring for good in 1958.

As a fighter against the Nazi regime, Schmitz tried desperately to raise consciousness of what the Nazis represented for the Jews of Berlin—and Germany was a whole—and cried out continually for Protestant Christianity to heed her warnings. On September 10, 1977, she died at the age of 84. Sadly—and shamefully—only seven people attended her funeral. In October 2011, in recognition for her efforts to save Jewish lives during the Holocaust, Elisabeth Schmitz was acknowledged by Yad Vashem as one of the Righteous among the Nations.

Scholl, Hans and Sophie (1918–1943 & 1921–1943)

Hans Scholl and his sister Sophie were a brother and sister at the forefront of organizing a resistance movement against the Nazi regime within Germany during World War II. The movement, known as the Weisse Rose (the White Rose), was largely centered on the University of Munich, where the Scholls were students.

Hans Scholl was born on September 22, 1918, in Ingersheim, the second of six children. Sophie Scholl was born on May 9, 1921, in Forchtenberg. Hans joined the Hitler Youth (Hitlerjugend), and Sophie joined the League of German Girls (Bund Deutscher Mädel), soon after Adolf Hitler came to power in 1933, and at first they were enthusiastic supporters of the Nazi regime. Their parents, however, were far less enamored with the Nazis and expressed their dissatisfaction to others.

The younger Scholls became increasingly disenchanted with the Nazi party during their years at the University of Munich. Hans became a medical student, and Sophie studied biology and philosophy. By the early 1940s they had developed a

Hans and Sophie Scholl, a brother and sister who, with others, organized the White Rose, an anti-Nazi movement centered among students at the University of Munich. They produced and distributed a series of leaflets condemning Nazism and calling on the German people to rise up against it. Hans and Sophie, together with Christoph Probst, were executed on February 22, 1943; others were later caught and also executed. (ADN/dpa/Corbis)

belief that Hitler and the Nazis were ruining the German nation and engaging in atrocities against Jews and others. They had also come to realize that all Germans had a duty to object to their government's policies and activities, and their attitudes were reinforced at home; in 1942 their father, Robert Scholl, was arrested for publicly doubting Germany's ability to win World War II.

In 1942, with a group of fellow students including Christoph Probst, Willi Graf, and Alexander Schmorell, and their professor Dr. Kurt Huber, the Scholls helped to spearhead the White Rose. The group members began posting and mailing various antigovernment posters and literature that publicized the atrocities perpetrated by Hitler's government, and they urged Germans to resist the government and its policies. One of those who met with them and assisted briefly in these early days was a Swedish Red Cross delegate, **Sture Linnér**.

The focus of these statements was a series of numbered pamphlets campaigning for the overthrow of Nazism and the revival of a new Germany dedicated to the pursuit of goodness and founded on the purest of Christian values. The group's opposition to Adolf Hitler and the Nazi party was essentially based on religious morality and humanitarianism, with little, if any, overt political motivation.

The name of their movement came from a novel that had inspired the Scholls when they were young. Their initial pamphlet, the first in a series of six, was secretly published in June 1942. The pamphlets attracted public attention, and copies were made and distributed widely. Problems arose regarding state-regulated supplies of paper and ink, which could only be overcome illegally, but eventually White Rose pamphlets were dispersed throughout Germany and Austria, denouncing the activities of the Nazi party and decrying the murder of innocent German citizens, including Jews. The activities of the group quickly drew the attention and ire of the Gestapo. Hans Scholl, Christoph Probst, and others were sent to fight on the Russian front from the summer of 1942 onward, exposing them to the horrors of the Holocaust and other wartime atrocities. This only encouraged their efforts to resist Nazi authority when they returned to Germany.

The range of the White Rose group expanded beyond the University of Munich. Students at the University of Hamburg also joined, and at its peak membership reached about 80 adherents.

In mid-February 1943 the White Rose arranged a small anti-Nazi demonstration in Munich. The members' ideals inspired them to an ever-increasing number of daring acts, such as a run through the buildings of the university during which leaflets condemning the Nazis were scattered liberally in the hallways. On February 18, 1943, a janitor who was a Nazi party member, Jakob Schmid, spotted the Scholls scattering copies of the sixth pamphlet from a balustrade in the atrium of the university. He raised the alarm, called the Gestapo, and had the Scholls and Probst arrested.

They were sent for a summary trial in the Volksgerichtshof (People's Court) on February 22, 1943, and stood before Judge Roland Freisler, who berated them for their activities. They were quickly indicted for treason, and, defiantly, they admitted their crimes. Inevitably found guilty, Hans and Sophie Scholl, together with Christoph Probst, were executed by beheading the same day. It was noted by witnesses that all three faced their deaths bravely, with Hans claiming as his last words, "Long live freedom!" Hans Scholl was 24, Sophie Scholl was 21, and Probst was 22. From arrest to execution took only four days.

Shortly afterward, numerous others associated with the White Rose were denounced, identified, and arrested by the Gestapo. Later that same year, other executions took place. Alexander Schmorell (age 25) and Dr. Kurt Huber (age 49) were both executed on July 13, 1943, and Willi Graf (age 25) on October 12, 1943. Another member, Hans Conrad Leipelt, who helped distribute the sixth leaflet in Hamburg, was executed on January 29, 1945, at the age of 23. Most of the other students convicted for their part in the group's activities received prison sentences; many were consigned to concentration camps.

The text of the sixth White Rose leaflet was picked up by **Helmuth James Graf von Moltke** and smuggled out of Germany, through Scandinavia, to the United Kingdom. In July 1943 tens of thousands of copies were air-dropped over Germany as "The Manifesto of the Students of Munich."

The White Rose movement and the story of the Scholls became the subject of numerous depictions in literature and film, most notably in two movies: *Die Weiße Rose* (directed by Michael Verhoeven, 1982), and *Sophie Scholl, Die letzten Tage* (directed by Marc Rothemund, 2005).

In death, the members of the White Rose became a spur to other anti-Nazi groups as well as to the political left throughout Germany. After World War II the movement began to be seen by Germans as an admirable example of resistance to evil. The Scholls have become revered as among Germany's greatest heroes (particularly among younger Germans), with the White Rose Foundation and White Rose International serving as contemporary organizations that seek to preserve the memory of the group and continue its tradition of "principled resistance."

The bravery of the Scholls and their friends has come to represent individual sacrifice in the midst of unspeakable oppression and evil.

Schonfeld, Solomon (1912–1984)

Solomon Schonfeld was a British rabbi who rescued thousands of Jews from Nazism before, during, and after the Holocaust.

Born on February 21, 1912, he was the son of Rabbi Dr. Victor Schonfeld. He studied at a yeshiva in Nitra, Czechoslovakia, where he was the student of Rabbi **Chaim Michael Dov Weissmandl**, who would later play his own part in the rescue of Jews in Slovakia. In 1940 Schonfeld married Judith Hertz, daughter of the chief rabbi of the United Kingdom, Dr. Joseph Hertz.

When Schonfeld was just 22 years of age he became rabbi of the Adath Yisroel synagogue in North London, succeeding his father and at the same time becoming principal of the Jewish Secondary School, the first Jewish day school in Britain.

In the aftermath of the November pogrom known as *Kristallnacht* (November 9–10, 1938), Julius Steinfeld, the head of Vienna's Agudath Israel community, contacted Schonfeld with the desperate plea that arrangements be made for a transport of children—a so-called *Kindertransport*—for as many Orthodox Jewish children as possible from Austria and Germany to Britain. Schonfeld met with Yacob Rosenheim and Harry Goodman, respectively the founder and secretary of World Agudath Israel, to discuss what could be done. Traveling to Vienna, Schonfeld helped Steinfeld organize a *Kindertransport* of close to 300 children.

Prior to the transport leaving, Schonfeld arranged for 1,200 German rabbis and other Jewish religious leaders, together with their families, to be brought to the UK. In this endeavor, he was helped by his appointment as executive director of a new organization, the Chief Rabbi's Religious Emergency Council (CRREC), which had been established by his father-in-law, Chief Rabbi Hertz, in 1938. In the years that followed, Schonfeld developed excellent relationships with certain

British officials who tried to offer him their support despite the more negative mood prevailing in Whitehall at this time.

Schonfeld personally rescued thousands of Jews. In the summer of 1942 he negotiated with the Colonial Office to issue more than 1,000 visas for Jews to enter the island of Mauritius. None arrived, but it was an indication of just how far he was prepared to go to secure some sort of protection for Jews. As it turned out, many of those with such papers managed to enter Palestine instead, having already been granted access to a British territory.

Schonfeld was also highly creative. In December 1942 he organized broad support within Parliament for a motion asking the government to declare that Britain would be prepared to offer temporary refuge within the British Empire for Jews desperate to leave Nazi-occupied Europe. The declaration also invited other Allied governments to consider similar action. It received broad support and was endorsed by senior Christian clergy and leading aristocrats in the House of Lords. It ultimately gained the backing of 177 members of Parliament, and although it failed in an overall vote, it was a strong indication of the kind of initiative Schonfeld was able to make, and of how far the reach of his efforts extended.

All in all, Rabbi Schonfeld arranged for more than 4,000 Jewish children to be brought to the UK, in addition to the religious leaders already mentioned. As an Orthodox rabbi, he sought to keep Orthodox children together in Orthodox homes whenever possible, while at the same time providing them with a Jewish religious education. To help achieve this, he established an organization called the National Council for Religious Education and then, in 1944, founded a new school, the Hasmonean High School, to help in furthering his religious day school aims. Among those he also sought to help were youths aged 16 to 18, who were ineligible for the *Kindertransports*. He brought them to the UK on the pretext that they were going to be studying in Jewish religious seminaries.

Schonfeld was a rabbi who lived his vocation and his faith. In 1940, after the refugees arrived in the UK and many were interned as "enemy aliens," he made a number of official visits to internment camps; he organized religious events for the Jewish festivals; and he worked to ensure that an uninterrupted supply of kosher food was available for those who were observant. Then in 1943 he amassed a treasure-trove of tinned kosher food in preparation for postwar distribution to the expected influx of survivors from Nazi Europe—at a time when the Holocaust was still raging and there was no certainty that any survivors would be left to feed.

After the war, Schonfeld rescued hundreds more Jewish children who had been living in hiding during the conflict. Many of them came from the communist-dominated countries of Eastern Europe. He also went into the displaced persons' camps searching for survivors, and brought many out.

Rabbi Schonfeld was something of a maverick both as a rabbi and a rescuer. He worked independently of any political or religious group, and preferred to work as a one-man committee. His successes can be measured in the thousands—a most remarkable case of what could be done to rescue Jews during the Holocaust when political considerations did not cloud the will and necessity to save lives.

Rabbi Solomon Schonfeld died of a long-term brain tumor, at the age of 72, on February 6, 1984. In 2013 he was recognized as a British Hero of the Holocaust.

Segerstedt, Torgny (1876–1945)

Torgny Segerstedt was a Swedish journalist who served as editor in chief of the newspaper *Handelstidningen*, one of Sweden's leading liberal newspapers, between 1917 and 1945. The son of a teacher, he was born in Karlstad in 1876 and educated at Lund University, where he taught the history of religion from 1904 to 1912. In 1913 he moved to Stockholm University, where he taught until joining the newspaper in 1917.

Segerstedt's resistance to Nazism began as soon as Adolf Hitler became chancellor of Germany in 1933. Through the pages of his paper he launched an unceasing campaign against Hitler, starting with the comment: "To force the politics and press of the entire world to deal with that character, that is unforgivable. Mr. Hitler is an insult." He continued with other articles, prompting a response within days from senior Nazi Hermann Göring, who protested that the tenor of Segerstedt's articles, if continued, could threaten relations between Germany and Sweden.

Segerstedt's criticism marks him as one of the earliest European journalists to recognize where Nazism could lead, identifying it as the cause of a new global conflict. In years to come, members of the Swedish government expressed concern at Segerstedt's condemnations, but he persisted nonetheless. As Nazi anti-Jewish measures intensified, he wrote in response to Sweden's silence on the passage of the Nuremberg Laws of 1935: "We are responsible for what we say and for what we do not say." Segerstedt opposed Sweden's participation at the Berlin Olympic Games in 1936, and he was critical of the Munich Agreement of September 1938, the high point of British and French appeasement of Hitler. The excesses of Nazism, culminating with the *Kristallnacht* pogrom of November 9–10, 1938, encouraged him to continue his campaign with relentless vigor.

On November 30, 1939, the Soviet Union—at that time allied to Germany—attacked Sweden's immediate neighbor, Finland. Then, on April 9, 1940, Norway and Denmark were invaded by Germany. With war encroaching on Scandinavia, the Swedish government, desperate not to antagonize the Nazis, began to fight hard to maintain its neutrality, and the introduction of press censorship resulted in Segerstedt's editorials being cut. His response was to leave blank columns as an indication to his readers that press freedom had been assaulted.

Across Nazi-occupied Scandinavia, Segerstedt's articles and the *Handelstidningen* newspaper were banned, a measure that only served to inspire resistance movements in Norway and Denmark. Indeed, in Norway the paper was smuggled into both countries, with the intention of letting the fighters know that they were not alone.

Throughout the war years Segerstedt continued to defy his government, which, in turn, held that he was too uncompromising in his sustained criticism of Nazi Germany. In 1940, at the request of the government, King Gustaf V called Segerstedt to Stockholm's Royal Palace and reproached the journalist for his irresponsibility. The king informed him: "If Sweden gets into the war, it will be your fault." When Segerstedt objected and tried to point out the morality of his stance, the king is reputed to have said: "We know why you are defending the Jews."

In this manner, Segerstedt's relationship with his Jewish mistress, Maja Forssman, was thrown in his face. Soon after this incident *Handelstidningen* began to lose its advertising sponsors, while certain editions of the newspaper were actually seized by the government amid threats from Berlin. Despite such pressure, Segerstedt never gave in, and he maintained his condemnation of Hitler and Nazi Germany.

Segerstedt's story relates one man's moral courage in the face of intense pressure to back down for the sake of state interests. At the same time that Prime Minister Per Albin Hansson, a longtime friend, pleaded with him not to drag Sweden into the war, he continued his writing—indeed, it has been estimated that Segerstedt wrote up to 10,000 articles across the span of his career. Of course, along the way he made many enemies. Several even played the antisemitic card in view of his relationship with Maja Forssman, sending him hate mail and calling him a "lackey" of the Jews.

On March 31, 1945, after a walk with his dogs (one of whom he named "Winston" in honor of the British prime minister), Segerstedt fell ill and died in Gothenburg.

He was recalled in an award-winning movie made in 2012, *The Last Sentence* (directed by Jan Troell; Swedish title, *Dom över död man*, or *Judgement on the Dead*), which paints a particularly sensitive picture of Segerstedt as a man of intense convictions who struggled with what he saw as his moral duty in a world of increasing immorality. Starring Jesper Christensen, the film shows a Segerstedt who is zealous in his opposition to Hitler, conflicted in his interpersonal relations with those around him, and a major hero of the opposition to Nazism—against the advice of his friends, the preferences of his government, and the demands of his king.

Sendler, Irena (1910–2008)

Irena Sendler was a Polish social worker who, as head of the children's section of the underground resistance movement Żegota, was instrumental in saving thousands of Jewish children from the Nazis.

Born Irena Krzyżanowska on February 15, 1910, her father was Dr. Stanisław Krzyżanowski, a physician and one of the earliest members of the Polish Socialist party (Polska Partia Socjalistyczna, or PPS). He had a profound influence on many of her ideas regarding social justice. She was born in Otwock, a short distance from Warsaw. When her father died in 1917, Jewish community leaders, out of gratitude for his efforts to reduce medical costs among poor Jews, offered to help pay for her education. She attended the University of Warsaw, studying Polish literature, and married Mieczysław Sendler. Although their marriage ended in divorce in 1947, she kept her married name for the rest of her life.

When Germany invaded Poland in September 1939, the 29-year-old Sendler was a senior administrator in the Warsaw Social Welfare Department, providing meals, financial aid, and other services for orphans, the elderly, the poor, and the destitute throughout the city. With the onset of war, and in view of the Nazi treatment of the Jews, she also began aiding Jews. Through her office she arranged for the provision of clothing, medicine, and financial aid. Jews receiving assistance were registered under fictitious Christian names, with more than 3,000 false documents being forged in order to help Jewish families in need. Once the ghetto into which the Jews had been forced was sealed in November 1940, however, the options for continuing this kind of aid effectively disappeared.

Despite this situation, Sendler was determined to continue providing aid to the Jews of the now-isolated ghetto. Therefore, when Żegota, the Council to Aid Jews, was established in October 1942, she was among its most enthusiastic supporters. Żegota existed under the auspices of the Polish government-in-exile and operated through the Polish resistance, with the express purpose of aiding the country's Jews and finding places of safety for them within occupied Poland.

Sendler saw her specific role as one of rescuing Jewish children. To do so, she needed to enter the heavily guarded ghetto on some sort of official business, and so she secured a pass from Warsaw's Epidemic Control Department. With pass in hand, she was able to visit the ghetto on a daily basis, enabling her to reestablish earlier contacts and thereby arrange the rescues that were so urgently needed. Żegota played a vital role in this enterprise. Two dozen other Żegota members helped get Jewish children out and assisted Jews remaining behind in the ghetto—hiding them, seeking hiding places for them, and paying for their upkeep and medical care. Overall, Żegota helped save up to 4,000 Polish Jews by also providing aid to those hiding on the Aryan side and in other parts of Poland.

In August 1943 Sendler—known by her nom de guerre, Jolanta—was appointed to head Żegota's Department for the Care of Jewish Children. This position enabled her to formalize her rescue activities, and with the help of each of the 10 centers of the Social Welfare Department, from which she recruited people to assist her, she issued hundreds of false documents with forged signatures, at least 400 on her own responsibility.

Sendler cooperated with others in Warsaw's Municipal Social Services Department and the RGO (Central Welfare Council), a Polish relief organization tolerated under German supervision. Her team then organized a smuggling operation, sneaking out babies and small children in ambulances and trams. Sometimes they were taken out in sacks or bags, or disguised as packages; others were hidden deep inside freight consignments. All and any means were taken to get the children out of the ghetto and to safety.

Children were then hidden with kindly Polish families, but finding homes willing to provide refuge was never easy. It was no mean thing to ask parents to risk the lives of their own children if the Nazis were to find out what they were doing. Often, Sendler relied on the good graces of the Church to provide assistance. Various Catholic convents were successfully prevailed upon to open their doors, and the Sisters of the Family of Mary orphanage enabled Jewish children to pass through with changed identities. Sendler retained the real names of the children by adopting a code only she understood. She kept the only record of their identities in a set of jars buried, ironically, not far from a German military barracks. These jars, which were located later, contained the names of 2,500 children. The exact number of children saved is unknown.

Not all were rescued by Sendler alone, but her group, comprising about 30 volunteers, managed collectively to achieve these remarkable rescues. So far as it was humanly possible, Żegota did its best to ensure that the children were returned to their Jewish families when the war ended, but unfortunately, all too often there were no family members left alive by 1945.

On October 20, 1943, Sendler's run came to an abrupt end when she was arrested. The Gestapo sought full disclosure of all Żegota operations regarding the hidden children, particularly their secret identities and their hidden locations. Interrogation and imprisonment led to torture. She had her legs broken and her feet crushed, but she refused to divulge anything that would give away the children or her co-conspirators. Sent to the notorious Pawiak prison, she was sentenced to death. Only at the last minute was her life spared, when Żegota activists managed to bribe one of the Gestapo officers. She escaped from prison, spent the rest of the war in hiding, and continued her work for Jewish children while heading the Children's Section of Żegota. With the end of the war she and her surviving helpers gathered as many of their records as could be located and passed them on to the general secretary of Żegota, Adolf Berman, at the Central Committee of Polish Jews.

On October 19, 1965, Israel's Yad Vashem recognized Irena Sendler as one of the Righteous among the Nations for her efforts on behalf of Jewish children, and in 1991 she was made an honorary citizen of Israel. She was awarded Poland's Order of the White Eagle on November 10, 2003, and in 2008 she appeared on a Polish commemorative silver coin. Later that same year, she was declared the 2003 recipient of the **Jan Karski** Award for Valor and Courage, and in 2007 she was nominated for the Nobel Peace Prize. Sendler died in Warsaw on May 12, 2008, at the age of 98.

Sheptytsky, Andrey (1865–1944)

Andrey Sheptytsky was the metropolitan archbishop of the Ukrainian Greek Catholic Church in Lvov (Lviv) between 1901 and 1944, harboring hundreds of Jews in his residence and in Greek Catholic monasteries during the Holocaust.

Born on July 29, 1865, in the village of Prylbychi, Galicia, he came from a family that had strong Polish, aristocratic, and Catholic roots, though with an Orthodox Ukrainian line stretching back many centuries. Sheptytsky received his education first at home and then in Kraków. He studied law in Kraków and Breslau (Wrocław), earning a doctorate in 1888, and then entered a Basilian monastery of the Ukrainian Greek Catholic Church and took the name Andrey, after Ukraine's patron saint. He was ordained on August 22, 1892, and then studied at the Jesuit Seminary in Kraków. There, in 1894, he received a second doctorate, in theology. On September 17, 1899, he was consecrated a bishop by Metropolitan Julian Sas-Kuilovsky, and the following year, on December 12, 1900, he was appointed metropolitan archbishop of Lvov.

During World War I Sheptytsky was arrested by the Russians due to his national origin in the Austro-Hungarian Empire. In March 1918, as a result of the Russian Revolution, he was released and returned to Ukraine—at that time a quasi-independent republic under German suzerainty.

Before World War II Sheptytsky became the de facto head of all Ukrainian aspirations, and where Jewish-Christian relations were concerned he had a long and sympathetic past from which to draw. While a student he had learned Hebrew; in his pastoral visits to mixed Ukrainian-Jewish villages he was met by local delegations, led by the town or village priest, who were followed by the local rabbi carrying the village Torah. Given the time and place, Sheptytsky's relationship with the Jews was strong.

That said, Sheptytsky's responses to the war were somewhat inconsistent. Following the Nazi invasion of Ukraine at the end of June 1941, the Organization of the Ukrainian Nationalists, led by Yaroslav Stetsko, declared an independent Ukrainian state. The Germans immediately crushed this state, but Sheptytsky had already issued a pastoral letter welcoming the Nazis as liberators from the Soviet yoke and recognizing Stetsko as de facto head of the new Ukrainian government. This gesture would throw a huge cloud over his subsequent actions, the more so as anti-Jewish pogroms broke out immediately after the declaration of independence was announced.

Sheptytsky knew of the pogroms; he had been informed of developments on either July 1 or 2 by Lvov's chief rabbi Ezekiel Lewin. The extent to which he tried to check them, however, is highly disputed. It is likely, in fact, that he might have had little control over what was happening in any case, given the mob nature of the riots.

How Sheptytsky responded to Chief Rabbi Lewin is unknown to this day. It is clear, however, that he offered sanctuary to Lewin and his family, and that Lewin accepted the offer on behalf of his children but refused it for himself, saying that his duty was to stay with his community. Later, he was arrested by Ukrainian militia and murdered. Sheptytsky took charge of two of Lewin's three sons (the other died in a Nazi camp), providing forged certificates of baptism, new identities, and instructions to his priests to train the boys to pray in Ukrainian. Both were to survive.

From early 1942 onward Sheptytsky provided a refuge to Jews through his Church, instructing monasteries and convents to follow his lead. From then until the liberation, no Jewish child was forcibly converted to Christianity, and all were to survive the Nazis. It has been calculated that Sheptytsky personally arranged for the hiding of 150 Jews—mostly children and about a dozen rabbis—in his official residence and throughout his monasteries.

He also protested the killing of Jews to high-ranking Nazis who made official visits to his residence, and he sent a letter to Reichsführer-SS Heinrich Himmler objecting to Nazi treatment of the Jews and the use of Ukrainians in anti-Jewish repressions. His letter included a request that Ukrainian police and militias be removed from duty in the camps. On November 21, 1942, he issued a strong pastoral letter to all Ukrainians denouncing killing. As a final indicator of his attitude toward Nazi antisemitic measures, he wrote a number of letters to Pope Pius XII advising him of the Nazis' "diabolical" nature.

While it seems clear that Sheptytsky sheltered Jews during the Holocaust, there is a great deal of ambiguity regarding his support for the Nazis. He did not sympathize with Nazi ideology, but initially thought that German rule would be better than that of the Soviets, and he appeared to hold hopes of exploiting the German presence in order to buttress a possible Ukrainian state. The invasion of Ukraine in the summer of 1941 did not at first shake this belief; indeed, it took nearly a year before he realized that Nazi occupation policies were even more brutal than those of the Soviets. It was only then that he really began to assist the Jews, leading some to ask whether or not his early support for the Nazis actually served to assist them during the first year of the Holocaust in Ukraine.

Adding to the complexity of Sheptytsky's response to the Nazis and, through that, to the Holocaust, is the support he gave to the creation, in April 1943, of the 14th Waffen-SS Grenadier Division ("Galician"), a German military formation initially made up of volunteers from Galicia with a Ukrainian ethnic background. Sheptytsky blessed the division and those who joined it—perhaps thinking that they could serve as the nucleus of a future Ukrainian army, perhaps in the hope that they could protect the country in the event of a German collapse and Soviet reconquest.

The gray area involving Sheptytsky during the Holocaust is thus highly complex. Many of those he saved have sought to have him recognized by Yad Vashem as one of the Righteous among the Nations, including former Polish foreign minister Adam Daniel Rotfeld, Nobel prize–winning chemist Roald Hoffmann, and Chief Rabbi David Kahane of the Israeli Air Force. In Israel, the Commission for the Designation of the Righteous has debated in considerable detail whether Sheptytsky's initial support for the Nazi occupation contributed to the murder of Jews in Ukraine, and has, as a result, continued to deny him as one of the Righteous among the Nations.

Sheptytsky's brother Klementiy was recognized by Yad Vashem as one of the Righteous among the Nations in 1995, and on June 27, 2001, he was beatified by Pope John Paul II.

On November 1, 1944, Andrey Sheptytsky died at the age of 79 in Lvov. In 1958 an initial investigation into the cause for his possible beatification and canonization commenced, and on July 16, 2015, Pope Francis signed a decree declaring him "venerable," an initial step in the sainthood process.

Shirer, William L. (1904–1993)

William Lawrence (Bill) Shirer was an American journalist, war correspondent, and historian. Born in Chicago in 1904, he attended Coe College in Cedar Rapids, Iowa, and in 1925 he moved to France to take up a position as European correspondent for the *Chicago Tribune*. In 1931 he married Theresa ("Tess") Stiberitz, an Austrian photographer. Between 1934 and 1940 Shirer lived and worked in Nazi Germany, working for the Berlin bureau of the Universal News Service until 1937, and then as European bureau chief of CBS radio based in Vienna, reporting to Edward R. Murrow.

Fluent in German, French, and Italian, Shirer thrived in his new environment. When the German annexation of Austria took place on March 12, 1938, Shirer, as the only American broadcaster in Vienna, was obliged to fly to London to report on what he had seen; he could not do so in Vienna itself, as CBS did not possess radio facilities there. With this as a precedent, he then reported on all the major developments in Europe that followed, including the Munich Agreement (September 30, 1938), the German annexation of what remained of Czechoslovakia (March 15, 1939), and the German invasion of Poland (September 1, 1939).

Throughout this time, Shirer was an acute observer of Nazi policies regarding the harassment of Jews, and almost as soon as he arrived in Germany he was conscious of the Nazi attempt to terminate the Jewish presence. In 1935 he reported on the Nuremberg Laws, which stripped Jews of their German citizenship and introduced other restrictions reducing them to second-class noncitizens. He continued his reports the following year when additional restrictions on Jews were made, and with each

William L. Shirer, a leading American journalist in prewar Europe. He and his wife Tess would often shelter Jews in their own home, and provide them with foreign currency and the means to escape the country for other lands of refuge. Upon leaving Germany in December 1940, he smuggled out voluminous notes and diaries that were subsequently published and did much to alert American public opinion as to why the Nazis had to be resisted in the future. (Bettmann/Corbis)

successive antisemitic measure he became more and more disgusted by what he witnessed.

Whenever possible, Shirer took a stand against the Nazis in his reportage but found himself in a difficult position. There was only so much on which he could report, as his outgoing dispatches were watched carefully by the Nazi state as a condition of his credentials being respected. While reporting the 1936 Olympics from Berlin, for example, he was publicly condemned by the Ministry of Propaganda for exposing the antisemitism he detested. He was threatened with expulsion and accused of being a "German hater," in what would not be an isolated reference.

The threat of expulsion dogged Shirer. He was concerned that if he went too far he could suffer the same fate as Dorothy Thompson, who in August 1934 was the first American journalist expelled from Nazi Germany for writing articles considered offensive to the regime. Shirer's reporting, therefore, was fenced in by a form of self-censorship; this practice became much more formalized once war broke out, when state-imposed censorship was introduced.

As foreigners, Bill and Tess Shirer did what they could to help the Jews they encountered, though the position of Tess Shirer, as an Austrian-born U.S. citizen, placed her in a precarious position. They put themselves at risk by sheltering Jews whom they knew personally, using their home as a refuge for those who had gone into hiding. Shirer exploited his contacts in the United States, as well as in the British, French, and Swiss embassies and consulates, in order to get visas for Jews trying desperately to leave Germany. Despite the ban on trading in foreign currency, he also worked to procure money to help tide Jews over once they managed to move to new countries.

Occasionally the Shirers would find themselves harboring a Jew who had just been released from a jail or concentration camp. In such circumstances, he related later, their guest would often have been badly beaten or mistreated, and they would care for him until he had recovered sufficiently to return to his family in something resembling a passable condition. For all his efforts at saving people, however, Shirer knew that his contribution was only a minor one, as most Jews could not avail themselves of the help he and his wife were able to provide.

As a journalist from a neutral country, Shirer was permitted to remain in Germany and report back to the United States. He covered the invasion of Denmark and Norway in April 1940, followed by Germany's further invasions of the Low Countries and France on and after May 10. He moved with the German armies as they progressed through France, and he was the only foreign correspondent to report in person to the American people on the French surrender at Compiègne on June 22, 1940.

Despite this access, he found himself increasingly frustrated by the Nazi state from which he was reporting. With Germany victorious on all fronts, Nazi propaganda minister Joseph Goebbels placed pressure on Shirer to broadcast official accounts of Germany's war efforts, rather than independent reports. Shirer began pestering CBS management in New York to relieve him of this assignment, and the situation was not helped when he learned that the Gestapo was waiting for him to slip up in one of his reports so they could arrest him for espionage. Finally, he managed to leave Germany in December 1940. As he left, he smuggled with him his diaries and notes from his time in Germany. These were to be published in 1941 as *Berlin Diary: The Journal of a Foreign Correspondent, 1934–1941*.

Much of what Shirer wrote did not refer specifically to Jews; he was too savvy to commit his thoughts to paper, and certainly not to broadcast them. Shirer's resistance to Nazism, where Jews were concerned, must be measured by his actions—and in this regard, his behavior spoke loudly. Underscoring his commitment to covering the crimes of Nazi Germany, he returned to Europe to report on the Nuremberg Trials in 1945.

Shirer's masterwork, although it appeared well after the end of the war, was his study of Nazi Germany, *The Rise and Fall of the Third Reich*, which appeared in 1961. One of the first major studies of its subject, it won the 1961 National Book Award for Nonfiction. The author of many other important works, Shirer died in Boston in 1993, at the age of 89.

Slachta, Margit (1884–1974)

Margit Slachta was a Hungarian pioneer in social service and a leading political figure in interwar Hungary. During the Holocaust, members of the religious order she founded, the Sisters of Social Service, worked to protect their Jewish neighbors while at the same time continuing their commitment to social justice.

Born in Kassa, Hungary, on September 18, 1884, she lived with her parents in the United States when she was a child but returned to Hungary before the turn of the century. Upon her return, she taught French and German at a Catholic school in Budapest. In 1908 she joined a religious community, the Society of the Social Mission. She became an activist for social causes, establishing the Union of Catholic Women, an organization to promote the female franchise in Hungary. As early as 1919 she organized the Catholic Women's party, and in 1920 she became the first woman elected to the Hungarian Parliament (for a term lasting two years), where she campaigned on behalf of women, children, families, and the safeguarding of workers' rights.

On May 12, 1923, Margit Slachta founded a new order, the Sisters of Social Service, whose members were dedicated to carrying out their commitment to care for those in need and combat the suffering around them. Over time, the Sisters became well known throughout Hungary for nursing, midwifery, and the care of orphans.

As an outspoken woman, committed Christian, and promoter of socially advanced causes, Slachta defied the spirit of the age. When Hungary began to introduce measures discriminating against Jews, it was inevitable that Mother Margit (as she was now called) would rebel against such developments. When the first anti-Jewish laws appeared in Hungary in 1938, she began publishing articles opposing official antisemitism in her newspaper, *Voice of the Spirit*. In 1943 the paper was suppressed, but Slachta continued to publish it underground. Sisters were instructed to familiarize themselves on Jewish matters and prepare accordingly.

Slachta's political activities increased as World War II began with the German invasion of Poland in September 1939, leading to waves of Jewish refugees. In 1940 Hungary joined the Axis Powers, and that fall, before the Nazis insisted on it, deportations of Jews began in certain regions of the country. Slachta responded immediately by agitating for these actions to stop at once, and in at least one region the deportations ceased as a result of her actions. Beyond this, she also provided shelter and protested against forced labor and antisemitic laws. In 1943 she even went to Rome to ask the Vatican to intervene and stop the persecution of Jews in Slovakia.

Slachta instructed her Sisters that they had a bounden duty to protect the Jews, even at the risk of their own lives. She considered it a theological matter, in view of the fact that the Jews were God's people, those from among whom Jesus was born and raised.

Between July 15 and August 12, 1941, approximately 20,000 Jews living in Hungary who could not prove legal residency since 1850 were deported to southern Poland, there to await their fate at the hands of the Germans. Slachta demanded that the process be stopped, protesting directly to Magdolna Purgly, the wife of Hungary's regent, Miklós Horthy.

When the Nazis occupied Hungary in March 1944, bringing the full weight of the Holocaust with them, the Sisters of Social Service began to arrange baptisms of convenience in the hope that doing so would spare Jews from deportation. As things got worse, the Sisters focused completely on helping the Jews. Giving of themselves selflessly, they hid at least 1,000 Jews and provided food and safe houses whenever they could. Following Slachta's lead, one of the sisters, **Sára Salkaházi**, took the admonition to offer her life for the Jews literally. She personally saved the lives of about 100 Jews, and as the persecution intensified during 1944 she redoubled her efforts to save as many as she could. Eventually, she was caught by Hungarian Arrow Cross soldiers and murdered on the banks of the Danube on December 27, 1944. Her body was never recovered.

In a singular act of defiance once the Nazis had invaded, Slachta began to live in the order's Mother House, located on Budapest's Thököly Street. The house itself acted as a place of refuge for Jews, but its location was both ironic and a challenge, as it was situated directly opposite the 14th District Arrow Cross party headquarters. At one point, gangs invaded the Mother House and carried out a brutal hunt for Jews, attacking Slachta as well as several of the Sisters. On this occasion she only narrowly avoided execution.

With the end of the war, Slachta once more became a member of the Hungarian Parliament during the democratic period prior to the communist takeover. At the end of 1948 she fled Hungary for the West, arriving in the United States on June 22, 1949. On January 6, 1974, she died, at the age of 89, in Buffalo, New York. In recognition for her work in hiding Jews, supplying basic goods, and providing false evidence to save Jewish lives during the Holocaust, she was recognized by Yad Vashem on February 18, 1969, as one of the Righteous among the Nations.

Smolar, Hersh (1905–1993)

Hersh Smolar was the editor of a Yiddish daily newspaper in Poland. After Operation Barbarossa in June 1941 he became a leading resistance fighter in the Minsk ghetto and, later, fought with partisans operating in the forests of Belorussia.

He was born in 1905 to a poor family in the town of Zambrów, northeastern Poland; his father, David Smolar, was a soda manufacturer. As a teenager, Smolar became active in the Communist party, organizing and leading Zambrów's left-wing Jewish Socialist Youth Association from 1918 to 1920, when he moved to the Soviet Union to escape anticommunist repression. He lived first in Kiev before moving to Moscow. In 1925 he joined the Communist party of the Soviet Union, and a year later became an elected member of the Central Jewish Bureau of the Central Committee of Komsomol. While in the Soviet Union he attended party-run universities and wrote for the Yiddish youth press.

In 1928 the Polish section of the Communist International sent him to work as a Comintern agent in Poland. He moved to Vilna (Vilnius), where he became party secretary to the Communist Party of Western Belarus (CPWB). He was arrested by the Polish authorities, however, and imprisoned for the next three years. In 1932 he returned to the CPWB and after 1934 became head of publications—in effect, chief of party propaganda. In 1936 he was arrested again and this time sentenced to six years in prison; it was only the outbreak of war and the invasion of eastern Poland by the Soviet Union in mid-September 1939 that secured his release.

With the onset of war Smolar moved to Soviet-occupied Białystok. There, he became editor of the communist journal *Białystokier Sztern* (*Białystok Star*) and gained some measure of prominence among Yiddish writers living there. On June 22, 1941, the Nazis invaded the Soviet Union. At the time, Smolar was in Minsk. When the Nazis established a ghetto there after the city was taken on June 28, 1941, Smolar took charge of the resistance. His major link was with another leader, **Mikhail Gebelev**, who was captured, tortured, and hanged on August 15, 1942.

Smolar led the underground movement in a ghetto housing tens of thousands of Jews. He and his cadres had an active underground printing press that continually advertised Soviet successes, hid non-Jewish communists and escaped Soviet prisoners of war, and worked to save Jewish lives using all means at their disposal.

Moreover, the ghetto resistance established links with partisan groups in the forests outside, and both worked jointly in operations directed by a unified Soviet command. Under these circumstances, there was an ongoing hemorrhaging of Jews from the ghetto into the forests, where they joined partisan groups by the thousands. Not only was this an effective way of fighting the German invaders but it also ensured Jewish survival. By the time the ghetto was liquidated on October 21, 1943, up to 10,000 Jews had escaped to join the partisans.

By the spring of 1942 Smolar was in hiding, hunted continually by the Nazis who knew that they had to capture him in order to staunch the flow of escapees and destroy the resistance. On April 1, 1942, the Gestapo issued an ultimatum to members of the Minsk Jewish Council (Judenrat) that they were to locate, apprehend, and turn Smolar over to them by noon that day or be executed themselves. Hiding in the hospital's infectious disease ward, disguised as a typhus patient, Smolar was told about the ultimatum by one of the Judenrat members, Hersh Ruditzer. While some were prepared to surrender Smolar on the basis that his single death would save the lives of many, others sought a more imaginative solution. Eventually, a sophisticated ruse made it appear that Smolar was already dead, and the Nazis accepted this explanation.

With this guarantee, he remained in hiding at the hospital for another four months. After this he was moved to another hiding place, until, in August 1942—when Gebelev was murdered, and the ghetto resistance was in danger of being destroyed completely—Smolar was forced to leave the ghetto and join the partisans. In this way he managed to escape just prior to the final liquidation of the ghetto in October 1943. He fought with partisans in the Naliboki Forest, where another resister, **Tuvia Bielski**, and his brothers were also active. Smolar became commissar of his own partisan group, attained the rank of lieutenant, and edited five underground newspapers published in Russian and Yiddish. By the time the Red Army retook Minsk on July 3, 1944, there were only a handful of Jewish survivors.

In 1946 Hersh Smolar published a memoir in Yiddish of the Minsk ghetto, *Fun Minsker geto* (published in English in 1989 as *The Minsk Ghetto: Soviet-Jewish Partisans against the Nazis*). After the war he received a number of decorations for his resistance and partisan activities, including the Partisan Cross, Order of Grunwald Cross Third Class, and the Cross of Valor. He led a very active postwar life as a leading communist in Poland and between 1946 and 1950 served as a member of the presidium of the Central Committee of Polish Jews. After an anti-Jewish campaign across 1967–1969, during which he was expelled from the Polish United Workers' party, he realized that his life in Poland was no longer viable. He left for Paris in 1970 on his way to Israel, where he arrived in 1971. There he worked at the National Library in Jerusalem and Tel Aviv University before retiring. In 1993 Hersh Smolar died at the age of 88.

Sommer, Margarete (1893–1965)

Margarete (Grete) Sommer was a German Catholic social worker who helped persecuted Jews in Berlin before and during World War II, facilitating the survival of many through her work with the Catholic aid agency Caritas and then directly through the diocesan office.

Born in Berlin's Schöneweide neighborhood on July 21, 1893, she completed her primary and secondary education before attending the University of Berlin, from which she earned a doctorate in 1924. She then taught at a number of different colleges. Her main employment was at the Social Welfare Institute of Pestalozzi-Fröbel House in Berlin, where she taught from 1927 until 1934. That year she was forced to resign after she refused to teach her students the Nazi laws regarding compulsory sterilization.

Following her dismissal from Pestalozzi, she worked at the Episcopal Diocesan Authority in Berlin, counseling "non-Aryan" Christians through Caritas Emergency Relief. In this way she was able to assist those who were forced to leave the Third Reich but needed professional help to do so. In 1939 she took on new responsibilities as diocesan instructor for the ministry to women, becoming increasingly involved in the work of the Berlin Episcopate relief agency founded in August 1938 at the initiative of Bishop **Konrad Graf von Preysing**.

In 1941 she became managing director of the Berlin diocesan authority, under the Cathedral provost, Father **Bernhard Lichtenberg**. After Lichtenberg's arrest by the Gestapo in October 1941, Sommer took charge of the welfare office's operations, work that Lichtenberg had been doing up to that point. She began coordinating Catholic aid for victims of Nazi racial persecution, providing them with food, clothing, and occasionally financial assistance. From other Catholic workers in various parts of the country she also began to gather information about Nazi antisemitic measures, such as deportations of Jews and living conditions in concentration camps. She employed this material in a series of reports, one of which, in August 1942, was conveyed to the Vatican under the title "Report on the Exodus of the Jews." Throughout this time her focus was on the welfare of "non-Aryan" Christians, though she also helped Jews escape. Her superior in all these initiatives was Bishop von Preysing, who gave her his full support and endorsement.

In 1943 Margarete Sommer and Bishop von Preysing drafted a statement for consideration by the German bishops, rebuking Hitler for human rights abuses and mass murder. Recalling the first words of the 1939 Papal Encyclical *Mit Brennender Sorge*, the draft began, "With deepest sorrow—yes even with holy indignation—have we German bishops learned of the deportation of non-Aryans in a manner that is scornful of all human rights. It is our holy duty to defend the unalienable rights of all men guaranteed by natural law." It was a very clear statement that, if accepted and read publicly, would have left the Nazi regime in no doubt as to the official attitude of the Catholic Church in Germany—regardless of what came from the Vatican. The statement was not, however, made public.

One further dimension of Sommer's efforts on behalf of Jews involved the employment of her legal skills to challenge the Third Reich's laws on mixed marriages. While she could not overturn the laws, she worked nonetheless to assist those in danger of having their marriages annulled in the event of the Jewish spouse being deported. A disbelieving Church had, until now, not accepted that the government would go ahead with its threat, but Sommer compiled and sent reports to the hierarchy explaining the situation in full. Again, Bishop von Preysing gave her his support, though they were unable stop the Nazis from going ahead with their plans.

After the war Sommer continued to work at the Episcopal diocesan authority in Berlin. With the liberation of the camps and the return of Jews looking to pick up the threads of their destroyed lives, the authority had much work to do in assisting survivors desperate for the kind of help she could provide.

Margarete Sommer died in Berlin on June 30, 1965, just one month short of her 72nd birthday. On May 5, 2003, she was posthumously recognized by Yad Vashem as one of the Righteous among the Nations for her work in rescuing Jewish lives during the Holocaust.

Soos, Géza (1912–1953)

Géza Soos was a member of the Hungarian resistance during World War II. Born in 1912, he became a member of the Reformed Church in Hungary, where he was head of the Soli Deo Gloria youth movement. Soos was a member of the Hungarian Foreign Ministry during the regency of Miklós Horthy, and a key resister in the secret Hungarian independence movement against the Nazi occupation of Hungary.

Between July 6 and July 15, at Evian-les-Bains, France, an international conference, called by U.S. president Franklin D. Roosevelt, took place to discuss the problem of what to do about Jewish refugees from Nazi Germany and Austria. Géza Soos, then in France representing Soli Deo Gloria at a conference, went to Evian, entirely on his own initiative, on July 5, 1938. From his attendance at this meeting he gained a measure of appreciation for the situation facing Jews under the Nazis, and from this point on he realized that he should be doing something to assist them. By 1942 he was working actively with the Good Shepherd Committee of the Reformed Church, and with their assistance hid many Jews, both families and individuals.

As a member of the Hungarian Foreign Service, Soos was part of a cohort dedicated to resisting the Nazis, including László (Leslie) Veress, Domokos Szent-Iványi, and Ferenc Vali. Perhaps his most important contact was the Swedish emissary **Raoul Wallenberg**, with whom he developed a close working relationship dedicated to saving Jews. Their personal connection is unclear; perhaps they became friends, but this is not certain. Their cooperation was, however, an efficient one. Soos was the first non-Swedish official Wallenberg encountered after his arrival in Budapest in July 1944; together the two experienced related dangers requiring them to hide out in different places each night in various safe houses.

Soos, who was Szent-Iványi's deputy both formally and within the Hungarian independence movement, is considered by some to be the Hungarian official who did the most to save Jews from deportation in 1944. At one point he acquired a motor vehicle with diplomatic plates enabling him to move Jews around Budapest to safe houses, and on another he appropriated a military aircraft and flew to Rome, where he engaged in discussions with the Allies in the hope of giving Budapest the status of an open city and negotiating a separate peace—and, by doing so, sparing the population from unnecessary suffering. Activities such as these placed his life at risk, but he did so in order to provide help to those in need.

Arguably, the most vital service undertaken by Soos occurred in the aftermath of **Rudolf Vrba** and Alfréd Wetzler's escape from Auschwitz on April 10, 1944. It seems that Soos obtained the German-language testimony through a member of the Budapest Jewish community, **Rezső Kasztner**. Soos gave it to József Éliás, head of the Good Shepherd Mission. Éliás's secretary, Mária Székely, then translated it into Hungarian and prepared six copies. These were in turn forwarded to diplomats and Jewish leaders in Hungary and overseas. In an attempt to generate attention at the highest levels in Hungary, Soos also passed the report to Countess Ilona Edelsheim-Gyulai, Horthy's daughter-in-law. Taken overall, this was the first time that a complete and authentic report of the extermination operations at Auschwitz was released to world leaders. Unfortunately, public acknowledgement of Vrba's testimony was delayed for political reasons, just as the full force of the Nazi killing process fell onto the Jews of Hungary. Arguments still reverberate as to whether the lives of hundreds of thousands of people could have been saved if the news from Soos had been made public and acted upon.

Nevertheless, when the Auschwitz report reached Horthy, he immediately acted to stop the deportations of Hungarian Jews to Auschwitz. While it is difficult to speculate as to why he did this, one suggestion could be that the intervention of Soos, through Ilona Edelsheim-Gyulai, played a role in his calculations.

Research into Soos's activities during the Nazi invasion and occupation of Hungary is difficult, as most of what he did was illegal when measured against his formal duty as a government official. Documentation, therefore, is rare. As in many similar cases of helping activities, the only ones who know of Soos's activities with any authority are those whom he helped directly—the survivors who owe him their lives.

When peace came in 1945, Soos returned to Hungary. The Soviet takeover of the country, however, placed him in an unsafe position, given than he had been a leading civil servant of the Horthy regime. Communists expected him to join the party, which he refused to do. In 1946, therefore, he left for Geneva, Switzerland, where he studied for his ordination as a pastor. At the same time, he edited Hungarian-language journals for distribution around Europe.

In 1953 Géza Soos and his wife, Ilona Tüdős, together with their five children, moved to the United States, where they settled in North Carolina. Two years later, at the age of just 41, Soos died in a road accident in what some asserted were suspicious (though unconfirmed) circumstances.

Sorkine, Charlotte (b. 1925)

Charlotte Sorkine Noshpitz was a French Jewish resister. She was born in Paris on February 15, 1925; her mother was born in Braila, Romania, and her father in Rogachev (Rahachow), Belorussia.

She was raised in a highly academic family; her grandfather, Wolf Louis Horowitz, was a professor of anthropology who spent much of his professional career at King's College, London. At the time of the Nazi invasion of France in 1940, neither of her parents had yet become French citizens. This made them vulnerable to anti-Jewish legislation from the collaborationist Vichy regime, which required that foreign nationals of Jewish background be interned and deported. Naturalized Jews, regardless of status, could have their citizenship revoked.

Given that Sorkine was very young when the Nazis came to power in 1933 in nearby Germany, she only vaguely understood that they represented some sort of danger to her and her family. She saw impoverished German Jewish refugees in Paris, and that was about it. During the summer of 1942, however, things changed. Sorkine, now a teenager, wept when her mother conveyed the news that from now on the family members would have to wear a yellow Jewish star on their clothes to indicate that they were Jewish. Sorkine saw at this point that she was adult enough to join in some sort of resistance to Nazi rule.

In July 1942 French police came on several occasions in the middle of the night looking for Sorkine's father, who was in hiding. On July 16, 1942, two officers came for her mother, who was arrested and taken to the center of Paris during the infamous roundup at the Velodrome d'Hiver (the Vel d'Hiv), during which more than 13,000 French Jews were incarcerated for five days without food or water, toilets or resting places. From there they went to the transit camp complex at Drancy before being moved on to their deaths at Auschwitz.

Moving to Nice to join her father and her brother, Leo Serge Lazare (then fighting as part of the French Resistance movement), Sorkine, at age 17, did some resistance work of her own. Realizing that to protect her father she would have to arrange his immediate departure from France, she made false papers for him as, of all things, a citizen of China. She told him that she would accompany him to safety in Switzerland but instead handed him over to a *passeur*, a member of the resistance who led people to safety across the border. He survived the war and was able to reunite with Sorkine after the liberation.

In Nice, Sorkine joined the Armée Juive (Jewish Army), a Zionist-focused resistance movement created during January 1942. It was established and led by **Abraham Polonski** and **Dovid Knut**, among others. Working under the direction of Maurice Loebenberg, a resister with a specialization in engraving whose work was dedicated to forging official papers for resistance fighters and escaping Jews, she guided men to Toulouse, where *passeurs* took them to the Spanish border. Once secure, some then went on to join the resistance in North Africa. On some occasions, Sorkine would even accompany these groups. As part of this work she assisted Loebenberg in creating thousands of false papers to assist in these people-smuggling activities.

On the evening of May 31, 1944, a German patrol arrested another Jewish resister, **Marianne Cohn**, near Annemasse, just 200 meters from the Swiss border. Cohn had taken hundreds of Jewish children across before the Gestapo captured, tortured, and killed her on the night of July 7–8, 1944. Sorkine not only knew about Cohn's activities but also assumed one of Cohn's duties after her death—transporting children. She continued the work of producing false documents, but in addition she received and transported weapons and money, and planted explosives in German areas.

On July 22, 1944, the Gestapo arrested 24 members of the Armée Juive. Sorkine managed to avoid this mass arrest and joined an independent liaison group, the Jewish Combat Organization. Through this she was able to actively participate in the liberation of Paris in August 1944.

After the war, Sorkine learned that her mother, Pauline Sorkine, had been murdered in Auschwitz, while her brother, Leo Serge Lazare, fought with the French Resistance and was killed by the Nazis in Silesia while working as a slave laborer, after being denounced. Sorkine herself survived the war and, after a period of readjustment to peacetime conditions, migrated to the United States. For her service in the French Resistance she was awarded the *Médaille de la Résistance*, the *Croix du Combattant Volontaire de la Resistance*, the *Médaille des Services Volontaires Dans la France Libre*, and the War Commemoration Medal.

Stöhr, Hermann (1898–1940)

Hermann Stöhr was a German pacifist who resisted Nazism before World War II and was executed as a conscientious objector to military service and for his opposition to the state.

Born in Stettin on January 4, 1898, Stöhr was the child of a conservative family of civil servants. When war broke out in 1914 he volunteered for military service at the age of just 16. Upon returning from the trenches, he had transformed into a pacifist. Between 1919 and 1922 he studied economics, law, and social policy at the University of Rostock, earning a PhD in 1922. He then moved to Berlin, where he worked under the guidance of Friedrich Siegmund-Schulze, professor of philosophy at the University of Berlin and a deeply committed Lutheran working for social causes and the peace movement.

Stöhr took a position as a secretary in the German branch of the International Fellowship of Reconciliation, cofounded by Siegmund-Schultze in August 1914 as an antiwar movement based on a common Protestant Christianity. He engaged in various journalistic activities on behalf of his mentor, writing pieces that were published internationally. In 1931, however, he lost his position and moved back to Stettin.

After the Nazis came to office in January 1933, Stöhr decided to take a stand against National Socialist Church policy by calling on the Protestant Churches to include victims of political persecution in their prayers of intercession, and also to show practical solidarity with the Jews. He went public in his opposition to Nazi calls for a boycott of Jewish businesses and to swastika flags being displayed in churches. He later joined the Confessing Church, a Protestant church in Nazi Germany that arose in opposition to government-sponsored efforts to Nazify organized Protestantism.

On February 28, 1939, Stöhr received his call-up for military service in the German navy, and was ordered to report to naval headquarters at Kiel. He replied immediately that, for reasons of conscience, he was forced to refuse armed service, though in its stead he requested to carry out labor service. This was declined, and he was then given two further call-up orders, on March 2 and August 22, 1939; on each of these occasions he also refused the call. On August 31, 1939, he was arrested and charged with desertion, and on November 1 a military court-martial was held in which he was sentenced to a year's imprisonment. At the end of 1939, while in prison, he refused to swear a compulsory oath to Adolf Hitler and rejected the possibility of any compromises. On January 9, 1940, his case came before a military court-martial, and on March 16, 1940, he was sentenced to death as a conscientious objector.

Stöhr's case was immediately the subject of a clemency request from the prison chaplain. It was rejected. When asked to intervene, the Church said it could not get involved in a case of this kind.

Sitting in the Wehrmacht remand prison in Berlin-Tegel, Stöhr awaited news of his execution date. He wrote his final letters to family and friends, at peace with his Christian faith and the teachings of Scripture. When told that the date of his execution had been set for June 6, 1940, he wrote a last letter in which he stated that no one should be sad about his fate, and that he faced "the end in gratitude and joy." As it turned out, his execution was delayed beyond the June 6 date, but he was finally beheaded in Berlin-Plötzensee prison on June 21, 1940. The burial took place in the cemetery of the Protestant St. John's church in Berlin-Wedding. During the funeral service the pastor, closely observed by the Gestapo, was prevented from speaking freely about Stöhr and was interrupted several times. The only invocation he was able to recite was the Lord's Prayer.

Studies into the fate of those who consistently refused military service show that there were at least 7 Catholics, 2 Quakers, 1 Mormon, 7 Seventh-Day Adventists, and about 7,000 Jehovah's Witnesses who were subjected to various forms of judicial persecution from the Nazi state for their beliefs. Only one Evangelical Protestant, however, was convicted and executed: Hermann Stöhr. In the history of resistance to Nazism and the Holocaust, his life and fate were practically forgotten until a German theologian and writer on religious matters, Eberhard Röhm, published a book in Stuttgart in 1985 entitled *Sterben für den Frieden. Spurensicherung: Hermann Stöhr (1898–1940) und die ökumenische Friedensbewegung (Dying for Peace. Forensics: Hermann Stöhr (1898–1940) and the Ecumenical Peace Movement)*. Röhm concluded that Stöhr, like another Protestant resister from the same period, Dietrich Bonhoeffer, "died for peace and justice," presenting an "unambiguous stance of conscientious objector" to the Nazis just at the time when no opposition was permitted.

Possibly on account of Eberhard Röhm's work in raising awareness about Hermann Stöhr, there was an aftermath to his case at the very end of the 20th century.

In December 1997 the Berlin Regional Court (Landgericht Berlin) reconsidered Stöhr's case and overthrew his 1940 conviction. The radical Christian loner who refused to bow to the Third Reich, who stood up for the Jews and said no when commanded to fight contrary to his most cherished beliefs, was exonerated. Since that time, a number of monuments, streets, and squares have been named in his honor.

Strobos, Tina (1920–2012)

Tina Strobos was a Dutch medical student in Amsterdam who, with her mother, helped save more than 100 Jews from the Nazis during World War II by giving them refuge on the upper floor of her Amsterdam home.

Born Tineke Buchter in Amsterdam on May 19, 1920, she was an only child. She came from an activist family: her mother, who raised Strobos after her divorce, was a socialist (and atheist) who had housed refugees during World War I; her grandmother (whom Strobos was later to describe as "the only person I know who scared the Gestapo") had been involved with the Dutch labor movement in the latter part of the 19th century.

When Germany invaded the Netherlands on May 10, 1940, Strobos was almost 20. A university student working toward a degree in medicine, she and her classmates refused to sign an oath of loyalty to Adolf Hitler, and the medical school was forced to close down; many students, including Strobos, then joined the underground movement.

At first, this involved assisting those fighting in the resistance. Strobos smuggled guns, explosives, and radios by hiding them in the basket of her bicycle as she rode around the countryside. As the nature of resistance transformed into acts of sabotage and targeted assassinations, however, her activities changed. Instead of engaging in or assisting with acts of physical violence, she found another outlet for her opposition to the Nazis—helping Jews.

Fluent in German, she would ride her bicycle relatively unmolested while at the same time carrying ration stamps to Jews hiding on farms. She created false identity papers in a variety of ways—sometimes she would steal legitimate documents from guests at her mother's boarding house; sometimes she would arrange for pickpockets at train stations to "lift" documents from travelers; on one occasion, when attending a family funeral, she even searched through mourners' coats looking for documents.

Her early motivation might have been found in the need to save her Jewish fiance, Abraham Pais, who later became a celebrated physicist serving as an assistant to Niels Bohr and working with Albert Einstein at Princeton University. Strobos arranged hiding places for Pais and other Jews in Amsterdam. When the Germans began forcing the Dutch Jews into a ghetto, Strobos found a place for

Pais's sister Annie and her husband, Hermann, to hide; sadly, they did not take up the opportunity, and Annie was later murdered at Sobibor. Strobos also found a refuge for Pais's parents on a farm outside Amsterdam, where they were able to survive the war.

Her relationship with Pais notwithstanding—and their marriage ultimately did not take place—Strobos's efforts did not stop there. In what became a conspiracy of goodness, she and her mother, Marie Schotte, helped shelter more than 100 Jewish refugees, in small groups, for short periods. In the upper floors and attic of their three-story boarding house, located at 282 Nieuwezijds Voorburgwal (just behind the royal palace, in the center of Amsterdam), they created a secret compartment that could hold up to four people behind a hard-to-spot door in the attic. While in this sanctuary, the refugees received food and medical care from Strobos, her mother, and her grandmother. Through her contacts in the resistance, as well as through her own earlier experiences, Strobos was able to provide false passports that would assist the Jews in the next step of their journey to safety.

The house was just a few blocks away from another safe house located at 263 Prinsengracht. This was where **Miep Gies** and others were hiding the family of Anne Frank, a young German-born diarist, while Tina Strobos was rescuing other Jews.

The work Strobos was doing was not without risks, of course. Her grandmother had a radio transmitter hidden in the house, which was used to pass messages from the underground to the Dutch military authorities in London, and discovery could have exposed the house at any moment. Indeed, the Gestapo, Dutch police, and Dutch Nazis searched the house on at least eight occasions, and Strobos herself was arrested and questioned by the Gestapo nine times. On one of these occasions, she was physically manhandled and left unconscious after being thrown against a wall. When asked later why she engaged in these hazardous actions, she said that in her view what she did was "just the right thing to do." Another time she admitted, "I never believed in God," but, rather, always "believed in the sacredness of life."

In 1946, with the end of the war and the liberation of the Netherlands, Strobos resumed her medical studies at the University of Amsterdam. Earning her degree, she went on to further study in London under the direction of Anna Freud, the celebrated psychoanalyst and daughter of Sigmund Freud, the father of psychoanalysis. In 1947 she married Robert Strobos, a neurologist, and together they had three children. They were later divorced, and she married Walter A. Chudson, an economist. In 1951 she migrated to the United States, where she became a U.S. citizen and practiced psychiatry in New York until the age of 89.

In 1989 Yad Vashem recognized Strobos and her mother, Marie Schotte, as Righteous among the Nations, and in 2009, in further recognition of her efforts to save Jewish lives, Strobos received a special award from the Holocaust and Human Rights Education Center of New York. On February 27, 2012, she died of cancer in Rye, New York, at the age of 91.

Sugihara, Chiune (1900–1986)

Chiune "Sempo" Sugihara was a Japanese diplomat who issued travel visas in direct defiance of his government's wishes, enabling more than 6,000 Jewish refugees to escape to safety from German-occupied Lithuania during World War II.

He was born on January 1, 1900, to Yoshimizu and Yatsu Sugihara in Yaotsu, Gifu prefecture. He was one of six children, with a sister and four brothers. Yoshimizu Sugihara raised his children under the strict code of ethics that characterized Japanese samurai tradition, but after finishing his secondary education with honors, Chiune Sugihara defied his father's wish that he enter the medical profession and instead enrolled at Waseda University in 1918 to study English literature. A year later he moved to a foreign language institute in Harbin, Manchuria, to study Russian, after first passing an overseas studies exam administered by Japan's Ministry of Foreign Affairs. He graduated in 1924 and began a diplomatic career by accepting a clerical position at the Japanese consulate in Harbin. While there, he continued to study the Russian language and also acquired proficiency in German.

In 1932 Sugihara was promoted to deputy consul in the Japanese Foreign Ministry in Manchuria. In that capacity, he successfully negotiated the purchase of the Northern Manchurian Railroad, a vital component of Manchuria's economic infrastructure, from the Soviet Union. He also converted to Orthodox Christianity during that time. In 1934 he resigned his consular post in protest at Japan's treatment of the Chinese in occupied Manchuria following the Manchurian invasion. He returned to Tokyo the following year, where he married Yukiko Kikuchi.

Chiune "Sempo" Sugihara, Japanese vice-consul in Kovno (Kaunas), Lithuania during 1939 and 1940. He issued thousands of travel visas to Jews, enabling them to transit through the Soviet Union to temporary refuge in Japan. From here, they could move safely to more permanent havens. He was forced to leave his diplomatic career after the war, possibly because of his disobedience in contravening Japanese immigration regulations back in 1940. (United States Holocaust Memorial Museum, courtesy of Hiroki Sugihara)

Sugihara received a new assignment in 1937, when he was sent to work in the Japanese embassy in Helsinki as interpreter and secretary. He remained there for two years, after which, in March 1939, he was sent to Kovno (Kaunas), then the capital of Lithuania, to open a new embassy there as vice-consul.

When Germany invaded Poland in September 1939 thousands of Jewish refugees fled to Lithuania to escape Nazi atrocities. On June 15, 1940, the Soviet Union invaded and occupied Lithuania, and Soviet authorities would not allow Jews to emigrate from Soviet-occupied territory without special travel documents. Although Germany and the Soviet Union were not yet at war, Soviet antisemitism was strong, and Nazi troops were very close to the border, prompting substantial numbers of Jews in Kovno to line up outside the Japanese embassy in hopes of securing transit visas to East Asia.

Soviet authorities then issued an order requiring that all foreign embassies vacate Lithuania by July 1940. Sugihara was able to negotiate a three-week extension, during which time he risked his career, and possibly his life, to issue more than 2,000 travel visas covering entire families and facilitating the escape of more than 6,000 Jewish refugees to Japanese territory. To make the situation of the refugees easier, the Dutch consul in Kovno, **Jan Zwartendijk**, worked at the same time to provide Jewish refugees with visas issued on his own initiative to the Dutch colony of Curaçao, which did not possess any restrictive entry requirements. The advantage of this lay in the fact that the Japanese government demanded that anyone granted a visa for Japan also have a visa to a third destination—in reality, then, Japan was only allowing Jews short-term transit privileges.

Aware that the Jews were in grave danger if they remained, Sugihara started granting visas without further consultation. He knew that his actions contravened official Japanese policy, but he proceeded regardless. Throughout July and August 1940, with help from his wife, Yukiko, he wrote out and signed thousands of visas by hand, barely pausing to eat or sleep. He handed out the last of these from the window of his train as it left Kovno station on September 1, 1940.

Many of the refugees he saved ended up in Shanghai, China, resulting in the growth of an already flourishing Jewish refugee community there. Despite the insistence of their German allies, the Japanese government proved unwilling to round up and murder Jews; in like manner, they did not follow through on their preliminary plans for mass deportation.

After the Kovno mission was closed, Sugihara was reassigned to Berlin and then Prague, where he served between March 1941 and late 1942. He then went to Königsberg and Bucharest, and remained in Romania through the end of World War II. His family's return to Japan was delayed, however, by a period of imprisonment in a Soviet internment camp, as Japan and the Soviet Union had been at war since August 9, 1945. Released in 1946, they traveled across the Soviet Union and returned to Japan. In 1947 the Japanese Ministry of Foreign Affairs asked Sugihara to resign—some, including his wife, asserted later that it was because of his disobedience in Kovno back in 1940.

In 1978 the government of Israel honored Sugihara for saving the lives of thousands of Jews during the Holocaust, and in 1985 Yad Vashem recognized him as one of the Righteous among the Nations. By this time he was too ill to travel to Israel, so Yukiko Sugihara and her son went to Jerusalem to accept the honor on his behalf. Chiune Sugihara and his descendants were then awarded honorary Israeli citizenship.

On July 31, 1986, he died at his residence in Fujisawa at the age of 86, recognized around the world and in his home country as one of Japan's foremost humanitarians.

Süskind, Walter (1906–1945)

Walter Süskind was a German-born Jewish businessman of Dutch background. Born on October 29, 1906, in Ludenscheid, Germany, he became a manager for the German company Bolak in 1929. In 1935 he married Johanna (known as Hannah) Natt, and in March 1938 they, together with their mothers, Fran Natt and Frieda Süskind, moved to Amsterdam. With other family members already in the United States, the intention was to migrate there later.

After the German invasion of the Netherlands in May 1940, however, the family became trapped. In July 1942 the Nazi-imposed Amsterdam Jewish Council (Joodse Raad) appointed Süskind, as one with management experience, to run the Hollandsche Schouwburg (Dutch Theater), which was renamed the Jüdische Schouwburg and utilized for the purpose of holding Dutch Jews prior to their deportation to the transit camp at Westerbork. From there—though it was not widely known—they were sent regularly to their deaths at Sobibor and Auschwitz.

Right opposite the Dutch Theater was a nursery, where the Nazis preferred to place young Jewish children. Süskind, together with another member of the theater administration, Felix Halverstad, and the director of the nursery, Henriette Henriques Pimentel, established a means whereby Jewish children could be rescued. Children were brought secretly to the Hervormde Kweekschool (Reformed Teacher Training College), two houses from the theater, and with the assistance of the college director, **Jan van Hulst**, passed through the garden and into the theater.

From within the Dutch Theater registry, Süskind and Halverstad then manipulated the records to show that these children were not registered; in this way, their names did not appear in any official capacity. They would sneak the children out from under the Nazis' gaze using a variety of ruses and whisk them off to safer locations outside the city. During the 18 months that Süskind was in charge of the Dutch Theater he saved the lives of some 600 Jewish children. In this he was helped by a number of different Dutch resistance groups.

Such rescue came at a price, however. In order to remain at his post he had to show himself to be an effective administrator of Nazi dictates, which meant organizing the deportation of thousands of Jews to the euphemistically named "East." Moreover, to achieve such effectiveness he was obliged to develop a relationship with the Nazi in charge of the deportations, Ferdinand aus der Fünten, at that time a senior officer of Amsterdam's Central Office for Jewish Emigration. Süskind was therefore seen by many to be a Jewish collaborator, the more so as he used his position to secure the safety of his wife and their daughter, Yvonne.

During the entire operation, Süskind and those around him were never betrayed or discovered by the Nazis, even as he worked seemingly hand-in-hand with aus der Fünten. Only a few people, moreover—those directly involved with the escapes—ever knew the details of Süskind's activities. Süskind experienced considerable turmoil over his role, particularly the dilemma over the issue of saving his family or saving others. Every leader of every Jewish Council throughout Europe was confronted with one fundamental question: should the Nazis be met with opposition at every turn, or should one collaborate with them if doing so makes it possible to save at least some lives? Does one become a traitor, or a hero? After his realization of what the Nazis were actually doing by sending transports to the East, Süskind sought to thwart their deportation plans so far (at least) as the children were concerned.

On September 2, 1944, time and luck ran out for the Süskind family. They were sent to Westerbork, but even there Süskind attempted to find a way to help people escape. In this endeavor, however, he failed. From Westerbork, in October 1944, the family was deported to Terezín (Theresienstadt). As this happened, a forged letter, purportedly from a high-ranking Nazi, was in Süskind's possession. It described how Süskind had been valuable to the Nazi administration in Amsterdam, and with it he hoped to secure some sort of guarantee for himself and his family. He attempted to present it to the commandant of Terezín, Karl Rahm, but a kapo got in the way and instead pushed him into a railcar headed for Auschwitz.

Johanna and Yvonne Süskind were murdered immediately upon arrival. The fate of Walter Süskind himself has been disputed. Most accounts argue that he died on February 28, 1945, on a death march somewhere in Central Europe, but another version claims that Dutch prisoners in Auschwitz, who believed he was a collaborator, murdered him.

In 2012 a Dutch film was made about the exploits of Walter Süskind. The eponymously titled *Süskind*, directed by Rudolf van den Berg, compares well, in several areas, to what is possibly the best known of all Holocaust movies, *Schindler's List* (directed by Steven Spielberg, 1993). In fact, a number of parallels can be drawn between the two stories. One vitally important difference, however, is that while **Oskar Schindler** was not Jewish, Walter Süskind certainly was. Unlike in

Schindler's List, there is nothing remotely resembling a happy ending in *Süskind*. The heartbreaking end of the movie mirrors the tragic reality that was Walter Süskind's own story.

Sylten, Werner (1893–1942)

Werner Sylten was a Protestant theologian, educator, and opponent of Nazism who was instrumental in saving the lives of numerous racially persecuted Christians of Jewish descent in Berlin.

Swiss by birth, he was born to German parents on August 9, 1893, in Hergiswil am See, Nidwalden. His father, a chemist from Königsberg (Kaliningrad), East Prussia, had converted from Judaism to Christianity before marrying a Protestant. Sylten, the eldest of five children, was educated in Berlin, Breslau (Wrocław), and Lohr am Main, Bavaria. He fought for Germany as a volunteer during World War I, after which, in 1920, he completed his theological studies and received ordination at the University of Marburg. He was influenced by liberal theology, supported a strong democracy, and had a commitment to social justice.

After ordination, he searched for positions in Göttingen and Hildesheim before settling as director of a Protestant girls' school at Bad Köstritz, Thuringia, in 1925. In 1933, with the advent of Nazism, he was forbidden from teaching because of his Jewish ancestry, and in 1936 the Church compulsorily dismissed him as a pastor on orders from the government.

Sylten was regarded by Nazi racial thinking as a *mischling*, that is, a person of mixed "Aryan" and Jewish descent. The Nuremberg race laws of 1935 codified the legal status of the *mischlinge*. Thus, those with four Jewish grandparents were "full Jews"; those with three Jewish grandparents were "three-quarter Jews"; those with two Jewish grandparents were considered "*Mischlinge* of the First Degree," provided they did not identify with the Jewish religion and were not married to Jewish spouses; and those with only one Jewish grandparent were "*Mischlinge* of the Second Degree." In 1935 Germans in the latter two categories were said to number anywhere between 100,000 and 350,000. For the most part, *Mischlinge* of the First Degree, such as Sylten, were classified as Jews; those of the Second Degree were absorbed into German society, albeit with restrictions and no little amount of discrimination.

In 1933 Sylten joined the Confessional Church with the assistance of Lutheran pastor Martin Niemöller and subsequently headed the Thuringian office of the Confessional Church in Bad Köstritz. Following the publication of a vicious attack on Sylten in the *Völkischer Beobachter* on September 20, 1935, the Thuringian minister of the interior dismissed him from his job and later expelled him from Thuringia. Sylten's wife, Hildegard, unable to stand the emotional pressure of these early years of Nazi persecution, committed suicide in 1935. With this double blow, and directly affected by the Nuremberg Laws, he was no longer able to serve a regular parish. He worked as executive director of the Thuringian Confessing Church office from May 1936 until March 1938, when it was shut down by police.

Later in 1938 he was offered a position by Pastor **Heinrich Grüber**, who maintained a Church Aid Office for Protestant Non-Aryans in Berlin to support those designated by the Nazis as "non-Aryan Christians." Sylten began work in December 1938. His position enabled him to give pastoral support to Protestant victims of Nazi racial oppression and help them find ways to emigrate. Through the Büro Grüber (Grüber Bureau), as it became known, he helped save the lives of more than 1,000 "non-Aryan Christians" by facilitating their safe departure from Germany.

After Grüber was arrested on December 19, 1940, Sylten took over management of the Aid Office until he finally had to close it down two months later. On February 25, 1941, he was arrested. After three months on remand at the Alexanderplatz police prison, he was sent to Dachau. There he had to do hard physical work, but this did not deter him from maintaining his ministry among the other prisoners. At one point he became seriously ill but refused to report himself as sick after realizing that doing so would mean deportation and certain death.

Pastor Grüber, who was in the camp with Sylten, arranged a bribe to ensure that he would not be placed on a transport list but could not save him indefinitely. Weak from continual forced labor and sick from a debilitating skin condition, Sylten was taken to the Nazi killing center at Hartheim Castle, near Linz, Austria, on an "invalid transport." So far as can be ascertained, he was gassed there on August 26, 1942.

On October 16, 1979, in recognition of his work on behalf of "non-Aryan Christians," Yad Vashem in Jerusalem recognized Werner Sylten as one of the Righteous among the Nations.

Szenes, Hannah (1921–1944)

Hannah Szenes was a Hungarian-born Jewish paratrooper trained in Palestine to rescue Jews during the Holocaust.

She was born into an assimilated family in Budapest on July 17, 1921. Her father, Béla Szenes, had been a well-known writer and playwright but died when she was six years old, leaving her and her brother, György, to be raised by their mother, Katharine. Following her famous father, she demonstrated literary talent, keeping a diary from the age of 13 until shortly before her death.

As a student she attended a high school for Protestant girls that also accepted Catholics and Jews, and it was here that she first experienced antisemitism. As she grew older, she sought to learn more about what it meant to be Jewish; she adopted Zionism as her political lodestone and joined Maccabea, a Hungarian

Hannah Szenes, an iconic Hungarian-born resistance fighter trained in Palestine by British forces and parachuted back into Europe in 1944. Determined to return to Hungary and assist the Jews then suffering the full onslaught of the Holocaust, she was arrested soon after crossing the border. Tried by a Hungarian court for treason and espionage, she was executed by a German firing squad. (United States Holocaust Memorial Museum, courtesy of Beit Hannah Senesh)

Zionist youth movement that helped to develop her skills in Hebrew and her love for *Eretz Yisrael* (the Land of Israel).

In 1939 Szenes finished school and made the decision to emigrate to what was then the British Mandate of Palestine. She studied first at the Girls' Agricultural School at Nahalal and then in 1941 settled at Kibbutz Sdot Yam, near Haifa. She continued the diary she had begun in Hungary, as well as writing poetry and even a play about kibbutz life. Her work included shifts in the communal kitchen and the kibbutz laundry.

In 1943 she joined the Palmach (the combat units of the Haganah) and was soon training for a special mission—a secret scheme that would see her join the British army and be parachuted into Nazi-occupied Europe. She would assist Allied efforts behind the lines and make contact with resistance fighters in an attempt to offer aid to European Jewry. At first she studied wireless operation procedures, and in January 1944 she moved to Egypt to be trained as a paratrooper. She was one of a unit of 33 people, comprising both sexes.

In mid-March 1944 they were dropped into Yugoslavia, where Szenes spent three months with Tito's partisans. Entering Hungary had to be put on hold for a time, as the parachute drop coincided directly with the German invasion of Hungary. Instead, Szenes worked with the partisans until the time was opportune to cross into Hungary.

On June 7, 1944, just as the deportation of the Hungarian Jews was at its most intense, Szenes decided to move into Hungary with the aim of reaching Budapest. It was an extremely dangerous time; in fact, her two partners on the mission, Yoel Palgi and Peretz Goldstein, both counseled against proceeding. In spite of their caution, she decided to go ahead alone. Within hours of crossing the border she was arrested by Hungarian gendarmes; finding her British military credentials and radio transmitter, they imprisoned and tortured her for the transmission code so they could track down all the other parachutists. She was tortured repeatedly for months but refused to divulge anything about her mission. When the authorities arrested her mother (who did not know that Szenes had moved to Palestine, or that she was back in Budapest on a secret military mission), she still would not speak.

Seeing themselves with little other option, the Hungarian fascist authorities tried her for treason and spying. The trial began on October 28, 1944, its outcome a foregone conclusion. Convicted as a spy, she was sentenced to death by a German (not Hungarian) firing squad on November 7, 1944. When facing her executioners she refused a blindfold. At the time of her death she was 23 years old.

In 1950 the remains of Hannah Szenes were taken to Israel and reburied in the military cemetery on Mount Herzl in Jerusalem. A tombstone was erected for her in November 2007 at her kibbutz in Sdot Yam, and with the end of the Cold War a Hungarian military court overturned the original decision and posthumously exonerated her.

Szenes's diary was published in Hebrew in 1946. Her poetry contains lines that have become iconic in Israeli literature, the best known of which is the poem "*Halikha LeKesariya*" ("A Walk to Caesarea"), commonly known as "*Eli, Eli*" ("My God, My God"), set to music by David Zahavi and sung or played in most Jewish remembrance services to this day. Another of her poems, "*Ashrei Hagafrur*" ("Blessed Is the Match"), equals it for recognition and has been quoted frequently since the Holocaust. Written after she was parachuted into Yugoslavia, the most crucial lines are:

> Blessed is the match consumed in kindling flame.
> Blessed is the flame that burns in the secret fastness of the heart.
> Blessed is the heart with strength to stop its beating for honor's sake.
> Blessed is the match consumed in kindling flame.

Hannah Szenes remains a national heroine in Israel, where she is representative of all that Israeli society seeks in terms of idealism and self-sacrifice in the face of adverse circumstances. As a resister, she was unable to achieve her objectives, but the symbolism of her actions was (and remains) immense.

Sztehló, Gabor (1909–1974)

Gabor Sztehló was a Christian minister in Budapest who rescued hundreds of Jewish children during the Holocaust.

The son of a lawyer, Marta Maria Jozefa, he was born in Budapest on September 29, 1909. He attended the Sopron Lutheran grammar school and in 1931 obtained a degree in Lutheran theology. The following year he was ordained a pastor. From 1933 to 1935 he served a congregation in Hatvani, northern Hungary, before moving to Nagytarcsa in central Hungary, where he was stationed between 1935 and 1942.

On October 20, 1942, under the direction of Pastor Gyula Muraközy and the sponsorship of the Universal Convent of the Reformed Church of Hungary, the Good Shepherd Mission (or Committee) was established. This became Hungary's major association of Jews converted to Protestantism. Its leadership was entrusted to Pastor József Éliás, himself of Jewish background. The Hungarian Evangelical Church became affiliated with the Committee in May 1944, when Bishop Sándor Raffay appointed Sztehló as its representative in charge of providing food, clothing, and succor to converts from Judaism and the dependents of those called up for forced labor. Before Hungary was occupied by Nazi Germany in March 1944, the Committee had already been helpful toward Jewish and non-Jewish refugees through providing assistance for those interned in various camps.

After Germany invaded Hungary, Sztehló and the Good Shepherd Committee began rescuing abandoned Jewish children. This intensified considerably in October 1944, after the antisemitic, fascist Arrow Cross party took power and unleashed a full anti-Jewish campaign of terror.

Éliás and Sztehló had prepared for this, seeing to it that the children in their care would be fed, housed, and looked after with the cooperation of the International Red Cross, which established a special department (Section B) especially for this purpose. Responsibility for the protection of the children fell almost exclusively on Sztehló's shoulders; Éliás, who had crossed its members too many times, was targeted by the Arrow Cross.

Most of those they helped were children of converts and Christian orphans, but Sztehló soon decided to extend his rescue activities to all Jewish children regardless of status. By Christmas, 32 homes had been designated as havens for children. One of these was the castle of Ney Ákos, the former director of railways in Hungary and a hero of World War I. Sztehló provided documents for approximately 1,500 children, stating that they were Gentiles and likely saving them from deportation and execution. While the Arrow Cross and police raided some of the homes, no harm came to any of the children housed in them.

On December 26, 1944, Soviet units began the encirclement of Budapest, signaling the start of a siege that would claim the lives of some 38,000 civilians. During the battle, many of Sztehló's homes were damaged, rendering them useless as shelters for the children. With the escalation in fighting, Sztehló moved 33 children to the basement of his own home, and he and his family protected them for nearly three weeks. The city surrendered to the Russians unconditionally on February 13, 1945, and Sztehló then managed to move the children to more permanent places until they were either claimed by their families—unfortunately, all too infrequently—or until Jewish organizations accepted them.

When liberation came and the war finally ended, Sztehló continued to care for children once it became known that their families had definitely succumbed to the Holocaust. He established a school in which the children not only received an education but also learned technical skills that would permit them to enter whatever the new society would look like. In 1951 the home was taken over by Hungary's communist regime.

Sztehló's family moved to Switzerland in 1956. Anxious to continue his work, he remained in Hungary and persisted in the development of charity homes as part of the work of the Lutheran Church. In 1961, however, during a visit to Switzerland, he suffered a stroke that necessitated him remaining there on medical advice. Upon recovery, he resumed his pastoral activities in his new home. When his passport expired, the Hungarian government did not renew it; he was not even permitted to return to Hungary as a visitor. It took more than 10 years before he finally received permission to return, but he died on May 28, 1974, just two months prior to his scheduled visit. He was cremated, and his ashes were returned for their final interment to Budapest's Farkasréti cemetery.

In 1972 Pastor Gabor Sztehló was recognized as one of the Righteous among the Nations by Yad Vashem for his work in saving the lives of Jewish children. He was the first Hungarian to be so acknowledged. Then, in 1973, the Swiss government nominated him for the Nobel Peace Prize. Overall, the acts of resistance undertaken by Gabor Sztehló saw some 1,600 Jewish children and 400 Jewish adults saved from the Holocaust.

Ten Boom, Corrie (1892–1993)

Cornelia (Corrie) ten Boom was a Dutch rescuer of Jews during the Holocaust, proceeding from a firm Christian belief that demanded she help those in need. It is estimated that overall she and her family saved the lives of more than 800 Jews.

She was born in Haarlem, near Amsterdam, on April 15, 1892, the youngest in a family of four children. She had two sisters, Betsie and Nollie, and a brother, Willem; their father, Casper, was a jeweler and watchmaker. Cornelia was named after her mother. Their home was always crowded, as ten Boom's three maternal aunts also lived with her family. In 1924 ten Boom, having learned at the feet of her father, became the first licensed female watchmaker in the Netherlands. As she became older, she established a youth club for teenage girls, ran a church for people with disabilities, raised foster children in her home, and engaged in other charitable works. After the Nazis invaded the Netherlands in May 1940, ten Boom was forced to close down the girls' youth club.

The ten Booms were members of the Dutch Reformed Church, and Corrie ten Boom came from a family tradition that had long championed Jewish causes. During the 19th century, her grandfather had supported efforts to improve Christian-Jewish relations, and her brother, Willem, a Dutch Reformed minister assigned to convert Jews, studied antisemitism and ran a nursing home, which in the late 1930s became a refuge for Jews fleeing Germany.

Within months of the German takeover, the social, political, and legal climate of the Netherlands was transformed. It did not take long for the ten Booms to become involved in resistance activities, with various extended family members taking a number of different underground roles. Corrie ten Boom became directly involved when she, her father, and her sister Betsie decided to hide Jews in the family home. She established contacts with members of the resistance, who assisted her through obtaining extra ration books and building a hiding place in the family home. This tiny secret room, built into ten Boom's bedroom behind a false wall, became a refuge for Jews, students, and political dissidents. It could hold up to six people, standing, and was serviced by a rudimentary ventilation system.

The "hiding place," also known as "*de Bejé*"—an abbreviation of their street address on the Barteljorisstraat, a shopping street in Haarlem—thus became a center of short-term rescue. From this start, ten Boom became a leader in what was nicknamed the "Beje movement," in which a series of safe houses was established throughout the Netherlands.

On February 28, 1944, a Dutch informant betrayed the ten Booms and denounced them to the Nazis. That same day the Gestapo raided the house, and ten Boom, her father, brother, sisters, and other family members, as well as some resistance fighters, were arrested. In total, the Gestapo arrested more than 30 people in the ten Boom family home. Although German soldiers searched the house thoroughly, they did not find the Jews who were at that moment concealed in the hiding place next to ten Boom's room. They remained there for nearly three days, until the Nazis gave up their surveillance, and Dutch resisters, who knew they were there, moved in and rescued them. By the end of the war, all but one survived.

The ten Booms were sent immediately to Scheveningen prison. Nollie and Willem ten Boom, and their nephew, Peter, were released straightaway, but Corrie and Betsie ten Boom, and their 84-year-old father, Casper ten Boom, remained incarcerated. Casper ten Boom died 10 days later after falling ill. Corrie and Betsie ten Boom stayed at Scheveningen until June 1944, when they were transferred to the concentration camp at Vught. In September 1944 they were deported to Ravensbrück, where Betsie ten Boom died on December 16, 1944.

Ten Boom was released from Ravensbrück on December 28, 1944, in what was believed to have been a clerical error. She traveled by train to Berlin, where she arrived on January 1, 1945. From there she made her way back to the Netherlands.

After the war, ten Boom set up a rehabilitation center for concentration camp survivors. In a Christian spirit of reconciliation, she also took in and sheltered those who had cooperated with the Germans during the occupation but were now homeless and without the means of making a living. She returned to Germany in 1946 and began a worldwide ministry that led to her appearance in more than 60 countries. As an evangelist and motivational speaker she would refer to her experiences in Ravensbrück, and as a social critic she protested the Vietnam War. Her main message focused on reconciliation as a means for overcoming the psychological scars left by war. She also wrote many inspirational books advocating a Christian message of love, goodwill, and human understanding through the embrace of Christ's message.

The main written work for which Corrie ten Boom is remembered is the story of her own family's confrontation with Nazism during World War II. Entitled *The Hiding Place*, the book appeared in 1971 and became a best seller. In 1975 it was made into a motion picture with the same name, directed by James F. Collier and starring Jeannette Clift as Corrie ten Boom and Julie Harris as her sister Betsie.

In recognition of her work during the war, Corrie ten Boom was knighted in 1962 by Queen Juliana, and on December 12, 1967, for her efforts in hiding Jews from arrest and deportation, she was recognized by Yad Vashem as one of the Righteous among the Nations. In 1977 ten Boom, now 85 years old, moved to the United States, where she settled in California. She died on April 15, 1983, her 91st birthday.

In resisting the Nazi persecution of the Jews, Corrie ten Boom suffered imprisonment, internment in a concentration camp, and the loss of family members. She followed both the letter and the spirit of her Christian beliefs, seeing that what had to be done was a duty to fulfill for all those purporting to be true Christians.

Tenenbaum, Mordechaj (1916–1943)

Mordechaj Tenenbaum was a resister in the Vilna ghetto, a member of the Żydowska Organizacja Bojowa (Jewish Combat Organization, or ŻOB) during the Warsaw Ghetto Uprising of April–May 1943, and a leader of the Białystok ghetto uprising of August that same year.

He was born in 1916 in Warsaw and studied at the University of Warsaw. From 1935 he was a member of the Socialist Union of Jewish Youth, or Frajhajt (Freedom) organization, which in turn was closely connected to the right wing of the Poale Zion movement. From 1938 onward he belonged to the Central Committee of Hechalutz, a Zionist association of Jewish youth whose aim was to train its members to settle in Palestine. With the outbreak of war in September 1939, Tenenbaum went first to Kovel and then to Vilna (Vilnius), where he was instrumental in organizing an anti-German underground resistance network after the Nazi invasion in 1941.

Outside Vilna, in March 1942 a group of Polish Jews calling themselves the Anti-Fascist Bloc was formed in the Warsaw Ghetto. It was an anti-Nazi alliance comprising left-wing Zionist groups, communists, and socialists. The Jewish Labor Bund did not join because its members were hoping instead for a broader socialist coalition that would embrace both Jews and non-Jewish Poles. The main instigators of the bloc were **Mordecai Anielewicz**, Józef Lewartowski, Josef Kaplan, Szachno Sagan, Jozef Sak, **Yitzhak Zuckerman**, and **Zivia Lubetkin**. The fighting arm of the Anti-Fascist Bloc evolved into the ŻOB.

Tenenbaum had returned to Warsaw from Vilna during 1942, but in October of that year, with forged documents and claiming to be a Tatar named Yussuf Tamaroff, the ŻOB sent him to Białystok. At that time Białystok was still relatively quiet, and it was planned that Tenenbaum's presence would give the underground there the time and opportunity to organize should there be any moves to liquidate the ghetto. Already that August, members of the Hashomer Hatzair youth movement, together with some from the Jewish Labor Bund, had created a resistance organization called Block A. Tenenbaum established a second organization, Block B. By the end of July 1943, a single anti-Nazi organization was formed, and serious planning began for a possible uprising. Tenenbaum became the commander, with **Daniel Moszkowicz** as his deputy.

A further initiative of Tenenbaum's tenure was to establish a Białystok equivalent of the Oneg Shabbat Archive set up in Warsaw by **Emanuel Ringelblum**. This was duly created and functioned until the destruction of the ghetto in April 1943, when it was hidden on the Aryan side to be recovered after the war.

An armed resistance movement in the ghetto was at first opposed by the head of the Białystok Jewish Council (Judenrat), Efraim Barasz, who, with other members of the organized Jewish community, held to the view that so long as Białystok remained useful to the German war effort the ghetto would not be harmed. Only after the Germans began the final liquidation of the ghetto on the night of August 15–16, 1943, did the resistance movement move into full operation. Numbering only a few hundred poorly armed fighters, the resisters struggled valiantly against overwhelming odds, but their efforts were doomed to failure and their struggle lasted little more than a day.

At first, and for a lengthy time, Tenenbaum's fate was not known. Later, it was shown that both he and Daniel Moszkowicz committed suicide once their bunker was surrounded, rather than surrender to the Germans. A date of August 20, 1943, has been recorded for Tenenbaum's death.

On April 18, 1945, Mordechaj Tenenbaum, this much traveled resister instrumental in three ghetto underground movements, was posthumously awarded the Order of Grunwald Cross, Third Class. Recognizing his efforts and leadership in the defense of the Białystok ghetto, and his resistance to the Nazis, the Białystok City Council on July 11, 2008, named a plaza in his honor, located on the site of the former ghetto.

Trocmé, André (1901–1971)

André Trocmé was a French Huguenot pastor who, with his wife Magda, directed a remarkable rescue effort of Jewish and other refugees in the village of Le Chambon-sur-Lignon and its surrounding areas, a rural mountainous region in south-central France known as the Plateau Vivarais-Lignon.

Born in Saint-Quentin-en-Tourmont in northern France on April 7, 1901, Trocmé was the son of a French father and German mother, and the product of a strict bourgeois Huguenot upbringing. As an eyewitness to the horrors of World War I he was shattered by its tremendous violence and the decimation of an entire generation, and he advocated for the resolution of conflict through nonviolent means. In 1926 he married the equally dedicated Magda Grilli di Cortona, whom he met while conducting graduate work at the Union Theological Seminary in New York. They would have four children: Nelly, Jean-Pierre, Jacques, and Daniel.

Trocmé became an outspoken proponent of nonviolence, making him a controversial figure in the French Protestant Church. Seeking to limit his influence, the Church sent him to the remote parish of Le Chambon, though once there he did not hesitate to impart his pacifist convictions. In 1938 he and Pastor Edouard Theis, who came to the village to assist him, opened the École Nouvelle Cévenole, a coeducational secondary school based on the principles of tolerance, pacifism, and internationalism. Trocmé's preaching was also politically shaded. He spoke out against Nazism in neighboring Germany, pointing out its discriminatory policies toward Jews. With the coming of World War II, his opposition toward the Nazis and his pacifism would be tested in a manner he did not anticipate.

In 1940 France capitulated to Germany in a few short weeks. On June 23, 1940, the day after the armistice was signed, Trocmé and Theis emphasized their views in a celebrated sermon directed squarely at their Protestant Huguenot congregation: "The duty of Christians is to resist the violence brought to bear on their consciences with the weapons of the spirit—we will resist whenever our adversaries try to force us to act against the commands of the Gospel. We will do so without fear, but also without pride and without hatred."

When the deportations of Jews began in France in 1942, Trocmé urged his congregation to give shelter to "the people of the Bible," the more so as the village and its outlying areas were quickly filled with hundreds of fleeing Jews. Trocmé showed the way by enjoining his congregation to take in refugees—particularly children—in need of sanctuary. From this point on the people of Le Chambon would prove over and over again that they were willing to open their doors courageously to Jews and other persecuted refugees.

Magda Trocmé also assisted refugees in their search for safe havens, connecting them with those prepared to take them in. While not part of any formal resistance network, the efforts of the Trocmés to assist Jews overlapped with the work of many others who were supporting rescue efforts in the area. As a result, large numbers of people found permanent shelter in and around Le Chambon, while others were sheltered temporarily until a way could be found to smuggle them across the border into Switzerland. They were housed with local townspeople and farmers, in public institutions, and in homes for children. There were many ways in which people provided help. Community members not only were prepared to accommodate the Jewish refugees but would also meet Jews (nicknamed "Testaments" by the villagers) who arrived at the local train station and spirit them away to new homes. Schools found ways to accommodate increased enrollments, and fabrications of school registers were made to appear as though the children—with changed names—had always been there. With very few dissenters, the entire community of Le Chambon, it seemed, banded together as one in order to rescue Jews.

While the people of Le Chambon were effectively hiding the children "in plain sight," the Vichy authorities learned of Trocmé's clandestine work. Accordingly, in January 1943 he and Theis, together with the local headmaster, Roger Darcissac, were arrested and imprisoned for several weeks in the St. Paul d'Eyjeaux internment camp for political prisoners, near Limoges. When he was arrested and first told to desist from his rescue activities, Trocmé made a famous statement: "These people came here for help and for shelter. I am their shepherd. A shepherd does not forsake his flock . . . I do not know what a Jew is. I know only human beings." After a period of imprisonment, the three men were released through the intervention of several individuals—including Trocmé's cousin Daniel Trocmé, who was also involved in refugee work in Le Chambon, and who was himself later arrested and deported to Majdanek, where he died in 1944.

Following his release Trocmé continued his efforts on behalf of Jews and others in Le Chambon, but he was forced to go into hiding for several months. His absence did not deter the residents of Le Chambon nor close down the rescue operation he had begun. Villagers continued welcoming persecuted Jews into their homes, providing sanctuary for them and enabling many to see out the war in relative safety.

No one knows precisely how many Jewish refugees were hidden or saved at Le Chambon during World War II. According to some estimates, about 3,500 Jewish refugees were saved; other estimates range as high as 5,000, taking into account those Jews who at least passed through Le Chambon and its vicinity, as well as those who remained for any length of time.

After the war, André and Magda Trocmé continued the cause of nonviolent resolution of problems. André Trocmé served as European secretary for the International Fellowship of Reconciliation, a nongovernmental pacifist organization founded in 1914 in response to the horrors of war in Europe. He spent his final years as pastor of a Reformed Church in Geneva.

On January 5, 1971, Yad Vashem recognized André Trocmé as one of the Righteous among the Nations, with his wife, Magda, receiving the same recognition on May 14, 1984. In an unprecedented move, Yad Vashem presented this honor to the entire village of Le Chambon-sur-Lignon in 1998.

Trocmé died on June 5, 1971, in Geneva, followed by his wife on October 10, 1996, in Paris. Both are buried in the family grave in Le Chambon.

U

Ülkümen, Selahattin (1914–2003)

Selahattin Ülkümen, born in 1914, was the Turkish consul-general on the German-occupied Greek island of Rhodes during World War II. Born in 1914, he managed to save the lives of 42 Jewish families threatened with death at the hands of the Nazis.

Jews had lived on Rhodes since the Jewish expulsion from Spain in 1492, at which time they were welcomed into the Ottoman Empire. When the Nazis occupied the island in September 1943, taking over from the Italians, Rhodes had a Jewish population of some 1,700. The occupation saw the Germans move to close the Turkish consulate, at that time the last remaining in Axis-controlled territory.

On July 19, 1944, the Gestapo ordered all the island's Jews to report for registration. Then, in late July, the Germans began deporting the Jewish population, and Ülkümen, distressed by what he was seeing, tried to save the lives of at least some of the people. Approaching the German commanding officer, General Ulrich Kleeman, he reminded him of Turkish neutrality and of the history that spanned the previous four centuries. With Rhodes a Turkish island since the 15th century, he argued, its Jewish inhabitants (including their spouses, whether Jewish or not) were Turkish citizens according to Turkish law, and thus should be spared deportation.

Kleeman's response was that no exceptions were to be made, and all Jews would have to go. Ülkümen's rejoinder was that he would advise the Turkish government if the Jews were not released and that an international incident would likely follow. After this, Kleeman agreed to spare those Jews who could verify their Turkish nationality or background. Ülkümen had clearly gone too far diplomatically, particularly as he was quoting a Turkish law that did not actually exist, but his ruse was effective—his action saved the lives of 42 Jewish families, numbering up to 200 individuals altogether.

Several personal dramas were resolved through Ülkümen's action. One man, Albert Franko, was saved when it was established that Franko's wife was a Turkish citizen. Although Franko was actually already on a deportation train, Ülkümen managed to have him taken off and returned to Rhodes.

In another case, a Turkish citizen living in Rhodes and married to an Italian citizen, Matilda Toriel, was rescued by Ülkümen through his intervention during the initial Nazi registration process. Although the Nazis had demanded that all Jews appear, Ülkümen approached Toriel and told her not to register until he could save her absent husband as well. When challenged by the Nazi authorities, he repeated that spouses of Turkish citizens were also citizens under Turkish law, and demanded his release. Again, this was a deception, but through it Ülkümen created a precedent, and with this he was able to save even more lives.

The remaining 1,700 Jews of Rhodes were not so fortunate. Almost all were deported to the Greek mainland, and from there to Auschwitz.

Ülkümen's audacity, sadly, had unfortunate consequences. The Nazis investigated the Turkish laws, saw that Ülkümen had played them for fools, and decided to punish him. An air raid was called in to bomb the Turkish consulate building, seriously injuring Ülkümen's pregnant wife, Mihrinissa. In August 1944, when Turkey broke diplomatic relations with Nazi Germany, they were deported to Piraeus and interned on the Greek mainland for the duration of the war. Mihrinissa, tragically, died from her injuries a week after giving birth to the couple's son, Mehmet.

Ülkümen returned to Turkey after the German surrender on May 8, 1945, and remained in the Turkish diplomatic service until his retirement. He never sought recognition for his bravery during the war years, and it was hardly ever mentioned.

On December 13, 1989, however, Yad Vashem recognized Ülkümen as one of the Righteous among the Nations. He became the first non-Christian (and first Muslim) to receive the award, forcing Yad Vashem to change its award from what had been "Righteous Christians" to "Righteous Gentiles"—the term that has been operational ever since. The man who became known as "the Turkish **Schindler**," at the age of 75, traveled to Jerusalem in order to plant a carob tree (the standard honor given to those named as Righteous) of his own in Yad Vashem's Garden of the Righteous.

Selahattin Ülkümen died in Istanbul on June 7, 2003, at the age of 89.

V

Veseli, Refik (1927–2000)

Refik Veseli was born in 1927 and raised in the rural village of Kruja in the mountains of Albania. He was a Muslim who saved the lives of a Jewish photographer and his family during the Holocaust. His story involves his whole family: his parents Vesel and Fatima, and their children Refik, Hamid, and Xhemal.

When Yugoslavia was invaded by Germany in April 1941, the Jewish family of Moshe (Mosa) and Gabriela Mandil and their children, Gavra and Irena, fled to Italian-occupied Kosovo. Between October 1941 and May 1942 they were imprisoned by the Italians in Pristina, but Moshe Mandil, a professional photographer, offered to take pictures of Italian soldiers—a measure that opened up a healthy relationship that eventually resulted in the family's release and transfer to Italian-occupied Albania. By the summer of 1943 they had settled in Tirana, where Mandil began working in the photography studio of one of his former students, Neshad Prizerini, whose apprentice was Refik Veseli.

Mandil befriended Veseli, who became concerned for the photographer and his family after the Nazis invaded in September 1943. Without hesitation, Veseli contacted his family and asked permission to spirit the Mandils

Refik Veseli, an Albanian Muslim who sheltered the Mandils, a Jewish family, during the Holocaust. Adopting the Albanian code of *Besa*, Veseli and his family, together with others in his village and around the country, protected those in need; as a result, over 1,800 Jews were rescued in Albania. In this image from October 1943 Veseli poses with one of the Mandil children, Gavra. (United States Holocaust Memorial Museum, courtesy of Gavra Mandil)

to their home, and then he guided them through the mountains to the Veseli home in Kruja.

Soon after their arrival, Veseli's brother Xhemal brought a second Jewish family from Tirana, Ruzhica and Yosef Ben Yosef, and Yosef's sister Finica. Two families together presented a space problem, so they were moved out of the Veselis' barn and dressed in Albanian peasant garb so they could hide "in plain sight." As members of the Kruja community, they were accepted by their neighbors as locals. When the Nazis came into the village looking for Jews or resisters, a curtain of silence fell across the village and they were not denounced. Moreover, in emulation of what the Veselis were doing, some other villagers also began giving sanctuary to Jews.

Together, the Mandils and the Finicas stayed with the Veselis from November 1943 until the Nazis were driven out in October 1944.

When looking for a reason behind the help offered by the Veselis and other members of the Kruja community, Albanians have pointed to a code of conduct known as *Besa*, which means "keeping a promise." In accordance with this code, people will keep their word and protect each other. The situation during the Holocaust was not an isolated incident, as *Besa* had been invoked on numerous occasions in the past—over time, Albanians had, for example, provided comfort to other neighboring peoples in need, including Italians, Greeks, Croats, and Hungarians.

Besa was best expressed by the example of Refik Veseli himself. Suspicious of the village's level of loyalty, the Nazis offered him (and others) a reward if he would point the Nazis in the direction of any Jews in the neighborhood. In accordance with the code of *Besa* his secret was kept, and no Jews were denounced. By maintaining his silence, of course, Veseli was risking his own life, but he took the risks and protected those to whom he was committed.

In one sense, Veseli's family was not all that unusual within the context of Albanian traditions. Albanians all over the country risked their lives to save Jews. In fact, in what is a remarkable statistic, Albania was the only country in Nazi-occupied Europe where the Jewish population actually *increased* during the Holocaust, with more than 1,800 Jews rescued in this almost exclusively Muslim country.

As for the first family whom Veseli sought to assist, the Mandils, their survival was guaranteed, and after the war they returned to their home city of Novi Sad, in Yugoslavia. Mandil resumed his career as a photographer, and in 1946 he invited Veseli to come and live with them in order to complete his apprenticeship as a photographer. He did so, remaining with the family until they migrated to Israel in 1948. Even then, Veseli sought to stay with them, but he was persuaded to return to Albania to be with his family.

In 1987 one of Moshe Mandil's children, Gavra Mandil—now an adult—wrote to Yad Vashem in Jerusalem and told the story of the Veseli family during World War II. He sought some sort of recognition for the goodness that had been offered them. After undertaking extensive research, Yad Vashem decided to recognize Vesel and Fatima Veseli and their children Refik, Hamid, and Xhemal as Righteous among the Nations. With this status, they became the first Albanians to be so recognized. In a highly symbolic gesture, the leader of Albania's hardline communist government, Ramiz Alia, permitted Refik Veseli and his wife to travel to Israel in order to attend the ceremony of recognition at Yad Vashem.

As an upstander, Veseli's action in saving Jews took place despite the risks and out of motives that were both noble and without any agenda, save that of putting the lives of those in need above baser interests.

Vrba, Rudolf (1924–2006)

Rudolf Vrba was a Slovak Jew who escaped from Auschwitz on April 7, 1944, and provided testimony detailing the enormity of the Holocaust in Eastern Europe.

He was born Walter Rosenberg in Topoľčany, Czechoslovakia, on September 11, 1924. His father, Elias Rosenberg, owned a sawmill. Walter Rosenberg was excluded from the local high school at the age of 15 because he was a Jew, so he began work as a laborer. He did his best to keep his head down in the early years of the war (and before that, Nazi occupation of the Slovak "protectorate"), but in 1942, when antisemitic measures intensified, he decided to try to join the Czechoslovak army-in-exile in Britain.

He only made it as far as the Hungarian border before he was picked up and handed over to Slovak authorities. Sent to a transit camp, he escaped but was soon apprehended. On June 15, 1942, he arrived at Majdanek and was then immediately transferred to Auschwitz, where he arrived on June 30. He was put to work exhuming bodies from mass graves (which were then cremated) and also worked as an orderly, tasked with sorting through the personal possessions of detainees destined for the gas chambers. He rose to become a camp registrar, and it was in this role that he began to calculate and, as he wrote later, "mentally record" statistics relating to those transported to the camp. Before long he was planning an escape.

On April 7, 1944, Rosenberg and fellow prisoner Alfréd Wetzler, also from Slovakia, managed to flee the death camp through a flaw in the otherwise impenetrable security system. They managed to return to Czechoslovakia, where they met with the Slovak Jewish Council at Žilina.

After a brief period to recover, they provided the Council with extremely detailed testimony of what was occurring at Auschwitz. The testimony, when transcribed and typed, totaled some 40 pages. It contained an exhaustive description of the geography and management of the camp, and of how the prisoners lived and died. It also gave a comprehensive list of every transport that had arrived at Auschwitz since 1942, chronicling each one's place of origin and how many people from each transport were murdered. The report also included sketches and information regarding the layout of the gas chambers. Rosenberg was later to state that much of his information about the operation of the gas chambers and crematoria came from *Sonderkommando* workers such as **Filip Müller**.

The report was copied and passed on to **Rezső Kasztner**, head of the Zionist Aid and Rescue Committee in Bratislava. He, in turn, passed it to **Gisi Fleischmann** and Rabbi **Chaim Michael Dov Weissmandl**, who arranged for a much a wider distribution, including Hungary's Foreign Ministry and the Vatican. British and American operatives saw copies as early as mid-June 1944, and it was broadcast in part by the BBC and condensed and printed in the *New York Times* on June 20.

After the report had been handed to the Slovak Jewish Council, Rosenberg was given a new identity and new papers in the name of Rudolf Vrba, which he legalized after the liberation. On August 29, 1944, the Slovak army revolted against the Nazis, and Vrba joined a Czechoslovak partisan unit in September 1944. He gave April 7, the day of his escape, as his birthdate.

When World War II ended, Vrba was celebrated as a national hero. He was awarded the Czechoslovak Medal for Bravery, the Order of Slovak National Insurrection, and the Order of Meritorious Fighter. Moving to Prague in 1945, he read biology and chemistry at Charles University and earned a doctorate in biochemistry. Chafing under the yoke of communism, however, he defected to Israel in 1958, and then moved to Britain in 1960, where he became a British citizen.

In 1963 he published his memoir, *Escape from Auschwitz: I Cannot Forgive*, which he wrote with the assistance of Irish journalist Alan Bestic. The book was based on a series of articles he wrote for the *Daily Herald*, timed to coincide with the 1961 trial of SS-Obersturmbannführer Adolf Eichmann in Israel. The book was translated into several languages, although, interestingly, it did not appear in Hebrew until 1998. During the trial itself, Vrba presented written testimony against Eichmann.

Vrba detailed not only his daring escape but also the mishandling of his report, which he considered a lost opportunity that might well have led to the deaths of more than 400,000 Hungarian Jews, who were deported to Auschwitz beginning in May 1944—less than a month after his escape. Vrba maintained that the Zionist Aid and Rescue Committee delayed passing on his testimony, in which he had warned of the Nazi plan to deport the Hungarian Jews. He also claimed that the Allies did not act quickly or forcefully enough given the information he had provided. For the remainder of his life, Vrba believed that more could have been done to mitigate the effects of the Holocaust.

Vrba moved to Canada in 1967, taking a faculty position at the University of British Columbia. He became a Canadian citizen in 1972. In 1985 he testified at the Toronto trial of Ernst Zündel, a publisher of Holocaust denial material who had been charged with knowingly publishing false information in an attempt to foment social or racial intolerance. When Zündel's defense attorney, Doug Christie, accused Vrba of having fabricated the events at Auschwitz, Vrba shot back that he had witnessed the evidence of unmistakable mass murder with his own eyes. The confrontation between the two was a memorable highlight of the trial for those who were there to see it.

Rudolf Vrba died of cancer, at the age of 81, on March 27, 2006, in Vancouver, British Columbia.

Wallenberg, Raoul (1912–1947)

Raoul Wallenberg was a Swedish diplomat who volunteered to go to Budapest in 1944 on behalf of the World Jewish Congress and the American War Refugee Board to save Jews threatened with deportation at the hands of the Nazis.

He was born in Stockholm on August 4, 1912, to Raoul Oscar Wallenberg, a Swedish naval officer, and Maj (Maria) Sofia Wallenberg, née Wising. The large Wallenberg family was one of the most famous in Sweden, comprising bankers, diplomats, industrialists, and politicians over several generations. Wallenberg's great-great grandfather, a man named Benedicks, was Jewish, a fact that Wallenberg remained proud of all his life.

After completing his compulsory military service, Wallenberg studied for a year in Paris before being sent, in 1931, to the University of Michigan, where he studied architecture and graduated with honors, winning a university medal for academic excellence. Upon returning to Sweden he learned that his American degree did not qualify him to practice as an architect, so he spent the next period of his life wandering through a variety of occupations in various places around the world: in a construction company in Cape Town, South Africa; at a branch office of the Holland Bank in Haifa, Palestine; and finally at an import-export company back in Sweden, the Central European Trading Company. Within eight months, he was a joint owner of the company and its international director.

This position not only gave him administrative experience but also enabled him to ascertain firsthand the nature of conditions in Germany and other Nazi-occupied countries. As a necessary part of his business dealings he also made numerous trips to Hungary. He learned to speak Hungarian and made many contacts in Budapest that would soon be useful for the purpose of saving lives.

As the war progressed and Hungary's earlier successes began to slip away, Germany decided that its ally should be occupied to ensure that it would not surrender, as Italy had in September 1943. Accordingly, on March 19, 1944, German troops invaded Hungary, and a pro-German puppet government was installed. For the Jews of Hungary—the last large Jewish community thus far untouched by the Holocaust—Nazi antisemitic measures now arrived like the eruption at Vesuvius. By May 1944 the mass deportation of Hungary's Jews was in full swing, at the average rate of 12,000 each day.

In 1944 the United States established the War Refugee Board (WRB) to try to save the remaining Jews of Europe. The WRB soon learned that attempts were being

Raoul Wallenberg, one of the best-known rescuers of Jews during the Holocaust. Sent by the Swedish government to Budapest, Hungary, in 1944 on an extraordinary mission to save Jews from deportation, his initiatives built on the efforts of fellow Swede Per Anger as well as other members of the Budapest diplomatic corps. Together, these efforts saved upwards of 100,000 Jews. (AP Photo/Pressens Bild)

made in Sweden to rescue Hungary's Jews, and it established a committee in Stockholm to discuss suitable candidates to lead a rescue mission in Budapest. Initially, Count Folke Bernadotte was proposed, but the Hungarian government rejected him. The next to be suggested was Raoul Wallenberg, already known to many Hungarians. He was approved by the committee, and by the end of June 1944 was appointed first secretary at the Swedish legation in Budapest. His was a singular mission—to start a rescue operation.

Wallenberg took up his position in July 1944, with the campaign against the Jews of Hungary at its height. Already more than 400,000 Jews from the countryside had been deported, mostly to Auschwitz. Budapest was about to be hit.

Together with fellow Swedish diplomat **Per Anger**, and building on the precedent established by the Swiss vice-consul in Budapest, **Carl Lutz**, he issued "protective passports" (*Schutzpässe*), which placed those holding them under Swedish protection. The Swedish legation negotiated with the Germans, for the bearers would be treated as Swedish citizens and exempt from wearing the yellow star. In no time at all, more than 700 passes had been issued, though Wallenberg saw an immediate need for a much greater number. He requested that the Swedish government send more of everything—people, money, and anything that could aid in the creation of a rescue infrastructure.

Even before Wallenberg had commenced his activities, **Valdemar Langlet**, the head of the Swedish Red Cross in Hungary, had already found ways to assist the Swedish legation. He rented buildings for the Red Cross and put Swedish signs on them to give the impression that somehow they were official diplomatic premises. Wallenberg then capitalized on this by renting 32 additional buildings and declaring them to have diplomatic immunity. Adorned with Swedish flags, they were then used as hiding places for Jews. It is estimated that these buildings eventually housed more than 10,000 people.

Wallenberg did not use traditional diplomacy, and he employed everything from bribes to threats of extortion to save lives. One way was by employing Jews in the Swedish legation offices. By the time the war ended, at least 340 Jews "worked" in the embassy, with another 700 living in the building. His "protective passes," moreover, had no official status whatsoever, though he created credibility for them through the confident manner in which he introduced them—such that Hungarian and German officials accepted them without demur. At the start of his mission, he was only given authority to issue 1,500 passes, but without waiting to be told otherwise he negotiated a further 1,000 and then kept going until he had raised the quota to 4,500.

With the war coming to an end and the Soviet Red Army advancing on Budapest during the late fall of 1944, the Nazis intensified their efforts to deport the remaining Jews. Wallenberg went to train stations where Jews were embarking, entered railcars with Jews inside, and handed out protective passes. He stood on tracks to make trains stop, after which he repeated the exercise. He was even known to climb on board carriage roofs and stuff protective passes into the air vents for the people inside.

When the Nazis began to deport large numbers of Jews on death marches, in conditions where freezing and starving Jews were subjected to brutal conditions, Wallenberg, like Lutz, Anger, and other members of the diplomatic community, was there, too. He accompanied the death marches for as long as he could, handing out more protective passes and demanding that those holding them be freed. On January 17, 1945, with the end of the war nigh and the liberation of Budapest close, Wallenberg was arrested by Soviet troops on charges of espionage. On his way out of the capital, he stopped at one of the "Swedish Houses" to give its inhabitants a final farewell. He was never seen in public again.

Just why he was arrested has remained a mystery, though one explanation is that, through his work with the War Refugee Board, the Soviets considered him to be an agent of the U.S. government, and therefore a spy. His fate was for a long time a matter of intense speculation. The actual locations of his imprisonment were never confirmed, and all information about his detention is essentially speculation. Even the date and circumstances of his death are uncertain. At first, the Soviet government denied that he had been arrested at all; then, when they confirmed it, they insisted that he died of a heart attack on July 17, 1947. After the downfall of communism and the end of the Cold War, a former member of the Politburo, Alexander Yakovlev, announced in 2000 that the KGB had executed Wallenberg in 1947 at Moscow's Lubyanka prison.

According to some estimates, Raoul Wallenberg's actions in Budapest during 1944 and early January 1945 saved the lives of more than 30,000 Jews. His influence, however, far exceeds this number. When Soviet forces liberated Budapest in February 1945, more than 100,000 Jews were still alive, mostly as a result of his efforts and those of other members of the diplomatic community, which, it has been argued, he was instrumental in mobilizing. According to Wallenberg's colleague at the Swedish embassy, Per Anger, Wallenberg is therefore responsible for saving those 100,000 lives.

Due to his efforts on behalf of the Hungarian Jews, Wallenberg has been celebrated throughout the world. He has been awarded the status of honorary citizen in the United States, Canada, Hungary, Australia, and Israel, and on November 26, 1963, Yad Vashem recognized him as one of the Righteous among the Nations. Monuments have been dedicated to him, and streets and squares named in his honor. When the United States Holocaust Memorial Museum was built in Washington, D.C., its street location was designated as 100 Raoul Wallenberg Place.

Wdowiński, Dawid (1895–1970)

Dawid Wdowiński was chairman of the right-wing Jewish Hatzohar party (an acronym of Hatzionim Harevizionistim, or Revisionist Zionists), a political movement founded by Ze'ev Jabotinsky and others in Paris in April 1925. Wdowiński was one of the founders and key leaders of the Żydowski Związek Wojskowy (Jewish Military Union, or ŻZW) before and during the Warsaw Ghetto Uprising.

Born to Jezajasza and Maria Wdowińskiego on February 25, 1895, in Będzin, Poland, he studied medicine and became a psychiatrist and neurologist. After the Nazi invasion of Poland in September 1939, he and several other Jewish former members of the Polish army, including Dawid Apfelbaum, a prewar army lieutenant, formed the ŻZW in the Warsaw Ghetto.

Wdowiński's formal title within the ŻZW was political chair; unlike most of the other operatives of the organization he was not a military commander, though his role served an important ideological function.

Political tensions between the ŻZW and the left-leaning Jewish Combat Organization (Żydowska Organizacja Bojowa, or ŻOB), led by **Mordecai Anielewicz**, **Yitzhak Zuckerman**, and **Marek Edelman**, threatened to derail prospects of unified anti-Nazi action, but with the onset of large-scale deportation offensives by the Nazis against the Jews of Warsaw, both groups saw little alternative but to mount a united opposition. When the Warsaw Ghetto rose in revolt in April 1943 the ŻOB had about 500 fighters and the ŻZW around 250—which grew to some 400 well-armed combatants, grouped in 11 units. Dawid Apfelbaum was in overall military command of the ŻZW.

Its members, many of whom came from the Revisionist movement's Betar youth wing, were connected with the Polish Home Army, and had a more nationalistic and right-wing perspective than the ŻOB. However, as it was the latter body that had greater numbers, more resources, and a more extensive youth basis, it became the ranking resistance organization in the ghetto and dominated with regard to strategy and time. While the fighting in the uprising was united—and the sacrifices were shared, with massive casualties from both groups—the rancor characterizing the relationship intensified even as the fight was taking place. Wdowiński and others claimed that the ŻOB refused to incorporate them into the overall command structure; the ŻOB, in turn, held that the nationalist ŻZW wanted to take over. That they managed to fight alongside each other was a development brought about through sheer necessity and the desperation of the situation.

ŻZW actions during the uprising took place on Muranowska Street (where ŻZW headquarters was located) and Miła Street; in actions near Zamenhof Street; and in the district around Nalewki Street, among other locations. When the ghetto resistance was finally broken, surviving ŻZW members fled through the sewers to the Aryan side of Warsaw and continued the fight alongside nationalist Poles there. With many of the military leaders of the ŻZW dead, Dawid Wdowiński was one of the last authority figures remaining by the end of the war.

After 1945 contested memories of the Warsaw Ghetto Uprising took hold. Surviving commanders of the ŻOB rarely, if ever, mentioned the ŻZW's role in the uprising, preferring to emphasize its proletarian nature. This fit in well with the changed political realities of Poland after the country's takeover by the Soviet Union, and with the political orientation of the socialist-Zionist youth movements from which the ŻOB was originally formed.

It left only Dawid Wdowiński to mount any sort of defense on behalf of his fellow-fighters from the ŻZW. In 1963, in New York, he published his memoirs, *And We Are Not Saved*. In this he gave his interpretation of his involvement with the ŻZW and the Warsaw Ghetto Uprising, writing the truth as he saw it in contrast to what had by now become conventional wisdom from the perspective of the ŻOB. Among other things, he noted the leftist political orientation of those who were not from the ŻZW or the Polish Home Army. He was equally opposed to any form of postwar Jewish reconciliation with Germany. The book was never translated into Polish, nor released in Poland.

Dawid Wdowiński died in 1970, at the age of 74.

Wegner, Armin T. (1886–1978)

Armin Theophil Wegner was one of the earliest voices to protest Adolf Hitler's treatment of the Jews, and the only popular author in Nazi Germany to publicly remonstrate against it.

Born on October 16, 1886, in the town of Elberfeld, Wuppertal, he was descended from an old aristocratic Prussian family with roots reaching back to the Crusades. He was educated in Zürich, Breslau, and Berlin, where he graduated with a doctorate in law. After graduating he took a range of jobs but always had a love for writing. By the age of 16 he had published his first book of poetry, and between 1909 and 1913 he established his reputation as one of Germany's most promising young poets.

With the outbreak of World War I he enlisted in the medical corps as a volunteer nurse in Poland and was decorated with an Iron Cross for assisting wounded troops under enemy fire. In April 1915 he was sent to the Ottoman Empire as a member of the German Sanitary Corps, with the rank of second lieutenant. Wegner's unit was stationed along the Baghdad Railway in Syria and Mesopotamia, where he witnessed death marches of Armenians during the Armenian genocide.

Between July and August 1915 he investigated the massacres more closely, traveling throughout the region, speaking to a wide range of people, collecting documents, making notes, and photographing everything he saw. He managed to send some of this material to Germany and the United States, but disclosing what he saw was forbidden, and the Germans arrested Wegner at the request of the Turks. In December 1916 he was recalled to Germany; although some of his photographs were confiscated and destroyed, he successfully smuggled out hundreds of negatives, which today provide an outstanding archive documenting and testifying to the veracity of the Armenian genocide.

In 1920 Wegner married German-Jewish author Lola (Leonore) Landau and became an activist for pacifist movements. In 1921 he testified in court on behalf of Soghomon Tehlirian, an Armenian who shot and killed former Ottoman minister of the interior Mehmed Talaat Pasha in Berlin on March 15, 1921.

A new book published in 1922, *Der Schrei von Ararat* (*The Scream from Ararat*), saw Wegner reach the peak of his popularity as a writer. In 1927 he and his wife made a trip to the Soviet Union and the Soviet republic of Armenia, and after this trip he wrote a new work, *Five Fingers over You*, in which he describes the underlying political violence of Soviet communism and predicted the extremes of Stalinism.

Back in Germany, Wegner then witnessed the onset of Nazism, predicting that the antisemitic policies of the Nazis would lead to the destruction of Germany's reputation, possibly forever. Noting how no one appeared to see what he was seeing, he felt he had to do something to avoid becoming complicit in the silence surrounding the intensifying persecution of the Jews. In 1933 he wrote a long open letter to Adolf Hitler in which he denounced Nazi antisemitism, and with this he became one of the earliest voices protesting Hitler's treatment of the Jews. The letter was written a few days after the failed nationwide boycott of Jewish businesses on April 1, 1933, but despite it being an open letter, no newspaper in Germany was willing to publish it. As a result, Wegner forwarded it directly to Nazi party headquarters in Munich.

The letter was received by the head of the party chancellery, Martin Bormann. A few weeks later Wegner was arrested by the Gestapo, imprisoned, and tortured brutally in the infamous Columbia House prison. He was then sent to concentration camps at Oranienburg, Börgermoor, and Lichtenburg; in all, he suffered imprisonment in seven camps and prisons before he was released and could flee to Rome, where he assumed the alias Percy Eckstein. After these experiences, he never felt at home again in Germany and remained in exile for the rest of his life.

On May 23, 1967, Yad Vashem recognized Armin Wegner as one of the Righteous among the Nations, and in 1968 he received an invitation to Armenia from the Catholicos of All Armenians to be awarded the Order of Saint Gregory the Illuminator.

He died in Rome, at the age of 92, on May 17, 1978, virtually forgotten by Germany. Some of his ashes were later taken to Armenia to be honored at a posthumous state funeral at Tsitsernakaberd, near the Armenian Genocide Memorial's perpetual flame.

Weidner, Johan Hendrik (1912–1994)

Johan Hendrik Weidner was a resister during World War II, whose work on behalf of the French underground proved to be vital. While most witnesses of the Holocaust were in fact bystanders, Weidner exemplified courage, compassion, and self-determination, putting his life and that of his family and friends in danger to establish the "Dutch-Paris" network and help victims escape Nazi persecution. His underground operation, running from the Netherlands through France and into surrounding neutral countries, successfully smuggled 800 people to safety during the German occupation.

Born in Brussels on October 22, 1912, Weidner was the oldest of four children. He grew up in Switzerland, near the French border at Collonges-sous-Salève, where his father was a minister at a Seventh-Day Adventist church and taught Latin and Greek at the Seventh-Day Adventist seminary. Through their father's example, Weidner and his siblings were taught from a young age to resist institutions that contradicted their religious values—during his childhood, his father sat willingly in jail every Sunday because the Swiss government required all children to attend school seven days a week, imprisoning parents for every school day missed. Weidner later explained that his father's unwavering principles were heavily influential in inspiring his rescue behavior during the war.

At the outbreak of World War II Weidner was living in Paris, but the German occupation of northern France caused him to flee Paris and resettle in Lyon. When the Nazis began to deport Jews (with the active assistance of Vichy authorities) he saw the necessity of developing an escape route to neutral Switzerland, so in 1941 he founded Dutch-Paris to facilitate his rescue activities. He used the knowledge of the Swiss border he had acquired while attending school, and his recollections of the territory around the University of Geneva, to create an escape route. His import/export textile business in Lyon allowed him to set up a subsidiary branch in Annecy that facilitated the procurement of necessary permits to reside near the border.

Driven by his conviction, Weidner often undertook the dangerous task of personally leading refugees across the border; every time he embarked on a trip, he would say the prayer: "My Father, help me to be kind to those I try to help. Where they have known only hatred, help me to be loving. And give me the confidence that this work will accomplish what you have placed me in the world to do." Over time, Dutch-Paris became one of the largest and most successful underground networks for helping Jews, downed Allied pilots, and prominent Dutch individuals escape to Switzerland.

Once the route to Switzerland was created, other resistance groups became interested in enlarging and improving Weidner's rescue effort. To compensate for the increase in the number of refugees receiving aid, Weidner created an escape route to Spain through the Pyrenees. Willem Visser 't Hooft, secretary of the World Council of Churches in Geneva, and Johan Bosch van Rosenthal, the Dutch minister in Bern, also became interested in Weidner's work and made financial contributions. It has been estimated that the escape route created through Dutch-Paris was responsible for the rescue of well over 1,000 people, including 800 Dutch Jews and more than 100 downed Allied pilots.

The network's success eventually led to Weidner becoming one of the most hunted men in the French underground, with the Gestapo offering a reward of 5 million francs for his arrest. Eventually, he was indeed arrested and tortured along with other resisters. The network's greatest loss occurred on February 10, 1943, when Suzy Kraay, a young agent, was caught and turned over to the Gestapo. Besides information she divulged during the course of interrogation and torture, a small notebook filled with contact information on the organization, including the names of 300 members, was found on her person. Kraay's vulnerability resulted in the deaths of Weidner's sister Gabrielle and 40 other members.

Nonetheless, the Dutch-Paris network continued its rescue efforts until May 1944, when Weidner was arrested for the last time. With perseverance, luck, and help from a prison guard, he was able to escape a day before his execution. Once free, he fled to Britain at the request of Allied command in London, as it was too dangerous for him to stay in France.

Even after the Dutch-Paris network collapsed, Weidner continued to resist the Nazis by fighting in the Dutch army (with the rank of captain) until the end of the war. Once the war ended, he continued his humanitarian operations through his work for the Dutch government, bringing war criminals to justice. In 1955 he migrated to the United States; he settled in southern California, married, and founded a successful food store chain, Weidner National Foods.

Weidner's wartime efforts saw him honored on many occasions after 1945. He received the United States Medal of Freedom; the French Legion of Honor, *Croix de Guerre*, and *Medaille de la Résistance*; the Order of the British Empire; the Dutch Order of Orange-Nassau; and the Belgian Order of Leopold. In Israel, he was recognized as one of the Righteous among the Nations, and at the opening of the United States Holocaust Memorial Museum in Washington, D.C. in 1993 he was one of seven persons chosen to light candles recognizing the rescuers.

The rescue efforts prompted by his compassion and resolute convictions made Weidner a Holocaust hero. He died on May 21, 1994, at the age of 82, but his legacy lives on through the lives and the descendants of those he saved.

Weidt, Otto (1883–1947)

Otto Weidt was the owner of a Berlin workshop for the blind, in which he protected his Jewish workers against deportation during the Holocaust.

He was born on May 2, 1883, to Max and Auguste Weidt, née Grell, in the north German city of Rostock. Upon finishing school he followed in his father's footsteps and became a paperhanger. After the family moved to Berlin, he became involved in working-class politics, with a special interest in anarchism. A hearing problem allowed him to avoid service during World War I, which was convenient in view of the fact that he was also a convinced pacifist.

Due to growing blindness by the 1930s he was forced to abandon his work as a paperhanger and instead learned the craft of brush making and broom binding. In 1936 he set up a brush- and broom-making workshop for the blind at Grossbeerenstrasse 92. In 1940 he moved to another location at Rosenthalerstrasse 39, in central Berlin, where he applied for and was assigned a workforce from the Jewish Home for the Blind. Practically all his employees were blind, deaf, or mute—and Jewish.

His small factory was considered important for the war effort, with one of his bigger clients being the Wehrmacht. Having the factory classified as "vital," therefore, enabled Weidt to continue in business with the workforce at his disposal, even though it was said that he never actually completed his orders for the army in full so as to keep the workshop operating. Up to 30 Jews were thus employed at any one time during the years between 1941 and 1943. Weidt also employed, as office workers, eight Jews without disabilities, which was, of course, strictly forbidden.

In the normal run of events, all Jewish labor had to be negotiated and approved through the labor employment office. Jews would for the most part be sent on forced labor rather than to civilian factories. Weidt, however, managed to procure his workforce by developing good relationships with the authorities, together with a mixture of bribery and flattery. In this way, he succeeded in keeping his workers and overriding the objections of government inspector Alfred Eschhaus, a notorious antisemite.

In 1942 the Gestapo began to pay careful attention to Weidt's factory and started arresting and deporting his employees. He confronted the Nazis face-to-face over this, emphasizing his workers' status as "protected" and producing appropriate documents (falsified, as it turned out), together with additional bribes. Of greatest use in the short term, perhaps, was a secure hiding place he created for his workers at the rear of the factory.

Once, when the Gestapo had arrested several of his workers, he went in person to where they were being held near the ancient Jewish cemetery on Grosse Hamburger Strasse. Facing down the SS officers guarding them, the half-blind Weidt succeeded in securing their release at the last minute. Like Moses leading the children of Israel, he then guided the group of blind and deaf Jews, walking through the streets of Berlin and all wearing their Jewish stars, back to the workshop on Rosenthalerstrasse.

When he was unable to secure the release of others who were deported to Terezín (Theresienstadt) with their families, Weidt made sure they were supported and somehow sustained. At considerable expense, he organized a supply of food parcels for up to 25 people and arranged for them to be delivered to the camp. All in all, more than 150 parcels arrived.

When Weidt received a tipoff that a major pogrom against the last Jews in Berlin was about to take place on February 27, 1943—the so-called *Fabrikaktion* (Factory Action), he made sure to keep the workshop closed so as not to present the Gestapo with a convenient concentration of Jews all in one place. He was, however, helpless to stop them being arrested in their homes, and many were deported to their deaths. Among those Weidt managed to save were Inge Deutschkron and Alice Licht, two sighted women who worked in the office, and Hans Israelowicz, who was arrested and imprisoned in the Jewish community building at Rosenstrasse 2-4 until the protest by the non-Jewish wives and mothers of those inside managed to get them released in March 1943.

Alice Licht was one of those who went to Terezín (in her case, to accompany her deported parents), and who Weidt supported through the provision of food parcels. When she was later deported to Auschwitz, Weidt, pretending to be on a business trip, actually went to the camp in June 1944 in an attempt to help her. Unable to gain access, he hid clothes and money for her nearby. When the inmates of the subcamp in which she was working were taken on a death march, Alice made her escape and eventually returned to Berlin in January 1945. She then lived in hiding with the Weidt family until the end of the war. Her parents never returned.

Weidt managed to obtain an Aryan work permit for Inge Deutschkron from a prostitute. This permit, unfortunately, had to be discarded three months later when the police arrested the prostitute, but in the meantime Deutschkron managed to survive and find a safe space for herself in the Weidt workshop.

After the war Otto Weidt established an orphanage for child survivors and a retirement home for those who were elderly. The Otto Weidt workshop remained functioning until 1952, when East Berlin communist police closed it down. By that stage, owing to Weidt's death of heart failure on December 22, 1947, it was managed by his widow, Else. At the time of his death, Weidt was 64 years of age.

On September 7, 1971, Yad Vashem recognized Otto Weidt posthumously as one of the Righteous among the Nations, and in 1993 Inge Deutschkron affixed a plaque honoring him on the site of the workshop. In 1999 a museum was opened there, the Museum Blindenwerkstatt Otto Weidt. Since 2005 the museum has been administered by Berlin's German Resistance Memorial Center (Gedenkstätte Deutscher Widerstand).

Weissmandl, Chaim Michael Dov (1903–1957)

Chaim Michael Dov Weissmandl resisted Nazism through his efforts to save the Jews of Slovakia from extermination during the Holocaust.

He was born in Debrecen, Hungary, on October 25, 1903. His father, Yosef Weissmandl, was a *shochet*, a person specially trained and licensed to slaughter animals and birds in accordance with Jewish religious law. Michael Dov Weissmandl was an acclaimed student in the Slovak *yeshivot* (Torah academies) of Sered and Tirnoy before moving to Nitra, in western Slovakia, in 1931; there he studied under Rabbi Shmuel Dovid Ungar and married Rabbi Ungar's daughter, Bracha Rachel, in 1937. He also went to the Bodleian Library in Oxford, where he examined Hebrew rabbinic manuscripts.

When World War II broke out on September 1, 1939, he returned to Slovakia from Oxford, where he began working for the Orthodox World Agudath Israel. His resistance activities commenced once Jews started being deported from Slovakia. He engaged non-Jewish emissaries to send food, clothing, and money to the deportees temporarily "settled" in the territories of the Generalgovernement established by the Nazis in Poland. In March 1942 deportations began from Slovakia to Auschwitz. Weissmandel and a distant relative, **Gisi Fleischmann**, together with members of the Slovak Jewish Council (Judenrat), founded what became known as the Pracovna Skupina (Working Group) and instigated an initiative called the Europa Plan. This plan involved bribing the SS envoy to Bratislava, Dieter Wisliceny, to stop the deportations.

An initial U.S. $20,000 ransom was paid to Wisliceny (which he reported to his superiors in Berlin), and it did halt the deportations for a time. With this small victory, Weissmandel considered the prospect of using this formula to save Jews more broadly. Unfortunately, the much larger sums he was hoping to receive—particularly from the American Jewish Joint Distribution Committee—were not forthcoming owing to wartime currency restrictions. He had sought a further U.S. $200,000 as a down payment on a $2 million ransom, but when this did not eventuate he took it as Western indifference to the fate of the Jews, not realizing that the funds could not have been transmitted. Moreover, there was no guarantee that the Nazis would not renege on any arrangements that might be made.

The Working Group did, however, manage to delay the mass deportation of Slovakian Jews for two years, from 1942 to 1944. It was also pivotal in distributing the so-called "Auschwitz Report" in the spring of 1944. Weissmandl and Fleischmann were among those who received the report from the Auschwitz escapees **Rudolf Vrba** and Alfréd Wetzler, who escaped on April 7. Their testimony contained a comprehensive description of the geography and management of the camp, and of how the prisoners lived and died, together with a full listing and dissection of every transport that had arrived at Auschwitz since 1942. The report included sketches and information about the layout of the gas chambers.

On May 27, 1944, two more Jews, Czesław Mordowicz and Arnošt Rosin, also escaped, and their report gave direct evidence of the extermination of the Hungarian Jews taking place at that time. The Working Group passed on this information to world leaders, the government of Slovakia, and the Catholic Church after Weissmandl had sent it to George Mantello, a Jewish diplomat working for the Salvadoran consulate in Geneva, Switzerland. Once it reached the West, this news prompted leaders, including U.S. president Franklin D. Roosevelt and British prime minister Winston Churchill, to threaten the Hungarian government with postwar justice if it did not stop the deportations.

Weissmandl also lobbied hard at this time for the train lines leading to Auschwitz, as well as for the camp itself, to be bombed by the Allied air forces. He was among the first to make such a demand.

In the fall of 1944 the deportations from Slovakia resumed, and Weissmandl and his family were sent to Auschwitz. As the train was en route, however, he escaped from the moving train by breaking the lock of the carriage in which he was traveling, and then jumping. In the process he broke his leg but managed to get away and hide in a secret bunker in Bratislava. His wife, Bracha Rachel, together with their five children, was killed at Auschwitz.

In Bratislava, Weissmandl was contacted by **Rezső Kasztner**, who was at that time negotiating with Adolf Eichmann in Budapest to "pay" for Jewish lives in trucks that would be supplied by the Allies. As a sign of goodwill, Eichmann agreed to allow one trainload of Jews to be routed through Switzerland and away from Auschwitz. Kasztner and his contact among the Nazis, SS-Untersturmführer Kurt Becher, organized for Weissmandl to be taken from his Bratislava hiding place on the "Kasztner train," which also included another Orthodox leader, Rabbi Joel Teitelbaum, head of the Satmar Hasidic dynasty.

After the war, Weissmandl moved to the United States. He remarried; his second wife was Leah Teitelbaum, with whom he had five children. In November 1946, Weissmandl and his brother-in-law, Rabbi Sholom Moshe Ungar, reestablished the Nitra Yeshiva from which he came, in Somerville, New Jersey. A year later, a large estate in Mount Kisco, New York, was purchased and the Yeshiva relocated.

As he aged, Weissmandl suffered poor health and depression over his losses and the trauma of the Holocaust. In late 1957 he suffered a severe heart attack, and on Friday, November 29, 1957, at the age of 54, he died at Mount Kisco. A memoir, *Min ha-Mezzar* (*From the Depths*), a bitter work highly condemnatory of the West during the Holocaust, was published posthumously in 1960.

Weltsch, Robert (1891–1982)

Robert Weltsch was the prewar editor of a twice-weekly Berlin Jewish newspaper, the *Jüdische Rundschau* (*Jewish Review*). He was born on June 20, 1891, in Prague to a long-established Jewish family; his father, Theodore Weltsch, was an active member of the Jewish community and played an important administrative role in communal organizations.

Robert Weltsch studied law at the Karl-Ferdinand German University of Prague, where he joined Bar Kochba, a Zionist student association to which many young Jewish intellectuals were attracted. He served as the association's leader in 1911–1912. Between 1910 and 1914 he published articles in German-language Zionist newspapers, an activity he continued after he began serving as an officer on the Russian front in the Austro-Hungarian army during World War I.

After the war, Weltsch was invited to Berlin to serve as editor-in-chief of the *Jüdische Rundschau*, where he would remain until he left Germany in 1938. A committed Zionist, Weltsch was keen to develop the idea of a joint Jewish-Arab commonwealth for Palestine, in which statehood was rarely discussed and never advocated. One of the reasons behind Weltsch's opposition to a singular Jewish state in Palestine stemmed from his reaction to any form of nationalism or chauvinism, which he attributed to the horrors of war he had witnessed in the trenches. Given this, he was fearful as to where the organized Zionist movement might lead. Accordingly, he became one of the leading lights of the movement *Brit Shalom*, which advocated a binational Arab-Jewish presence in Palestine focusing on ideals such as political equality, cultural autonomy, and socioeconomic coexistence. This stance led to hostility toward him from some circles within the Zionist movement, and periodically there were moves to have him removed as editor of the *Jüdische Rundschau*. These were unsuccessful, however, and he retained the post until he departed Berlin.

As one who was in many respects a semi-official voice of German Jewry through the pages of his highly influential newspaper, Weltsch saw that he had an important responsibility to somehow accommodate Nazi antisemitic measures while at the same time showing that the Jewish community would not be cowed. On April 1,

1933, the Nazis organized a boycott of all Jewish shops, banks, offices, and department stores. This was arguably the first overtly antisemitic measure adopted by the new Nazi government, and it was a failure. The German public mostly ignored the boycott, forcing it to be called off within three days.

Weltsch, alert to the future possibilities that the boycott signified, reacted by publishing an article on April 4, which became famous as one of the earliest Jewish responses to Nazi anti-Jewish persecution. Entitled *"Tragt ihn mit Stolz, den gelben Fleck!"* (well known by its English title "Wear It with Pride, the Yellow Badge"), Weltsch's editorial was a call for the Jews of Germany to recognize the reality of their situation and confront their changed situation with dignity and in solidarity.

He wrote that, in light of the new regime, "Today the Jews cannot speak except as Jews. Anything else is utterly senseless. . . . We live in a new period . . . indicating that the world of our previous concepts has collapsed. That may be painful for many, but in this world only those will be able to survive who are able to look reality in the eye." He continued, in italics, that in view of the Jewish self-deception that they would always be accepted as Germans, *"It is not true that the Jews betrayed Germany. If they betrayed anyone, it was themselves, the Jews.* Because the Jew did not display his Judaism with pride, because he tried to avoid the Jewish issue, he must bear part of the blame for the degradation of the Jews."

He noted that during the boycott a number of antisemitic signs appeared on the streets. "One often saw," he wrote, "windows bearing a large Magen David, the Shield of David the King. It was intended as dishonor." In light of this new realization, in which "the Jew is marked as a Jew" with "the yellow badge," he now called upon the Jews of Germany to "take it up, the Shield of David, and wear it with pride!"

The prescience his statement displayed was acute, as the Nazis did not actually require Jews to wear yellow armbands with the Star of David until September 19, 1941. Rather, Weltsch was referring to a German-Jewish community that had, until that time, seen itself as a thoroughly integrated part of German society. Now that the Jews were being marked out, he was alerting them to the need to unite in view of what was now their "difference" from mainstream society—a metaphoric "yellow star," so to speak.

During these early years of the Third Reich Weltsch made a number of trips to Palestine, reporting back to the *Jüdische Rundschau* on what he saw there. He tried to encourage the Jews to leave Germany, though still unconvinced that Palestine was the right place for them. Still, he foresaw that whatever befell Germany's Jews would, soon enough, extend across all of Europe, so perhaps any refuge—including Palestine—would have to be considered, as a war would mean that all the Jews in Germany "would be lost." He acknowledged that with things getting worse by the day he would be lucky to escape with his life—something he was able to do in September 1938, immediately prior to the *Kristallnacht* pogrom of November 9–10, when he left Germany for Palestine.

He worked there for many years as a correspondent for the newspaper *Haaretz*, and in 1945 he moved to London as the newspaper's European correspondent, covering the Nuremberg Trials during 1945–1946. While in London, Weltsch also edited the *Yearbook of the Leo Baeck Institute* from 1956 to 1978. This quickly became a high-class academic periodical publishing scholarly articles focusing on German-Jewish history. He remained in London as a political journalist until his return to Jerusalem in 1978, where he died on December 22, 1982, at the age of 91.

Westerweel, Johan (1899–1944)

Johan Gerard (Joop) Westerweel was a Dutch resister and rescuer of Jews during World War II.

He was born in the small city of Zutphen on January 25, 1899, and as a young man developed a belief in nonviolent resistance. He became a teacher in the Dutch East Indies, but as a conscientious objector he was expelled from the colony for refusing to be drafted into the army. His pacifism became the basis of his moral compass, with a strict Christian upbringing implanting in him a sense of universal justice and a belief in the basic goodness of humanity.

In 1940 Westerweel and his wife, Wilhelmina (Wil, or Willy), moved to Rotterdam, where he had been offered a position as principal of a Montessori school. In earlier appointments he had already come into contact with Jewish refugee children, most of whom arrived from Germany during the 1930s. In Rotterdam Westerweel began his resistance activities against the Nazis, who had occupied the Netherlands since May 1940.

He could not reconcile his humanistic worldview with what he was seeing around him, as Jews were being segregated from non-Jews, and Dutch society was becoming fragmented by the Nazi occupation. He gathered a group of people from among his family and friends with a view to developing a network that would try to save Jewish lives and mitigate the worst effects of Nazi antisemitism. They would come to be known as the "Westerweel group."

He organized for German and Polish Jewish refugees to be received into safe houses and found the means to enable their children's education to continue. As time went on, Dutch Jews also began to help out, particularly teenagers and those in their early 20s, who were often members of such Zionist youth groups as Hechalutz. Many of the *Halutzim*, as they were called, comprising youth aged between 15 and 19, originated from Central and Eastern Europe, and had come to the Netherlands before the war to undertake agricultural training before migrating to Palestine.

Members of the Westerweel group included Wil Westerweel, Joachim Simon (known as "Schuschu"), Letty Rudelsheim, Giel Salome, Frans Gerritsen and his wife, Henny Gerritsen-Kouffeld, Jan Smit, Paula Welt Kaufman, Menachem Pinkhof, and Miriam Pinkhof.

By 1942 Joop Westerweel had organized a rescue network so effective that anywhere between 300 and 400 people had been helped, many hiding or escaping to Palestine. Throughout this time, he and his wife continued to live in the open, with Westerweel teaching and his four children going about their daily routines in school.

In December 1943 the Germans arrested Wil Westerweel during an attempt to free one of the *Hehalutz* members, Lettie Rudelsheim, from the Scheveningen prison. She was taken to the Vught concentration camp, where she remained incarcerated for nearly a year. She was later transferred to Ravensbrück, where she was put to work at hard labor. Although severely weakened by her experience, she survived the war and was repatriated to Sweden as part of a prisoner exchange, and finally returned to Holland after the war. Immediately after his wife's arrest, Westerweel arranged for their children to go into hiding. He then quit his position at the school and went underground.

One of those with whom he worked in the Westerweel group was Bouke Koning, a young man who had begun rescue work on his own initiative before joining with Westerweel in the summer of 1942. Among his tasks was accompanying refugees across the Belgian border, from where they headed southward. On March 11, 1944, while escorting two young Jewish women to the frontier, Koning and Westerweel were arrested, the latter returning to the Netherlands having just visited a large number of young Jews hidden in the Pyrenees. At first he was taken to Rotterdam, where he was imprisoned at the police station on Haagseveer. He was severely tortured for information regarding his network and resistance activities prior to being transferred to the concentration camp at Vught, where he was again tortured.

It soon became clear to him that his life was forfeit and that one day he would be executed for his continued refusal to provide the Gestapo with any information. In July 1944 he wrote a poem entitled "*Avond in de Cel*" ("Evening in the Cell"), which was sent out of the camp. It was to be his last communication with the outside world. On August 11, 1944, Joop Westerweel, with four others, was executed at Vught. Wil Westerweel, at that time still at Vught, was forced to witness her husband's execution.

After the war Joop Westerweel was remembered fondly by the Dutch government. A number of streets were named in his honor, as well as a school and other public spaces. In March 1947 the Joop Westerweel Park was built, and on June 16, 1964, Joop and Wil Westerweel were recognized by Yad Vashem as Righteous among the Nations.

Winton, Nicholas (1909–2015)

Sir Nicholas Winton was a British stockbroker who organized a rescue operation that brought 669 children, almost all of them Jewish, from Czechoslovakia to safety in Britain before the outbreak of World War II.

He was born Nicholas Wertheim (some sources say Wertheimer) on May 19, 1909, in West Hampstead, England. His parents were Rudolf and Barbara Wertheim, German Jews who had come to London in 1907. In an effort to acculturate, they changed their name to Winton, converted to Christianity, and ensured that their son was baptized into the Church of England. Rudolf Wertheim-Winton, a successful banker, saw that his family wanted for nothing, and Nicholas Winton was raised to a life of some comfort. After attending the Stowe School in Buckingham (where he began but left without graduating), Winton followed in his father's footsteps as a banker, learning his profession by working in banks in Hamburg, London, Berlin, and Paris. In 1931, after working for the Banque Nationale de Crédit in Paris, he returned to England and began his career as a stockbroker at the London Stock Exchange.

As a young man Winton held progressive views on a number of issues, aligning himself with many matters close to the agenda of the Labour party. He was opposed to the Conservative government's policy of appeasement, and expressed apprehension over German Nazism.

In December 1938 Winton was about to leave for a Christmas skiing holiday in Switzerland when he received a phone call from his friend Martin Blake—a teacher at London's Westminster School and an associate of the British Committee for Refugees from Czechoslovakia—asking him to forego his vacation and instead come immediately to Prague. The British Committee had been established in October 1938 to provide assistance for refugees created by Germany's annexation of the Sudeten regions after the Munich Agreement the previous month. Winton was happy to do so, and upon his arrival in Prague Blake introduced him to his colleague, Doreen Wariner, and arranged for him to visit refugee camps filled with Jews and political prisoners.

Winton was appalled by what he saw, and Blake and Wariner invited him to assist in helping Jews. He decided to act and soon established an organization to aid Jewish children at risk.

The timing could not have been more opportune. On the night of November 9–10, 1938, the Nazis launched the pogrom that became known as *Kristallnacht*, and Winton learned that in the aftermath the British government had approved a measure to allow the entry of Jewish refugees younger than 17, on the proviso that they had a place to stay and landing money of £50 for their eventual return home. He then also learned of how some Jewish relief organizations in Britain were planning to rescue German and Austrian Jewish children on what became known as the *Kindertransport* ("children's transport") program. This initiative eventually brought some 10,000 unaccompanied children to safety in Britain.

Winton was told, however, that whereas the *Kindertransport* initiative applied to Germany and Austria, there was no organization in Prague to deal with Jewish refugee children. Accordingly, he put together a small team to organize a rescue operation for children in the Czech lands. Without authorization, he established a Children's Section of the British Committee for Refugees from Czechoslovakia, and began taking applications from parents in Prague. Racing against the clock to find foster homes in Britain, raise funds, and obtain exit papers, Winton opened an office on Vorsilska Street in which his appointees, Trevor Chadwick and Bill Barazetti, worked continually to assist the thousands of parents who soon began lining up to find a safe haven for their children. After Winton returned to Britain, leaving Chadwick in charge in Prague, he contacted a number of foreign governments, asking if they would be prepared to accept the children. Only Sweden and Britain agreed to do so.

In trying to save as many children as possible, Winton worked to arrange facilities for their reception in Britain. He faced many obstacles. The Dutch government had closed its borders to Jewish refugees after the *Kristallnacht*, and Winton knew he would have to negotiate an agreement to provide the children transit through Holland for embarkation to Britain. He also had to find foster homes so that he could assure the Dutch authorities that the children had somewhere to go and would not remain in the Netherlands. To secure places in British homes and hostels, he placed newspaper advertisements seeking families prepared to accept the children, and then made arrangements for their transportation. He also had to raise money to fund transport and the British government's £50 pound guarantee required for each child.

At every turn he was successful, and on March 14, 1939—one day prior to the German occupation of the Czech lands—the first of Winton's transports left Prague by plane for London. He then arranged another seven transports, which left Prague by train across Germany to the Netherlands, and then by ferry to Britain. In London, the children were met by their British foster parents. The last trainload of children to arrive in Britain from Prague left on August 2, 1939.

One further group of 250, the biggest thus far, was scheduled to leave Prague on September 1, 1939. They did not make it. On that day Germany invaded Poland, and all German borders were closed. Two days later, Britain and Germany were at war, and all further rescue activities ceased. The train carrying the 250 children was shunted out of sight, and the children were never seen again. Overall, Nicholas Winton found homes in Britain for 669 children, many of whose parents would later perish at Auschwitz.

After the war, Winton's rescue efforts remained practically unknown and unremembered. In 1988 his wife, Grete—whom he had married in 1948 and who knew nothing of this earlier episode in his life—found a scrapbook from 1939 chronicling the full story. His attitude was that he did not think anyone would be interested.

Winton's achievements were recognized around the world, particularly in Britain and the Czech Republic. In 1993 Queen Elizabeth II awarded him an MBE (Member of the British Empire), and on October 28, 1998, the president of the Czech Republic, Václav Havel, recognized his achievement with the award of the Order of T. G. Masaryk. Queen Elizabeth then went further than her earlier award and knighted him on December 31, 2002, for his services to humanity. In 2008 the Czech government nominated Winton for the 2008 Nobel Peace Prize, and in 2010 he was named a Hero of the Holocaust by the British government. On October 28, 2014, Czech president Miloš Zeman awarded him the highest honor of the Czech Republic, the Order of the White Lion, and finally, on February 23, 2015, he was awarded the Freedom of the City of London. Winton's Jewish birth disqualified him from being declared Righteous among the Nations by Yad Vashem.

Sir Nicholas Winton died peacefully in his sleep on the morning of July 1, 2015, at Wexham Park Hospital in Slough. He was 106 years old.

Wittenberg, Yitzhak (1907–1943)

Yitzhak Wittenberg was the first commander of the Fareynikte Partizaner Organizatsye (United Partisan Organization, or FPO), a Jewish resistance organization in the Vilna ghetto. He was born into a working-class family in 1907 and became a tailor by trade. From a young age he was a member of the Communist party, until it was banned in 1938.

When the Soviets occupied Vilna (Vilnius) between June 1940 and June 1941, Wittenberg distinguished himself as an activist on behalf of the party, and so, after the invasion of Lithuania by the Germans on June 24, 1941, and the establishment of a ghetto in Vilna by September of that year, he became a vital leader of the ghetto resistance.

In December 1941 a number of meetings were held in which a resistance movement was established. At this time it was decided to fight and remain in the ghetto rather than try to escape. Three weeks later, on January 21, 1942, a further meeting was held at the home of Josef Glazman. Representatives from the major youth groups met: **Abba Kovner**, from Hashomer Hatzair; Glazman, from Betar; Wittenberg and Chyena Borowska, representing the communists; and Nissan Reznik of Hanoar Hazioni. Other groups came into the movement later. This became the United Partisan Organization, or FPO, with Wittenberg as its commander. His staff included Glazman, Kovner, Reznik, and Avraham (Abrasha) Havoynic.

The main aim of the FPO was to prepare for armed resistance in the event of the ghetto being liquidated, as well as to spread the idea of resistance to other ghettos. It was organized into two battalions, each composed of 100 to 120 fighters. It sent emissaries to Grodno, Białystok, and Warsaw to promote the idea of resistance as well as to inform them of the mass extermination of the Jews in Vilna. An attempt was also made to send several female emissaries (*kashariyot*) into the Soviet Union, but they were arrested by the Germans before they reached safety. Most managed to escape, however, and made their way back to Vilna.

At its height, the FPO had some 300 organized members. They carried out acts of sabotage beyond the ghetto confines, such as the mining of railway lines. Before they had the opportunity to mount a large-scale uprising, however, fate intervened. In early 1943 a Polish communist by the name of Kozlovsky was captured by the Gestapo. Under extreme torture, he was forced to divulge the names of any other resisters, and one, a Lithuanian partisan named Vitas, was revealed. Vitas was also captured, and when tortured he surrendered Wittenberg's name.

Jacob Gens, the chairman of the Vilna Jewish Council (Judenrat), knew of the FPO's existence and maintained contact with Wittenberg and other leaders. On July 8, 1943, when the Germans learned about the existence of the FPO, they ordered Gens to find Wittenberg and deliver him to them. Gens might have privately sympathized with the ideals of the resistance but held that its existence endangered the continued existence of the ghetto. Thus, on the night of July 15, Gens, together with Salek Desler, chief of the Jewish police, called Wittenberg and others from the underground to his office for a "meeting." It was, of course, a trap; after a few moments, armed SS men appeared with machine guns drawn. Desler identified Wittenberg, who was immediately arrested.

Members of the FPO, who had accompanied the leaders to the meeting and were waiting outside, attacked the Gestapo and rescued him. Furious, the Nazis told Gens that if he did not bring Wittenberg back at once they would liquidate the ghetto. Ghetto inhabitants now took a stand. Terrified, they demanded that Wittenberg be handed over, lest they and their families be deported to their deaths. The choice was clear—surrender Wittenberg or civil war would break out in the ghetto.

During the day Wittenberg met with members of the leadership group. He thought of taking his life, but word came from Gens that the Germans had demanded him alive. Abba Kovner told Wittenberg the sad truth that either he hand himself over or the FPO would be forced to fight the people who were demanding that he give himself up. Wittenberg would not tolerate the idea of Jew fighting Jew while the Nazis looked on, and so, regrettably, he handed command over to Kovner and went out into the street with the words "*Ich gehe*" ("I go"), and gave himself up to the Jewish police. Gens accepted the surrender in person.

Wittenberg was taken out of the ghetto and handed across to the Germans, who placed him in a cell. When they came to begin his interrogation the next day, they found him dead. He had taken poison—some said it was smuggled to him by Gens—in order to avoid the torture that was awaiting him.

Wittenberg's death now caused a rift in the FPO, with some arguing that the ghetto could not be defended because most Jews were not prepared to fight. The best way to resist the Nazis, many felt, was through escaping to the forest where they would join the partisans. The first group of 21 left on July 24, 1943, calling themselves the "Leon" unit in honor of Wittenberg's resistance codename. Others remained.

Six weeks later, on September 1, 1943, the Nazis liquidated the ghetto. Led by Kovner, the remaining FPO commanders issued a call for the Jews not to go "like sheep to slaughter" and rose in revolt. The fighters, however, had little support from those around them and saw that they were fighting alone. Escaping to the forests through the sewers, they were met by those who had joined the partisans earlier and were already under Soviet command.

Most of those in the ghetto who did not join the revolt—the majority—were sent to labor camps in Estonia, where they were eventually killed by the SS.

Wrobel, Eta (1916–2008)

Eta Wrobel was a commander of Jewish partisans in the forests of central Poland during the Holocaust.

She was born Eta Chajt into a solidly middle-class family of 10 in Łuków, eastern Poland, on December 28, 1916. In early 1940, soon after the war began, she started working as a clerk in an employment agency but quickly began her resistance activities by creating false identity papers for Jews in the work office set up by German Reserve Police Battalion 101 in Łuków. She also smuggled guns she had stolen from Nazis in Łódź, and somehow got them to Łuków. She was, however, eventually denounced and arrested by the Gestapo.

Imprisoned in Lublin, she was beaten and tortured in order to divulge the names of other resisters. She held out for 10 months before being released for work duties, building the death camp at nearby Majdanek. This was highly unusual, as Jews were at no time ever permitted to do such work, but she had assistance from outside the prison through the intervention of another prisoner's family. On the way to the worksite, she managed to slip away from the wagon on which she was riding and ran into the forest. There, she was met by her father, who had escaped the destruction of the Łuków ghetto.

The ghetto had been established in May 1941 and was destroyed before the end of 1942. By then the population had grown to nearly 12,000. Deportations, mainly to Treblinka, took place in early October and early November, while some 2,200 Jews were shot locally into pits. Whatever remained of the ghetto was transformed into a slave labor camp, but over the next few months thousands of those who had survived the initial deportations, and others who had been relocated there from elsewhere, were shot dead or transported to Treblinka. Only about 150 Jews of Łuków survived the Holocaust.

Under these circumstances, it was ironic that Wrobel could count herself as one of the survivors of the Łuków ghetto, given that she had already been imprisoned by the Gestapo. Having fled to the woods, she then helped organize an all-Jewish partisan unit numbering about 80, which because of her innate military skills, she ultimately commanded. She was active on missions with men and made important strategic decisions under which the unit would steal German supplies, set mines, and engage in skirmishing.

The unit lived rough. They slept in cramped quarters and had no access to medical attention. Unlike the other seven women in the unit, she refused to cook or clean. On one mission she was shot in the leg and went to see a friendly Polish doctor. The bullet was difficult to remove, and he kept asking her to come back when the swelling went down. But after continued intense pain and sustained swelling over several months, the doctor eventually gave her a knife and a bottle of alcohol, and she dug the bullet out herself. It was said that this experience was beneficial in other ways, as she then learned how to remove bullets from wounded fellow partisans.

In July 1944 the Soviet army liberated Łuków. Wrobel came out of hiding and was asked if she was interested in becoming the mayor of Łuków. She readily accepted this offer on the grounds that by doing so she could make a positive difference for the future. On December 20, 1944, she was married, and in 1947 she and her husband, Henry, moved to the United States, settling first in Brooklyn before moving to New Jersey. They raised three children, who in turn produced nine grandchildren. Wrobel, for her part, was the only child in her family to survive the Holocaust.

After settling in the United States, Wrobel spent much of her time engaging in community activities, such as raising money to assist in anti-cancer initiatives. In later life she traveled throughout New Jersey, educating schoolchildren about her experiences and generally imparting to them a lifetime of accumulated wisdom wrung from the most testing of conditions. In 2006, at the age of 90, she wrote her memoir, a book entitled *My Life My Way*, written in conjunction with Jeanette Friedman.

Eta Wrobel died on May 26, 2008, in Highland, New York, at the age of 92. Before her death, she summarized her years with the partisans by saying, "The biggest resistance that we could have done to the Germans was to survive."

Żabiński, Jan (1897–1974)

Dr. Jan Żabiński was a Polish Christian zookeeper who, with his wife Antonina Żabińska, née Erdman, protected hundreds of Jews by hiding them in the zoo precincts during World War II.

Born on April 8, 1897, in Warsaw, Żabiński grew up in Jewish neighborhoods and attended Jewish schools, even though he was not Jewish. A Catholic whose father raised him as a staunch atheist in a working-class Jewish neighborhood, he studied agriculture and zoology at university. In 1931 he married Antonina Erdman, who had been born in St. Petersburg in 1908 and whose parents had been killed during the Russian Revolution. By the time World War II began with the Nazi invasion of Poland on September 1, 1939, Żabiński was director of the Warsaw Zoo and a teacher of geography in the private Kreczmara high school. He was a well-known author of many popular books about animals and biology.

When war came, the zoo suffered heavy bombardment. Many of the animal cages were blown open, and animals roamed around the city until they had to be shot by Polish troops. Upon their arrival in the city, the Germans appointed Żabiński as superintendent of Warsaw's public parks, providing him with an opportunity to visit the Warsaw Ghetto under the pretext of inspecting the trees and small public garden inside. This provided a further chance to keep in touch with Jews he had known before the war, whom he provided with a means of escape. He extended this help to others—those with whom he shared professional connections, as well as strangers who needed his help.

In trying to find some sort of accommodation for those he was rescuing, Żabiński and his wife considered the one clear option available to them—to employ the zoo cages that had been left empty of animals as a result of the Nazi occupation. These, Żabiński realized, would make excellent hiding places. In ensuing months and years, these cages became temporary shelter for hundreds of Jews until more permanent places of refuge could be found. And, along the way, the Żabińskis found an unknowing ally to assist them from among the Germans.

A Nazi named Lutz Heck, who was a zoologist, animal researcher, and director of the Berlin Zoo, brought Nazi ideology into animal breeding through the development of a program that attempted to revivify such extinct "German" species as the aurochs (*Bos primigenius*) and the tarpan horse (*Equus ferus ferus*). He used the closed Warsaw Zoo as his laboratory, and thus with his authority the zoo remained open. Heck was far from being an altruist; he was known to be cruel toward some of the animals, and he certainly had no specific love for the Warsaw Zoo, often stealing the most valuable animals and taking them to German zoos. Still, by enabling it to remain open, Heck gave Żabiński (whose codename in the Polish resistance was Francis, for Francis of Assisi, patron saint of animals) a place where he could engage in his rescue work, right under the noses of the very people who were seeking the Jews' death.

The Żabińskis also took Jews into their own home located at the zoo. Antonina Żabińska and their son, Ryszard, took care of the Jews' personal needs, providing warm clothing and food, while Jan Żabiński sought documents that could protect them outside. The underground organization known as Żegota—a codename for the Polish Council to Aid Jews (Rada Pomocy Żydom)—provided funds to assist Żabiński in caring for those he had rescued. At the same time as he was hiding Jews, Jan Żabiński became a leader and active member of the underground Polish Home Army (Armia Krajowa, or AK). He taught biology at an underground university and continued smuggling food into the Warsaw Ghetto even as he was trying to save lives in the zoo. In addition, he conducted active military work as a bomb maker, and went on missions sabotaging trains. He eventually fought in the Warsaw Uprising of 1944, was wounded, taken as a prisoner of war, and removed to Germany.

Throughout the war, Antonina Żabińska kept a diary; after the ghetto was liquidated in 1943, she went into hiding and continued to work on it, recording events for posterity. As the fighting in and around Warsaw intensified during the Warsaw Uprising of 1944, she gave one of her notebooks to her husband. He buried it in the zoo grounds, where it was retrieved in April 1945 by author Rachel Auerbach, who later arranged for it to be published.

In the course of the Nazi occupation, Jan and Antonina Żabiński helped to save the lives of approximately 300 Jewish men, women, and children. In recognition of this feat, on September 21, 1965, Yad Vashem recognized them as Righteous among the Nations, and the following month they were present for the conferring ceremony, during which they planted a tree on the Mount of Remembrance in Jerusalem.

When asked several years later about his motivation in helping so many people, at such risk to himself and his family, Jan Żabiński replied that his actions were based on the "progressive-humanistic upbringing" he received at home and at school. He said that he was never able to find any logical reasons for why people hated Jews, only "artificially formed ones." For her part, Antonina Żabińska, whose parents had been murdered by the Bolsheviks, was aware of where politically motivated violence could lead. She believed that every living thing is entitled to life and respect, making her incapable of turning away from suffering.

Antonina Żabińska died on March 19, 1971, in Warsaw; Jan Żabiński died on July 26, 1974, also in Warsaw. In 2007 Antonina Żabińska's wartime diary formed the basis of a best-selling book entitled *The Zookeeper's Wife* by Diane Ackerman, an American writer.

Zilberberg, Rachel (1920–1943)

Rachel Zilberberg was a key member of the Jewish resistance during the Warsaw Ghetto Uprising, losing her life in the command bunker at Miła 18 on May 8, 1943.

Known also as Sarenka, she was born in Warsaw on January 5, 1920, to Alexander and Masha Zilberberg, Orthodox Jews who owned a dairy goods store. She was an active member of the Zionist-socialist youth movement Hashomer Hatzair, where she was friends with **Mordecai Anielewicz**. While enrolled at the Jewish gymnasium (high school) she was an exceptional student, not only in academics but also in sports. She received her matriculation certificate around the same time that Poland was invaded by Germany in September 1939.

With the outbreak of war she and her sister Ruth moved to Vilna (Vilnius) in order to escape the Nazis. There she entered into an active kibbutz life with Hashomer Hatzair, along with her boyfriend Moshe Kopito, also a close friend of Anielewicz. On February 22, 1941, Kopito and Zilberberg's daughter Maya was born in Vilna.

With the onset of Operation Barbarossa on June 22, 1941, the Jews of Lithuania found themselves right in the path of the advancing onslaught. Vilna was occupied by the German army on June 24, 1941, and by July Einsatzgruppen (mobile killing squads), aided by Lithuanian auxiliaries, killed 5,000 Jewish men in the Ponary Forest just outside of Vilna. At the end of August 1941 Germans killed another 3,500 Jews at Ponary, and the killing continued such that by the end of 1941 the Einsatzgruppen had murdered at least 40,000 Jews there.

Zilberberg managed to escape the hunts accompanying these mass murders, first by hiding with other members of Hashomer Hatzair and then through finding short-term sanctuary in the "Little Sisters" convent in a forest about four miles outside of Vilna. She then went into the forest with **Abba Kovner** and some 15 to 20 others.

One day Kopito, while trying to buy milk and supplies for baby Maya, was killed by the Nazis. Zilberberg placed Maya with a friendly doctor in a Vilna orphanage under the name Yodviga Sogak, and was then persuaded by Hashomer Hatzair leaders to return to Warsaw. Another member of Hashomer Hatzair, Chaika Grossman, was to accompany her and oversee her transfer to a family in the ghetto; there, it was intended that she would continue her youth leadership work.

Zilberberg returned to the Warsaw Ghetto in January 1942. Once there, she related all she had seen and learned about the massacres at Ponary, providing detailed information that, owing to the sealed existence of the ghetto inhabitants, was new and alarming news. In view of this, she was desperate to motivate those around her to the urgency of inciting rebellion against the Nazis from inside the ghetto. Many of those she had earlier led in youth activities were keen to follow her. Others, such as Mira Fuchrer, agreed; Fuchrer then convinced her boyfriend, Anielewicz, that rebellion was the appropriate course for the Jews of Warsaw to follow, too. Eventually, due largely to Zilberberg's entreaties, all saw the urgency of what faced the ghetto.

When the Warsaw Ghetto Uprising broke out on April 19, 1943, Zilberberg was one of the leaders of the Jewish Combat Organization (Żydowska Organizacja Bojowa, or ŻOB), which largely comprised members from Hashomer Hatzair and other left-wing youth movements. Together with Anielewicz, Fuchrer, and many others present in Miła 18 on May 8, 1943—up to 300, by all accounts— Zilberberg refused to surrender after the Nazis had located the command bunker. With the Germans pumping in tear gas, some attempted to break out through one of the remaining exits, but it was a forlorn hope. One of those who did manage to survive was another Hashomer Hatzair leader, **Tova (Tosia) Altman**, who got out of the bunker and escaped into the sewers and into the Aryan side on or by May 10. She was killed before the month was out, handed over by Polish police to the Nazis.

Those remaining in the bunker saw no other alternative—rather than surrender, they took their own lives. Many of the bodies were never recovered or identified, though Zilberberg was one of those recognized. Having fallen in combat, her name is now engraved on a memorial stone at Miła 18, together with the names of 50 other Jewish fighters who died and whose identities have been established.

Maya, the daughter Zilberberg handed over in Vilna, has never been traced.

Zimetbaum, Mala (1918–1944)

Mala Zimetbaum was a Jewish woman from Belgium best remembered as the first female prisoner to escape from Auschwitz extermination camp.

She was born on January 26, 1918, in Brzesko, Poland, the fifth daughter in a large family. In 1928 they all emigrated from Poland and settled in Antwerp, Belgium. Zimetbaum, an excellent student, became proficient in several languages (Flemish, French, German, English, and Polish) but was forced to leave school because of the family's difficult economic circumstances. She went to work, first as a seamstress for a major fashion house, and then in one of Antwerp's many diamond factories.

On or about July 22, 1942, she was arrested for the first time by the SS. She was released but arrested a second time during a roundup on September 11–12, 1942. She was sent to the transit camp at Mechelen/Malines, and then, on September 15, to Auschwitz. She reached what would be her final destination two days later. After arrival, and having survived the preliminary selection process, she was sent to the women's camp at Birkenau, with the registration number 19880.

Owing to her proficiency in languages, Zimetbaum was chosen to serve as a "runner," or courier, and a translator for the SS. This position came with privileges—she could move relatively freely between different parts of the camp and could speak up on behalf of her fellow inmates. She was also able to smuggle tiny items between compounds. Zimetbaum's attitude toward her privileged position was that she had been given a gift with which to help those around her and thereby save lives. It also gave her an opportunity to make connections with the camp resistance movement.

Her tasks included working in the camp hospital, where she could warn of forthcoming selections among those patients too weak to continue working, or those who seemed less likely to recover quickly. She tried to ensure that they would leave the hospital as soon as possible if she knew that a selection was imminent. She also had responsibility for assigning to new work details those who had been sick once they had been released from the hospital. This gave her some measure of discretion in allocating less demanding work to those women who were physically unable to handle harder forms of labor.

Among the prisoners Zimetbaum met was a Pole, Edward (Edek) Galiński. He was brought to Auschwitz as an early Polish political prisoner, having arrived on June 14, 1940. Determined to escape, he had made attempts before he met Zimetbaum, though nothing had materialized. After he met her, however, things changed. The two fell in love, and Zimetbaum said she was prepared to escape with him—her motive being to let the world know about Auschwitz in order for the killing to stop.

On Saturday, June 24, 1944, they made their escape. Galiński wore an SS uniform and carried a gun obtained from Edward Lubusch, a member of the SS guard detachment known to assist prisoners. Disguised as a guard, Galiński led Zimetbaum, as a prisoner being led to work, out of the camp by showing a bogus SS pass. They succeeded in escaping to a nearby town, but on July 6, 1944, they were captured by a German patrol. Returned to Auschwitz, they were sent to Block 11, the punishment block, where they underwent a long period of interrogation and torture. The Gestapo was particularly interested in learning who their conspirators were in the escape, and in particular, who provided them with the SS uniform. They remained true to their promise to Lubusch and did not break under the torture.

On September 15, 1944, Zimetbaum and Galiński were executed. Orders were received at Birkenau that the executions were to take place at the same time, though in the men's and women's camp respectively.

As he was hanged, Galiński shouted, defiantly, "Long live Poland." Zimetbaum's death has become shrouded in legend. According to one version, she was brought forward toward the gallows by SS-Unterscharführer Johan Ruiters, and as her sentence was read out by SS officer Maria Mandl she took a razor blade hidden in her hair and slit her wrists. As blood poured from the wounds, she slapped Ruiters, who attempted to stop her. This resulted in the other SS officers closing in on her and beating her as they attempted to take the razor blade away.

It is here that reality becomes mixed with fable. With the blood draining away her life, some accounts assert that she shouted at Ruiters, saying that she was dying a hero while he would die a dog. Others assert that she shouted at the prisoners assembled to witness her execution that they should revolt. Another claimed that she told the prisoners they would soon be liberated. Even the precise circumstances of her death are uncertain. In some accounts, she was taken to the camp hospital and died on the way to the crematorium. One account has it that an SS officer said that an order had arrived from Berlin that she was to be burned alive in the crematorium. Other accounts hold that she was poisoned or shot to death at the crematorium entrance, while yet others say that she actually was thrown into the furnace alive.

Notwithstanding the differences between the various versions of Zimetbaum's death, it is clear that she was a remarkable young woman. Her courage in the face of the Nazi terror; her willingness to put herself at risk in order to ease the suffering of those around her (and even to save lives); her attempt to escape in order to tell the world the truth about Auschwitz; even the love she managed to find in the midst of the horror—all these point to a woman who refused to allow the Nazi evil to prevail. Her resistance was truly inspirational to all those around her and remains so today, making Mala Zimetbaum a genuine heroine of the Holocaust.

Zuckerman, Yitzhak (1915–1981)

Yitzhak Zuckerman, also known as Antek, was a key leader of the Żydowska Organizacja Bojowa (Jewish Combat Organization, or ŻOB) in the Warsaw Ghetto, and one of the few survivors of the Warsaw Ghetto Uprising of April–May, 1943.

Born in Vilna in 1915, he attended a Hebrew high school before moving to Warsaw in 1938 to work for the Dror Hechalutz Zionist youth movement. As a young man he embraced socialism as well as Zionism.

Soon after Germany invaded Poland in September 1939, Zuckerman fled to Soviet-occupied eastern Poland, where he organized Zionist youth groups. In April 1940 he returned to Warsaw to stimulate resistance to the Nazis. It was at this time that he met another underground leader, **Zivia Lubetkin**, and the two fell in love.

When the Germans launched mass deportations from Warsaw during the summer of 1942, Zuckerman was among the first calling for armed resistance. This would prove to be difficult to achieve, largely on account of opposition from members of the Warsaw Jewish Council (Judenrat), in particular its chairman, Adam Czerniaków. On July 22, 1942, the Nazis began what they termed *Grossaktion Warschau* (Great Action Warsaw), an operation dedicated to the mass extermination of Jews from the Warsaw Ghetto. After Czerniaków's suicide on July 23, 1942, events developed at a rapid pace.

A meeting was called involving several leading members of the organized Jewish community, including Yitzhak Zuckerman, **David Guzik**, and **Emanuel Ringelblum**, among many others. Opinions were divided. Representatives of the left-wing Zionist parties and Hechalutz called for some form of active intervention; others preferred to wait and see what would happen next. Not willing to wait and simply postpone the inevitable, Hechalutz and its youth movement branches, Hashomer Hatzair, Dror, and Akiva, held a meeting on July 28, 1942, in which it was decided to go ahead and establish a Jewish Combat Organization (Żydowska Organizacja Bojowa, or ŻOB). They formed a command group comprising Shmuer Bresler, Zuckerman, Zivia Lubetkin, **Mordechaj Tenenbaum**, and Josef Kaplan. A delegation was sent to make contact with the Polish underground and obtain weapons on the Aryan side of Warsaw. This included **Tova (Tosia) Altman**, Frumke Plotnicka, Leah Perlstein, and Izrael Chaim (known as "Arie" and "Jurek") Wilner. In November 1942 **Mordecai Anielewicz** was elected as commander in chief. Zuckerman became one of his three co-commanders and also helped lead a political affiliate founded at the same time, the Jewish National Committee (Żydowski Komitet Narodowy).

On December 22, 1942, Zuckerman, Miriem (Gole) Mire, and Adolf Liebeskind were sent by the ŻOB to Kraków to meet with resistance fighters there. While in the city, they took part in an attack on a café that was frequented by the SS and the Gestapo. Liebeskind was killed. There is debate regarding Mire's fate. Some say she was killed soon afterward; others assert she played a part in the Warsaw Ghetto Uprising in the spring of 1943. Zuckerman, although shot in the leg, managed to escape and return to Warsaw.

Back in Warsaw, Zuckerman became the unofficial armorer of the ŻOB. He negotiated through contacts he had made with external resistance groups, attempting to procure rifles, pistols, ammunition, and grenades. These were smuggled into the ghetto via the Warsaw sewers, and his ongoing negotiations meant that he had a good idea of how he might navigate the labyrinth in the future. When the Nazis initiated another round of deportations in January 1943, it was Zuckerman who led the ŻOB in fighting back against the Germans. This, however, was but a prelude of things to come.

Zuckerman spent a lot of his time outside the ghetto, and when the uprising began on April 19, 1943, he found himself on the wrong side of the wall. The ŻOB had been preparing for a revolt should the time arrive when hope for all other alternatives was lost. From his position, Zuckerman did all he could to spread word of the revolt and what the Jews in the ghetto were facing, and he smuggled in any additional weapons he was able to obtain. By now, however, many suppliers had decided to curtail arms transfers for the Jews.

With the defeat of the uprising and the death of the other main leaders on or around May 8, 1943, Zuckerman returned to the ghetto as the sole surviving commander. He led some 75 ŻOB fighters (including Zivia Lubetkin), together with some of the few survivors of the Żydowski Związek Wojskowy (Jewish Military Union, or ŻZW), through the sewers and onto the Aryan side. While there, he wrote an important report on the ŻOB's role during the uprising, which he managed to send to London. He also maintained his military command role, leading a group of Jewish guerrillas in the Polish underground during the Warsaw Revolt that began on August 1, 1944.

After the war, Yitzhak Zuckerman and Zivia Lubetkin became involved in the Bricha movement, an underground network that helped survivors reach the Mediterranean coast on their way to Palestine. In 1947 he and Lubetkin married and settled in Israel, and in 1949, along with others who had been ghetto resisters and partisans in Poland and Lithuania, they founded Kibbutz Lohamei Hagetaot (Ghetto Fighters Kibbutz); there, a memorial museum, Ghetto Fighters' House, was established. In 1961 the Zuckermans were prosecution witnesses at the trial of Adolf Eichmann.

When Yitzhak Zuckerman died in Israel on June 17, 1981, he was buried at Kibbutz Lohamei Hagetaot, recognized by all as a hero of the Jewish people. Among the many mourners present to pay their respects on the day was Israeli president Yitzhak Navon.

Zwartendijk, Jan (1896–1976)

Jan Zwartendijk was a Dutch businessman and diplomat stationed in Lithuania during World War II, during which he created conditions enabling thousands of Jews to obtain lifesaving visas for foreign countries.

Born in Rotterdam on July 29, 1896, he worked for the Dutch Philips electrical company, and in May 1939 he became director of operations in Lithuania, running a small plant of 20 workers. On June 19, 1940, he became acting Dutch consul in Kovno (Kaunas), representing the interests of a Dutch government that by now had gone into exile in London due to the German invasion of the Netherlands the previous month. The Philips Company, furthermore, was no longer able to engage in the export of its goods to Lithuania due to restrictions imposed by the war.

As consul, Zwartendijk was subordinate to the more formal and senior jurisdiction of the Dutch ambassador to nearby Latvia, L. P. J. de Decker. In July 1940, on his own initiative, de Decker had issued a visa enabling Pessla Lewin, a Dutch-born Jewish woman holding Polish citizenship, to be admitted to a Dutch colony in the West Indies. The visa was marked: "Surinam, Curaçao, and other possessions of the Netherlands in the Americas, no entry visa is required." With this notation in her passport, Lewin's husband, Dr. Isaac Lewin, approached Zwartendijk in Kovno with the request that he write the same statement in his identity papers. This, the first of what became known as the "Curaçao visas," was duly noted on July 22, 1940.

Zwartendijk already had a reasonable understanding of what Nazi antisemitic measures could look like, as he had spent time in Hamburg during the 1930s. He appreciated de Decker's action and adopted it as his own—and even extended its reach. Little wonder, then, that when Lithuanian Jews learned of de Decker's precedent they began to approach Zwartendijk, asking that the same sort of visas be made available to them. He was more than receptive, and with de Decker's approval he started issuing visas to others. Word of this amazing exception, in an international climate where visas were usually not available, spread like wildfire, and Jews escaping from German-occupied Poland also began to approach Zwartendijk. Between July 23 and August 3, 1940, Zwartendijk issued up to 2,345 Curaçao visas.

He was far from sure that the Curaçao notations would secure the refugees' freedom, particularly in view of the fact that in all cases permission from the respective colonial governors was necessary before a prospective immigrant could enter the territory. Nonetheless, he made every effort to help. When the process was still being developed, he wrote and signed each visa by hand, but with the intensification of applications he had a rubber stamp made, giving the visas a more official look. The stamp simply said "No Visa to Curaçao Necessary."

Jan Zwartendijk, a Dutch citizen who, when acting in an honorary capacity as a diplomatic representative of the Netherlands in Lithuania in 1940, created a loophole in the immigration regulations that permitted thousands of Jews to obtain life-saving visas. He is pictured here with his son and daughter in Kovno (Kaunas), sometime in 1939 or 1940. (United States Holocaust Memorial Museum, courtesy of Dr. Jan Zwartendyk)

On August 3, 1940, the Soviet authorities in Lithuania forced Zwartendijk's consulate in Kovno to close down and confiscated his office at Philips. Indeed, all embassies and consulates in Kovno were closed, meaning that Zwartendijk's issuing of Curaçao visas came to an end. Just before closing down he burned whatever official consular papers he had generated, destroying all evidence of the deeds he had undertaken on behalf of Jews. He then returned to the Netherlands with his family, where he remained for the rest of the war, still working for Philips. It has been speculated that he might have acted as a British contact for the Dutch underground, though this has not been confirmed.

Granting the Curaçao visas was more significant than it first appeared. An important consequence was that the Japanese consul in Lithuania, **Chiune Sugihara**, aware that the Jews had a visa from a third country, was able to provide them with a transit visa through Japan. Sugihara's consulate issued close to 2,000 such visas, enabling the holders to move through the Soviet Union and into Japan. Sugihara knew that Zwartendijk's visas were not legitimate, but he issued his own transit visas in any case. This was certainly against Japanese rules, but his attitude was that doing so would save lives—which, for him, was more important. The Japanese authorities subsequently permitted every Jew holding one of these permits to land.

After the war, Zwartendijk never told anyone about what he had done. In fact, not even the Dutch government was aware of his actions until 1963.

Jan Zwartendijk died in 1976, in Eindhoven. On October 6, 1997, Yad Vashem posthumously recognized him as one of the Righteous among the Nations for his efforts on behalf of the Jewish refugees in Kovno back in 1940. Then, on September 10, 2012, Zwartendijk was awarded one further accolade, the Life Saving Cross of the Republic of Lithuania, a decoration for those who attempt to save life regardless of the dangers to their own personal safety.

Zygielbojm, Shmuel (1895–1943)

Shmuel Zygielbojm was a Jewish-Polish socialist politician who committed suicide in London in the aftermath of the Warsaw Ghetto Uprising during the spring of 1943. His suicide was in protest of the Allied governments' failure to do anything meaningful to assist the Jews during the Holocaust, and it was a powerful symbol of resistance in the face of inaction.

Zygielbojm was born to a poor family on February 21, 1895, in the Polish village of Borowica. He was one of 10 children. At the beginning of World War I, he and his family moved to the city of Chełm, and during the war years he became involved in the Jewish labor movement. Joining the Labor Bund, he rose quickly through the leadership, and in 1924 he was elected to the Bund's Central Committee in Warsaw. By 1936, after a number of years as editor of the Jewish labor movement's journal *Arbeiter Fragen* (*Worker's Issues*), he was sent to Łódź on behalf of the movement to organize Jewish workers there.

With the Nazi invasion of Poland on September 1, 1939, Zygielbojm returned to Warsaw, where he became a member of the defense committee that functioned during the siege and defense of the capital. He also served at this time as editor of the *Folkszeitung* (*People's Newspaper*).

Once the city had been conquered and occupied, the Nazis demanded a dozen hostages from the Polish population who would be held responsible for the maintenance of order in the city. The mayor of Warsaw, Stefan Starzynski, advised the Jewish community to offer up a worker as one of the hostages, and he named a woman, one Ester Ivinska. Zygielbojm, horrified at the idea of a civilian woman being so endangered, suggested himself instead. He thus became one of two Jewish hostages, along with prominent industrialist, social worker, and philanthropist Abraham Gepner. Upon his release, Zygielbojm was called upon to represent the Bund in the newly established (and Nazi-imposed) Warsaw Judenrat (Jewish Council).

At the same time, he began to organize an underground movement. Despite being a member of the Judenrat, Zygielbojm resisted the very idea of the ghetto, and he called on Jews to remain in their homes and not move into the ghetto until they were forced to.

This level of opposition was brought to the attention of the Germans, who summoned him for interrogation. Instead, he went into hiding. His involvement in the formal resistance movement did not, therefore, last long; his fellow party members, recognizing his value as an organizer and publicist and concerned for his welfare, thought it better that he leave Poland. In December 1939, therefore, he was spirited out of the country and moved to still-neutral Belgium. Speaking to a Socialist International meeting in Brussels, he described at firsthand his observations of the persecution of the Jews—one of the earliest accounts during the war of the Nazi brutalities to reach the West. After the Nazi invasion of Belgium in May 1940, he moved to France; later still, he went to the United States. In both countries he worked to raise awareness of what was happening to the Jews of Poland. In March 1942 he went to London, where he joined the National Council of the Polish government-in-exile.

In May 1942 Zygielbojm received a report from the Bund that had been smuggled out from Warsaw. It was one of the first statements providing detailed information of the carnage. Even by this stage, the report calculated a figure of 700,000 murdered Jews, and it provided the names and locations of killing sites and extermination camps. Then, on December 2, 1942, Zygielbojm met with **Jan Karski**, who had been covertly brought into the Warsaw Ghetto to report at firsthand what was taking place there. Upon speaking with Karski, Zygielbojm was at once unnerved and more determined than ever to bring this news to the attention of Allied governments so that some sort of concrete action would follow.

Worse was to come. From April 19, 1943 onward, an uprising of the remaining Jews took place in the Warsaw Ghetto, leading to its destruction and the annihilation of its last inhabitants. News of the uprising was quick to reach London, and compounding Zygielbojm's despair was information he received that his wife, Manya, and 16-year-old son, Tuvia, had been killed by the Nazis.

On May 12, 1943, in a final act of protest at the seeming Allied indifference to the fate of the Jews, Zygielbojm committed suicide in London. He left two letters—one for the Polish president, Władysław Raczkiewicz, and one for Prime Minister Władysław Sikorski. His message was straightforward—the Nazis were the ones doing the killing, but it was the Allies who had brought the Jews into their status of worthlessness. "The responsibility for the crime of the murder of the whole Jewish nationality in Poland," he wrote, rested indirectly "upon the whole of humanity, on the peoples of the Allied nations and on their governments, who up to this day have not taken any real steps to halt this crime." Chillingly, he then placed his own death alongside those of the heroes in the Warsaw Ghetto: "I cannot continue to live and to be silent while the remnants of Polish Jewry, whose representative I am, are being murdered. My comrades in the Warsaw ghetto fell with arms in their hands in the last heroic battle. I was not permitted to fall like them, together with them, but I belong with them, to their mass grave." He concluded: "By my death, I wish to give expression to my most profound protest against the inaction in which the world watches and permits the destruction of the Jewish people."

In what was his final act of resistance, and in symbolic unity with those murdered in the Holocaust, Zygielbojm's body was then cremated, in accord with his own expressed wishes.

Primary Source Documents

The documents that follow represent a snapshot of resistance expressions prevailing during the Holocaust. Resistance activities of all types flourished across the entire period of the Third Reich, as the many examples shown in this book demonstrate. Often, however, records of those activities are hard to locate owing to the clandestine nature of the undertakings involved. Sometimes, records were not kept at all, for fear of various initiatives being exposed or denounced. This section attempts to provide a varied range of sources that will give readers an idea of the types of resistance documents that can be accessed, whether from upstanders, partisans, ghetto fighters, concentration or death camp prisoners, or survivors.

1. Robert Weltsch, "Wear It with Pride, the Yellow Badge" (April 4, 1933)

In March 1933 the newly installed Nazi government issued a call for a nationwide boycott of all Jewish businesses, to take place on April 1, 1933. In response, Robert Weltsch, editor of the national Jewish newspaper Jüdische Rundschau, wrote an editorial pointing out to his readers that life would henceforth be altered—perhaps irretrievably—for Germany's Jews. His article, one of the first statements of Jewish assertiveness in the face of Nazi provocation, argues that Jews should not simply acquiesce to Nazi antisemitism.

The first of April, 1933, will remain an important date in the history of German Jewry—indeed, in the history of the entire Jewish people. The events of that day have aspects that are not only political and economic, but moral and spiritual as well. The political and economic implications have been widely discussed in the press, though of course the need for agitation has frequently obscured objective understanding. To speak of the *moral* aspect, that is our task. For however much the Jewish question is now debated, nobody except ourselves can express what is to be said on these events from the Jewish point of view, what is happening in the soul of the German Jew. Today the Jews cannot speak except as Jews. Anything else is utterly senseless. . . . Gone is the fatal misapprehension of many Jews that

Jewish interests can be pressed under some other cover. On April 1 the German Jews learned a lesson which penetrates far more deeply than even their embittered and now triumphant opponents could assume. . . .

We live in a new period; the national revolution of the German people is a signal that is visible from afar, indicating that the world of our previous concepts has collapsed. That may be painful for many, but in this world only those will be able to survive who are able to look reality in the eye. We stand in the midst of tremendous changes in intellectual, political, social and economic life. It is for us to see how the Jews will react.

April 1, 1933, can become the day of Jewish awakening and Jewish rebirth. If the Jews will it. If the Jews are mature and have greatness in them. If the Jews are not as they are represented to be by their opponents.

The Jews, under attack, must learn to acknowledge themselves.

Even in these days of most profound disturbance, when the stormiest of emotions have visited our hearts in face of the unprecedented display of the universal slander of the entire Jewish population of a great and cultural country, we must first of all maintain: composure. Even if we stand shattered by the events of these days we must not lose heart and must examine the situation without any attempt to deceive ourselves. One would like to recommend in these days that the document that stood at the cradle of Zionism, Theodor Herzl's "Jewish State," be distributed in hundreds of thousands of copies among Jews and non-Jews. . . .

They accuse us today of treason against the German people: The National-Socialist Press calls us the "enemy of the Nation," and leaves us defenseless.

It is not true that the Jews betrayed Germany. If they betrayed anyone, it was themselves, the Jews.

Because the Jew did not display his Judaism with pride, because he tried to avoid the Jewish issue, he must bear part of the blame for the degradation of the Jews.

Despite all the bitterness that we must feel in full measure when we read the National-Socialist boycott proclamations and unjust accusations, there is one point for which we may be grateful to the boycott Committee. Para. 3 of the directives reads: "The reference is . . . of course to businesses owned by members of the Jewish race. Religion plays no part here. Businessmen who were baptized Catholic or Protestant, or Jews who left their Community remain Jews for the purpose of this Order." This is a [painful] reminder for all those who betrayed their Judaism. Those who steal away from the Community in order to benefit their personal position should not collect the wages of their betrayal. In taking up this position against the renegades there is the beginning of a clarification. The Jew who denies his Judaism is no better a citizen than his fellow who avows it openly. It is shameful to be a renegade, but as long as the world around us rewarded it, it appeared an advantage. Now even that is no longer an advantage. The Jew is marked as a Jew. He gets the yellow badge.

A powerful symbol is to be found in the fact that the boycott leadership gave orders that a sign "with a yellow badge on a black background" was to be pasted on the boycotted shops. This regulation is intended as a brand, a sign of contempt. We will take it up and make of it a badge of honor.

Many Jews suffered a crushing experience on Saturday. Suddenly they were revealed as Jews, not as a matter of inner avowal, not in loyalty to their own community, not in pride in a great past and great achievements, but by the impress of a red placard with a yellow patch. The patrols moved from house to house, stuck their placards on shops and signboards, daubed the windows, and for 24 hours the German Jews were exhibited in the stocks, so to speak. In addition to other signs and inscriptions one often saw windows bearing a large Magen David, the Shield of David the King. It was intended as dishonor. Jews, take it up, the Shield of David, and wear it with pride!

Source: Robert Weltsch, *Jüdische Rundschau*, No. 27, April 4, 1933. From Yitzhak Arad, Yisrael Gutman, and Abraham Margaliot, eds., *Documents on the Holocaust, Jerusalem: Yad Vashem* (1981), pp. 44–47. Reproduced by permission of Yad Vashem Publications.

Commentary

Robert Weltsch was the prewar editor of the twice-weekly *Jüdische Rundschau* (*Jewish Review*). When the newly installed Nazi government organized a boycott of all Jewish businesses on April 1, 1933, it was its first official overtly antisemitic measure.

Weltsch reacted by writing an editorial on April 4 that became famous as one of the earliest Jewish responses to Nazi anti-Jewish persecution. Entitled "Tragt ihn mit Stolz, den gelben Fleck!" ("Wear It with Pride, the Yellow Badge"), it is a call for the Jews of Germany to recognize their changed situation with dignity and in solidarity.

He writes that in light of the new regime, "Today the Jews cannot speak except as Jews. Anything else is utterly senseless. . . . We live in a new period . . . indicating that the world of our previous concepts has collapsed. That may be painful for many, but in this world only those will be able to survive who are able to look reality in the eye." In view of their earlier self-deception that they would always be accepted as Germans, "*It is not true that the Jews betrayed Germany. If they betrayed anyone, it was themselves, the Jews.* Because the Jew did not display his Judaism with pride, because he tried to avoid the Jewish issue, he must bear part of the blame for the degradation of the Jews."

With this in mind, if they were to be stigmatized, they should accept the mark of that stigma. Noting that during the boycott a number of antisemitic signs and Stars of David appeared on the streets in opposition to the Jews, Weltsch enjoins his readers to "take it up, the Shield of David, and wear it with pride!"

2. Armin T. Wegner, Open Letter to Adolf Hitler (April 11, 1933)

In the aftermath of the Nazi takeover, the failed boycott of Jewish businesses, and the intensification of Nazi antisemitic rhetoric, Armin T. Wegner, a writer with a well-established reputation as an advocate of human rights, wrote in impassioned terms to Adolf Hitler asking that he rein in the regime's rapidly developing extremism. The letter, recently translated into English by Silvia Samuelli, was a plea for restraint made on the ground of humanitarianism and also a commentary on the impact Hitler's agenda would have on the image of Germany and Germans in the future.

Mr. Reich Chancellor,

With your statement on March 29 of this year, the Government decreed that all Jewish citizens be forbidden to carry on with their commercial enterprises. Offensive words like "swindlers," "don't buy," "death to the Jews," "go back to Jerusalem" appeared on shop windows, men holding clubs and guns guarded the doors, and for ten hours the capital turned into a theatre for the solace of the masses. Eventually, satisfied with such punishment and derision, the boycott was lifted and the city and the streets went back to their routine activities.

But is the aftermath not even worse? Judges, attorneys, doctors are discharged from their well-paid posts, schools are closed for their sons and daughters, high school teachers are expelled and sent on leave—a concession which can rouse no suspicion—theatre directors, actors and singers are deprived of their stages, publishers are forbidden to print their newspapers, every book written by a Jewish poet and writer is confiscated to silence the guardians of the moral order.

It is Judaism that is the target rather than business; it is the noblest values of the human community that are under attack.

You state, Mr. Reich Chancellor, that Germans have been framed and blamed by their neighbors of unworthy actions for which they are not responsible, but have not mistakes and a bad reputation always preceded honor and glory? Have the Jews not taught us how to bear slander as a badge of honor? It is not by mere chance that so many Jews live on German soil, but it is, rather, the result of a common destiny! This great but unhappy people, after centuries of wandering, after being expelled from Spain and refused by France, has been given hospitality by Germany for about one thousand years. The Jew spontaneously went to where his life was safest or where he could satisfy his desire for culture; when Germany, destroyed and surrounded by so many enemies, offered a shelter to the victims of persecution, she was only complying with the principle of freedom she herself was fighting for. And now shall one thousand years be erased forever?

We have always given other nations the best of ourselves, in the West, in South America, in Russia. A lifelong wanderer over the earth, the German was always strongly drawn to his unhappy fatherland, which accumulated more and more possessions overseas. The German settlers, bridge engineers and businessmen have all contributed to the good name and the growing wealth of every nation. And for these merits have we not been denigrated before the First Great War and even now?

So, we who so often have experienced injustice, are we going to inflict the same grief on others who, like us, do not deserve it? Justice has always been a source of pride of all people; if Germany has become a great nation in the world, we owe it to the Jews, too. Have they not always showed themselves grateful for the protection offered them?

Do you remember Albert Einstein, a German Jew, a scientist who revolutionized the concept of space, a man who, like Copernicus, devoted himself to the study of the universe, giving us a new image of the world? Do you remember Albert Ballin, a German Jew who created the greatest ship line to the West? It was from Germany that the largest ship in the world set sail to the land of freedom. And yet unable to cope with the shame of his king leaving the country, he committed suicide! Do you remember Emil Rathenau, a German Jew, who turned the General Company for the production of electric energy into a world enterprise? And what about Haber, a German Jew who with his compressor extracted nitrogen from the air? And what about Ehrlich, a German Jew, a doctor who with his treatment defeated syphilis, a deadly disease found among our people? And what about the 16-year-old girl who won the World Championship in fencing in Amsterdam, gaining a victory for Germany? She was also Jewish, the daughter of an attorney, one of those we are now going to expel from our courts.

Do you remember all the people—I would have to fill many sheets of paper just to list their names—whose intelligence and zeal have left their mark on our history? So, I ask, have all these men and women acted as Jews or as Germans?

Have writers and poets written a history of German or of Jewish thought? Have their actors cultivated the German language or a foreign language? Have their great advocates of a new social doctrine been prophets for the Jews or for the Germans? Have their unfortunately unheeded warnings been addressed to the Jews or to the Germans?

We have accepted the sacrifice of blood shed during the war by 12,000 Jews. How can we now—if our hearts still harbor the slightest sense of justice—deprive their parents, children, brothers, grandchildren, their women and sisters of something rightly deserved for generations, namely, the right to a fatherland and a home? How unfortunate are these people who loved the country that welcomed them even more than themselves! Are we not bound by the same feelings and the same inner doubts? And being so similar to us, has the Jew not helped spread German customs and the German language as far as remote Russia? In the Jewish lanes of Polish villages German medieval songs can still be heard; the Jews' ancestors sent away centuries ago stole no gold from those lands, just the touching melodies they still sing, which we have forgotten.

If a German needs help in a foreign land, if he looks for someone who speaks his own language, where can he find him? In the chemist's shop of a Caucasian Jew, or in the tailor's shop near the well in an Arabian desert. In Poland Jewish families that had identified themselves with German culture have been robbed and thrown into prison. After their taking refuge in Germany, are we going to mete out the same fate as before? What wretched love! They cannot believe those who say that the Jews are foreigners and, therefore, are incapable of loving our fatherland. Isn't the German people itself a melting pot of different origins, Frank, Frisian and Wend? Was Napoleon not from Corsica? Are you yourself not from a neighboring country? If you could have seen, as I did, the tears of the Jewish mothers, the anguish on the fathers' pale faces, the children's eyes, you would have understood the strong attachment of a people once forced to endless wandering, because they feel a stronger tie to their land than those who have never lost it.

"I love Germany," I heard a boy and a girl say to their parents who, appalled by the present threatening situation, wanted to leave the country. "Go without us," they told their parents, "we prefer to die here rather be happy in a foreign country." Is such a strong feeling not to be admired?

Mr. Reich Chancellor!

It is not only a question of the destiny of our Jewish brothers. The very destiny of Germany is at stake! In the name of the people for whom I have the right and no less the duty to speak, as if they were of my own flesh and blood, as a German who has not been given the gift of speech to be a silent accomplice and whose heart is quivering with indignation, I address myself to you: Put a stop to all this!

Judaism survived the Babylonian captivity, slavery in Egypt, the Inquisition in Spain, the misfortunes of the Crusades, and the 17th-century persecutions in Russia. The same stubborn will that allowed the Jews to survive and become an ancient people will help them overcome this danger. But as a result of this, shame and misfortune will befall Germany and for a long time will not be forgotten! In fact who is going to pay for the evil we are now inciting on the Jews if not ourselves?

If the Jews have a share in our culture and have increased our wealth, then if we destroy them, their ruin will necessarily result in the ruin of German riches.

History teaches us that those nations that expelled the Jews paid for their crimes by incurring contempt and impoverishment. To tell the truth, they are not being thrown into the gutter as they were at the beginning. In public they are apparently respected but, even more painfully, they are robbed, in secret. I do not know how much of what is rumored is actually true. Whole areas of the city are being plundered, houses covered in graffiti during the night, and trucks waving pennons, full of singing and shouting soldiers drive through the streets of the city, while we all stare with dismay at this growing tide which is now threatening to drag down everything with it.

In this, the most difficult hour awaiting mankind, newspapers and illustrations humiliate and deride. One hundred years after Goethe and Lessing, we are regressing to superstition, source of the most miserable sufferings of all times.

Anxiety and insecurity are on the increase, together with despair, terror and suicides!

And while a part of the population—hoping to profit from these events that their conscience could never justify—approves them. Nevertheless, all the responsibility lies with the government which, with cold determination, goes ahead with its policies. All it is worse and less justifiable than a slaughter since it is the result of a deliberate action taken in cold blood. As such it cannot but end with the self-destruction of our people.

So what will the results be? The moral principle of justice is now replaced by one's racial origins. Till now the division of labor has been based on a person's capability of carrying out a job, not on creed or on race. You yourself have praised creativity as the most precious virtue of a people; you yourself have praised thinkers and inventors as the noblest resources of a nation.

From now on, any inept and unscrupulous person will be able to say to himself, "I can perform this task just because I am not a Jew; my being German is enough." And hiding behind this shield she or he may even get away with an evil action. Once chatterers and servile people, just to enter a new master's service, submit to a new unfamiliar doctrine, for which you and your friends have endangered life and honor, then warrants of arrest are released, families are denounced according to the whims of the evil-minded people. Their persecution is tolerated if it helps get rid of a bothersome rival. Can the mere participation in a war decide an individual's skill?

If Walter Rathenau, who was a minister in Germany during one of the most difficult post-war periods, were still alive, he could not be a doctor or an attorney for he never fought on a battlefield. However, he rescued his country from an early defeat by organizing the war economy in a way not previously contemplated by the government. He exposed himself to the bullet which hit him in a time of peace with no less courage than if he had been hit on the battlefield.

Distinction between good and evil has vanished, and, as a result, has not the community of a nation been brought into question? You may argue that our German blood prevents us from acting dishonorably. No doubt origins and heritage bring obligations with them; but, in my opinion, we have greater obligations to fight "for" than "against" the Jews. True, in recent times the Jews may not have given many heroes to their fatherland on the battlefield if compared to the fighting troops of our people. But they have made up for this with wise men, martyrs and saints. Even the saviors of an awakened people should admit that they cannot do without such saints; their voices have never failed to remind us of the most ancient prophecies and the highest moral law on earth.

So why then are these extraordinary outsiders being persecuted? Why are they so much hated throughout the world? Only because this people has placed law and justice above all else, because they have loved and respected law as if it were a bride, and because nobody is more hated than the upholders of justice by those who want injustice.

Mr. Reich Chancellor, nations and individuals are estranged from each other; this is the worst evil. Have the Germans ever tried to consider something they have avoided like leprosy from their youth onwards, a prejudice spreading now even among some Jews who are beginning to be ashamed of their wonderful origins? Yes, the people you and your friends are now fighting in Germany—if we are to believe your words—are no longer Jews, but renegades overwhelmed by greed and sensuality, people who have lost their faith and forgotten their duties, rejected both by their Jewish brothers and by the Germans.

Have the Germans by any chance acted better? How about the custodians of great wealth? Do they not blame the Jews only because they would like to be in their shoes? Have the German citizens, by any chance, lowered interest rates on loans and house rents? Is it possible to punish the mistakes of a few hundred who in the ancient struggle of this people between holiness and sin have betrayed the deepest yearnings of their race and thereby sacrificed hosts of innocent lives? Have we not rejected the revenge of the group in favor of the responsibility of the individual? In your speeches you often mention God Almighty; was it not perhaps the Omnipotent Himself who blended this dispersed people with the Germans like salt in bread dough? Are they not socially and morally necessary for us? Does their inborn integrity not let us distinguish the merits and faults of our own nature more clearly? You say that Germany is in a state of need. But instead of defending the cause of all the oppressed, you are now attempting to soothe the suffering of one part of the population with the suffering of another. Some even say that blaming the Jews would be necessary for the salvation of the fatherland.

Nevertheless there is no fatherland without justice! There is one Jew for every hundred Germans, how could he be stronger? A powerful people does not sink so low as to leave defenseless people at the mercy of the hatred of the frustrated.

You tell us of Jews whose presumptuousness apparently stirs up hostility. Has this by any chance happened without our help? When the Jews contributed to the spread of revolutionary ideas, does not their rebellion originate in their being treated unjustly? Did we not offend them ever since we were young? Does not a common destiny entail a common right and a common guilt as well? I contest the insane belief that all the evil in the world comes from the Jews. I contest it on the basis of law, the evidence of a century-old history. If I am now addressing these words to you, it is simply because I can find no other way to be heard. Not as a friend of the Jews, but as a friend of the Germans, of Prussian origin, in the light of the dangers looming up over Germany. Now when everyone is silent, I no longer want to be silent.

The masses can easily change their minds. They may soon condemn what they are now passionately fostering. Even if a long time should pass, the hour of freedom for the victims of persecution is approaching together with the punishment of criminals. The day shall come when the Germans will judge their actions from the depth of their hearts. The first of April will then be remembered as a day of shame by all. If Germany had really been slandered, would it need these policies just to defend a clear conscience?

We are told that abroad they are no longer worried. Why then are persecutions still being carried out secretly? Was there no simpler way to face slanderous rumors about our crimes without humiliating the Jews? Could we not have given them signs of friendship instead? Would not bad reputations disappear immediately were there evidence of love and common sense? Is a good action not always the best conversion?

Mr. Reich Chancellor, I am sending you words that spring from a torn and tormented heart. They are not only mine; it is rather the voice of destiny warning you through my mouth. Protect Germany by protecting the Jews. Do not allow people around you to mislead you! You are badly advised! Question your conscience as you did when walking through a freed world on your way home from the war when you decided to start your battles on your own. Admitting a mistake has always been a quality of great spirits. There are now clear signs of what the people need. Let those who have been dismissed return to their places of work; send back the doctors to the hospitals, judges to the courts; open the schools to the children and heal their mothers' grieving hearts and the whole nation will thank you. Because even if Germany might be able to do without the Jews, she cannot do without her virtue. "There is only one true faith," wisely warns Immanuel Kant from the crypt of his hundred-year-old tomb, "even if there may be many different creeds." Keeping this doctrine in mind will allow you also to understand those you are now fighting. What would Germany be without truth, beauty and justice?

One day, should towns be just a heap of rubble, should the race die out, should voices of tolerance be silenced forever, the mountains of our fatherland would still rise to the sky and the eternal forests would rustle on. But they would no longer breathe our fathers' air, that of freedom and justice. With shame and scorn they would tell of a race that not only thoughtlessly jeopardized the destiny of the country but also brought eternal dishonor upon its memory. When we demand justice, we want dignity.

I beg you! Defend nobility of mind, pride and conscience without which we cannot live. Defend the dignity of the German people!

Source: *Journal of Genocide Research* 2 (1) (2000): 139–144 (translated by Silvia Samuelli). Reprinted by permission of the publisher (Taylor & Francis Ltd., http://www.tandfonline.com).

Commentary

Armin Wegner was one of the earliest voices to protest Adolf Hitler's treatment of the Jews, and the only popular author in Nazi Germany to publicly remonstrate against it.

Witnessing the onset of Nazism before January 1933, he foresaw that the Nazis' antisemitic policies would lead to the destruction of Germany's reputation, possibly forever. His long open letter to Adolf Hitler, in which he denounces Nazi antisemitism, makes him one of the earliest voices protesting Hitler's treatment of the Jews. In despair he writes: "Distinction between good and evil has vanished."

The letter was written a few days after the failed nationwide boycott of Jewish businesses on April 1, 1933. Although an open letter intended to be read by everyone, no newspaper in Germany was willing to publish it for fear of retribution; upon realizing this, Wegner instead forwarded it directly to Nazi party headquarters in Munich, where it was received by the head of the party chancellery, Martin Bormann.

A few weeks later Wegner was arrested by the Gestapo, imprisoned, and tortured brutally in the infamous Columbia House prison. He was then sent to concentration camps at Oranienburg, Börgermoor, and Lichtenburg, among other places. After these experiences, he never felt at home again in Germany and remained in exile in Italy for the rest of his life. Hitler presumably never saw the letter, but even if he did, it made no difference to the softening of any of his policies.

3. Interrogation of Father Bernhard Lichtenberg by the Gestapo (October 25, 1941)

Official Church opposition to Nazi antisemitism came in a number of forms, but individual clergy were often arrested more for their resistance to anti-Church measures than for their support for Jews. One who stood out in the latter regard was Father Bernhard Lichtenberg, provost of St. Hedwig's Cathedral in Berlin. This document, a record of his interrogation by the Gestapo in October 1941, has been specially translated into English for the first time by Lori Boegershausen. It shows a man not only prepared to stand by his religious convictions but also willing to suffer the same fate as those he was defending.

I was born in Ohlau as the son of the businessman August Lichtenberg, and there I attended primary and high school. My three brothers attended the same school. One of them holds the position of a lawyer and a notary now, while the second is a teacher in retirement, and the third brother has already passed on. I graduated with a degree from school in Ohlau. From 1895 to 1898, I studied theology, including one semester at the University in Innsbruck and six additional semesters at the University in Breslau. Upon the completion of the final stages of schooling, I entered the seminary in Breslau and was ordained as a priest in 1899. The first job I received was minister at the Jacobus-Church in Weisse.

In 1900, I was transferred to Berlin, where I became the minister of St. Mauritius-Lichtenberg. During this time, I studied economics at the University in Berlin for three semesters and worked in Charlottenberg as chaplain at St. Michael-Berlin until 1905. Then I was a parish priest in Berlin-Friedrichsfelde, to which Karlshorst also belonged. In 1911, I became a parish priest in Pankow and in 1913, I was appointed as a priest at the Sacred Heart Church in Charlottenburg. I practiced these activities from 1930. During World War I, I was also the military chaplain for the third regiment under Queen Elizabeth in Charlottenberg. In 1917, I travelled to the Eastern Front on behalf of the Reich War Office Press. I was invited by the Reich War Office Press and had no information on the purpose of the trip. As for decorations, I received the Red Cross Medal.

In 1930 or 1931 I was ordained in the newly built cathedral at St. Hedwig's in Berlin. At the same time, I oversaw the Cathedral Priests. After the death of the Vicar General Dr. Steinmann, I became the superior. In about 1926, Pope Pius XI appointed me as the papal chamberlain. Pope Pius XI appointed me to continue apostolic prothonotary A.I.P. I continue my activity and practice in St. Hedwig to the present day as I stand in my office directly under the Bishop of Berlin.

Politics:

In political terms, before the dissolution of parties in 1933 and since before the World War, I was a member of the Centre Party. In Charlottenberg I was an alderman as a member of the civil fraction, and in Berlin an alderman as a member of the Centre Party. This activity took place 1930–31. Also, I was a member of the Peace Federal German Catholics in Berlin. As this association allied themselves to the "union of the denomination for Peace," I became a member of the bureau of this association.

Concerning my attitude to the NSDAP, the National Socialistic State and its leading men, upon asking, I explain the following: In the section, "Belief and Organization" of the book *Mein Kampf*, page 507, 2nd paragraph, he states:

> *A philosophy filled with infernal intolerance will only be broken by a new idea, driven forward by the same spirit, championed by the same mighty will, and at the same time pure and absolutely genuine in itself.*
>
> *The individual may establish with pain today that with the appearance of Christianity the first spiritual terror entered into the far freer ancient world, but he will not be able to deny the act that since then the world has been afflicted and constrained by this coercion, and that coercion is broken only by more coercion, and terror with only terror. Only then can a new state of affairs be created.*

Since this book is written according to your National Socialist belief, as understood from the quoted excerpt, as a Catholic priest I reject this belief and refer it as de facto from the book.

My attitude for the existing National Socialist State draws on the attitude of the Apostle Paul as expressed in Romans chapter 13. Since a Catholic edition of the New Testament is currently not available in this space, I will quote from my mind.

> *There is no power except from God, and that is ordained of God....*
> *The authority is God's servant for good...*

So I want to have said that I recognize the state as such. But I cannot, as a Catholic priest, say yes and amen to any government order from the outset. I ask for my letter to Reich physician leader, Dr. Oontil to compare, as I have sent over a copy to the State Police.

If the tendency of such government orders and measures go against the revealed doctrine of Christianity and therefore against my priestly conscience, I will follow my conscience and *take into account* all consequences for me personally which result from it. It follows from that that I inwardly reject the evacuation and all of its resulting phenomena, because it is directed against the main Commandment of Christianity, "thou shalt love thy neighbor as thyself." And I also recognize the Jew as my neighbor, who possesses an undying soul created after the image and *likeness* of God. Since I cannot prevent this government order, I was determined to accompany the deported Jews and Jewish Christians in the removal, and to serve as their pastor. I use this opportunity to ask the Secret State Police to give me this permission.

To the point: In connection with the above opinion there's also the "*Vermeldung*," a leaflet written by me: "if you see this mark ... J-u-d-e." I had the intention to announce this leaflet the following Sunday (October 26th, 1941) in all of the services at St. Hedwig's Church. If that cannot happen, the reason will be my resulting detention.

To the third question, how I view the leading men of the state, I must allow myself a digression: I recognize Adolf Hitler as head of the Reich. If I have made numerous written remarks with red pencil in the book *Mein Kampf* that was brought to me, this should not be considered a criticism of the person "Adolf Hitler," but rather only of the train of ideas that I don't understand. The personality of Adolf Hitler is, to me as a minister, just as sacred as any other human being. That's why I also include Adolf Hitler in my morning prayer by name.

If I maintain that the written remarks in the book *Mein Kampf* that I made are not a criticism of Adolf Hitler's train of ideas, but rather in places a criticism of his person and through that revealing his person in the constructed German Fatherland state, to that I have the following to say: The actions of a person are the consequences of his principles. If the principles are false, the actions will not be right. That is true even for Adolf Hitler. In my above interrogation I have already been allowed to point out some false principles of Adolf Hitler's. That's why the actions arising from them will not be right.

I fight against false principles, from which false deeds must follow; one thinks about the removal of religious education from schools, fight against the Cross (same as the removal of crosses from schools), removal of Sacraments, secularization of marriage, intentional killing of allegedly unworthy life (euthanasia), persecution of the Jews, etc.

QUESTION: Did you also express this viewpoint down from the pulpit?
ANSWER: Yes.
QUESTION: Then you admit that you do not approve of the government actions?
ANSWER: I do not approve of those resulting from the measures following the above principles.
QUESTION: It should also be clear to you that because of the above-mentioned views that were publicly represented by you, there may be a concern of the national community?
ANSWER: This concern can only be prevented if one refrains from unjust measures.
QUESTION: So you put the rights of the Church before the rights of the State.
ANSWER: Christ the Lord did not give the right to teach, to give sacraments, and to give moral commandments to the State, but rather to the Church.
QUESTION: So that means that the activities carried out by the State, like, for example, the evacuation of the Jews, are not within the scope of the State's powers.
ANSWER: The discussion was, as previously stated, not only persecution of the Jews, but many other measures that contradicted Christian moral law.
QUESTION: You allegedly made the following utterances in the hour of prayer on Friday, the 29th of August, 1941: *We pray for the Jews, we pray for the prisoners in the concentration camps and especially for the armed brothers.* The word "Bolshevism" was also supposedly used in that context.
ANSWER: I pray every evening with my congregation, among other things, for the hard-pressed non-Aryan Christians, for the Jews, for the prisoners in the concentration camps, especially for the imprisoned priests and religious officials, especially for the priests of our diocese, for nonbelievers, for people in despair and who attempt suicide, for the millions of nameless and stateless refugees, for the fighting, wounded and dying soldiers on both sides, for the bombed cities in allied and enemy countries and so on, and in the passage of the general church prayer, for the Fatherland and the leaders of the people.

It is true that on the 29th of August 1941, on a Friday, in the evening at 7:30 after the Stations of the Cross, I carried out the above-mentioned intercessions. The rapporteur on the events of that night must surely have been interrogated, if he believes he heard "Bolsheviks" in the intercessions. But I would not hesitate to also include the Bolsheviks in the daily prayer, so that they could be cured of their madness. The term "Bolshevism" did not appear in the reading, either, because that time we read the writing of St. Augustine on the City of God, and in the fourth century AD the term was not yet common.

By subsequent reflection, wondering why the rapporteur has come to the idea about my evening prayer that I pray for Bolshevism, I have come to the following view. I used to pray in my evening prayer for the end of housing shortage and unemployment, although there was no more unemployment in Germany, but my prayer was indeed Catholic, i.e. in general, and I thought I should keep at the request, because in other countries there is still unemployment and housing shortage. So I am accustomed to pray, even now, for the beleaguered Mexican, Russian and Spanish people, because of the persecution of Christians that prevailed in these countries.

Perhaps the rapporteur, at the mention of the Russian people, had thought of Bolshevism, and believed I meant that I prayed for the growth of Bolshevism.

Signed: Bernhard Lichtenberg

Source: *Protokoll der Vernehmung Lichtenbergs in Polizeihaft durch die Geheime Staatspolizei, Berlin*, 25 Oktober 1941 (Brandenburgisches Landeshauptarchiv, Rep. 12 C, Nr. 19106, fol. 12r–17r).

Commentary

Bernhard Lichtenberg was a German Catholic priest who preached against the Nazis from the pulpit, supported by his bishop, Berlin's Konrad von Preysing. After several anti-Nazi sermons over a long period, he was finally denounced by two female students who had heard him pray publicly for Jews and concentration camp inmates. On October 23, 1941, he was arrested by the Gestapo, who, upon searching his rooms, found a statement he was planning to read from the pulpit the following Sunday. It was a call for his congregation to ignore Nazi proclamations against the Jews.

This document is the Gestapo transcript of his interrogation, incorporating statements in which he explains his motivations for acting the way he has. Not only does he refuse to retract his words but he even condemns Hitler's *Mein Kampf* as antithetical to Christianity, and recognizing where his defiance will lead, notes his determination "to accompany the deported Jews and Jewish Christians, and to serve as their pastor." He is conscious of the import of his actions and where they can lead, and is willing to go wherever the victims are being sent. He will suffer their fate and asks the Gestapo "to give me this permission." He was aware, moreover, that this request would mean transfer to the Łódź ghetto.

With little other alternative, the Nazi authorities ordered that he be sent to Dachau, where all anti-Nazi priests were imprisoned. On November 5, 1943, while in transit and awaiting his final transport to the camp, he collapsed and died, according to the Gestapo.

4. Resistance Proclamation, Vilna Ghetto (January 1, 1942)

It was Abba Kovner who was credited with first using the phrase "sheep to the slaughter" when trying to raise consciousness and develop a resistance mentality in the Vilna ghetto. In this document, Kovner's phrase has been picked up by a Jewish youth group and is repeated as a rallying cry for others. The statement is at once a recounting of history and also a call to arms; as such, it is a powerful early call for resistance in the ghetto, set against the backdrop of the horrific massacres in the nearby Ponary Forest.

They Shall Not Take Us Like Sheep to the Slaughter!

Jewish Youth, do not be led astray. Of the 80,000 Jews in the "Jerusalem of Lithuania" only 20,000 have remained. Before our eyes they tore from us our parents, our brothers and sisters. Where are the hundreds of men who were taken away for work by the Lithuanian "Snatchers"? Where are the naked women and children who were taken from us in the night of terror of the *provokatzia*?

Where are the Jews [who were taken away on] the Day of Atonement?

Where are our brothers from the second ghetto?

All those who were taken away from the ghetto never came back.

All the roads of the Gestapo lead to Ponary.

And Ponary is death.

Doubters! Cast off all illusions. Your children, your husbands and your wives are no longer alive.

Ponary is not a camp—all are shot there.

Hitler aims to destroy all the Jews of Europe. The Jews of Lithuania are fated to be the first in line.

Let us not go as sheep to slaughter!

It is true that we are weak and defenseless, but resistance is the only reply to the enemy!

Brothers! It is better to fall as free fighters than to live by the grace of the murderers.

Resist! To the last breath.

Source: Moreshet Archive, Mordechai Anielevich Memorial. Used by permission.

Commentary

In July 1941, less than a month after the Germans occupied Vilna, 6,000 Jewish men were rounded up by the SS, taken to the Ponary Forest, and shot. Another 8,000 men and women were shot at Ponary at the end of August, after which tens of thousands of Jews from surrounding areas were crowded into the Vilna ghetto.

Abba Kovner, a leading partisan in Vilna, realized that a revolt would be necessary—if not to stop the killing, then at least to hinder the Germans. He started building a ghetto defense force, and in December 1941 a number of meetings were held in which a resistance movement was established. The resistance leaders decided to remain in the ghetto and fight rather than try to escape. On New Year's Eve, before a gathering of 150 Jews at Straszuna 2, in a public soup kitchen, this document was issued, dated January 1, 1942.

It is here that the phrase "sheep to the slaughter" enters the annals of resistance language, as Kovner tries desperately to rouse the population and alert them to the necessity of fighting back against the Nazis. If not, then the only alternative will be that everyone ends up in the Ponary Forest, suffering the same fate as those who went before them.

Kovner's words struck a chord with many in the Jewish youth movements, particularly his penultimate exhortation: "It is better to fall as free fighters than to live by the grace of the murderers."

Within three weeks, the Faraynigte Partizaner Organizatzye (United Partisan Organization, or FPO) had been formed—one of the first ghetto resistance organizations to be established.

5. Final Report of German Jewish Youth Movement (March 1942)

As the situation for German Jews continued to deteriorate with the war situation, almost all Jewish institutions were closed down. This process, which began in the 1930s, was unrelenting all the way to the end of the war, until the only establishment remaining was the Berlin Jewish Hospital. Here we see a final farewell from Germany's Zionist youth, in a report on the situation transmitted to other young Zionists in Palestine.

To our Members in the Countries of the Diaspora and in the Land of Israel,

Even though we do not know whether, in fact this letter will ever reach you, we will write it in the hope that at least one of us will remain alive and hand it over to you when the day comes. It is already a few weeks since our troop discussed the approach of Scouts' Day. Shall we be able to celebrate it in the accustomed manner this year, too? For we are living in very different times. Many of our members are no longer with us. They have already been taken to Poland, a place where an unknown fate awaits them. But the Jewish Scout is told never to despair, and we are therefore determined that, *despite everything*, we shall meet this year, to honor this special day. We therefore met on that Wednesday afternoon in one of the classrooms of the school in Wilsnacker Street. Despite the danger involved almost all came in their white shirts (under jackets), and there was an atmosphere of high spirits and joy in the room. We had gathered together all the Jewish scouts who still remained in Berlin, boys and girls, about 50 altogether, from all circles. As guests of honor we had Herbert Growald and Fanny Bergas, from the *Hakhshara* (training) Kibbutz at Neuendorf, and also Alfred Selbiger, a member of the Movement's leadership. We sat in a big circle, and the room echoed to the sound of our singing "Be Prepared . . ." and all the other songs. The candles flickered gaily and the members looked into the flames.

After that one of our members, Mary Simon, read us a story about trees and plants in our Jewish Homeland which made us forget the dangers and the sorrows. After that we sang again, and several poems were read. . . . We stood to attention to sing the anthem of the Movement. When we unfolded the flag after that—we gave the Scouts' salute and sang the song of the flag: "Carry it to Zion, the Banner and the Flag." . . . Then one of our members, Erwin Tichauer, stepped forward—at first we had no idea what he was about to do—and read to his group the names of all those who had been taken from us during the past months, since the deportations had begun, and as he read each name the members replied as one: "Here," that is to say, that even those who were missing were with us on this occasion, for we are always with them in our thoughts, just as they are surely with us in their thoughts. . . .

At this difficult time we send our good wishes to all of you, outside. Do not forget us, just as we will not forget you—those already living in the Land of Israel and building our future, and those who are living a free life in other countries. We will all be united in spirit until the day comes when we can once more all be together. We send our good wishes and send you Shalom! Be of good courage!

Source: Y. Schwersenz, *Mahteret Halutzim be-Germanya Hanazit* (*Pioneer Underground in Nazi Germany*) (Tel Aviv, 1969), pp. 55–57.

Commentary

Nazism was an ideology for youth. All the major Nazi leaders were young when compared to the statesmen of the day elsewhere; Adolf Hitler himself was only 43 when he became chancellor of Germany. Most Nazi propaganda was youth-directed, and the two Nazi youth organizations, the Hitler Youth and the League of German Girls, were created specifically for the purpose of establishing a new Germany.

In this environment, no competition was permitted. Thus, very soon after the Nazi ascent to office, all non-Nazi youth organizations were compulsorily disbanded. The Catholic youth movements were the last holdouts, lasting much longer than all others.

For the Jewish youth organizations, on the other hand, there was no chance of negotiating a stay of execution. They were outlawed almost immediately, their activities proscribed. There was thus little alternative but for young Jews to continue meeting in secret, and it is remarkable that they managed to do so for such long periods.

This document is a report on Jewish Scouts' Day, as undertaken through Young Maccabi, a Jewish youth movement with a specific interest in promoting the physical education of the young generation. Dated March 1942 and emanating from Berlin, it is essentially a farewell message trying to show that its secret resistance has come to an end. There was little more that could be done to keep the youth movement going; not only was it banned by the Nazis and operating underground, but numbers had also fallen drastically owing to earlier emigration and, more recently, deportations. In light of what the future held for these young people, this is a sad report to read.

6. Anton Schmid to Steffi Schmid (April 13, 1942)

Sergeant Anton Schmid, an Austrian soldier serving in the Wehrmacht, was stationed in Vilna after the Nazi occupation of Lithuania. For saving Jews from the massacres of the Ponary Forest during 1942, he was first cautioned, and then after repeated offenses, sentenced to death. In this, his final letter to his wife, Steffi, prior to his execution, he explains his reasons for engaging in these lifesaving activities, even as he laments losing his beloved wife and apologizes for putting her through the ordeal to come.

My dear Steffi,

Thinking of you in joy and in sorrow, I am informing you, my dearest, that my verdict has been announced today and that I must part from this world, am sentenced to death.

Please remain strong and trust in our dear God who decides the fate of each one of us. I could not change anything any more, otherwise I would have spared you and Gerta all this. Please forgive me, therefore, I did not want to cause you this pain, but unfortunately it cannot be changed any more. I am ready to die since this is the will of God and His will be done. You must resign yourself to this. I ask you again, please forget the pain which I inflicted upon you, my dear ones, and keep quiet about it.

After all, I have only saved human beings, even if they were Jews, and this was my death. Just as I have always done everything for other people, I have also sacrificed everything for other people. Everything else you will hear, because a comrade will visit you and he will tell you how the court judges. Please do read the letters 1–4 which you are sure to receive, you will understand from them that I had intended it differently, but I considered you, my dear ones.

My dear ones, I beg you again, please forget me, it had to be this way, fate has willed it like that. I am concluding these last lines which I am still writing to you and I send many greetings and kisses to the two of you and to you my dearest one in this world and in the other world where I shall be soon in God's hand and I remain your ever loving.

Toni

> **Source:** Letter from Anton Schmid to Steffi Schmid, 4/13/1942. Yehudit Kleinman and Reuven Dafni, eds., *Final Letters—From the Yad Vashem Archive* (London, 1991), pp. 102–104. O.6/49. Reproduced by permission of Yad Vashem Publications.

Commentary

Anton Schmid was an Austrian soldier conscripted to serve in the Wehrmacht during World War II. During this time, while stationed in Vilna, he rescued hundreds of Jews.

After the Nazi invasion of the Soviet Union in June 1941 he was transferred to Nazi-occupied Lithuania, and was soon stationed near Vilna (Vilnius). For Schmid it was unthinkable not to find a way to go to the Jews' aid and protect those imprisoned in the ghetto. He hid Jews, supplied them with false papers, and arranged their escape. His efforts saved the lives of up to 250 men, women, and children.

In January 1942 he was arrested, and on February 25, 1942, summarily court-martialed for high treason. The death penalty was the only possible outcome, and on April 13, 1942, he was executed by firing squad.

The night before his execution, from his prison cell, he wrote a final letter to his wife, Steffi. In this he writes, "I only acted as a human being and did not want to hurt anyone." He also writes that his only crime was to have "saved human beings." Noting the refrain that accompanied his actions all his life, he reminds Steffi, "Just as I have always done everything for other people, I have also sacrificed everything for other people."

This is an especially poignant letter, made more painful by the realization that it took decades for his reputation to be restored and the German government to acknowledge the injustice he suffered for resisting the Nazis and doing the right thing.

7. The White Rose Movement, Second Leaflet (1942)

The White Rose Movement, centered on the University of Munich, produced six anti-Nazi leaflets that were distributed throughout Germany by various means. In this document, the second leaflet (undated, like the rest), reference is made to the fate of the Jews, examples of which were witnessed by White Rose members when they were on active service in the Soviet Union. The document asserts that this is further evidence of why the Nazi regime must be destroyed, if Germany is to live proudly in the future.

It is impossible to engage in intellectual discourse with National Socialism because it is not an intellectually defensible program. It is false to speak of a National Socialist philosophy, for if there were such an entity, one would have to try by means of analysis and discussion either to prove its validity or to combat it. In actuality, however, we face a totally different situation.

At its very inception this movement depended on the deception and betrayal of one's fellow man; even at that time it was inwardly corrupt and could support itself only by constant lies. After all, Hitler states in an early edition of "his" book (a book written in the worst German I have ever read, in spite of the fact that it has been elevated to the position of the Bible in this nation of poets and thinkers): "It is unbelievable, to what extent one must betray a people in order to rule it."

If at the start this cancerous growth in the nation was not particularly noticeable, it was only because there were still enough forces at work that operated for the good, so that it was kept under control. As it grew larger, however, and finally in an ultimate spurt of growth attained ruling power, the tumor broke open, as it were, and infected the whole body. The greater part of its former opponents went into hiding. The German intellectuals fled to their cellars, there, like plants struggling in the dark, away from light and sun, gradually to choke to death.

Now the end is at hand. Now it is our task to find one another again, to spread information from person to person, to keep a steady purpose, and to allow ourselves no rest until the last man is persuaded of the urgent need of his struggle against this system. When thus a wave of unrest goes through the land, when "it is in the air," when many join the cause, then in a great final effort this system can be shaken off. After all, an end in terror is preferable to terror without end.

We are not in a position to draw up a final judgment about the meaning of our history. But if this catastrophe can be used to further the public welfare, it will be only by virtue of the fact that we are cleansed by suffering; that we yearn for the light in the midst of deepest night, summon our strength, and finally help in shaking off the yoke which weighs on our world.

We do not want to discuss here the question of the Jews, nor do we want in this leaflet to compose a defense or apology. No, only by way of example do we want to cite the fact that since the conquest of Poland three hundred thousand Jews have been murdered in this country in the most bestial way. Here we see the most frightful crime against human dignity, a crime that is unparalleled in the whole of history. For Jews, too, are human beings—no matter what position we take with respect to the Jewish question—and a crime of this dimension has been perpetrated against human beings.

Someone may say that the Jews deserved their fate. This assertion would be a monstrous impertinence; but let us assume that someone said this—what position has he then taken toward the fact that the entire Polish aristocratic youth is being annihilated? (May God grant that this program has not fully achieved its aim as yet!) All male offspring of the houses of the nobility between the ages of fifteen and twenty were transported to concentration camps in Germany and sentenced to forced labor, and the girls of this age group were sent to Norway, into the bordellos of the SS!

Why tell you these things, since you are fully aware of them—or if not of these, then of other equally grave crimes committed by this frightful sub-humanity? Because here we touch on a problem which involves us deeply and forces us all to take thought. Why do the German people behave so apathetically in the face of all these abominable crimes, crimes so unworthy of the human race? Hardly anyone thinks about that. It is accepted as fact and put out of mind. The German people slumber on in their dull, stupid sleep and encourage these fascist criminals; they give them the opportunity to carry on their depredations; and of course they do so. Is this a sign that the Germans are brutalized in their simplest human feelings, that no chord within them cried out at the sight of such deeds, that they have sunk into a fatal consciencelessness from which they will never, never awake?

It seems to be so, and will certainly be so, if the German does not at least start up out of his stupor, if he does not protest wherever and whenever he can against this clique of criminals, if he shows no sympathy for these hundreds of thousands of victims. He must evidence not only sympathy; no, much more: a sense of complicity in guilt. For through his apathetic behavior he gives these evil men the opportunity to act as they do; he tolerates this "government" which has taken upon itself such an infinitely great burden of guilt; indeed, he himself is to blame for the fact that it came about at all! Each man wants to be exonerated of a guilt of this kind, each one continues on his way with the most placid, the calmest conscience. But he cannot be exonerated; he is guilty, guilty, guilty!

It is not too late, however, to do away with this most reprehensible of all miscarriages of government, so as to avoid being burdened with even greater guilt. Now, when in recent years our eyes have been opened, when we know exactly who our adversary is, it is high time to root out this brown horde. Up until the outbreak of the war the larger part of the German people were blinded; the Nazis did not show themselves in their true aspect. But now, now that we have recognized them for what they are, it must be the sole and first duty, the holiest duty of every German to destroy these beasts.

> If the people are barely aware that the government exists, they are happy. When the government is felt to be oppressive, they are broken. Good fortune, alas! builds itself upon misery. Good fortune, alas! is the mask of misery. What will come of this? We cannot foresee the end. Order is upset and turns to disorder, good becomes evil. The people are confused. Is it not so, day in, day out, from the beginning?
>
> The wise man is therefore angular, though he does not injure others: he has sharp corners, though he does not harm; he is upright but not gruff. He is clear-minded, but he does not try to be brilliant.
>
> —Lao Tzu

Whoever undertakes to rule the kingdom and to shape it according to his whim—I foresee that he will fail to reach his goal. That is all.

The kingdom is a living being. It cannot be constructed, in truth! He who tries to manipulate it will spoil it, he who tries to put it under his power will lose it.

Therefore: Some creatures go out in front, others follow, some have warm breath, others cold, some are strong, some weak, some attain abundance, other succumb.

The wise man will accordingly forswear excess, he will avoid arrogance and not overreach."

—Lao Tzu

Please make as many copies as possible of this leaflet and distribute them.

Source: Available online at http://www.holocaustresearchproject.org/revolt/wrleaflets.html. Used by permission of the Holocaust Education and Archive Research Team.

Commentary

The anti-Nazi White Rose movement bought together a number of students, together with their professor, from the University of Munich. The six pamphlets they produced and distributed campaigned for the overthrow of Nazism and the revival of a new Germany, dedicated to the pursuit of moral goodness and founded on Christian values.

The document here is the second in the series, written by White Rose member Alexander Schmorell. The leaflet does not engage directly with all issues relating to the Jews but notes that "we want to cite the fact that since the conquest of Poland three hundred thousand Jews have been murdered in this country in the most bestial way," and that this was "the most frightful crime against human dignity, a crime that is unparalleled in the whole of history." The leaflet comments on the fact that "Jews, too, are human beings," and that "a crime of this dimension has been perpetrated against human beings."

The leaflet also expresses the view that while this is happening "the German people slumber on in dull, stupid sleep and encourage the fascist criminals." And why do they do it? Because, it says, each person wants to be "exonerated of guilt." The White Rose perspective, on the other hand, is explicit: in often-quoted words, the leaflet proclaimed that no one can be exonerated; all are "guilty, guilty, guilty!"

The significance of the second leaflet is to be found in the fact that it is simultaneously a condemnation of German policies toward minorities and a call to action against the regime coming from members of the next generation—young people who, the Nazis would have preferred to think, had been inoculated against thoughts of this kind.

8. Testimony of Sidney Simon, Forest Partisan (2009)

When war came to Belorussia in July 1941, Sidney Simon and his family were taken by the Nazis to a ghetto. One of five children, he was then 14 years old. After a period of terror at the hands of the Nazis the family escaped the ghetto and sought sanctuary in the woods, where Simon joined the partisans until aligning with the Soviet army. His memoir, recounting his experiences both as a partisan and with the Soviets, provides an account of how and when Jewish opposition could take place, through the lens of what has become known as "forest resistance."

My brother Mojshe belonged to a group of about twenty or twenty-two men. When Mojshe heard about the liquidation, he went to the woods with this group of men to meet up with the partisans.

After a short time as a partisan Mojshe was killed by the Germans and the police. The Germans had surrounded a clearing. As the partisan group went through this clearing that they had thought was safe, the Germans opened fire from all four sides. The partisans didn't have a chance. One partisan, Jankel Orzhechowski, survived by jumping into the bushes when he wasn't noticed.

After our family escaped the ghetto, we met Jankel. Jankel told us that my brother had escaped; Jankel said he had seen Mojshe running, running. My father and I didn't believe Jankel, but he insisted this was the truth. Out of pain and concern to make Jankel tell us the truth, as if to stab himself, my father grabbed a knife, which I immediately took away from him. Jankel continued lying. He lied to protect my parents from pain.

A few days later—this was after Mojshe had left—my family escaped the ghetto because we were warned that, on April 28, 1942, all the Jews in the Žetel Ghetto were to be taken outside the ghetto, massacred, and buried. We went into a hiding place under a small stable—8' by 12'. My brother, Richard, sisters Katie and Ida, my parents, and three more people—neighbors—hid there. We made a shallow, square box and filled this with manure. Under this we made a hole. We would get in the hole and pull the box over the hole to cover our hiding place. The Germans would open the door then look around, but they didn't see anything but manure. We stayed there until night on the day the ghetto was liquidated. We heard a lot of explosions.

My father looked through the hole of the pipe we used for air and said, "They just got your mother's sister Bashe Malke, her husband Shimen, and the baby (two or three months old)." They had hidden in another place under the floor of a house. My father continued, "They took them outside; she is holding the baby. Oh G-d, a German is choking the baby to death in his mother's arms. Now he is killing Bashe! And her husband is watching. The German beast killed Bashe's husband." Can you imagine the brutality of this!

Then we found that my cousin, Hirshe Leizer, the Hebrew teacher, who had been with us and was married to Civia, and now with a little baby, was hiding too. The baby started to cry. The others said, "Smother the baby or they'll find us." Hirshe said, "I am not killing my baby. I'll go out." He went out, and they killed him; they threw in hand grenades and everybody was murdered, including Civia and the baby....

This horror was our life every day. I never dreamed we would ever get out. This goes for the ghetto, the partisans, and whatever else I went through.

Night came. Father said, "I am going to walk out first. If you hear shooting, don't come out." He left. There were no shots. We did not wait. Without hesitation, my mother, then the children, and then the neighbors followed my father and so left the hiding place. It was dark but flames flared occasionally. My father took a stick and held it over his shoulder so if anybody saw this they would think he had a rifle.

We made it to the woods and slept there. We saw no partisans. We had no food, except wild berries. At night my mother went to the village from house to house asking for a slice of bread. She would not let us go because it was too dangerous. I saw my mother leaving and I didn't know if she would ever come back. Life was treacherous.

We were looking for a place to settle. We saw a place close to houses. But could the occupants be trusted? Would they betray us? This place was not far from a house occupied by a family named Shavel. We felt safe even though we were not close to him. He could give us news about the Germans. He couldn't give us much food, however, because he was poor.

Finally the Germans decided to go into the woods and kill the "Stalin dogs," what the Germans called the partisans. Everybody heard the news and abandoned their hiding places. We ran deeper into the forest. We had to run through creeks. My boots got wet. It had been rainy and the ground was deep with mud; then it turned cold and the ground froze. My feet were frostbitten. They swelled so much that they had to cut my boots off.

The Germans were still searching in the woods; we were short of places to hide. To be safe we dug an underground shelter that we shored up with saplings so that it wouldn't cave in. There were steps going up to the door. Inside there were bunks. We made torches from moss and sticks, lighting these with a flint stone. Sometimes we would inhale soot, the residue of these torches. Eight or nine people, including my family, lived in this bunker—Majewski, his wife, and a baby, Sanford. The baby caused us anxiety because if the baby cried our bunker could have been discovered. The father said, "If you want my baby killed, *you* kill him." So one of them put pillows over the baby's face. When they lifted the pillows, the baby was still breathing. They say that this baby was meant to live. After this, they agreed not to kill the baby, no matter what happened. The parents wanted to give their baby to a non-Jew; however, this man saw that the mother was having a hard time giving the baby away, so he said no. *That baby, Sanford, is alive today with a family of his own. We were invited to his wedding.*

When the Germans were in the woods looking for Jews, all the others from the bunker, except me, would leave the bunker and go deeper into the woods to flee. I could not leave; because of my frostbitten feet, I could not walk. When they left they would cover the opening of the shelter with wood to which they had attached moss and pieces of branches to camouflage the opening. I would be in the bunker hiding. I would hear the Germans calling to each other. I often would hear horses trotting and whinnying. Once a horse stepped right near me. If his hoof had been any closer, he and his rider would have been in the hole with me and I would have been killed. I had to wait in the bunker until the rest returned.

When the Germans were not searching for Jews and we were all in the bunker, I would sometimes climb out and put my feet in the sun. That seemed to help with the sores and cracks in my feet. During the night my feet would crack again. The next day I would start over again with my feet in the sun. I could feel the reforming during the day and then at night it would crack again. I would wrap my feet in burlap potato bags—these were dirty—full of mud and sand, but they were all I had. It was a wonder my feet did not become infected. In my old age, my feet are numb from the frostbite and I have trouble walking.

I tried to keep clean, using the snow to wash and rinse myself. We had to wear the same clothes all the time. In the spring when it was warmer, I would bathe and wash my clothes in a creek.

We had to move deeper into the woods to hide from the Germans who continued searching for Jews. I had to walk, leaning on two sticks, like crutches. I was in pain and very thirsty. One day I was so thirsty that when I saw a spot where a horse had urinated and the snow had melted, I knelt down and sucked the melted snow.

With me I had a hand grenade without the lever and a gun without ammunition. These were of no use to me but I kept them, hoping, I guess, that I would run into ammunition for the gun and a lever to arm the grenade. Eventually my feet were somewhat better. We continued hiding in the woods. We would still go to the villagers to ask for some food. We would go out and get potatoes and bread and bring these back. Sometimes the partisans would drop off some food.

That was our life for a while until one day a group of partisans came along to see us and give us information, dropping off some potatoes. They had heard that someone had buried a gun in the vicinity, so they had come along and dug up the gun. It had been buried in the woods, wrapped in an oiled cloth. While they were visiting with us, they asked me if I wanted to be a partisan. I said, "Yes, but I don't have a good gun nor any ammunition." To be allowed to join the partisans a person would usually need to bring a gun and ammunition or they didn't want him. But they said they had an extra rifle. They gave me the rifle—the buried one.

The partisans also received weapons from Russian planes that dropped ammunition and dynamite attached to parachutes. At the same time, they would also drop a

Russian officer who made sure the partisans received the ammunition. For the time being, he became part of the partisans group.

The partisans would then make signal fires for the planes—in different designs at different times—so that they not only would know where to drop the supplies but also so that the Germans would not anticipate where they would be dropping the supplies. On rare occasions the planes circled but did not drop any supplies, as if they had intelligence that the drop was unsafe. This was disturbing to us, waiting for supplies that were desperately needed.

The partisans told me to ask my father if I could join them. I walked up to my father and said, "I would like to become a partisan. They have a rifle for me." He said, "My son, do what you think is right and G-d should watch over you." Thus, I joined the partisans.

Source: Sidney Simon with Maryann McLoughlin, *In the Birch Woods of Belarus: A Partisan's Revenge*, ed. Rosalie Simon and Maryann McLoughlin (Richard Stockton College, 2009), pp. 34–38. Used by permission of Maryann McLoughlin.

Commentary

Examples of what might be termed "forest resistance" includes Jews who had been persecuted by the Nazis living under conditions much more extreme than those of regular soldiers in organized armies. Mostly they were civilians who either joined those possessing military training or learned about combat in situ. Either way, not all those who made it into the forest were armed or trained to fight, while many were not prepared or disposed psychologically to do so.

Sidney Simon's account brings up several aspects of the Holocaust. In addition to showing that not all Jews who went into the ghettos died, we also see important evidence of the role that Jewish partisans played in resisting the Nazis. A necessary part of that role inevitably involved an interrelationship between Jewish and Soviet partisans, which did not always run smoothly. Protection for Jews in the forest was never guaranteed, though on an individual level male Jews in good health could be welcomed into Soviet partisan units. Jewish women, children, and the elderly were not usually made welcome but considered to be "useless mouths" that could make no worthwhile contribution to the war effort.

One of the features of Simon's story relates to the manner in which he and his family managed to avoid capture just before the liquidation of the Žetel ghetto on April 28, 1942. Hiding in a carefully constructed wooden bunker concealed by a pile of manure, they watched from their hiding place the unfolding horror "that was our life every day." While the camouflage saved their lives, the ordeal of witnessing was exacted at a heavy emotional price and left Simon with a legacy of inner distress, which comes through clearly in the account. It was while living this forest existence that Simon made the transition from forest dweller to forest fighter.

9. Emanuel Ringelblum on the *Kashariyot* in the Polish Ghettos (May 19, 1942)

The various resistance movements in the Polish ghettos needed to find a way to keep in touch with each other, not an easy matter in a situation where the ghettos were effectively sealed by the Nazis, guarded by both German troops and Jewish police, and ostensibly self-governed through the Jewish Councils (Judenräte). In this document, tribute is paid to the brave young Jewish women (kashariyot) who were sent out to enable communication between the various ghettos.

The heroic girls, Chaika [Grosman], Frumke [Plotnicka] and others—theirs is a story that calls for the pen of a great writer. They are venturesome, courageous girls who travel here and there across Poland to cities and towns, carrying Aryan papers which describe them as Polish or Ukrainian. One of them even wears a cross, which she never leaves off and misses when she is in the ghetto. Day by day they face the greatest danger, relying completely on their Aryan appearance and the kerchiefs they tie around their heads. They accept the most dangerous missions and carry them out without a murmur, without a moment's hesitation. If there is a need for someone to travel to Vilna, Białystok, Lvov, Kowel, Lublin, Czestochowa, or Radom to smuggle in such forbidden goods as illegal publications, goods, money, they do it all as though it were the most natural thing. If there are comrades to be rescued in Vilna, Lublin, or other cities, they take the job on themselves. Nothing deters them, nothing stops them. If it is necessary to make friends with the German responsible for a train, so as to travel beyond the borders of the Government-General, which is only allowed for people with special permits—they do it quite simply, as though it were their profession. They travel from city to city, where no representative of any Jewish institution has reached, such as Volhynia and Lithuania. They were the first to bring the news of the tragedy in Vilna. They were the first to take back messages of greeting and encouragement to the survivors in Vilna. How many times were they arrested and searched? But their luck held. "Those who go on an errand of mercy will meet no evil." With what modesty and simplicity do they deliver their reports on what they accomplished during their travels on trains where Christians, men and women, were picked up and taken away for work in Germany. Jewish women have written a shining page in the history of the present World War. The Chaijkes and the Frumkes will take first place in this history. These girls do not know what it is to rest. They have hardly arrived from Czestochowa where they took forbidden goods, and in a few hours they would move on again: they do it without a moment's hesitation, without a minute's rest.

Source: E. Ringelblum, notes from the Ghetto, Underground Couriers in the Polish Ghettos, 1942-sign. ARG I 445. Courtesy of the Jewish Historical Institute in Warsaw, Poland.

Commentary

The story of the female couriers (*kashariyot*) in Nazi-occupied Europe is a story of resistance that has been overshadowed by more overt examples of armed resistance in the ghettos and forests. It is, however, a remarkable story, in which Jewish girls and young women braved danger and death to serve as the lifeline between Jewish communities. They traveled on illegal missions for the Jewish resistance in Nazi-occupied Eastern Europe, using false papers to conceal their true identities.

Disguised as non-Jews, they would transport the sort of things required by Jewish communities to sustain some sort of autonomous existence, smuggling them across borders and into ghettos: identity documents, underground newspapers, money, medicine, military intelligence, ammunition and weapons, and even other Jews.

This document is taken from the diary of Warsaw's distinguished historian Emanuel Ringelblum, who, on May 19, 1942, immortalized the bravery of the *kashariyot* through an entry which resonates today. The *kashariyot* were seen as fearless heroes whose death-defying activities were a source of great pride. Ringelblum predicts that the *kashariyot* will be viewed as leading figures by future historians, though his prediction, unfortunately, has not been entirely accurate as they have to some degree been passed over in discussions of resistance during the Holocaust.

Ringelblum notes well the importance of the courageous *kashariyot*, recognizing the significance of their work and showing the extent of his admiration for their bravery. He also gives them a central role in history, writing that their exploits "have written a shining page" in Jewish history during the present war, and noting that "the Chaijkas and Frumkes will take first place in this history."

10. Dutch Protest at the Deportation of Jews (July 1942)

Discriminatory measures against Dutch Jews began in February 1941, but they were at first held back because of the famous protest strike that crippled the city of Amsterdam. By July 1942 the Nazis were no longer holding back from their deportation plans, with transports being assembled and channeled through the transit camp at Westerbork prior to being sent to Sobibor (or, later, Auschwitz). In this document, one of the many circulating at this time, a plea is made urging Dutch citizens to protest the deportation of the Jews and take concrete steps to deny the Germans in their genocidal aims.

FELLOW CITIZENS!

THE TIME HAS COME!

After a long line of inhumane decrees during the past weeks: the yellow star; the surrender of bicycles; the prohibition to enter houses of non-Jews; the prohibition to use the telephone, street-cars or trains; the prohibition to shop in non-Jewish stores except during specified hours, etc., now the crowning blow has been struck:

THE DEPORTATION OF ALL JEWS BETWEEN THE AGES OF 16 AND 42!

During the night of July 15, 1942 around 1:50 a.m., the first group had to report at Amsterdam's Central Station. Thereafter, every day 1,200 Jews will have to do likewise. From Westerbork in Drenthe where the unfortunate people are being screened, approximately 4,000 Jews altogether are being deported each time. The trains for this purpose stand ready. Specialists from Prague well versed as executioners have gone there in order to expedite the deportations as much as possible. In this manner, a total of approximately 120,000 Jewish Dutch citizens will be taken away.

Such are the sober facts. They compare in brutality and matter-of-factness only with the instructions of the Egyptian Pharaoh who had all male children killed, and with Herod, that anti-Semite, who had all infants in Bethlehem killed in order to kill Jesus. Now, several thousand years later, Hitler and his henchmen have found their place in this company. Official Polish reports have found their place in this company. Official Polish reports name the figure of 700,000 Jews who have already perished in the clutches of the Germans. Our Jewish fellow citizens will suffer a like fate. True, the lot of the non-Jewish workers (Dutch) is hard; but when it comes to the Jews, we are dealing with the realization of threats which the Nazis have hurled at Jews again and again—their destruction and annihilation.

FELLOW CITIZENS!

The Dutch people have taken note of the anti-Jewish measure with disgust and outrage. To be sure, our people must pay heavily for the fact that they did not refuse to sign the Declaration on Jews so ingenuously presented to them. It is our joint guilt—that of the Jewish Council not excepted—that our enemies now dispose over a complete Jewish administration.

All prior German measures had aimed at isolating the Jews from the rest of the Dutch, to make contact impossible, and to kill our sentiments concerning living side by side and in solidarity. They [the Germans] have succeeded much better than we know ourselves or are probably willing to admit. The Jews have to be killed in secrecy and we, the witnesses, must remain deaf, blind, and silent. We may not listen to their moans, watch their misery, may not voice our abhorrence and our pity. God and history will condemn us and hold us partly responsible for this mass murder if we now remain silent and simply look on.

Holland has been hit hard and is deeply humiliated. Now we must bring proof that even under pressure we have not lost our honor, that our conscience has not been struck dumb, that our faith has not been paralyzed. For this reason we expect that every citizen will sabotage preparations and executions of this deportation. Remember the February strikes of 1941, when a nation, provoked to the utmost limit, showed what it can do if it only wants to do it. We expect general secretaries, mayors, [and] high officials to lay their jobs on the line and not to cooperate any longer with the German occupation power. Whoever remains glued to his office chair will have a tough time after the liberation to justify his attitude. We are counting on it that all who are in a position to do so, notably public officials, police, railway officials etc., will sabotage these inhumane Nazi measures.

One final word: We urge all Dutch citizens to protest to the address of the Commander in Chief of the German Army in the Netherlands, Lieutenant General of the Air Force Christiansen.

Source: "Landgenoten! De Slag is gevallen!" IP17.13/MIP041. Nederlands Instituut voor Oorlogsdocumentatie. Used by permission.

Commentary

In 1941 most Dutch Jews were living in Amsterdam, their population numbers having been boosted significantly in the prewar years due to an influx of Jews from Germany.

Starting in January 1942 some Dutch Jews from towns and cities outside Amsterdam were forced to move to the city, while others were deported to the Dutch internment camp at Westerbork. All non-Dutch Jews were also sent to Westerbork. On July 15, 1942, the Germans took direct control of the camp.

In June 1942 the Nazis decided to deport up to 40,000 Dutch Jews to extermination camps in "the East," with Westerbork serving as the major collection and transit point for Dutch Jews prior to their deportation to Sobibor and Auschwitz. The first two transports, comprising 2,000 Jews, were deported on July 15–16, 1942. During the course of that year, nearly 38,000 Jews were deported, and overall some 98 trains transported more than 100,000 Dutch Jews to camps in the Reich and Poland between July 1942 and September 1944.

The Dutch people were not oblivious to these developments, and protests did take place. At this time most people in Amsterdam still remembered the February 1941 strike in Amsterdam that crippled the city for two full days.

This document, from July 1942, expresses the view of many who were opposed to the deportations. The first paragraph reminds readers of the various measures against Jews that were enacted during 1941; now, it says, enough is enough, and the hope is expressed that anyone capable of sabotaging the Nazi actions against the Jews will do so.

11. Handbill: Call for Resistance in the Warsaw Ghetto (January 1943)

In January 1943 it seemed as though the Nazis were about to commence their final liquidation of the Warsaw Ghetto. Faced with this challenge, the Żydowska Organizacja Bojowa (Jewish Combat Organization, or ŻOB) was established under the leadership of Mordecai Anielewicz. The call for resistance issued at the same time was intended to inspire members of the ghetto population into joining the ŻOB in resisting the Nazis—not to defeat them, but to ensure that no more deportations would take place.

We are rising up for war!

We are of those who have set themselves the aim of awakening the people. Our wish is to take this watchword to the people:

Awake and fight!

Do not despair of the road to escape!

Know that escape is not to be found by walking to your death passively, like sheep to the slaughter. It is to be found in something much greater: in war!

Whoever defends himself has a chance of being saved! Whoever gives up self-defense from the outset—he has lost already!

Nothing awaits him except only a hideous death in the suffocation-machine of Treblinka.

Let the people awake to war!

Find the courage in your soul for desperate action!

Put an end to our terrible acceptance of such phrases as:

We are all under sentence of death! It is a lie!!!

We also were destined to live! We too have a right to life!

One only needs to know how to fight for it!

It is great to live when life is given to you *willingly*!

But there is an art to life just when they are trying to rob you of this life!

Let the people awaken and fight for its life!

Let every mother be a lioness defending her young!

Let no father stand by and see the blood of his children in silence!

Let not the first act of our destruction be repeated!

An end to despair and lack of faith!

An end to the spirit of slavery amongst us!

Let the tyrant pay with the blood of his body for every soul in Israel!

Let every house become a fortress for us!

Let the people awaken to war!

In war lies your salvation!

Whoever defends himself has a hope of escape!

We are rising in the name of war for the lives of the helpless masses whom we seek to save, whom we must arouse to action! It is not for ourselves alone that we wish to fight. We will be entitled to save ourselves only when we have completed our duty! *As long as the life of a Jew is still in danger, even one, single, life, we have to be ready to fight!!!!*

Our watchword is:

Not even one more Jew is to find his end in Treblinka!

Out with the traitors to the people!
War for life or death on the conqueror to our last breath!
Be prepared to act!
Be ready!

Source: Leaflets of Jewish Fighting Organization, Calls for Resistance, 1943-sign. ARG II 426. Courtesy of the Jewish Historical Institute in Warsaw, Poland.

Commentary

For comments on this document, see #12, **Statement: Call for Resistance in the Warsaw Ghetto (January 1943)**, below.

12. Statement: Call for Resistance in the Warsaw Ghetto (January 1943)

Similarly to Document #11, this document is also a call for resistance issued by the ŻOB in January 1943. Rather than a programmatic listing, however, this statement was placed in narrative form and intended to be a more reasoned explanation for the need to resist the Nazis.

To the Jewish Masses in the Ghetto

On January 22, 1943, six months will have passed since the deportations from Warsaw began. We all remember well the days of terror during which 300,000 of our brothers and sisters were cruelly put to death in the death camp of Treblinka. Six months have passed of life in constant fear of death, not knowing what the next day may bring. We have received information from all sides about the destruction of the Jews in the Government-General, in Germany, in the occupied territories. When we listen to this bitter news we wait for our own hour to come, every day and every moment. Today we must understand that the Nazi murderers have let us live only because they want to make use of our capacity to work to our last drop of blood and sweat, to our last breath. We are slaves. And when the slaves are no longer profitable, they are killed. Everyone among us must understand that, and everyone must remember it always.

During the past few weeks certain people have spread stories about letters that were said to have been received from Jews deported from Warsaw, who were said to be in labor camps near Minsk or Bobruisk. *Jews in your masses, do not believe these tales. They are spread by Jews who are working for the Gestapo.* The blood-stained murderers have a particular aim in doing this: to reassure the Jewish population in order that the next deportation can be carried out without difficulty, with a minimum of force and without losses to the Germans. They want the Jews not to prepare hiding-places and not to resist. Jews, do not repeat these lying tales.

Do not help the [Nazi] agents. The Gestapo's dastardly people will get their just deserts. *Jews in your masses,* the hour is near. You must be prepared to resist, not to give yourself up like sheep to slaughter. *Not even one Jew must go to the train. People who cannot resist actively must offer passive resistance, that is, by hiding.* We have now received information from Lvov that the Jewish Police there itself carried out the deportation of 3,000 Jews. Such things will not happen again in Warsaw. The killing of Lejkin proves it. Now our slogan must be:

Let everyone be ready to die like a man!

> **Source:** Leaflets of Jewish Fighting Organization, Calls for Resistance, 1943-sign. ARG II 426. Courtesy of the Jewish Historical Institute in Warsaw, Poland.

Commentary

This document and #11, above, are illustrations of the kind of propaganda employed by the Żydowska Organizacja Bojowa (Jewish Combat Organization, or ŻOB) at the outset of its operations.

In January 1943 there were only 60,000 Jews left in the Warsaw Ghetto. They were what remained of the approximately 440,000 Jews who had at one time been confined there. At the start of the great deportation during the summer of 1942, Adam Czerniaków, the head of the Judenrat, had committed suicide rather than continue handing over lists of Jews to be slaughtered. This left the way clear for the ŻOB to assume a leadership role in the ghetto.

On Monday, January 18, 1943, German troops entered the ghetto to round up Jews for deportation. At this time the plan was to take another 8,000 people, but from the ŻOB's perspective enough was enough. Believing this was the start of the final liquidation, they issued the call to arms for physical confrontation with the Nazis. What resulted was four days of Jewish armed resistance in the ghetto, sending a clear signal to the Germans that they would be challenged in the future.

The two documents here, #11 and #12, provide excellent glimpses into how the fighters viewed the situation. Expressions such as "sheep to the slaughter," first employed by Abba Kovner in Vilna, were reprised in document #11, which was a sheet printed off and distributed widely. Expressed in a series of short, sharp admonitions, it left little room for doubt that the time had come for physical resistance, and that arms must be taken up now. The number of exclamations at the end of some of the sentences points to a clear urgency on the part of the ŻOB communications department.

Document #12, on the other hand, is written in a way that is more measured, offering a rationale for resistance in a clear and lucid format that reads more like a manifesto. It is intended to appeal to those who might have harbored doubts beforehand, working to explain why this is the only option remaining for the inhabitants of the ghetto. It ends by saying that now is the time to stand up, and "be ready to die" with dignity and defiance.

The four days of this first uprising in January 1943 were significant. At the time, they showed the Jews of Warsaw that it was possible to fight back against the Nazis (even if doing so did not defeat them, liberate the ghetto, or drive them out of Poland). The important thing was that now, for the first time, both the Nazis and the Jews realized that passive acquiescence to deportation and mass murder was no longer how the ghetto would respond.

13. Mordecai Anielewicz to Yitzhak Zuckerman (April 23, 1943)

Mordecai Anielewicz was 24 years old when the Warsaw Ghetto rose in revolt. On April 23, with the struggle against the Nazis faltering, he wrote what would be his final letter to his co-commander, Yitzhak Zuckerman, who was at that time on the Aryan side attempting to procure weapons, supplies, and food. The letter has become an iconic statement of the resistance, made more poignant by the knowledge that Anielewicz, having seen his dream of self-defense in the ghetto come true, would not live to see the final defeat of the Nazis.

It is impossible to put into words what we have been through. One thing is clear, what happened exceeded our boldest dreams. The Germans ran twice from the ghetto. One of our companies held out for 40 minutes and another for more than 6 hours. The mine set in the "brushmakers" area exploded. Several of our companies attacked the dispersing Germans. Our losses in manpower are minimal. That is also an achievement. Y. [Yechiel] fell. He fell a hero, at the machine-gun. *I feel that great things are happening and what we dared do is of great, enormous importance....*

Beginning from today we shall shift over to the partisan tactic. Three battle companies will move out tonight, with two tasks: reconnaissance and obtaining arms. Do you remember, short-range weapons are of no use to us.

We use such weapons only rarely. What we need urgently: grenades, rifles, machine-guns and explosives.

It is impossible to describe the conditions under which the Jews of the ghetto are now living. Only a few will be able to hold out. The remainder will die sooner or later. Their fate is decided. In almost all the hiding places in which thousands are concealing themselves it is not possible to light a candle for lack of air.

With the aid of our transmitter we heard the marvelous report on our fighting by the "Shavit" radio station. The fact that we are remembered beyond the ghetto walls encourages us in our struggle. Peace go with you, my friend!

Perhaps we may still meet again! The dream of my life has risen to become fact. Self-defense in the ghetto will have been a reality. Jewish armed resistance and revenge are facts. I have been a witness to the magnificent, heroic fighting of Jewish men in battle.

M. Anielewicz
Ghetto, April 23, 1943

Source: [M. Kann], *"Na oczach swiata"* ("In the Eyes of the World") (Zamosc, 1932 [i.e., Warsaw, 1943]), pp. 33–34. Online at the Jewish Virtual Library, http://www.jewishvirtuallibrary.org/jsource/Holocaust/Anielewiczlet.html. Used by permission of the American-Israeli Cooperative Enterprise (AICE).

Commentary

Mordecai Anielewicz was the leader of the 1943 Warsaw Ghetto Uprising. He was instrumental, with several others, in forming the Jewish Combat Organization (Żydowska Organizacja Bojowa, or ŻOB), established in 1942 to resist continued Nazi deportations from the ghetto. In November 1942 he became commander in chief of the ŻOB.

On April 19, 1943, no fewer than 2,000 Nazis moved into the ghetto to begin the deportation of the remaining 60,000 or so Jews still there. For Anielewicz and the fighters of the ŻOB, this was the moment for resistance.

The ŻOB was not well armed (though in a better state than many other ghetto resistance organizations) but achieved a remarkable victory on the first day, inflicting Nazi losses and generating a retreat that left behind weapons that could be used by the fighters. The Nazis eventually managed to reverse the situation, and on May 8 they captured ŻOB headquarters at Miła 18. At this time Anielewicz and many of the other resisters died, either by their own hand or as a result of gas piped into the bunker by the Nazis.

This document is Anielewicz's last communication, a letter to his comrade Yitzhak Zuckerman, who was then outside the ghetto trying desperately to attract additional support from non-Jewish Poles. Anielewicz writes words that have since become iconic in the annals of the resistance movement: "The dream of my life has risen to become fact. Self-defense in the ghetto will have been a reality." In view of the times, this was a demonstration of Jewish dignity and defiance in the face of overwhelming odds.

14. Shmuel Zygielbojm to Władysław Raczkiewicz and Władysław Sikorski (May 11, 1943)

Immediately after the fall of the ŻOB command bunker at Miła 18, Shmuel Zygielbojm, secretary general of the Jewish Section of Poland's Central Committee of

Trade Unions and a member of the Polish National Council in London, wrote an impassioned open letter to the president and prime minister of Poland, then also in exile in London. It was his suicide letter; devastated at the fate of his comrades in Warsaw, he hoped that his death would serve to raise consciousness and provoke Allied action on behalf of the beleaguered Jews of Poland.

Mr. President,
Mr. Prime Minister,

I am taking the liberty of addressing to you, Sirs, these my last words, and through you to the Polish Government and the people of Poland, and to the governments and people of the Allies, and to the conscience of the whole world:

The latest news that has reached us from Poland makes it clear beyond any doubt that the Germans are now murdering the last remnants of the Jews in Poland with unbridled cruelty. Behind the walls of the ghetto the last act of this tragedy is now being played out.

The responsibility for the crime of the murder of the whole Jewish nationality in Poland rests first of all on those who are carrying it out, but indirectly it falls also upon the whole of humanity, on the peoples of the Allied nations and on their governments, who up to this day have not taken any real steps to halt this crime. By looking on passively upon this murder of defenseless millions—tortured children, women and men—they have become partners to the responsibility.

I am obliged to state that although the Polish Government contributed largely to the arousing of public opinion in the world, it still did not do enough. It did not do anything that was not routine, that might have been appropriate to the dimensions of the tragedy taking place in Poland.

Of close to 3.5 million Polish Jews and about 700,000 Jews who have been deported to Poland from other countries, there were, according to the official figures of the Bund transmitted by the Representative of the Government, only 300,000 still alive in April of this year. And the murder continues without end.

I cannot continue to live and to be silent while the remnants of Polish Jewry, whose representative I am, are being murdered. My comrades in the Warsaw ghetto fell with arms in their hands in the last heroic battle. I was not permitted to fall like them, together with them, but I belong with them, to their mass grave.

By my death, I wish to give expression to my most profound protest against the inaction in which the world watches and permits the destruction of the Jewish people.

I know that there is no great value to the life of a man, especially today. But since I did not succeed in achieving it in my lifetime, perhaps I shall be able by my death to contribute to the arousing from lethargy of those who could and must act in order that even now, perhaps at the last moment, the handful of Polish Jews who are still alive can be saved from certain destruction.

My life belongs to the Jewish people of Poland, and therefore I hand it over to them now. I yearn that the remnant that has remained of the millions of Polish Jews may live to see liberation together with the Polish masses, and that it shall be permitted to breathe freely in Poland and in a world of freedom and socialistic justice, in compensation for the inhuman suffering and torture inflicted on them. And I believe that such a Poland will arise and such a world will come about. I am certain that the President and the Prime Minister will send out these words of mine to all those to whom they are addressed, and that the Polish Government will embark immediately on diplomatic action and explanation of the situation, in order to save the living remnant of the Polish Jews from destruction.

I take leave of you with greetings, from everybody, and from everything that was dear to me and that I loved.

S. Zygielbojm

> **Source:** Letter from Shmul Zygielbojm to Raczkiewicz and Sikorski, May 11, 1943. Yad Vashem Archives, O.55/5 (pp. 15–16). Reproduced by permission of Yad Vashem Publications.

Commentary

Shmuel Zygielbojm was a Polish-Jewish socialist politician, spirited out of Warsaw after the Nazi invasion of Poland in 1939. By March 1942 he was in London, where he joined the National Council of the Polish government-in-exile.

After a series of communiqués informing him of the destruction of the Jews then taking place in Warsaw (and Poland, generally), he learned almost immediately when the Warsaw Ghetto Uprising had broken out. An already despairing Zygielbojm learned at the same time that his wife, Manya, and 16-year-old son, Tuvia, had been killed.

On May 12, 1943, he committed suicide in London. The letters he left were for Polish president Władysław Raczkiewicz and Polish prime minister Władysław Sikorski. His message, as can be seen in this document, was straightforward. "The responsibility for the crime of the murder of the whole Jewish nationality in Poland" rests indirectly "upon the whole of humanity, on the peoples of the Allied nations and on their governments, who up to this day have not taken any real steps to halt this crime."

Chillingly, he places his own death alongside those of the heroes in the Warsaw Ghetto: "I cannot continue to live and to be silent while the remnants of Polish Jewry, whose representative I am, are being murdered. My comrades in the Warsaw ghetto fell with arms in their hands in the last heroic battle. I was not permitted to fall like them, together with them, but I belong with them, to their mass grave." He concludes: "By my death, I wish to give expression to my most profound protest against the inaction in which the world watches and permits the destruction of the Jewish people."

15. *The Pioneer* (Warsaw), "The Ghetto Fights On" (May 12, 1943)

The attitude of the non-Jewish population to the fighting in the Warsaw Ghetto was mixed. Much ink has been spilled chronicling the ambivalence—if not hostility—felt by some Warsaw Poles toward the Jews. But as this document shows, not all Poles felt this way. Taken from an underground Polish newspaper, it gives a very positive view of the armed struggle of the Jews, praising them for showing the way to all Poles in their resistance to the Nazis.

The armed struggle offered the Germans by inhabitants of the Warsaw Ghetto has moved public opinion not only throughout Poland but will no doubt resound in the public opinion of other nations fighting for the dignity of human rights. As far as the fate of the fighting Jews is concerned, their struggle is, for all we know, rather hopeless. A few may, perhaps, succeed and survive. Against this background of Jewish tragedy, it is all the more resolutely and all the more convincingly that their determined protest stands out—a protest against the ultimate humiliation and maltreatment of man which the Germans dared undertake toward the Jewish population, thereby defying the fundamentals of law and culture.

This valiant and fierce armed resistance against an incomparably stronger oppressive foe is by no means a defence reflex of a victim. It is indeed, and quite indubitably, a conscious act of strong will, undertaken for the cause of human honour and dignity. Therefore, we owe full respect and good will to the fighters of the Warsaw Ghetto.

For us Poles the armed protest of the Warsaw Ghetto has special significance. On the premises of Polish statehood, we condemn German crimes against Jews, not only for humanitarian and cultural reasons, but also because the aggressor's unprecedented, barbarous persecution of Jews who are citizens of the Polish state, directly undermines the Polish *raison d'état*. The Ghetto fighters have risen to the task of Polish citizenry by defending their dignity and extending the front of the struggle against the aggressor.

Thus, while it is impossible at this juncture to offer an exhaustive evaluation of the immediate and ulterior consequences of the armed stand of the Warsaw Ghetto, we must nevertheless regard the participants in this rising as fighters against our common foe and *ipso facto* deserving of assistance on the part of the Polish community, wherever such assistance should prove possible and useful.

The armed resistance of the Warsaw Jews puts in a fix the German thugs who have been hypocritically professing a holy war against the "oriental barbarians." Echoes of the strife in the Warsaw Ghetto should appeal in an incomparably stronger manner to the conscience of the free nations of the world than the tacit, passive submission to mass slaughter by hundreds of thousands of exterminated Jews; these echoes will in an incomparably more pronounced fashion visualize the whole terror of German savagery and atrocities, the like of which the civilized world must not suffer in the future.

The Germans' battle must be deepened still further by the fact that the proud, vain "conquerors of the world," who feel absolutely at ease when it comes to bullying defenceless victims, have proved pitifully clumsy warriors in this real drawn-out battle against a handful of those whom they regard as inferior pariahs. They have had to rely on artillery and tanks in this battle. . . . This long war against the Warsaw Ghetto, which has already been termed sarcastically as the Germans' "Third Front," automatically bring to mind reflections ridiculing and discrediting their talents at conducting war and government.

The Ghetto fights on. The Polish society, which has been nurtured in the cult of fighting for honour and liberty, no doubt appreciates the significance and solemn splendour of the armed stand of the Warsaw Jews; they desire this stand to become a turning point in the martyrdom and humiliation which the Jewish population in the Polish lands has been suffering from the hands of the aggressor.

Source: *The Pioneer* (Warsaw Polish underground newspaper), May 12, 1943, in Wladyslaw Bartoszewski and Zofia Lewin, ed., *Righteous among Nations: How Poles Helped the Jews, 1939–1945* (London: Earlscourt Publications, 1969), pp. 678–680. Used by permission of The Wylie Agency LLC.

Commentary

The attitude of Poles toward the Warsaw Ghetto Uprising during April–May 1943 has been much discussed, with polarized attitudes on both sides ranging from how helpful the Poles were to how indifferent—when not outright hostile—their response was.

At the time, Polish attitudes toward the Jews ranged widely, increasingly so as the city of Warsaw became enveloped in smoke from the fires raging in the ghetto during the Holy Week of Easter that accompanied the first days of the revolt.

Wherever possible, everyday routines in Warsaw were maintained, with an ongoing attempt to retain or reclaim some measure of normality in the midst of the destructive Nazi occupation. Given this, people did their best to go about their everyday activities, with many glad that at least they were better off than their Jewish neighbors.

Yitzhak Zuckerman, of the Jewish Combat Organization, was later to write that the Polish "street" during the days of the revolt was essentially pro-Jewish and that there was, in general, a sympathetic atmosphere for the Jewish fighters on the other side of the wall.

This document, from an underground Polish newspaper, is indicative of the kind of attitude to which Zuckerman was referring. The Polish underground press was full of excitement and wonder at what the Jews were doing, and in the view of the

Pioneer "we owe full respect and good will to the fighters of the Warsaw Ghetto." An article like this serves as a corrective, in part, to the notion of a universally held hostility on the part of the Poles toward the Jews during the Holocaust.

16. Unaish Hilari, "The Jewish Partisan" (1954)

The world of partisan fighters saw life stripped bare. In and around the vicinity of Slonim, not far from Grodno, Belorussia, partisan activity was especially intense, as was resistance in the Slonim ghetto before its brutal liquidation in November 1941. In this document, a memoir written by Borya Udkofsky, focus is made on a remarkable comrade known by the name of Unaish Hilari. The attitudes and actions of Hilari show him to be an especially effective partisan fighter, with an approach ready-made for guerrilla warfare.

The first of the Jewish young folk of Slonim and its vicinity who had decided to make a stand and fight the German invader, attached themselves to a group of Partisans known as the Supiet unit. They brought enough ammunition with them to arm themselves and also some other Partisans. They took the machineguns out of the city in parts, and reassembled them in the forest. At that time we were in the Forest of Rapolofka.

Our first baptism of fire was when we attacked the police station in Divinovitz, a city about 40 kilometres from our camp. In this action Stephan Stephanovich led us, and he carried it out very successfully. We destroyed the station house, shot most of the garrison, and took many of the police prisoners. We lost not one man. It was our first experience of combat, and our first taste of sweet revenge on our enemies.

Our Russian comrades-in-arms could understand how we felt, and sympathized with us. Great was our excitement and pride when the group commander made mention of the bravery of the Jewish Partisans in the Order of the Day.

As time passed, our group was sent to the neighbouring forest of Bulli. Partisan units had been active there for a long time, most of them White Russians from among the people who lived nearby. Jews, left over as refugees after the German advance, were also among them. We were able to help to organize and train groups of new Jewish Partisans.

The people of White Russia (Belorussia) were not enthusiastic about the fighting capabilities of the Jewish Partisans. It was clear to us that only through deeds would we be able to convince them. So we always pioneered in actions against the enemy. Our anxiety to defend our Jewish honor, and our hatred of the murderers, inspired us to the most heroic and dangerous deeds. Especially was this so of Unaish Hilari—to him I shall especially dedicate this next narration.

Unaish was a tinsmith by profession. He had come to Slonim in 1939 with a stream of refugees from Poland. He was among the first to go into the forest, and there I met him. He was wonderfully good-natured and well-mannered, always ready to help, known and beloved by everyone.

Between one action and another, comrades would come to him with requests: to fix the magazine of a revolver, to fix a spring, etc., etc.: and he always tried to fulfill the requests.

He was completely disciplined, but burned with anger if he didn't receive an assignment in every action. His mind could not be at peace when he had to remain in camp while his friends and comrades went on dangerous missions. His commanders and leaders eventually yielded, and so he participated in all of the missions and actions of our group.

My group received an order to cut the telephone wires on the road from Slonim to Rozansi, and Unaish was among those who went on this mission. With great enthusiasm he started to get the tools together, and look over the ammunition. Unaish and I left in the same wagon. He had everything in order and just as it was supposed to be: belt taut, rifle clean and shining. All of us were burning with excitement, looking forward to the action.

Two hundred metres from the road we left our wagons. Unaish and I were about 50 metres ahead of the others. We reached the road, crossed it quickly and were ready to start. The men were deployed so that they were covered from the front and from the rear. Everyone started the work of destruction. Unaish, his gun on his shoulder, was faster than all of us. We sawed through the foot of the pole, but it was stubborn. Just then the pole fell over and Unaish started for the next pole working his pliers like the experienced tin smith he was.

We had carried out our instructions, but we didn't feel enough had been done. Time was in our favor, so we continued cutting the wire. Suddenly we heard wagons approaching. Several people suggested that we should get a move on, but we stayed on working at the wires, remaining out of sight. Maybe it was some Germans passing by—and we would have an opportunity to accomplish some additional work. But they were only farm wagons. We let the farmers go by and we continued our destruction of the telephone lines. Finally we were ready to return. Unaish was very satisfied; he had found salvation for his soul, and he hummed a Hebrew song.

Here is another story about Unaish in another action. It was a very hot summer day; people were sleeping in their tents after a night of battle. Unaish alone sat up, belted with grenades, as was his custom. And as always, he was busy with his ammunition. Suddenly a Partisan galloped up on horseback and broke into the tent of the General Staff. It was one of the watchmen stationed at the edge of the forest. A moment later, there was a general alarm.

Within a few minutes about 60 Partisans were moving along the road leading to the village of Harotsek; eight Jews of my group were with them, and Unaish among them. The message had come that 40 German soldiers and many policemen had surrounded the village, and were confiscating cattle and preparing to leave. We rushed to stop them and prevent the robbery.

Quietly we moved toward the village, which was as deserted as a cemetery. We could see the police under the direction of the Germans, leading the cattle away. Our orders were to block the road leading to the village.

Unaish was already lying down, finding a good position from which to fire on them. He pulled his hat down and put the bullets in it, ready for reloading. And he loaded his rifle and had his fingers on the trigger ready to fire. The Germans seemed to feel that we were around and they sent two fellows to see that the road was clear. It was just as though, like dogs, they smelled danger.

Our orders were not to shoot! To let them pass! About 200 meters from our wagons, two cars jammed full of Germans moved along. They rode as though alerted, their weapons in their hands. When the first car came very close to us the order was given: "Fire." The machineguns from the center of our group and from both ends started to do their work. Unaish himself worked like a machine, loading his rifle and firing one bullet after the other, with careful aim, but non-stop. He got up, ran forward and prepared to throw a grenade. The Germans were confused and started to shoot without aiming. Many of them were already wounded and they jumped from the cars.

The first car was set afire by one of our flame throwers. The second one was smashed by a grenade. After the Germans had jumped from the cars, they continued to shoot while retreating. Unaish started to pursue them: it was difficult to hold him back. His enthusiasm carried all of us with him. Every time a German fell dead, wild laughter would break out of his mouth.

In the midst of this, a field-artillery piece started firing on our left flank and most of us instantly moved back. One of us tried to find refuge behind a tree, but Unaish stared at him with his eyes bulging out, and the man stopped where he was as though paralyzed. Then I heard the voice of Unaish saying, "Comrade Commander, allow me to go over to the cars. Perhaps there is some ammunition in them. It's really a waste if ammunition is burned."

But it wasn't logical to send him to raid a burning car that might blow up at any minute, the blast would make him fly into the air in bits. Besides, maybe a German was hiding in the back of that truck.

In that battle 18 Germans fell, and Germans never again appeared in that village.

In the next two and a half years I was with Unaish in action many times under different conditions, and he always had to be held back and prevented from making foolhardy displays of bravery. Finally he fell in battle, and this is how he died: in one of the villages there was a road junction just outside the railroad station. The Germans set up a garrison there, manned by many people from the village. They were able to stop us from any action. So our General Staff decided to wipe them out. We knew that it would not be easy, because the position was well fortified and there was no opening or weak point where we could launch an attack.

The battle was long and brutal. In the beginning we made use of our small cannon, a .45 millimeter. Unaish was among the first to break into the village.

He fought crazily; he fired point blank and he threw grenades so that they were exploding all around him.

Finally the battle was over. The safe nest of the enemy had been destroyed. But just then Unaish saw a German officer escaping from the village. He ran after him against an order to remain in his place. After a while we found his body near the body of the German officer. He must have been hit by a stray bullet, and his blood, his clean, pure, in fact his holy blood was mixed with the blood of the German. Our group really won fame in this encounter. Five of us had fallen.

Unaish was placed in a wagon drawn by a dark horse. A blanket of flowers made by his friends and comrades was spread over the wagon box. The commander of the group took formal farewell of the departed.

In deep silence we walked our five friends and comrades to their common grave. We looked for the last time on the face of Unaish, who had been so dear to us. We parted from him forever. A volley of shots was fired over the grave of Unaish as he went on his last journey. His memory will remain in the hearts of many of us. We knew how he felt towards us as Jewish Partisans and as soldiers, and the honor he gave us on that account. But the source of that honor was heroic action, like the deeds of Unaish, which earned respect and glory. These people died to give us an example, a criterion, so that we would be the kind of people Unaish was.

Source: Meyer Barkai, trans. and ed., *The Fighting Ghettos* (first published in Hebrew as *Sefer Milchamot Hagetaot*, ed. Izhak Zuckerman and Moshe Basak [Tel Aviv: Ghetto Fighters House and Kibbutz Hameuchad, 1954]) (Philadelphia and New York: J. B. Lippincott Company, 1962), pp. 211–216.

Commentary

Jewish partisan fighters lived under conditions that were somewhat unregimented, though of necessity highly disciplined. The issues they faced were driven by desperation and frequently accompanied by a lack of weapons, food, shelter, and supplies. There was often little or no time for strategic planning, little chance of external support, and usually a deficiency in military leadership. The fighters were also repeatedly hampered by a concern for local civilian lives relative to their own combat operations.

Jewish partisan warfare saw a very distinctive type of resistance movement. Unlike other underground organizations, Jews had to fight for their lives or, at least, for whatever lives could be saved. Yet not all resistance groups were identical, and not all fighters were of the same cast, as shown by the example of Borya Udofsky's comrade, Unaish Hilari, who is described as one who "burned with anger if he didn't receive an assignment in every action."

Slonim, in the Grodno region of Belorussia, saw major massacres of the Jewish population, with 70 percent killed in a single Nazi operation on November 14, 1941. A second mass murder of those remaining took place in 1942.

Hilari, who was not originally from Slonim, took it upon himself to be the town's avenging angel. As described by Udofsky, his sacrifice and his memory "will remain in the hearts" of all those who knew him and were there to see him in action—"so that we would be the kind of people Unaish was."

17. Tadeusz Pankiewicz: "The 'Eagle' Pharmacy in the Kraków Ghetto"

Tadeusz Pankiewicz, a Polish pharmacist, found that his shop was situated on the "wrong" side of Kraków when the Nazis created the ghetto. Given the option to leave, he refused on the grounds that he served his community and that now, more than ever, it was likely to need his services. This document, part of his memoir of the "Eagle" pharmacy during the time of the ghetto's existence, tells us much about how even the smallest act of goodness could also be an act of resistance.

The "Eagle" Pharmacy was placed by fate in the very heart of the Jewish quarter, where it became witness to the inhuman deportations, monstrous crimes, and the incessant debasing of human dignity by the Nazis. All sorts of people gathered there for their daily political discussions, and often some ghetto inhabitants spent the night hiding out from police round-ups and arrests. This was where many personal human tragedies were enacted, farewells were said by those on their way to certain death; this was where the ones who were saved reported, and finally this is where the Gestapo agents received their secret confidents in the duty room.

This small town, walled off and fenced off by wire, was ravaged by death in the most varied forms. Every day, every hour, human life was in danger of extermination. Any form of normal treatment was out of the question under such conditions. Heart medicines, tranquillizers and sleep-inducing potions were the most popular of all drugs. Of course, this is quite apart from the bandages and dressings which were most in demand during the Nazi excesses, the evictions and the round-ups. It must be stressed that sleeping drugs were in most cases used for other purposes than those foreseen by the pharmacopoeia.

When the Jewish quarter was being created in 1941 the "Eagle" Pharmacy, located at 18 Zgoda Place in Podgórze, was one of the four pharmacies of the quarter within the area of the ghetto. I, its owner, became one of the few Poles working there and the only one to live there throughout the existence of the ghetto and the occupation. After losing my home I moved into the pharmacy's duty room when we had been ordered to be on duty day and night. The "Eagle" Pharmacy was fully entitled to receive the same type of drugs as other pharmacies which were outside of the Jewish district. Relatively speaking, the supplies were adequate, especially as supplies of medicines for the Jewish population were mainly in the hands of Dr Weichert who was in charge of the drugs and provisions from the Red Cross in Geneva.

The unusual character of the "Eagle" Pharmacy, however, did not consist solely in the fact that it was in the hands of a Pole who lived and worked there, nor of the fact that he himself, as well as the two women employees (also Poles), had a right to enter and leave the ghetto. The unusual character lay mostly in the fact that it was the daily meeting place, not of ill people, but of people who were thirsty for political news from the front and from the world, that the German and Polish press was read there, that while tea or coffee was sipped, comments were exchanged on the news brought in by the Underground, and this is where the latest radio communiqués were discussed. We had numerous guests all the time, including many very interesting, exceptional people who forgot their daily problems and worries for a time during these very lively discussions. Among the regular callers were many doctors, lawyers, journalists, painters and musicians.

In the pharmacy a well-known Lvov lawyer and enthusiastic amateur mathematician, Dr Rappaport, worked out the proof for a mathematical problem which had been regarded as insoluble. It was there that he presented his solution to a professor of Mathematics from the Jagiellonian University whom I had brought into the ghetto. This event was described in detail in the quarterly mathematical publication which was put out under the auspices of the University. In this same pharmacy an outstanding Jewish poet, Gebirtig, recited his verses and sang songs he had written; here, too, a noted Jewish painter, Neumann, often painted his works, making use of the spacious pharmacy premises.

After every major event, after every police round-up, after every "operation" or deportation, our acquaintances directed their first steps towards the pharmacy. It gave a certain guarantee of safety for those seeking refuge, for it had one entrance from the street and two exits at the back of the building leading to the courtyard onto other streets. There was also an excellent hiding place which we had built inside the front room. The oldest, invaluable Pentateuch scrolls survived the war in it and right after the war they were handed over to the Jewish Historical Commission in Cracow.

After the destruction of the ghetto the pharmacy actually lost any reason for existence. It seemed to me that after two years in the ghetto I myself had been deported into the land of the dead, as it were. The town had become depopulated and a place where the footsteps of any stray person gave rise to fear, where the sight of a human being sent chills up one's spine. After two days of compulsory sitting in the pharmacy I walked around this deserted town, listening to the echo of my own footsteps. It was dark when I was returning to the pharmacy. The meanness of the surroundings, dark empty streets and squares, filled me with a strange uneasiness. Every open gate, every window left open in those dead houses heightened my disquiet. There were moments when I felt I was having hallucinations: someone quickly ran through an entrance, someone lit a match in a window, someone opened a window; I heard a whistle, a small card thrown by an unseen hand fell at my feet. No, these were not hallucinations. They were reality. Someone was still living in this building, someone was hiding in fear of someone else. I picked up the paper and hurried my steps. The things I had seen and lived through were still too fresh in my mind and in my thoughts for me to stop and calmly consider the contents and the meaning of this bit of paper, to remember the place where these secret signals had come from.

Before re-entering the pharmacy I heard the shuffle of someone's quiet footsteps and a knock on the pane. I ran into the gateway. There was complete silence. In the corridor I stumbled over the corpse of a man. I heaved a sigh of relief when I finally reached the pharmacy. I went to the window to look out into the square I knew so well so as to be able to believe the reality of what I had experienced. I found it difficult to go to sleep that night. The sensations of emptiness and silence were making me nervous. I kept having the impression that I could hear the soft echo of someone's steps, a door squeaking somewhere, a knocking on a window-pane. For many days after that, whenever I walked about the ghetto, I kept hearing similar sounds. Then I knew for certain that these were no deceiving spirits, people were giving an indication that they were alive, that they needed help.

But it was not all that simple to give help. It was dangerous to stop in front of an empty building, or to try to get in touch with someone who was hiding, for this might be noticed by the German police and the all-too-eager Jewish OD-men only a very few of whom could be trusted. In the meantime, the unfortunate ones simply had to be helped. I then decided to ask for help from two OD-men I knew well. I told them in detail where I had heard the sounds, about the place where the card with a plea for help had been dropped down to me. They did whatever they could. When the furniture was being taken away from the isolation clinic and from the hospital on Józefińska St. to barracks in Plaszów, they smuggled out a few children. Sometimes, some of the older ones joined groups of prisoners from the camp who came to clean up the ghetto buildings and returned to the barracks, together with the prisoners. At first, this escaped the notice of the Germans for the returning prisoners were not counted too accurately. Later the situation changed because some of those being taken to work had escaped.

One day, while sitting in the pharmacy, I heard soft footsteps in the corridor leading to it. Someone was sneaking in. A light knock at the door and then the sound of steps going away. I felt a bit uneasy. Then a moment later I heard a knock at the window from the courtyard side. I went to the window and I saw the shadow of a man running and then I again heard the sound of muffled steps in the corridor. I opened the door. A small boy was standing in front of me: "Please help me, sir!"

"Who are you?" I asked. "Where are you hiding out?"

The haggard, dirty face of the boy showed fear and the stamp of previous experiences. His name was Teufel. Before the war his father had owned a stationery shop on Szewska St., and he was working in the *Gemeinschaft* (guild) of this same trade in the ghetto. On 13 March he had marched off along with others to the barracks in Plaszów, and the boy with an aunt and her small child were hiding out in the cellar in a hole they had made in a pile of coal. They had not eaten for several days. The aunt was very ill and the child was dying. They had experienced some horrible moments. Several times the Germans had passed very close to the hiding place, and they were terrified that the Germans would find them, for the child had given a cry. And now they were asking for help.

I gave him everything I had to eat and I promised to tell the father about their existence. A few days later the aunt joined a group of working people and got to the barracks, the boy was taken out of the ghetto in a cupboard from the hospital. The child died. . . .

In the tragic history of the ghetto the two pharmacy employees must be mentioned for their meritorious deed: pharmacists Irena Droździkowska and Helena Krywaniuk, who, all this time and at the risk of their lives, have given assistance to the maltreated and humiliated Jews, by their behavior giving expression to a belief in the triumph of justice and humanitarianism.

Source: Wladyslaw Bartoszewski and Zofia Lewin, *Righteous among Nations: How the Poles Helped the Jews, 1939–1945* (London: Earlscourt Publications, 1969), pp. 222–227. Used by permission of The Wylie Agency LLC.

Commentary

Tadeusz Pankiewicz was a Polish pharmacist in the city of Kraków. In 1933 he assumed control of the "Under the Eagle" pharmacy that had been established by his father in 1910.

In March 1941 the Nazis demanded that Pankiewicz leave the ghetto district of Podgórze, as it was being closed off. Pankiewicz saw that this would deprive his Jewish customers of the services of a pharmacist, particularly after the other non-Jewish pharmacists in the area had gone. He sought and received permission to stay. In 1947 he wrote a memoir of his wartime experiences entitled *Apteka w getcie krakowskim* (*The Cracow Ghetto Pharmacy*), part of which has been extracted here.

Pankiewicz describes the context within which the pharmacy was operating, noting the unusual circumstances in which he, a Pole, oversaw a location in which "it was the daily meeting place, not of ill people, but of people who were thirsty for political news from the front and from the world, that the German and Polish press was read there, that while tea or coffee was sipped, comments were exchanged on the news brought in by the Underground, and this is where the latest radio communiqués were discussed." In short, he shows how this had become a social hub for the Jews of the ghetto.

The document also gives an indication of how Pankiewicz was able both to help Jews and at the same time resist the Nazis, through covering for those in hiding and providing them with succor. For two and a half years the pharmacy remained open, during which time Pankiewicz and his staff risked their lives constantly to undertake frequent covert operations. Not only did they permit the store to remain open, but they smuggled food and passed on information, often not waiting for the couriers to arrive.

18. Yankiel Wiernik on the Revolt at Treblinka (August 2, 1943)

The prisoner revolt at Treblinka was carefully planned down to the last detail. On August 2, 1943, after having built an arsenal consisting of hand grenades and rifles stolen from the camp armory, between 150 and 200 inmates rose in a coordinated action, rushed the fence, and attempted a breakthrough. Yankiel Wiernik was one of the few survivors, and in this document he relates the events surrounding the revolt. Most clearly, he shows how he was able to live through it, make it through to the forest—and live.

The final, irrevocable date for the outbreak of the revolt was set for August 2, and we instinctively felt that this would really be the day. We got busy with our preparations, checking whether everything was in readiness and whether each of our men knew the part he had to play. It so happened that I did not go to Camp No. 1 for several days because I was busy constructing an octagonal building with a suspended roof, resembling a guard station, that was to house a well. I was also constructing a portable building in Camp No. 2 which could be taken apart and which I subsequently had to move to Camp No. 1, where it was supposed to remain permanently. I was becoming impatient because I was unable to get in touch with Camp No. 1 and zero hour was approaching.

August 2, 1943, was a sizzling hot day. The sun shone brightly through the small, grated windows of our barrack. We had practically no sleep that night; dawn found us wide awake and tense. Each of us realized the importance of the moment and thought only of gaining freedom. We were sick of our miserable existence, and all that mattered was to take revenge on our tormentors and to escape. As for myself, all I hoped for was to be able to crawl into some quiet patch of woodland and get some quiet, restful sleep.

At the same time, we were fully aware of the difficulties we would have to overcome. Observation towers, manned by armed guards, stood all around the camp, and the camp itself was teeming with Germans and Ukrainians armed with rifles, machine guns and revolvers. They would lock us up in our barracks as early as 12 noon. The camp was surrounded by several rows of fences and trenches.

However, we decided to risk it, come what may. We had had enough of the tortures, of the horrible sights. I, for one, was determined to live to present to the world a description of the inferno and a sketch of the layout of that accursed hellhole. This resolve had given me the strength to struggle against the hangmen and the endurance to bear the misery. Somehow I felt that I would survive our break for freedom.

A presentiment of the coming storm was in the air and our nerves were at high tension. The Germans and the Ukrainians noticed nothing unusual. Having wiped out millions of people, they did not feel they had to fear a paltry handful of men such as we. They barked orders which were obeyed as usual. But those of us who belonged to the committee were worried because we had no instructions about the timing of the outbreak. I was fidgety. I kept on working but all the time I worried that we might fail to establish contact which, in turn, would mean that we would perish miserably and in vain.

However, I found a way of communicating with Camp No. 1. My superior, Loeffler, was no longer there; he had been replaced by a new man whose name I did not know. We nicknamed him "Brown Shirt." He was very kind to me. I walked up to him and asked him for some boards. Boards were stored in Camp No. 1 and he, not wanting to interrupt our work, went off with some workers to get them. The boards were brought. I inspected and measured them, and then said they weren't right for the job. I volunteered to go over myself to select the material I needed, but I made a wry face as if I did not like the idea. And so I went to the storage shed with my superior, all the while shaking with excitement. I felt that unless I made the most of this opportunity, all would be lost.

Presently I found myself in Camp No. 1 and nervously looked around, appraising our chances. Three other men were with me. The storage shed was guarded by a Jew about 50 years of age, wearing spectacles. Because he was an inmate of Camp No. 1, I knew nothing about him, but he was a participant in the conspiracy. My three helpers engaged the German superior in a conversation to divert his attention, while I pretended to be selecting boards. I deliberately went away from the others, continuing to select boards. Suddenly, someone whispered in my ear: "Today, at 5:30 p.m." I turned around casually and saw the Jewish guard of the storage shed before me. He repeated these words and added: "There will be a signal."

In feverish haste I collected whatever boards were nearest to me, told my comrades to pick them up and started to work, trembling with fear lest I betray my emotions. Thus time went by until noon, when all hands returned from work. Again our committee met furtively and the word was passed around. I asked everyone to keep cool and remember their individual assignments. The younger ones among us were greatly agitated. As I looked at our group, I began to believe that we would really win.

Volunteers for the afternoon work shift were then selected. We assigned the weaker and less capable men to the first shift because it had no task to perform. The first afternoon shift returned from work at 3 p.m. The men we had picked then went to work, thirty in number. They were the bravest, the pluckiest and the strongest in the lot. Their task was to pave the way for the others to escape. A crew was also picked for fetching water from the well. At around 5 p.m. there suddenly was a great need for water. The gate leading to the well was opened wide and the number of water carriers was considerably augmented.

All those assigned to work with the corpses wore only striped overalls. A penalty of 25 lashes was meted out for wearing any other clothing while doing this particular job. On that day, however, the men wore their clothes under their overalls. Before escaping, they would have to get rid of the overalls, which would have given them away at once.

We remained in our barracks, sitting close together and exchanging glances; every few minutes someone would remark that the time was drawing near. Our emotions at that point defied description. We silently bade farewell to the spot where the ashes of our brethren were buried. Sorrow and suffering had bound us to Treblinka, but we were still alive and wanted to escape from this place where so many innocent victims had perished. The long processions, those ghastly caravans of death, were still before our eyes, crying out for vengeance. We knew what lay hidden beneath the surface of this soil. We were the only ones left alive to tell the story. Silently, we took our leave of the ashes of our fellow Jews and vowed that, out of their blood, an avenger would arise.

Suddenly we heard the signal—a shot fired into the air.

We leaped to our feet. Everyone fell to his prearranged task and performed it with meticulous care. Among the most difficult tasks was to lure the Ukrainians from the watchtowers. Once they began shooting at us from above, we would have no chance of escaping alive. We knew that gold held an immense attraction for them, and they had been doing business with the Jews all the time. So, when the shot rang out, one of the Jews sneaked up to the tower and showed the Ukrainian guard a gold coin. The Ukrainian completely forgot that he was on guard duty. He dropped his machine gun and hastily clambered down to pry the piece of gold from the Jew. They grabbed him, finished him off and took his revolver. The guards in the other towers were also dispatched quickly.

Every German and Ukrainian whom we met on our way out was killed. The attack was so sudden that before the Germans were able to gather their wits, the road to freedom lay wide open before us. Weapons were snatched from the guard station and each one of us grabbed all the arms he could. As soon as the signal shot rang out, the guard at the well had been killed and his weapons taken from him. We all ran out of our barracks and took the stations that had been assigned to us. Within a matter of minutes, fires were raging all around. We had done our duty well.

I grabbed some guns and let fly right and left, but when I saw that the road to escape stood open, I picked up an ax and a saw, and ran. At first we were in control of the situation. However, within a short time pursuit got under way from every direction, from Malkinia, Kosow and from the Treblinka Penal Camp. It seemed that when they saw the fires and heard the shooting, they sent help at once.

Our objective was to reach the woods, but the closest patch was five miles away. We ran across swamps, meadows and ditches, with bullets pursuing us fast and furious. Every second counted. All that mattered was to reach the woods because the Germans would not want to follow us there.

Just as I thought I was safe, running straight ahead as fast as I could, I suddenly heard the command "Halt!" right behind me. By then I was exhausted but I ran faster just the same. The woods were just ahead of me, only a few leaps away. I strained all my will power to keep going. The pursuer was gaining and I could hear him running close behind me.

Then I heard a shot; in the same instant I felt a sharp pain in my left shoulder. I turned around and saw a guard from the Treblinka Penal Camp. He again aimed his pistol at me. I knew something about firearms and I noticed that the weapon had jammed. I took advantage of this and deliberately slowed down. I pulled the ax from my belt. My pursuer—a Ukrainian guard—ran up to me yelling in Ukrainian: "Stop or I'll shoot!" I came up close to him and struck him with my ax across the left side of his chest. He collapsed at my feet with a vile path.

I was free and ran into the woods. After penetrating a little deeper into the thicket, I sat down among the bushes. From the distance I heard a lot of shooting. Believe it or not, the bullet had not really hurt me. It had gone through all of my clothing and stopped at my shoulder, leaving a mark. I was alone. At last, I was able to rest.

Source: Yankiel Wiernik, *A Year in Treblinka: An Inmate Who Escaped Tells the Day-to-Day Facts of One Year of His Torturous Experiences* (New York: American Representation of the General Jewish Workers Union of Poland, 1945). Located online at http://www.zchor.org/treblink/wiernik.htm.

Commentary

Yankiel Wiernik was a Jewish prisoner at Treblinka, closely involved in the uprising at the camp on August 2, 1943.

Born in Poland in 1889, he had been a member of the Jewish Labor Bund and was put to work in Treblinka as a member of the *Sonderkommando*, removing bodies from gas chambers and burying them in mass graves or consigning them to cremation. Wiernik escaped Treblinka during the prisoner revolt of which Berek Lajcher was one of the principal leaders.

After his escape, Wiernik wrote a report on the camp, how it operated, and the rebellion. It was entitled *Rok w Treblince* (*A Year in Treblinka*) and was published through the combined efforts of the Jewish National Committee (Żydowski Komitet Narodowy), the Jewish Labor Bund, and the Polish Council to Aid Jews (Żegota). It appeared a year after the rebellion, in 1944, with a circulation of 2,000 copies.

Smuggled out of occupied Poland, it went first to London and then to the United States, where it was translated into English and Yiddish and published by the American Representation of the General Jewish Workers Union of Poland. It was translated into Hebrew by Yitzhak Zuckerman and distributed throughout Palestine after the war by the Histadrut trade union movement.

Wiernik's was the earliest (and, for several decades, only) account of the Treblinka uprising. For many years, then, it was the authoritative source regarding the events of August 2, 1943. Subsequent recollections have to a large degree corroborated Wiernik's version of the story, which, in view of how few survivors there were and how many have since died without leaving their own narratives, is destined to remain the uprising's premier record.

19. Call for Revolt in the Vilna Ghetto (September 1, 1943)

Led by Yitzhak Wittenberg and (after his death) Abba Kovner, the Fareynikte Partizaner Organizatsye (United Partisan Organization, or FPO) was inspired by the Warsaw Ghetto fighters who rose in rebellion in April 1943. After Kovner's declaration that the Jews would not go "like sheep to the slaughter," the FPO rose against the Nazis on September 1, 1943. This document is the FPO's proclamation to the people of Vilna to rise with them, to avenge their loved ones who had been murdered in the Ponary Forest, and to drive the Nazis from their city.

Jews, Prepare for Armed Resistance!

The German and Lithuanian hangmen have reached the gates of the ghetto. They will murder us all. They will take us, group by group, through the gates.

That is how they took them in their hundreds on the Day of Atonement.

And that is how they took them at the time of the White, the Yellow and the Pink Papers.

That is how they took our brothers, sisters, fathers, mothers, our children.

That is how they took tens of thousands away to their death.

But we will not go!

We will not let them take us like animals to slaughter.

Jews, prepare for armed resistance!

Do not believe the false assurances of the murderers, do not believe the words of the traitors. Whoever is taken through the gate of the ghetto has only one road ahead—Ponary. *And Ponary is death.*

Jews, we have nothing to lose.

Death is certain. Who can still believe that he will survive when the murderers kill systematically? The hand of the hangman will reach out to each of us. Neither hiding nor cowardice will save our lives.

Only armed resistance can save our lives and honor.

Brothers, it is better to fall in battle in the ghetto than to be led like sheep to Ponary.

Know that in the ghetto there is an organized Jewish force which will rise up with arms in its hands.

Rise up for the armed resistance!

Don't hide in the *malines*. You will fall there like mice in the hands of the murderers. Jewish masses.

Out into the streets!
Those who have no arms get hold of an axe.
Those who haven't an axe take hold of an iron bar or a cudgel!
- For our murdered children,
- For our murdered parents,
- For Ponary.

Strike the murderers!
In every street, in every yard, in every room, within the ghetto and outside the ghetto.
Strike the dogs!
Jews, we have nothing to lose. *We can save our lives only if we kill the murderers.*
Long live liberty! Long live armed resistance!
Death to the murderers!

Command Staff
United Partisans Organization—F.P.O. (Fareynegte Partizaner Organizatsye)
Vilna Ghetto
September 1, 1943

Source: Moreshet Archive, Mordechai Anielevich Memorial. Used by permission.

Commentary

Early on September 1, 1943, the Vilna ghetto was surrounded by German and Estonian security forces, who began arresting Jewish men and removing them from the ghetto. The Germans demanded that the Jewish Council (Judenrat) provide 3,000 men and 2,000 women for deportation to Estonia.

Immediately, the Fareynikte Partizaner Organizatsye (United Partisan Organization, or FPO), led by Yitzhak Wittenberg, issued a general call to arms. The result saw many fighters step forward, but about 100 who had mobilized around the arms caches were surrounded by German troops before they managed to arm themselves. Their subsequent removal was a bitter blow to the already small FPO force.

This document is a notice that the FPO published calling on the Jews of the ghetto to resist. It is a powerful, emotional call, drawing attention to the immediacy of the situation in urging that "the hangmen" had already "reached the gates of the ghetto." The notice exhorted the inhabitants, "They will take us, group by group, through the gates," and argued that the Jews would have to "prepare for armed resistance."

Unfortunately for the FPO, the ghetto inhabitants did not respond. Yechiel Scheinbaum, a fighter who led his own underground force known as the "Yechiel Group," was one of the first casualties, and the leader of the Judenrat, Jacob Gens, refused to support the revolt. As a result, the fighters were defeated quickly, and the proclamation calling the Jews to arms became irrelevant. All that was left was for the remaining fighters to escape to the forest, where they could join the partisans and continue the war from there. The ghetto itself was liquidated on September 23, 1943, with few survivors.

20. Alexander Pechersky on the Sobibor Revolt (October 14, 1943)

The Sobibor Revolt of October 14, 1943, was the biggest uprising in any of the Nazi death or concentration camps. Prior to the arrival just a few weeks earlier of a Soviet officer, Alexander Pechersky, together with several of his soldiers—all Jewish—there seemed little chance that the prisoners would have the military knowhow or leadership to mount a successful rebellion. After the war Pechersky gave his account of the Sobibor Revolt, reproduced here in full.

I was born in Kremenchug in 1919, but spent my childhood in Rostov. After I finished my secondary studies I entered a music school. Music and theatre were the most important things in my life. I directed amateur dramatic circles and took a great interest in the arts.

In 1941 I joined the army with the rank of second lieutenant, and was soon promoted to first lieutenant. Taken prisoner in October 1941, I caught typhus, but concealed the disease, fearing to be killed.

In May 1942, I tried to escape with four other prisoners, but we were caught and were sent first to the disciplinary camp of Borysov and then to Minsk. During a medical examination it was discovered that I was Jewish. I was locked up with other Jews in a place nicknamed "the Jewish cellar," where we spent ten days in complete darkness.

We were allowed 100 grams of bread a day and a jug of water. Then on September 20 1942 we were transferred to the labour camp of Sheroka Street in Minsk, where I lived until my deportation to Sobibor.

In September 1943 we were told that Jews would be transferred to Germany, but that families would not be separated. At 4 a.m. a silent crowd left Minsk, the men on foot, women and children in trucks.

We gathered at the railway station where a freight train awaited us. Seventy people were crowded into a boxcar, and after four days we reached Sobibor. We stopped during the night and were given water. The doors opened, and facing us, was a poster Sonderkommando Sobibor.

Tired and hungry, we left the car. Armed SS officers stood there and Oberscharfuhrer Gomerski shouted, "Cabinet makers and carpenters with no families forward."

Eighty men were led into the camp and locked in a barrack. Older prisoners informed us about Sobibor. We had all fought in the war and suffered in labour camps but we were so horrified about Sobibor that we could not sleep that night.

Shlomo Leitman, a Polish Jew from Sheroka, was lying at my side. "What will become of us?" he asked. I didn't answer pretending to sleep. I couldn't get over my reaction and was thinking of Nelly, a little girl who travelled in my boxcar and who was, no doubt, dead already. I thought of my own daughter Elochka.

On September 24, I wrote in my diary: "We are in the camp of Sobibor, we rise at 5:00 a.m., get a litre of warm water, but no bread, at 5:30 we are counted, at 6:00 we leave for work, in columns of threes, Russian Jews are in front, then Poles, Czech and Dutch."

I remember when the SS man Frenzel ordered us to sing, Cybulski was walking at my side. "What shall we sing?" he asked and I answered, "We only know one song: *Yesli Zavtra Voyna*." It was a patriotic Russian song and it gave us hope for freedom.

Soldiers led us to the Nordlager, a new section of the camp. Nine barracks were already built there and others were under construction. Our group was split in two, one part was sent to build, the other to cut wood. On our first day of work, fifteen people got twenty-five lashes each for incompetence.

On September 25, we unloaded coal all day and were given only twenty minutes for lunch. The cook was unable to feed us all in such a short time. Frenzel was furious and ordered the cook to sit down. Then he whipped him while whistling a marching tune. The soup tasted as though it had been mixed with blood and although we were very hungry, many of us were unable to eat.

Our arrival at the camp made a great impression on the older prisoners: they knew well that the war was going on, but had never seen the men who fought in it. And these newcomers could handle arms!

We were approached by men and women who made us understand that their wish was to get out of hell. I couldn't speak Yiddish so Shlomo Leitman who was born in Warsaw, acted as interpreter. We could understand some Polish as it resembles Russian.

I wanted to know the topography of Sobibor. Camp Number 1 where we lived, included workshops and kitchens. Camp Number 2 the reception centre of the new arrivals, had storage for the belongings stolen from the prisoners; a corridor led to Camp Number 3 and its gas chambers.

On September 26, twenty-five prisoners were whipped, a young Dutchman tall and lean, was chopping wood, but was not strong enough for the task. The SS guard hit him on the head. Astonished I stopped working. Furious, the guard shouted, "I give you five minutes to chop this wood, if you fail, you will get twenty-five lashes."

I hit the wood as though it were his head. "You did it in four and a half minutes," said the Nazi looking at his watch. He offered me a cigarette. "Thanks, I don't smoke," I replied.

27 September. We were still working at the Nordlager. At 9 a.m. Kali-Mali, from Sheroka, whose real name was Shubayev, told me, "All the Germans have left, only the Kapo is here, why?"

I answered, "I don't know, but let us see where we are." A prisoner informed us, "If they are not here, it means that a convoy has just arrived, look over there at the Camp Number 3." We heard a terrible scream from a woman, followed by children wailing, "Mother, mother." And, as if to add to the horror, the bawling of geese joined the human wailing.

A farmyard was established in the camp to enrich the menus of the SS men, and the bawling of the geese covered the shrieks of the victims.

My helplessness at these crimes horrified me; Shlomo Leitman and Boris Cybulski were livid, "Sasha, let us escape, we are only 200 metres from the forest, we can cut the barbed wire with our axes and run," said Boris. "We must escape all together and soon: winter is near and snow is not our friend," he added.

On September 28, one week after I arrived at the camp, I knew everything about the hell of Sobibor. Camp Number 4 was on a hill: each section was surrounded with barbed wire and was mined. I was informed of the exact place occupied by the personnel, the guards and the arsenal.

Next day, the 600 prisoners, men and women were taken to the station to unload eight cars of bricks. Each of us was forced to run and fetch eight bricks; the one who failed was whipped twenty-five times. We finished our work in less than an hour and we returned to our commandos. The reason for the haste, a new convoy was just entering the station.

Our group of eighty men was finally led to Camp Number 4, I was working near Shlomo; another prisoner from Sheroka approached me and whispered, "We have decided to escape; there are only five SS officers, and we can wipe them out. The forest is near."

I replied, "Easier said than done, the five guards are not together. When you finish with one, the second shoots at us; and how shall we cross the minefields? Wait the time is near."

At night, Baruch (Leon Feldhendler) told me, "It is not the first time that we have planned to finish with Sobibor, but very few of us know how to use arms. Lead us, and we shall follow you." His intelligent face inspired trust and gave me courage. I asked him to form a group of the most reliable prisoners.

On October 7, I gave to Baruch (Feldhendler) my first instructions on how to dig a tunnel. "The carpenters' workshop is at the end of the camp, five metres from the barbed wire; the net of three rows of barbed wire occupies four metres to fifteen metres; let us add seven metres, the length of the barrack.

We shall start digging under the stove and the tunnel will be no more than thirty-five metres long and eighty centimetres deep, because of the danger of mines. We shall have at least twenty cubic metres of earth to hide, and shall leave that earth under the floorboards. The job must be done only at night."

We all agreed to start working: the digging of the tunnel would take us fifteen to twenty days. But the plan presented weak spots: between 11 p.m. and 5 a.m. six hundred persons had to pass in Indian file the thirty-five meters of the tunnel and run a good distance from the camp in order to avoid the posse of the SS.

I said, "I also have other ideas, meanwhile, let us prepare our first arms: seventy well whetted knives or razor blades." Barauch (Feldhendler) said that the Kapos were interested in our plans and could be very helpful, since they walked freely in the camp. I thought that their help was vital. "All right, I accept," I said.

October 8, 1943. A new transport arrived. Janek, the carpenters' supervisor, needed three prisoners to help him. Shlomo, another prisoner and I were chosen and sent to Camp Number 1. That same evening, Baruch (Feldhendler) brought Shlomo seventy well whetted knives.

October 9: Grisha, who was caught sitting while cleaning wood, got twenty-five lashes. It was a bad day, thirty of our people had been flogged for various transgressions and we were exhausted. In the evening Kali-Mali came to the barracks, out of breath.

He informed me that Grisha and seven of our men were ready to escape and asked us to join them. "Come with us, the site near the barbed wire is badly lit, we will kill the guard with an axe and then we will run to the forest." We went to find Grisha, and I explained to him that reprisals would be terrible even if his plan succeeded. I had to use threats before I persuaded him to plan only a collective escape.

October 10: I saw an SS officer with his arm in a sling. I was told that it was Greischutz back from his leave. He had been wounded in a Russian air raid. Later, Shlomo and I met the Kapo Brzecki who knew that we were preparing something. "Take me with you; together we shall accomplish more. I know the end awaits us all," he said, and he also asked us to include the Kapo Geniek. I answered, "Could you kill a Nazi?" He thought for a moment, and replied, "Yes, if it is necessary for our cause."

October 11: That morning, we heard screams followed by shots. We were locked up in the barracks and guards stood around us. The shooting lasted a long time and seemed to be coming from the Nordlager. We feared the prisoners had tried to escape before we were ready. Soon we learned the cause of the fusillade, a group of new prisoners already undressed, had revolted and had tried to run in the direction of the barbed wire.

The guards began to shoot and killed many of them instantly. The others were dragged to Camp Number 3. That day, the crematorium burned longer than usual. Huge flames rose up in the grey autumn sky and the camp was lit with strange colours. Helpless and distressed, we looked at the bodies of our brothers and sisters.

October 12: It was a terrible day: eighteen of our friends, many from Sheroka, were sick. Several SS men, under the direction of Frenzel, entered our barrack and asked the patients to follow them. Among them was a young Dutch prisoner with his wife, and the unfortunate man could hardly walk. The woman was running after the group screaming, "Murderers, I know where you are taking my husband. I can't live without him! Assassins, murderers." She died with the group.

Shlomo and I ordered a meeting for 9:00 p.m., at the carpenters' workshop. Baruch (Feldhendler), Shlomo, Janek, the tailors Joseph and Jacob, Moniek and others were present. We posted a sentry at the entrance. Moniek went to fetch Brzecki and, when both returned, I asked Brzecki again if he had thought over the consequences of his decision; if the plan failed, he would be the first to die.

He said, "I know it, but we must get rid of the SS officers and this should take one hour, if we could do it in less time, so much the better. For that purpose, we need efficient and determined men, since one moment's hesitation would be fatal, and I know some capable people, who can do the job."

At 3:00 p.m. Brzecki was to lead three of his men to Camp Number 2 under any pretext that he would find himself. Their task would consist of liquidating the four officers present. Baruch (Feldhendler) would lead the SS men to a place where the prisoners would be waiting, and would prevent anyone from leaving Camp Number 2 once the action had begun.

At exactly 4 o'clock, another team would cut the telephone wires from Camp Number 2 to the guards' quarters. The same team would hide those wires in such a way as to make it impossible to reconnect the telephone on the same day. At the same time, we were to start killing SS officers; they would be invited, one by one, into the workshops where two of our men would execute them. At 4:30 p.m. everything would be finished.

At the same time Brzecki and Geniek would assemble the prisoners for the usual evening roll call. In front would be the Soviet prisoners who were to take over the arsenal and the rest of us would cover them. Once the arsenal was open, armed men would head the group and kill the guards at the gate. If they resisted we would fight with the arms taken from the officers.

Near the workshops and the officers' villas was a mesh of barbed wire. There the ground was mined, but less dangerous. Stones were to be thrown in order to destroy the mines.

These were the details of the plan: I added that I had long discussions with Shlomo and I couldn't think of anything better. I asked everybody to think it over again, and a new meeting was planned for the next day, under the strictest secrecy.

Just before the revolt, an idea occurred to me and I wanted to check if it was right. Having observed the behaviour of the guards for a long time, I knew that every morning each of them got five bullets for his rifle. I also noticed that, with the changing of each guard, the bullets were handed over to the next guard. This meant that the guards who were not on duty had no bullets.

In order to check my findings, I asked Brzecki to find an excuse to send me to the guards' barracks. On October 13 at 10:00 a.m., the carpentry workshop got an order to send a man to the barracks in order to repair the doors. Janek sent me there and, while I was visiting the rooms, I was glad to see that my idea was correct.

October 14: On the night of October 13 we distributed knives and hatchets, as well as warm clothes. I was to remain in the carpentry workshop where, from the window, I could watch what was happening in Camp Number 3. In the next barrack, Shlomo and a team of twenty men were repairing our wooden beds.

According to our plan, at 4:00 and at 4:15 p.m., two SS men were to appear at the tailors' workshop. At the same time, two officers, Greischutz and Getzinger, were in another workshop. Frenzel was supervising the building of some cupboards.

Rosenfeld's job was to kill him. Friedrich Gaulstich would enter the carpentry workshop where Shlomo would be waiting. Other SS officers of Camp Number 2 were to be enticed into different workshops.

Each of us had his task: Shubayev, aged twenty-five, a railway engineer from Rostov, a good and simple buddy, would go to the tailors' workshop with Moniek. Cybulski, a thirty-five-year-old driver, a former truck driver from Donbass, and accompanied by Michael and Bunio. Guided by Brzecki, they were to go to Camp Number 2 to meet Baruch (Feldhendler).

At 2 p.m., SS Unterscharfuhrer Walter Ryba came to Brzecki; he had a machine gun, and that worried me. That morning Frenzel noticed that Janek was better dressed than usual, but Geniek reassured us. Brzecki had to go to Camp Number 4 with other prisoners in order to stack wood. The guard took his machine gun only because he was the sole supervisor.

Geniek was to lead the four men to Camp Number 2. At first he asked us to postpone it to the next day, but that was impossible. Although the details of our plan were known only to the committee and a small group, the other prisoners felt that something was going to happen and kept asking: "Well, when will it be?"

On the eve of October 14th, the older people said prayers; it was Yom Kippur, the Day of Atonement. Some inmates told them, "Better pray for Sasha to help you." They answered, "We are praying to God to help Sasha."

We had another reason for not postponing our plan: On October 14 Gomerski was on vacation. The Lagerfuhrer Frenzel was a bastard but, compared to Gomerski, he seemed a choirboy. "Tomorrow may be too late," I said to Geniek, "we have to do what we decided, and you must obey."

At 3:20 p.m. Geniek came to Cybulski's barrack with Shlomo and the two others. Two officers were killed by Wajspapier in the shoemakers' barrack while Jacob was giving them their boots. At 4:15 I heard that Cybulski, Michael and Baruch (Feldhendler) had accomplished their mission at Camp Number 2. At 4 p.m. I had met Luka, the Dutch girl and told her, "The officers will soon be dead, be ready to escape." As she trembled, I added, "What we are doing is the only way to survive, we have no right to give up living, we must avenge ourselves."

At 4.30 p.m., Brzecki returned from Camp Number 4 with the commando and Unterscharfuhrer Gaulstich arrived soon afterwards. Shlomo told him, "We have done the repairs in the barracks, now the workers do not know what to do." The SS man went in: Shlomo's hatchet awaited him.

Frenzel didn't come, and later we learned that SS officer Ryba had been killed in the garage. Now it was vital to leave; Brzecki whistled and prisoners were directed to Camp Number 1 in a disorderly way. This infuriated the guard, a Volksdeutsch from the Volga region; he was killed with an axe.

A new group coming from Camp Number 2 entered Camp Number 1 where prisoners were just learning what was happening. A Ukrainian guard began to shoot, a mighty "Hurrah" was heard. "Forward, forward," shouted the prisoners.

They were running towards the gate, shooting with rifles, cutting barbed wire with pliers. We crossed a minefield and many lost their lives. My group marched towards the quarter where the SS lived, and several of us were killed. Between the camp and the forest there was an immense clearing and here, too, many fell.

At last, we got to the forest, but Shlomo and Luka were missing. We walked all night in a column, one by one. I was up front, followed by Cybulski, while Arkady brought up the rear. We were all silent; from time to time, a light was visible in the sky.

After walking three kilometres we reached a canal that was five or six metres wide and quite deep. Suddenly we saw a group of men. Arkady went crawling off to investigate. He found Shubayev and many other friends. Together we built a bridge with tree trunks, and then I learned that Shlomo had been wounded while escaping. Unable to run, he asked to be put to death. Of course nobody listened to him and he stayed behind with other prisoners.

Our group numbered fifty-seven people. After walking another five kilometres, we heard the noise of a train. We were on the edge of a wood, an area of bushes in front of us. Dawn was approaching and we needed a safe place to hide. I knew the Nazis were after us and we thought that a group of trees near a railway wouldn't attract the attention of our enemy. We decided to remain there during the day, camouflaged by branches.

At dawn, it was raining. Arkady and Cybulski left to explore the terrain on one side, Shubayev and I on the other. We found an abandoned site near the forest. Cybulski and Arkady reached the railway line. Poles were working there, but without a guard. We hid and posted two sentries nearby; these sentries were to be changed every three hours. All day, planes were flying over our heads. We heard the voices of the Polish workers.

At night, we saw two men looking for something; we understood that they were fugitives who had returned from the direction of Bug. "Why haven't you crossed the river?" I asked. They told us that they had been near a village where they learned that soldiers were sent along the Bug River to check all points.

I asked if they had met Luka, and they assured me that they had seen her in the forest, leaving for Chelm with Polish Jews. We formed a new column, Cybulski and I leading, Arkady and Shubayev in the rear. After five kilometres we reached the forest, but we couldn't find enough food so we decided to split into small groups, each taking a different direction. My unit included, Shubayev, Cybulski, Arkady, Michael Itzkovich and Simon Mazurkewich.

We set off eastwards, guided by the stars. We walked at night, and hid during the day. Our objective was to cross the Bug River. We approached little villages to beg for food and to ask our way. We were often told, "Prisoners escaped from Sobibor where people are being burned, they are looking for fugitives."

We reached the village of Stawki, a kilometre and a half from the Bug River. We had spent the day in the forest and, at sunset, three of us entered a hut. A thirty-year-old peasant was cutting and gathering tobacco leaves, an old man was near a stove. In a corner, a baby's cradle was hanging from the ceiling, and a young woman was rocking it. "Good evening, may we come in?"

"Come in, come in," answered the young man. "Draw the curtains," said Cybulski. We sat down, everyone was quiet. "Could you tell us where to cross the Bug?" asked Shubayev. "I don't know," said the young man. "You must know, you have been living here long enough. We know that there are places where the water is low, and the crossing easy," I said. "If you are so sure, then go. We know nothing, and we have no right to go near rivers."

We talked a little longer, and told them that we were escaped war prisoners and wished to return home. At last the young man said, "I shall show you the direction, but I won't go to the river. Find it yourselves, be careful, it is guarded everywhere since prisoners escaped from a camp where soap is made with human fat. The fugitives are being chased everywhere, even underground. If you are lucky, you will get to the other side. I wish you luck."

"Let's go before the moon rises." "Wait," said the young woman, "take some bread for the way." We thanked them and the old man blessed us with the sign of the cross. The same night, October 19 we crossed the Bug. On the 22nd, eight days after the uprising, we met a unit of partisans of the Voroshilov detachment.

A new chapter began.

Source: Available online at http://www.holocaustresearchproject.org/revolt/pechersky.html. Used by permission of the Holocaust Education and Archive Research Team.

Commentary

Alexander "Sasha" Pechersky was a Jewish soldier in the Soviet army and, with Leon Feldhendler, the leader of the Sobibor Revolt on October 14, 1943. This was arguably the most successful uprising and mass escape of Jews from a Nazi death camp during the Holocaust.

On September 22, 1943, Pechersky had been deported to Sobibor from Minsk, along with nearly 2,000 Jewish civilians, most of whom were murdered on arrival. Pechersky and about 80 others were selected to live and work as slave labor.

The revolt at Sobibor took place after Pechersky had studied the camp routine and layout carefully, and then planned out a strategy. It was not going to be easy to achieve a mass breakout, however. Until the arrival of Pechersky and his men, most of the inmates had been tailors, teachers, and civilians from domestic walks of life, with no military or tactical training. Yet when the revolt took place it was so successful that the camp had to close down after the breakout.

Whereas prior to Pechersky's arrival the prisoners had tried hard to think of ways to escape, it only took 22 days from the time of Pechersky's arrival until the revolt.

Afterward, Pechersky gave his account of what happened on a number of occasions. The document here is a description of the events leading up to revolt and the event itself, which Pechersky outlines in some detail. He is keen to include many of those who worked to bring about the revolt, and by doing so shows that it was a broad-based endeavor that involved more than just the Soviet soldiers.

21. Hirsh Glik, "The Partisan Song" (1943)

The iconic anthem of anti-Nazi resistance, "Zog Nit Keynmol" ("Never Say"), often simply referred to as "The Partisan Song," was penned in Yiddish by Hirsh Glik, a poet from Vilna. Set to a marching beat by Soviet composers Dmitry and Daniel Pokrass, it is used today at most Holocaust commemorations around the world and is a defiant statement of challenge and endurance in the face of oppression.

Never say that you are walking the final road,
Though leaden skies obscure blue days;
The hour we have been longing for will still come,
Our steps will drum—we are here!
From green palm-land to distant land of snow,
We arrive with our pain, with our sorrow,
And where a spurt of our blood has fallen,
There will sprout our strength, our courage.
The morning sun will tinge our today with gold,
And yesterday will vanish with the enemy,
But if the sun and the dawn are delayed—
Like a watchword this song will go from generation to generation.
This song is written with blood and not with lead,
It's not a song about a bird that is free,
A people, between falling walls,
Sang this song with pistols in their hands.
So never say that you are walking the final road
Though leaden skies obscure blue days.
The hour we have been longing for will still come—
Our steps will drum—we are here!

Source: U.S. Holocaust Memorial Museum in Washington, D.C., *Music of the Holocaust*. Available online at http://www.ushmm.org/information/exhibitions/online-features/collections-highlights/music-of-the-holocaust-highlights-from-the-collection/music-of-the-holocaust/never-say-that-you-have-reached-the-final-road. Used by permission.

Commentary

Hirsch Glik was a Jewish poet and partisan born in 1922 in Vilna. After the German invasion of the Soviet Union in 1941 he was imprisoned in the Vilna ghetto, where he became a member of the Fareynikte Partizaner Organizatsye (United Partisan Organization, or FPO).

In 1943 he wrote his most famous work, a Yiddish resistance march entitled "*Zog Nit Keynmol, az du geyst dem letstn veg*," also referred to as the "*Partizaner Lid*," or "Partisan Song." Glik's lyrics were set to music from a prewar Soviet song written by Dmitri and Daniel Pokrass, and in practically no time at all it was adopted by Jewish partisan groups throughout Eastern Europe, where it became a symbol of their resistance efforts against the Nazis. After the war, it became one of the major anthems of Holocaust survivors, and today it is sung in memorial services around the world.

The title of the song, "Never Say," derives from the first line, "Never say that you are walking the final road"—the idea being an upbeat one in which only positive thoughts can prevail despite all that is happening around.

Glik was inspired to write the song after he received news, in Vilna, about the uprising in the Warsaw Ghetto during April–May 1943. When the Vilna ghetto was being liquidated in October 1943 and the ghetto's own short-lived uprising collapsed, he managed to flee but was soon captured and deported, along with most of the other Vilna ghetto residents, to a concentration camp in Estonia. With the advance of the Soviet army in July 1944, Glik escaped but was never seen again. It is presumed that he was killed by the Germans in August 1944.

22. Ruth Andreas-Friedrich, Diary (March 31, 1945)

Ruth Andreas-Friedrich, a non-Jewish opponent of the Nazis, kept a diary throughout the war years. Highly secret, it would probably have led to her death if found. In this short entry, written as the Soviets were closing in on Berlin, she confides the hope that Nazi Germany will lose the war and that the Allies will occupy her city.

The final victory: when the Allies march through the Brandenburg Gate. And once again I think, as so often: what an absurdity, for a German to pray for the enemies' victory! A strange patriotism that can wish for nothing better than the conquering of one's own country!

Source: German Resistance Memorial Center, Berlin, *Resistance against National Socialism* (2014), p. 18. Used by permission.

Commentary

Ruth Andreas-Friedrich was a citizen of Berlin throughout the Nazi period, and an active contributor to an informal resistance group.

Throughout much of this time she kept a detailed diary, published in English in 1947 as *Berlin Underground, 1938–1945*. The diary offered a vivid portrait, not only of life in Berlin, but also of the attempts Andreas-Friedrich made to ease the lot of the Jews. The diary also gave her observations of daily life under the Nazis, in which she showed the stifling nature of everyday existence and how difficult it was to offer any sort of substitutes.

In this short extract, we see a reflection of something no patriot should ever have to anticipate: the defeat—nay, the conquest—of her own country in war. After so many years of Nazi rule, however, coupled with a war destructive of human lives, ambitions, and hopes, and in which every civil right had been removed completely, Andreas-Friedrich found little other alternative. Wishing for Nazi Germany's defeat, she could contemplate a new future; without that wish, there could be no possibility of things ever getting better, and life would be nothing but an unfillable void.

23. Kurt Gerstein, Report (May 4, 1945)

Kurt Gerstein was an SS officer with responsibility for the delivery of large quantities of Zyklon B to Auschwitz and other camps, who witnessed gassings of Jews at Bełżec and Treblinka. By April 1945, as defeat loomed for the Third Reich, he surrendered to the Allies. Transferred to Paris, he wrote his final account, now known as the Gerstein Report, in which he made a full disclosure of what he had witnessed as an SS officer. The following document is his report.

On 10 March 1941 I joined the SS. I received my basic training in Hamburg-Langenhorn, in Arnhem (Holland), and in Oranienburg. In Holland I immediately contacted the Dutch resistance movement (graduate engineer Ubbink, Doesburg).

Because of my dual studies I was soon taken over by the technical-medical service and allotted to the SS-Führungshauptamt, Amtsgruppe D, Sanitätswesen der Waffen-SS Abteilung Hygiene. I completed the training in a course together with 40 physicians. At the Hygienedienst I could determine my activities for myself. I constructed mobile and stationary disinfection facilities for the troops, for prisoner-of-war camps, and concentration camps. With this I had great success and was from then on undeservedly considered as a kind of technical genius. Indeed it turned out well at least to some extent, by getting the horrible epidemic typhus wave in 1941 in the camps under control. Because of my successes I soon became Leutnant and then Oberleutnant. . . .

In January 1942 I became head of the department of health engineering and in addition in a double function for the same sector I was taken over by the Reichsarzt

SS und Polizei. In this function I took over the whole technical disinfection service including disinfection with highly toxic gases.

In this capacity I was visited on 8 June 1942 by the until then unknown to me SS-Sturmführer Günther from Reichssicherheitshauptamt Berlin W, Kurfürstenstraße. Günther arrived in civil clothing. He gave me the order to immediately obtain 100 kg prussic acid for a very secret Reichs order, and to drive with it by car to an undisclosed location which would be only known by the driver. Then some weeks later we drove to Prague. I understood little of the nature of the order but accepted it because here was an accidental opportunity to do something which I had longed for for a long time—to be able to view inside these objects.

In addition I was recognized as such an authority and considered so competent as an expert on prussic acid, that in every case it would have been very easy for me to declare on some pretext that the prussic acid was unsuitable—because of decomposition or the like—in order to prevent its use for the real killing purpose. Together with us traveled—merely by chance— Professor Dr. med. Pfannenstiel, SS-Obersturmbannführer, full Professor of Hygienics at the University of Marburg/Lahn.

Then we drove by car to Lublin where the SS-Gruppenführer Globocnik awaited us. In the factory in Collin I had intentionally intimated that the acid was destined for the killing of human beings. A man appeared in the afternoon who was very interested in the vehicle and, after being noticed, promptly fled at a breakneck tempo. Globocnik said: "This whole affair is one of the most secret things of all in this time, one can say the most secret of all. Whoever talks about it will be shot on the spot. Only yesterday two blabbers have been shot." Then he explained to us:

"Actually"—that was on 17 August 1942—"we are running three facilities," namely:

- Belzec, at the country road and railway line Lublin-Lemberg, at the demarcation line with Russia. Maximum output 15,000 persons daily.
- Treblinka, 120 km northeast of Warsaw. Maximum output 25,000 persons daily.
- Sobibor, also in Poland, I don't know exactly where. 20,000 persons maximum output daily.
- Then in preparation—Majdanek near Lublin.

Belzec, Treblinka, and Majdanek I have visited personally in detail, together with the leader of these facilities, Polizeihauptmann Wirth.

Globocnik consulted me alone and said: "It is your task in particular to disinfect the extensive amounts of textiles. The whole Spinnstoffsammlung [= Collection of spun material in Germany] has only been gathered in order to explain the origin of the clothing material for the Ostarbeiter [eastern workers] etc, and to present it as an offering of the German nation. In reality the yield of our facilities is 10–20 times larger than that of the whole Spinnstoffsammlung."

Thereafter I discussed with the most efficient companies the possibility of disinfecting such amounts of textiles—it consisted of an accumulated stock of approximately 40 million kgs = 60 complete freight trains—in the existing laundries and disinfection facilities. However it was absolutely impossible to place such huge orders. I used all these negotiations to make known in a skillful way or at least to intimate, the fact of the killing of the Jews. In the end it was sufficient for Globocnik that everything was sprinkled with a bit of Detenolin so that it at least smelled of disinfection. That was then carried out.

"Your other and far more important task is the changeover of our gas chambers which actually work with diesel exhaust fumes into a better and quicker system. I think especially of prussic acid. The day before yesterday the Führer and Himmler were here. On their order I have to personally take you there, I am not to issue written certificates and admittance cards to anybody!"

Then Pfannenstiel asked: "What did the Führer say?" Glob: "Quicker, carry out the whole action quicker." Pfannenstiel's attendant, Ministerialrat Dr. Herbert Lindner, then asked: "Mr. Globocnik, do you think it is good and proper to bury all the corpses instead of cremating them? A generation could come after us which doesn't understand all this!"

Then Globocnik said: "Gentlemen, if ever a generation will come after us which is so weak and soft-hearted that it doesn't understand our task, then indeed the whole of National Socialism has been in vain. To the contrary, in my opinion one should bury bronze plates on which it is recorded that we have had the courage to carry out this great and so necessary work."

The Führer: "Good, Globocnik, this is indeed also my opinion!" Later the alternative option was accepted. Then the corpses were cremated on large roasts, improvised from rails, with the aid of petrol and diesel oil.

The next day we drove to Belzec. A small special station had been created for this purpose at a hill, hard north of the road Lublin-Lemberg, in the left angle of the demarcation line. South of the road some houses with the inscription "Sonderkommando Belzec der Waffen-SS." Because the actual chief of the whole killing facilities, Polizeihauptmann Wirth, was not yet there, Globocnik introduced me to SS-Hauptsturmführer Obermeyer (from Pirmasens). That afternoon he let me see only that which he simply had to show me. That day I didn't see any corpses, just the smell of the whole region was stinking to high heaven in a hot August, and millions of flies were everywhere.

Near to the small double-track station was a large barrack, the so-called "cloakroom," with a large counter for valuables. Then followed the barber's room with approximately 100 chairs, the barber room. Then an alley in the open air, below birches, fenced in to the right and left by double barbed wire with inscriptions: "To the inhalation- and bath rooms!" In front of us a sort of bath house with geraniums, then a small staircase, and then to the right and left 3 rooms each, 5 x 5 meters, 1.90 meters high, with wooden doors like garages. At the back wall, not quite visible in the dark, larger wooden ramp doors. On the roof as a "clever, little joke" the Star of David. In front of the building an inscription: Hackenholt-Foundation. More I couldn't see that afternoon.

The next morning, shortly before 7 a.m. someone announced to me: "In ten minutes the first transport will come!" In fact the first train arrived after some minutes, from the direction of Lemberg. 45 wagons with 6,700 people of whom 1,450 were already dead on arrival. Behind the barred hatches children as well as men and women looked out, terribly pale and nervous, their eyes full of the fear of death. The train comes in: 200 Ukrainians fling open the doors and whip the people out of the wagons with their leather whips.

A large loudspeaker gives the further orders: "Undress completely, also remove artificial limbs, spectacles etc." Handing over valuables at the counter, without receiving a voucher or a receipt. The shoes carefully bound together (because of the Spinnstoffsammlung), because on the almost 25 metre high heap nobody would have been able to find the matching shoes again. Then the women and girls to the barber who, with two, three scissor strokes is cutting off all hair and collecting it in potato sacks. "That is for special purposes in the submarines, for seals or the like!" the SS-Unterscharführer who is on duty there says to me.

Then the procession starts moving. In front a very lovely young girl; so all of them go along the alley, all naked, men, women, children, without artificial limbs. I myself stand together with Hauptmann Wirth on top of the ramp between the gas chambers. Mothers with babies at their breast, they come onward, hesitate, enter the death chambers! At the corner a strong SS man stands who, with a voice like a pastor, says to the poor people: "There is not the least chance that something will happen to you! You must only take a deep breath in the chamber, that widens the lungs; this inhalation is necessary because of the illnesses and epidemics." On the question of what would happen to them he answered: "Yes, of course, the men have to work, building houses and roads but the women don't need to work. Only if they wish they can help in housekeeping or in the kitchen."

For some of these poor people this gave a little glimmer of hope, enough to go the few steps to the chambers without resistance. The majority are aware, the smell tells them of their fate! So they climb the small staircase, and then they see everything. Mothers with little children at the breast, little naked children, adults, men, women, all naked—they hesitate but they enter the death chambers, pushed forward by those behind them or driven by the leather whips of the SS.

The majority without saying a word. A Jewess of about 40 years of age, with flaming eyes, calls down vengeance on the head of the murderers for the blood which is shed here. She gets 5 or 6 slashes with the riding crop into her face from Hauptmann Wirth personally, then she also disappears into the chamber. Many people pray. I pray with them, I press myself in a corner and shout loudly to my and their God. How gladly I would have entered the chamber together with them, how gladly I would have died the same death as them. Then they would have found a uniformed SS man in their chambers—the case would have been understood and treated as an accident, one man quietly missing. Still I am not allowed to do this. First I must tell what I am experiencing here!

The chambers fill. "Pack well!"—Hauptmann Wirth has ordered. The people stand on each other's feet. 700–800 on 25 square meters, in 45 cubic meters! The SS physically squeezes them together, as far as is possible.

The doors close. At the same time the others are waiting outside in the open air, naked. Someone tells me: "The same in winter!" "Yes, but they could catch their death of cold," I say. "Yes, exactly what they are here for!" says an SS man to me in his Low German. Now I finally understand why the whole installation is called the Hackenholt-Foundation. Hackenholt is the driver of the diesel engine, a little technician, also the builder of the facility.

The people are brought to death with the diesel exhaust fumes. But the diesel doesn't work! Hauptmann Wirth comes. One can see that he feels embarrassed that that happens just today, when I am here. That's right, I see everything! And I wait. My stop watch has honestly registered everything. 50 minutes, 70 minutes—the diesel doesn't start! The people are waiting in their gas chambers. In vain! One can hear them crying, sobbing . . . Hauptmann Wirth hits the Ukrainian who is helping Unterscharführer Hackenholt 12, 13 times in the face.

After two hours and 49 minutes—the stop watch has registered everything well—the diesel starts. Until this moment the people live in these 4 chambers, four times 750 people in 4 times 45 cubic meters! Again 25 minutes pass. Right, many are dead now. One can see that through the small window in which the electric light illuminates the chambers for a moment. After 28 minutes only a few are still alive. Finally, after 32 minutes, everyone is dead!

From the other side men from the work command open the wooden doors. They have been promised—even Jews—freedom, and some one-thousandth of all valuables found, for their terrible service. Like basalt pillars the dead stand inside, pressed together in the chambers. In any event there was no space to fall down or even bend forward. Even in death one can still tell the families. They still hold hands, tensed in death, so that one can barely tear them apart in order to empty the chamber for the next batch. The corpses are thrown out, wet from sweat and urine, soiled by excrement, menstrual blood on their legs.

Children's corpses fly through the air. There is no time. The riding crops of the Ukrainians lash down on the work commands. Two dozen dentists open mouths with hooks and look for gold. Gold to the left, without gold to the right. Other dentists break gold teeth and crowns out of jaws with pliers and hammers.

Among all this Hauptmann Wirth is running around. He is in his element. Some workers search the genitals and anus of the corpses for gold, diamonds, and valuables. Wirth calls me to him: "Lift this can full of gold teeth, that is only from yesterday and the day before yesterday!" In an incredibly vulgar and incorrect diction he said to me: "You won't believe what we find in gold and diamonds every day"—he pronounced it (in German Brillanten) with two L—"and in dollars. But see for yourself!" And now he led me to a jeweller who managed all these treasures, and let me see all this. Then someone showed me a former head of the Kaufhaus des Westens in Berlin, and a violinist: "That was a Hauptmann of the Austrian Army, knight of the Iron Cross 1st class who is now camp elder of the Jewish work command!"

The naked corpses were carried on wooden stretchers to pits only a few meters away, measuring 100 x 20 x 12 meters. After a few days the corpses welled up and a short time later they collapsed, so that one could throw a new layer of bodies upon them. Then ten centimeters of sand were spread over the pit, so that a few heads and arms still rose from it here and there. At such a place I saw Jews climbing over the corpses and working. One told me that by mistake those who arrived dead had not been stripped. Of course this has to be done later because of the Spinnstoffsammlung and valuables which otherwise they would take with them into the grave.

Neither in Belzec nor in Treblinka was any trouble taken over registering or counting the dead. The numbers were only estimates of a wagon's content. . . . Hauptmann Wirth asked me not to propose changes in Berlin re his facilities, and to let it remain as it is, being well established and well-tried. I supervised the burial of the prussic acid because it allegedly had decomposed.

The next day—19 August 1942—we drove in the car of Hauptmann Wirth to Treblinka, 120 km north northeast of Warsaw. The equipment was nearly the same as, but much larger than in Belzec. Eight gas chambers and real mountains of suitcases, textiles, and clothes. In our honour a banquet was given in old German style in the communal room. The meal was simple but everything was available in sufficient quantity. Himmler himself had ordered that the men of these commandos received as much meat, butter and other things, especially alcohol, as they wanted.

Then we drove in the car to Warsaw. I met the secretary of the Swedish legation in Berlin, Baron von Otter in the train when I tried in vain to get a bed in a sleeping car. Still under the immediate impression of the terrible events, I told him everything with the entreaty to inform his government and the Allies of all of this immediately because each day's delay must cost the lives of further thousands and tens of thousands.

He asked me for a reference, as to which I specified Generalsuperintendent Dr. Otto Dibelius, Berlin, Brüderweg 2, Lichterfelde-West, an intimate friend of the pastor Martin Niemöller and member of the church resistance movement against Nazism. I met Mr. von Otter twice again in the Swedish legation. Meanwhile he had reported to Stockholm and informed me that this report has had considerable influence on Swedish-German relations. At the same time I tried to report to the Papal Nuncio in Berlin. There I was asked if I am a soldier. Then any further conversation with me was refused and I was asked to leave the embassy of His Holiness. While leaving the embassy, I was shadowed by a policeman on a bicycle who shortly passed me, got off, and then absolutely incomprehensibly, let me go.

Then I reported all this to hundreds of personages, among others the company lawyer of the Catholic bishop of Berlin, Dr. Winter, with the special entreaty to forward it to the Holy See. I must also add that SS-Sturmbannführer Günther from the Reichssicherheitshauptamt—I think he is the son of the Race-Günther—again demanded from me very large amounts of prussic acid in early 1944 for a very sinister purpose. On the Kurfürsten-Street in Berlin he showed me a shed in which he intended to store the prussic acid. I consequently explained to him that I cannot take sole responsibility. It was approximately several wagon loads, enough to kill millions of people. He told me that he himself doesn't know whether the poison would still be needed; when, for whom, in which way etc. But it has to be permanently kept available.

Later I often thought about the words of Goebbels. I can believe that they wanted to kill a majority of the German nation, surely including the clergy or the unpopular officers. It should happen in a kind of reading rooms or club rooms, so far as I gathered from the questions re the technical realization that Günther asked me. It could also be that he intended to kill the foreign workers or prisoners of war—I don't know. In every case I managed to ensure that the prussic acid disappeared for some purpose of disinfection after arrival in the two concentration camps Oranienburg and Auschwitz.

That was somewhat dangerous for me but I could have easily said that the poison had already been in a dangerous condition of decomposition. I am sure that Günther tried to get the poison in order to probably kill millions of persons. It was sufficient for approximately 8 million people, 8,500 kgs. I have authorized invoices for 2,175 kgs. I always allowed the invoices to be authorised in my name, allegedly for the sake of discretion, but in truth because of being free to dispose of the poison and being able to allow it to disappear. Above all I avoided presentation of invoices again and again, delaying payment and putting off companies until later.

As for the rest I avoided appearing in concentration camps too often because it was sometimes usual to hang people or to carry out executions in honor of the visitors.

All my statements are true, word-for-word. I am fully aware of the extraordinary tragedy of my record before God and the whole of mankind, and take it on my oath that nothing of all this that I have registered has been made-up or invented but everything is exactly the truth.

Kurt Gerstein

> **Source:** U.S. National Archives, Judge Advocate General Law Library, 1944–1949 (Entry 135), RG 153, Box 91, 100-1125.

Commentary

Kurt Gerstein was a deeply devoted Christian from Westphalia, and a member of the Waffen-SS Hygiene Institute. He had served two periods of detention for defying Nazi authority on the grounds of his Christian principles and was dismissed from membership in the Nazi party before being reinstated.

In early 1941 he joined the SS and rose to become head of Technical Disinfection Services. On August 17, 1942, he went to Bełżec death camp, where he witnessed the gassing of up to 3,000 Jews; the next day he went to Treblinka and saw what was happening there.

On April 22, 1945, unable any longer to continue in the simultaneous roles of unwilling mass murderer and witness, he defected to the Allies, making his way through to French lines in Reutlingen. He was well received, and given the opportunity to write a full report of what he had done and seen. On July 25, 1945, while still in French custody, he was found dead in his cell, an alleged suicide.

In his report, he writes that he was moved the join the SS in early 1941, in order "to see things from the inside." He surely did so. After witnessing the gassing at Bełżec, he was told by SS major Christian Wirths, the commandant: "There are not ten people alive, who have seen or will see as much as you." Gerstein's report became perhaps the most horrifying eyewitness account of the Holocaust. In order to alert the world he then told as many people as possible what he had seen; with the writing of the report, a permanent record was created, much of it unscientific and exaggerated, but basically correct as verified by other Nazis after the war.

24. Statement of Support, Siegbert Lewin, Regarding Otto Weidt (1946)

The Otto Weidt brush-making factory in Berlin-Mitte was a tiny haven in which blind and deaf-mute Jews were concealed safely during World War II. After the war, several of those whose lives had been safeguarded by Weidt testified on his behalf. In this document one of his blind Jewish workers, Siegbert Lewin, offers a statement in which he outlines just how far Weidt's workshop helped protect the Jews employed there, in a remarkable example of anti-Nazi resistance and affirmation of life.

I, the undersigned, the brush-maker Siegbert Lewin, Berlin-Köpenick, Kinzeallee 12, have worked from 1941 to the present day as foreman and brush maker in the firm of Mr. Otto Weidt, Otto Weidt's Workshop for the Blind, Berlin C.2, Rosenthalerstr. 39. I am Jewish, but have a mixed marriage and was consequently not affected in the same way by the intense persecution that my fellow Jews had to suffer as "full Jews."

I can testify that my boss and his wife were probably the only two people in Berlin who took on the task of helping and caring for people of my faith to such an extent. Up to 60 or 65 people worked in our workshop. In the worst period, that is, from the beginning of 1942 to the end of 1943, half of them were almost continually in danger, and during police searches my boss always hid them in a special room in the workshop. These house searches occurred two or three times a week. Mr. and Mrs. Weidt not only looked after Jews living in hiding, they also packed up countless parcels every week and sent them to different concentration camps all over the place. Whether food, textiles, shoes or other useful items, time and again it was always the Weidts who collected things and gave help.

Almost every week Mr. Weidt sent certain persons to towns outside Berlin including Freienwalde, Angermünde, and Stettin, to buy up vegetables and potatoes that were then distributed to the victims of persecution entirely cost-free. I'm proud to have worked in this workshop. It gave me the chance to make a modest contribution toward helping fellow members of my faith. For months on end, big buckets of syrup were purchased and the workers in the workshop were always given equal portions for free.

As far as I know, there was no other firm in Berlin that operated in the same way as this firm, where I am still working to this day.

The above statement has been read out to me because I am blind myself, and was transcribed by a member of staff. As well as myself, two comrades who have also been working in the firm from 1941 up until now will co-sign this statement, and it is an immense pleasure for us to be able to do this for our boss.

Siegbert Lewin

The above statement is co-signed by:

Martin Jacobson
Simon Weiss

Source: BLHA, Rep. 12C Berlin II, Nr. 19106. Used by permission.

Commentary

Siegbert Lewin was born in 1902. He was blind, and after moving to Berlin worked as a brush maker at Otto Weidt's workshop at Rosenthalerstrasse 39. Although Jewish, he was spared from deportation because his wife, Lidia Walther, came from a Protestant family.

Weidt's workshop protected his Jewish workers from deportation. The small brush- and broom-making factory had been established in 1936, and in 1940 he applied for and was assigned a workforce from the Jewish Home for the Blind. Practically all his employees were blind, deaf, or mute—and Jewish.

The factory was considered important for the war effort, with one of his bigger clients being the Wehrmacht. Having it classified as "vital" enabled Weidt to continue in business with the workforce at his disposal. Up to 30 Jews were thus employed at any one time during the years between 1941 and 1943, together with eight sighted Jews employed as office workers.

In the summer of 1946 Otto Weidt made an application to be recognized as a "victim of fascism" given his efforts on behalf of Jews during World War II. Siegbert Lewin, in support of Weidt, made a sworn statement describing how Weidt had helped protect him and the other blind Jewish workers in the factory, noting that when the Nazis came to conduct house searches "two or three times a week," Otto and Else Weidt would not only look after Jews in hiding, but also collect "countless parcels" and send them "to different concentration camps all over the place."

Lewin's statement on behalf of Weidt was countersigned by two other blind workers in the workshop, Martin Jacobson and Simon Weiss.

Chronology

The items in this chronology have been tailored toward an emphasis on resistance during the Holocaust, though inevitably there have been some general dates that have had to be included in order to enhance historical context.

1933
January 30: Adolf Hitler is appointed chancellor of Germany
February 27–28: Reichstag fire; arrests of political opponents of the Nazis begin almost immediately
March 20: Dachau concentration camp is established
April 1: Jewish businesses are boycotted across Germany
April 4: **Robert Weltsch** writes an article in the *Jüdische Rundschau* entitled "Wear It with Pride, the Yellow Badge"
April 11: Nazis issue a decree defining who is a non-Aryan
May 10: Books written by Jews and "undesirables" are publicly burned

1934
June 30: *Sturmabteilung* (SA) leadership is purged during the "Night of the Long Knives"
August 2: German president Paul von Hindenburg dies; Hitler declares the office of president abolished and names himself Führer

1935
September 15: The Nuremberg Laws on Race are announced
December 31: Jews holding civil service positions in Germany are dismissed

1936
February 4: David Frankfurter, a young Jewish student, assassinates Wilhelm Gustloff, leader of the Nazi party in Switzerland
March 21: Papal encyclical *Mit Brennender Sorge* issued by Pope Pius XI
May 8: Revised version of memorandum on Jewish situation in Germany presented by **Elisabeth Schmitz** to the Third Confessing Synod; fails to gain any support

June 13: **August Landmesser** protests Nazi regime by refusing to give Nazi salute in the presence of Hitler
August 1: Summer Olympic Games begin in Berlin

1937
January 26: A new law is passed prohibiting Jews from working in any office
July 19: Buchenwald concentration camp is established

1938
March 12: The *Anschluss* (Union) of Austria with Germany; all German antisemitic decrees are immediately applied in Austria
July 6–14: International conference on refugees held at Evian, France; no definite action follows to alleviate the situation of Jews
August 1: Nazi Office of Jewish Emigration established to speed up the pace of Jewish emigration from Germany
August 8: Mauthausen concentration camp established in Austria
August 11: Nazis destroy the Nuremberg synagogue
August 17: Nazis require Jewish women to add "Sarah" and men to add "Israel" to their names on all legal documents
August 19: Swiss government refuses entry to Austrian Jews seeking sanctuary; from this point on, border guard **Paul Grüninger** disobeys regulation, saving the lives of thousands
September 27: German Jews banned from practicing law
September 29–30: Munich Conference: Britain and France surrender the Sudetenland of Czechoslovakia to Germany by negotiation
October 5: Passports belonging to German Jews are marked with the letter "J" to indicate their identity
November 7: Ernst vom Rath, third secretary in the German embassy in Paris, is shot and mortally wounded by Herschel Grynszpan; vom Rath dies on November 9, precipitating *Kristallnacht*
November 9–10: *Kristallnacht* pogrom occurs in Germany and Austria. Nazi figures give 91 Jews killed, and up to 10,000 are arrested; 267 synagogues are destroyed; figures are likely much higher
November 16: Jewish children are forbidden from attending German schools

1939
March 15: Germany invades Czechoslovakia
August 23: The Nazi-Soviet Non-Aggression Pact is signed
September 1: Germany invades Poland
September 3: France and Britain declare war against Germany
September 17: Soviet Union invades Poland

September 21: Reinhard Heydrich orders Einsatzgruppen commanders to establish ghettos in German-occupied Poland
September 27: Warsaw surrenders; Jewish Councils are established in Poland
November 23: Yellow stars required to be worn by Polish Jews over age 10
November 28: First ghetto in Poland is established in Piotrków

1940

February 8: Łódź ghetto is established
April 9: Denmark and Norway invaded by Germany
April 9: Himmler issues a directive to establish a concentration camp at Auschwitz
April 30: The Łódź ghetto is sealed off from the outside world
May 10: France, the Netherlands, Belgium, and Luxembourg are invaded by Germany
May 20: Auschwitz concentration camp established for Polish political prisoners
June 4: Neuengamme concentration camp opens
June 10: Italy declares war on Britain and France
June 15: Soviet Union occupies Latvia, Lithuania, and Estonia
June 22: France surrenders; Philippe Pétain leads collaborationist government at Vichy
July: **Chiune Sugihara** of the Japanese embassy is permitted to extend his stay in Lithuania; during this time he issues more than 2,000 travel visas to Jewish refugees
July 17: The first anti-Jewish measures are taken in Vichy France
July 22: First "Curaçao visa" issued by **Jan Zwartendijk** in Kovno, Lithuania
August 17: The Jewish resistance group Fortress Juive is organized in France; it later becomes Armée Juive
September 27: Tripartite (Axis) Pact signed by Germany, Italy, and Japan
October 3: Vichy France passes its own version of the Nuremberg Laws
October 7: Nazis invade Romania
October 16: Germans officially establish the Warsaw Ghetto
November: **Emanuel Ringelblum** establishes the Oneg Shabbat Archive in the Warsaw Ghetto
November 15–16: Warsaw Ghetto is sealed
November 20–24: Hungary, Romania, and Slovakia join the Axis

1941

January 2: Attempted coup in Romania by Iron Guard against government of Marshal Ion Antonescu
January 21–26: Romanian Iron Guard annihilates hundreds of Jews
February 9: Dutch Nazis riot against Amsterdam Jews

February 21: Some 398 Jewish men are taken from Amsterdam and sent to Buchenwald
February 25: An anti-Nazi strike is held in Amsterdam protesting deportations of Jews, led by **Willem Kraan** and Piet Nak
March 1: Construction of Birkenau begins
April 6: Nazis invade Yugoslavia and Greece
April 21: Natzweiler-Struthof concentration camp opens in France
May 14: More than 13,000 Jews, including 4,000 Jewish children, are rounded up in Paris at the Vel d'Hiv
June 22: Operation Barbarossa—Germany invades Soviet Union
June 27: Białystok occupied by Nazis; Białystok ghetto established
July 2: Ukrainian nationalists murder thousands in Lvov
July 17: Einsatzgruppen ordered to execute captured communists and Jews during Soviet campaign
July 20: Minsk ghetto established
July 31: Adolf Eichmann appointed to prepare the "Final Solution"
September: **Varian Fry** deported back to the United States after aiding the rescue of nearly 4,000 Jews and others
September 6: The Vilna ghetto is established
September 19: Jews in Germany are ordered to wear yellow armbands bearing the Star of David
October 7: Birkenau is established as the primary mass murder site of Auschwitz
November 24: Terezín (Theresienstadt) ghetto/concentration camp established
December 7: Japan attacks Pearl Harbor, drawing the United States into World War II
December 8: Chełmno extermination camp becomes fully operational
December 11: Germany and Italy declare war on the United States
December 31: **Abba Kovner** addresses the resistance in Vilna and makes the statement "We will not be led like sheep to the slaughter!"

1942

January 10: Armée Juive (Jewish Army) created in France
January 20: Wannsee Conference takes place in Berlin
March 1: Extermination by gas begins at Sobibor
March 17: Mass killings begin at Bełżec extermination camp
May: In France, a new resistance organization, the Mouvement de Jeunesse Sioniste (Zionist Youth Movement) is created
May 18: **Herbert Baum**'s group of resisters in Berlin sets fire to "The Soviet Paradise" exhibition; all are caught and executed
May 21: **Sven Norrman** smuggles a consignment of documents and negatives to Sweden with full particulars of the alienation of 700,000 Polish Jews at the hands of the Nazis

June: First anti-Nazi resistance pamphlet published by the White Rose group of **Hans and Sophie Scholl**

June: Jewish partisan units established in the forests of Belorussia and the Baltic States

June 1: Jews in France, Holland, Belgium, Croatia, Slovakia, and Romania ordered to wear yellow stars

June 1: Treblinka extermination camp begins operation

June 29–30: Following acts of armed resistance by Jewish partisans in the ghetto of Slonim, the Nazis set the ghetto on fire; they spend the next two weeks murdering 7,000–10,000 Jews

July 14: Mass deportation of Dutch and Belgian Jews to Auschwitz begins

July 16: More than 4,000 children are taken from Paris and sent to Auschwitz; overall, some 12,887 Jews in Paris pass through Drancy

July 22: Mass deportation of Jews from the Warsaw Ghetto to Treblinka begins

July 23: Adam Czerniakow commits suicide in Warsaw

July 28: The Jewish Combat Organization is formed in the Warsaw Ghetto

August 17: **Kurt Gerstein** visits Bełżec death camp; witnesses the gassing of up to 3,000 Jews

September 2–3: Revolt of the Łachwa ghetto, arguably the first ghetto revolt of the Holocaust

October 22: SS put down a revolt at Sachsenhausen by a group of Jews about to be sent to Auschwitz

October 28: First transport of Jews from Terezín (Theresienstadt) to Auschwitz

December 24: Armed operations by the Jewish Combat Organization against German troops in Kraków

1943

January 17: **Konrad Graf von Preysing**, bishop of Berlin, threatens to resign over the collaborative behavior of the German Catholic bishops

January 18–21: Renewed deportations of Jews from the Warsaw Ghetto begin following a visit from Himmler; Warsaw Ghetto fighters of the Jewish Combat Organization fire upon German troops

January 22: Deportations from the Warsaw Ghetto end, following the deaths of 50 Nazi soldiers

February 22: Christoph Probst, **Hans Scholl**, and **Sophie Scholl** are executed after admitting to distributing White Rose pamphlets

February 27: *Fabrikaktion* (Factory Action); the roundup and deportation of the last Jews in Berlin

February 27–March 6: Rosenstrasse protest in Berlin by non-Jewish wives and mothers against imprisonment of their Jewish husbands and children

March 8–9: **Dimitar Peshev** stops deportation of Bulgarian Jews before the process begins

March 13–14: Liquidation of the Kraków ghetto
March 23: Nazi deportation of Greek Jews begins
April 5: Approximately 4,000 Jews are massacred in the Ponary Forest, outside Vilna
April 19: New deportations from the Warsaw Ghetto; first day of Warsaw Ghetto Uprising
May 8: Nazi forces capture the Jewish Combat Organization's command bunker at Miła 18; **Mordecai Anielewicz** is among the dead found there
May 12: **Shmuel Zygielbojm** commits suicide in London
May 16: SS general Jürgen Stroop reports that the "Jewish quarter of Warsaw is no more"
May 19: Nazis declare Berlin to be *Judenfrei* ("cleansed of Jews")
Summer: Armed resistance by Jews in Będzin, Białystok, Częstochowa, Lvov, and Tarnów ghettos
June 2: 3,000 Jews killed following resistance in Lvov; another 7,000 are sent to Janowska
June 11: Himmler orders liquidation of all ghettos in occupied Poland
June 25–26: Częstochowa ghetto revolt
July 25: Fall of fascist regime in Italy; Mussolini dismissed by King Victor Emmanuel III
August 2: Treblinka uprising
August 15–16: Uprising of the Białystok ghetto
September 8: Italy surrenders to the Allies and declares war against Germany
October 1–2: German police begin deportations of Danish Jews; Danes respond with a rescue effort that saves the lives of 90 percent of the Jewish population
October 14: Sobibor uprising
October 16: Major Nazi raid and *razzia* (roundup) against the Jews of Rome
October 21: Minsk Ghetto liquidated
November 2–4: **Itzhak Katzenelson** writes *The Song of the Murdered Jewish People*

1944

March 14: **Hannah Szenes** and others parachuted into Yugoslavia
March 19: Germany begins its occupation of Hungary
April 7: **Rudolf Vrba** and Alfréd Wetzler escape from Auschwitz, bringing details of mass extermination of the Jews
May 15: Beginning of the deportation of Jews from Hungary to Auschwitz
May 16: Germans offer to free 1 million Jews in exchange for 10,000 trucks
June 7: **Hannah Szenes** slips into Hungary with aims to reach Budapest and is arrested immediately
June 30: Departure of "**Kasztner** Train" from Budapest
July 9: **Raoul Wallenberg** arrives in Hungary

July 11: Deportations from Hungary are halted by order of Regent Miklós Horthy
July 20: German officers fail to assassinate Hitler in Bomb Plot
August 1–October 4: Warsaw Revolt
August 6: Łódź, the last Jewish ghetto in Poland, is liquidated with 60,000 Jews sent to Auschwitz
August 25: Paris is liberated
September 15: Execution of **Mala Zimetbaum** and Edek Galiński at Auschwitz
October 7: *Sonderkommando* revolt at Auschwitz
November 7: **Hannah Szenes** convicted as a spy and executed by German firing squad
November 19: The Vatican and four other neutral powers in Budapest issue a collective protest to the Hungarian government calling for the suspension of Jewish deportation
December 24–29: Hungarian Arrow Cross fascists attack Jews in Budapest

1945

January 5: **Roza Robota**, Estusia Wajcblum, Ala Gertner, and Regina Safirsztajn, accused of supplying gunpowder to the Auschwitz *Sonderkommando*, are executed
January 17: **Raoul Wallenberg** arrested by Soviet forces for espionage
January 28: Soviet forces liberate Auschwitz
April 9: Evacuation of Mauthausen begins
April 11: American forces liberate Buchenwald
April 15: British forces liberate Bergen-Belsen
April 27: Soviet forces liberate Sachsenhausen
April 29: American forces liberate Dachau; Soviet forces liberate Ravensbrück
April 30: Hitler commits suicide
May 2: Soviet forces capture Berlin
May 3: Terezín (Theresienstadt) is surrendered to the International Committee of the Red Cross
May 5: American forces liberate Mauthausen
May 7: Germany surrenders to the Allies in Reims
May 9: Wilhelm Keitel signs surrender documents in Berlin
July 25: **Kurt Gerstein** found hanged in his cell in a French prison

Bibliography

The bibliography that follows is intended as a starting point for researchers and students of the Holocaust, with a specific focus on resistance in all its forms. It does not pretend to be a complete listing of all works relating to upstanders, partisans, or survivors, nor could it be within the scope of a listing of this size. New works are appearing literally every day, but at a bare minimum the works in this listing could form the core of any research project.

Where possible, I have added the names of those featured in this book alongside works where they feature. Unfortunately, there are still many stories remaining to be told or further developed, which is why not all the people featured in this volume have yet had studies done on their remarkable contributions when resisting the Holocaust.

Ackerman, Diane. *The Zookeeper's Wife: A War Story*. New York: Norton, 2007. [**Żabiński**]

Ainsztein, Reuben. *Jewish Resistance in Nazi-Occupied Eastern Europe: With a Historical Survey of the Jew as Fighter and Soldier in the Diaspora*. New York: Harper and Row, 1974. [**Anielewicz; Edelman; Feldhendler; Ringelblum; Tenenbaum; Wittenberg; Zuckerman**]

Arad, Yitzhak. *Belzec, Sobibor, Treblinka: The Operation Reinhard Death Camps*. Bloomington: Indiana University Press, 1999. [**Pechersky**]

Arens, Moshe. *Flags over the Warsaw Ghetto: The Untold Story of the Warsaw Ghetto Uprising*. New York: Gefen, 2011.

Baker, Leonard. *Days of Sorrow and Pain: Leo Baeck and the Berlin Jews*. New York: Macmillan, 1978. [**Baeck**]

Barkai, Meyer, ed. *The Fighting Ghettos*. Philadelphia: Lippincott, 1962.

Bartoszewski, Wladyslaw, and Zofia Lewin, eds. *Righteous among Nations: How Poles Helped the Jews, 1939–1945*. London: Earlscourt Publications, 1969.

Bartrop, Paul R. "The Premier as Advocate: A. G. Ogilvie, Tasmania and the Refugee Crisis, 1938–39." *Tasmanian Historical Research Association Papers and Proceedings*, vol. 35, no. 2 (June 1988): 49–57. [**Ogilvie**]

Beck, Gad. *An Underground Jew: Memoirs of a Gay Jew in Nazi Berlin*. Madison: University of Wisconsin Press, 1999. [**Beck**]

Bierman, John. *Righteous Gentile: The Story of Raoul Wallenberg, Missing Hero of the Holocaust*. New York: Viking, 1981. [**Wallenberg**]

Blaichman, Frank. *Rather Die Fighting: A Memoir of World War II*. New York: Arcade, 2009. [**Blaichman**]

Bourke, Eoin. "Wilhelm Krützfeld and Other 'Good' Constables in Police Station 16 in Hackescher Markt, Berlin." In *Representing the "Good German" in Literature and Culture after 1945: Altruism and Moral Ambiguity*, ed. Pól Ó Dochartaigh and Christiane Schönfeld, 66–84. Rochester, N.Y.: Camden House, 2013. [**Krützfeld**]

Brothers, Eric. *Berlin Ghetto: Herbert Baum and the Anti-Fascist Resistance*. Stroud: Spellmount, 2012. [**Baum**]

Brzezinski, Matthew. *Isaac's Army: A Story of Courage and Survival in Nazi-Occupied Poland*. New York: Random House, 2012. [**Zuckerman**]

Castle, John. *The Password Is Courage*. London: Souvenir Press, 1954. [**Coward**]

Coleman, Fred. *The Marcel Network: How One French Couple Saved 527 Children from the Holocaust*. Washington, D.C.: Potomac Books, 2013. [**Abadi**]

Cox, John. *Circles of Resistance: Jewish, Leftist, and Youth Dissidence in Nazi Germany*. New York: Peter Lang, 2009. [**Baum**]

Crowe, David M. *Oskar Schindler: The Untold Account of His Life, Wartime Activities, and the True Story behind the List*. Boulder: Westview Press, 2004. [**Schindler**]

Deaglio, Enrico. *The Banality of Goodness: The Story of Giorgio Perlasca*. Notre Dame, Ind.: University of Notre Dame Press, 1998. [**Perlasca**]

Dippel, John H. *Bound upon a Wheel of Fire: Why So Many German Jews Made the Tragic Decision to Remain in Nazi Germany*. New York: Basic Books, 1996. [**Baeck; Weltsch**]

Dohnányi, Ilona von. *Ernst von Dohnányi: A Song of Life*. Ed. James A. Grymes. Bloomington: Indiana University Press, 2002. [**Dohnányi**]

Dumbach, Annette E., and Jud Newborn. *Shattering the German Night: The Story of the White Rose*. Boston: Little, Brown and Co., 1986. [**Scholl**]

Edelman, Marek. *The Ghetto Fights*. London: Bookmarks, 2013. [**Edelman**]

Epstein, Barbara. *The Minsk Ghetto, 1941–1943: Jewish Resistance and Soviet Internationalism*. Berkeley: University of California Press, 2008. [**Gebelev; Smolar**]

Fensch, Thomas, ed. *Oskar Schindler and His List: The Man, the Book, the Film, the Holocaust and Its Survivors*. Forest Dale, Vt.: Paul S. Eriksson, 1995. [**Schindler**]

Fleming, Brian. *The Vatican Pimpernel: The World War II Exploits of the Monsignor Who Saved over 6,500 Lives*. New York: Skyhorse Publishing, 2012. [**O'Flaherty**]

Fogelman, Eva. *Conscience and Courage: Rescuers of Jews during the Holocaust*. New York: Anchor Books/Doubleday, 1994.

Fralon, José-Alain. *A Good Man in Evil Times: Aristides de Sousa Mendes—the Unknown Hero Who Saved Countless Lives in World War II*. London: Viking, 2000. [**De Sousa Mendes**]

Friedländer, Saul. *The Ambiguity of Good*. New York: Knopf, 1969. [**Gerstein**]

Friedman, Philip. *Their Brothers' Keepers*. New York: Holocaust Library, 1978.

Friedman, Philip, ed. *Martyrs and Fighters: The Epic of the Warsaw Ghetto*. New York: Praeger, 1954.

Gallagher, J. P. *The Scarlet and the Black: The True Story of Monsignor Hugh O'Flaherty, Hero of the Vatican Underground*. San Francisco: Ignatius Press, 2009. [**O'Flaherty**]

Gies, Miep, and Alison Leslie Gold. *Anne Frank Remembered: The Story of the Woman Who Helped to Hide the Frank Family*. New York: Simon and Schuster, 1987. [**Gies**]

Gilbert, Martin. *The Righteous: The Unsung Heroes of the Holocaust*. London: Doubleday, 2002.

Glass, James M. *Jewish Resistance during the Holocaust: Moral Uses of Violence and Will*. London: Palgrave Macmillan, 2004.

Good, Michael. *The Search for Major Plagge: The Nazi Who Saved Jews*. New York: Fordham University Press, 2005. [**Plagge**]

Grose, Peter. *A Good Place to Hide: How One French Community Saved Thousands of People during World War II*. New York: Pegasus Books, 2015. [**Trocmé**]

Grunwald-Spier, Agnes. *The Other Schindlers: Why Some People Chose to Save Jews in the Holocaust*. Stroud, UK: The History Press, 2010.

Gushee, David P. *Righteous Gentiles of the Holocaust: Genocide and Moral Obligation*, 2nd ed. St. Paul: Paragon House, 2003.

Gutman, Israel. *Resistance: The Warsaw Ghetto Uprising*. Boston: Houghton Mifflin, 1994.

Gutman, Israel, ed. *The Encyclopedia of the Righteous among the Nations: Rescuers of Jews during the Holocaust*. 10 vols. Jerusalem: Yad Vashem, 2003–2011.

Hallie, Philip. *Lest Innocent Blood Be Shed*. London: Michael Joseph, 1979. [**Trocmé**]

Hanser, Richard. *A Noble Treason: The Story of Sophie Scholl and the White Rose Revolt against Hitler vs the Revolt of the Munich Students against Hitler*. San Francisco: Ignatius Press, 1979. [**Scholl**]

Hébert, Valerie. "Disguised Resistance? The Story of Kurt Gerstein." *Holocaust and Genocide Studies*, vol. 20, no. 1 (Spring 2006): 1–33. [**Gerstein**]

Hellman, Peter. *Avenue of the Righteous*. London: Dent, 1981.

Hughes, Jon. "From Hitler's Champion to German of the Century: On the Representation and Reinvention of Max Schmeling." In *Representing the "Good German" in Literature and Culture after 1945: Altruism and Moral Ambiguity*, ed. Pól Ó Dochartaigh and Christiane Schönfeld, 66–84. Rochester, N.Y.: Camden House, 2013. [**Schmeling**]

Jagendorf, Siegfried. *Jagendorf's Foundry: Memoir of the Romanian Holocaust, 1941–1944*. New York: HarperCollins, 1991. [**Jagendorf**]

Jangfeldt, Bengt. *The Hero of Budapest: The Triumph and Tragedy of Raoul Wallenberg*. London: I. B. Tauris, 2014. [**Wallenberg**]

Jens, Inge, ed. *At the Heart of the White Rose: Letters and Diaries of Hans and Sophie Scholl*. New York: Harper and Row, 1987. [**Scholl**]

Joffroy, Pierre. *A Spy for God: The Ordeal of Kurt Gerstein*. New York: Harcourt Brace Jovanovich, 1970. [**Gerstein**]

Kassow, Samuel D. *Who Will Write Our History? Emanuel Ringelblum, the Warsaw Ghetto, and the Oyneg Shabes Archive*. Bloomington: Indiana University Press, 2007. [**Ringelblum**]

Kershaw, Alex. *The Envoy: The Epic Rescue of the Last Jews of Europe in the Desperate Closing Months of World War II*. Boston: Da Capo Press, 2010. [**Wallenberg**]

Kidder, Annemarie S. *Ultimate Price: Testimonies of Christians Who Resisted the Third Reich*. Maryknoll, N.Y.: Orbis Books, 2012. [**Lichtenberg; Scholl**]

Klaphek, Elisa. *Fraulein Rabbiner Jonas: The Story of the First Woman Rabbi*. [**Jonas**]

Krall, Hanna. *Shielding the Flame: An Intimate Conversation with Dr. Marek Edelman, the Last Surviving Leader of the Warsaw Ghetto Uprising*. New York: Henry Holt, 1986. [**Edelman**]

Kruk, Hermann. *The Last Days of the Jerusalem of Lithuania: Chronicles from the Vilna Ghetto and the Camps, 1939–1944*. New Haven: Yale University Press, 2002. [**Kruk**]

Landau, David J. *Caged*. Sydney: Pan Australia, 2000.

Langbein, Hermann. *Against All Hope: Resistance in the Nazi Concentration Camps, 1938–1945*. New York: Paragon House, 1994. [**Langbein**]

Langlet, Valdemar. *Reign of Terror: The Budapest Memoirs of Valdemar Langlet, 1944–1945*. New York: Skyhorse Books, 2012. [**Langlet**]

Large, David Clay, ed. *Contending with Hitler: Varieties of German Resistance in the Third Reich*. New York: Cambridge University Press, 1991.

Latour, Anny. *The Jewish Resistance in France (1940–1944)*. New York: Holocaust Library, 1970.

Lazare, Lucien. *Rescue as Resistance: How Jewish Organizations Fought the Holocaust in France*. New York: Columbia University Press, 1996.

Lefenfeld, Nancy. *The Fate of Others: Rescuing Jewish Children on the French-Swiss Border*. Clarksville, Md.: Timbrel Press, 2013. [**Cohn; Racine**]

Lifton, Robert Jay. *The Nazi Doctors: Medical Killing and the Psychology of Genocide*. New York: Basic Books, 1986. [**Münch**]

Micheels, Louis J. *Doctor 117641: A Holocaust Memoir*. New Haven, Conn.: Yale University Press, 1989. [**Münch**]

Moltke, Helmuth James von. *Letters to Freya, 1939–1945*. New York: Alfred A. Knopf, 1990. [**Moltke**]

Moorehead, Caroline. *Village of Secrets: Defying the Nazis in Vichy France*. New York: HarperCollins, 2014. [**Trocmé**]

Monroe, Kristen Renwick. *Ethics in an Age of Terror and Genocide: Identity and Moral Choice*. Princeton, N.J.: Princeton University Press, 2012.

Monroe, Kristen Renwick. *The Hand of Compassion: Portraits of Moral Choice during the Holocaust*. Princeton, N.J.: Princeton University Press, 2004.

Müller, Filip. *Auschwitz Inferno: The Testimony of a Sonderkommando*. London: Routledge and Kegan Paul, 1979. [**Müller**]

Nelson, David Conley. *Moroni and the Swastika: Mormons in Nazi Germany*. Norman: University of Oklahoma Press, 2015. [**Hübener**]

Newman, Richard, with Karen Kirtley. *Alma Rosé: Vienna to Auschwitz*. Pompton Plains, N.J.: Amadeus Press, 2000. [**Rosé**]

Oliner, Pearl M. *Saving the Forsaken: Religious Culture and the Rescue of Jews in Nazi Europe*. New Haven, Conn.: Yale University Press, 2004.

Oliner, Samuel, and Kathleen Lee. *Who Shall Live: The Wilhelm Bachner Story*. Chicago: Academy Chicago, 1996. [**Bachner**]

Oliner, Samuel P., and Pearl M. Oliner. *The Altruistic Personality: Rescuers of Jews in Nazi Europe*. New York: Free Press, 1988.

Paldiel, Mordecai. *Churches and the Holocaust: Unholy Teaching, Good Samaritans, and Reconciliation*. New York: KTAV, 2006.

Paldiel, Mordecai. *Diplomat Heroes of the Holocaust*. New York: Yeshiva University/KTAV, 2007. [**Anger; Born; De Sousa Mendes; De Souza Dantas; Duckwitz; Foley; Ho Feng-Shan; Langlet; Lutz; Perlasca; Rotta; Sanz Briz; Sugihara; Ülkümen; Wallenberg; Zwartendijk**]

Paldiel, Mordecai. *The Path of the Righteous: Gentile Rescuers of Jews during the Holocaust.* Hoboken, N.J.: KTAV, 1993. [**Bogaard; Damaskinos; De Sousa Mendes; Kowalski; Lutz; Père Marie-Benoît; Schindler; Sendler; Slachta; Sugihara; Sztehló; Trocmé; Veseli; Wallenberg; Wegner; Westerweel; Żabiński**]

Paldiel, Mordecai. *Saving the Jews: Amazing Stories of Men and Women Who Defied the "Final Solution."* Rockville, Md.: Schreiber Publishing, 2000. [**Abadi; Calmeyer; Foley; Fry; Gerstein; Karski; Perlasca; Rotta; Sheptytsky; Süskind; Ülkümen; Veseli; Wegner; Zwartendijk**]

Pankiewicz, Tadeusz. *The Cracow Ghetto Pharmacy.* Washington, D.C.: Holocaust Library, 1987. [**Pankiewicz**]

Pilecki, Witold. *The Auschwitz Volunteer: Beyond Bravery.* Los Angeles: Aquila Polonica, 2012. [**Pilecki**]

Press, Eyal. *Beautiful Souls: Saying No, Breaking Ranks, and Heeding the Voice of Conscience in Dark Times.* New York: Farrar, Straus and Giroux, 2012. [**Grüninger**]

Rittner, Carol, and Sondra Myers, eds. *The Courage to Care: Rescuers of Jews during the Holocaust.* New York: New York University Press, 1986.

Roe, Michael. *Albert Ogilvie and Stymie Gaha: World-wise Tasmanians.* Hobart: Parliament of Tasmania, 2008. [**Ogilvie**]

Schmeling, Max. *Max Schmeling: An Autobiography.* Chicago: Bonus Books, 1998. [**Schmeling**]

Scrase, David, Wolfgang Mieder, and Katherine Quimby Johnson, eds. *Making a Difference, Rescue and Assistance during the Holocaust: Essays in Honor of Marion Pritchard.* Burlington, Vt.: Center for Holocaust Studies, University of Vermont, 2004. [**Pritchard**]

Silent Witness. Prod. Angela Kaye. Reporter Iain Guest. BBC-TV, 1988. [**Linnér**]

Silver, Daniel B. *Refuge in Hell: How Berlin's Jewish Hospital Outlasted the Nazis.* Boston: Houghton Mifflin, 2003. [**Lustig**]

Silver, Eric. *The Book of the Just: The Unsung Heroes Who Rescued Jews from Hitler.* New York: Grove Press, 1992. [**Born; Coward; Damaskinos; De Sousa Mendes; Duckwitz; Maltzan; Perlasca; Schindler; Schmeling; Schmid; Sugihara; Sztehló; Trocmé; Ülkümen; Veseli**]

Silverman, Emily Leah. *Edith Stein and Regina Jonas: Religious Visionaries in the Time of the Death Camps.* [**Jonas**]

Smith, Lyn. *Heroes of the Holocaust: Ordinary Britons Who Risked Their Lives to Make a Difference.* London: Edbury Press, 2012. [**Alice; Coward; Foley; Winton**]

Snyder, Louis L. *Hitler's German Enemies: Portraits of Heroes Who Fought the Nazis.* New York: Hippocrene Books, 1990. [**Moltke; Scholl**]

Stegelmann, Katharina. *Staying Human: The Story of a Quiet WWII Hero.* New York: Skyhorse Publishing, 2015. [**Drossel**]

Stern, Fritz, and Elisabeth Sifton. *No Ordinary Men: Dietrich Bonhoeffer and Hans von Dohnanyi, Resisters against Hitler in Church and State.* New York: New York Review Books Collections, 2013. [**Dohnányi**]

Suhl, Yuri, ed. *They Fought Back: The Story of the Jewish Resistance in Nazi Europe.* New York: Crown Publishers, 1967. [**Atlas; Baum; Gildenman; Pechersky; Robota; Rufeisen; Zimetbaum**]

Tammeus, Bill, and Rabbi Jacques Cukierkorn. *They Were Just People: Stories of Rescue in Poland during the Holocaust.* Columbia: University of Missouri Press, 2009.

Tec, Nechama. *Defiance: The Bielski Partisans.* New York: Oxford University Press, 1993. [**Bielski**]

Tec, Nechama. *In the Lion's Den: The Life of Oswald Rufeisen.* Oxford: Oxford University Press, 1990. [**Rufeisen**]

Tec, Nechama. *Resistance: Jews and Christians Who Defied the Nazi Terror.* Oxford: Oxford University Press, 2013.

Tec, Nechama. *When Light Pierced the Darkness: Christian Rescuers of Jews in Nazi-Occupied Poland.* New York: Oxford University Press, 1986.

Thalhammer, Kristina E., et al. *Courageous Resistance: The Power of Ordinary People.* New York: Palgrave Macmillan, 2007.

Tomaszewski, Irene, and Tecia Werbowski. *Code Name: Żegota: Rescuing Jews in Occupied Poland, 1942–1945.* Santa Barbara, Calif.: Praeger, 2010.

Trunk, Isaiah. *Jewish Responses to Nazi Persecution: Collective and Individual Behavior in Extremis.* New York: Stein and Day, 1979.

Tschuy, Theo. *Dangerous Diplomacy: The Story of Carl Lutz, Rescuer of 62,000 Hungarian Jews.* Grand Rapids, Mich.: William B. Eerdmans Publishing, 2000. [**Lutz**]

Tushnet, Leonard. *To Die with Honor: The Uprising of the Jews in the Warsaw Ghetto.* New York: Citadel Press, 1965.

Vargo, Marc E. *Women of the Resistance: Eight Who Defied the Third Reich.* Jefferson, N.C.: McFarland, 2012. [**Scholl; Sugihara; Szenes**]

Von Kellenbach, Katharine. "Denial and Defiance in the Work of Rabbi Regina Jonas." In *In God's Name: Genocide and Religion in the Twentieth Century*, ed. Omer Bartov and Phyllis Mack. New York: Berghahn Books, 2001. [**Jonas**]

Vromen, Susan. *Hidden Children of the Holocaust: Belgian Nuns and Their Daring Rescue of Young Jews from the Nazis.* Oxford: Oxford University Press, 2008.

Wallenberg, Raoul. *Letters and Dispatches, 1924–1944.* New York: Arcade, 1995. [**Wallenberg**]

Wette, Wolfram. *The Wehrmacht: History, Myth, Reality.* Cambridge, Mass.: Harvard University Press, 2007. [**Schmid**]

Wetzler, Alfréd. *Escape from Hell: The True Story of the Auschwitz Protocol.* New York: Berghahn, 2007. [**Vrba**]

Wick, Steve. *The Long Night: William L. Shirer and the Rise and Fall of the Third Reich.* New York: Palgrave Macmillan, 2011. [**Shirer**]

Wood, E. Thomas, and Stanisław M. Jankowski. *Karski: How One Man Tried to Stop the Holocaust.* Lubbock, Tex.: Texas Tech University Press, 2014. [**Karski**]

Wyllie, James. *Goering and Goering: Hitler's Henchman and His Anti-Nazi Brother.* Stroud, UK: The History Press, 2006. [**Göring**]

Yad Vashem. *Jewish Resistance during the Holocaust: Proceedings of the Conference on Manifestations of Jewish Resistance, Jerusalem, April 7–11, 1968.* Jerusalem: Yad Vashem, 1971.

Zimmerman, Joshua D. *The Polish Underground and the Jews, 1939–1945.* Cambridge: Cambridge University Press, 2015. [**Sendler**]

Zuckerman, Yitzhak. *A Surplus of Memory: Chronicle of the Warsaw Ghetto Uprising*. Berkeley: University of California Press, 1993. [**Altman; Anielewicz; Edelman; Guzik; Katzenelson; Kovner; Lubetkin; Meed; Ringelblum; Tenenbaum; Zuckerman**]

Zucotti, Susan. *Père Marie-Benoît and Jewish Rescue: How a French Priest Together with Jewish Friends Saved Thousands during the Holocaust*. Bloomington: Indiana University Press, 2013. [**Père Marie-Benoît**]

Internet Resources

The Internet is an extraordinarily rich repository for researching all forms of resistance during the Holocaust, though the mandatory caution must be made: not all websites are trustworthy, accurate, or committed to historical accuracy. The following list of websites, arranged alphabetically, provide resources that are both authoritative and comprehensive. Researchers looking for more specific information will in some instances need to move beyond these, and in certain cases be prepared to consult websites in languages other than English.

Beit Lohamei HaGetaot: Ghetto Fighters' House Museum
http://www.gfh.org.il/Eng/

European Holocaust Research Infrastructure
http://www.ehri-project.eu/

Holocaust Education and Archive Research Team
http://www.holocaustresearchproject.org/

Jewish Foundation for the Righteous
https://jfr.org/

Jewish Partisan Educational Foundation
http://www.jewishpartisans.org/

Jewish Virtual Library
https://www.jewishvirtuallibrary.org/

United States Holocaust Memorial Museum
http://www.ushmm.org/

Yad Vashem
http://www.yadvashem.org/

YIVO Encyclopedia of Jews in Eastern Europe
http://www.yivoencyclopedia.org/

Index

Boldface page numbers indicate main entries.

Abadi, Moussa, **1–3**, 223
Abwehr, 56–57
Ackerman, Diane, 324
Adath Yisroel synagogue, 253
Adler, Anita, 247
Adler, Herman, 247
Adler, Ruth, 130
Ákos, Ney, 284
Albania, 295–297
Albeck, Hanoch, 116
Albert I (Belgium), 65
Albrecht, Hilde, 242
Alice, Princess Andrew of Greece and Denmark, **3–5**, 67
All Quiet on the Western Front, 160
Alsina, 52
Altenburg, Günther, 49
Altman, Anka, 5
Altman, Gustav, 5
Altman, Tova (Tosia), **5–7**, 326, 329
American Jewish Joint Distribution Center, 214, 311
American Jewish Joint Distribution Committee, 71
American Relief Center, 75
Amitié Chrétienne (Christian Friendship), 85
Anadi, Nassim, 1
And We Are Not Saved, 305
Andreas-Friedrich, Ruth, **7–8**; diary, 397–398
Andriessen, Mari, 143
Anger, Per, **8–11**, 156, 219, 302, 304
Anielewicz, Mordecai, 5, **11–13**, 63–64, 141, 166, 289, 325–326, 365; letter to Yitzhak Zuckerman, 368–369
Anti-Defamation League, 159
Antonescu, Ion, 114
Antyfaszystowska Organizacjz Bojowa (Anti-Fascist Military Organization, AOB), xx, 184
Apfelbaum, Dawid, 304
Apteka Pod Orlem (Under the Eagle) pharmacy, 199, 378–382
Apteka w getcie krakowskim (The Cracow Ghetto Pharmacy), 200, 381
Arbeiter Fragen (Worker's Issues), 332
Arendt, Hannah, 18, 75
Arkin, Alan, 70, 202
Armée Juive (Jewish Army, AJ), 132, 214–215, 271–272
Armenian genocide, 306–307
Armenian Genocide Memorial, 307
Armia Krajowa (Polish Home Army, AK), 6, 12, 28, 64–65, 124–126, 154, 191–192, 324
Armia Ludowa (People's Army/AL), 6, 32, 64
Arnold, Friedrich, 57
Atlantic Monthly, 74
Atlas, Icheskel, xxii, **13–14**

Au Revoir les Enfants, 203
Auerbach, Rachel, 225
Aus der Fünten, Ferdinand, 279
Auschwitz, 2, 27–29, 71–72, 98, 110, 117, 131, 134, 169, 171, 188–189, 209–212, 226–227, 270, 278, 294, 297–299, 318, 326–327, 398, 404; II, xxi; III (Monowitz), 44; Crematorium III, xxi; Crematorium IV, xxi; E715 labor detachment camp, 44; liberation, 189; Report, 71–72, 156, 312; *revier*, 154; *Sonderkommando*, xxi, 177, 226–227, 298; women's orchestra, 227–229
Auschwitz Military Council, 154
Austria; *Anschluss*, 92, 103, 121–122, 247; German occupation of, 86–87, 103, 113–116, 153–155; Jews in, 103–104
Australia, 195–197

BBC, 298
Bachner, Wilhelm, **15–16**
Baeck, Leo, **16–18**, 73, 89, 117, 168
Baeck, Samuel, 17
Baer, Max, 244
Baleanu, Ion, 115
Balkan Wars, 48
Ballin, Albert, 339
Baneth, Edward, 116
Bar Kochba, 313
Barasz, Efraim, 184, 290
Barazetti, Bill, 318
Bartali, Andrea, 20
Bartali, Gino, **19–20**, 47
Barth, Karl, 249
Baruk, Jakob, 208
Barzilai, Elias, 49
Bas, Maurice, 203
Basilica di San Clemente, 194
Battle of France, 58
Battleground Berlin: Diaries, 1945–1948, 8
Baum, Herbert, xix, **20–22**
Baum, Marianne (Cohn), xix, 20–22, 222
Bauminger, Avi Hersch, 6
Becher, Kurt, 128

Beck, Gad, **22–24**
Beck, Margot, 23
Beitz, Berthold, **24–26**
Beitz, Else, 26
Beje movement, 287–288
Belgium, 333; Jews in, 65–67, 118–120; resistance movement, 118–120
Bell, Jamie, 31
Bellgardt, Otto, 146–147
Belzec extermination camp, 25, 79, 399, 403
Benedict XVI, 28, 238
Benghabrit, Si Kaddour, **26–27**
Bennett, Edward, 183
Berg, Rudolf van den, 279
Bergau transfer camp, 177
Berlin Diary: The Journal of a Foreign Correspondence, 1934–1941, 263
Berlin Hochschule, 54
Berlin Regional Court, 274
Berlin Underground, 1938–1945, 398
Berlin Zoo, 323
Berman, Adolf, 258
Bernadotte, Folke, 302
Bernovits, Vilma, 238
Bertram, Adolf Cardinal, 160, 216
Besa, 296
Beskidian Oil Company, 24
Bestic, Alan, 298
Betar movement, 11, 138, 304–305, 319; Revisionist, 164
Bettinger, Franzikus von, 215
Bialek, Marutizio, 36
Bialystok ghetto, 167; Jewish Council (Judenrat), 290; uprising, 183–185
Białystokier Sztern (Białystok Star), 266
Bielecki, Jerry, **27–29**
Bielski, Alexander, 29–30
Bielski, Aron, xxii, 29–31
Bielski, Asael, xxi–xxii, 30–31
Bielski, Beila, 29
Bielski, David, 29
Bielski, Tuvia, xxi–xxii, **29–31**, 233, 267
Bielski, Zus, xxii, 30–31
Bialustok ghetto, xx

Bingham, Hiram IV, 75
Birgy, Rolande, 42
Birkenau camp, 226, 326
Bismark, Otto von, 146
Black Front, 101
Blaichman, Frank, **31–33**
Blake, Martin, 317
Blatt, Thomas "Toivi," 70
Bloch, Ferdinand (Felix), 98
Block A, 289
Blomberg, Digne, 155
Boegershausen, 344
Bogaard, Aagji, 34
Bogaard, Antheunius, 33–34
Bogaard, Johannes, xxiv, **33–34**
Bogaard, Johannes "Grandpa," 34
Bogaard, Klaasje, 34
Bogaard, Metje, 34
Bogaard, Willem, 33–34
Bogarde, Dirk, 45
Bogdush, Israel, 14
Bohr, Niels, 274
Bonhoeffer, Christel, 56–57
Bonhoeffer, Dietrich, 55–57, 273
Bonhoeffer, Klaus, 55–56
Boris III (Bulgaria), 208
Borkowska, Anna, 137
Bormann, Martin, 56, 122, 306
Born, Friedrich, **34–36**, 173, 207, 231, 239
Bornstein, Isaac, 94
Bornstein, Samuel, 14
Boros-Gutman, Anna, 99–100
Borovko, Nina, 155
Borowska, Chyena, 138, 319
Borromeo, Giovanni, xxiv, **36–38**
Boryslaw, 26
Bosnia, 135–137; *Pinkas,* 136
Bosnian National Museum, 136
Böro Grüber (Grüber Bureau), 89, 281
Bratislava, 90–91, 298
Bratislava Working Group, 70–72; Auschwitz Report, 71–72, 156, 312
Brazilian Foreign Ministry, 52
Bricha (Flight), 166

Brit Shalom, 313
Britain, 72–74, 255, 317–319
British Committee for Refugees from Czechoslovakia, 317
Brunner, Alois, 72
Bruno, Borel, 140
Bucharest pogrom, 114
Buchfuehrer, Helene, 15
Bucholtz, Leah, 141
Buchter, Tineke. *See* Strobos, Tina
Budapest Academy, 54–55
Budapest ghetto, 55
Budapest Philharmonic Orchestra, 54–55
Büdische Jugend, 101
Bulat, Boris, 14
Bulak, Pavel, 14
Bulgaria, 208–209; Law for the Protection of the Nation, 208
Bunel, Lucien-Louis. *See* Père Jacques
Busnelli, Sandra, 48

Cahn, Ernst, 142
Calmeyer, Hans, **39–41**
Calmeyer Foundation, 40–41
Canaris, Wilhelm, 57, 181
Cantoni, Raffaele, 47
Caratis Emergency Relief, 267
Carpathian Oil Company, 24–25
Casals, Pablo, 75
Cassuto, Nathan, 19, 47
Castle, John, 45
Cattedrale di Santa Maria del Fiore, 48
Central Committee of Polish Jews, 267
Central Council of Jews (Germany), 26
Central Islamic Institute (Berlin), 99
Central Jewish Bureau of the Central Committee of Komsomol, 265
Chadwick, Trevor, 318
Chagall, Marc, 75
Chaillet, Pierre, 85
Chen Jie, 103
Chiam, Izrael, 329
Chevra Kadisha, 90
Chiang Kai-shek (Jiang Jieshi), 103
Chicago Tribune, 261

Chief Rabbi's Religious Emergency Council (CRREC), 253
China, 103–104
Chinese Lutheran Church, 104
Chorazycki, Julian, 149
Christian Association of Auschwitz Families, 28
Christian Democratic Appeal (CDA), 107
Christian Historical Union (CHU), 107
Christian Sisterhood of Martha and Mary, 4
Christie, Doug, 299
Chudson, Walter A., 275
Chug Chaluzi (Clan of Pioneers), 23–24
Church Aid Office for Protestant Non-Aryans, 281
Church of Jesus Christ of Latter-day Saints (LDS), 104–106
Ciechanów ghetto, 226
Cleven, Alwine, 88
Clift, Jeannette, 288
Cohen, David, 107
Cohen, Gustave, 1
Cohen, Haimaki, 4
Cohen, Jacques, 4–5
Cohen, Michel, 4
Cohen, Rachel, 4
Cohen, Tilda, 4
Cohen, Virrie (Virginia), 107
Cohn, Marianne, **41–43**, 271
Collier, James F., 288
Columbia House prison, 307, 344
Comité de Défense des Juifs (Committee for the Protection of Jews, CDJ), 118
Committee to Aid Refugees, 85
Communist International, 266
Communist Party of Austria, 153
Communist Party of Belgium, 118
Communist Party of the Netherlands, 142
Communist Party of West Belarus (CPWB), 266
Convent of St. Mary Magdalene, 4
Courier from Poland: The Story of a Secret State, 126
Coward, Charles, **43–45**

Craig, Daniel, 31
Cristensen, Jesper, 256
Cybulska, Cyla, 27–28
Cyrankiewica, Józef, 211
Czech Skoda Works, 87
Czechoslovakia, 17–18, 297–298, 317–319; Jewish Council, 18; Ministry of Slovak Affairs, 90; resistance movement, 88
Czerniaków, Adam, 11, 328, 367

D'Annunzio, Gabriele, 206
Dachau, 153, 159, 188–189, 281; priest block, 204
Daily Herald, 298
Dalla Costa, Elia, 19, **47–48**
Dam, Jan Van, 106
Damaskinos, Archbishop of Athens, **48–50**
Damiecki, Mateusz, 29
Danek-Czort, Aurelia, 199
Danielsson, Carl Ivan, 8–9, 156
Darcissac, Roger, 291
Das Wesen des Judenstums (The Essence of Judaism), 17
Davenport, Miriam, 75
Davidovitc, Erna, 97, 99
De Decker, L. P. J., 330–331
De Dokwerker, 143
De Gaulle, Charles, 236
De Lequerica, José Félix, 239
De Sousa, Maria Angelina Coelho, 50
De Sousa Mendes, Aristides, **50–52**, 220
De Sousa Mendes, José, 50
De Souza Dantas, Luis Martins, **52–54**
De Streel, Edouard, 66
Deaglio, Enrico, 207
Deffaugt, Jean, 42
Defiance, 31
Deichmann, Freya, 180
Delasem (Delegazione Assistenza Emigranti Ebrei, Delegation for the Assistance of Jewish Emigrants), 205
Delattre, Sylvia. *See* Abadi, Moussa
Delp, Alfred, 167

Der Schrei von Ararat (The Scream from Ararat), 306
Der Stürmer, 101
Desler, Salek, 320
Deutsche Emalwarenfabrik (German Enamelware Factory), 241
Deutsche Jugenschaft, 101
Deutsche Technische Hochschule (German Institute of Technology), 101
Deutsches Volkstheater, 153
Deutschkron, Inge, 310
Diamant, Cesia, 15
Die verlorene Zeit (The Lost Time), 28–29
Die Weisse Rose, 253
Die Wiener Walzermädeln (The Waltz-Girls of Vienna), 227–228
Die Wormundschaftsakte 1935–58 (The Guardianship Documents, 1935–1958), 153
Die Zeit, 153
Dienemann, Max, 117
Dieses Volk: Jüdische Existenz (This People Israel: The Meaning of Jewish Existence), 18
Dodd, William E., 102
Dohnányi, Christoph von, 57
Dohnányi, Ernő, **54–55**, 56
Dohnányi, Hans von, **55–57**
Dohnányi, Klaus von, 57
Dohnányi–Bayer, Barbara von, 57
Donati, Angelo, 205
Dornelles Vargas, Getúlio, 53
Dos Lid funem Oysgehargen Yidishn Folk (The Song of the Murdered Jewish People), 130
Drancy transit camp, 131, 271
Drozdzikowska, Irena, 199, 381
Dror Hechalutz Zionist movement, 129, 328–329
Drossel, Heinz, **57–59**, 219
Duckwitz, Georg Ferdinand, **59–61**
Düsseldorf detention center, 168
Dutch-Paris network, 307–309
Dwyer, Alice, 29

Eckler, Ingrid, 152–153
Eckler, Irene, 152–153
Eckler, Irma, 150, 152–153
Eckstein, Ze'ev, 128
École Nouvelle Cévenole, 291
Edelman, Cecylia, 63
Edelman, Marek, 6, **63–65**
Edelman, Natan, 63
Edelsheim-Gyulai, Ilona, 270
Eichman, Adolf, 71–72, 90, 98, 127–128, 140, 167, 170, 202, 298
Einstein, Albert, 274, 339
Éliás, József, 269
Elik, Eliyahu Lifshovitz, 14
Elinger, Jetty, 70
Elisabeth, Queen Mother of the Belgians, **65–67**
Elizabeth II of England, 4, 319
Emergency Rescue Committee, 74
Epenstein, Hermann von, 86
Episcopal Diocesan Authority (Berlin), 267
Epstein, Roland, 221–222
Ernst, Max, 75
Ernst von Dohnányi: A Song of Life, 54–55
Errázuriz, María, **67–68**
Escape from Auschwitz: I Cannot Forgive, 298
Escape from Sobibor, 70, 202
Eschhaus, Alfred, 309
Estonia, 138
Evert, Angelos, 49

Factory Action (*Fabrikaktion*), 109, 171, 310
Falkenhausen, Alexander von, 66
False papers, xxii, 7, 24, 27–28, 33, 40, 51, 73, 133–134, 157, 257–258, 271, 279, 321; baptism certificates, 134, 204–206, 230–231; Curaçao visas, 330–331; diplomatic visas, 52–54; passports, 92–93, 239–240; Vatican-issued, 231–232
Farago, György, 54

Fareynikte Partizaner Organizatsye (United Partisan Organization, FPO), xix–xx, 138–139, 319–321, 350, 386–387, 397
Feldhendler, Leon, **69–70**, 201, 390–392
Fénelon, Fania, 228
Ferenczy, György, 54
Feuchtwanger, Lion, 75
Feydeaus, Jacques, 68
Filov, Bogdan, 208
Fischer, Elizabeth, 127
Fischer, Jósef, 127
Fischer, Julia, 70
Five Fingers Over You, 306
Flesch, Carl, 54
Fleischmann, Gisi, **70–72**, 298, 311–312
Fliess, Julius, 57
Florida State University's School of Music, 55
Folcia, Marta, 48
Foley, Frank, **72–74**
Foley, Katherine, 73
Folkszeitung, 332
Foll, Hattil Spencer, 196
Forssman, Maja, 256
Fortner, Johann, 136
Forty Years of My Diplomatic Life, 104
France, 3, 270–271; German occupation of, 1, 50, 203–204, 215–224, 235–237, 291; Jews in, 1–3, 41–43, 52–54, 235–237, 291
Franciscan Sisters of Christian Charity, 121
Frank, Anne, 81–82, 275
Frank, Otto, 82
Frankl, Viktor, 117
Franko, Albert, 293
Franz Liszt Academy of Music, 54
Freiburger Rundbrief (Freiberg Circular), 168
Freisler, Roland, 181, 252
French Resistance, 26–27, 41–43, 67–68, 85–86, 131, 204–206, 214–215, 221–222, 271–272
Frenkel, Yedidya, 141
Freud, Anna, 275

Freud, Sigmund, 275
Freudiger, Fülop von, 127
Friedman, Jeanette, 322
Fritta, Bedrich, 98
Fritta, Tomás, 99
Fry, Varian, 74–76, 412
Fuchrer, Mira, 11–12, 166, 325–326
Fun Minsker geto (The Minks Ghetto: Soviet-Jewish Partisans against the Nazis), 78, 267

Gabrovski, Petar, 209
Gaha, John Francis "Stymie," 195
Galinski, Edward, 327
Gebelev, Mihail, xx, **77–78**, 266
General Jewish Workers Union of Poland, 385
Geneva Conventions, 181
Gens, Jacob, 138, 320
George III (Greece), 50
Gerlier, Pierre-Marie, 85
German Jewish Youth Movement, 350–352
German Resistance Memorial Center (Gedenkstätte Deutscher Widerstand), 311
German Sports Press Authority, 246
Germany: Criminal Code, 23; Moabit prison, 22; Plötzensee prison, 101–102, 105, 181; Soviet occupation of, 171–172; "The Soviet Paradise," exhibition, 21–22
Gerritsen, Frans, 316
Gerritsen-Kouffeld, Henny, 316
Gerstein, Elfriede, 81
Gerstein, Kurt, 16, **78–81**, 398–405, 413, 415
Gertner, Ala, 226–227
Ghetto Fighters' House, 131, 167, 330
Gies, Miep, **81–83**, 219, 275
Gildenman, Moshe "Uncle Misha," xxii, **83–84**
Gildenman, Simke, 84
Girls' Agricultural School at Nahalal, 282
Giterman, Isaac, 94

Glasberg, Alexandre, **84–86**
Glazman, Josef, 138, 319
Glick, Hirsch, 396–39
Gloria, Soli Deo, 269
Goebbels, Joseph, 21–23, 56, 109–110, 244, 404
Goeth, Amon, 200
Gold, Jack, 70, 202
Gold, Mary Jayne, 75
Goldenberg, Giorgio, 20
Goldstein, Peretz, 282
Good Shepherd Committee of the Reformed Church, 269, 284
Goodman, Harry, 253
Gorbachev, Mikhail, 10
Göring, Albert, **86–88**
Göring, Hermann, 86–87, 244, 255
Graf, Willi, 251–252
Great Mosque of Paris (France), 26–27
Greece, 3–5 ; Jews in, 48–50, 239–240
Gregor, Hans, 16
Gröber, Conrad, 168
Groboys, Sarra, 131
Grohé, Josef, 183
Grosman, Chaika, 167, 325, 361
Grossaktion Warschau (Great Action Warsaw), 94, 328
Grüber, Ernst, 88
Grüber, Heinrich, **88–90**, 281
Gruber, Samuel, 32
Gruenwald, Malchiel, 128
Grünhut, Aron, **90–91**
Grünhut, Benny, 91
Grüninger, Paul, **91–93**, 410
Gryn, Netanel "Tony," 221
Grynszpan, Herschel, 145
Grynszpan, Yehiel, 32–33
Gurs internment camp, 168
Gürtner, Franz, 56
Gustav V of Sweden, 156, 192, 256
Guzik, David, **93–95**, 130, 328

Haaretz, 132, 138, 315
"Halikka LeKersariya," 283
Halpern, Jacques-France, 203
Halverstad, Felix, 278
Hamas, Steve, 244
Hamburg Social Authority, 104
Hammarskjöld, Dag, 163
Handelstidningen, 255–256
Hanoar Hazioni, 138, 319
Hansson, Per Albin, 60, 256
Harris, Julie, 288
Hashomer Hatzair, 5, 11, 137, 226, 289, 319, 325–326, 329; Bet Leadership, 5; Fourth World Convention, 5
Hass, Jack, 58
Hass, Leo, **97–99**
Hass, Lucy, 58
Hass, Margot, 58
Hassan, Mervat, 100
Havoynic, Avraham (Abrasha), 319
Hebrew Immigrant Aid Society (HIAS), 71
Hebrew Union College (Ohio, U.S.), 18
Hechalutz, 315–316
Hechalutz, Holohem, 6
Heck, Lutz, 323–324
Hedtoft, Hans, 60
Heiden, Konrad, 75
Helldorf, Wolf-Heinrich Graf von, 146
Heller, Yom-Tov Lipmann, 129
Helmy, Mohammed, **99–100**
Henriques, Carl Bertelsmann, 60
Herben, Jan, 217
Hermann, Sophie, 97
Hernádi, Lajos, 54
Hertz, Joseph, 253
Hertz, Judith, 253
Hervormede Kweekschool (Reformed Teacher Training College), 106, 278
Herzl, Theodor, 336
Hess, Rudolf, 73, 151
The Hiding Place, 288
Hilari, Unaish, 374–378
Hillbring, Walter, 175
Himmler, Heinrich, 66, 192, 260
Hirsch, Helmut, **100–102**
Hirsch, Sigfried, 102
Hirsch, Kaete, 100
Hirsch, Marta, 100

Hirsch, Siegfried, 100
Hirschel, Hans, 176
Hirschfeld, Marianne, 58
Hitler, Adolf, xx, 12, 23, 56–57, 66, 86, 102, 110, 121, 151, 161, 180–181, 235, 244, 245, 251, 255–256, 268, 273–274, 305–306, 345–346, 351, 354; open letter to Hitler from Armin T. Wegner, 338–344
Hitler Youth, 23, 104, 250, 351
HKP (Heereskraftpark) 562 camp, 212–213
Ho Feng-Shan, **102–104**
Hochschule für die Wissenschaft des Judentums (Higher Institute for Jewish Studies), 116
Hoess, Rudolf, 177
Hoffman, Roald, 261
Höfler, Hermann, 70
Hollandsche Schouwburg (Dutch Theater), 278–279
Holocaust and Human Rights Center of New York, 275
Homosexuality, 22–24, 53
Hooft, Willem Visser 't, 308
Horowitz, Wolf Louis, 270
Horthy, Miklós, 230, 264
Hound & Horn, 74
Hübener, Gerhard, 104–105
Hübener, Helmuth, **104–106**
Huber, Kurt, 251–252
Hughes, Eileen Avery, 74
Hulst, Jan van, **106–107**, 278
Humboldt State University, 16, 180
Hungarian Academy of Fine Arts, 133
Hungarian Catholic Working Women's Movement, 237
Hungarian Chamber of Music, 54
Hungarian College of Fire Arts, 134
Hungary, 27, 263, 269–270, 301; Arrow Cross, 156–157, 231, 237–238, 265, 284; Catholic Women's party, 264; Foreign Service, 269; German occupation, 8–10, 126–129, 172–174, 229–232, 230, 265, 284–285; Jews in, 9, 34–36, 54–55, 155–157, 173, 206–207, 237–239, 281–285, 301–303; resistance, 269; Soviet liberation of, 55, 303–304

I. G. Farben, 44
Ich Boxte mich durchs Leben (Max Schmeling: An Autobiography), 246
Il Morbo di K, 37
Innitzer, Theodor, 122
Inside the Gestapo: A Jewish Woman's Secret War, 183
Inter-Denominational Working Group for Peace, 160
International Auschwitz Committee, 155
International Boxing Hall of Fame, 246
International Committee of the Red Cross (ICRC), 34, 44, 66, 98, 231, 239; letters of protection (*Schutzbriefe*), 35, 34–36, 173; -protected homes, 35–36
International Fellowship of Reconciliation, 272, 292
International Ghetto, 231–232
Iskra, 6
Israel: Mapai (Labor) Party, 128; War of Independence, 140
Israel, Charlotte, xiv, **109–111**
Israel, Julius, 109–111
Italy, 19, 36–38, 193–194
Itzhak Katzenelson Holocaust and Jewish Resistance Heritage Museum, 131
Ivinska, Ester, 332–333

Jacobs, Joe, 244–245
Jacobson, Martin, 407
Jaeger, Maximilian, 174
Japan, 276–278
Jefroykin, Dika, 214
Jagendorf, Abraham, 113
Jagendorf, Hilda, 113–114
Jagendorf, Siegfried, **113–116**
Jan Karski Award for Valor and Courage, 258
Jaruzelski, Wojciech, 65
Jewish Adult Education Center (Berlin), 24

Jewish Agency for Palestine, 214
Jewish Brigade (Palestine), 95
Jewish Colonization Association (ICA), 71
Jewish Historical Commission (Poland), 379
Jewish Historical Institute (Zydowski Instytut Historyczny, ZIH), 226
Jewish Home for the Blind, 309, 406
Jewish Hospital (Berlin), 169–171
Jewish Labor Bund, 143, 178, 289, 332
Jewish National Committee (Zydowski Komitet Narodowy, ZKN), 166, 329, 385
The Jewish Resistance in France, 41–42
Jewish Socialist Youth Association, 265
Jewish Teachers' Association, 179
Jewish Theological Seminary (Breslau), 17
Joachim, Hans, 21
John XXIII, 231
John Paul II, 122, 161, 261
Joint Distribution Committee (JDC), 93–94, 130, 224
Jonas, Regina, **116–117**
Jonas, Sara, 116
Jonas, Wolf, 116
Jospa, Hertz, 118
Jospa, Yvonne, **118–120**
Jozefa, Marta Maria, 284
Jüdische Rundschau, xix, 313–314; "Wear It with Pride, the Yellow Badge," 335–337
Juliana, Queen of the Netherlands, 90
July Bomb Plot, 57
Justice, Anna, 29

Kafka, Anton, 121
Kafka, Helene, **121–122**
Kahane, David, 261
Kamionska ghetto, 31–32
Kampfgruppe Auschwitz (Auschwitz Combat Group), 154, 211
Kant, Immanuel, 343
Kapito, Moshe, 325
Kaplan, Chaim A., **122–124**
Kaplan, Josef, 289, 329
Kappler, Herbert, 194
Karl-Ferdinand German University of Prague, 313
Karski, Jan, **124–126**, 219, 333
Kasariyot, 361–362
Kasztner, Rezső, 72, **126–129**, 269, 298, 312, 414
Katran, Farida, 1
Katzenelson, Benjamin, 129
Katzenelson, Hinda, 129
Katzenelson, Itzhak, **129–131**, 414
Katzenelson, Zvi, 130
Kaufman, Paula Welt, 316
Kazinetz, Isay Pavlovich, 77
Kellenbach, Katherina von, 117
Kempner, Vitka, 139–140
Kibbutz Lohamei Hagetaot, 167, 330
Kibbutz Sdot Yam, 282–283
Kikuchi, Yukiko, 276–278
Kinderaktion, 213
Kindertransport, 91, 253–255, 317–319
Kirschenbaum, Menachem, 94
Kirstein, Lincoln, 74
Kittel, Bruno, 212
Kleeman, Ulrich, 293
Klooger concentration camp, 144–145
Knut, Dovid, **131–133**, 214, 271
Köbel, Eberhard "Tusk," 101
Kochmann, Sala, 21
Kodály, Zoltán, 54–55
Koessler, Hans von, 54
Koffán, Károly, **133–134**
Koffán, Keska, 133–134
Kohn, Alfred, 142
Kor, Eva Mozes, 189
Korczak, Rozka, 139
Korkut, Dervis, **135–137**
Korkut, Servet, 137
Kovács, Laszlo, 87, 134
Kovner, Abba, xx, **137–140**, 167, 319–321, 325, 348–350, 386, 412
Kovner, Israel, 137
Kowalski, Władysław, **140–141**, 369–371

Kozalchik, Yakov, 227
Kraan, Willem, **142–143**, 412
Kraay, Suzy, 308
Kraków ghetto, 6, 199–200, 378–382
Kramer, Josef, 229
Krasnostawski, Moshe, 83
Kreisau Circle, 180–181
Kreutz, Benedikt, 168
Kristallnacht (Night of Broken Glass) pogrom, 17, 20, 73, 89, 97, 103, 104, 118, 145–147, 161, 243, 245, 253, 255, 315, 318
Kruk, Herman, 143–145
Krützfeld, Wilhelm, **145–147**
Krywaniuk, Helena, 199, 381
Krzyzanowska, Stanislaw, 257
Kto ratuje jedno zycie... (He Who Saves One Life), 28
Kuhn-Leitz, Cornelia, 159
Kuhn-Leitz, Elsie, 157, 159
Kunwald, Elisabeth, 55

La banalità del bene (The Banality of Goodness), 207
La Main Forte (The Strong Hand), 214
La Pira, Giorgio, 48
Lachwa ghetto revolt, xix, 163–165
L'affirmation, 132
Lagedi concentration camp, 144–145
Lainz General Hospital, 121
Lajcher, Berek, **149–150**
Landau, Lola (Leonore), 306
Landmesser, August, xxiv, **150–153**, 410
Landmesser, August Frand, 150
Langbein, Hermann, **153–155**, 211
Langlet, Nina, 157
Langlet, Valdemar, 8, **155–157**, 302
Lao Tzu, 355–356
Lasker-Wallfisch, Anita, 228
The Last Days of the Jerusalem of Lithuania: Chronicles from the Vilna Ghetto and the Camps, 145
The Last Sentence, 256
Latour, Anny, 41–42
Laufer, Julius, 24

Law for the Protection of German Blood and Honor, 151
Lazare, Leo Serge, 272
League of German Girls, 250, 351
Lederman, Charles, 235
Lee, Kathleen, 16
Lehi (Stern Gang), 128
Leica Camera Company, 157
Leica Freedom Train, 157–159
Leipelt, Hans Conrad, 252
Leitman, Shlomo, 389, 392–393
Leitz, Ernst I, 157
Leitz, Ernst II, **157–159**
Leizer, Hirsche, 358
Leo Baeck Institute, 18
Levitte, Simon, 214
Lewartowski, Józef, 289
Lewin, David, 245
Lewin, Ezekiel, 259–260
Lewin, Isaac, 330
Lewin, Siefbert, 405–407
Licht, Alice, 310
Lichtenberg, Bernhard, **159–162**, 167, 216, 268; interrogation by the Gestapo, 344–348
Liebeskind, Aharon, 6
Lifton, Robert Jay, 190
Linder, Menahem, 225
Linnér, Sture, xxiv, 3, **162–163**
Lipshovitz, Gershon, 14
Lipshovitz, Taibe, 14
Lithuania: German occupation of, 247, 276–278, 353; Jews in, 138, 143–145, 330–331; Soviet occupation of, 143–145, 319
Little Sisters convent, 325
Loenberg, Maurice, 271
Logothetopoulos, Constantinos, 49
London, Jerry, 194
Lopatyn, Dov, xix, **163–165**
Lospinoso, Guido, 205
Louis, Joe, 245–246
Löwenberger Arbeitsgemeinschaften (Löwenberg working groups), 180
Lubetkin, Zivia, 6, **165–167**, 289, 328

Lubusch, Edward, 327
Luckner, Gertrude, **167–169**
Luisengymnasium Berlin, 248
Lustig, Walter, **169–172**
Lutz, Carl, 35, 134, **172–174**, 231, 302
Lutz, Gertrude, 174
Lyons, Joseph, 196

Maccabea, 281–282
MacKay, George, 31
Mädchenorchester von Auschwitz (Girl Orchestra of Auschwitz), 228
Mahler, Gustav, 227
Malke, Bashe, 357
Malke, Shimen, 357
Malle, Louis, 203
Maltzan, Maria von, **175–176**
Maly Trostenets, 78
Mandel, Maria, 229
Mandil, Gabriela, 295
Mandil, Gavra, 295–296
Mandil, Irena, 295
Mandil, Moshe (Mosa), 295
Mandl, Maria, 327
Mann, Daniel, 229
Mann, Franceska, **176–178**
Mann, Heinrich, 75
Marcel Network, 1–3
Mauthausen concentration camp, 133, 203–204
Mechelen/Malines camp, 65–66
Meed, Benjamin, 179
Meed, Vladka, **178–179**
Mein Kampf, 161, 345–346
Meinecke, Friedrich, 248
Melchior, Marcus, 60
Menche, Chaskiel, 70
Meneghello, Giacomo, 47
Mengele, Josef, 188, 229
Menkes, Yosef, 128
Mentello, George, 72
Mészáros, André, 133–134
Metaxas, Ioannis (John), 48
Meusel, Marga, 249
Meyer, Gerd, 21

Michel, Hans-Helmut, 203
Miedzyrzecka, Czeslaw. *See* Benjamin Meed
Mihalev, Petar, 209
Min ha-Mezzar (From the Depths), 313
Minsk ghetto, xx, 77–78, 266–267, 366
Mir ghetto, 232–233
Mir yeshiva, 122
Mischlinge, 23, 40, 109, 280
Mit Brennender Sorge (With Burning Anxiety), 216, 268
Mohn, Heinrich, 105
Molodaya mysl' (Young Thought), 131
Moltke, Helmuth James Graf von, **179–182**, 216, 252
Monte, Joe, 243
Morávek, Jan, 87–88
Mordowicz, Czeslaw, 312
Morganstern, Yochanan, 94
Morrow, Edward R., 261
Moszkiewiez, Hélène, **182–183**
Moskowitz, Daniel, xx, **183–185**, 289–290
Mossad, 86
Mountbatten, George, 3
Mountbatten, Louis, 3
Mouvement de Jeunesse Sioniste (Zionist Youth Movement, MJS), 214, 221–222
Muckermann, Friedrich, 175
Mühfelder, Karl, 250
Müller, Filip, 177, **185–187**, 298
Münch, Hans, **187–190**
Munich Agreement, 97, 255, 261, 317
Muraközy, Gyula, 284
Museum Blindenwekstatt Otto Weidt, 311
Mussolini, Benito, 19, 193
My Life My Way, 322
Myrgren, Erik, 175

Näff, Roslï, 36
Nak, Piet, 143
Nakam (Avengers), 139
National Council for Religious Education, 254

National Liberation Committee (Comité français de Libération nationale), 215
National Museum of Natural History (Paris), 203
National Jewish Party, 127
Natt, Johanna "Hannah," 278
Navon, Yitzhak, 330
The Nazi Doctors, 190
Neged Hazerem (Against the Stream), 11
Nejman, Mordka, 196
Netherlands, 80; Central Off ice for Jewish Emigration, 279; Dutch protest at the deportation of Jews, 362–364; German occupation, 59–61, 217–219, 274–275, 278–280, 307–309; Jews in, 33–34, 39–41, 59–61, 106–107, 142–143, 287–288, 307–309, 362–364; Jewish Council (Joodse Raad), 106–107; underground movement, 34, 39–41, 217–219; Willem Kraanstraat, 143
Neuberger, George, 102
Neue-Bremm reprisal camp, 203
Neuengamme camp, 155
Neusel, Walter, 246
Neustadt, Leib, 94
New Synagogue, 145–147
New York Times, 25, 298
Niemöller, Martin, 88, 280
Night of the Long Knives, 56
Nisko labor camp, 97
Nitra Yeshiva, 312–313
Noah camp, 236
Noar (Youth), 126
Nobel Peace Prize, 259, 285, 319
Norrman, Sven, **191–192**, 412
North Western Reform Synagogue (London), 18
Northern Manchurian Railroad, 276
Notes from the Warsaw Ghetto, 225
Notes on the Refugees in Zbaszyn, 224
Novitch, Miriam, 130
Nuremberg Laws, 23, 101, 110, 152, 169–170, 172, 249, 255, 261, 280–281
Nuremberg Trials, 44, 87–88, 200, 202, 315

O'Flaherty, Hugh, **193–194**
O'Flaherty, James, 193
O'Flaherty, Margaret, 193
Ogilvie, Albert, **195–197**
Oliner, Samuel P., 16
Olympic Games, 255, 262
On Both Sides of the Wall, 179
Ondra, Anny, 246
Oneg Shabbat archives, 94, 224–226, 289
Open School of Art (Budapest), 133
Operation Barbarossa, 13, 24, 164, 181, 184, 232
Operation Bernhard, 98
Operation Ezra and Nehemiah, 86
Operation Reinhard, 70, 150
Organisation Juive de Combat (Jewish Company Organization, OJC), 215
Organization of the Ukrainian Nationalists, 259
Orsenigo, Cesare, 80
Orthodox World Agudath Israel, 311
Oster, Hans, 56, 181
Otter, Göran von, 79, 81, 403
Otto Weidt workshop, 310–311, 405–407

Pagine Ebraica, 20
Pais, Abraham, 274
Palgi, Yoel, 282
Pankiewicz, Jozef, 199
Pankiewicz, Tadeusz, **199–200**; "The 'Eagle' Pharmacy in the Kraków Ghetto," 378–382
Papandreou, Dimitrios. *See* Damaskinos, Archbishop of Athens
Papos, Mira, 135–137
"The Partisan Song," 396–397
Pasha, Mehmed Talaat, 306
Passeurs, 42
The Password Is Courage, 45
Paul Grüninger Foundation, 93
Peace Association of German Catholics, 160, 167
Pechersky, Alexander "Sasha," xxi, 69, **200–202**, 388–396
Peck, Gregory, 194

Peltel, Feigele. *See* Vladka Meed
Peltel, Hanna, 178
Peltel, Schlomo, 178
Pelzl, Emilie, 240
Penteli Monastery (Athens), 48
Père Jacques, **202–204**
Père Marie-Benoît, **204–206**, 236
Perlasca, Giorgio, 35, 173, **206–207**, 231, 240
Perlestein, Leah, 329
Peshev, Dimitar, **208–209**, 208, 413
Pèteul, Pierre. *See* Père Marie-Benoit
Petit Collège Saint-Thérèse de l'Enfant-Jésus, 203
Pfannenstiel, Wilhelm, 81
Pfarrernotbund (Emergency Association for Protestant Pastors), 88
Philip, Prince of Greece and Denmark, 3–4
Pilecki, Andrzej, 210
Pilecki, Józef, 210
Pilecki, Maria, 210
Pilecki, Witold, 154, **209–212**
Pilecki, Zofia, 210
Pilzer, Oskar, 87
Pinsky, Gertrude, 95
Pinkhof, Menachem, 316
Pinkhof, Miriam, 316
The Pioneer, 372–374
Pius IX, 47, 193, 205, 216, 229–231, 260
Plagge, Karl, **212–213**
Playing for Time, 229
Plazlo labor camp, 200
Plimpton, Martha, 183
Plotnicka, Frumke, 329, 361
Plummer, Christopher, 194
Pokrass, Daniel, 396
Pokrass, Dmitry, 396
Polak, Erica, 218
Polak, Fred, 217
Poland, 24–26, 27–29; Central Committee of Trade Unions, 370; Communist Party, 183; Dereczyn massacre, 14; Epidemic Control Department, 257; German occupation of, xix, 11, 63, 123–124, 137–140, 144, 149–150, 158–159, 166, 209–212, 230–232, 241–243, 264–265, 277, 289, 318–319, 332–334, 385; Jewish Council (Judenrat), 11, 138, 164–165, 184, 328, 333, 361, 367, 287; Jews in, 1, 11–13, 29–33, 93–95, 129–131, 149–150, 163–165, 176–178, 209–212, 224–226, 230–233, 240–243, 256–259, 264, 289–290, 324, 369–371; Jewish Council (Judenrat), 32, 69, 163; Knyszyn Forest, 185; Ministry of Agriculture, 141; Municipal Social Services Department (Warsaw), 258; Naliboki Forest, xxii, 29–31, 233, 267; National Army, 70; Ponary Forest, 232, 247, 349–350; Soviet occupation of, 13–14, 28–33, 83–84, 166, 232–233; *Umschlagplatz,* 63; underground, 6, 95, 124–126, 209–212, 257–259, 289–290; Warsaw Swedes, 191–192; Worker's Defense Committee, 65
Polish National Council in London, 370
Polish-Soviet War, 149, 210
Polonski, Abraham, 132, **214–215**, 271
Polonski, Eugénie, 214
Pomeranc, Cesia, 33
Poons, Karel, 218
Portugal, 51–52, 94
Pracovna Skupina (Working Group), 311–312
Preysing, Konrad Graf von, 161, **215–217**, 268, 413
Prison de Pax, 42
Pritchard, Marion van Binsbergen, **217–219**
Prizerini, Neshad, 295
Probst, Christoph, 251–252
Prodolliet, Arnest, 92
Propper de Callejón, Eduardo, **219–220**
Pruslin, Matvey, 77
Purgly, Magdolna, 264

Rachel, Braca, 311–312
Racine, Mila, 42, **221–222**
Raczkiewicz, Władysław, 333–334, 369–371

Raffay, Sándor, 284
Rahm, Karl, 279
Raiscko Institute, 189
Rathenau, Emil, 339
Rathenau, Walter, 341
Rather Die Fighting: A Memoir of World War II, 33
Ravensbrück camp, 152, 168, 316
Récébedou camp, 236
Reeder, Eggert, 66
Reich Security Main Office, 127
Reichsmusikkamer, 54
Reichsleiter Rosenberg Taskforce, 144
Reichsverband der Juden in Deutschland (Reich Association of Jews in Germany), 17, 89, 171
Remilleaux, Laurent, 85
Rémond, Paul, 1–2, **222–224**
Resistuta, Maria. *See* Helene Kafka
Reznik, Nissan, 138, 319
Rhodes, 294
Ribère, Germaine, 85
Ricotti, Cipriano, 47–48
Ridovics, László, 133–134
Ringelblum, Emanuel, 94, **224–226**, 289, 328, 411; on the *Kasariyot* in the Polish ghetto, 361–362
The Rise and Fall of the Third Reich, 263
Risko, Johnny, 243
Robert Koch Hospital, 99
Robota, Roza, **226–227**, 415
Rochczyn, Isaac, xix, 164
Röhm, Eberhard, 273
Roitman, Paul, 214
Rok w Treblince (A Year in Treblinka), 385
Romania, 114–116
Rome ghetto, 36–38, 194
Roncalli, Angela. *See* John XXIII
Roosevelt, Franklin D., 126, 269, 312
Rosé, Alma, **227–229**
Rosé, Arnold, 227
Rosenberg, Kurt, 158
Rosenberg's Center for the Study of Jewry without Jews, 144
Rosenheim, Yacob, 253

Rosenstock-Abadi, Odette, 1–2
Rosenstrausse protest, 109–111
Rosenthal, Johan Bosch van, 308
Rosin, Arnost, 312
Rotfeld, Adam, 261
Rothenmund, Marc, 253
Rotta, Angelo, 35, 173, 207, **229–232**, 240
Royal National Hungarian Academy of Music, 54
Rubin, Phillip, 140
Rudelsheim, Letty, 316
Rufeisen, Oswald, **232–233**
Ruiter, Johan, 327
Russian Revolution, 84, 131
Rykestrasse Synagogue, 147

Sabyriv, Alexander, 84
Sacerdoti, Vittorio Emanuele, 36–37
Sachsenhausen concentration camp, 73, 98
Safirsztajn, Regina, 226–227
Sagan, Szachno, 289
St. Hedwig's Cathedral (Berlin), 161
St. Mary's College (Maryland), 117
Sak, Josef, 94, 289
Saliège, Jules-Géraud, **235–237**
Salkaházi, Sára, **237–238**, 265
Salome, Giel, 316
San Giovanni Calibita church, 36
Sanz Briz, Ángel, 206, 231, **238–240**
Sarajevo Haggadah, 135–137
Sargent, Joseph, 229
The Scarlet and the Black, 194
Scharping, Rudolf, 248
Scheveningen prison, 288
Schillinger, Josef, 177
Schindler, Oskar, 53, 100, 128, **240–243**, 279
Schindler's List, 200, 240, 243, 279–280
Schiper, Ignacy (Yitzhak), 94
Schlosser, Maurice, 203
Schmeling, Max, xxiv, **243–246**
Schmid, Anton, 212–213, **246–248**; letter to Steffi Schmid, 352–353
Schmid, Jakob, 252
Schmid, Stefi, 246, 248, 352–353

Schmitz, August, 248
Schmitz, Elisabeth, **248–250**, 409
Schmorell, Alexander, 251
Schneider, Antón, 92
Schnibbe, Karl-Heinz, 105
Scholem, Gershom, 18
Scholl, Hans and Sophie, 163, **250–253**, 413
Schonfeld, Solomon, **253–255**
Schonfeld, Victor, 253
School of Jewish Studies (Berlin), 17
Schotte, Marie, 275
Schriabina, Alexander, 131
Schriabina, Ariadna, 131–132
Schreiber, Liev, 31
Schulhof, Andrew, 54
Scroll of Agony, 123
Segerstedt, Torgny, xxiv, **255–256**
Seidel, Norman, 196
Seitz, Walter, 8
Seiwaldstätter, Brunhilde, 88
Sendler, Irena, **256–259**
Sendler, Mieczyslaw, 257
Sered concentration camp, 72
Serédi, Jusztinián György, 231
Sergiani, Enrico, 48
Sergiani, Luigina, 48
Serly, Tibor, 55
Shalev, Avner, 220
Sharkey, Jack, 243–244
Sheptytsky, Andrey, **259–261**
Shermer, Dan, 128
Shirer, William L., **261–263**
Siegmund-Schulz, Friedrich, 272
Siemens-Schuckert Werke, 20–21, 114–115
Sikelianos, Angelos, 49
Sikorski, Władysław, 192, 333–334
Sima, Horia, 114
Simon, Joachim, 316
Simon, Mary, 351
Simon, Mojshe, 357
Simon, Sidney, 357–360
Slachta, Margit, 237, **263–265**
Slovakia, 70-72, 264, 311
Smit, Jan, 316

Smolar, David, 265
Smolar, Hersh, xx, 77, **265–267**
Soares, Mário, 52
Sobibor camp, 278; revolt, xxi, 69–70, 200–202, 388–396
Social Welfare Institute of Pestalozzi-Fröbel House (Berlin), 267
Socialist Movement of Jewish Youth, 289
Society of the Sisters of Social Service, 237–238, 264
Society of the Social Mission, 264
Solf, Hanna, 175
Solf Circle, 181
Sommer, Margaret, 216, 267–268
Sonnenfeldt, Richard, 87
Soos, Géza, **269–270**
Sophie, Princess of Greece and Denmark, 4
Sophie Scholl, Die letzten Tage, 253
Sorkine, Charlotte, 222, **270–272**
Sorkine, Pauline, 272
Soutou, Jean-Marie, 85
Soviet Union; German invasion of, 13, 77, 114, 200–202, 247, 353
Spanish Civil War, 153, 206, 238
Spanish Houses, 239–240
Spielberg, Steven, 200, 240, 243, 279
Starzynski, Stefan, 332
Stephanovich, Stephan, 374
Steinfeld, Julius, 253
Stella Maris Carmelite Monastery, 233
Sterben für Frieden. Spurensicherung: Herman Stöhr (1898–1940) und die ökumenische Friedensbewegung, 273
Stern, Itzhak, 241
Sternberg Centre for Judaism, 74
Stetsko, Yaroslav, 259
Stiberitz, Theresa "Tess," 261–262
Stöhr, Hermann, **272–274**
Strobos, Robert, 275
Strobos, Tina, **274–275**
Stroop, Jürgen, 13, 64
Stumfohl, Lambert, 122
Sugihara, Chiune, **276–278**, 331–332, 411
Sugihara, Yatsu, 276

Sugihara, Yoshimizu, 276
Surmacki, Władysław, 210
Süskind, 279–280
Süskind, Walter, 106, **278–280**
Süskind, Yvonne, 279
Sweden, 79, 251, 255–256; Jews in, 60–61; *Schutzpässe*, 10, 134; Swedish Foreign Ministry, 156; visas for, 8–11
Swedish Houses, 303
Swedish-Hungarian Association, 157
Switzerland, 24, 54, 91–92, 174; Red Cross, 34–36, 155–157; safe conduct documents, 173; Swiss Federal Department of Foreign Trade, 35
Sylten, Hidegard, 280–281
Sylten, Werner, 89, **280–281**
Szalasi, Ferenc, 206
Székely, Mária, 269
Szenes, Béla, 281
Szenes, György, 281
Szenes, Hannah, **281–282**, 414–415
Szent-Iványi, Domokos, 269
Szentiványi, Lajos, 133–134
Szinyei-Merse, Jeno, 55
Sztehló, Gabor, 35, **283–285**
Szturmann, Frieda, 99–100

Tajna Armia Polska (Polish Secret Army, TAP), 210
Taubman, Rachel (Rosa), 137
Tedesco, Claudio, 38
Tedesco, Luciana, 38
Tehlirian, Soghomon, 306
Teitelbaum, Joel, 127, 312
Teitelbaum, Leah, 312
Ten Boom, Betsie, 288
Ten Boom, Casper, 287–288
Ten Boom, Corrie, **287–289**
Ten Boom, Nollie, 287–288
Ten Boom, Willem, 287–288
Tenenbaum, Mordechaj, xx, 130, 183–184, 247, **289–290**, 329, 414
Terezín/Theresienstadt concentration camp, 17–18, 97–99, 117, 168–169, 171, 310

Thierack, Otto Georg, 105
Thies, Eduoard, 290–291
Third Confessing Synod, 249
Thomán, István, 54
Thompson, Dorothy, 262
Tiefenbrunn, Franziska "Fanny," 86
Toriel, Matilda, 293
Trading with the Enemy Act, 71
Treblinka death camp, xx–xxi, 11, 63, 80, 94, 178, 184, 209, 321, 366, 399, 403; revolt, 149–150, 382–385
Trocmé, André, **290–292**
Trocmé, Daniel, 290, 292
Trocmé, Jacques, 290
Trocmé, Jean–Pierre, 290
Trocmé, Magda, 290–292
Trocmé, Nelly, 290
Troell, Jan, 256
Tüdös, Ilona, 270
Turk, Elsie, 159
Turnatoria foundry, 115

Ubbink, J. H., 80
Udkofsky, Borya, 374–378
Uj Kelet, 126
Ukrane, 259–261
Ülkümen, Mehmet, 294
Ülkümen, Mihrinissa, 294
Ülkümen, Selahattin, **293–294**
Uncle Emil network, 8
An Underground Life: Memoirs of a Gay Jew in Nazi Berlin, 24
Ungar, Moshe, 312
Ungar, Otto, 98
Ungar, Shmuel Dovid, 311
Union des Anciens Résistants Juifs de Belgique (Union of Former Belgium Jewish Resistance Members), 119
Union of German Rabbis (Allgemeiner Deutscher Rabbinerverband), 17
United Palestine Appeal, 127
United States Holocaust Memorial Museum (USHMM), xxix, 304, 309
Universal Convent of the Reformed Church of Hungary, 284

Universal News Service, 261
University of Amsterdam, 275
University of Berlin, 272
University of British Columbia, 298
University of Hamburg, 252
University of Michigan, 301
University of Munich, 250, 252, 353, 356
University of Rome, 36
University of Rostock, 272
University of Warsaw, 257, 289
Uzcudun, Paulino, 243

Vaada Etzel Vehatzalah (Jewish Relief and Rescue Committee), 127
Vali, Ferenc, 269
Varian's War, 76
Vatican, 80, 193–194, 205, 231–232, 240, 298; "Report on the Exodus," 268
Velodrome d'Hiver (the Vel d'Hiv), 271
Veres, László "Leslie," 269
Verhoeven, Michael, 253
Veseli, Fatima, 295, 297
Veseli, Hamid, 295, 297
Veseli, Refik, **295–297**
Veseli, Vesel, 295, 297
Veseli, Xhemal, 295–296
Vespignani, Benedetta, 48
Vilna ghetto, 143–145, 184, 212–213, 247, 289, 319, 325, 353, 396–397; Call for Revolt in the Vilna Ghetto, 386–388; Library, 144–145; Resistance Proclamation, 348–350
Vital war workers, 24–25
Vittal camp, 131
Voice of the Spirit, 264
Völkischer Beobachter, 280
Volksgerichtshof (People's Court), 102, 105, 122, 181, 252
Vom Rath, Ernst, 145
Vrba, Rudolf, 72, 156, 269, **297–299**, 312
Vrije Universiteit Amsterdam (VU University), 106–107
Vught concentration camp, 316

Waffen-SS Institute for Hygiene, 79, 188
Wajcblum, Estusia, 226–227
Wallenberg, Maj (Maria) Sofia, 301
Wallenberg, Raoul, 8–10, 134, 156–157, 173–174, 207, 219, 220, 231, 240, 269, **301–304**, 414–415
Wallenberg, Raoul Oscar, 301
Walther, Irene, 21
Walter, Lidia, 406
Wandervogel movement, 7, 94
War Refugee Board (WRB), 301–302
Wariner, Doreen, 317
Warsaw Ghetto, 5, 7, 16, 122–126, 129–131, 140, 177, 191–192, 224–226, 397; Handbill: Call for Resistance in the Warsaw Ghetto, 364–366; Statement: Call for Resistance in the Warsaw Ghetto, 366–368; Uprising, xx, xxvi, 11, 63–65, 130, 140–141, 166, 178, 266, 304–305, 325–326, 328–330, 332–334, 364–369, 372–374, 386
Warsaw Ghetto Resistance Organization, 179
Warsaw University, 149
Warsaw Zoo, 324
Wartenburg, Peer Graf Yorck von, 180
Waseda University, 276
Wasser, Bluma, 225
Wasser, Hersh, 225
Wassermann, Oskar, 160
Wdowiński, Dawid, **304–305**
Weber, Bruno, 188
Wegner, Armin T., **305–307**; open letter to Adolf Hitler, 338–344
Węgrow ghetto, 149
Wehrmacjt remand prison, 273
Weichsel-Union-Metallwerke, 226–227
Weidner, Johan Hendrik, **307–309**
Weidt, Auguste, 309
Weidt, Else, 311
Weidt, Max, 309
Weidt, Otto, 146–147, **309–311**; statement of support from Siegbert Lewin, 405–407
Weiler, Lucien, 203

Weiner, Leo, 55
Weiss, Simon, 407
Weissmandl, Chaim Michael Dov, 71, 253, 298, **311–313**
Weissmandl, Yosef, 311
Weltguck (World Look), 175
Weltsch, Robert, xix, 18, **313–315**, 409; "Wear It with Pride, the Yellow Badge," 335–337
Weltsch, Theodore, 313
Werfel, Franz, 75
Wertheim, Barbara, 317
Wertheim, Rudolf, 317
Wesse, Suzanne, 21
Westerweel, Johan, **315–316**
Westerweel, Wilhelmina, 315–316
Westerweel group, 315–316
Wetzler, Alfréd, 72, 156, 269, 297, 312
Weyl, Max, 116
White Rose Foundation, 253
White Rose Movement, xix, 122, 163, 250–253; Second Leaflet, 353–356
White Rose International, 253
Who Shall Live: The Wilhelm Bachner Story, 16
Wiernik, Yankiel, 382–385
Winton, Grete, 318
Winton, Nicholas, 91, 219, **317–319**
Wirth, Christian, 81
Wirths, Eduard, 153
Wislicenty, Dieter, 311
Wittenberg, Yitzhak, 138, **319–321**, 386–387
Włodarkiewicz, Jan Henryk, 210
Wobbe, Rudi, 105
A Woman at War, 183
Women's International Zionist Organization (WIZO), 221
Working Girls' Homes, 237–238
World Council of Churches, 308
World Jewish Conference, 301
World Union for Progressive Judaism, 18
World War I, 26, 36, 88, 91–92, 100, 170, 175, 204, 208, 248, 259, 280, 284, 290, 306, 309, 313, 332

Wrobel, Eta, xxii, **321–322**
Wrobel, Henry, 322
Wurzel, Nathan, 241

Yad Vashem, xxix, 4, 8, 73; Department of the Righteous, 100; Righteous among the Nations, 8, 10, 20, 26, 28, 34, 35–36, 38, 40, 42, 45–46, 48, 49, 52, 54, 57, 59, 61, 67–68, 74, 76, 86, 93, 100, 104, 107, 126, 134, 137, 141, 143, 155, 157, 159, 161, 169, 174, 176, 204, 206–207, 209, 213, 219, 220, 224, 232, 235, 237–238, 240, 243, 248, 250, 258, 261, 265, 268, 275, 278, 281, 285, 288, 292, 294, 297, 304, 307, 311, 316, 319, 324, 332
Yakovlev, Alexander, 303
Yearbook of the Leo Baeck Institute, 315
Yiddish Grosser Library, 143
Yiddish Kultur Organizatsye, 225
YIVO Institute, 145
Yoffe, Moshe, 78
Yom Kippur War, 169
Yosef, Finica Ben, 296
Yosef, Ruzhica Ben, 296
Yosef, Yosef Ben, 296
Young Communist League (Germany), 20
Young Maccabi, 352

Żabiński, Antonina, 323–324
Żabiński, Jan, **323–324**
Żabiński, Ryszard, 324
Zachár, Ilona, 54–55
Zahavi, David, 283
Zander, Arthur, 104
Żegota, 256–259, 324
Zemon, Milos, 319
Zilberberg, Rachel, 11–12, 166, 185, **325–326**
Zima, Emanuel, 91
Zimetbaum, Mala, **326–328**, 415
Zionist Aid and Rescue Committee, 72, 298
Zionist Organization, 127

Zionist Organization of France, 214
Ziss, Meier, 70
The Zookeeper's Wife, 324
Zuckerman, Roni, 167
Zuckerman, Yitzhak, 6, 12–13, 166, 289, **328–330**, 373, 385; letter from Mordecai Anielewicz, 368–369
Zündel, Ernst, 298–299
Zwartendijk, Jan, 277, **330–332**, 411
Zwiazek Organizacji Wojskowej (Union of Military Organization, ZOW), 154, 210–211
Zybszynska, Iza, 192

Zydowska Organizacja Bojawa (Jewish Combat Organization, ZOB), xxii, 6, 12, 63–64, 94, 130, 141, 165–167, 178, 272, 289–290, 304–305, 326, 328–330, 364–369, 373
Zydowska Samopomoc Spoleczna (Jewish Social Aid), 225
Zydowski Zwiazek Wojskowy (Jewish Military Union, ZZW), 304–305, 329
Zygielbojm, Shmuel, **332–334**, 414; Letter to Władysław Raczkierwicz and Władysław Sikorski, 369–371
Zyklon B, 79–80, 188–190, 398

About the Author

Dr. Paul Bartrop is an award-winning scholar of the Holocaust and genocide. He is Professor of History and Director of the Center for Judaic, Holocaust, and Genocide Studies at Florida Gulf Coast University in Fort Myers, Florida.

In 2011–2012 he was the Ida E. King Distinguished Visiting Professor of Holocaust and Genocide Studies at Richard Stockton College in New Jersey.

Between 1997 and 2011 he taught in, and was head of, the Department of History at Bialik College in Melbourne, Victoria, Australia. Concurrently, he was for many years an honorary fellow in the faculty of Arts and Education at Deakin University in Melbourne.

He has previously been a scholar-in-residence at the Martin-Springer Institute for Teaching the Holocaust, Tolerance, and Humanitarian Values at Northern Arizona University, and a visiting professor at Virginia Commonwealth University. In Australia, he also taught at the University of South Australia and Monash University.

He is the author or editor of 14 books, including the following published works with ABC-CLIO: *Bosnian Genocide: The Essential Reference Guide* (2016); *Modern Genocide: The Definitive Resource and Document Collection* (2015); *Encountering Genocide: Personal Accounts from Victims, Perpetrators, and Witnesses* (2014); and *An Encyclopedia of Contemporary Genocide Biography: Portraits of Evil and Good* (2012), which was awarded recognition by *Choice* as "Outstanding Academic Title 2013."

In addition, he has published numerous scholarly articles in journals and books. He has been a member of the International Association of Genocide Scholars and was for many years the Australian representative on the International Committee of the Annual Scholars' Conference on the Holocaust and the Churches. He is a past member of the editorial advisory board of the international journal *Genocide Studies and Prevention*; a member of the editorial advisory board of the journal *Holocaust and Genocide Studies*; a member of the advisory board of the Genocide Education Project, California; and senior consultant to the Jewish Holocaust Centre, Melbourne. Dr. Bartrop is currently vice president of the Midwest Jewish Studies Association, and is a past president of the Australian Association of Jewish Studies.

www.ingramcontent.com/pod-product-compliance
Lightning Source LLC
Chambersburg PA
CBHW060504300426
44112CB00017B/2541